McGraw-Hill Ryerson

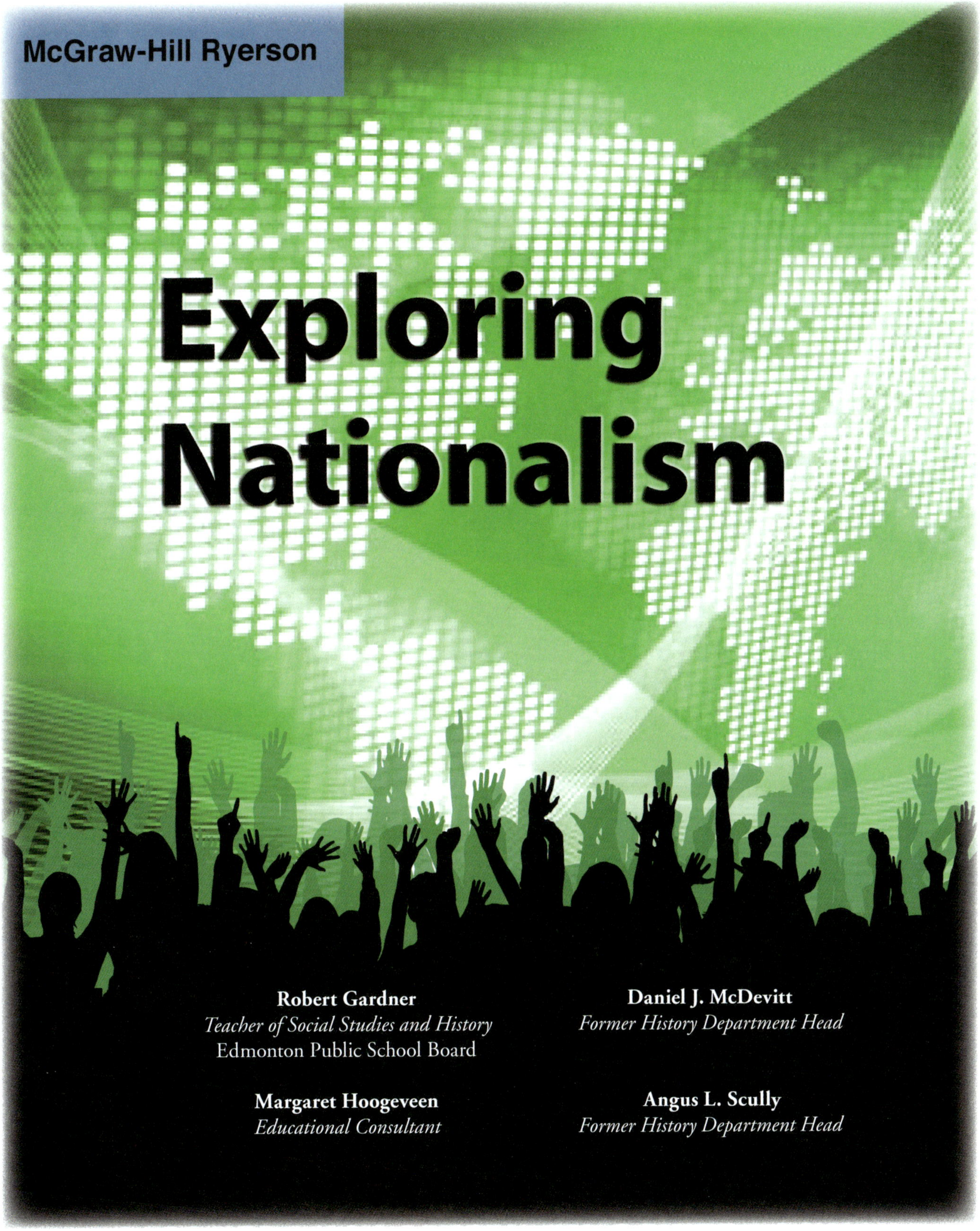

Exploring Nationalism

Robert Gardner
Teacher of Social Studies and History
Edmonton Public School Board

Daniel J. McDevitt
Former History Department Head

Margaret Hoogeveen
Educational Consultant

Angus L. Scully
Former History Department Head

Toronto Montréal Boston Burr Ridge, IL Dubuque, IA Madison, WI New York
San Francisco St. Louis Bangkok Bogotá Caracas Kuala Lumpur Lisbon London
Madrid Mexico City Milan New Delhi Santiago Seoul Singapore Sydney Taipei

The McGraw·Hill Companies

COPIES OF THIS BOOK MAY BE OBTAINED BY CONTACTING

McGraw-Hill Ryerson Ltd.

WEB SITE

http://www.mcgrawhill.ca

E-MAIL

orders@mcgrawhill.ca

TOLL-FREE FAX

1-800-463-5885

TOLL-FREE, CALL

1-800-565-5758

OR BY MAILING YOUR ORDER TO

McGraw-Hill Ryerson
Order Department
300 Water Street
Whitby, ON L1N 9B6

Please quote the ISBN and title when placing your order.

Student text ISBN

978-0-07-074028-0

Exploring Nationalism

ISBN-13: 978-0-07-074028-0
ISBN-10: 0-07-074028-3

http://www.mcgrawhill.ca

2 3 4 5 6 7 8 9 10 TCP 6 5 4 3 2 1 0 9 8

Printed and bound in Canada

PROJECT MANAGER: Joseph Gladstone
PROJECT EDITOR AND DEVELOPMENTAL EDITOR: Dyanne Rivers
DEVELOPMENTAL EDITOR: Maryrose O'Neill
ADDITIONAL WRITING: Jill Colyer, Meaghan Craven, Joseph Gladstone, Maryrose O'Neill, Dyanne Rivers, Sheila Wawanash
MANAGER, EDITORIAL SERVICES: Crystal Shortt
SUPERVISING EDITOR: Janie Deneau
COPY EDITOR: Sheila Wawanash
PHOTO RESEARCH / PERMISSIONS: Linda Tanaka
EDITORIAL ASSISTANT: Erin Hartley
MANAGER, PRODUCTION SERVICES: Yolanda Pigden
PRODUCTION CO-ORDINATOR: Madeleine Harrington
INTERIOR DESIGN: First Image
ELECTRONIC PAGE MAKE-UP: First Image
MAP DESIGNER: Gary Birchall
COVER DESIGN: Cathie Ellis
COVER IMAGES: Courtesy of Shutterstock Inc.

Table of Contents

Tour of the Textbook viii

Prologue

Exploring Nationalism 1
What Is Nationalism? 2
Your Exploration of Nationalism 3
What Is an Issue? 4
Critical Thinking 6
Powerful Questions 7
Habits of Mind 8
The Inquiry Process 9
Steps in the Inquiry Process 10
Terms Used in *Exploring Nationalism* 12

Related Issue 1
To What Extent Should Nation Be the Foundation of Identity?

The Big Picture 15
Your Challenge *Create a coat of arms to show how your understandings of the concept of nation shape — and are shaped by — your identity* 16

Chapter 1 Nation and Identity 18
Chapter Issue *To what extent are nation and identity related?* 19

What are some concepts of nation? 20
The View from Here *Johann Gottlieb Fichte, Ernest Renan, and Benedict Anderson on what makes a nation a nation* 22
What are some understandings of nation? 25
How can nation be understood as a civic concept? 30
Making a Difference *Mustafa Kemal Atatürk — Founding the Turkish Nation* 33
Focus on Skills *Developing Effective Inquiry Questions* 34
How do people express their identity through nation? 36
Taking Turns *How is nation a part of who you are?* 37
Think . . . Participate . . . Research . . . Communicate 40

Chapter 2 Shaping Nationalism 42
Chapter Issue *To what extent do external and internal factors shape nationalism?* 43

What are some factors that shape nationalism? 44
Focus on Skills *Detecting Rhetoric and Bias in Historical Writing* 48
The View from Here *Various solutions to the problems facing the people of 18th-century France* 51
GeoReality *The Disastrous Russian Campaign* 54
How have people responded to some factors that shape nationalism? 56
How have people in Canada responded to some factors that shape nationalism? 59
Making a Difference *Victoria Callihoo — The Métis Queen Victoria* 60
Taking Turns *Have your people's stories helped shape Canadian nationalism?* 63
Think . . . Participate . . . Research . . . Communicate 64

Chapter 3 Reconciling Nationalist Loyalties . . . 66
Chapter Issue *To what extent should people reconcile their contending nationalist loyalties?* . . . 67
How do nationalist loyalties shape people's choices? . . . 68
What choices have people made to affirm nationalist loyalties? . . . 70
Making a Difference *Kiviaq — Championing a People's Rights* . . . 71
How can nationalist loyalties create conflict? . . . 75
Taking Turns *Do contending nationalist loyalties create conflict for you?* . . . 76
Impact *Québec — Focus of Francophone Nationalism in Canada* . . . 78
Focus on Skills *Analyzing Information from Many Sources* . . . 80
How have people reconciled contending nationalist loyalties? . . . 82
The View from Here *Shawn Brant, Marilyn Jensen, and Doug Cuthand on the National Day of Action, 2007* . . . 85
Think . . . Participate . . . Research . . . Communicate . . . 86

Chapter 4 Reconciling Nationalist and Non-Nationalist Loyalties . . . 88
Chapter Issue *To what extent should people reconcile their contending nationalist and non-nationalist loyalties?* . . . 89
What are non-nationalist loyalties? . . . 90
How can nationalist and non-nationalist loyalties compete? . . . 92
Spinbuster *Identifying Spin in the News* . . . 94
The View from Here *Melody Lepine, Don Thompson, Peter Lougheed, and Richard Schneider on development of the oil sands* . . . 99
Focus on Skills *Defending an Informed Position* . . . 100
How have people reconciled contending nationalist and non-nationalist loyalties? . . . 102
Making a Difference *Sandra Lovelace Nicholas — Fighting for First Nations Women* . . . 104
Taking Turns *Is it important to your identity to reconcile your nationalist and non-nationalist loyalties?* . . . 107
Think . . . Participate . . . Research . . . Communicate . . . 108

Related Issue 2
To What Extent Should National Interest Be Pursued?
The Big Picture . . . 111
Your Challenge *Research and present an investigative report on a nationalist movement* . . . 112

Chapter 5 National Interest and Foreign Policy . . . 114
Chapter Issue *To what extent do national interest and foreign policy shape each other?* . . . 115
How are nationalism and national interest related? . . . 116
Focus on Skills *Building Consensus* . . . 120
How has national interest shaped foreign policy? . . . 122
Making a Difference *Woodrow Wilson — Visionary or Dreamer?* . . . 124
The View from Here *John Maynard Keynes, Joachim von Ribbentrop, and Margaret MacMillan on the Treaty of Versailles* . . . 125
GeoReality *Oil and National Interest in Iraq* . . . 128
How has foreign policy shaped national interest? . . . 130
Taking Turns *Has Canadian foreign policy in Afghanistan supported the national interests of the Afghan people?* . . . 133
Think . . . Participate . . . Research . . . Communicate . . . 134

Chapter 6 Nationalism and Ultranationalism . . . 136
Chapter Issue *To what extent can nationalism lead to ultranationalism?* . . . 137
What is ultranationalism? . . . 138
How does ultranationalism develop? . . . 141
Focus on Skills *Assessing the Validity of Information* . . . 142

Taking Turns *How might a crisis affect people's sense of nationalism and national identity?* 144
Spinbuster *Analyzing Propaganda* 146
How have people responded to ultranationalism? 149
Making a Difference *Joy Kogawa — Shedding Light on a Shameful Story* 153
The View from Here *Sima Wali, Karin von Hippel, and Michael Ignatieff on nation building* 155
Think ... Participate ... Research ... Communicate 156

Chapter 7 Ultranationalism and Crimes against Humanity 158
Chapter Issue *To what extent can the pursuit of ultranationalism lead to crimes against humanity?* 159

What are crimes against humanity? 160
How has ultranationalism caused crimes against humanity? 163
Impact *Shoah — The Holocaust* 166
The View from Here *Leó Szilárd, Mitsuo Okamoto, and Oliver Kamm on whether dropping the atomic bomb was justified* 169
What are some contemporary consequences of ultranationalism? 170
Making a Difference *Louise Arbour — Speaking Out for Human Rights* 172
Focus on Skills *Analyzing Cause-and-Effect Relationships* 174
Taking Turns *Are crimes against humanity a thing of the past or could they happen again?* 177
Think ... Participate ... Research ... Communicate 178

Chapter 8 National Self-Determination 180
Chapter Issue To *what extent should national self-determination be pursued?* 181

What is national self-determination? 182
What are some effects of pursuing national self-determination? 184
Focus on Skills *Predicting Likely Outcomes* 188
What are some effects on Canada of pursuing national self-determination? 193
Making a Difference *Zacharias Kunuk — Telling the Truth of What Happened* 195
The View from Here *Stephen Harper, Phil Fontaine, and Clément Chartier on pursuing national self-determination within Canada and Québec* 198
What are some unintended consequences of the pursuit of national self-determination? 199
Taking Turns *How has the pursuit of national self-determination affected you?* 201
Think ... Participate ... Research ... Communicate 202

Related Issue 3
To What Extent Should Internationalism Be Pursued?
The Big Picture 205
Your Challenge *Participate in a roleplay of an international summit convened to respond to the international water crisis* 206

Chapter 9 Nations, Nation-States, and Internationalism 208
Chapter Issue *To what extent does involvement in international affairs benefit nations and states?* 209

What are some common motives of nations and states? 210
The View from Here *Robert I. Rotberg, Erin Simpson, and Jean-Pierre Lindiro Kabirigi on what happens when states fail to meet citizens' needs* 215
GeoReality *Botswana and Zimbabwe — Similar Geography, Different Results* 216
Focus on Skills *Decision Making and Problem Solving* 218
How do the motives of nations and states shape their responses to the world? 220
Taking Turns *Is isolationism a valid response to world issues?* 221
What are some understandings of internationalism? 223
Making a Difference *Clara Hughes — Supporting Children's Right to Play* 225
How does internationalism benefit nations and states? 226
Think ... Participate ... Research ... Communicate 228

Chapter 10 Foreign Policy and Internationalism ... 230
Chapter Issue *To what extent can foreign policy promote internationalism?* ... 231
How do countries set foreign policy? ... 232
The View from Here *Joe Clark, Bill Graham, and Wilfried von Bredow on factors that influence foreign policy* ... 234
How can states promote internationalism through foreign policy? ... 236
Focus on Skills *Persuading, Compromising, and Negotiating to Resolve Conflicts and Differences* ... 240
Making a Difference *Jenna Hoyt — The Power of One* ... 243
How does Canadian foreign policy try to balance national interest and internationalism? ... 245
Impact *Canada and Peacekeeping — Myth and Reality* ... 246
Taking Turns *In a globalizing world, should national interest be the focus of foreign policy?* ... 249
Think . . . Participate . . . Research . . . Communicate ... 250

Chapter 11 Internationalism and Nationalism ... 252
Chapter Issue *To what extent do efforts to promote internationalism through world organizations affect nationalism?* ... 253
How have changing world conditions promoted the need for internationalism? ... 254
How have the United Nations' changing international responses affected nationalism? ... 257
Spinbuster *Analyzing Spin in Official Documents* ... 259
Focus on Skills *Using Debate to Persuasively Express Informed Views* ... 262
How do the responses of various international organizations affect nationalism? ... 264
Making a Difference *Mary Simon — A Life Devoted to Activism* ... 267
Taking Turns *How much sovereignty should Canada be willing to give up for the sake of pursuing internationalism?* ... 268
The View from Here *Eric Kierans, Andrew Herod, and J. Michael Adams and Angelo Carfagna on whether internationalism is the only logical response in a globalized world* ... 269
Think . . . Participate . . . Research . . . Communicate ... 270

Chapter 12 Internationalism and Global Issues ... 272
Chapter Issue *To what extent can internationalism effectively address contemporary global issues?* ... 273
What are some contemporary global issues? ... 274
How has internationalism been used to address contemporary global issues? ... 278
Making a Difference *Sheila Watt-Cloutier — Defending the Right to Be Cold* ... 283
Focus on Skills *Communicating Effectively to Express a Point of View* ... 286
Is internationalism always the most effective way of addressing contemporary global issues? ... 288
Taking Turns *Is internationalism the only way to address contemporary global issues?* ... 289
The View from Here *Gareth Evans, Srgjan Kerim, and Shashi Tharoor on whether the UN will remain a useful tool for dealing with global issues in the 21st century* ... 291
Think . . . Participate . . . Research . . . Communicate ... 292

Related Issue 4
To What Extent Should Individuals and Groups in Canada Embrace a National Identity?
The Big Picture ... 295
Your Challenge *Participate in a four-corners debate on the related-issue question, then develop a class consensus on the course issue* ... 296

Chapter 13 Visions of Canada ... 298
Chapter Issue *To what extent have visions of Canadian identity evolved?* ... 299
What is Canada? ... 300
Focus on Skills *Comparing Various Narratives* ... 302
How and why did early visions of Canada emerge? ... 304

The View from Here *Shingwaukonse, Antoine-Aimé Dorion, and Thomas D'Arcy McGee on visions of Canada before Confederation* ... 306
To what extent did various early visions of Canada meet people's needs? ... 308
Taking Turns *What vision of Canada meets your needs?* ... 310
Impact *The Ukrainian Experience in Canada* ... 312
How is the evolution of various visions of Canada reflected in the country today? ... 316
Making a Difference *Neil Bissoondath — Challenging Multiculturalism* ... 317
Think... Participate... Research... Communicate ... 318

Chapter 14 Canadian Identity ... 320
Chapter Issue *To what extent have attempts to promote a national identity been successful?* ... 321

How have symbols and myths been used to promote a national identity? ... 322
Making a Difference *Jowi Taylor and George Rizsanyi — The Six String Nation Guitar* ... 323
How have institutions been used to promote a national identity in Canada? ... 325
Spinbuster *Identifying Spin in Commercial and Corporate Communications* ... 329
Focus on Skills *Writing for Different Purposes and Audiences* ... 330
How can government programs and initiatives be used to promote a national identity? ... 332
How can individuals promote a national identity? ... 336
Taking Turns *Is promoting a national identity my responsibility?* ... 337
The View from Here *James Outram, Peter C. Newman, and Dan George on whether Canadians will stop identifying with the outdoors* ... 339
Think... Participate... Research... Communicate ... 340

Chapter 15 The Quest for Canadian Unity ... 342
Chapter Issue *To what extent should Canadian national unity be promoted?* ... 343

What is national unity? ... 344
Making a Difference *Maude Barlow — Passionately Dedicated to Canadian Unity* ... 345
How does the nature of Canada affect national unity? ... 347
The View from Here *Angus Reid, Jean Chrétien, and Ovide Mercredi on bringing Québec into the Constitution* ... 353
Focus on Skills *Confirming or Revising Your View or Opinion* ... 354
GeoReality *Nunavik and the New North* ... 358
How has the changing face of Canada affected national unity? ... 360
Taking Turns *Is economic globalization likely to increase — or decrease — Canadians' sense of national unity?* ... 363
Think... Participate... Research... Communicate ... 364

Chapter 16 Visions of National Identity ... 366
Chapter Issue *To what extent should I embrace a national identity?* ... 367

What are some possible visions of nation? ... 368
What are some possible visions of Canada? ... 371
Making a Difference *Zarqa Nawaz — Breaking Down Stereotypes* ... 373
The View from Here *Michael Adams, Gilles Duceppe, and Will Kymlicka on multiculturalism* ... 377
Taking Turns *Is North American integration a sound idea?* ... 379
Focus on Skills *Honing Oral, Written, and Visual Literacy* ... 382
What is your vision of national identity? ... 384
Think... Participate... Research... Communicate ... 386

Glossary ... 388
Index ... 392
Credits ... 402

Tour of the Textbook

Welcome to *Exploring Nationalism*. These pages provide you with a guided tour of the textbook and are designed to help you understand how *Exploring Nationalism* is set up to help you complete this course successfully.

By the time you finish *Exploring Nationalism*, you will be in a position to respond to the key question for this course: To what extent should we embrace nationalism? As you progress through the book, keep this question in mind as you think about the ideas, points of view, perspectives, and insights you encounter. They will help you formulate a response to this question.

Cover

The cover of *Exploring Nationalism* shows people silhouetted against a stylized map. These images symbolize the concept behind this textbook.

Examine the images carefully. Why do you suppose the artist showed a crowd of people? Why are the people shown with arms raised? Are they angry? Cheering something? Asking for help? Feeling other emotions? Is it important to draw a conclusion about what they are feeling — or should this be left open to interpretation?

And what do you see in the stylized map? What continents and countries are shown? Why do you suppose the artist chose this particular perspective on the world? What does this choice suggest about the content of *Exploring Nationalism*?

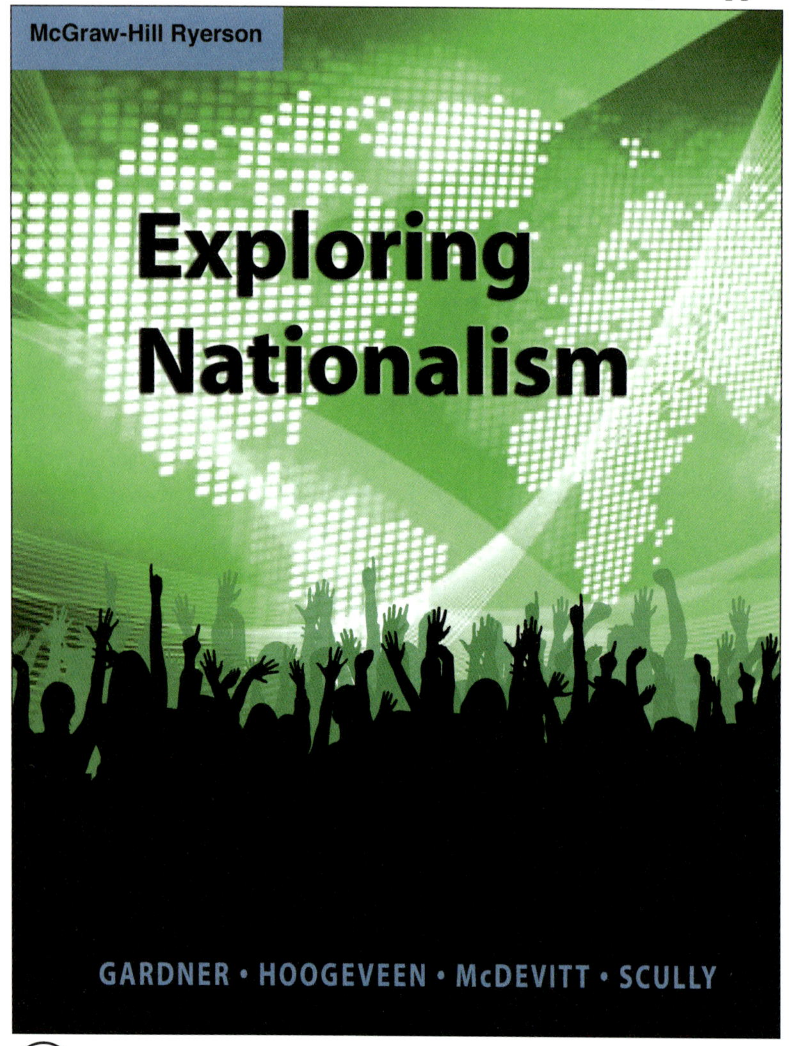

Why might the artist have chosen these particular images for the cover of a textbook that explores nationalism?

The key course-issue question — To what extent should we embrace nationalism? — demands that you analyze the concepts of nation and nationalism, as well as the many different identities that "we" may represent. As you do this, you will discover that nationalism is much more than an emotional response to nationalistic symbols, such as a flag or a national anthem. As the cover suggests, nationalism is open to interpretation, but it also suggests that you, and other people, shape this interpretation.

The title, *Exploring Nationalism*, also communicates a message. It tells you that you are embarking on an exploration that will involve many different points of view and perspectives on nationalism. As you progress through this exploration, allow your mind to remain open to new and exciting ideas and be ready to question your understandings of nationalism and its effect on you — and the world.

How This Book Is Organized

The table of contents shows how *Exploring Nationalism* is organized. The book is divided into four related issues. Each related issue includes four chapters. The section labelled "Looking Ahead" includes three or four questions that serve as the basis of each chapter's exploration of the chapter issue.

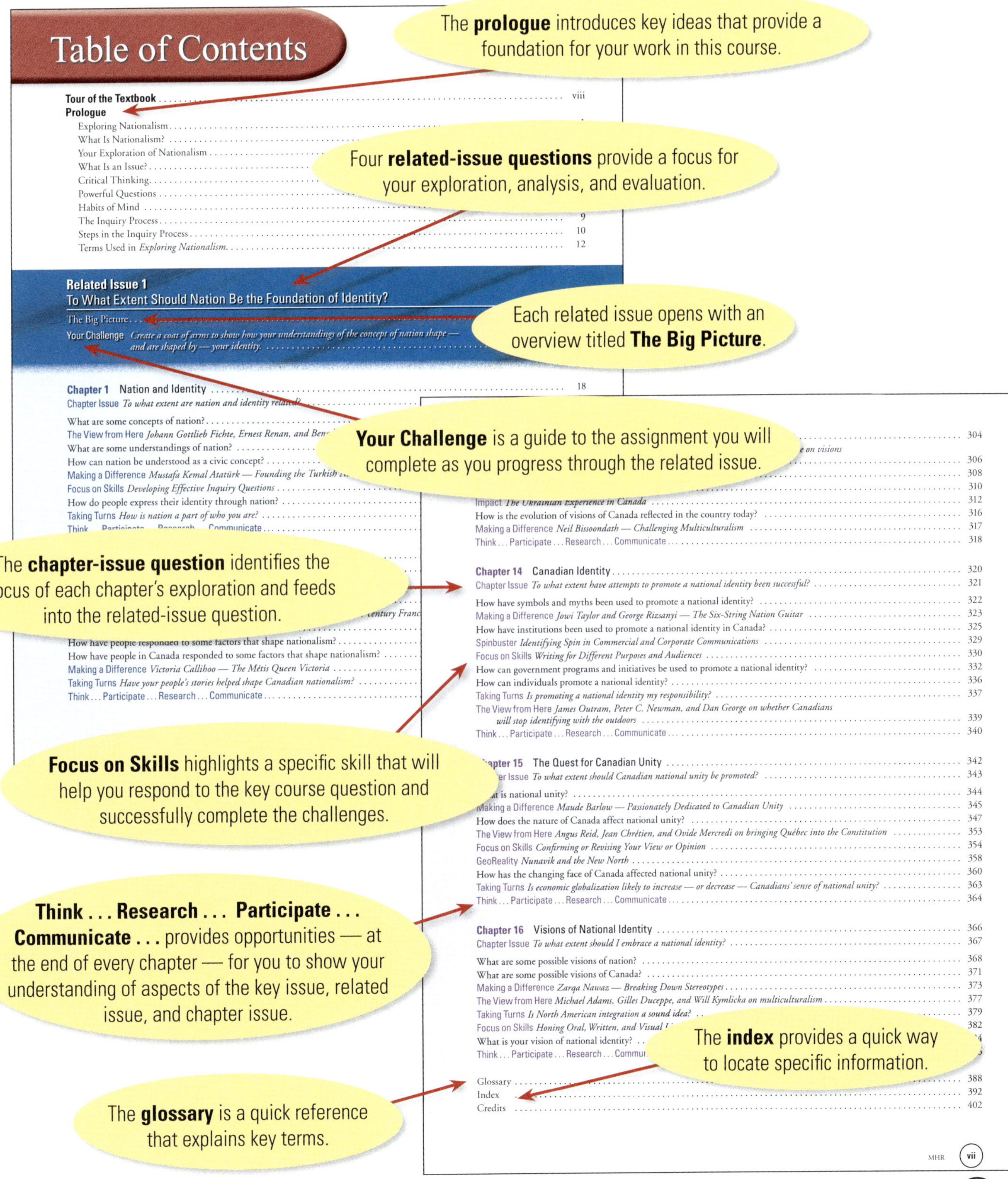

The Big Picture

The Big Picture provides an overview of your journey of exploration through the related issue. Like a trailer for a movie, this opening two-page spread touches on the highlights of the related issue and prepares you for the "feature presentation."

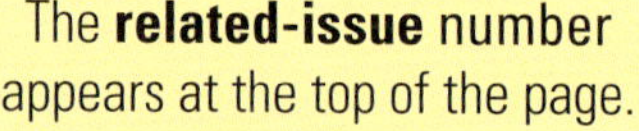

The **related-issue** number appears at the top of the page.

The **related issue** provides the focus for the following four chapters.

The **colour bar** identifies the related issue throughout the four chapters of the section.

RELATED ISSUE 2

To what extent should national interest be pursued?

Key Issue
To what extent should we embrace nationalism?

Related Issue 1	Related Issue 2	Related Issue 3	Related Issue 4
To what extent should nation be the foundation of identity?	To what extent should national interest be pursued?	To what extent should internationalism be pursued?	To what extent should individuals and groups in Canada embrace a national identity?

Chapter 5	Chapter 6	Chapter 7	Chapter 8
National Interest and Foreign Policy	Nationalism and Ultranationalism	Ultranationalism and Crimes against Humanity	National Self-Determination
To what extent do national interest and foreign policy shape each other?	To what extent can nationalism lead to ultranationalism?	To what extent can the pursuit of ultranationalism lead to crimes against humanity?	To what extent should national self-determination be pursued?
How are nationalism and national interest related? How has national interest shaped foreign policy? How has foreign policy shaped national interest?	What is ultranationalism? How does ultranationalism develop? How have people responded to ultranationalism?	What are crimes against humanity? How has ultranationalism caused crimes against humanity? What are some contemporary consequences of ultranationalism?	What is national self-determination? What are some effects of pursuing national self-determination? What are some effects on Canada of pursuing national self-determination? What are some unintended consequences of pursuing national self-determination?

THE BIG PICTURE

Your personal interests, such as your career choices and your health and well-being, are not fixed. They change constantly — as you change, as your needs change, and as the world around you changes.

You can control some of the events that shape your decisions about what is in your interests. If, for example, you plan to become a health care professional, you can choose an educational path that will improve your chances of achieving this goal.

But not everything that affects your interests is in your control. An unexpected accident, an inheritance, or a life-altering emotional experience may prompt a change in the focus of your interests. You may suddenly need to leave school, adopt a different lifestyle, or develop new interests that have a deeper and more personal meaning. In addition, your ideas about what is in your interests may change as you mature. But no matter how you change, pursuing a course that is in your interests requires planning, thought, and an understanding of the changing influences that affect you.

Like you, countries and nations also have interests, and these interests, too, are shaped by events, some of which cannot be controlled. A global epidemic such as SARS, for example, requires an immediate response that may lead to a shift in priorities. But other interests, such as achieving economic prosperity, can be more closely controlled through specific actions and policies.

In Related Issue 1, you explored understandings of nation, nationalism, and identity. In this related issue, you will expand this understanding by exploring and analyzing the links that connect nationalism, national interest, ultranationalism, crimes against humanity, and the pursuit of national self-determination.

The chart on the preceding page shows how you will progress through the chapters of Related Issue 2. As you explore this related issue, you will come to appreciate

- that pursuing national interest can result in both positive and negative outcomes
- how ideas about national interest can change as circumstances change
- that points of view and perspectives on national interest differ, and that these differences often affect decisions about how national interest should be pursued
- that the pursuit of national interest may involve pursuing national self-determination

111

The **key issue** reminds you of the overarching issue for the course.

The **organization chart** maps the structure of the entire related issue.

Visuals provide clues about what will be covered in the related issue.

Your Challenge

Each related issue presents a challenge. The challenge appears at the beginning of the related issue so you know ahead of time what assignment you may be required to complete. This helps you think about, develop, and prepare the ideas and materials you will need to successfully complete the challenge as you progress through the related issue.

Specific instructions explain what the challenge involves.

The **Checklist for Success** is a quick review of how various elements of your challenge may be evaluated. This checklist is based on the evaluation rubric and provides a self-assessment tool to help you complete the challenge successfully.

Your Challenge

Create a coat of arms to show how your understandings of the concept of nation shape — and are shaped by — your identity, and be prepared to explain how your coat of arms represents your response to the question for this related issue:

To what extent should nation be the foundation of identity?

✔ Checklist for Success

Use this checklist to ensure that your finished product includes everything necessary to be successful.

My Knowledge and Understanding

- ☑ My symbols illustrate my understanding of the connections between my identity and nation.
- ☑ My criteria indicate my understanding of the related-issue question.
- ☑ My notes show the underlying meaning of my coat of arms.
- ☑ My responses to questions show my understanding of the purpose of this challenge.

My Selection, Analysis, and Evaluation of Information

- ☑ My criteria guided my research.
- ☑ My coat of arms is based on my criteria.
- ☑ My symbols, information, and notes reflect my understanding of the related-issue question.

My Coat of Arms

- ☑ My coat of arms is interesting and engaging.
- ☑ My notes are complete and support my coat of arms.
- ☑ My use of language and references is appropriate.
- ☑ My responses to questions are positive and constructive.

Your Coat of Arms

A coat of arms presents the heritage, goals, values, and aspirations of the individual or collective it represents. When Michaëlle Jean, for example, was appointed governor general of Canada in 2005, she created the personal coat of arms shown on the following page.

Each element of Jean's coat of arms sends a message about who she is, and each element of your coat of arms should do the same. This message may reflect past glories and connections, and it may also provide a basis for future actions. A coat of arms says, "This is who I am, in body and soul." A motto often makes this meaning clear.

As you progress through the four chapters of this related issue, you will develop understandings of nation — and how this concept influences, and is influenced by, aspects of your individual and collective identity. You will use these understandings to create and present a coat of arms representing you or a collective you choose.

You may present your coat of arms in one of several forms:

- a computer-generated graphic
- a collage
- a drawing or painting
- a combination of forms or one you choose yourself

You will also prepare notes to attach to your presentation. These notes may be presented in a separate booklet, on separate screens if you are using computer software, or in another format of your choice. Your notes will help others understand your coat of arms.

Your notes will conclude with your personal response to the related-issue question.

What Your Coat of Arms Will Include

To show the relationship between your identity and your understandings of nation, you will develop symbols to place on your coat of arms. For each symbol, your notes should include

- a description
- the reason for your choice
- an explanation of the connection(s) between the symbol, your identity, and your understandings of nation

Keep in mind that you may decide that nation should not play a role as a foundation of your identity. If this is the case, the symbols you choose should reflect this position.

16

Creating and Assembling Your Coat of Arms

Step 1

Decide on the form your coat of arms will take. This will affect the symbols you include.

Decide whether your coat of arms will represent you, your family, or another collective.

Step 2

Think about the symbols Michaëlle Jean included on her coat of arms and how these symbols reflect her feelings about the connections between her identity and nation. What criteria do you think Jean might have used when choosing these symbols?

Develop two or three criteria to help you decide which connections you will highlight on your coat of arms. On the basis of the criteria you choose, prepare a motto that expresses their purpose and meaning. You may revise your criteria as you work through the related issue.

As you progress through this related issue, keep notes about the aspects of nation and identity that best fit your criteria. You may wish to keep your notes in a chart similar to the one shown.

Step 3

As you complete each chapter and add more notes to your chart, share your work with a partner and your teacher. Use this feedback to revise and refine your coat of arms.

Step 4

At the conclusion of the related issue, organize your symbols, notes, and information into your final presentation: a coat of arms. Be prepared to respond to questions about the meaning and purpose of the symbols you have used — and how they show your response to the related-issue question.

Notes for My Coat of Arms

Criterion	Evidence	Possible Symbol
What aspects of nation inspire feelings of pride?	Singing "O Canada." I'm Canadian, but my heritage is Sri Lankan, so I was proud when Sri Lanka made it to the 2007 Cricket World Cup final.	Maple leaf Sri Lankan lion

Governor General Michaëlle Jean's Personal Coat of Arms

1. Sand dollar — A sea creature found on Canada's Atlantic and Pacific shores. For Jean, this creature is a talisman.
2. Royal crown — Symbolizes Jean's role as the queen's representative in Canada and the governor general's duty to serve all Canadians.
3. Conch shell and broken chain — Refers to a sculpture that stands in the main square of Port au Prince, Haiti, Jean's birthplace. The sculpture, by Albert Mangonès, shows an escaped slave blowing a conch shell as a call to arms to other slaves around the island. For Jean, this represents her ancestors' victory over slavery and is a call for freedom for everyone.
4. Simbi — These two wise water spirits are drawn from Haitian culture. They comfort souls and purify troubled waters. For Jean, they also represent the important role of women in working toward social justice.
5. Palm tree — A symbol of peace in Haiti.
6. Pine tree — A symbol of the natural riches of Canada.
7. Briser les solitudes — A motto that means "breaking down solitudes." This French motto represents Jean's goal as governor general.
8. Desiderantes meliorem patriam — These Latin words mean "They desire a better country" and are the motto of the Order of Canada.
9. Insignia of the Order of Canada — As governor general, Jean presents the Order of Canada to people who have contributed to making Canada a better country.

17

Steps provide specific instructions for organizing, developing, and completing your challenge.

An **illustration** provides an organizer or an example of part of the challenge to help you organize your work or envision what your completed challenge might look like.

Chapter Openers

Every chapter opens with a two-page spread. On the left page is a visual or collage of visuals designed to provide insight into the related and chapter issues, as well as to spark thought and discussion.

The **course issue** is always identified at the top of the page.

The **chapter number** and **title** appear below the colour bar.

The **visuals** provide a point of view or perspective on the related and chapter issues.

TO WHAT EXTENT SHOULD WE EMBRACE NATIONALISM?

CHAPTER 10 Foreign Policy and Internationalism

Figure 10-1 This collage shows various views of Canada's peacekeeping monument near Parliament Hill in Ottawa. Canada is the only country that has created a monument to peacekeeping forces. The name of the monument, *Reconciliation*, illustrates the central purpose of peacekeeping: to keep the peace long enough for reconciliation to take place.

The **chapter issue** is presented in the colour bar across the top of the page. This is the focus of the chapter.

An **introduction** provides insight into the visuals.

Questions guide you to think about the visuals and explore their connections to the chapter and related issues.

CHAPTER ISSUE

To what extent can foreign policy promote internationalism?

Reconciliation, Canada's peacekeeping monument, was designed by sculptor Jack Harman, urban designer Richard Henriquez, and landscape architect Cornelia Oberlander. The monument depicts three peacekeepers — two men and a woman — keeping watch from a wall amid the debris of war. In front of them, a grove of young trees symbolizes peace. In 1988, United Nations peacekeepers won the Nobel Peace Prize for 40 years of tireless effort to keep the peace in various parts of the world. This monument commemorates Canada's contribution to those missions.

Examine the collage carefully, then respond to the following questions:

- What is your initial response to the collage of the peacekeeping monument? Does your sense of national identity influence your response?
- What does the existence of the peacekeeping monument say about Canada?
- Why is the name of this monument significant? What other names might have been chosen for this monument?
- The peacekeeping monument is located in Ottawa, Canada's capital and a city that hosts many tourists. What message might this monument convey to visitors from other countries?

KEY TERMS

economic sanctions

collective security

gross national income

tied aid

Key Terms alert you to vocabulary that is important to understanding concepts. These terms are explained in the chapter and in the glossary.

Looking Ahead

In this chapter, you will develop responses to the following questions as you explore the extent to which foreign policy can promote internationalism:

- How do countries set foreign policy?
- How can states promote internationalism through foreign policy?
- How does Canadian foreign policy try to balance national interest and internationalism?

Looking Ahead sets out the inquiry questions that form the focus of the explorations in the chapter. You will find these questions repeated as the main headings in the chapter.

My Journal on Nationalism

Look again at the photograph of the earth rising. Think about how you could use photographs to express your current ideas about nationalism. Date your ideas and keep them in your journal, notebook, learning log, portfolio, or computer file so that you can return to them as you progress this course.

My Journal on Nationalism encourages you to rethink, re-evaluate, and reshape your evolving understandings of nationalism.

231

Special Features

The special features present information, data, ideas, and issues in different ways.

In the psychological sense, there is no Canadian nation as there is an American or French nation. There is a legal and geographical entity, but the nation does not exist. For there are no objects that all Canadians share as objects of national feeling.

— *Charles Hanley, in* Nationalism in Canada, *1966*

Voices

A quotation that supports an idea or provides an alternative point of view or perspective.

Web Connection

To find out more about the Great Depression, go to this web site and follow the links.

www.ExploringNationalism.ca

Web Connection

The web address in this feature takes you to a central site that provides connections that will expand your research and exploration of an issue.

When immigrants become Canadian citizens, they are required to repeat the following oath:

I swear [or affirm] that I will be faithful and bear true allegiance to Her Majesty Queen Elizabeth the Second, Queen of Canada, Her Heirs and Successors, and that I will faithfully observe the laws of Canada and fulfil my duties as a Canadian citizen.

FYI

These are interesting facts and ideas that enhance your understanding of the issues. This feature often provides a broader context for exploring the issues.

CheckBack

You read about the rise of Turkish nationalism in Chapter 1.

CheckForward

You will read more about Rwanda and Roméo Dallaire in Chapter 10.

CheckForward and CheckBack

These icons appear at various points. They direct you to chapters where the ideas you are reading about are explored further.

Activity Icon

Quick activities designed to help you think about and explore the issues you are reading about.

With a partner, return to the chapter-opening photograph of the seal hunt protest (Figure 4-1, p. 88) and choose one character or group mentioned in the questions on page 89. Or choose the Ryan Smyth fan mentioned on page 90.

Discuss the loyalties involved in the situation you chose and create a web or other graphic to show them visually. Use colour and shape to indicate which loyalties are nationalist and which are non-nationalist. Identify contending loyalties by adding connecting lines or another graphic element. Use a numbering system or another method to rate the importance of each loyalty shown. Add a title and a legend to your graphic, and be prepared to explain your judgments.

Explain your graphic to a small group and respond to their questions and comments.

Reflect and Respond

These activities conclude each inquiry section by encouraging you to reflect on aspects of the related issue, the chapter issue, and the inquiry question. They provide opportunities to assess your understanding and review ideas from various points of view and perspectives.

How might a crisis affect people's sense of nationalism and national identity?

The students responding to this question are Pearl, who lives in St. Albert and whose great-great-great grandfather immigrated from China to work on the Canadian Pacific Railway; Blair, who lives in Edmonton and whose heritage is Ukrainian, Scottish, and German; and Amanthi, who lives in Edson and whose parents immigrated from Sri Lanka.

My great-grandfather was born in Canada, but he had family in China — and they have told him what it was like when Japan invaded. China was in such chaos that he didn't hear from some of his relatives for years. Sometimes he worried that they had all been killed. He told me that people were really scared, and yeah, some people betrayed their friends and neighbours to get on the good side of the Japanese. But lots of people didn't. People helped one another whenever they could. Even strangers. So in some ways, the hardships drew people together — and deepened their sense of Chinese national identity.

The way my great-uncle Dmytro tells it, what people in Ukraine went through in 1932 to '33 was caused by Stalin's fear of Ukrainians' strong nationalist loyalties — and these ties still exist, even though we're scattered in different countries. Ukrainians were resisting Stalin in the 1930s, and to force them to do what he wanted, he took the grain from the farmers. He just let them starve. That famine was definitely created by someone who hated my nation, but it sure didn't destroy it. Just the opposite.

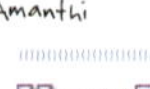

I liked what Louise Arbour said about what people do in a crisis. If you didn't have food or a safe place to live, you might not be so concerned about things like equality and freedom — and even national identity. You'd have more important concerns. In some ways, just talking about national identity is a luxury that people like us here in Canada enjoy. I'll bet that if we lived in a one-party state that controlled the media, we wouldn't even hear a voice like Arbour's. If what she said wasn't what the government wanted people to hear, then her words wouldn't be broadcast in the media or put in a textbook.

Your Turn How would you respond to the question Pearl, Blair, and Amanthi are answering? Explain the reasons for your answer.

Taking Turns

In every chapter, three students respond to a question suggested by the focus of the chapter. "Your Turn" invites your response to the same question.

Focus on Skills
A two-page feature that highlights a specific skill in every chapter. Honing these skills will help you achieve success in this course, in other educational programs, and in many aspects of life.

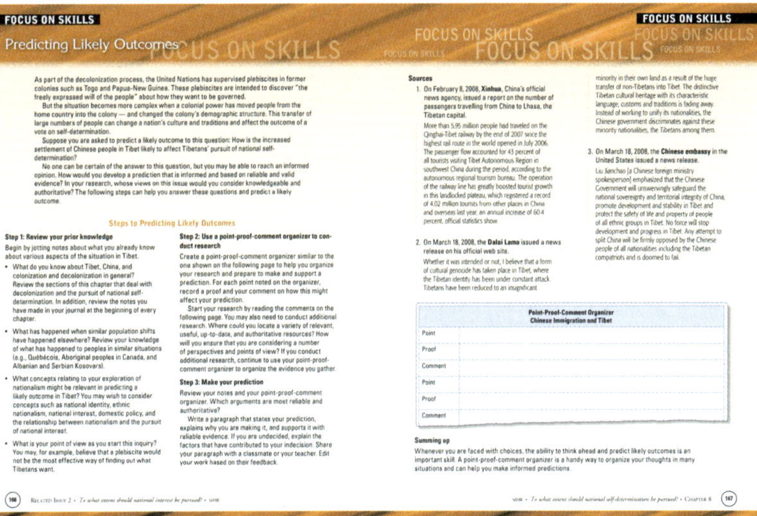

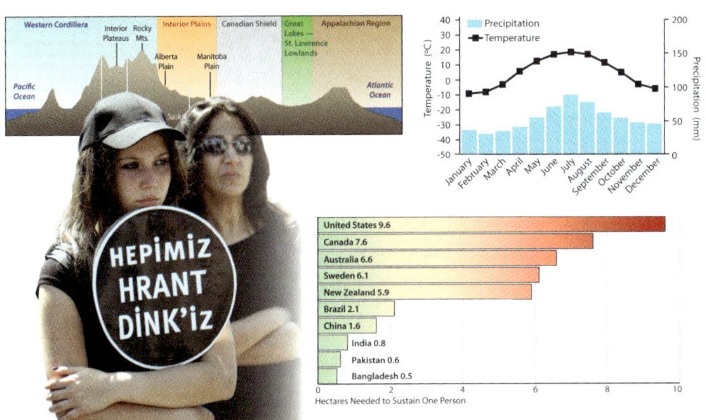

Photographs, charts, graphs, and other visuals
These visuals support your learning and provide context for the material being studied. The photo captions often include challenging questions designed to stimulate thought and reflection.

Should people stop looking back to past events and focus on the present and the future?

Up for Discussion
Questions in the margin are designed to provoke thought and discussion by challenging an aspect of the narrative and encouraging you to examine the way you view issues.

Hudson Bay
Canada
Baffin Island
Victoria Island
Banks Island
Queen Elizabeth Islands
United States
Atlantic Ocean
Greenland (Denmark)
Ellesmere Island
Arctic Ocean
Bering Sea
North Pole
Lomonosov Ridge
Norway
Russia
Legend
Area beyond National Zones (Administered by International Seabed Authority)
Equidistance Line between Adjacent Countries
Agreed National Border
Northwest Passage
sea level
200 m
1000 m
2000 m
3000 m
4000 m
5000 m
6000 m
7000 m
sea depth
0 500 1000 1500
kilometres

Maps
Show where events happened, provide information in a graphic format, and expand the meaning and context of the ideas and issues you are exploring.

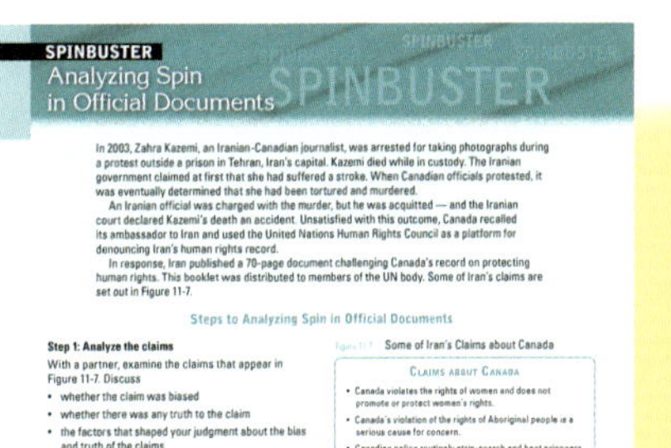

Spinbuster
Helps you understand how the media and others shape ideas and influence public opinion, enabling you to effectively analyze and evaluate information from a variety of sources.

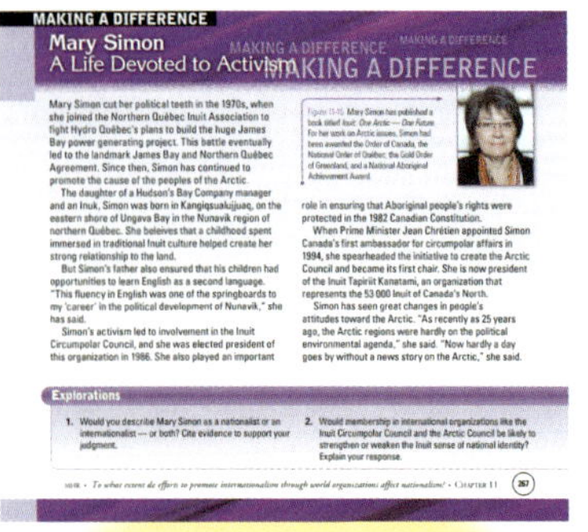

Making a Difference
Presents a brief, highly focused examination of an individual or organization whose contributions have shaped — or been shaped by — an issue. They often show how one person can bring about change.

Impact
Focuses on a specific aspect of an issue. These features highlight how a group, place, person, or event has shaped — and been shaped by — the issue and encourage you to think critically about issues.

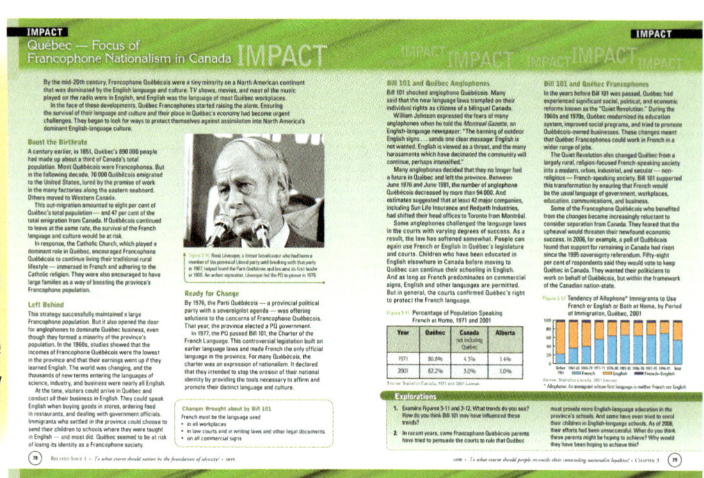

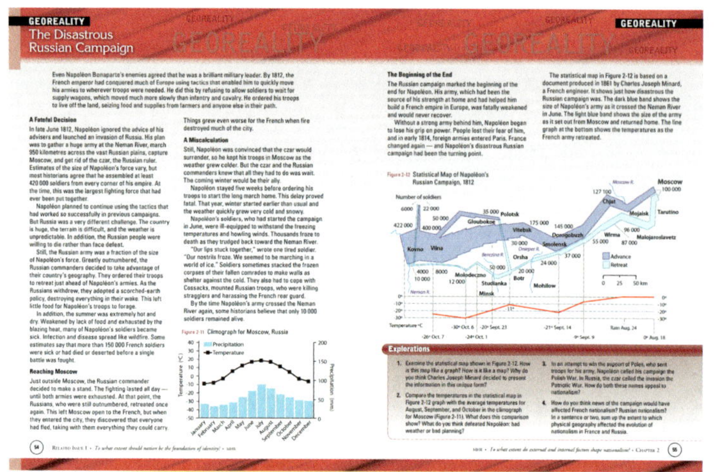

The View from Here
A one-page feature that provides an opportunity to deepen your understanding of an issue by exploring, analyzing, and evaluating what various people have written or said about it.

GeoReality
Presents geographic perspectives that focus on the connections between nationalism and human, economic, and physical geography. These features help you understand how conflict and co-operation are shaped — and shaped by — geographic factors.

Think . . . Participate . . . Research . . . Communicate . . .
End-of-chapter activities that help reinforce skills and enhance your understanding of the issues as you explore, analyze, evaluate, and debate your responses. In many cases, they shine a different light on some of the issues raised in the chapter.

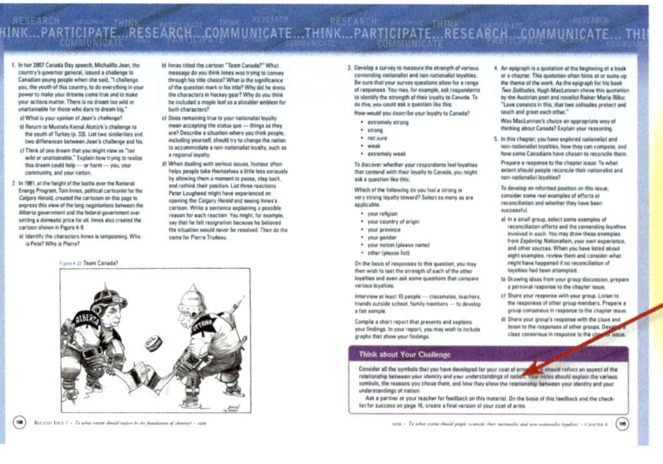

Think about Your Challenge
A reminder of the challenge you are preparing to complete as you progress through the related issue. It provides tips to help you consider approaches and stage your work so that you can achieve success.

PROLOGUE

Exploring Nationalism

CheckForward

You will explore ideas about nation and identity in Chapters 1 to 4.

Exploring Nationalism is built around a single key issue: To what extent should we embrace nationalism?

Before you can address this issue, you must first arrive at an understanding of what nationalism is — and as you progress through this course, you will discover that thinkers have defined this term in various ways. These definitions often place a particular spin on nationalism and reveal people's opinions about whether it is a positive or negative force in the world.

You will also come to understand how nationalism is linked to ideas about nation and identity and to recognize the forces that shape — and are shaped by — nationalism. In addition, you will explore, analyze, and evaluate aspects of internationalism, as well as ultranationalism.

As your understandings of nationalism and related concepts expand, you will develop your own ideas about this phenomenon, and these ideas will equip you to make a reasoned judgment in response to the key-issue question.

Nationalism: The Word

The concept of nation is at the heart of any exploration of nationalism. "Nation" is a root word — and a root concept — from which many other words and concepts, including "nationalism," can be created by adding prefixes or suffixes.

Many of the words based on the root word "nation" are shown in Figure P-1. Examine this concept map and identify some of the prefixes (e.g., inter-) and suffixes (e.g., -al) that have been added to the word "nation." Explain how each changes its meaning.

As you progress through this course, you will encounter many terms — like "nationalism" — that include the suffix "-ism." When you see this suffix, you know you are looking at a noun. This suffix often signals that the noun in question refers to an ideology — a system of ideas about how society should work (e.g., "conservatism," "feminism," "imperialism"). In the case of "nationalism," this suffix signals that this word is referring to an ideology about nation.

On the basis of your knowledge of the meaning of the prefixes "inter-," "ultra-" and "supra-" and the meaning of the suffix "-ism," predict the meaning of the words "internationalism," "ultranationalism," and "supranationalism." Keep your predictions in a journal, learning log, portfolio, or computer file so that you can refer to and refine them as you progress through this course.

Figure P-1 Nation and Related Words

What Is Nationalism?

Definitions of Nationalism

Oxford Canadian Dictionary
1 a patriotic feeling, principles, etc. **b** an extreme form of this. **2** a policy of national independence.

George Orwell in "Notes on Nationalism," 1945
[Nationalism is] the habit of identifying oneself with a single nation or other unit, placing it beyond good and evil and recognising no other duty than that of advancing its interests . . . Nationalism . . . is inseparable from the desire for power. The abiding purpose of every nationalist is to secure more power and more prestige, *not* for himself but for the nation or other unit in which he has chosen to sink his own individuality.

Ernest Gellner in *Nations and Nationalism*, 1983
Nationalism is a political principle which holds that the political and the national unit should be congruent [match].

Michael Ignatieff in *Blood and Belonging*, 1993
Nationalism is a doctrine which holds (1) that the world's peoples are divided into nations, (2) that these nations should have the right to self-determination, and (3) that full self-determination requires statehood.

Adrian Hastings in *The Construction of Nationhood: Ethnicity, Religion and Nationalism*, 1996
[Nationalism] arises chiefly where and when a particular ethnicity or nation feels itself threatened in regard to its own proper character, extent or importance, either by external attack or by the state system of which it has hitherto formed part; but nationalism can also be stoked up to fuel the expansionist imperialism of a powerful nation-state, though this is still likely to be done under the guise of an imagined threat or grievance.

As this course unfolds and you learn more about nationalism, you are likely to find that your views on this phenomenon will change. To help you keep track of these changes, a brief activity titled "My Journal on Nationalism" begins every chapter and asks you to note your current understandings of nationalism.

At the end of the course, you can use this record to trace the evolution of your thinking about nationalism. This process will help you respond to the key-issue question, which is also one focus of the challenge for Related Issue 4.

Points of View* and Perspectives* on Nationalism

The word "nationalism" did not even exist in English till the middle of the 19th century — and thinkers have been debating its meaning ever since. Just as thinkers disagree on the meaning of "nationalism," they also disagree on when peoples began to feel a sense of nation and nationalism.

- Some believe that the concepts of nation and nationalism have existed for as long as human beings, even if peoples did not use these words to describe the sense of belonging they felt.
- Others believe that nations and nationalism have existed for a very long time, though peoples have felt and expressed these concepts in different ways at different times. Some argue that these ideas are rooted in early societies, such as Ancient Greece and Rome or the China of Emperor Shi Huangdi, who united the country for a brief time in the third century BCE.
- Still others believe that ideas about nation and nationalism are relatively recent. But even these thinkers disagree on how recent. Some, for example, argue that current ideas about nationalism began in the 18th century with the American and French revolutions.

To develop a sense of the range of points of view and perspectives on "nationalism," scan the definitions in the margin of this page. How are they similar? How are they different? Why do you suppose the range is so broad? If you were required, right now, to choose one of these definitions to defend, which would you select? Explain the reasons for your judgment.

Think about this choice — and the reasons for your judgment — when you write the first entry in your journal on nationalism. You will do this at the beginning of Chapter 1.

As you progress through this course and learn more about how you, your community, your country, and the world are affected by nationalism, you will encounter many more points of view and perspectives on this phenomenon — and you will also develop the skills necessary to draw your own conclusions about the extent to which you should embrace it.

* Alberta Education has defined "point of view" as a view held by a single person. A "perspective" refers to the shared view of a group or collective. These usages are reflected in *Exploring Nationalism*.

Your Exploration of Nationalism

Exploring Nationalism provides you with many opportunities to explore, analyze, and evaluate points of view and perspectives on nationalism. Your goal as you progress through the course is to draw on these points of view and perspectives to develop a response to the key-issue question: To what extent should we embrace nationalism?

To help guide your exploration, analysis, and evaluation of possible responses to this question, four related issues are identified. Each evolves from — and feeds into — the key-issue question.

Within each related issue, four chapters each focus on an issue that evolves from — and feeds into — the related-issue question. And within each chapter, inquiry questions are designed to guide your exploration, analysis, and evaluation of topics raised by the chapter-issue question, the related-issue question, and the key-issue question.

The following chart shows the relationship between the issue and inquiry questions. To examine these questions in greater detail, turn to the table of contents.

Figure P-2 Structure of *Exploring Nationalism*

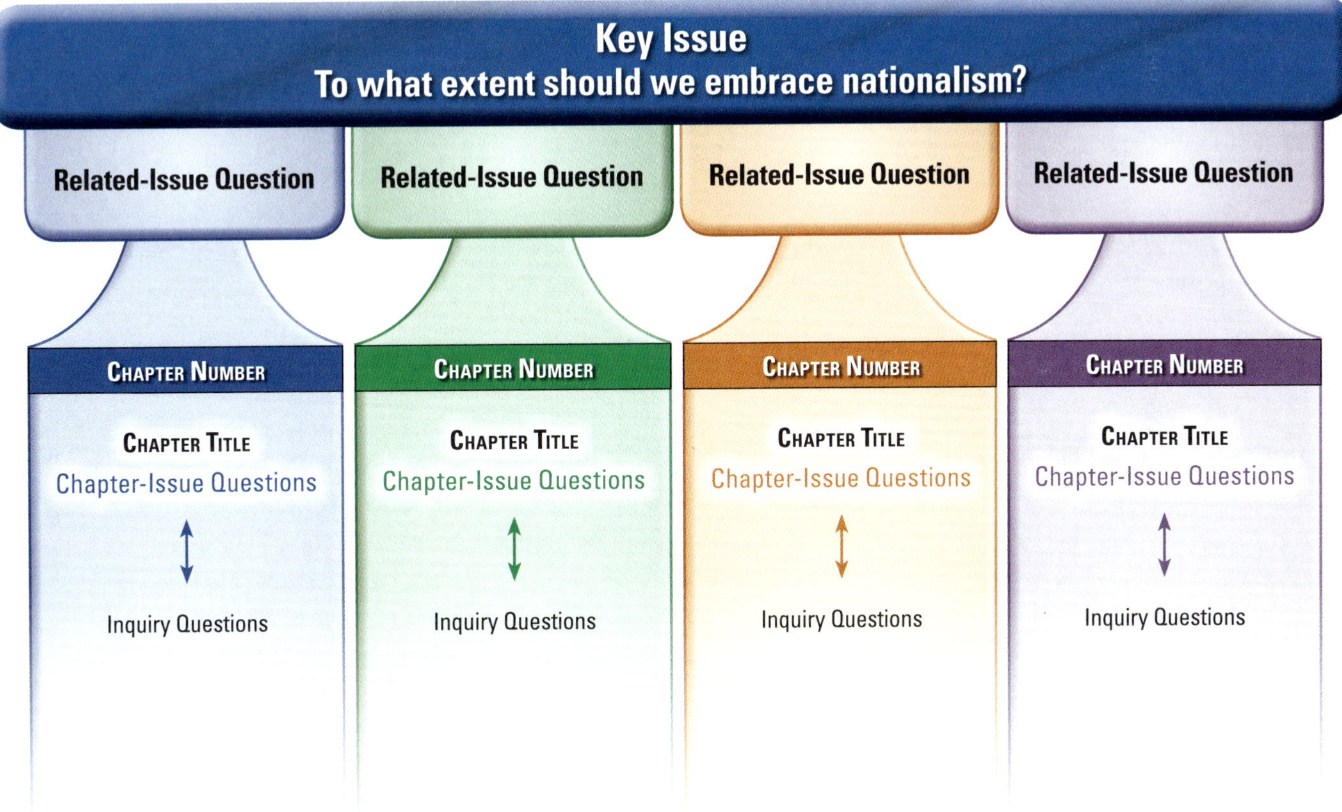

What Is an Issue?

Figure P-2 shows how issue questions provide a framework for *Exploring Nationalism* — but what is an issue?

An issue is a question or situation that involves thoughtful, well-informed, and well-meaning people in honest and sincere dialogue over a response or solution. An issue can also be a dilemma that requires people to make a choice or decision that involves responsible action. Most issues have no easy — or even correct — solutions, but a response or decision is required nonetheless.

An issue is more than simply a disagreement. People can disagree over whether they enjoyed a movie or which hockey team they support, but these disagreements are not issues because no decision, action, or change in policy is expected as a result.

Climate change, for example, is *not* an issue, though there may be disagreement over whether it exists. What to do about climate change *is* an issue because thoughtful people might arrive at different decisions and propose radically different solutions. As a result, clarifying the issue question is very important — because the term "issue" may be used carelessly.

Figure P-3 At the ceremony that opens the Olympics, members of national teams traditionally wear their country's uniform and march into the stadium as a group behind their country's flag. This photograph shows the Canadian Olympic team in 2004.

Dealing with issues requires you to gather information, analyze various points of view and perspectives, and develop criteria for making judgments. This process requires you to consider values, beliefs, worldviews, past experiences, and expected outcomes.

Elements of Issues

Deconstructing the elements of issues — separating them into component parts so that they can be analyzed — can help you understand the debate over issues and develop a process for arriving at an informed judgment about ways of resolving them. Many issues involve a combination of the following elements.

Policy — What should individuals, organizations, groups, or governments do? These questions involve taking action or making a change. They require you to think about solutions that are in the best interests of the community or society. Here is an example:

Should the federal government try to meet the targets set out in the Kyoto Protocol?

If the answer is yes, the government would make the change that is in the best interests of the broader community and develop a policy or pass a law to bring about the change.

Values — What is good or bad, right or wrong, more or less important or desirable? These questions involve ethical and moral conduct or beliefs. They require you to think about value systems and ask yourself, Why do I believe certain things? Here is an example:

Should violent video games be banned?

Answers to these questions provide a basis for improving the quality of life. Governments or groups would act in accordance with some general goals of society.

Definition — What is the meaning of a word or term? These questions explore how language is used and how concepts are understood. They require you to think about how to classify or categorize ideas. Here is an example:

Does a market economy offer the best hope for prosperity?

Responses to questions like these may turn on how terms are defined or understood. In the example, it may be important to define the terms "market economy" and "prosperity." The way terms are defined often dictates the action that is taken — or whether action is taken at all.

Fact — What is true or correct? These questions concern the truth of a matter. They require you to examine and weigh evidence. Is the information correct? Here is an example:

Is extracting oil from the tar sands damaging the environment beyond repair?

These are difficult issues because they involve "facts." There may be legitimate disagreement over how to weigh the factual evidence and what evidence to accept or reject.

History — Was an action justified, or did an event have a positive outcome? These questions examine the merits of past actions or events to inform future choices. They require you to judge — in context — decisions made in the past. Here is an example:

Should the United States and its allies have invaded Iraq?

The way past events are interpreted often influences contemporary decisions.

Figure P-4 At the ceremony that closes the Olympics, athletes from all countries traditionally mingle as they march into the stadium together. In this photograph, an athlete displays the flags of various countries during the closing ceremonies. Think about this tradition and the one displayed in Figure P-3 on the previous page. What statement do you think these Olympic traditions make about nationalism? What elements of issues are involved in this question?

Practise Identifying and Asking Issue Questions

With a partner, examine the following questions and classify the issue elements involved in each. You do not need to answer the questions. Discuss whether any of the questions involve more than one issue element. Then, for each category, work together to create an issue question of your own. Each of your questions may include more than one issue element.

1. Is nationalism a positive or negative force in the world?
2. Was Pierre Trudeau's National Energy Program a power grab by Ottawa?
3. Is pursuing nationhood a legitimate goal?
4. Should Canada accept more immigrants to strengthen the economy?
5. Is the concept of nation irrelevant in today's globalized world?

Critical Thinking

Figure P-5 Criteria and Critical Thinking

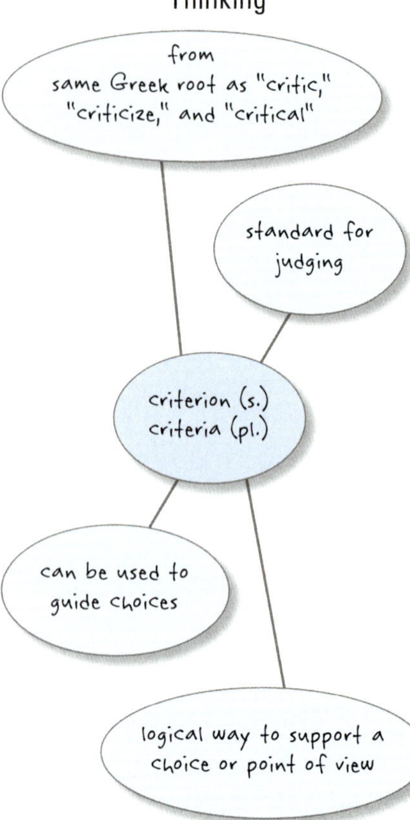

When you weigh evidence, analyze points of view and perspectives, and evaluate consequences in response to issue questions, you are engaging in the process of critical thinking. Critical thinking requires you to make reasoned judgments about issues by considering evidence and using clear criteria to guide your decisions.

An effective critical thinker

- considers all relevant evidence
- develops criteria for making reasoned judgments
- makes judgments on the basis of these criteria
- works on developing the character traits, or habits of mind (see p. 8), that promote effective decision making

You make choices every day — at school, at home, with friends, and at work. You may, for example, be called upon to decide whether to participate in an after-school activity, whether to support a friend in school elections, or how to plan your courses for the year. Using criteria to guide your decisions will help you succeed in school, but the benefits of using criteria to make reasoned judgments go well beyond the social studies classroom. Developing effective criteria will ensure that you make the most effective choices when faced with challenges in all aspects of your life.

Choosing Criteria

When developing criteria to guide your judgments

- keep the number of criteria manageable: a minimum of two and a maximum of four
- be sure the criteria reflect only the most important or relevant considerations
- be prepared to alter your criteria if circumstances change (e.g., if new evidence comes to light or if an event or another person's judgment changes your view)

What Criteria Would You Use?

The following cases are imaginary, but they will help you practise your skill at developing criteria to make reasoned judgments. In the first case, two criteria are already filled in. You should choose at least one more criterion. In the second case, only one criterion is filled in. You should choose at least two more criteria. In each case, turn your criteria into questions.

CASE 1

Your school's environment club has brainstormed to create a list of worthy projects. Now, club members must choose one. The selected project should

- be achievable over the course of the school year (Can the project's goals be achieved over the course of the year?)
- be something that will draw widespread student support (Will the project draw widespread student support?)
-
-

CASE 2

Your friends and classmates have decided to nominate you for a position on your school's student government. You must decide whether to accept the nomination. Your decision depends on

- whether you can adjust the hours of your part-time job so that you can attend meetings (Can I adjust the hours of my part-time job so that I can attend meetings?)
-
-
-

Powerful Questions

Asking questions is a key element of learning — and powerful questions require more than a one-word or yes-or-no response. Powerful questions help you uncover trends, understand relationships, and recognize forces that contribute to continuity and bring about change.

Asking powerful questions helps you think critically and provides a focus for all research and inquiry. A powerful question is one that requires a decision or judgment in response — and this decision or judgment should be based on clearly established criteria or evidence.

Powerful questions

- generate curiosity, encourage creativity, and lead to more questions
- are open-ended — they do not have one correct answer and may even have no "correct" answer
- require answers that promote deeper understanding
- are thought-provoking, requiring you to make choices, decisions, and judgments that can be supported by evidence or criteria

Exploring Nationalism is built around powerful questions. These are the issue questions that provide the structure for this textbook and set out the key course issue, each of the four related issues, and each chapter issue.

Powerful questions often begin with words and phrases like the following. Be careful, though. These words and phrases do not always signal that a question is powerful — and they are not the only words and phrases that can begin powerful questions. It is important to read the question carefully and decide whether it requires you to make a judgment in response.

- Which . . . (e.g., Which form of government is more effective — democracy or dictatorship?)
- What if . . . (e.g., What if John A. Macdonald had not pushed for a cross-country railway?)
- How . . . (e.g., How can a nation such as the Québécois exist within a nation-state such as Canada?)
- Why . . . (e.g., Why is asserting Arctic sovereignty important?)
- Should . . . (e.g., Should the pace of development in the oil sands be slowed down?)
- To what extent (how much) . . . (e.g., To what extent has nationalism been a negative force in the world?)

Powerful Questions

When formulating powerful questions, think about the following:

What . . .
is worth knowing?
is uncertain?
is unclear and needs explanation?
requires exploration?
requires a decision or judgment?
leads to deeper understanding?
connects to other familiar events or developments?
incorporates existing knowledge?
sparks imagination? (e.g., What if . . . ?)
engages people's interest?
requires a shift in point of view or perspective?
makes people think?
requires people to express an informed opinion?

Practise Identifying and Asking Powerful Questions

As you progress through *Exploring Nationalism*, you will be asked to respond to powerful questions — and to develop powerful questions of your own. With a partner, discuss the following questions about Canada and the North Atlantic Treaty Organization and decide which are powerful and which are not.

1. When did the Canadian government decide to join NATO?
2. Why did Canada decide to join NATO?
3. Why should Canada continue to belong to NATO?
4. What is the most important benefit or drawback of Canada's membership in NATO?
5. To what extent does membership in NATO reduce Canadian sovereignty?

Now, choose a topic (e.g., participating in Earth Hour, bullying). Imagine that a speaker will visit your school to discuss this topic. Create three powerful questions to ask your guest.

Habits of Mind

Certain character traits — or habits of mind — promote critical thinking and effective decision making. Whether you are completing a social studies assignment or dealing with other challenges, these habits of mind can help you achieve success at school and in life.

I'm an active thinker.

I explore alternatives and consider their strengths and weaknesses.

I persevere. The first — or most obvious — solution is not always the best.

I resist pressure to adopt opinions just because they are popular.

I think about how I'm thinking about an issue.

I'm curious.

I do not take everything at face value. I investigate beyond the obvious.

I take time to think about things and explore unanswered questions.

I look for various sources of information and expert opinions.

I'm flexible.

I'm willing to change my tactics or approach.

I allow my beliefs to change until I have enough evidence to support a definite point of view.

I don't reject ideas just because they are contrary to my point of view.

I'm ready to compromise and take my thinking in new directions.

I'm open-minded.

I'm open to the views of others, especially when their views are different from my own.

I judge ideas on the basis of their strengths and weaknesses.

I identify and examine my own biases.

I explore beyond my personal interests and biases.

I'm empathetic.

I listen to and try to understand others' points of view.

I don't pass judgment until I've gathered enough information.

I'm aware of the effects of my actions on others.

I choose my words carefully and try to use respectful language.

I'm collaborative.

I'm willing to work with others to brainstorm and combine ideas.

I judge the message, not the messenger.

I'm prepared to give — and take — constructive feedback.

I make sure everyone has opportunities to contribute and share ideas.

I'm thoughtful.

I think before I act. I consider the consequences of various alternatives.

I think about my own thinking and examine my biases.

I set goals and understand what I'm trying to achieve. I try to visualize what success will look like.

I recognize that my success is not based on another's failure.

I'm respectful.

I listen carefully to others.

I'm aware of the limits of my knowledge and avoid claiming to know more than I do.

I judge ideas based on their strengths and weaknesses.

I understand that there are seldom single correct answers.

The Inquiry Process

The key-issue question for this course — To what extent should we embrace nationalism? — is a powerful question that presents an issue. To gather the information necessary to respond thoughtfully to this question — and many others — you will need to engage in the inquiry process.

The inquiry process involves formulating an issue question, developing criteria for judgment, developing inquiry questions, creating an inquiry plan, investigating to collect and organize ideas and concepts, analyzing and evaluating information and evidence, reflecting on the evidence and making informed judgments based on clear criteria, and communicating these judgments. Variety and depth are the keys to this process.

As you engage in the inquiry process, you will come to understand that ideas and events that occurred in the past often contributed to present-day points of view and perspectives on nation and nationalism — and you will learn to analyze and evaluate how effectively these ideas and events contributed to both continuity and change.

Examine Figure P-6, which illustrates the inquiry process. Why do you think an arrow connects Step 8 to Step 1? What is the significance of this?

Figure P-6 Steps in the Inquiry Process

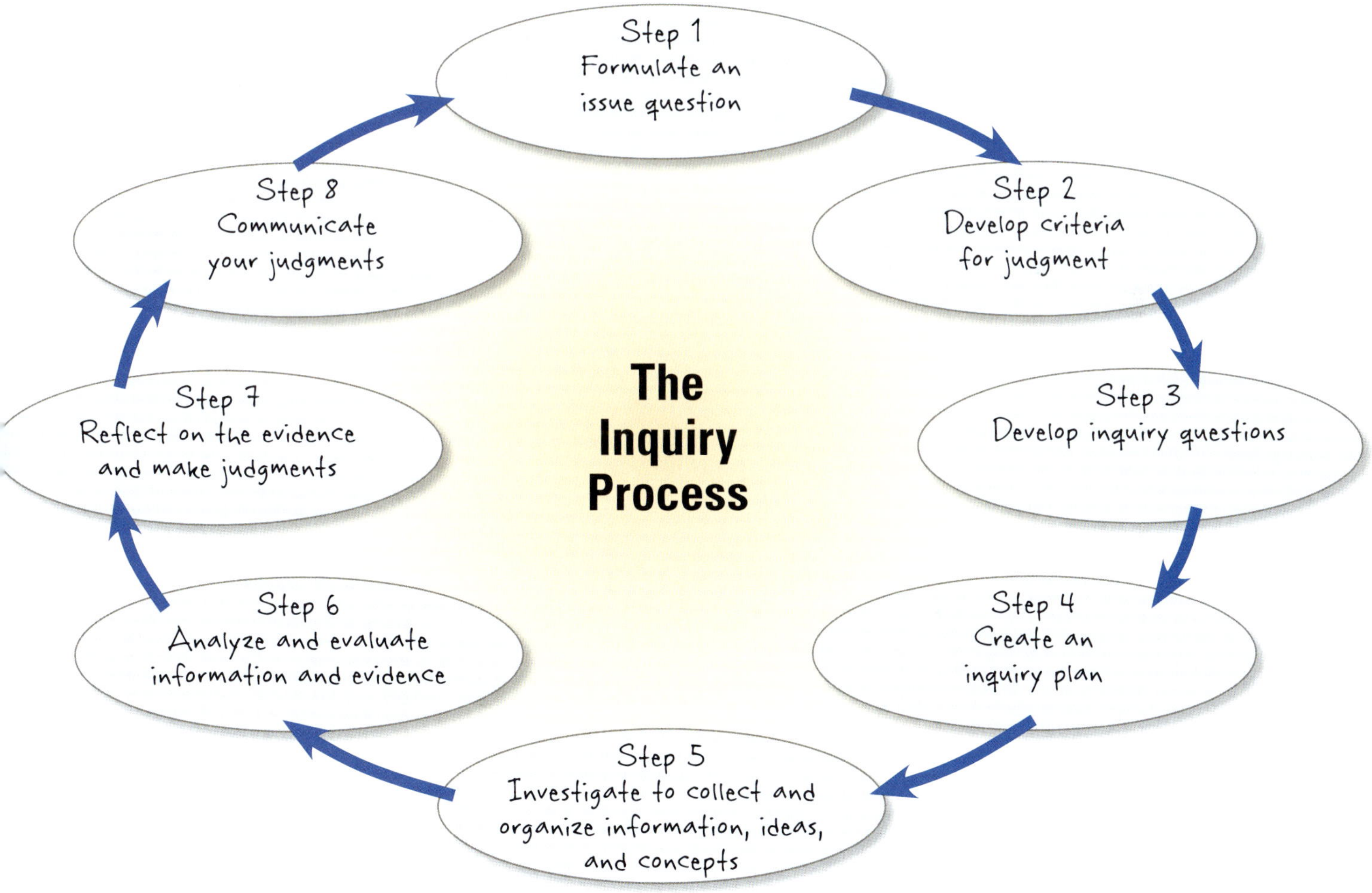

Steps in the Inquiry Process

As you go through the steps of the inquiry process, think about your thinking — to ensure that you are cultivating the habits of mind that will make you a more effective critical thinker. The checklist at the bottom of page 11 can help you do this.

Thoughtful reflection about your own thinking processes is an important part of every stage of the inquiry process. It helps you keep the central issue or challenge in mind as you conduct research, organize evidence, and draw conclusions. Reflection also helps you confirm your conclusions or revise your line of inquiry by asking new questions.

Step 1: Formulate an issue question

The inquiry process begins with a powerful issue question that inspires you to build on your prior knowledge and gather and explore the information needed to develop a response. *Exploring Nationalism* is built around issue questions, but your teacher may also pose issue questions — or you may create your own (see pp. 4–5).

Step 2: Develop criteria for judgment

Think about the issue question that is the focus of your inquiry and draft three or four criteria (see p. 6) you might use to guide the informed judgments you will make in response. At this stage, your criteria should be flexible. Be prepared to revise them as the process unfolds and you gather new information and follow new paths of inquiry.

Step 3: Develop inquiry questions

Examine and deconstruct the issue question. This deconstruction may provide the first of your inquiry questions.

Then explore a general source, such as *Exploring Nationalism* or an encyclopedia entry, to develop an overview of the issue. Think about what you have read and create a list of inquiry questions to guide your investigation and help you gather the information and evidence you need to make an informed judgment in response to the issue question.

Step 4: Create an inquiry plan

Once you have formulated your inquiry questions, decide where, when, and how you will conduct your inquiry. This may involve setting a schedule for completing various phases of your exploration, deciding where and how you will conduct your research, and listing sources that you might consult.

Step 5: Investigate to collect and organize concepts

Start your investigation. As you gather information and connect it to your prior knowledge, you will create new knowledge and new thoughts, ideas, and theories.

Keep a careful record of your sources so that you can refer to them and include them in an accurate and complete bibliography. At this stage, you will also begin to think about the most effective way of communicating your learning to your audience.

Step 6: Analyze and evaluate information and evidence

Analyzing and evaluating information and evidence is a continuing process. As you gather information, highlight ideas and concepts that relate most directly to the issue question and your criteria for judgment. Keep an open mind. If your analysis reveals that you need to change tactics or direction, be prepared to refine or redirect your questions, clarify ideas, and revise your criteria.

Step 7: Reflect on the evidence and make judgments

Using your criteria and the evidence you have gathered, make informed judgments in response to the issue question. Be prepared to support your judgments with solid evidence.

Step 8: Communicate your judgments

By sharing your ideas and conclusions with your teacher and other students — and listening carefully as they share with you — you will be able to refine your ideas and reflect on the process you followed to solve a problem and arrive at a judgment on an issue.

✔ Critical Thinking Checklist

- ☑ I am thinking actively.
(e.g., I am exploring alternatives and considering their strengths and weaknesses.)
- ☑ I am being curious.
(e.g., I am taking time to think about things and explore unanswered questions.)
- ☑ I am being flexible.
(e.g., I am allowing my beliefs to change until I have enough evidence to support a specific judgment.)
- ☑ I am keeping an open mind.
(e.g., I am judging ideas on the basis of their strengths and weaknesses.)
- ☑ I am being collaborative.
(e.g., I am working with others to brainstorm and combine ideas.)
- ☑ I am being empathetic.
(e.g., I am not passing judgment until I have gathered enough information.)
- ☑ I am being respectful.
(e.g., I am aware of the limits of my knowledge and avoid claiming to know more than I do.)
- ☑ I am being thoughtful.
(e.g., I am thinking about my own thinking and examining my biases.)

Terms Used in *Exploring Nationalism*

As people have become sensitive to the power of language to reinforce negative stereotypes and to exclude individuals and groups, English has changed. Language has become more inclusive as people have come to recognize the importance of respecting diversity — and of showing this respect through their choice of words.

Developed and Developing, North and South

Economists and others now use terms such as "developing country" to describe countries whose economies are not as strong as those of the wealthy democracies of North America and Europe. These wealthy democracies are often called "developed countries."

The term "global North" is also used to describe developed countries, while the "global South" is used to describe developing countries.

No firm guidelines exist for classifying a country as developed or developing. The map in Figure P-7, for example, shows the approximate division of the world into developed and developing countries.

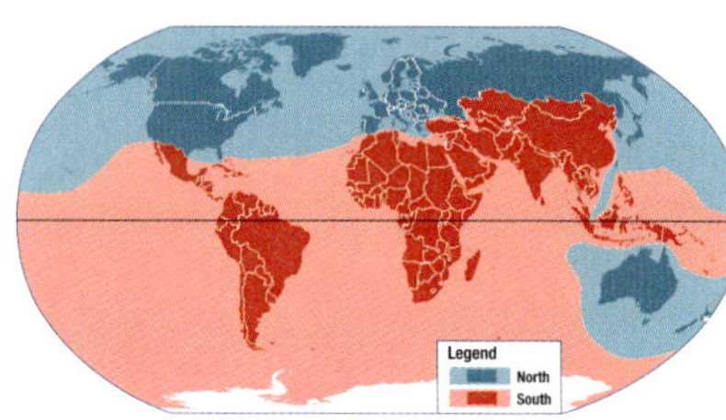

Figure P-7 The Global North and the Global South

Multiculturalism and Pluralism

You will encounter the terms **multiculturalism** and **pluralism** many times as you explore nationalism. Multiculturalism is a belief, doctrine, or policy that embraces the idea of ethnic or cultural diversity and promotes a culturally pluralistic society. And pluralism is a belief or doctrine that a society should reflect an inclusive approach that encourages diversity. It assumes that diversity is beneficial and that diverse groups, whether these are cultural, religious, spiritual, ideological, gender, linguistic, environmental, or philosophical, should enjoy autonomy.

Francophone References

Exploring Nationalism includes many references to Francophones — people whose first language is French. Canada is an officially bilingual country, as Francophone colonists were one of Canada's founding peoples. Though Québec is home to most Canadian Francophones, Canada's other provinces and three territories also have Francophone populations. Francophones may also have immigrated to Canada from other French-speaking countries, such as France, Haiti, Rwanda, Lebanon, and Sénégal.

Aboriginal References

When Europeans arrived in Canada, they often imposed their own names on the First Peoples they met. In Eastern Canada, for example, the French gave the name "Huron," an old French term for "boar's head," to the Ouendat. The term referred to the bristly hairstyles worn by Ouendat men.

In recent years, many First Nations, Métis, and Inuit have reclaimed names derived from their own language and prefer to be known by these names. These are the terms used in *Exploring Nationalism*. Though considerable variation in spelling and usage continues to occur, the chart on the following page provides a guide to many of these names. This list is not comprehensive.

Research Tip

When conducting research into Aboriginal peoples, be prepared to encounter various names and to check both alternative names and alternative spellings.

First Nations, Métis, and Inuit Names	
Contemporary Name	Alternative Names
A'aninin	Gros Ventre, White Clay People, Aaninen
Aamskaapipikani	South Peigan, South Piikani, Blackfeet
Anishinabé or Saulteaux	Ojibway, Ojibwa, Anishinaabe, Anishnabe, Anishnabeg, Bungee
Apsaroke	Crow
Asakiwaki	Sauk
Baffinland Inuit	Eskimo
Cayuga	Cayuga
Cree or Nehiyaw	Cris
Dakelh	Carrier
Dakota	Sioux
Dene Suliné	Chipewyan, Dene Souline, Denesuline
Dené Tha'	Dene Dháa, Slavey
Dunne-za	Beaver, South Slave
Gitxsan	Tsimshian, Gitksan
Haida	Haida
Haisla	Kitimat
Heiltsuk	Bella Bella
Innu	Montahfais, Montagnais-Naskapi
Inuit	Eskimo
Inuvialuit	Western Inuit, Eskimo
Haudenosaunee	Iroquois
Kainai	Blood
Kaska Dena	Kaska
Kichesiprini	Algonquin
Kitlinermiut	Copper Inuit, Eskimo
Ktunaxa	Kutenai, Kootenay
Kwakwaka'wakw	Kwakiutl, Kwagiud, Kwakwawaw, Kwagiulth
Labrador Inuit	Sikumiut, Eskimo
Lakota	Sioux
Gwich'in	Loucheaux, Kutchin, Tukudh
Meshwahkihaki	Fox
Métis	Half-breed, Country-born, Mixed-blood
Mi'kmaw (sing.), Mi'kmaq (pl.)	Micmac, Mi'maq, Micmaw
Mohawk	Mohawk
Nakoda	Stoney, Assiniboine, Nakota
Nakota	Assiniboine
Nisga'a	Nishga, Nisga
Netsilingmiut	Netsulik Inuit, Eskimo
Nlaka'pamux	Thompson, Couteau
Nuu-chah-nulth	Nootka
Nuxalk	Bella Coola
Odawa	Ottawa
Okanagan	Okanagan
Oneida, Six Nations Confederacy	Oneida
Onondaga, Six Nations Confederacy	Onondaga
Ouendat	Huron
Oweekeno	Kwakiutl, Kwagiud, Kwakwawaw, Kwagiulth
Piikani	Peigan, Pikuni, North Peigan
Qairnirmiut	Caribou Inuit, Eskimo
Secwepemc	Shuswap
Sekani	Sekani
Seneca, Six Nations Confederacy	Seneca
Siksika, Blackfoot Confederacy	Blackfoot
Stl'atl'imx	Lilloet
Sylix	Lake Okanagan
Tagish	Tagish
Tahltan	Tahltan
Thcho	Dogrib
Tlingit	Tlingit
Tsilhqot'in	Chilcotin
Tsimshian	Tsimshian
Tsuu T'ina	Sarsi, Sarcee
Tuscarora, Six Nations Confederacy	Tuscarora
Tutchone	Tuchone
Ulliniwek	Illinois
Wet'suwet'en	Babine Carrier
Woods Cree	Wood Cree, Woodland Cree

RELATED ISSUE 1

To what extent should nation be the foundation of identity?

Key Issue
To what extent should we embrace nationalism?

Related Issue 1
To what extent should nation be the foundation of identity?

Related Issue 2
To what extent should national interest be pursued?

Related Issue 3
To what extent should internationalism be pursued?

Related Issue 4
To what extent should individuals and groups in Canada embrace a national identity?

This chart shows how you will progress through this related issue. Within each chapter, inquiry questions will help guide your exploration of responses to the chapter issue, related issue, and key course issue.

Chapter 1

Nation and Identity

To what extent are nation and identity related?

What are some concepts of nation?

What are some understandings of nation?

How can nation be understood as a civic concept?

How do people express their identity through nation?

Chapter 2

Shaping Nationalism

To what extent should internal and external factors shape nationalism?

What are some factors that shape nationalism?

How have people responded to some factors that shape nationalism?

How have people in Canada responded to some factors that shape nationalism?

Chapter 3

Reconciling Nationalist Loyalties

To what extent should people reconcile their contending nationalist loyalties?

How do nationalist loyalties shape people's choices?

What choices have people made to affirm nationalist loyalties?

How can nationalist loyalties create conflict?

How have people reconciled contending nationalist loyalties?

Chapter 4

Reconciling Nationalist and Non-Nationalist Loyalties

To what extent should people reconcile their contending nationalist and non-nationalist loyalties?

What are non-nationalist loyalties?

How can nationalist and non-nationalist loyalties compete?

How have people reconciled contending nationalist and non-nationalist loyalties?

The Big Picture

Who you are — and who you are likely to become — is not always easy to figure out or express. People change over time as they are influenced by new, different, and varied experiences and ideas. Sometimes the influences that shape identity cannot be clearly seen or understood. These influences may take the form of emotions, thoughts, and vague feelings. The emotions stirred, for example, when you see a specific image, such as a flag, or hear a specific piece of music, perhaps one associated with a family member or close friend, can shape your identity: who you are. The reverse is also true. Your evolving sense of identity can shape the events, people, and issues around you.

In similar ways, nations and states grow, change, and respond to forces within and outside themselves as they mature and develop individual identities.

The prologue introduced various ideas about nation and nation-state — and how these ideas may be expressed through nationalism. In the four chapters of this related issue, you will analyze and evaluate these ideas more fully as you explore their relationship to identity, both personal and collective.

One important idea involves distinguishing between nation and nation-state, or country. You will explore the idea that a nation can exist without specific borders, while a nation-state cannot — a sense of nation often emerges from a collective that is united in some way, while a nation-state often includes various nations. Expressing the feelings and "soul" of the nation or nation-state is one form of nationalism. Nationalism can also become a vehicle to exploit the feelings of the people of a nation or nation-state, for good or evil.

The chart on the previous page shows how you will progress through the chapters of Related Issue 1. As you explore this related issue, you will come to appreciate

- that many understandings of nation, nation-state, and nationalism exist and that these understandings may change over time
- that the relationships among identity, nation, nation-state, and nationalism are complex and dynamic
- how the forces of nationalism have shaped and continue to shape Canada and the world
- why peoples promote their identities through nationalism

Your Challenge

Create a coat of arms to show how your understandings of the concept of nation shape — and are shaped by — your identity, and be prepared to explain how your coat of arms represents your response to the question for this related issue:

To what extent should nation be the foundation of identity?

Checklist for Success

Use this checklist to ensure that your finished product includes everything necessary to be successful.

My Knowledge and Understanding

☑ My symbols illustrate my understanding of the connections between my identity and nation.

☑ My criteria indicate my understanding of the related-issue question.

☑ My notes show the underlying meaning of my coat of arms.

☑ My responses to questions show my understanding of the purpose of this challenge.

My Selection, Analysis, and Evaluation of Information

☑ My criteria guided my research.

☑ My coat of arms is based on my criteria.

☑ My symbols, information, and notes reflect my understanding of the related-issue question.

My Coat of Arms

☑ My coat of arms is interesting and engaging.

☑ My notes are complete and support my coat of arms.

☑ My use of language and references is appropriate.

☑ My responses to questions are positive and constructive.

Your Coat of Arms

A coat of arms presents the heritage, goals, values, and aspirations of the individual or collective it represents. When Michaëlle Jean, for example, was appointed governor general of Canada in 2005, she created the personal coat of arms shown on the following page.

Each element of Jean's coat of arms sends a message about who she is, and each element of your coat of arms should do the same. This message may reflect past glories and connections, and it may also provide a basis for future actions. A coat of arms says, "This is who I am, in body and soul." A motto often makes this meaning clear.

As you progress through the four chapters of this related issue, you will develop understandings of nation — and how this concept influences, and is influenced by, aspects of your individual and collective identity. You will use these understandings to create and present a coat of arms representing you or a collective you choose.

You may present your coat of arms in one of several forms:

- a computer-generated graphic
- a collage
- a drawing or painting
- a combination of forms or one you choose yourself

You will also prepare notes to attach to your presentation. These notes may be presented in a separate booklet, on separate screens if you are using computer software, or in another format of your choice. Your notes will help others understand your coat of arms.

Your notes will conclude with your personal response to the related-issue question.

What Your Coat of Arms Will Include

To show the relationship between your identity and your understandings of nation, you will develop symbols to place on your coat of arms. For each symbol, your notes should include

- a description
- the reason for your choice
- an explanation of the connection(s) between the symbol, your identity, and your understandings of nation

Keep in mind that you may decide that nation should not play a role as a foundation of your identity. If this is the case, the symbols you choose should reflect this position.

Creating and Assembling Your Coat of Arms

Step 1

Decide on the form your coat of arms will take. This will affect the symbols you include.

Decide whether your coat of arms will represent you, or your family, or another collective.

Step 2

Think about the symbols Michaëlle Jean included on her coat of arms and how these symbols reflect her feelings about the connections between her identity and nation. What criteria do you think Jean might have used when choosing these symbols?

Develop two or three criteria to help you decide which connections you will highlight on your coat of arms. On the basis of the criteria you choose, prepare a motto that expresses their purpose and meaning. You may revise your criteria as you work through the related issue.

As you progress through this related issue, keep notes about the aspects of nation and identity that best fit your criteria. You may wish to keep your notes in a chart similar to the one shown.

Step 3

As you complete each chapter and add more notes to your chart, share your work with a partner and your teacher. Use this feedback to revise and refine your coat of arms.

Step 4

At the conclusion of the related issue, organize your symbols, notes, and information into your final presentation: a coat of arms. Be prepared to respond to questions about the meaning and purpose of the symbols you have used — and how they show your response to the related-issue question.

Notes for My Coat of Arms

Criterion	Evidence	Possible Symbol
What aspects of nation inspire feelings of pride?	Singing "O Canada." I'm Canadian, but my heritage is Sri Lankan, so I was proud when Sri Lanka made it to the 2007 Cricket World Cup final.	Maple leaf Sri Lankan lion

Governor General Michaëlle Jean's Personal Coat of Arms

1. **Sand dollar** — A sea creature found on Canada's Atlantic and Pacific shores. For Jean, this creature is a talisman.
2. **Royal crown** — Symbolizes Jean's role as the queen's representative in Canada and the governor general's duty to serve all Canadians.
3. **Conch shell and broken chain** — Refers to a sculpture that stands in the main square of Port au Prince, Haiti, Jean's birthplace. The sculpture, by Albert Mangonès, shows an escaped slave blowing a conch shell as a call to arms to other slaves around the island. For Jean, this represents her ancestors' victory over slavery and is a call for freedom for everyone.
4. **Simbi** — These two wise water spirits are drawn from Haitian culture. They comfort souls and purify troubled waters. For Jean, they also represent the important role of women in working toward social justice.
5. **Palm tree** — A symbol of peace in Haiti.
6. **Pine tree** — A symbol of the natural riches of Canada.
7. **Briser les solitudes** — A motto that means "breaking down solitudes." This French motto represents Jean's goal as governor general.
8. **Desiderantes meliorem patriam** — These Latin words mean "They desire a better country" and are the motto of the Order of Canada.
9. **Insignia of the Order of Canada** — As governor general, Jean presents the Order of Canada to people who have contributed to making Canada a better country.

CHAPTER 1 Nation and Identity

Figure 1-1 Canadian artist and filmmaker Joyce Wieland, shown at right, created this quilt, called *Confedspread,* for Expo 67, Canada's coming-of-age party. This world's fair, which took place in 1967 in Montréal, commemorated the 100th anniversary of Confederation. The celebration filled many Canadians with pride and marked a particularly optimistic time in Canadian history.

CHAPTER ISSUE
To what extent are nation and identity related?

JOYCE WIELAND WAS A PROLIFIC CANADIAN ARTIST in the prime of her career when she created *Confedspread*, the quilt shown on the previous page. Wieland was proud of her reputation as a cultural activist who both celebrated the Canadian identity and highlighted women's issues at a time when the art world was dominated by men.

Examine *Confedspread* carefully, then respond to the following questions:

- What words did Wieland combine to form the title of the quilt?
- What elements of Wieland's quilt symbolize her pride in her Canadian identity?
- What elements of the quilt represent the Canadian landscape?
- If you removed the flags from Wieland's quilt, would it still represent nation and identity for Canadians?
- How did Wieland's choice to represent her feelings in the form of a quilt make a statement about her identity?
- If you were preparing a similar piece to represent your collective and individual identity in Canada today, what would you include? How would these choices represent your ideas about Canada?
- What would you need to add to the quilt to reflect your identity in Canada?

KEY TERMS

nation-state

international

patriotism

ethnic

self-determination

sovereignty

civic nation

ethnic nationalism

LOOKING AHEAD

In this chapter, you will develop responses to the following questions as you explore the extent to which identity and nation are related:

- What are some concepts of nation?
- What are some understandings of nation?
- How can nation be understood as a civic concept?
- How do people express their identity through nation?

My Journal on Nationalism

Follow Joyce Wieland's example and use words or images — or both — to express your current ideas about nation and identity. Date your ideas and keep them in a notebook, learning log, portfolio, or computer file so that you can return to them as you progress through this course.

What are some concepts of nation?

When people talk about nation, they often mean different things. Some people, for example, view "country" and "nation" as synonyms. Others think the two words mean different things. They believe that a country is defined by physical territory that is managed by a central government, while the idea of nation has nothing to do with physical borders or a government. They believe that "nation" refers to a shared state of mind or shared characteristics such as beliefs, language, religion, traditions, cultures, and customs.

What does "nation" mean to you? What are some words that describe your concept of nation? Does your concept of nation involve physical borders or a state of mind — or both?

Are military monuments such as the Canadian National Vimy Memorial appropriate symbols of nationhood?

Nation as Us

"Every nation has a creation story to tell." With these words, Canadian prime minister Stephen Harper began his speech to 15 000 people — dignitaries, soldiers, students, and civilians — who had gathered in France on April 9, 2007, for the ceremony rededicating the Canadian National Vimy Memorial.

The occasion marked the 90th anniversary of the Battle of Vimy Ridge, which took place on April 9, 1917, during World War I. Until then, Canadian soldiers had always fought with British forces. At Vimy, they fought together under a Canadian commander for the first time — and won a vital military position that the armies of Britain and France had failed to capture.

For many Canadians, the victory was an achievement that symbolized the country's coming of age as a nation. Vimy gave many people a sense that when Canadians united, they could tackle, and achieve, great things. It gave Canadians a pride in "us" — and many Canadians continue to feel this pride today.

Do you agree with Prime Minister Harper's view that Vimy represents Canada's "creation story"? Think about what you know about Canadian history. What other events might contend with Vimy as Canada's creation story?

Figure 1-2 The Vimy Memorial took 11 years to build and stands on land granted to Canada by France to use forever. Carved into the memorial are the names of 11 285 Canadian soldiers who fought in World War I but whose bodies were never found.

Figure 1-3 Métis fiddler Sierra Noble of Winnipeg played "The Warrior's Lament" at the Vimy Memorial rededication ceremony and at other memorial events in France. Noble, who was 17 at the time, was deeply moved by the experience. "I don't know how I didn't start to cry," she said later. "There was such pride to be there."

Country and Nation

The distinction between "country" and "nation" can be confusing, especially because other widely used terms seem to suggest that the two words are synonyms. Here are some examples:

- "**Nation-state**" means "country."
- "**International**" means "between countries or nation-states."
- "Nationalism" means, among other things, "striving for a country."
- Only countries can be members of the United Nations.

Although the word "nation" has been part of the English language for hundreds of years, it was originally a Latin word that meant "people" or "race." As a result, many people believe that the concept of nation refers to people and is different from the idea of country, or nation-state.

Think about Canada, for example. Canada can be thought of as a country — or nation-state — that extends from sea to sea to sea. It has physical borders and a single federal government that manages this vast territory on behalf of the people who live here. But Canada can also be thought of as a nation made up of people who share similar values and beliefs and are passionate about affirming and promoting them. Some people believe that Canada is a multi-nation state.

Do you think of Canada as merely a country — the place where you live and where everyone shares the same federal government? Or do you view Canada as your nation? Is the idea of Canada and being Canadian part of your identity?

In the psychological sense, there is no Canadian nation as there is an American or French nation. There is a legal and geographical entity, but the nation does not exist. For there are no objects that all Canadians share as objects of national feeling.

— *Charles Hanley, in* Nationalism in Canada, *1966*

Would you or the people who attended the Vimy Memorial rededication ceremony in April 2007 agree with Charles Hanley's words in "Voices"?

Nation as a Concept

The study of nation as a concept began a little more than two centuries ago. Ever since, sociologists, political scientists, anthropologists, historians, and other academics have tried to understand how this idea unites — and divides — people. Many of these academics have tried to define "nation" and to develop criteria to help them decide when a nation *is* a nation. The web on this page shows some of their views. Which view(s) do you agree with?

Figure 1-4 Some Understandings of Nation

nation

- The nation is the people.
- Nation emerges from a feeling of belonging.
- The nation expresses the soul of the people.
- The nation is an imagined political community.
- The nation exists when a people want self-government.

THE VIEW FROM HERE

What makes a nation a nation? For more than 200 years, thinkers have grappled with this question. Here is how three people have responded — at three different times.

One of the first to consider what makes a nation was **JOHANN GOTTLIEB FICHTE**, a German philosopher. In the early 1800s — when Germany was not a single country but a collection of small states — Fichte wrote that a nation is defined by shared linguistic, ethnic, and cultural origins.

> The first, original, and truly natural boundaries of states are beyond doubt their internal boundaries. Those who speak the same language are joined to each other by a multitude of invisible bonds . . . ; they understand each other and . . . they belong together and are by nature one and an inseparable whole . . . From this internal boundary, which is drawn by the spiritual nature of man himself, the marking of the external boundary by dwelling place results . . . and in the natural view of things it is not because men dwell between certain mountains and rivers that they are a people, but . . . men dwell together . . . because they were a people already by a law of nature which is much higher.

ERNEST RENAN was a 19th-century French philosopher who believed that the concept of nation includes, but goes beyond, the idea of shared roots.

> A nation is a soul, a spiritual principle. Two things, which in truth are but one, constitute this soul or spiritual principle. One lies in the past, one in the present. One is the possession in common of a rich legacy of memories; the other is present-day consent, the desire to live together, the will to perpetuate the value of the heritage that one has received in an undivided form. Man . . . does not improvise . . . To have common glories in the past and to have a common will in the present; to have performed great deeds together, to wish to perform still more – these are the essential conditions for being a people.

BENEDICT ANDERSON is an Irish specialist in international studies. In *Imagined Communities: Reflections on the Origin and Spread of Nationalism*, Anderson envisions a nation as an imagined political community. This description is often used today.

> [Nation] is an imagined political community – and imagined as both inherently limited and sovereign.
>
> It is *imagined* because the members of even the smallest nation will never know most of their fellow-members, meet them, or even hear of them, yet in the minds of each lives the image of their communion . . .
>
> The nation is imagined as *limited* because even the largest of them encompassing perhaps a billion living human beings, has finite, if elastic boundaries, beyond which lie other nations . . .
>
> It is imagined as *sovereign* because the concept was born in an age in which Enlightenment and Revolution were destroying the legitimacy of the divinely ordained, hierarchical dynastic realm . . . The gauge and emblem of this freedom is the sovereign state.
>
> Finally, it is imagined as a *community*, because, regardless of the actual inequality and exploitation that may prevail in each, the nation is always conceived as a deep, horizontal comradeship.

Explorations

1. Which description most accurately and completely describes your understanding of nation? Explain the reasons for your choice.
2. Which description do you think most accurately describes your understanding of Canada? Explain the reasons for your choice. Is this choice different from the one you made in response to Question 1? Explain why or why not.

Nation as a Collective Concept

When Johann Gottlieb Fichte, Ernest Renan, and Benedict Anderson — the thinkers quoted in "The View from Here" — wrote about nation, they used expressions such as "an inseparable whole," "common glories," "common will," and "community." These words and phrases suggest that the idea of a collective — or group — identity underlies the concept of nation.

Think about the groups and collectives you belong to. They may start with your family and school, and extend to many other collectives, including linguistic, religious, and social collectives. Though not all these collectives form the basis of a nation, thinkers agree that a sense of collective identity is essential to a sense of nation.

Paying attention to language can help you identify the collective aspect of nation. When retelling the tale of Snow White, for example, Arthur Quiller-Couch wrote: "As soon as the palace guns announced [the birth of a daughter], the whole nation went wild with delight . . . Even strangers meeting in the street fell upon each other's neck, exclaiming: 'Our Queen has a daughter! Yes, yes — Our Queen has a daughter! Long live the little Princess!'"

Quiller-Couch's description is revealing in two ways. First, think about why he used the phrase "the whole nation." Did he mean a government? A territory? The people? Then examine how Quiller-Couch described people's words about the queen. Strangers greeted one another saying "our queen," not "the queen" or "my queen." What does this choice of words suggest about the links between nation and collective identity?

Using terms like "we," "us," and "our" shows that people are thinking collectively. As you continue your exploration of nation and nationalism, watch for collective language like this.

An English lady on the Rhine [a river in Germany], hearing a German speaking of her party [of English visitors] as foreigners, exclaimed, "No, we are not foreigners; we are English; it is you that are foreigners."

— Ralph Waldo Emerson, American writer and philosopher, commenting in the early 20th century on the traits of the English

Does using collective language like "we," "us," and "our" automatically place people in opposition to "them"?

Figure 1-5 Hockey fans like these, who were attending an NHL playoff game in Calgary, sometimes describe themselves collectively as the "Flames nation" or "Oilers nation." When they do this, what collective identity are they expressing? Is this an appropriate use of the term "nation"?

I love America more than any other country in this world: and exactly for this reason, I insist on the right to criticize her perpetually.

— James Baldwin, American writer, in Notes of a Native Son, *1955*

Nation as a Patriotic Concept

Many of the thousands of Canadians who attended the Vimy Memorial rededication ceremony in April 2007 were expressing their **patriotism** — love of their country. They were also commemorating the patriotism of the soldiers who fought, and especially those who died, in World War I.

People express patriotism in different ways. James Baldwin, for example, whose words are quoted in "Voices," was a black American. Baldwin expressed his patriotism by criticizing American society.

To be patriotic, is it necessary to support everything your nation does? Can speaking out against a situation be, as James Baldwin points out in "Voices," an important aspect of patriotism?

One Expression of Patriotism

In 2007, Historica, an organization dedicated to exploring Canadian history, posted a patriotism-related question on its online forum. The question asked high school students whether they would die for their country.

Is dying for one's nation the highest expression of patriotism?

The response was mixed. "No, I would not die for my country!!!" wrote Lesley M of Corner Brook, Newfoundland and Labrador. "I would protest and argue and discuss and get royally angry for my country. I don't really want to die for it. Dying seems a bit counterproductive to me."

But Robert R of Oshawa, Ontario, said, "Yes, I would die for my country. I love my country and every Canadian citizen. To me, Canada is one of the greatest countries in the world."

And Susan M of Marystown, Newfoundland and Labrador, said that her response would not necessarily be clear cut. "For me the answer would depend on the circumstances. If I was fighting for my country for a cause I believe in, I wouldn't mind dying for Canada," she wrote. "However, if the cause we were fighting for was something that I didn't believe in, I would not be willing to die for my country. As I said, it all depends on the circumstances."

Reflect and Respond

Think about the understandings of nation that you have encountered so far — and which of these understandings most effectively express your own ideas. Jot down some of your ideas.

Then create a mind map with yourself at the centre. Organize your ideas in bubbles around this centre. Use size, colour, and shape to highlight the understandings of nation that are most important to your identity. Add a legend to explain your use of size, shape, and colour.

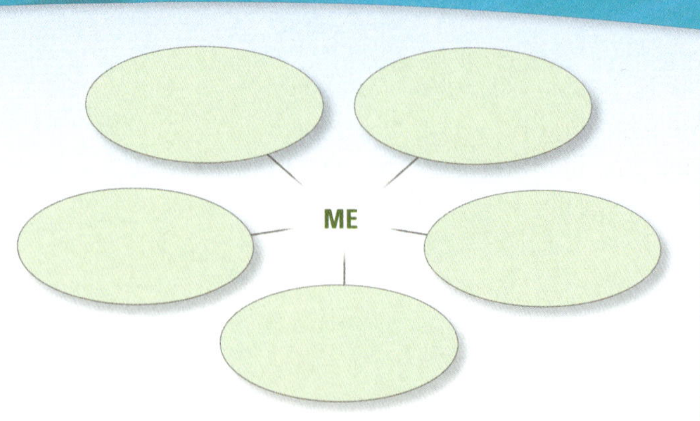

What are some understandings of nation?

Peter Russell, a Canadian constitutional expert, believes that the term "nation" refers collectively to a people rather than to a country. "[The word 'nation'] has a long, pre-modern existence as a term to designate a people who have an identifiable culture, history, language, etc.," Russell told an interviewer.

Like Russell, many scholars believe that people with a similar worldview and ideas about themselves make up a nation. These collective ideas can develop from shared linguistic, ethnic, cultural, religious, spiritual, geographic, and political understandings.

Tremblay is the most common last name in Québec, where most Tremblays are descended from a 17th-century couple who married and had 10 children. But this situation is changing as more and more Francophone immigrants from countries such as Vietnam make new homes in Québec. In Montréal, Québec's largest city, statisticians predicted in 2007 that people named Nguyen — a common Vietnamese last name — may soon outnumber Tremblays.

Linguistic Understandings of Nation

Experts estimate that English is the first language of more than 380 million people around the world. But few would suggest that the world's English speakers make up a single nation. Still, as Johann Gottlieb Fichte pointed out in "The View from Here," a common language can sometimes create a feeling of belonging so powerful that it inspires a sense of nation.

Samuel Johnson, the 18th-century English writer who compiled the first English dictionary, said, "Languages are the pedigrees of nations." Johnson's words express many people's belief that language helps create a shared worldview that gives people a sense of nation. Language plays an important role in creating the mindset of a distinct people, because language influences how people see the world. It creates a mental universe that is shared by the people who speak a language fluently.

This linguistic understanding of nation is very strong in Québec. The feeling of belonging to a linguistic nation is shared by Francophones across Canada. In Québec, French is the first language of more than 80 per cent of people. Many Québécois also share a history and cultural roots: their ancestors immigrated from northern France in the 17th and 18th centuries. In many cases, they also share a religion: Catholicism.

In recent years, many Francophones from countries such as Haiti, Lebanon, and Vietnam, where French is either an official language or widely spoken, have immigrated to Québec. These immigrants do not share a common cultural background with Francophones whose families have lived in Québec for generations, but they have swelled the number of people whose first language is French.

In November 2006, the Conservative government of Prime Minister Stephen Harper created a sensation when it passed a motion recognizing that "the Québécois form a nation within a united Canada." The carefully worded motion referred to Québécois — the people — rather than to Québec — the geographic and political entity.

Why do you suppose Harper chose to call the Québécois, but not Québec, a nation? How significant is Harper's distinction between Québécois and Québec?

Figure 1-6 Every year, Québécois celebrate Fête nationale on June 24. This holiday originally combined summer solstice celebrations with a Catholic festival marking the feast day of St-Jean-Baptiste, who is considered the patron saint of French Canada. In 1977, the Québec government officially named this holiday Fête nationale. What difference might this change make to the way this festival is celebrated? What is the significance of the word "nationale" in the name of this holiday?

Ethnic Understandings of Nation

If someone mentioned the Ukrainian nation, you would probably conclude that she or he was talking about people who live in the European country of Ukraine and whose language, culture, and ancestors are Ukrainian. Although many people of Ukrainian heritage, including many Albertans, do not live in Ukraine, and although some citizens of Ukraine are not of Ukrainian heritage, your conclusion would be generally accurate. Many nations come into being because people share the same **ethnic** — racial, cultural, or linguistic — characteristics. The Korean, Japanese, Somali, and Norwegian nations, for example, are based largely on ethnicity.

Many people support the idea of basing nation on a common ethnicity because they believe that this will protect a people's collective identity. But others believe that this idea is dangerous because people may come to loathe and fear people they think of as "other." In extreme cases, this can lead to racism and intolerance.

Koreans have developed a sense of nation based on shared blood and ancestry. The Korean nation was "racialized" through a belief in a common prehistoric origin, producing an intense sense of collective oneness. Koreans . . . believe that they all belong to a "unitary nation" *(danil minjok)*, one that is ethnically homogenous and racially distinctive.

— Gi-Wook Shin, a director at the Walter H. Shorenstein Asia-Pacific Research Center, 2006

Cultural Understandings of Nation

Culture — the ways of life that a people share — can also inspire a sense of nation. The cultural aspects of nation are often closely related to ethnicity, but this is not always the case. In Canada, for example, the cultures of First Nations are often distinct from one another. The culture of the Haida people, whose traditional territory is on the West Coast, is different from the cultures of First Nations of the Prairies.

Figure 1-7 This Korean woman is walking past a street vendor in Seoul, the capital of South Korea. Each of the people in this photograph is a distinct individual, yet most share certain ethnic characteristics, such as language and customs. What might be the benefits of living in a community with people who share these characteristics?

Figure 1-8 Nicole Nicholas (left) is a Haida teenager who grew up in British Columbia, where her people created totem poles as a form of spiritual, cultural, and artistic expression. Joe Big Tobacco (right) is a Siksika, shown dancing at a powwow sponsored by the Blackfoot Canadian Cultural Society. These young people share an Aboriginal heritage, but they are from different areas with distinct cultural traditions that have been shaped, in part, by the land they inhabit..

Religious Understandings of Nation

Religion can also form an important understanding of nation. The Jewish nation, for example, has existed for about 3000 years. For most of this time, Jews did not have a territory of their own. Then, in 1948, the country of Israel officially came into being.

Though Jewish communities had existed in various countries around the world, communication between them was limited by both geography and politics. As a result, these various Jewish communities often developed their own distinct culture and language. Jews might speak, for example, Hebrew, Yiddish, Ladino, and other languages. Despite these differences, the Jewish sense of nation survived, at least to some extent, as a result of people's shared religious beliefs.

Geographic Understandings of Nation

Compare a political map of the world with a relief map, and you will see — in broad terms — the effects of geography on the development of nations. Mountains, oceans, and deserts are physical barriers that often forced peoples to develop in isolation from other peoples. Take Tibet, for example. For thousands of years, Tibetans were isolated on the vast Tibetan plateau. As a result, they developed a distinct language and culture, as well as religious beliefs and their own forms of government.

Examine the map of Tibet in Figure 1-10. What physical features isolated the people of the Tibetan plateau? How might this isolation have influenced Tibetans' collective identity as expressed through their language, culture, religion, and forms of government?

Israel is the very embodiment of Jewish continuity: It is the only nation on earth that inhabits the same land, bears the same name, speaks the same language, and worships the same God that it did 3000 years ago. You dig the soil and you find pottery from Davidic times, coins from Bar Kokhba, and 2000-year-old scrolls written in a script remarkably like the one that today advertises ice cream at the corner candy store.

— Charles Krauthammer, Pulitzer Prize–winning political commentator, 1998

Figure 1-9 On July 1, 2006, the Qinghai–Tibet Railway carried its first passengers between Golmud, in the Chinese province of Qinghai, and Lhasa, the capital of Tibet. In its first year, this rail line transported more than 1.5 million people into Tibet. How might this development affect the collective identity of Tibetans?

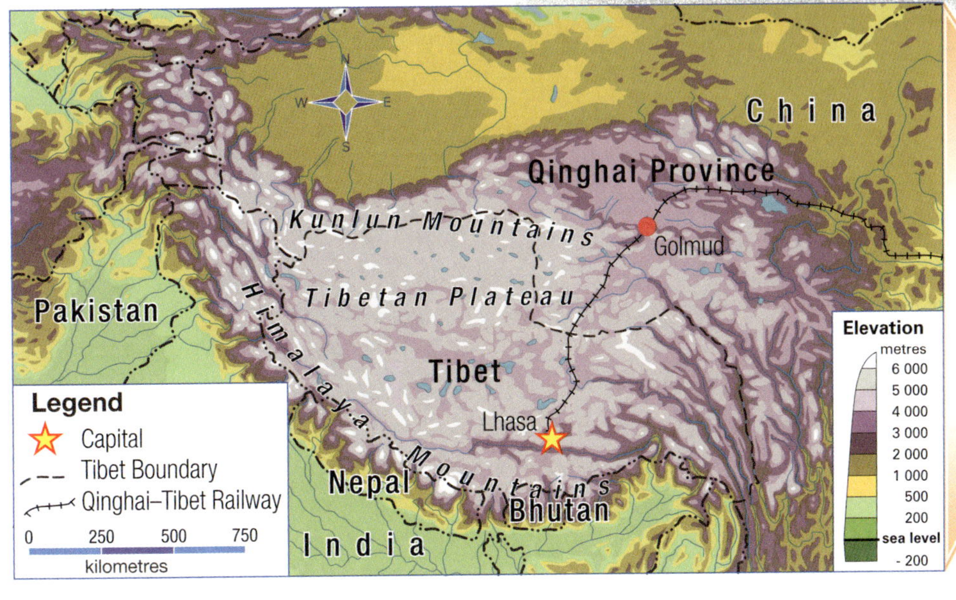

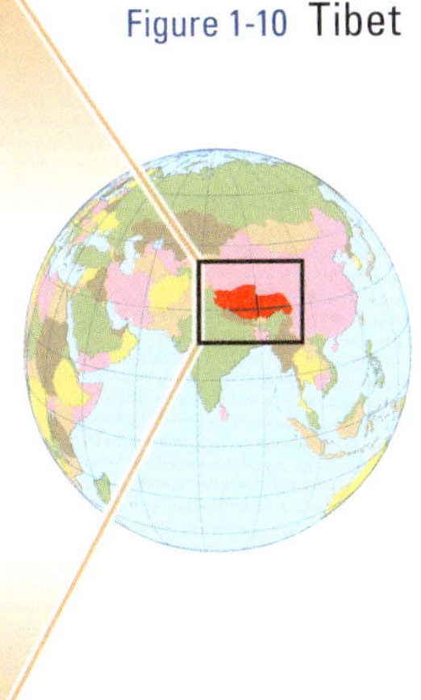

Figure 1-10 Tibet

Not Just a Platform for My Dance

this land is not
just a place to set my house my car
my fence
this land is not
just a plot to bury my dead my seed
this land is
my tongue my eyes my mouth
this headstrong grass and relenting
willow
these flat-footed fields and
applauding leaves
these frank winds and
electric sky
are my prayer
they are my medicine
and they become my song
this land is not
just a platform for my dance

— Marilyn Dumont, Métis poet, in A Really Good Brown Girl, *1996*

Nation and Relationship to Land

Land can influence the development of nations in ways that go far beyond the isolation created by geographic barriers. Different geographic areas, for example, provide different resources, which influence the way people live. What are some geographic influences that affect your life?

"Spirit of place" is a phrase that is often used to describe the spiritual connection between human beings and a particular place. In *Nitsitapiisinni: The Story of the Blackfoot People*, the writers described the unique relationship between the Siksika people and their traditional territory, which lies east of the Rocky Mountains in what is now southern Alberta and Saskatchewan and the American state of Montana:

> Our sacred sites are places where significant things happened to our ancestors. This is where the ancient stories took place. These sites are uniquely important to us. They tell us that our ancient stories are true. They tell us that we belong to this place in a way that no other human being can.
>
> Our sacred geography shows us our path through life. By following this path, our people will live long and productive lives.

Examine the preceding quotation, as well as Figure 1-11 and Marilyn Dumont's poem. With a partner, create a graphic organizer or another image to depict the connections between geography and people's relationship to the land.

Spiritual Understandings of Nation

A people's relationship with the land is sometimes bound up with spiritual connections that unite them. Southern Alberta and Saskatchewan, as well as northern Montana, for example, contain many sites that are sacred to Siksika. These sites help bind people to the land and are an important aspect of their spiritual identity.

Figure 1-11 Siksika Sacred Places

Spiritual ties also connect Jews, Christians, and Muslims to the city of Jerusalem. For people of all three faiths, Jerusalem is a holy city.

Jerusalem's Temple Mount, for example, is the holiest Jewish religious site. Two ancient temples stood on this site. Many important Jewish religious traditions are associated with these temples, which were destroyed by warfare. Jews believe that a third temple will be built on the site when the Messiah — the promised deliverer of Jews — arrives on Earth.

The Temple Mount is also important to Christians because New Testament stories describe the association of Jesus with the Jewish temple that was located there. And the site is sacred to Muslims, who call it "Noble Sanctuary." Long after the Jewish temples had been destroyed, two Muslim religious shrines, the Dome of the Rock and the Al-Aqsa Mosque, were built there.

Political Understandings of Nation

In 1965, the United Nations General Assembly was debating what to do about the Chinese takeover of Tibet. The takeover had started in 1949, and Tibetans had been living under Chinese control for about 15 years.

The debate revolved around whether Tibet was a nation. During the discussion, Frank Aiken, the Irish ambassador to the UN, argued that Tibet was indeed a nation. As proof, he cited Tibetan history: "For thousands of years, or for a couple of thousand years at any rate, [Tibet] was as free and as fully in control of its own affairs as any nation in this Assembly."

Aiken's criterion was political. He reasoned that if Tibetans had controlled their own political affairs for thousands of years, then Tibet must be a nation. This view is shared by many. They believe that when deciding whether a people are a nation, the *desire* for **self-determination** — the power to control one's own affairs — is an important consideration. This consideration may be more important than actual **sovereignty** — the political authority to control one's own affairs.

If they do not have sovereignty, do Tibetans have the right to call themselves a nation?

In 1975, the Dene Nation of the Northwest Territories expressed this idea in a declaration. The declaration insisted on the right of the Dene to be regarded by the world as a nation. The declaration also said:

> The Dene find themselves as part of a country. That country is Canada. But the Government of Canada is not the Government of the Dene. The Government of the N.W.T. is not the government of the Dene. These governments were not the choice of the Dene, they were imposed on the Dene . . .
>
> Our plea to the world is to help us in our struggle to find a place in the world community where we can exercise our right to self-determination as a distinct people and as a Nation.
>
> What we seek then is independence and self-determination within the country of Canada.

Web Connection

Many Tibetans believe that their nation is an independent country and have set up a government in exile. To find out more about Tibet and its government in exile, go to this web site and follow the links.

www.ExploringNationalism.ca

The Métis Nation, as an Indigenous peoples, developed its own identity, language, culture, way of life, and self-government prior to Canada's crystallization as a nation-state . . . Based on this existence, the Métis Nation possesses the inherent right of self-determination and self-government.

— Clément Chartier, president of the Métis Nation, in The Métis Nation, *2007*

Reflect and Respond

Create a chart like the one shown. In the first column, list the understandings of nation explored in this section. In the second column, identify one people for whom this understanding is particularly important. In the third column, rate each understanding on a scale of 1 to 5 (1 = not very important; 5 = very important).

Then choose two peoples you identified in the second column and think about how their rating might compare with yours. Explain the reasons for the similarities or differences.

Understandings of Nation

Understanding	People for Whom Understanding Is Important	My Rating of Importance 1 = Not very important 5 = Very important

How can nation be understood as a civic concept?

When did Canada become a nation? In 1867, with Confederation? In 1917, at Vimy Ridge? In 1982, when the Constitution was proclaimed? On another date? Or not yet?

An early draft of the Constitution Act, 1982, opened with the words "We, the people of Canada . . ." This phrase was later taken out, because some people disagreed with it.

Consider what the deleted phrase implies — that Canada is a nation. Some people, such as Charles Hanley, who was quoted in "Voices" on page 21, disagree with the idea of Canada as a nation. What do you think? Try testing Canada against the criteria established in the previous section of this chapter. Is language, for example, a foundation of Canada? Is ethnicity? Religion? Geography?

As a result of this test, you may conclude — like Hanley — that Canada is not a nation. But other people disagree. John Ibbitson, for example, is a columnist and political commentator who believes that Canada works as a nation precisely because it is not built on any one understanding.

Ibbitson opened his 2005 book, *The Polite Revolution: Perfecting the Canadian Dream*, with these words: "Some time, not too long ago, while no one was watching, Canada became the world's most successful country."

Web Connection

To find out more about the Charter of Rights and Freedoms, go to this web site and follow the links.

www.ExploringNationalism.ca

Shared Values and Beliefs Expressed in Law

The Charter of Rights and Freedoms forms the first 34 clauses of Canada's Constitution. The Charter begins with these words: "Whereas Canada is founded upon principles that recognize the supremacy of God and the rule of law . . ."

Figure 1-12 Charter of Rights and Freedoms

Section 2
Fundamental Freedoms

2. Everyone has the following fundamental freedoms:
   a) freedom of conscience and religion;
   b) freedom of thought, belief, opinion and expression, including freedom of the press and other media of communication;
   c) freedom of peaceful assembly; and
   d) freedom of association.

The phrase "rule of law" is important because laws reflect the kind of society that people want to live in. Laws can be rules about littering, speeding on roads, and committing serious crimes, but they can also go much farther — and in the Canadian Constitution, they do. They express the values and beliefs that Canadians choose to embrace and agree to abide by as a condition of citizenship.

These values and beliefs are enshrined — included so that they will always be preserved and protected — in the Constitution so that they cannot be changed by a simple act of Parliament. Changing the Constitution is a complicated process that requires widespread agreement. Why do you suppose the complex amending process was set up?

The fundamental freedoms set out in Section 2 of the Charter express the foundational values and beliefs of Canadians. When people, no matter what their ethnicity, culture, and language, agree to live according to particular values and beliefs expressed as laws, they have created a **civic nation**.

The Making of a Civic Nation

"Civic" is an adjective that refers to citizens, who are a key element of a civic nation. "Civic government" refers to government by citizens, and "civic involvement" refers to the involvement of citizens. Your community, for example, may have a publicly funded civic centre, a place where citizens can participate in local government and take part in public events.

One understanding of the concept of civic nation combines two key elements: citizens — and their shared values and beliefs. A civic nation emerges from the choice of citizens to live together according to shared principles. A civic nation-state gives people the opportunity to live together under laws that reflect their shared values and beliefs and a similar worldview. When they do this successfully, they become a civic nation.

Ethnic nationalism claims . . . that an individual's deepest attachments are inherited, not chosen. It is the national community that defines the individual, not the individuals who define the national community.

— *Michael Ignatieff, politician, political scientist, and historian, in* Blood and Belonging: Journeys into the New Nationalism, *1995*

People agree to abide by shared laws.

↓

Mutual respect for laws enables people to live together peacefully.

This is what politician, political scientist, and historian Michael Ignatieff believes. In his book *Blood and Belonging*, Ignatieff wrote: "[Civic nationalism] maintains that the nation should be composed of all those — regardless of race, colour, creed, gender, language, or ethnicity — who subscribe to the nation's political creed. This nationalism is called civic because it envisages the nation as a community of equal, rights-bearing citizens, united in patriotic attachment to a shared set of political practices and values."

Figure 1-13 A Hindu woman carries a Québec flag as she marches in a Canada Day parade in Montréal. On the basis of this photograph, what conclusion might you draw about the idea of Canada as a civic nation?

Canada as a Civic Nation

Canadians do not share a religion, spiritual beliefs, language, ethnicity, or culture — but in a civic nation-state, these commonalities may not matter. The only important criterion may be, as Ignatieff wrote, an agreement to live together according to certain rules.

In *The Polite Revolution*, John Ibbitson suggested that Canadians' choice to live together as a civic nation is the reason the myth — even the joke — of Canadian politeness has arisen. But he also said that, joke or not, this politeness is at the core of what Canadians are. "It is the means by which we accommodate each other," he wrote. "It is the secret recipe for a nation of different cultures, languages and customs whose citizens all get along. Canadians have used politeness to foment a social revolution. And from that revolution our Canada has emerged — young, creative, polyglot, open-minded, forward-looking, fabulous."

➡ Do you agree with Ibbitson's portrayal of Canada as a civic nation? Explain your response.

Nation and Nation-State

Civic nationalism — of the French, British, and American type — defines the nation not in terms of ethnicity but in terms of willingness to adhere to its civic values. Allegiance is essentially directed toward the state and its civic institutions and values. Ethnic nationalism — of the German and Polish type — defines the nation in terms of ethnic origins and birth. Allegiance is directed primarily at the nation, at the traditions, values, and cultures incarnated in a people's history.

— *Michael Ignatieff, politician, political scientist, and historian, in* Blood and Belonging: Journeys into the New Nationalism, *1995*

One understanding of the term "civic nationalism" suggests that a sense of nation emerges from the creation of a nation-state. When a people or a number of peoples choose to live together according to certain laws, a nation emerges — and the character of this nation evolves over time.

Britain is an example of a civic nation that has emerged this way. Britain began as a nation-state made up of four nations: the Irish, Scottish, English, and Welsh peoples. Today, people of these four nations continue to live within the British nation-state, or country, but immigrants from other nations are also included. All these peoples form a British civic nation on the basis of shared values and beliefs, as well as other common ground that has evolved over time.

Compare your understanding of Canada with the model of the British civic nation. How is the idea of Canada as a civic nation similar to — or different from — the British model?

Civic nationalism is different from **ethnic nationalism**, which is founded on shared ethnicity, culture, and language. In the early 19th century, for example, German-speaking peoples lived in a number of relatively small kingdoms, duchies, principalities, and city states. But supporters of the idea of a single German nation-state believed that the German nation consisted of all people of German descent, including those living in Czechoslovakia, Austria, Switzerland, and elsewhere. In 1871, people in the small German-speaking states, such as Bavaria, Prussia and Saxony, united to form the nation-state of Germany.

How Forms of Nationalism Emerge

Ethnic Nationalism	Civic Nationalism
Pre-existing characteristics or traditions lead to a shared sense of nation.	A group of people or peoples choose to live together in a nation-state according to shared values and beliefs, often expressed in a constitution.

The people may then create a nation-state if they choose to live together with others who share their sense of nation.	The characteristics of the nation evolve over time, as common beliefs and values enable people to respect their differences.

Reflect and Respond

Think about the idea of a civic nation. Which comes first, the nation-state or the nation? Are they the same thing? Do they exist at the same time?

Use Canada and another nation-state as examples to support your response.

MAKING A DIFFERENCE

Mustafa Kemal Atatürk
Founding the Turkish Nation

During World War I, the Ottoman Empire, which was ruled by a Turkish sultan, fought on the side of Germany. When the war ended in victory for the Allies, the sultan surrendered. Control of Ottoman territories, including large parts of present-day Turkey, was parcelled out to Britain, France, Greece, and Italy.

The sultan agreed to the peace settlement — but other Turks did not. One of those who disagreed was Mustafa Kemal.

During the war, Kemal had successfully led Turkish troops in resisting an Allied invasion at Gallipoli. For this exploit and others, Turks viewed him as a hero. Kemal envisioned Turkey as a new nation: an independent republic controlled by the people rather than by sultans, religious leaders, and foreign countries.

Kemal's charismatic style drew many Turks to his cause, and in 1919, the Turkish War of Independence began. This struggle lasted three years, but by 1922, all foreign troops, as well as the sultan, had fled the country.

Kemal was elected president, a position he held till his death in 1938. He and his supporters set about transforming Turkey into a nation whose people's values were similar to those of many European countries.

- All Turkish citizens were granted the right to vote.
- Old Ottoman laws, which had been based on religious laws, were replaced by new laws.
- Traditional dress was discouraged, and European-style dress was required in public.
- Women gained the same political and social rights as men.
- Turkish became the country's official language — and Turkish script was changed to an alphabet more like the Roman letters used in European languages.
- An education system designed to promote tolerance was developed.

Figure 1-14 The Turkish people revered Mustafa Kemal so much that they gave him an additional last name: Atatürk, which means "father of the Turks." In this poster by the multimedia artist Ateş Akkor, Atatürk is pictured at the top. To the right are his own words: "My biggest success is the Turkish Republic." The words on the sign say, "This is how we established the republic."

Kemal also believed that the Turkish republic should exist in peace alongside other nations. Many Turks view his greatest achievement as encouraging them to switch their loyalty from a ruler to their nation.

In 1927, Kemal gave a famous speech designed to arouse the patriotism of Turkish young people. Here are some of his words:

> Turkish youth!
>
> Your first duty is to project and preserve the Turkish independence and the Turkish Republic forever. This is the very foundation of your existence and your future. This foundation is your most precious treasure . . . Youth of Turkey's future, even in [terrible] circumstances, it is your duty to save the Turkish independence and republic. You will find the strength you need in your noble blood.

Explorations

1. In your own words, explain the meaning of the words on the sign depicted in the poster in Figure 1-14: This is how we established the republic.
2. Was Mustafa Kemal Atatürk's vision of a Turkish republic based on the notion of an ethnic nation or a civic nation — or both?
3. Reread Atatürk's message to Turkish youth. What responsibility was he assigning to Turkish young people? Do you think a Canadian leader would direct a similar message to Canadian young people? If he or she did, how would you respond? Why?

FOCUS ON SKILLS

Developing Effective Inquiry Questions

FOCUS ON SKILLS

Many great thinkers believe that asking questions is the key to developing understanding and knowledge. The French anthropologist Claude Lévi-Strauss, for example, once said, "The scientific mind does not so much provide the right answers as ask the right questions."

But how do you know when you are asking the "right questions"? In the prologue, you learned about powerful questions. Issue questions — the kind that provide the structure of *Exploring Nationalism* — are powerful questions. Asking effective inquiry questions can help you guide your responses to these powerful questions.

Think about Turkey, for example. Suppose you are conducting research to develop responses to this issue question: Should laws require Turks to wear Western-style dress?

In a group, follow these steps to develop effective inquiry questions that will help guide your exploration of the issue question.

Steps to Developing Effective Inquiry Questions

Step 1: Conduct a quescussion

Write the issue question where everyone in the group can see it.

Warm up your thinking process by working with a group to conduct a "quescussion," a term that combines the words "question" and "discussion."

This idea-generating strategy was developed by Paul Bidwell of the University of Saskatchewan. Its goal is to open your mind to original, creative ideas by holding a discussion in which the participants can only ask questions. To ensure that only questions are asked, say "Statement!" if a group member makes a statement rather than asking a question.

Appoint a recorder to note group members' questions on a sheet of chart paper and start the quescussion.

Step 2: Choose a few effective inquiry questions

Examine the group's questions and choose three to five that you think might work as inquiry questions. In some cases, you may wish to revise a question generated during the quescussion to tighten the focus or the approach.

Use the criteria shown on the following page to help your group develop its list of questions.

Step 3: Select the most effective inquiry question.

As a group, choose the inquiry question that you believe most closely matches the criteria set out in Step 2.

Rules for a Quescussion

- As in a brainstorming session, speak up whenever you like — but do not interrupt others.
- Feed off the ideas of others.
- Ask questions that deal with feelings, not just facts (e.g., How might adopting Western-style dress create conflicts for some Turks?).
- Ask "why" questions (e.g., Why would Atatürk make this law about Western-style dress?), "if . . . then . . ." questions (e.g., If Turks dress more like Europeans, will they then be more European?), and "because" questions (e.g., Because Turks dress like Europeans, will they think more like Europeans?).

FOCUS ON SKILLS FOCUS ON SKILLS
OCUS ON SKILLS FOCUS ON SKILLS FOCUS ON SKILLS

Step 4: Revise your question

Appoint a spokesperson to present your group's question to the class and to explain why you chose it. Invite your classmates to comment on your question, then rejoin your group and discuss the feedback received. Revisit your question and decide whether you wish to revise it.

Step 5: Assess the effectiveness of your inquiry question

If you wish, you may assess the effectiveness of your inquiry question by conducting preliminary research on the Internet or in the library. As you do this, you may find it necessary to revise your question. Meet with your group to discuss possible revisions.

Creating Effective Inquiry Questions Checklist

Criterion	Question 1	Question 2	Question 3	Question 4	Question 5
• Does the question seek information?					
• Is the question relevant to the topic or issue question?					
• Responses can be found through research.					
• You don't already know the answer.					
• There may not be a right or wrong answer.					
• The question is focused and specific, not general and sprawling.					
• The question is connected to the issue you want to explore.					
• The question will help you find a variety of points of view and perspectives.					
• You find the question interesting, and you would really like to explore it.					

Summing Up

As you progress through this course, you will encounter many opportunities to develop, select, and revise inquiry questions. Following Steps 1 to 4 can help you do this.

How do people express their identity through nation?

The desire to belong is one of the strongest desires a human being can feel. Think, for example, about the sense of belonging you feel when you are part of a group such as your family, your friends, your school, or your community.

The idea of nation has the power to spark feelings of belonging to a much larger collective, and there are many similarities and areas of overlap between collective identity and national identity. This is largely because factors, such as language and religion, often inspire a sense of collective identity — and a sense of national identity.

[When I am among my own people], they understand me, as I understand them; and this understanding creates within me a sense of being somebody in the world.

— Isaiah Berlin, philosopher and historian, in "Two Concepts of Liberty," 1958

National identity is a kind of collective identity that is shared by large groups of people. In his book *Personal Identity, National Identity and International Relations*, psychologist William Bloom set out his understanding of national identity: "National identity describes that condition in which a mass of people have made the same identification with national symbols — have internalized the symbols of the nation — so that they may act as one psychological group when there is a threat to, or the possibility of enhancement of, these symbols of nationalism."

When Bloom wrote that people have internalized the symbols of nation, he meant that they had taken in these symbols and made them — consciously or unconsciously — part of themselves, their personality, and their beliefs.

Examine the graphic in Figure 1-15. It shows statements that a Lethbridge teenager of Indian heritage might make and how these might reflect her individual, collective, and national identities. Think about the language she uses. When does she use "I"? When does she use "we"? How do these words reflect the difference between individual, collective, and national identities?

Figure 1-15 Expressions of Individual, Collective, and National Identity

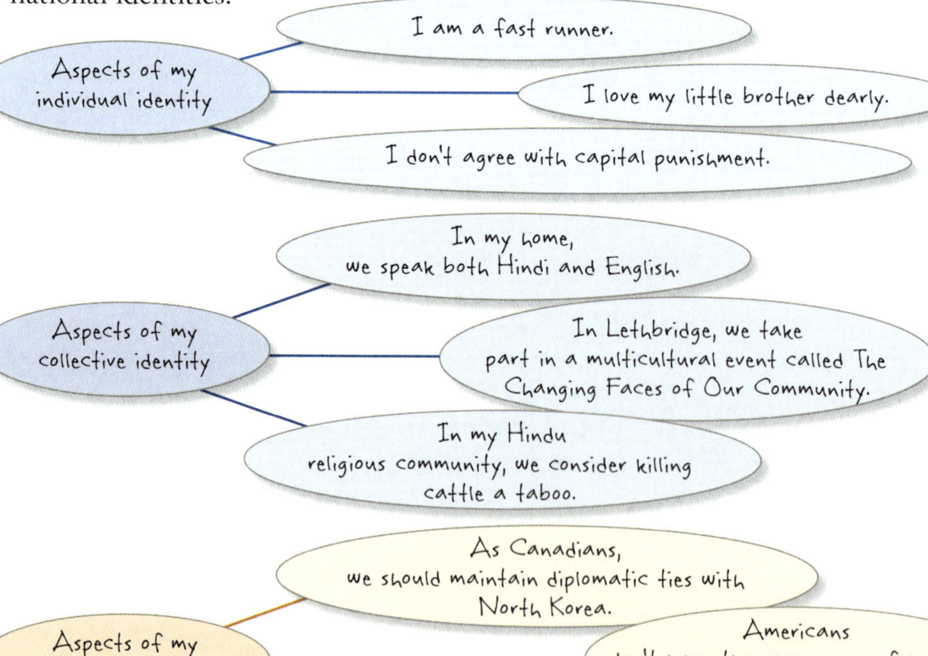

The Evolution of National Identity

The degree of connection people feel between their collective identities and their national identities depends to an extent on how their nation came into being and the extent to which it has evolved.

- A nation can develop because people feel strong shared bonds and wish to decide their own future. In this case, the feeling of collective identity is there in the beginning, and this helps create feelings of nationalism.
- Alternatively, a nation can come into being because people who belong to diverse collectives decide that they wish to live together in a nation-state according to shared values and beliefs. Mutual respect is the foundation of the nation-state — and a new nation may or may not emerge from this.

When I'm in Alberta, I'm an Edmontonian or a Calgarian; when I'm in Ottawa, I'm an Albertan or westerner; but when I'm in Washington or Singapore or Sydney, I'm Canadian.

— Preston Manning, founder of the Reform Party, in The Globe and Mail, *2007*

Taking Turns

How is nation a part of who you are?

The students responding to this question are Harley, a member of the Kainai Nation near Lethbridge; Jean, a Francophone student who lives in Calgary; and Violet, a Métis who is a member of the Paddle Prairie Métis Settlement.

Harley

I think two nations are part of who I am. The first is Kainai. The Kainai and other First Nations people have lived here longer than any other Albertans. Just last week, my grandmother took me to Áísínai'pi. I hadn't been there before, but my grandmother has told me stories about the ancient times. I will take my children and grandchildren there some day, because I want them to know our history, too.

I feel as if Canada is part of me, too, but these feelings are mixed. My grandfather fought in the Second World War because he wanted us all to live in peace here in Canada. He was a proud Canadian, and we are proud of him. He was a great Canadian — and a great Kainai.

Jean

My friend Wadji is a Francophone from Lebanon, which went through a long civil war. We sometimes talk about how his sense of Canada as part of his identity seems much stronger than mine.

I tend to think of my nation as Franco-Alberta, but Wadji identifies more with Canada. Even though I was born here and he wasn't, and even though we go to the same Francophone school, his goal is to join the English-speaking culture. He sees this as a way of blending in and becoming "Canadian," but I think people can be Canadian in many different ways. Affirming and promoting your own culture is just one of them.

Violet

For me, the answer isn't clear. Right now, I identify with the Métis people in our settlement, but I'm also thinking a lot about what will happen when I graduate from high school. A lot of kids leave Paddle Prairie to go to college or to get jobs in other places — and don't come back except to visit. They're still Métis, but they've made their lives somewhere else. And when that happens, I think being Canadian starts to become as important to them as being Métis. I want to be a biologist, so I plan to go to university. After that, if I want to work as a biologist, I'll probably have to move away. Will my feelings about nation change? I'm kind of scared — and sad — that they will.

How would you respond to the question Harley, Jean, and Violet are answering? Explain the reasons for your response. How does your identification with a nation or nations reflect one or more of your aspects of collective identity?

Figure 1-16 Comedian Seth Rogen is one of the latest in a long line of comedians who have helped boost Canada's reputation as a pretty funny country. Rogen co-wrote and starred in the 2007 blockbuster teen comedy *Superbad*. Is the Canadians-are-funny myth accurate? Does this myth affect your identity? How?

Myths and National Identity

National myths — shared stories, ideas, and beliefs that may or may not be accurate — are key to creating a sense of nation. These national myths can include everything from ancient traditional stories to beliefs about what makes a nation special. Many myths reach back into unrecorded history and have been passed on orally through generations. These shared stories, such as fairy tales and true stories of heroism or bravery, connect people with their past and shape the way they look at the world.

Although myths may or may not be accurate, they often include truths about who people think they are. Myths help people connect their sense of themselves — their identity — to the much larger group of people who form the nation.

Think about the stories told in your family, perhaps at family gatherings or other special family events. How do these stories connect you with your family's past and shape your family's shared view of the world?

Changing Myths

A nation's myths are not static. In the case of a nation founded on a common ethnicity, the myths may change and evolve over time. In the case of a civic nation, the creation and evolution of myths are what lead to a growing sense of a common collective identity among all citizens.

In the case of Canada, for example, one recently created myth suggests that Canadians are funny — and that this collective sense of humour has helped generate an unusually large number of comedians who have achieved international fame. "During the past few decades," wrote Scott Feschuk in *Reader's Digest Canada*, "Canada has definitively emerged as the class clown of the global schoolhouse: Many of today's funniest American comedians are in fact Canadian — a list that includes Jim Carrey, Mike Myers, Martin Short, Eugene Levy, Catherine O'Hara, Dave Foley, Samantha Bee, Norm Macdonald, Leslie Nielsen, Michael J. Fox, Tom Green and Dan Aykroyd."

The relationship between citizens and national identity is often reciprocal — it goes both ways. Myths influence the sense of national identity of people born into a nation or who immigrate to a nation — and these people in turn influence the myths of the nation. Do you, for example, think your identity is partly influenced by Canada's reputation as a comedy powerhouse?

Figure 1-17 Canoeists head out for a paddle on Moraine Lake in Banff National Park. The great Canadian outdoors is part of the Canadian myth of coureurs de bois, early gold seekers, and outdoor enthusiasts. Stories of coping with a harsh environment — including giant mosquitoes, freezing temperatures, and playing hockey on outdoor rinks — recur in Canadian literature. Do you think a passion for the outdoors is part of the Canadian national identity? Is it part of your identity? In what way?

National Myths and Canadian Identity

In addition to myths of Canada as a country of funny people who spend a lot of time participating in outdoor activities, many Canadians embrace the idea of Canada as a hockey nation. Since 1994, hockey has been Canada's official winter sport, and in 2004, a national survey by Pepsi-Cola Canada found that 82 per cent of those polled agreed that all children living in Canada should have an opportunity to play hockey if they want to. And 79 per cent of respondents identified the history or tradition of hockey as the factor that makes the game so important to Canadians.

Hockey also says Canada to many people in other countries. When, for example, the Canadian men's hockey team finished out of the medals at the 2006 Winter Olympics in Turin, Italy, an American reporter wrote: "In Canada . . . the birthplace of hockey where the game is a religion, the early exit will be viewed as nothing short of a national disaster."

CHECKFORWARD

You will explore more about national myths and how they shape Canadian identity in Chapter 14.

Canada has no fewer than six distinct seasons: Tax; Hockey; More Hockey; Still More Hockey; Summer (also known as the July Long Weekend, also known as "Was that it?"); and finally, Good God, Isn't the Hockey Season Over by Now?!

— *Will Ferguson and Ian Ferguson, in* How to Be a Canadian, *2001*

Reinventing an Iconic Canadian Sport

At one time, hockey was considered a sport for young men only. Now, this Canadian game is played by people of all ages, including women such as Sheema Khan, who was born in India but immigrated to Montréal with her family at the age of three. Khan is Muslim and wears a hijab. In a column in *The Globe and Mail*, she described how co-workers greeted the news that she had grown up playing hockey:

> All of a sudden, eyes looked up in disbelief. "You played hockey?" asked a friend incredulously. "Yes," I replied with a smile, thinking, "Doesn't every Canadian play hockey at some point in their life?" And then it hit me. Muslim women, especially hijabis [women who wear head scarves], aren't expected to be interested in sports, let alone play. Perhaps a calming sport like croquet. But hockey?
>
> Come on! I grew up cheering the Montreal Canadiens . . . [and] playing street hockey, driveway hockey and table hockey.

Figure 1-18 Team Canada's Carla MacLeod of Calgary scores a goal against Sweden at the 2005 world women's hockey championship. How have MacLeod and Sheema Khan, whose experience is described on this page, helped change the way hockey is viewed? How do these changes show an evolution in Canadian identity?

Khan went on to play intramural hockey at McGill University and later started a women's intramural league when she was studying at Harvard University in the United States. As a child in the early 1970s, Khan had admired Montréal Canadien goalie Ken Dryden, and she still loves hockey — but with one difference. "Now," she wrote, "I imagine myself as Hayley Wickenheiser, scoring with only seconds left to play."

On another occasion, Khan expressed her thoughts about wearing a hijab while playing the Canadian game: "We have various notions of what defines 'Canadian' identity . . . and we are now facing a choice of whether such definitions can include beliefs and customs which have not been part of historical markers of national identity." What did Khan mean? How was she challenging and changing ideas about Canadian identity?

1. Review Figure 1-15 on page 36, then create a similar graphic that includes statements about aspects of your individual, collective, and national identity. As you do this, think about the things that make you who you are. Your statements could, for example, express individual characteristics or your beliefs and values. They could express customs or ways of thinking that you share with others in a collective, and they could express patriotic feelings you have in common with others in a nation.

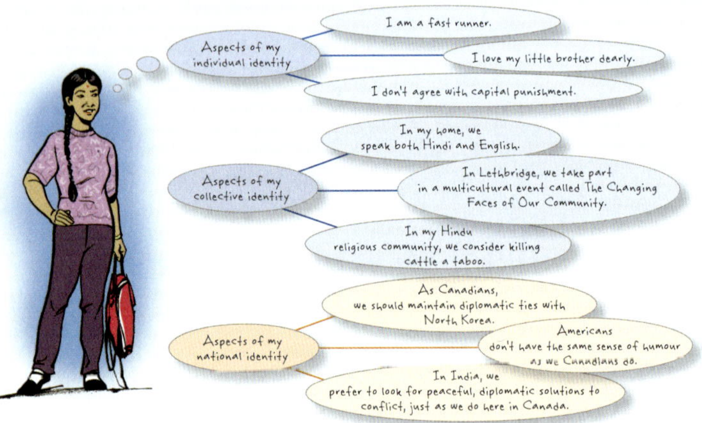

2. In his book *Identity and Violence*, Nobel Prize–winning economist Amartya Sen described the complexity of identity and loyalty:

> The same person can be, without any contradiction, an American citizen, of Caribbean origin, with African ancestry, a Christian, a liberal, a woman, a vegetarian, a long-distance runner, a historian, a schoolteacher, a novelist, a feminist, a heterosexual, a believer in gay and lesbian rights, a theatre lover, an environmental activist, a tennis fan, a jazz musician and someone who is deeply committed to the view that there are intelligent beings in outer space with whom it is extremely urgent to talk.

a) List as many aspects of your identities — individual, collective, and national — as you can. Don't limit yourself. See if you can create a list as long as the one put together by Sen.

b) Rank the various aspects you have listed by numbering them in order of importance (1 = most important; 5 = least important). If several share the same degree of importance, assign them the same number. This means, for example, that your list might include more than one aspect ranked 4.

c) Provide the criteria you used to decide on the rankings — even if you did not formally record your criteria.

d) Share your list with a partner. Note the similarities and differences. You and your partner probably have much in common (e.g., age, neighbourhood, education, and language). Write a short paragraph explaining why there are differences between your list and your partner's.

e) Remove the two most important aspects of your identities from your list. In what ways — both profound and trivial — might your life be altered by this change in your identity? Provide at least three examples of the changes.

3. Over the course of this chapter, you have explored various aspects of nation and nation-state — and how they are connected to identity. These explorations have helped you develop responses to the chapter-issue question: To what extent are nation and identity related?

a) Develop two or three criteria you would use to help you decide which aspects of nation most affect your identity. Select the aspects of nation that best meet your criteria. If you completed Question 2, review the list you compiled — and the criteria you identified — in your response to this question.

b) Share your list with a partner. If necessary, revise your list when you finish this discussion.

c) With your partner, develop and evaluate the strength of the connection between the aspects of nation you selected and your identity.

d) In a sentence or two, write your answer to the chapter-issue question. If you do not feel comfortable about writing a definitive answer, use words and phrases such as "in some cases . . ." "often . . ." and "though not everyone agrees . . ." to qualify your response.

4. Joseph Montferrand (1802–1864) was a Canadien logger who worked on the Ottawa River. Over the years, he became a larger-than-life folk hero. To Canadien loggers, he was a hero who defended them against their English bosses. To English speakers, he was a symbol of the strength and hardiness of early Canadian settlers. Over time, stories about Montferrand's exploits grew into tall tales about Joe Mufferaw, an English version of his name.

   In the 1970s, Stompin' Tom Connors wrote and recorded a song about Joe Mufferaw. The following are some verses:

   > Big Joe Mufferaw paddled into Mattawa
   > all the way from Ottawa in just one day
   > Hey-Hey
   > On the river Ottawa the best man we ever saw
   > was Big Joe Mufferaw, the old folks say
   > Come and listen and I'll tell you what the old folks say
   >
   > And they say Big Joe put out a forest fire,
   > halfway between Renfrew and old Arnprior
   > He was fifty miles away down around Smith Falls
   > but he drowneded out the fire with five spit balls.

   The verses of Stompin' Tom's song glorify Mufferaw's strength and concern for community well-being. With a partner, choose one important aspect of identity that is closely related to nation (e.g., bravery, civic involvement, obeying laws, questioning, compassion, helpfulness). Develop a tall tale using Joe Mufferaw or a character of your own choosing or invention to highlight the importance of the characteristic you and your partner chose.

   Share your tall tale with the class by telling the story, creating a comic strip, or writing and playing a song — or in some other interesting way.

Figure 1-19 Bernie Bedore wrote two books highlighting tall tales about Joe Mufferaw. Both were illustrated by Yüksel Hassan, a Canadian of Turkish heritage.

Think about Your Challenge

Look back at the challenge for this related issue. It asks you to create a coat of arms that represents your response to the related-issue question: To what extent should nation be the foundation of identity?

Review the material in this chapter and the activities you completed as you progressed through the chapter. Make notes about ideas that could be useful in completing the challenge. Your notes might include

- your current thoughts on the aspects of your identity that most affect — or are most affected by — nation, nation-state, and nationalism
- ideas about symbols that will represent your understandings of the connections between your identity and nation, nation-state, or nationalism
- some critical questions you might use to analyze and evaluate the information you will explore and use in your coat of arms

CHAPTER 2 Shaping Nationalism

Figure 2-1 When the people of France started a revolution in 1789, their battle cry was "Liberté, égalité, fraternité!" — "Liberty, equality, brotherhood!" These words became important symbols for the French, who built a nation on these principles. The cartoon depicts an imaginary young woman called Marianne who became a popular symbol of liberty. But the French are now bitterly divided over how their nation should evolve. This cartoon comments on the direction the nation seems to be taking.

CHAPTER ISSUE
To what extent do external and internal factors shape nationalism?

IN THE FALL OF 2005, riots erupted in some Paris suburbs and continued for 20 nights. The riots focused attention on the struggle of some young people — many of them French citizens born into families who had immigrated from former French colonies — to be included in French society.

In the view of many, French society and laws discriminate against non-white citizens and immigrants, who often have trouble finding jobs. As a result, they may live in suburban slums with little hope of improving their lives.

The cartoon on the facing page was created by Arcadio Esquivel and ran in the Panamanian newspaper *La Prensa* in the fall of 2005. Examine this cartoon in light of what you learned in Chapter 1 about ethnic and civic nationalism.

- What message is conveyed by the flaming banner?
- Why do you suppose Marianne is running? Do you think she is fleeing something or running toward something? What might it be?
- What elements in the cartoon represent ethnic nationalism? What elements represent civic nationalism?
- Does Esquivel favour the idea of an ethnic nation or a civic nation? What elements of the cartoon support your response?
- Do you believe that the concepts of ethnic nation and civic nation can coexist? Explain the reasons for your response.
- Does someone like Esquivel, who is not part of the nation he is commenting on, have a right — or even a responsibility — to judge what people in other nations do? Why or why not?

KEY TERMS

collective consciousness

rhetoric

LOOKING AHEAD

In this chapter, you will develop responses to the following questions as you explore the extent to which internal and external factors shape nationalism:

- What are some factors that shape nationalism?
- How have people responded to some factors that shape nationalism?
- How have people in Canada responded to some factors that shape nationalism?

My Journal on Nationalism

Use words or images — or both — to express your current ideas about nation, identity, and nationalism. Date your ideas and keep them in your journal, notebook, learning log, portfolio, or computer file so that you can return to them as you progress through this course.

What are some factors that shape nationalism?

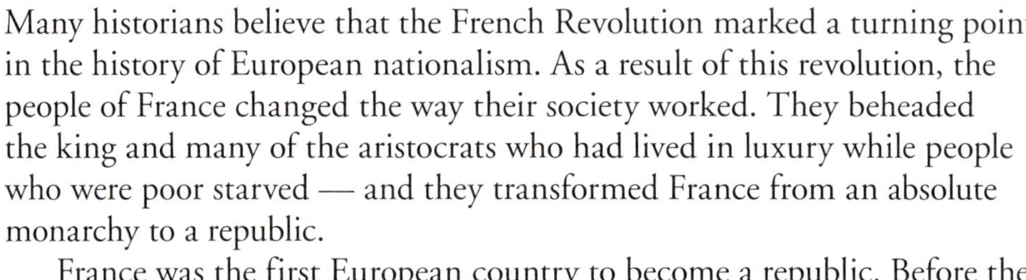

Voices

Sovereign power resides in my person alone. To me alone belongs all legislative power with neither any responsibility to others nor any division of that power. Public order, in all its entirety, emanates from me, and the rights and interests of the nation are necessarily bound up with my own and rest only in my hands.

— Louis XV, grandfather of King Louis XVI of France, 1766

Many historians believe that the French Revolution marked a turning point in the history of European nationalism. As a result of this revolution, the people of France changed the way their society worked. They beheaded the king and many of the aristocrats who had lived in luxury while people who were poor starved — and they transformed France from an absolute monarchy to a republic.

France was the first European country to become a republic. Before the revolution, the king had been the focus of many French people's sense of nation. But the revolution changed this. People began to focus their loyalty on the idea of themselves — the people — as the nation.

Think about the words of Louis XV in "Voices" and Benedict Anderson's definition of nation as an "imagined political community" (p. 22). Use the ideas of these two men to explain why the French Revolution might be considered a turning point in the history of European nationalism.

The French Revolution, and the events that followed, was an eruption that shows how nationalism can be shaped by external factors. These external factors can be historical, social, economic, geographic, and political. But these factors do not operate in isolation. In France, they overlapped, combined, and built on one another to create a sense of nation — and to shape the development of French nationalism.

Figure 2-2 This print shows the executioner preparing the guillotine to execute Louis XVI, the French king, in 1793. Louis's public execution drew a huge crowd. The people shouted, "Vive la nation!" and "Vive la république!" — "Long live the nation!" and "Long live the republic!" How did their words show a shift in loyalty?

Some Historical Factors That Shaped French Nationalism

No single event caused the French Revolution. The path to revolution was a long process that unfolded over decades. Still, a single event can often capture a people's collective imagination and inspire them to take action. In the case of France in 1789, this event was the storming of the Bastille.

The Bastille was a Paris prison where, it was rumoured, the king locked up people who spoke out against him. On July 14, 1789, about 600 angry Parisians successfully attacked the Bastille and took control of this symbol of tyranny. This event is usually considered the beginning of the French Revolution, and July 14 is now celebrated as a national holiday in France.

Figure 2-3 In 1789, Jean-Pierre Houel painted this famous picture of the storming of the Bastille — a royal fortress that had been converted into a prison. Why do you suppose this structure might have become the focus of people's anger?

The Bastille as a Nationalist Symbol

As news of the storming of the Bastille spread, it inspired other French people to take up arms against the king and the nobility. In subsequent years, this event entered the French people's **collective consciousness** — an internal consciousness, or awareness, shared by many — as a defining moment in their history as a nation. It became a central part of their national myth because it said, "We are a nation. We can govern ourselves — in our own interests."

Since then, the symbolic importance of the storming of the Bastille has extended far beyond France. More than two centuries later, the event continues to inspire people by reminding them that the actions of ordinary citizens can start a chain of events that lead to great change.

Read "FYI" on this page. The fact that the Bastille contained no political prisoners at that time has not affected its status as a symbol of French nationalism. Does this matter? Should this fact make a difference in the status of the fall of the Bastille as a powerful nationalist symbol? What aspects of the storming of the Bastille made this event so important?

When the Parisian citizens entered the Bastille, they found only seven prisoners — four counterfeiters, two men who had been declared insane, and a young aristocrat who was locked up because he had displeased his father.

Some Social Factors That Shaped French Nationalism

The term "social factors" refers to the relationships among people in a society. These factors include

- who should be considered important and who should not
- who should lead and who should follow
- who should be included and who should be excluded
- how groups should work out conflicts and respond to challenges

Before the French Revolution, France was divided into a strict social order that was defined largely by birth. The monarch and aristocrats, who also made up much of the high-ranking clergy in the Catholic Church, held most of the power.

In 1789, this ruling elite made up about four per cent of France's total estimated population of 26 million. The remaining 96 per cent were considered common people. The ruling elite paid few taxes, but their power enabled them to accumulate great wealth by collecting taxes, rents, and other fees from the common people.

Figure 2-5 This political cartoon was created in 1789, the year the French Revolution began. It shows a chained, blindfolded, and naked common man carrying an aristocrat, a bishop of the Catholic Church, and a judge on his back. What statement about French society was the cartoonist making?

Figure 2-4 A tourist visiting Havana, Cuba, sports a T-shirt bearing the image of Ernesto "Che" Guevara. Like events, people can become powerful symbols of nationalism. Born in Argentina, Guevara helped Fidel Castro lead a successful revolution in Cuba before being executed in Bolivia in 1967. In death, Guevara has become a legend. Name some other people and events that have become powerful symbols of nation and nationalism.

France as the Centre of New Ideas

During the 1700s, France was a cultural centre of Europe. Paris, the country's capital, provided fertile ground for developing new ideas. In the city's cafés, as well as salons — gatherings held in private homes and public buildings — writers, artists, philosophers, and others gathered to question the established order and to discuss ideas such as liberty, happiness, religious freedom, and individual rights.

These intellectuals used the mass media of the day — books, pamphlets, and newspapers — to spread their ideas. One of the most famous writers and thinkers was François-Marie Arouet, better known by his pen name, Voltaire. A wit who often poked fun at the nobility, Voltaire once said, "In general, the art of government consists in taking as much money as possible from one class of citizens to give to another." On two occasions, Voltaire was thrown into the Bastille for insulting aristocrats.

Voltaire also said, "Man is free at the moment he wishes to be." Do you agree? Why might this statement have angered aristocrats? How might it have helped inspire French nationalism?

Figure 2-6 This illustration shows Voltaire on a staircase as he leaves a salon. Women played an important role in salons, often hosting regular gatherings and turning them into fashionable events where people practised the art of conversation and debate.

A Growing Middle Class

The common people of France included a growing middle class called the bourgeoisie. Members of this group usually lived in towns and cities, where they had become prosperous in business or by practising a craft or profession. They were often well-travelled and well-educated, and many had absorbed new ideas about individual rights. Voltaire's father, for example, was an educated man whose work as a public official placed him squarely in the bourgeoisie.

Most members of the bourgeoisie were aware that in Britain, the power of the monarch had been limited by a parliament — and that in Britain's American colonies, a revolutionary war had led to the creation of an independent republic, the United States, in 1783. They were also aware of scientific discoveries that challenged old beliefs about the way the world worked.

The French bourgeoisie provided the audience for the new ideas that were spread through the mass media. These ideas changed the way people thought of themselves and of their relationships with other groups, but these people could do little to change French society. They were excluded from decision-making power.

Create a web diagram with the words "People's New Sense of the French Nation" at the centre. To this, link the various social factors that helped shape new ideas about the French nation. Under each factor, write one or two points explaining its role.

Some Economic Factors That Shaped French Nationalism

During the 18th century, France was almost constantly at war with its traditional rival, Britain, as well as other European countries. These conflicts, which included some support for the rebels in the American War of Independence, were costly — and largely unsuccessful.

As a result, the French economy was in chaos by the late 1780s. The decades of war had drained the treasury, and the country was nearly bankrupt. To raise money, Louis XVI decided that the people, including French aristocrats, should pay more taxes.

But the aristocrats blocked Louis XVI's plan. In desperation, Louis called a meeting of the Estates General to address the economic crisis. This French version of a parliament seldom met. In fact, when Louis called the meeting, the Estates General had not gathered in more than 170 years.

Read "Voices" and "FYI" on this page. What do Voltaire's words suggest about the level of French public support in 1759 for war against Britain? How might this affect nationalism in France? How might it affect nationalism among French people in New France?

The Seven Years' War was one of Louis XV's costliest defeats. This war (1756–1763) involved Canada, where the British won an important victory at the Battle of the Plains of Abraham in 1759. The treaty that ended the war officially gave New France to the British — and changed the course of Canadian history.

You know that [Britain and France] have been at war over a few acres of snow near Canada, and that they are spending on this fine struggle more than Canada itself is worth.

— *Voltaire, in* Candide, *1759*

The Estates General

The Estates General comprised elected representatives of three separate estates, or social groups:

- First Estate — clergy
- Second Estate — aristocrats
- Third Estate — common people

In the past, the three estates had always met and voted separately. The majority vote of each estate was then expressed as a single vote, so the First and Second Estates could always outnumber the Third Estate by 2 to 1.

When the Estates General met in June 1789, Louis XVI's plan to persuade them to approve new taxes backfired. Members of the Third Estate, who were mostly lawyers and other members of the bourgeoisie, were determined to change the system and create a constitution that set out equal rights for all men. They declared themselves the National Assembly and swore the Tennis Court Oath, saying that they were the only group who represented the nation.

This act of defiance, as well as news that Louis was gathering troops, inspired Parisians to storm the Bastille a few days later. As news of this event spread, people in other parts of France rose up against the nobles and clergy who had controlled them — and the revolution started.

Return to the web diagram you created earlier and revise it to show how economic factors contributed to new ideas about the French nation.

Figure 2-7 In June 1789, the Third Estate and some clergy who had joined them went to their meeting hall. But the door was locked. Suspecting a plot, they rushed to a nearby indoor tennis court. There, they swore the Tennis Court Oath, vowing to stay put until they had created a constitution that placed power in the hands of the people. What elements in this painting of the scene might be designed to inspire a sense of nationalism?

Detecting Rhetoric and Bias in Historical Writing

FOCUS ON SKILLS

To "sell" ideas to others, writers and speakers often use **rhetoric** — the art of shaping language to influence the thoughts and actions of an audience.

Rhetoric usually contains subtle biases — and detecting an author's bias can help readers decide whether, and how, they are being manipulated. The bias indicates the conclusion(s) an author hopes readers will reach.

During the French Revolution, some high-ranking Catholic clergy, who were members of the First Estate, joined the Third Estate in supporting the principles of liberty, equality, and fraternity. One of these was Emmanuel-Joseph Sieyès.

Sieyès was an abbé — a senior church official — who became one of the revolutionary leaders. He had mastered the art of rhetoric, and he used this skill to inspire people to join the revolutionary cause. The following excerpts are from Sieyès's pamphlet titled *What Is the Third Estate?* It was published in January 1789 and, within a few months, had sold 30 000 copies.

> The plan of this book is fairly simple. We must ask ourselves three questions.
>
> 1. What is the Third Estate? *Everything.*
>
> 2. What has it been until now in the political order? *Nothing.*
>
> 3. What does it want to be? *Something . . .*
>
> Who . . . shall dare to say that the Third Estate has not within itself all that is necessary for the formation of a complete nation? It is the strong and robust man who has one arm still shackled. If the privileged order [aristocrats] should be abolished, the nation would be nothing less, but something more. Therefore, what is the Third Estate? Everything; but an everything shackled and oppressed. What would it be without the privileged order? Everything, but an everything free and flourishing. Nothing can succeed without it, everything would be infinitely better without the others . . .
>
> The Third Estate embraces, then, all that which belongs to the nation; and all that which is not the Third Estate cannot be regarded as being of the nation.
>
> What is the Third Estate?
>
> It is everything.

The following steps can help you analyze and evaluate the rhetoric and bias in this piece of writing.

Steps to Detecting Rhetoric and Bias in Historical Writing

Step 1: Research the context

To understand any piece of historical writing, it is essential to find out about the speaker, the times, and the context in which a piece was written. To understand the excerpts from Sieyès's pamphlet, for example, it helps to understand the social structure of pre-revolutionary France. It also helps to know that although Sieyès was a senior church official — and was, therefore, considered a member of the powerful First Estate — he had been deeply influenced by ideas about individual rights and equality, and had joined the representatives of the Third Estate in the National Assembly.

What else might you want to discover about this man to help you understand him and the context of his writing? With a partner, create three inquiry questions that might help guide this research.

You might, for example, want to know whether Sieyès published other similar works, what thinkers influenced his work most profoundly, how people responded to his writing, and whether other members of the Third Estate published similar works.

Use the Internet, your school library, or *Exploring Nationalism* to develop responses to your questions.

Step 2: Develop an overall impression of the piece

Reread the excerpt on the previous page, jotting down the thoughts and ideas that come to mind. While reading, did you feel inspired? Angry? Another emotion? What thoughts jumped out at you? Did you find yourself agreeing or disagreeing with Sieyès? Why?

These notes will help you recall your first impression of the piece.

Step 3: Identify examples of rhetoric

Guiding readers to a specific conclusion is the purpose of rhetoric. Given what you have learned about Sieyès, what conclusion(s) do you think he hoped readers would come to after reading his pamphlet?

Read the excerpt again to find out whether and how Sieyès used rhetoric to help achieve his goal of guiding readers to a specific conclusion. To help you do this, ask yourself questions like those on the chart titled "Identifying Rhetoric" on this page.

Step 4: Identify how bias contributes to rhetoric

Bias is a tool that writers use to enhance their rhetoric. Bias is sometimes obvious, but more often it is subtle — hidden in word choices and images.

Read the excerpt again to detect the subtle biases included in Sieyès's rhetoric. To help you do this, ask yourself questions like those shown on the chart titled "Identifying Bias." Add at least one more question — and your responses — to the chart.

IDENTIFYING RHETORIC		
Question	**Response**	**Example(s)**
Does the author use simple, memorable words?		
Does the author repeat key terms or phrases?		
Does the author create one or more images that stick in the mind?		
Does the author use emotional language?		
Does the author keep the message simple and straightforward?		

IDENTIFYING BIAS		
Question	**Response**	**Example(s)**
Does specific vocabulary create bias? Identify the basis of the bias.		
Do the facts selected tilt your conclusion(s) in a specific direction?		
Do the examples selected favour one group over another?		
Are any groups singled out and shown in a particularly positive or negative light?		
Are counter-arguments included?		
Does the author use stereotyping or overgeneralizing?		
Does the author appeal to emotions rather than reason?		

Vocabulary Tip

When thinking about bias, it helps to understand two key words: **stereotyping** and **overgeneralizing**.

- **Stereotyping** occurs when someone places people in categories according to preconceived beliefs about how members of a particular group think or behave. Saying that Canadians have a great sense of humour is an example of stereotyping.
- **Overgeneralizing** occurs when someone draws a conclusion based on too little information. Meeting a Canadian with a great sense of humour and concluding that all Canadians have a great sense of humour is an example of overgeneralizing.

Summing Up

As you progress through this course, you will encounter many examples of historical writing. You can use these steps to help you detect rhetoric and bias in people's written and spoken words. Detecting rhetoric and bias helps you analyze and evaluate historical writing by understanding its messages and how it was shaped to guide people to reach a specific conclusion.

Some Geographic Factors That Shaped French Nationalism

At the same time as Louis XVI was demanding that people pay more taxes, large parts of France were suffering severe weather. The winter of 1788–1789 was bitterly cold, with piles of snow that blocked roads and made trade and travel impossible. When the snow melted, it caused floods in some areas. Then, in the spring and summer of 1789, parts of the country were hit by drought — a long period of dry weather.

These conditions combined to destroy grain crops and create a shortage. As the shortage worsened, the price of flour rose. As a result, many people could no longer afford to buy bread, which was a staple of their diet.

Riots occurred in the countryside as hungry people attacked wagons carrying grain to markets and seized grain supplies. In this tense atmosphere, rumours abounded. One of them suggested that aristocrats were preparing to attack people who were poor. How might a rumour like this have contributed to revolution?

FYI

In August 1788, Parisians paid nine sous for a two-kilogram loaf of bread. By February 1789, the price had risen to 14.5 sous. A labourer who was lucky enough to have a full-time job might earn between 20 and 35 sous a day.

Is armed rebellion justified when people believe that government actions are causing their hardships?

Famine Feeds Rumour

Louis XVI had married Marie Antoinette, a member of the Austrian royal family. In the past, Austria and France had often been at war, and many people distrusted the queen. She was viewed as a foreigner, and some even believed that she was a spy for the Austrian government.

As the bread shortage in France became worse and the poor starved, more and more people came to resent the extravagance of the French royal court. Many blamed Marie Antoinette for the lavish spending and making the country's financial problems even worse. As a result, they willingly believed a widespread rumour about her response when she was asked how people who couldn't afford to buy bread were to survive. She was said to have answered, "Let them eat cake."

The rumour was untrue; Marie Antoinette never said this. But the story was repeated, and for many people, it came to symbolize the huge gap between the royal family and the common people. As people became disillusioned with the monarchy, rumours like this fanned the flames of revolution and helped turn people toward new ideas about nation.

Return once more to the sketch you created earlier and revise it to show how geographic factors contributed to new ideas about the French nation.

Figure 2-8 Kirsten Dunst played Marie Antoinette, wife of Louis XVI, in a 2006 movie. The marriage of Marie Antoinette and Louis was arranged by their parents when she was 14 and he was 15. The two royal families hoped that the marriage would lead to lasting peace between their countries. Merging royal families through marriage was a common way of gaining influence over the affairs of another country.

THE VIEW FROM HERE

THE VIEW FROM HERE

THE VIEW FROM HERE

THE VIEW FROM HERE

According to French tradition, the people presented *cahiers de doléances* — lists of grievances — to delegates representing them at the Estates General. The *cahiers* also included proposed solutions to the problems. So when Louis XVI called the meeting of the Estates General, people in cities, towns, and villages across France began drawing up and debating their *cahiers.*

The *cahiers* describe people's concerns — and show how deeply divided French society was in 1789. The following are excerpts from a few of them.

From Ménouville, a rural community near Paris

> We beg His Majesty to have pity on our farmland because of the hail we have had.
>
> Also we have a great deal of waste land which is covered with juniper, and this causes much trouble on account of the rabbits which are very numerous; it is this that makes us unable to pay the dues we owe to His Majesty . . .
>
> We have one small meadow which only produces sour hay. The animals refuse to eat it. This is why we cannot raise stock . . .
>
> We state that there should not be any tax men; there could be a levy [tax] put on drinks so that everyone would be free.

From the bourgeoisie of Lauris in southern France

> To close off employment possibilities and respectable occupations to the most numerous and useful class is like killing genius and talents, and forcing them to run away from an ungrateful home. However, in our current constitution, only nobles enjoy all prerogatives like landed wealth, honours, dignities, graces, pensions, retirements, responsibility for government, and free schools . . . These [privileges] constitute the favours the State lavishes exclusively on the nobility, at the expense of the Third Estate.

From the clergy of Blois, a town near Orléans, southwest of Paris

> The clergy of the *bailliage* of Blois have never believed that the constitution needed reform. Nothing is wanting to assure the welfare of king and people except that the present constitution should be religiously and inviolably observed.

From the nobility of Blois

> The misfortune of France arises from the fact that it has never had a fixed constitution . . . The principles of this constitution should be simple; they may be reduced to two: security for person, security for property . . .
>
> Art. I. In order to assure the exercise of this first and most sacred of the rights of man, we ask that no citizen may be exiled, arrested or held prisoner except in cases contemplated by the law and in accordance with a decree originating in the regular courts of justice.
>
> Art. 2. A tax is a partition [a dividing up] of property.
>
> This partition ought not to be otherwise than voluntary; in any other case the rights of property are violated: Hence it is the indefeasible and inalienable right of the nation to consent to its taxes.

Explorations

1. Create a chart like the one shown at right. On the chart, list each group and the action(s) it proposed. Rate the argument(s) presented as strong or weak. In the final column, write a point-form note supporting your rating.
2. Write a series of points or sentences explaining how these documents show the great divide between the three estates — and how they contributed to the tensions between the estates.

Grievances and Recommendations

Group	Proposed Action(s)	Rating of Argument		Reason(s) for Rating
		Strong	Weak	

Some Political Factors That Shaped French Nationalism

Who has the right to decide when a government must be overthrown?

By late summer 1789, the National Assembly had put the finishing touches on the Declaration of the Rights of Man and of the Citizen. This political action, which abolished the traditional privileges enjoyed by the monarch, the clergy, and the aristocracy, sparked a bloody struggle that eventually led to the creation of a French nation based on new principles. It established France as a secular — non-religious — republic.

The 17 articles of the declaration set out these principles and became the basis of the new French constitution. This document has influenced all subsequent declarations and charters of rights.

Read the first four articles of the Declaration of the Rights of Man and of the Citizen in Figure 2-9. Who was excluded from this statement of the rights of the people of the nation? Compare the wording of this document with the wording of the Canadian Charter of Rights and Freedoms in Figure 1-12 (p. 30). What similarities and differences do you notice?

Web Connection

To read the entire Declaration of the Rights of Man and of the Citizen, go to this web site and follow the links.

www.ExploringNationalism.ca

Reaction outside France

As the revolution took hold in France, the ruling elites in other countries watched with growing fear. They were afraid that the events in France might inspire people in their own country to take similar actions.

Many French royalists — people who supported the king — had fled to neighbouring countries. Their stories of ill treatment at the hands of the revolutionaries fuelled the fears of ruling elites outside France. As a result, other countries, such as Austria, sent forces to invade France in an attempt to restore the power of the monarchy. Do you think these actions would have weakened or strengthened French nationalism? Why?

The revolutionaries successfully fought these invasions. But in response to outside threats and to ensure that the gains made during the revolution would not be lost, they executed Louis XVI and Marie Antoinette in 1793.

Figure 2-9 Declaration of the Rights of Man and of the Citizen

The representatives of the French people, organized as a National Assembly, believing that the ignorance, neglect, or contempt of the rights of man are the sole cause of public calamities and of the corruption of governments, have determined to set forth in a solemn declaration the natural, unalienable, and sacred rights of man . . .

Articles:

1. *Men are born and remain free and equal in rights. Social distinctions may be founded only upon the general good.*
2. *The aim of all political association is the preservation of the natural and imprescriptible [unchangeable or obvious] rights of man. These rights are liberty, property, security, and resistance to oppression.*
3. *The principle of all sovereignty resides essentially in the nation. No body or individual may exercise any authority which does not proceed directly from the nation.*
4. *Liberty consists in the freedom to do everything which injures no one else; hence the exercise of the natural rights of each man has no limits except those which assure to the other members of the society the enjoyment of the same rights. These limits can only be determined by law.*

The Revolution Becomes Extreme

Not everyone in France agreed with the way the revolution was being carried out. Many people were horrified by some of the brutal acts that were taking place and by the execution of the king and queen. Fearing opposition within the country, revolutionary leaders began a crackdown that became known as the Reign of Terror.

This period lasted for about 11 months in 1793 and 1794. The constitution was suspended and anyone who criticized the revolution was targeted. About 200 000 people were arrested, and 17 000 were sentenced to death.

Olympe de Gouges was one of them. Like many other women, de Gouges had played an active role in the early days of the revolution. She wrote plays and pamphlets supporting the revolutionaries. But in 1791, she challenged revolutionary leaders by pointing out that the Declaration of the Rights of Man excluded women. To remedy the situation, she wrote a pamphlet titled the *Declaration of the Rights of Woman and of the Female Citizen*. She also disagreed with executing the king, and when the Reign of Terror began in 1793, she was arrested, found guilty of treason, and beheaded.

Oh, you, pride of my country
Who saw kings at your feet
Your life has just ended
But you cannot die in us

— *François Georgin, French painter and poet, 1833*

It is the fashion of the day to glorify Bonaparte's victories . . . It is forgotten that everyone used to lament [his] victories, forgotten that the people, the courts, the generals, the intimates of Napoléon were all weary of his oppression and his conquests. . .

— *Vicomte de Chateaubriand, in* Mémoires d'outre-tombe, *1848–1850*

The Rise of Napoléon

Although the Reign of Terror ended in 1794, the revolutionaries split into factions — small groups within a larger group. For the next several years, French governments were unstable as these factions struggled for power. Finally, in 1799, Napoléon Bonaparte emerged as a leader who united the French and brought order to the country.

Napoléon did this — and conquered most of Europe — by launching a series of wars. In the end, though, he was defeated at the Battle of Waterloo by the British and their allies. He died in exile in 1821.

Many people remember Napoléon as an inspirational leader. His wartime victories helped strengthen French national pride. He modernized the government and laid the foundations for public education. The rule of law he established is the basis of the legal system in France today — and it also influenced the system of civil law now used in Québec.

But others remember him as a dictator whose wars cost the lives of a million French people. About three million Russian, German, British, Italian and Spanish soldiers also died in these wars.

Figure 2-10 Olympe de Gouges was the daughter of a butcher. Her hopes that revolution would bring equality for women were dashed when it became apparent that the revolutionary principle of equality applied only to men.

Reflect and Respond

The French Revolution shifted French citizens' collective consciousness to the idea that they, the people, are the nation. On the basis of what you have read about the revolution, which factors — historical, social, economic, geographic, or political — do you think exerted the most powerful influence in reshaping French ideas about nation? Explain the criteria you used to make your choice.

Think about Canada today. Does the factor you chose exert an equally powerful influence in Canada? If so, how? If not, why not?

GEOREALITY

The Disastrous Russian Campaign

Even Napoléon Bonaparte's enemies agreed that he was a brilliant military leader. By 1812, the French emperor had conquered much of Europe using tactics that enabled him to quickly move his armies to wherever troops were needed. He did this by refusing to allow soldiers to wait for supply wagons, which moved much more slowly than infantry and cavalry. He ordered his troops to live off the land, seizing food and supplies from farmers and anyone else in their path.

A Fateful Decision

In late June 1812, Napoléon ignored the advice of his advisers and launched an invasion of Russia. His plan was to gather a huge army at the Neman River, march 950 kilometres across the vast Russian plains, capture Moscow, and get rid of the czar, the Russian ruler. Estimates of the size of Napoléon's force vary, but most historians agree that he assembled at least 420 000 soldiers from every corner of his empire. At the time, this was the largest fighting force that had ever been put together.

Napoléon planned to continue using the tactics that had worked so successfully in previous campaigns. But Russia was a very different challenge. The country is huge, the terrain is difficult, and the weather is unpredictable. In addition, the Russian people were willing to die rather than face defeat.

Still, the Russian army was a fraction of the size of Napoléon's force. Greatly outnumbered, the Russian commanders decided to take advantage of their country's geography. They ordered their troops to retreat just ahead of Napoléon's armies. As the Russians withdrew, they adopted a scorched-earth policy, destroying everything in their wake. This left little food for Napoléon's troops to forage.

In addition, the summer was extremely hot and dry. Weakened by lack of food and exhausted by the blazing heat, many of Napoléon's soldiers became sick. Infection and disease spread like wildfire. Some estimates say that more than 150 000 French soldiers were sick or had died or deserted before a single battle was fought.

Reaching Moscow

Just outside Moscow, the Russian commander decided to make a stand. The fighting lasted all day — until both armies were exhausted. At that point, the Russians, who were still outnumbered, retreated once again. This left Moscow open to the French, but when they entered the city, they discovered that everyone had fled, taking with them everything they could carry. Things grew even worse for the French when fire destroyed much of the city.

A Miscalculation

Still, Napoléon was convinced that the czar would surrender, so he kept his troops in Moscow as the weather grew colder. But the czar and the Russian commanders knew that all they had to do was wait. The coming winter would be their ally.

Napoléon stayed five weeks before ordering his troops to start the long march home. This delay proved fatal. That year, winter started earlier than usual and the weather quickly grew very cold and snowy.

Napoléon's soldiers, who had started the campaign in June, were ill-equipped to withstand the freezing temperatures and howling winds. Thousands froze to death as they trudged back toward the Neman River.

"Our lips stuck together," wrote one tired soldier. "Our nostrils froze. We seemed to be marching in a world of ice." Soldiers sometimes stacked the frozen corpses of their fallen comrades to make walls as shelter against the cold. They also had to cope with Cossacks, mounted Russian troops, who were killing stragglers and harassing the French rear guard.

By the time Napoléon's army crossed the Neman River again, some historians believe that only 10 000 soldiers remained alive.

Figure 2-11 Climograph for Moscow, Russia

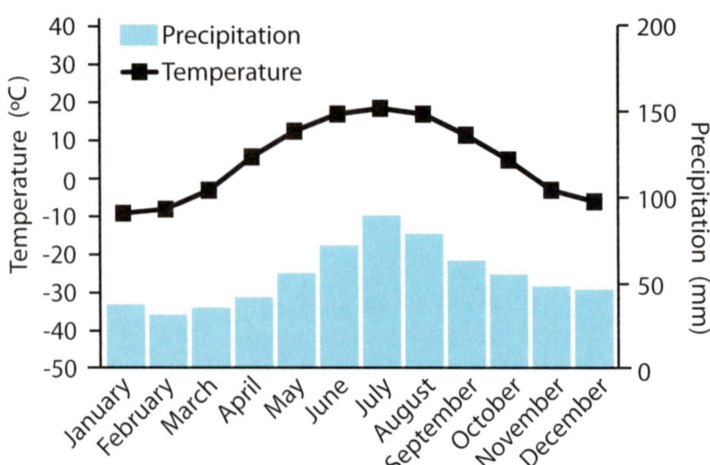

The Beginning of the End

The Russian campaign marked the beginning of the end for Napoléon. His army, which had been the source of his strength at home and had helped him build a French empire in Europe, was fatally weakened and would never recover.

Without a strong army behind him, Napoléon began to lose his grip on power. People lost their fear of him, and in early 1814, foreign armies entered Paris. France changed again — and Napoléon's disastrous Russian campaign had been the turning point.

The statistical map in Figure 2-12 is based on a document produced in 1861 by Charles Joseph Minard, a French engineer. It shows just how disastrous the Russian campaign was. The dark blue band shows the size of Napoléon's army as it crossed the Neman River in June. The light blue band shows the size of the army as it set out from Moscow and returned home. The line graph at the bottom shows the temperatures as the French army retreated.

Figure 2-12 Statistical Map of Napoléon's Russian Campaign, 1812

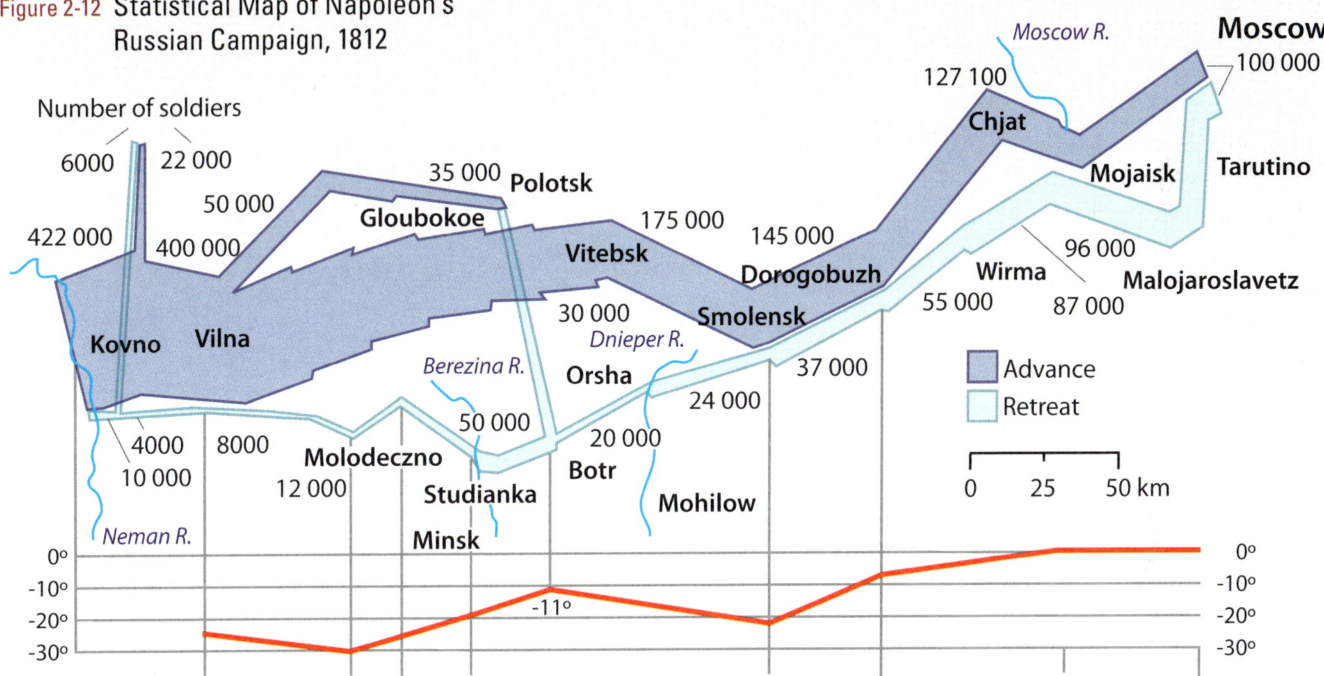

Explorations

1. Examine the statistical map shown in Figure 2-12. How is this map like a graph? How is it like a map? Why do you think Charles Joseph Minard decided to present the information in this unique form?
2. Compare the temperatures in the statistical map in Figure 2-12 with the average temperatures for August, September, and October in the climograph for Moscow (Figure 2-11). What does this comparison show? What do you think defeated Napoléon: bad weather or bad planning?
3. In an attempt to win the support of Poles, who sent troops for his army, Napoléon called his campaign the Polish War. In Russia, the czar called the invasion the Patriotic War. How do both these names appeal to nationalism?
4. How do you think news of the campaign would have affected French nationalism? Russian nationalism? In a sentence or two, sum up the extent to which physical geography affected the evolution of nationalism in France and Russia.

How have people responded to some factors that shape nationalism?

Is requiring people to study their country's history a positive way of ensuring that citizens develop shared memories? Or is it nothing but a way of manipulating citizens' nationalistic feelings?

Think about the actors, musicians, and athletes you admire. You may, for example, be a fan of Nelly Furtado's music. You may admire the exploits of a hockey player like Ryan Smyth, or eagerly follow the career of Jacques Villeneuve.

All these people are Canadians. You may take pride in their achievements — and the achievements of other Canadians. This pride may inspire you to feel a greater sense of nationalism. If this is the case, it means that you have internalized your feelings of nationalism.

Nationalism and Remembering

The glue that holds a community or a nation together is often made up of shared memories: memories of friendship, kindness, acceptance, belonging, support, sacrifice, courage, and success.

As the French Revolution and the Napoléonic era unfolded, French people developed a collective consciousness that grew out of their shared memory of — and shared pride in — specific events. This often happened even if people had not been involved in the event. The storming of the Bastille is an example. Only about 600 revolutionaries took part in this event, but it became a powerful historical symbol for people across France.

Figure 2-13 Jacques-Louis David created this famous painting of Napoléon crossing the Alps to commemorate an important French military victory. In reality, Napoléon rode a donkey across the Alps. What might have motivated David to portray the event this way?

Events such as the storming of the Bastille become symbols because they help people share a sense of belonging to a nation. People also develop other symbols that help them share a sense of belonging. Shortly after the Bastille was stormed, for example, the revolutionaries started wearing red, white, and blue cockades, or badges, to identify themselves as revolutionaries. This cockade became such a powerful symbol that its colours were later chosen for the French flag.

Individuals can also become important national symbols. Nearly 200 years after Napoléon Bonaparte's death, for example, he remains a powerful nationalistic symbol for the French. Napoléon viewed his military conquests as a mission to extend to all of Europe the revolutionary principles that had taken root in France. He explained his actions by saying, "I fought the decrepit monarchies of the old regime because the alternative was the destruction of [everything I and the revolution had achieved in France]."

To many French, Napoléon is a revered national hero who tried to abolish monarchies throughout Europe. But many British and others who fought, and eventually defeated, the French general view him as a power-hungry dictator who caused great suffering. How would these differing views have been shaped by the sense of nation of the people involved?

Challenging the Defining Histories of France

A nation's myths — its history — are often told by the dominant cultural group. In some cases, new generations begin to notice that these stories do not match the current reality. In 1789, French citizens rejected an absolute monarch as the focus of their idea of nation and based their nation on the principles of liberty, equality, and brotherhood. But today, many French citizens are questioning whether these words truly symbolize their nation. They do not believe that all French citizens are treated equally and have the same rights.

In the past, French people — like people in many countries — subjected many groups of immigrants to discrimination. In the 19th century, for example, Belgians who worked in France's coal, iron, and steel industries were often called *pots de beurre* (butter pots) or *vermines* (vermin). Italian and Polish immigrant workers were often scorned for their religious devotion, and Polish miners were forcibly returned to Poland during the 1930s.

Immigrants and Racisim

French citizens from France's former North African colonies of Algeria, Morocco, and Tunisia have experienced racism more recently. Many of these people, who are Muslims, were welcomed to France when immigrant labour was needed. From 1945 to 1974, for example, France had a fairly open immigration policy because the country needed workers to help rebuild after World War II. Many of these immigrants became French citizens.

But when a severe energy crisis hit in 1973, the French economy slowed. As jobs became harder to find, the country began shutting its doors to immigrants. By that time, however, the country's Muslim population had grown, and unlike other minorities, the members of this group were quite visible. Today, about six million French citizens are Muslims. Many of them live in low-income suburbs of Paris, Lille, Lyon, Marseille, and other cities.

Citizenship and French Nationalism

Some people began to suggest that the country's Muslim minority was threatening the French national identity. In recent years, the country has passed strict laws governing who can — and cannot — become a citizen. In 2004, another law came into effect after heated debate. It forbids the wearing of "conspicuous" religious apparel in state schools. The banned items include Jewish yarmulkes, Sikh turbans, large Christian crosses, and Muslim headscarves.

Read the comments in "Voices." Does the debate over headscarves and other religious apparel suggest that France's national ideals of liberty, equality, and brotherhood no longer apply — or that they are as strong as ever?

Where I live, in a small town in France, girls and young women are intimidated by Muslim men, who oblige them to wear the scarf. These Muslim women are often isolated, and need some protection. The law to outlaw the veil goes some way towards addressing this need.

— Rachida Ziouche, journalist and daughter of an Algerian imam, or religious leader, 2004

I think they have got it right in France. Civil servants and schoolgirls should not wear the veil. Personally, I am against it, it is a symbol of the inferior status of women in Muslim countries.

— Binnaz Toprak, political science professor in Turkey, 2004

Muslims in France believe they are being targeted. They fear the law banning scarves in schools will open the door to all kinds of discrimination. The French debate about the issue is so passionate that Muslims fear a new type of Islamaphobia.

— Tariq Ramadan, Islamic studies and philosophy professor in Switzerland, 2004

Web Connection

To read more about the issues involved in the headscarf ban in France, go the following web site and follow the links.

www.ExploringNationalism.ca

Story and Nationalism in the United States

Stories like the storming of the Bastille inform people of their roots, help shape their identity, and remind them of what they are capable of achieving. In the United States, for example, many Americans view the story of the Boston Tea Party of 1773 as a defining moment in their national history.

In 1773, Britain controlled 13 colonies along what is today the eastern seaboard of the United States. Like France during the 18th century, Britain had spent a lot of money on wars — and King George III and the British Parliament wanted to recover some of the costs. One of their strategies was to raise taxes in the American colonies. They also planned to be stricter about collecting existing taxes.

No violent story like the storming of the Bastille or the Boston Tea Party is attached to Canada's independence. Does this make a difference in the way Canadians view themselves as a nation?

These plans angered many colonists. They had no say in the way they were taxed because they did not elect representatives to the British Parliament. As a result, they said that Parliament had no right to tax them, and one of their slogans became "No taxation without representation." Facing this strong opposition, the British backed away from many of their taxation plans.

Figure 2-14 The Boston Tea Party, pictured here, drew thousands of spectators. Although British warships were also in the harbour, they did not try to stop the colonists. Was doing nothing a wise decision? Explain your response.

The Boston Tea Party

The British still needed money. So in 1773, Parliament decided to get around the colonists' objections by changing the way tea was taxed. They believed that the colonists would agree to pay this tax rather than go without tea, which was a very popular drink.

But the colonists surprised them. When three ships loaded with tea arrived in Boston, some of the colonists disguised themselves as American Indians, forced their way onto the ships, and dumped the tea into the harbour.

At the time, tea was very expensive, and the colonists' action cost British merchants a great deal of money. The British responded by shutting down the port of Boston so that no ships could come or go.

This incident is often identified as the spark that started the American Revolution, a violent conflict that led to the creation of an independent United States. Awareness of this story sets a tone for Americans. It supports their vision of themselves as a freedom-loving people who will not tolerate tyranny.

Reflect and Respond

Return to the web diagram you created earlier in this chapter and review the kinds of factors that can shape nationalism. Choose either the American Revolution or the religious-apparel debate in France.

Which two nationalism-shaping factors do you think exerted the greatest influence on the event you chose? Explain why you chose these two factors and how they were the driving forces behind the event.

How have people in Canada responded to some factors that shape nationalism?

Like the French and Americans, Canadians respond to national myths that seem to suggest a national character. One myth that has entered the collective consciousness of many Canadians involves the building of the Canadian Pacific Railway.

This project is forever linked to John A. Macdonald, Canada's first prime minister, who envisioned this national dream: an iron road that would unite the country. And on January 1, 1967, the first day of Canada's centennial year, singer-songwriter Gordon Lightfoot cemented the symbolic importance of this railway when he performed "The Canadian Railroad Trilogy" for the first time.

Figure 2-15 Canada's railway companies launched aggressive advertising campaigns to attract passengers. In 1925, the CPR used this poster to attract tourists to its western destinations. Do you think this advertising campaign exploited an existing national myth or helped create a new one?

In his song, Lightfoot paid tribute to the navvies — workers — who laboured in gruelling, dangerous conditions to build the railway. Among the navvies who helped drive the track through the Rocky Mountains were 6000 Chinese labourers who had been recruited to work on this treacherous stretch, where avalanches, rock slides, and cave-ins were everyday hazards. Despite the danger, the Chinese navvies earned less than half the wages of other workers. In the first year alone, 200 of them died of injuries and diseases such as scurvy.

For many Canadians, construction of the CPR represented a heroic achievement that shows how perseverance could triumph over a harsh environment. Does the story of the exploitation of the Chinese navvies affect the way you view this Canadian myth?

Defining Canada's Stories

For a long time, people of British heritage formed the dominant cultural group in Canada. In 1911, for example, more than 55 per cent of Canadians were of British background. As a result, many of Canada's stories were shaped by people whose worldview was British.

At Confederation in 1867, Canada's form of government — parliamentary democracy — was based on the British model. Britain's flag, the Union Jack, was also Canada's flag until 1965. British history was taught in schools, and Canadians often observed British traditions, such as celebrating British holidays.

Read the lines from Pauline Johnson's poem "Canadian Born" in "Voices." Note the year it was written. Johnson's words reflected a widely held view in Canada. Whose view is she presenting? What do her words tell you about the focus of Canadian nationalism at the beginning of the 20th century? What influenced Johnson's point of view?

Canadian Born

We first saw light in Canada, the land
beloved of God;
We are the pulse of Canada, its
marrow and its blood;
And we, the men of Canada, can face
the world and brag
That we were born in Canada beneath
the British flag.

— E. Pauline Johnson, or Tekahionwake, poet of Mohawk and English heritage, in "Canadian Born," 1903

Challenging Canadian Myths

During the 20th century, some Canadians began to challenge the British worldview that dominated the country. Immigrants from non-British countries, Francophones, and Aboriginal peoples struggled to make their voices heard and to affirm their place in the Canadian mosaic.

Is it the duty of every new generation to challenge Canada's national myths?

As they did this, they challenged some of the stories that had become part of the consciousness of many Canadians. Stories of "discovering" Canada's West and carving a cross-country railway out of the "wilderness" are examples.

Whose perspective is ignored when words like "discovering" and "wilderness," which refers to an uncultivated and uninhabited area, are used when talking about Canada's history? How might these words change when the stories are told from different points of view or perspectives?

MAKING A DIFFERENCE

Victoria Callihoo
The Métis Queen Victoria

MAKING A DIFFERENCE MAKING A DIFFERENCE MAKING A DIFFERENCE

Victoria Callihoo was in her 90s when she realized that she was one of the last Métis to remember a way of life that had vanished from Alberta. To ensure that the old stories were not lost, she resolved to record her people's culture and customs as her contribution to the history of a proud nation.

Callihoo had been born six years before Confederation in Lac Ste. Anne, a Métis community in what was then Rupert's Land. She took part in her first buffalo hunt when she was 13, travelling in a Red River cart with her mother, a Cree medicine woman. Her mother cared for the men who were injured while running buffalo — and she passed her knowledge of Aboriginal medicine to her daughter.

In one of her articles, Callihoo described the great buffalo herds as a dark, solid, moving mass. "We, of those days, never could believe the buffalo would ever be killed off, for there were thousands and thousands," she wrote.

In addition to describing what life was like while she was growing up, Callihoo recorded tales from even earlier times. These were stories that had passed into her people's oral tradition and that had been told to her when she was a child.

Figure 2-16 Victoria Belcourt Callihoo's family background included Métis and Cree. She and her husband, Louis Callihoo, had 12 children and often worked as teamsters for the Hudson's Bay Company.

Callihoo was proud of her Métis culture — and her writing reflected this pride. She said that she enjoyed even the more difficult aspects of traditional life: spreading a sleeping robe on a tipi floor, starting a fire without matches, and spending days making pemmican and preparing buffalo hides.

Among her people, Callihoo became a respected historian who was affectionately called the Métis Queen Victoria. When she died in 1966 at the age of 104, she was deeply mourned.

Explorations

1. Victoria Callihoo lived through a century of great change. What role do you think a sense of nation played in her decision to tell her people's stories?
2. How would Callihoo's stories help support her people's struggle to challenge predominantly European views of Canadian history and affirm their own identity?

First Nations and Métis Nationalism

In the early 20th century, Duncan Campbell Scott headed the federal Department of Indian Affairs. Scott viewed Aboriginal peoples as a "problem" that would be solved only by complete assimilation. "Our objective is to continue until there is not a single Indian in Canada that has not been absorbed into the body politic and there is no Indian question, and no Indian Department," he once said.

Although Aboriginal peoples resisted this plan, Scott's attitude reflected a widely held view that lasted well into the second half of the 20th century. Then, in 1968, Prime Minister Pierre Trudeau captured the imagination of many Canadians when he expressed a vision of Canada as a "just society."

But a year later, Trudeau and Jean Chrétien, who was minister of Indian affairs in Trudeau's government, introduced a controversial proposal to end the federal government's treaty obligations. Once again, the goal was to assimilate Aboriginal peoples.

My nation was ignored in your history textbooks.

— *Chief Dan George, Tsleil-Waututh First Nation, British Columbia, 1967*

After World War II, former British prime minister Winston Churchill referred to an "iron curtain" that divided the Communist countries controlled by the USSR and the Western European democracies. Harold Cardinal's reference to a "buckskin curtain" drew on this metaphor.

The Unjust Society

Trudeau and Chrétien's proposal, which was called a White Paper, proved to be a turning point for First Nations and other Aboriginal peoples. Aboriginal leaders were outraged. Harold Cardinal, an Alberta Cree leader, responded by publishing a book titled *The Unjust Society.* In it, Cardinal described what he called the "buckskin curtain" that divided First Nations and the rest of Canadian society. Referring to the popular idea of Canada as the product of two founding nations — British and French — Cardinal wrote: "Our people look on with concern when the Canadian government talks about 'the two founding peoples' without giving recognition to the role played by the Indian even before the founding of a nation-state known as Canada."

Cardinal's book became a bestseller that focused the attention of both Aboriginal and non-Aboriginal people on the struggle of First Nations, Métis, and Inuit to affirm and promote their identity. The outcry forced Trudeau and Chrétien to abandon their proposal — and strengthened the resolve of many Aboriginal people to promote their own national identity. The debate that resulted led to the recognition of Aboriginal and treaty rights in the Canadian Constitution of 1982.

The debate over the Trudeau–Chrétien proposal changed ideas about Canada. Today, it is widely acknowledged that the country was built by three founding peoples: British, French, and Aboriginal. Read Chief Dan George's comment in "Voices" and note the date. Would George's comment apply to the same extent today? Why is it important for a people's stories to be told?

Figure 2-17 Harold Cardinal, who led the Indian Association of Alberta at the time, speaks to Prime Minister Pierre Trudeau and other cabinet ministers at a 1970 meeting in Ottawa. These meetings marked one of the first times Aboriginal leaders and cabinet members had talked face to face. In 2001, Cardinal's efforts to affirm the rights of Aboriginal peoples were recognized when he received a National Aboriginal Achievement Award.

Inuit Perspectives on Nationalism

The Aboriginal people are, by tradition, a people of the land. Their very nature is tied strongly to the land, and any answer to the economic problems must include their remaining on the land.

— Rae Stephenson of Old Crow, Yukon, to the Royal Commission on Aboriginal Peoples, 1992

The political experience of Canada's Inuit was different from that of First Nations and Métis peoples. The Inuit signed no treaties with British or Canadian governments, and many continued to follow their traditional way of life until well into the 20th century. Like other Aboriginal peoples, however, they have been affected by government policies and other factors, such as global climate change.

In the 1930s, for example, the animal populations that were essential to the survival of the Inuit declined and many people faced starvation. As a result, the federal government introduced a relocation program. The Inuit, who had always lived in small, nomadic hunting groups, were moved, sometimes by force, to permanent communities, largely to make it easier for the government to provide services, such as schools.

The government policy ignored the importance of the Inuit way of life, which was built on sharing and focused on their relationship to the land. As a result, relocation created many social problems that remain unresolved. Many Inuit came to believe that achieving self-government was the only way they could begin to solve these problems, and they began working toward this goal.

Since 1975, the federal government and various Inuit groups have reached agreement on several land claims. The most recent of these was an agreement that created the new territory of Nunavut, which means "our land," in 1999. Under this agreement, the 30 000 people who live in Nunavut achieved a form of self-government.

Since then, Nunavut has become an important symbol for all Aboriginal peoples who are trying to assert their right to self-determination. Does the fact that the people of Nunavut enjoy a degree of self-government weaken or strengthen the Canadian confederation? Explain your response.

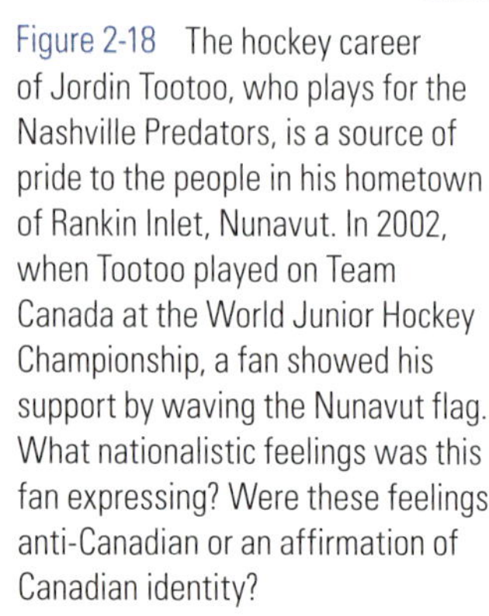

Figure 2-18 The hockey career of Jordin Tootoo, who plays for the Nashville Predators, is a source of pride to the people in his hometown of Rankin Inlet, Nunavut. In 2002, when Tootoo played on Team Canada at the World Junior Hockey Championship, a fan showed his support by waving the Nunavut flag. What nationalistic feelings was this fan expressing? Were these feelings anti-Canadian or an affirmation of Canadian identity?

Québécois Nationalism

In 2000, Michael Ignatieff wrote that Canada's "national experience had been bedevilled (as well as enriched) by the fact that English and French Canada do not share the same history of 1759." Ignatieff was referring to the Battle of the Plains of Abraham, in which French forces were defeated by the British during the Seven Years' War. When the war ended, the British took over New France and the course of Canadian history changed.

Until 1759, the dominant culture in Québec was French. Since then, Québécois — Francophones of Québec origin — have struggled to maintain their language, culture, and identity in a largely anglophone — English-speaking — country. As this struggle unfolded, Québécois developed a strong sense of themselves as a nation, a reality that was recognized by Prime Minister Stephen Harper in 2006.

CHECKFORWARD

You will read more about Québécois nationalism in Chapters 3, 4, 13, 15, and 16.

The tension between anglophones and Francophones has left its mark on Canada. Ignatieff wrote that "for more than 200 years, Canadian politics has been defined by the quarrel over the meaning of the battle on the Plains of Abraham. It is sentimental illusion to suppose that the two communities will ever agree on what it means. At best, we will agree to disagree; we will continue the argument. And the argument — provided it remains civil — will not prevent us from living together and sharing political institutions."

Do you believe, like Ignatieff, that agreeing to disagree is the best that Canadians can hope for?

Should people stop looking back to past events and focus on the present and the future?

Taking Turns

Have your people's stories helped shape Canadian nationalism?

The students responding to this question are Violet, a Métis who is a member of the Paddle Prairie Métis Settlement; Pearl, who lives in St. Albert and whose great-great-great grandfather immigrated from China to work on the Canadian Pacific Railway; and Rick, who was born in the United States but moved to Fort McMurray with his family when he was 10.

Violet

I'm Métis, but people sometimes wonder why I have an English name. My ancestors were Cree and English, not French like so many other Métis. They worked in the fur trade for the Hudson's Bay Company, and my great-great-great grandfather helped build the North West Mounted Police fort in Calgary before it became a city. He also put in a lot of years transporting goods from Fort Garry — that's Winnipeg today — to Fort Edmonton. Seeing as the fur trade and the Mounties are both symbols of Canada, then I'd say, yes, my people's stories helped shape Canadian nationalism.

Pearl

My great-great-great grandfather was one of the navvies who helped build the CPR, so his story played a big role in shaping Canadian nationalism. When people talk about this railway, they mention the bigwigs like John A. Macdonald and his big dream of Canada, but they don't think about the sweat and hard work of the people who built this country, railway tie by railway tie! This isn't really a big deal for me, because I just live my life — but I sure hate it when people whose families haven't been here as long as mine think I'm an immigrant.

Rick

I just came to Canada from the United States a few years ago, so I can't really say that my people's stories shaped Canadian nationalism in the past. But if I think about it, I can say that my family's story is shaping Canadian nationalism right now. My family — and all kinds of other immigrants — are building a civic nation where people are proud to live together according to the laws set out in documents like the Charter of Rights and Freedoms. So I would say that my family is adding a new story that enriches Canadian nationalism.

Your Turn

How would you respond to the question Violet, Pearl, and Rick are answering? Explain the reasons for your answer.

1. Consider the communities — real and imagined — to which you feel a sense of belonging and loyalty. You may, for example, feel loyalty to Canada, to your religious or spiritual community, to your family, and to your school. But do all these communities inspire feelings of nationalism in you? To what extent do nationalist feelings shape your identity? Do you, for example, have strong nationalist feelings about a country other than Canada? Along with Canada?
   a) In descending order of importance, list the loyalties that define your identity (i.e., place the loyalty that inspires the strongest feelings first on your list, the next second, and so on).
   b) Next to each loyalty, estimate its strength as a percentage. If Canada, for example, is number 1 on your list and your feelings are very strong, you might estimate it at 65 per cent. Because these estimates are percentages, the total should add up to 100.
   c) Translate your percentages into a pie chart that shows the loyalties that make up your identity. Your chart might resemble the one shown.
   d) Add a title and legend to your chart. Include a caption that identifies the degree of nationalism involved in your loyalties and the extent to which nationalism shapes your identity.
   e) Write a short paragraph explaining how you reached your conclusions.

2. The factors that influence people's nationalism stem from a variety of sources and act with varying degrees of strength. Some factors, such as the feelings inspired by national symbols, are internal and others are external. What factors shape your feelings of nationalism? Are you moved, for example, when you hear the national anthem? Do you feel proud to live in a country that supports universal access to medical care?
   a) Work with a partner to list five factors that you think influence your feelings of national identity. Discuss and list them from most important to least important. Beside each category, state why you chose it and why you assigned its ranking.
   b) Share your list with another pair. Work together to create a single list that all four of you agree on.
   c) Share this list with other groups and reach a class consensus on the five influences you think are most important.
   d) On your own, copy the list developed by the class onto a chart like the one shown. In the first column, record each influence in order from most to least important. In the second column, use a scale of 1 to 5 (1 = agree strongly; 5 = disagree strongly) to identify how strongly you agree with the class's ranking. In the final column, write a personal example that illustrates the influence. An example has been filled in for you.

Figure 2-19 Graphing My Loyalties

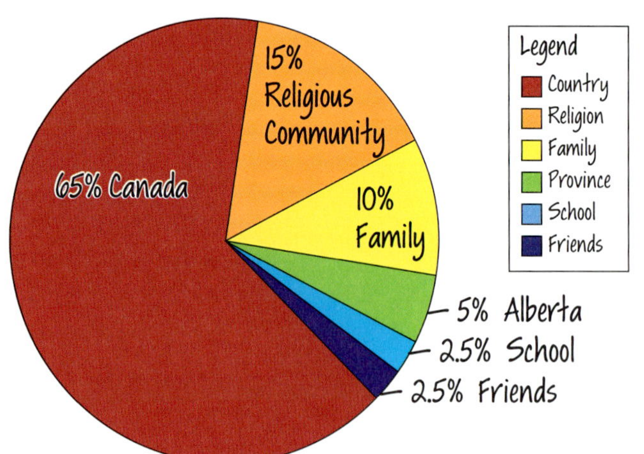

My loyalty to Canada makes up a large part of my identity. As a result, I would say that I am a strong Canadian nationalist.

Class Consensus Influences That Shape National Identity		
Influence	**Agree or Disagree** 1 = Agree strongly 5 = Disagree strongly	**Personal Example**
1. Social - universal medical care	2	I feel inspired to defend Canadian medicare when people criticize the system.
2.		
3.		
4.		
5.		

3. The following are excerpts from a translation of the *Declaration of the Rights of Woman and of the Female Citizen*, which was written by Olympe de Gouges, an outspoken social activist during the French Revolution. Her views were condemned by the revolutionaries during the Reign of Terror, and she was executed in 1793.
   a) Follow the steps set out in "Focus on Skills" (pp. 48–49) to determine the purpose of this document and to analyze its use of rhetoric and bias.
   b) Compare this document with the excerpts from the Declaration of the Rights of Man and of the Citizen (p. 52). List similarities and differences in a chart. Then write a short paragraph to explain whether de Gouges was building on — or challenging — the ideas included in the Declaration of the Rights of Man.
   c) Think about whether historical, social, economic, geographic, and political factors played a role in preventing de Gouges's vision of her nation from being accepted in late 18th-century France. Be specific.
   d) Has de Gouges's vision become a reality in Canada today? Identify and explain two factors that you think affected this outcome.

Declaration of the Rights of Woman and of the Female Citizen

Article 1: Woman is born free and lives equal to man in her rights. Social distinctions can be based only on the common utility.

Article 2: The purpose of any political association is the conservation of the natural and imprescriptible [absolute] rights of woman and man; these rights are liberty, property, security, and especially resistance to oppression.

Article 3: The principle of all sovereignty rests essentially with the nation, which is nothing but the union of woman and man; no body and no individual can exercise any authority which does not come expressly from it (the nation).

Article 6: The law must be the expression of the general will; all female and male citizens must contribute either personally or through their representatives to its formation; it must be the same for all: male and female citizens, being equal in the eyes of the law, must be equally admitted to all honours, positions, and public employment according to their capacity and without other distinctions besides those of their virtues and talents.

Article 10: No one is to be disquieted for his very basic opinions; woman has the right to mount the scaffold; she must equally have the right to mount the rostrum [speaker's platform], provided that her demonstrations do not disturb the legally established public order.

Think about Your Challenge

Look back at the challenge for this related issue. It asks you to create a coat of arms that represents your response to the related-issue question: To what extent should nation be the foundation of identity?

Decide on the format you intend to use to display your coat of arms. On the basis of this decision, start choosing symbols you will incorporate into your coat of arms and think about their purpose. Set up a chart to track the symbol: where you found it, its relative importance in your overall design, its purpose, and its relationship to nationalism and your identity.

CHAPTER 3 Reconciling Nationalist Loyalties

Figure 3-1 According to an old saying, everybody loves a parade — and the photographs on this page seem to suggest that this is true. All show people at parades that are celebrating an aspect of a group's collective identity. Which parade would you be most interested in attending? Does your choice reflect an aspect of your identity or a desire to enjoy a celebration of other people's identity — or something else?

CHAPTER ISSUE

To what extent should people reconcile their contending nationalist loyalties?

MOST PARADES, like those shown in the photographs on the previous page, are lighthearted expressions of aspects of a community's collective identity. A parade gives people a chance to say, "Hey, everyone, look at us!" Whether the parade includes marching bands, calypso music, Irish dancers, Chinese dragons, or rodeo stars on horses, it is an opportunity for people to express aspects of their identity — with a little fun thrown in.

A parade may also provide a way for members of a community to connect with others, who may or may not be part of that community.

Examine the photographs on the previous page, then respond to the following questions:

- If a nationalist loyalty is a commitment to one's nation, which, if any, of the pictured parades express nationalist loyalties?
- If a non-nationalist loyalty is a commitment to other aspects of people's identity, which, if any, of the pictured parades express non-nationalist loyalties?
- Can the same parade express both nationalist and non-nationalist loyalties? Explain your response.
- Which parades express loyalties — nationalist or non-nationalist — that you embrace?
- Would you attend a parade that does not directly express a loyalty you embrace? Why or why not?
- Would you attend a parade that expresses a loyalty that conflicts with your own? Why or why not?

KEY TERMS

contending loyalties

cultural pluralism

reasonable accommodation

sovereignists

federalists

reconciliation

royal commission

LOOKING AHEAD

In this chapter, you will develop responses to the following questions as you explore the extent to which people should reconcile their nationalist loyalties:

- How do nationalist loyalties shape people's choices?
- What choices have people made to affirm nationalist loyalties?
- How can nationalist loyalties create conflict?
- How have people reconciled contending nationalist loyalties?

My Journal on Nationalism

Examine a calendar that lists Canadian holidays. Select a pair of holidays that seem to celebrate contending nationalist loyalties. Could someone celebrate both? Responding to this question may help you think of ideas to use as you express your evolving point of view on nationalism. Record these ideas in your journal, notebook, learning log, portfolio, or computer file. Date your ideas so that you can return to them as you progress through this course.

How do nationalist loyalties shape people's choices?

One synonym for loyalty is "commitment" — the act of staying true to an idea, a cause, a nation, a person, or even yourself. People sometimes demonstrate their loyalty publicly. British prime minister Winston Churchill did this during World War II, when he vowed in a famous speech that Britain would "never surrender" to Hitler and fascism. But loyalty does not need to be displayed publicly. It can be low-key and long term, as in the quiet commitment of two people who are united in a lifelong relationship.

Other synonyms for loyalty are "allegiance," "faithfulness," "devotion," "fidelity," "steadfastness," and "attachment." Which of these synonyms best reflects what loyalty means to you? Think of an example in your own life to illustrate the synonym you chose. If it is not too personal, explain your example to a partner — or you may record it in your journal.

We shall not flag or fail. We shall go on to the end. We shall fight in France, we shall fight on the seas and oceans, we shall fight with growing confidence and growing strength in the air. We shall defend our island, whatever the cost may be. We shall fight on the beaches, we shall fight on the landing-grounds, we shall fight in the fields and in the streets, we shall fight in the hills. We shall never surrender!

— Winston Churchill, prime minister of Britain, in a speech to the British House of Commons, June 1940

Loyalties and Choices

When you are faced with a choice, loyalties can play a role in the decisions you make. Choices based on loyalty can range from easy decisions that require little thought to difficult decisions that require great sacrifice. Suppose, for example, that a friend asks you to help her defend herself against an unfair accusation. Would showing your loyalty to your friend in this way be a hard choice to make?

Then suppose that two good friends of yours are running for the same office on your school's students' council. Both expect your support. You are torn because you feel loyalty to both, but you can vote for only one of them. In a situation like this, how would you decide which loyalty is most important?

Some circumstances make it harder to be loyal than others, especially when showing loyalty seems to conflict with your own interests. Think, for example, about people who choose to become police officers and firefighters or to join the armed forces. Or people who make sacrifices to volunteer with groups such as Médecins Sans Frontières — Doctors Without Borders. How might choices to join organizations like these test a person's loyalties?

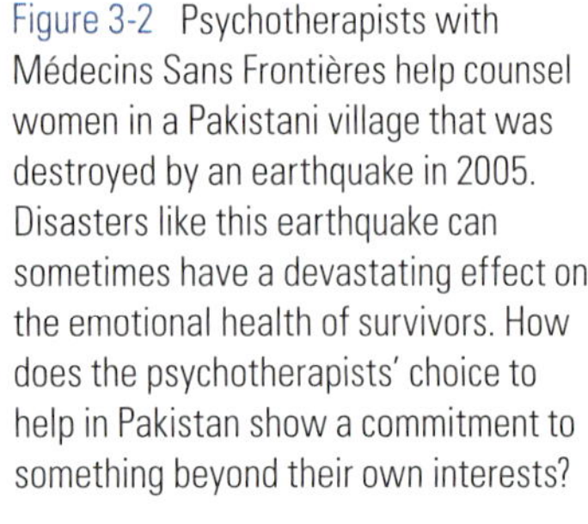

Figure 3-2 Psychotherapists with Médecins Sans Frontières help counsel women in a Pakistani village that was destroyed by an earthquake in 2005. Disasters like this earthquake can sometimes have a devastating effect on the emotional health of survivors. How does the psychotherapists' choice to help in Pakistan show a commitment to something beyond their own interests?

Patriotism and Loyalty

Patriotism can be understood as love of one's country or nation. Like love of people, patriotism shows itself in many kinds of behaviour, including loyalty. Love of people has inspired behaviour as varied as offering a gift of flowers and risking one's own life to protect loved ones. Similarly, patriotism has been known to inspire behaviour as varied as marching in a parade and risking one's life to defend the nation. Like love, patriotism is an emotion. Loyalty is a behaviour that can stem from patriotism.

Figure 3-3 People line Highway 401 to honour Master Warrant Officer Mario Mercier and Master Corporal Christian Duchesne, soldiers who were killed in Afghanistan in August 2007. Planes carrying bodies home from Afghanistan land at the military airfield in Trenton, Ontario. The bodies are then transported to Toronto, where autopsies are performed. At the urging of the public, the stretch of road between Trenton and Toronto was renamed the Highway of Heroes. What aspect(s) of nationalism does renaming this highway represent?

Nationalist Loyalties and Choices

Nationalist loyalties rarely demand extreme sacrifice, such as that made by some Canadian soldiers who served in Afghanistan. Still, these loyalties can strongly affect people's decisions.

If you, for example, feel loyalty to the Québécois nation, you might choose to attend a parade celebrating la Fête nationale on June 24th. If you feel loyalty to the Siksika nation, you might choose to attend a powwow to express your sense of community If you feel loyalty to the country of Madagascar, you might choose to periodically check the Internet for the latest news from that country. If you feel loyalty to Canada, you might choose to join a political campaign to help a candidate win election.

How Contending Loyalties Can Affect Choices

When you are faced with **contending loyalties** — loyalties that compete — choosing between them can be difficult. Suppose, for example, that you are invited to a friend's birthday lunch on Saturday. The invitation conflicts with your commitment to attend your younger sister's hockey game and your commitment to help members of your study group prepare a presentation for class on Monday morning. What loyalties might be involved in each of these commitments?

If you cannot rearrange plans, you must make a choice — and the importance you attach to various loyalties will play a role in this choice. Different people feel different loyalties that often contend for time, money, and emotions. Just as your life changes from day to day, so, too, do your loyalties and their relative importance to you. The same can be true when people feel loyalty to more than one nation.

Could a homecoming parade for Canadian soldiers be both a protest against war and a display of patriotism?

Reflect and Respond

In a small group, develop a scenario in which a person must choose among several loyalties. Identify the loyalties involved, as well as three possible courses of action. Create a list of criteria to help the person decide which loyalty should come first when making this particular decision. On your own, test the three options against your criteria and make a decision. Then return to the group, compare your results, and discuss how loyalties often shape the choices people make.

WHAT CHOICES HAVE PEOPLE MADE TO AFFIRM NATIONALIST LOYALTIES?

At some point, most people take action to declare or affirm a loyalty. When you were younger, for example, you might have traded friendship bracelets. As a high school student, you might wear a school ring or a T-shirt to show your commitment to your school community.

In the same way, people affirm their nationalist loyalties by taking specific actions — either individually or in a group. As an individual, you might, for example, wear a maple leaf pin while travelling. In a group, you might stand to sing the national anthem at hockey games and other gatherings.

Affirming First Nations Loyalties

Was changing the name of the National Indian Brotherhood to the Assembly of First Nations really a significant action?

In 1982, First Nations chose to affirm their status as nations by restructuring and reorganizing the National Indian Brotherhood — and renaming it the Assembly of First Nations. The AFN, they declared, is an association of the leaders of First Nation governments.

First Nations have insisted on maintaining their status as nations so that they can deal with the Canadian government on a nation-to-nation basis. Treaties, which were agreements between First Nations and the monarch, illustrate this relationship. Treaty 7, for example, was signed in 1877 and applies to a large part of southern Alberta. This treaty specifies that it is an agreement between "Her Majesty the Queen [Victoria] and the Blackfeet, Blood, Piegan, Sarcee, Stony, and Other Indian Tribes."

All in an Inuit Place Name

FYI

Some other Inuktitut place names and their meanings are

- Arviat — place of the bowhead whale
- Inuvik — place of man
- Pangnirtung — place of the bull caribou
- Qausuittuq — place with no dawn
- Tununiq — place that faces away from the sun
- Tuktoyaktuk — place where there are caribou
- Taloyoak — big caribou blind (stone corral)

Names can be useful tools for affirming nationalist loyalties. The Inuit of South Baffin Island, for example, have started the South Baffin Place Names Project to record traditional Inuktitut place names. Inuktitut is the language of the Inuit. Inuktitut names were often ignored by Europeans, who gave their own names to places in the North.

Iqaluit, for example, is the capital of Nunavut. But for decades, it was known as Frobisher Bay — after Martin Frobisher, a 16th-century English adventurer who landed there while seeking the Northwest Passage. In 1987, the name was changed back to Iqaluit, which means "place of fish."

Like Iqaluit, other Inuit place names often reveal important information. Qimmisarnaq, for example, means "the place where you have to unhitch your dogs to go down." Many places in the North are now reverting to their original Inuktitut names.

The South Baffin Place Names Project plans to produce a map of the place names collected from Elders. How would this map be useful to Inuit? How might it affect Inuit perspectives on nationalism? What could it teach non-Inuit?

Students from the Nunavut Sivuniksavut training program are helping another naming initiative by combing through historical photographs at Library and Archives Canada in Ottawa. Called Project Naming, the goal of this program is to discover the identity of the many unnamed Inuit depicted in a huge collection of historical photographs taken in the North.

Names and Inuit Identity

Many Inuit have also returned to using their Inuit names. Traditionally, Inuit had just one name. But in the late 1930s, the Canadian government decided that this made it too difficult to keep track of people and assigned a personal number to all Inuit.

For the next three decades, these numbers were used in dealing with the federal government. Some Inuit tell stories of teachers who used students' numbers rather than their names when taking attendance, and of letters that were addressed to a number, not a name. In 1969, the number system was abolished — and the Inuit were told that they must choose a last name in addition to their birth name.

Many governments assign numbers to citizens. You have a health card number, for example. Is assigning numbers simply a tool that promotes efficiency — or is there something sinister about it? Explain your response.

To the Canadian government . . . I was Annie E7-121 . . . E stood for east and W stood for west. We were given a small disc looped on a sturdy string, brown with black lettering. I only learned about last names when I went to school in Toronto in the early 1960s. My foster parents let me use their family name, so in Toronto I went by Annie Cotterill.

— Ann Meekitjuk Hanson, journalist, broadcaster, and commissioner of Nunavut, 1999

MAKING A DIFFERENCE

Kiviaq Championing a People's Rights

In 1936, an Inuit boy was born in a hunting camp near Chesterfield Inlet, Nunavut. His Inuit number was E5-776. Three years later, his new stepfather moved the boy, one of the boy's sisters, and their mother to Edmonton. There, the stepfather gave the boy a new name: David Ward.

David Ward's childhood was miserable. His father forbade the family to speak Inuktitut at home, and the boy felt isolated and lost. "I lived in total confusion," he told Jim Bell of the *Nunatsiaq News.*

Bullied by other kids, he learned to box — and eventually became a Canadian champion. As a young man, he was also a talented football player who earned a spot on the Edmonton Eskimos, but his gridiron career was cut short by injury. He went on to be elected to Edmonton city council and later hosted a radio open-line show. In the 1980s, he returned to school to study law and became the first Inuit lawyer in Canada.

Only after hanging out his shingle as a lawyer did he begin to explore his Inuit heritage. He discovered family members in the North and applied to change his name to the one he had been given at birth: Kiviaq. This should have been a simple matter, but Kiviaq wanted to observe the Inuit tradition of using only one name — and this sparked a long legal battle with the federal government because officials demanded that he choose a first and last name.

Figure 3-4 In his younger days, Kiviaq was a prizefighter who won 108 of 112 career matches. In 2006, Inuit filmmaker Zacharias Kunuk produced a 60-minute documentary — titled *Kiviaq versus Canada* — about this Inuk's struggle to affirm Inuit traditions and rights.

As a lawyer, Kiviaq was able to fight this battle, and in 2001, he won the right to be known by his birth name alone.

Since then, Kiviaq has worked actively on behalf of the Inuit. In 2004, he started his latest struggle — a lawsuit demanding that Inuit be granted the same rights as First Nations, who have access to a long list of benefits, including money for post-secondary education. The former boxer describes this battle, which remains unresolved, as the biggest fight of his life.

Explorations

1. Zacharias Kunuk's documentary about Kiviaq is titled *Kiviaq versus Canada*. Does this title effectively capture the idea of contending nationalist loyalties? Explain why you do — or do not — think so.
2. For much of his life, Kiviaq had little contact with the Inuit. Even now, he cannot visit his family in Nunavut because he suffers from an illness that is made worse by the motion of moving vehicles. Does a person need to be immersed in a nation to be loyal to it? Explain your response.

National Loyalties in a Multicultural Society

CHECKBACK

You explored the concept of a civic nation in Chapter 1.

Most immigrants are aware that Canada is a civic nation — and this is a reason many people choose to immigrate to this country. They know that the law guarantees them the same rights as all other Canadian citizens.

Many newcomers are also attracted by Canada's reputation for **cultural pluralism** — encouraging collectives to affirm and promote their unique cultural identity. In Canada, multiculturalism is official policy. It is Canada's version of cultural pluralism. Diversity is celebrated, and all citizens are encouraged to honour their cultural heritage.

But the vision of Canada as a bilingual and multicultural society has also sparked debate about how far a pluralistic nation should go to accommodate and protect the rights of minorities. George Jonas, a Canadian writer and columnist who immigrated from Hungary, believes that Canada has gone too far and that multiculturalism has diminished the idea of Canada as a nation.

"One result of the multicultural model was a retreat from the principle that immigration should serve the interests of the host country first," Jonas wrote in *Great Questions of Canada*. "The host country came to be viewed less and less as a nation, a legitimate entity with its own culture, and more and more as a political framework for various coexisting cultures. Newcomers were encouraged not to regard themselves as immigrants seeking to fit, but as explorers, if not conquistadores, whose quest was to carve out a congenial niche in Canada for their own tribes, languages, customs, or religions."

Others disagree with Jonas. In *The Polite Revolution*, for example, John Ibbitson said that multiculturalism is Canada's strength. "What matters about the Canadian mythical self-image is that we finally have one: that after years of muddle and confusion . . . a picture of Canada emerged in the minds of Canadians, a picture of tolerance and diversity and creativity and good humour . . . that makes Canadians feel, on most days, good about themselves," Ibbitson wrote. "This is something that, until recently, we lacked. In some countries, it's called patriotism. It feels good."

Read the citizenship oath in "FYI." Is it necessary for immigrants to reject their cultural values and beliefs when they become Canadian citizens? Does the oath of citizenship require immigrants to reject other nationalist loyalties?

FYI

When immigrants become Canadian citizens, they are required to repeat the following oath:

I swear [or affirm] that I will be faithful and bear true allegiance to Her Majesty Queen Elizabeth the Second, Queen of Canada, Her Heirs and Successors, and that I will faithfully observe the laws of Canada and fulfil my duties as a Canadian citizen.

Should Canada demand that immigrants renounce past nationalist loyalties when they choose to become Canadian citizens?

Figure 3-5 Fans celebrate with the Argentinian soccer team after their 2–1 victory over the Czech Republic in the final game of the 2007 FIFA World Youth Championship. This tournament took place in Canada. Why do you think Canadians of Argentinian heritage felt comfortable about displaying their loyalty to Argentina in this way?

Expressing Non-Canadian Nationalist Loyalties

If you have ever changed schools, you will understand that it can take a while to feel as if you fit in. At first, you may be nervous about expressing loyalties that are part of your identity. A student who has moved to Calgary from Edmonton, for example, might not feel comfortable about publicly rooting for the Oilers or the Eskimos. But in time, this can change.

The same can be true of new Canadians. At first, immigrants may be more concerned with fitting in to their new environment. But in time, they come to feel more comfortable about expressing non-Canadian nationalist loyalties.

New Canadians from Madagascar, for example, might send humanitarian aid to their former homeland, cheer for Malagasy athletes at the Olympics, or join a Malagasy cultural organization. All these actions are ways of affirming a nationalist loyalty within a Canadian context.

Canada has never been a melting pot; more like a tossed salad.

— Arnold Edinborough, writer, editor, and founder of the Council for Business and the Arts in Canada, 1973

The Dhillon case was not the first time the RCMP had changed its traditional dress code. In 1974, when women were first allowed to become full-fledged constables, they were required to wear the standard red serge jacket with a skirt and high heels. In 1989, the rules changed again so that women could wear the same uniform as men.

Putting Multiculturalism to the Test

The vision of Canada as a diverse society has always sparked debate over how much immigrants should try to fit in. In recent decades, this debate has often focused on **reasonable accommodation** — a legal and constitutional concept that requires Canadian public institutions to adapt to the religious and cultural practices of minorities as long as these practices do not violate other rights and freedoms.

In the early 1980s, for example, a Sikh employee of the Canadian National Railway challenged a company safety rule requiring construction workers to wear hard hats. To put on a hard hat, the worker would have had to violate his religious beliefs by removing his turban. For many Sikhs, religious symbols carry a strong link to their sense of nation. In this case, the Supreme Court of Canada ruled that safety came first and that wearing a turban instead of a hard hat is not a reasonable accommodation.

A few years later, Baltej Singh Dhillon launched a similar challenge. Dhillon, an immigrant from Malaysia, was accepted into the RCMP's training program. But the force wanted him to cut his hair, shave his beard, and remove his turban so he could wear the Stetson that has been part of the Mountie uniform since 1873. For many Canadians, the RCMP uniform is a national symbol.

Dhillon argued that wearing a turban is a religious duty for Khalsa Sikh men. In 1990, the federal government agreed that allowing Sikh RCMP officers to wear a turban rather than a Stetson is a reasonable accommodation. Dhillon became a full-fledged RCMP officer — and the RCMP uniform evolved to accommodate new symbols.

Does changing a nation's symbols reduce citizens' nationalist loyalties?

Figure 3-6 Wearing a turban and sporting a beard, Baltej Singh Dhillon stands with classmates at his 1991 RCMP graduation ceremony. "What is it to be Canadian, I think, ultimately becomes what it is to be a citizen of this earth," Singh said in a CBC interview. "And Canada is, I believe, a petri dish for this world . . . we are a test sample. And how we do as a country is going to be judged globally." What do you think Dhillon meant?

Reasonable Accommodation and Nationalist Loyalties

Ever since Confederation, people have disagreed over whether the idea now known as reasonable accommodation supports or undercuts the shared sense of Canadian identity and belonging that is essential to developing nationalist loyalties. In 2006, for example, Prime Minister Stephen Harper told a United Nations forum that "Canada's diversity, properly nurtured, is our greatest strength." And the web site of the Department of Canadian Heritage says that in Canada, differences among people have been not only accepted, but also recognized as a source of strength.

The web site goes on to say, "It is in building a peaceful, harmonious society that diversity plays its most dynamic role. It challenges [Canadians] to adapt and relate to one another *despite* our differences, which encourages understanding, flexibility and compromise. This makes us resilient — able to accommodate different points of view and see different ways to solve problems."

But not everyone supports this view. Some commentators, such as writer George Jonas, former Reform Party and Canadian Alliance party leader Preston Manning, novelist and cultural commentator Neil Bissoondath, and University of Lethbridge sociologist Reginald Bibby, believe that Canada's multiculturalism policy divides Canadians and interferes with their developing a shared nationalist loyalty. Bibby, for example, has asked, "If what [Canadians] have in common is our diversity, do we really have anything in common at all?"

Web Connection

To find out more about multiculturalism and diversity in Canada, go to this web site and follow the links.

www.ExploringNationalism.ca

CheckForward

You will read more about reasonable accommodation in Chapter 16.

Figure 3-7 In 2003, Suzan Meyers, who was born in the United States, and Hawraa Hassouni, who was born in Iraq, became Canadian citizens and celebrated the occasion together. Though these two women were born into different cultures, both are now Canadians. If you were one of these women, what might have inspired you to make the choice to become a Canadian?

Reflect and Respond

Many people argue that Canadian governments and institutions, such as the RCMP, should make "reasonable" efforts to accommodate the varied religious and cultural practices of new Canadians. Changing the RCMP dress code to allow Baltej Singh Dhillon to wear a turban rather than a Stetson is an example of an accommodation that is considered reasonable.

List three key arguments in favour of making reasonable accommodations — and three arguments that show possible drawbacks.

How can nationalist loyalties create conflict?

When people's choices enable them to include more than one nationalist loyalty in their identity, these loyalties are compatible — they can coexist without conflicting. If you are a new Canadian citizen, for example, you might feel a strong loyalty to Canada at the same time as you feel a strong loyalty to your original homeland. You might show these loyalties by choosing both to keep up with the news from your country of origin and to attend a Canada Day celebration. Your two loyalties can coexist without causing you turmoil.

But nationalist loyalties are not always compatible. Their goals sometimes conflict. If you feel a strong loyalty to Canada at the same time as you feel a strong loyalty to Québec — and your loyalty to Québec leads you to believe that the province should become independent — you would have a hard time making choices that would satisfy both these loyalties.

With a partner, read the words of Alice Munro's fictional character in "Voices." Munro's character is explaining her contradictory feelings about her husband. Discuss the insights this excerpt might provide into the turmoil that contending nationalist loyalties can create.

I wished that I could get my feelings about Andrew to come together into a serviceable and dependable feeling. I have even tried writing two lists, one of things I liked about him, one of things I disliked . . . as if I hoped to prove something, to come to a conclusion one way or the other. But I gave it up when I saw that all it proved was what I already knew — that I had violent contradictions.

— Alice Munro, Canadian author, in "Miles City, Montana," 1986

On the morning of July 1, 1916, about 780 soldiers of the Newfoundland Regiment were ordered to advance against heavy machine gun and artillery fire at Beaumont-Hamel, France; 324 were killed, and hundreds more were wounded. Only 68 were able to report for duty the next morning. This battle marked the opening day of the disastrous Battle of the Somme, which lasted for months and was a dark time for the Allies.

July 1 in Newfoundland

Across the country, Canadians celebrate Canada Day in different ways. The celebrations vary from serious and patriotic to wild and wacky. But things are different for many Newfoundlanders. When they wake up on July 1, some may plan to attend a Canada Day celebration — but they may also plan to attend Memorial Day ceremonies.

In his online blog, Newfoundland-born comedian Rick Mercer described the mixed emotions Newfoundlanders may feel on July 1: "In one of those great Newfoundland-in-Confederation ironies, Canada Day is actually an official day of mourning in Newfoundland. You see, Canada just happens to celebrate its birthday on the anniversary of the bloodiest day in Newfoundland history."

When he wrote about the "bloodiest day in Newfoundland history," Mercer was referring to the Battle of Beaumont-Hamel, which occurred in 1916 during World War I. At the time, Newfoundland was a self-governing British dominion that had not yet joined Canada. The Newfoundland Regiment was nearly wiped out in this battle, which is as symbolic for Newfoundlanders as Vimy Ridge is for other Canadians.

Figure 3-8 These young soldiers signed up with the Newfoundland Regiment during World War I. Most were just a few years older than you are now. What contending loyalties might Newfoundlanders feel on July 1?

Contending Loyalties and Conflict

Contending nationalist loyalties can create conflict between peoples for many reasons. When two peoples, for example, want to live in the same territory and cannot reconcile — settle or resolve — their conflicting loyalties by diplomatic means, the result may be violence. This is the case in Israel, where both Jewish Israelis and Palestinians wish to control the same territory, to which both have historical, religious, spiritual, cultural, and geographic ties. Nationalist loyalties can also come into conflict as a result of other equally strong forces, such as language rights, human rights, and natural resources. What loyalties, if any, would you consider worth fighting for? Explain your response.

Do contending nationalist loyalties create conflict for you?

The students responding to this question are Amanthi, who lives in Edson and whose parents immigrated from Sri Lanka; Blair, who lives in Edmonton and whose heritage is Ukrainian, Scottish, and German; and Rick, who was born in the United States but moved to Fort McMurray with his family when he was 10.

Absolutely. My mother is the Canadian patriot in the family. We've just moved into a new house here in Edson, and Mum is decorating everything to be as "Canadian" as she can make it. My dad couldn't care less. He spends his evenings glued to his computer. He was a police officer in Sri Lanka, and he still e-mails his old pals every night. My parents are always arguing about how much time he spends on his computer — and about how much Mum spends on redecorating. But I think these arguments are really about their changing nationalist loyalties.

If I get the question, it's talking about allegiances to different nations, and my loyalty is to Canada — 100 per cent. My heritage is a bit of a mixed bag. I have ancestors who were Scottish, German, and Ukrainian. Some were farm folk, but most of them lived — and died — right here in Strathcona. At World Cup time, I might root for Scotland or Germany because of family ties, but if a Canadian team ever made the tournament, I'd be decked out in red and white for sure.

Contending loyalties? Are you kidding? I grew up in the United States, where you swear allegiance to the flag every day in school! When we went to baseball games, people actually sang the national anthem. And every July 4, my family draped a big flag across the porch. Why? Because we were good Americans — and weren't embarrassed to show it. Now I'm a dual citizen, American and Canadian, or maybe I should say Canadian and American. Which comes first? Sometimes, I'm not sure. There are lots of great things about Canada. But it really bugs me when my friends slag Americans for warmongering. Talk about stereotyping! I'm always explaining that there are just as many points of view on war and terrorism in the United States as there are in Canada. So, yeah, sometimes it's hard to separate my feelings for my birth country and my adopted country.

How would you respond to the question Amanthi, Blair, and Rick are answering? Which of the three are experiencing contending loyalties that affect their own identity? Which are experiencing conflict between people as a result of contending nationalist loyalties? Do you think these conflicts can be resolved?

Contending Loyalties in Québec

Québécois have a long history of grappling with contending nationalist loyalties. In 1995, a referendum on separating from Canada forced them to choose between their loyalty to Québec and their loyalty to Canada. An extraordinary 93.5 per cent of Québécois voted in this referendum. The results, in which the no side eked out a narrow victory, revealed that voters were nearly equally divided over how to reconcile these contending loyalties.

Figure 3-9 Québec Sovereignty Referendum Results, 1995

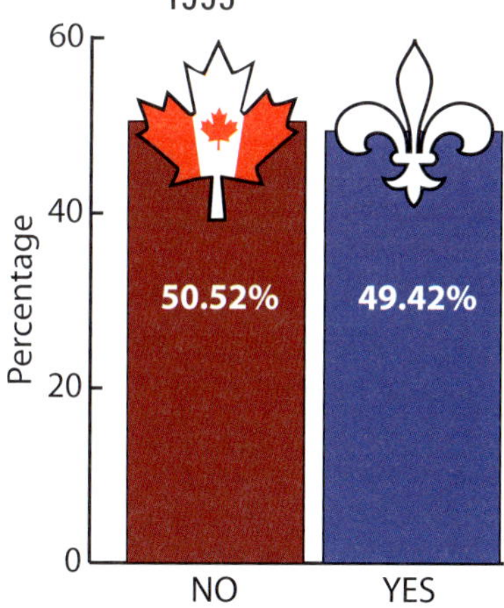

The Sovereignty Debate

Sovereignists — people who support the idea of Québec's becoming an independent nation-state — believe that Québécois must control their own destiny. Lucien Bouchard, who was premier of the province from 1996 to 2001, summed up this perspective when he said, "In Québéc, we are a people, we are a nation, and as a nation we have a fundamental right to keep, maintain, and protect our territory." He also said that "Canada is divisible because it is not a real country. There are two peoples, two nations, and two territories. And this one is ours."

Who was Bouchard talking about when he said "we" and "our"? How might the Aboriginal peoples of Québec view his words? What about immigrants? Québec anglophones? Canadian Francophones living outside Québec?

Many Québécois who oppose sovereignty — sometimes called **federalists** because they believe that Québec should remain a Canadian province — say that the Québécois identity is inseparable from the Canadian identity. Raymond Giroux, editorial writer for *Le Soleil*, expressed this idea when he wrote:

> Our Canada was born in 1534, not in 1867. Therein lies the deep Canadian misunderstanding. There lies, also, the source of the division in Québec, torn between its old continental nationalism and its more recent, narrower, territorial nationalism.
>
> Do not forget that our ancestors roamed the Prairies, were the first among the European explorers to see the Rockies and travel the Mississippi River, wrote "O Canada," and used the maple leaf as a national symbol. It is not an easy task to eradicate a few centuries of national history. So even in a time of real political turmoil, Québécois still consider themselves Canadians and are not ready for what they see as a shameful retreat to the present boundaries of Québéc.

Many people, including Québécois, believed that the referendum question was not clear enough. Here is what the question asked:

Do you agree that Québec should become sovereign after having made a formal offer to Canada for a new economic and political partnership within the scope of the bill respecting the future of Québec and of the agreement signed on June 12, 1995?

Is the Québec sovereignty movement an example of ethnic nationalism?

Reflect and Respond

Work with a small group to create a slogan or symbol that celebrates Canada as a nation that draws its identity and strength from its diversity. Share your group's idea with other groups and the class.

Note the similarities among the slogans and symbols. As a class, discuss the significance of these similarities.

IMPACT

Québec — Focus of Francophone Nationalism in Canada

IMPACT

By the mid-20th century, Francophone Québécois were a tiny minority on a North American continent that was dominated by the English language and culture. TV shows, movies, and most of the music played on the radio were in English, and English was the language of most Québec workplaces.

In the face of these developments, Québec Francophones started raising the alarm. Ensuring the survival of their language and culture and their place in Québec's economy had become urgent challenges. They began to look for ways to protect themselves against assimilation into North America's dominant English-language culture.

Boost the Birthrate

A century earlier, in 1851, Québec's 890 000 people had made up about a third of Canada's total population. Most Québécois were Francophones. But in the following decade, 70 000 Québécois emigrated to the United States, lured by the promise of work in the many factories along the eastern seaboard. Others moved to Western Canada.

This out-migration amounted to eight per cent of Québec's total population — and 47 per cent of the total emigration from Canada. If Québécois continued to leave at the same rate, the survival of the French language and culture would be at risk.

In response, the Catholic Church, which played a dominant role in Québec, encouraged Francophone Québécois to continue living their traditional rural lifestyle — immersed in French and adhering to the Catholic religion. They were also encouraged to have large families as a way of boosting the province's Francophone population.

Left Behind

This strategy successfully maintained a large Francophone population. But it also opened the door for anglophones to dominate Québec business, even though they formed a minority of the province's population. In the 1960s, studies showed that the incomes of Francophone Québécois were the lowest in the province and that their earnings went up if they learned English. The world was changing, and the thousands of new terms entering the languages of science, industry, and business were nearly all English.

At the time, visitors could arrive in Québec and conduct all their business in English. They could speak English when buying goods in stores, ordering food in restaurants, and dealing with government officials. Immigrants who settled in the province could choose to send their children to schools where they were taught in English — and most did. Québec seemed to be at risk of losing its identity as a Francophone society.

Figure 3-10 René Lévesque, a former broadcaster who had been a member of the provincial Liberal party until breaking with that party in 1967, helped found the Parti Québécois and became its first leader in 1968. An ardent separatist, Lévesque led the PQ to power in 1976.

Ready for Change

By 1976, the Parti Québécois — a provincial political party with a sovereignist agenda — was offering solutions to the concerns of Francophone Québécois. That year, the province elected a PQ government.

In 1977, the PQ passed Bill 101, the Charter of the French Language. This controversial legislation built on earlier language laws and made French the only official language in the province. For many Québécois, the charter was an expression of nationalism. It declared that they intended to stop the erosion of their national identity by providing the tools necessary to affirm and promote their distinct language and culture.

Changes Brought about by Bill 101

French must be the language used
- in all workplaces
- in law courts and in writing laws and other legal documents
- on all commercial signs

IMPACT IMPACT IMPACT IMPACT IMPACT IMPACT IMPACT

Bill 101 and Québec Anglophones

Bill 101 shocked anglophone Québécois. Many said that the new language laws trampled on their individual rights as citizens of a bilingual Canada.

William Johnson expressed the fears of many anglophones when he told the *Montreal Gazette*, an English-language newspaper: "The banning of outdoor English signs . . . sends one clear message: English is not wanted, English is viewed as a threat, and the many harassments which have decimated the community will continue, perhaps intensified."

Many anglophones decided that they no longer had a future in Québec and left the province. Between June 1976 and June 1981, the number of anglophone Québécois decreased by more than 94 000. And estimates suggested that at least 42 major companies, including Sun Life Insurance and Redpath Industries, had shifted their head offices to Toronto from Montréal.

Some anglophones challenged the language laws in the courts with varying degrees of success. As a result, the law has softened somewhat. People can again use French or English in Québec's legislature and courts. Children who have been educated in English elsewhere in Canada before moving to Québec can continue their schooling in English. And as long as French predominates on commercial signs, English and other languages are permitted. But in general, the courts confirmed Québec's right to protect the French language.

Figure 3-11 Percentage of Population Speaking French at Home, 1971 and 2001

Year	Québec	Canada not including Québec	Alberta
1971	80.8%	4.3%	1.4%
2001	82.2%	3.0%	1.0%

Source: Statistics Canada, 1971 and 2001 Census

Bill 101 and Québec Francophones

In the years before Bill 101 was passed, Québec had experienced significant social, political, and economic reforms known as the "Quiet Revolution." During the 1960s and 1970s, Québec modernized its education system, improved social programs, and tried to promote Québécois-owned businesses. These changes meant that Québec Francophones could work in French in a wider range of jobs.

The Quiet Revolution also changed Québec from a largely rural, religion-focused French-speaking society into a modern, urban, industrial, and secular — non-religious — French-speaking society. Bill 101 supported this transformation by ensuring that French would be the usual language of government, workplaces, education, communications, and business.

Some of the Francophone Québécois who benefited from the changes became increasingly reluctant to consider separation from Canada. They feared that the upheaval would threaten their newfound economic success. In 2006, for example, a poll of Québécois found that support for remaining in Canada had risen since the 1995 sovereignty referendum. Fifty-eight per cent of respondents said they would vote to keep Québec in Canada. They wanted their politicians to work on behalf of Québécois, but within the framework of the Canadian nation-state.

Figure 3-12 Tendency of Allophone* Immigrants to Use French or English or Both at Home, by Period of Immigration, Québec, 2001

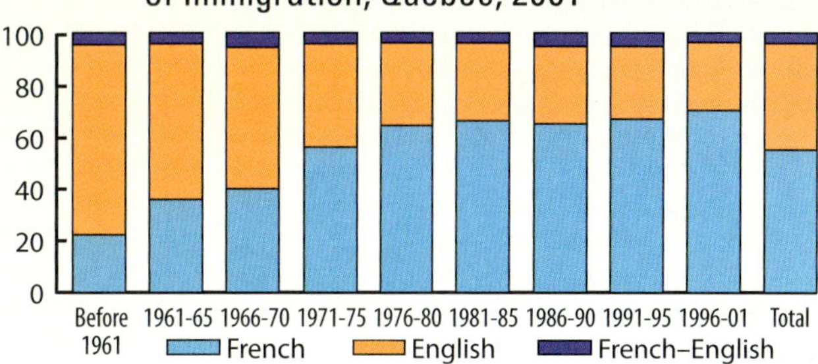

Source: Statistics Canada, 2001 Census

* Allophone: An immigrant whose first language is neither French nor English.

Explorations

1. Examine Figures 3-11 and 3-12. What trends do you see? How do you think Bill 101 may have influenced these trends?
2. In recent years, some Francophone Québécois parents have tried to persuade the courts to rule that Québec must provide more English-language education in the province's schools. And some have even tried to enrol their children in English-language schools. As of 2008, their efforts had been unsuccessful. What do you think these parents might be hoping to achieve? Why would they have been hoping to achieve this?

Analyzing Information from Many Sources

FOCUS ON SKILLS

In 2007, on the 30th anniversary of the passage of Bill 101, the *Montreal Gazette* published Robert Libman's comments on Québec's language laws. An anglophone Québécois, Libman helped found the Equality Party, which promoted using French and English equally. He said that the language laws have devastated Québec's English-speaking community. The following excerpt discusses how he believes the law has affected Montréal:

> In the 1970s, Montreal was Canada's most populous city, the country's head office capital, and the economic hub of our nation. Radio great Ted Tevan called us the City of Champions with Montreal sports teams thriving in their respective leagues. But today, Montreal's economy does not even compete in the same league as Toronto. We lag behind other Canadian cities as well, due in no small measure to one of the largest population displacements in North American history. Montreal has lost hundreds of thousands of people, young educated college and university graduates, taxpayers, property owners, tenants and consumers.

Libman's comments present one view of how Bill 101 has affected nationalist loyalties. But if you wished to explore this topic more deeply, you would also need to analyze a broader range of sources. The following steps can help you do this.

Steps to Analyzing Information from Many Sources

Step 1: Consider many points of view and perspectives

With a partner, examine various aspects of the issue and list people it might affect. On the basis of this list, create a list of sources you could consult to gather a wide range of points of view and perspectives. You might begin with a general source, such as *Exploring Nationalism*, to develop an overview of the topic. What other sources might you explore?

Step 2: Analyze sources by assessing their authority and validity

A chart like the one on this page can help you analyze sources by using criteria to assess the authority and validity of the information. With your partner, examine the questions on the chart and discuss how your response to each might affect your judgment of a source's authority and validity.

With your partner, reread the excerpt from Libman's comments at the beginning of this page. Work together to fill in a chart analyzing his views.

When you finish, discuss and compare your analysis with that of another pair. Revise your responses if you believe this is justified.

Then, with your partner, read the excerpts on the following page and fill out a similar chart for each.

Step 3: Select the most authoritative sources

With your partner, rank your assessments from most to least authoritative and valid. Discuss and compare your ranking with those of another pair. Revise your rankings if you believe this is justified. Compare your rankings with those of other groups. Once again, revise your rankings if necessary.

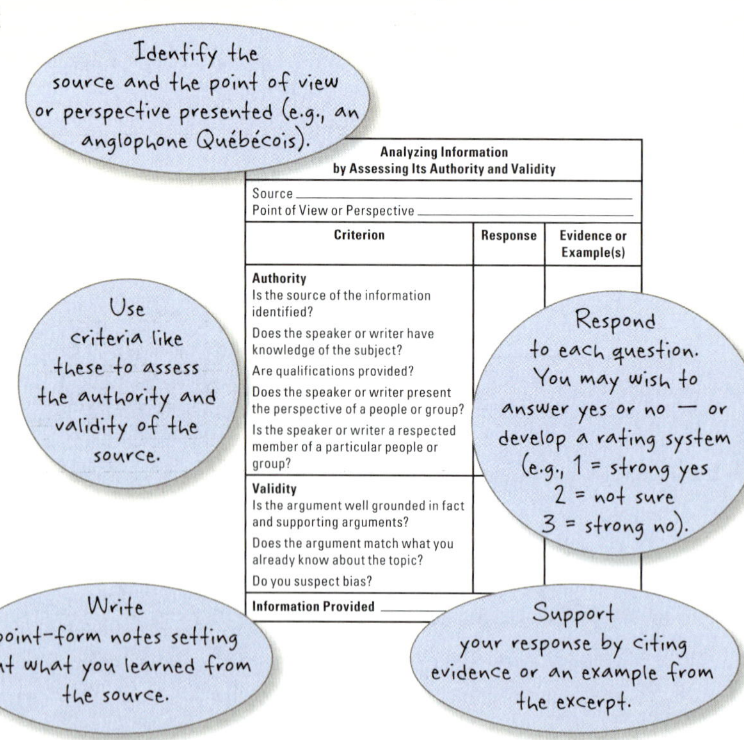

Analyzing Information by Assessing Its Authority and Validity

Source ______

Point of View or Perspective ______

Criterion	Response	Evidence or Example(s)
Authority		
Is the source of the information identified?		
Does the speaker or writer have knowledge of the subject?		
Are qualifications provided?		
Does the speaker or writer present the perspective of a people or group?		
Is the speaker or writer a respected member of a particular people or group?		
Validity		
Is the argument well grounded in fact and supporting arguments?		
Does the argument match what you already know about the topic?		
Do you suspect bias?		

Information Provided ______

Excerpt 1 — From a 1988 decision of the Supreme Court of Canada on a challenge to Bill 101

In the period prior to the enactment of the legislation at issue, the *"visage linguistique"* [language face] of Québec often gave the impression that English had become as significant as French. This *"visage linguistique"* reinforced the concern among francophones that English was gaining in importance, that the French language was threatened and that it would ultimately disappear. It strongly suggested to young and ambitious francophones that the language of success was almost exclusively English. It confirmed to anglophones that there was no great need to learn the majority language. And it suggested to immigrants that the prudent course lay in joining the anglophone community.

Excerpt 2 — From a *Montreal Gazette* article by André Burelle, a former constitutional adviser to the governments of Pierre Trudeau and Brian Mulroney

Those who oppose legislation to protect a language in public life must acknowledge that absolute freedom of choice is another way of saying that the strongest will prevail and English would have a monopoly in North America. According to the highest court in Switzerland, freedom of language under the Swiss constitution is compatible with a law of the Zurich canton that forbids francophone parents from sending their children to private French schools and makes it compulsory to send them to German public schools. Even in the United States, California has recently adopted a proposal that forbids bilingual teaching (English–Spanish) in public schools in order to favour a quicker integration of Spanish immigrants.

If these practices are seen as necessary and legitimate in liberal countries such as Switzerland and the United States, how could Bill 101 be condemned in Quebec, where French is a threatened language?

Excerpt 3 — From the manifesto of the Mouvement Québec français, an umbrella group founded in 1970 to protect the French language

All nations wish to live in their language. So does Québec wish to live in French. That is what our ancestors wanted. And this is what we wish for ourselves. That is what those who will come after us will also want . . .

What is happening presently under our eyes, and on our territory, is the fight that opposes one of the most threatened nations to one of the most ambitious giants of History who, not satisfied to have established its language on its territory, is actively seeking to spread it everywhere, around us and even among us . . .

The time is ripe. We must act, and do it immediately. The Mouvement Québec français invites us all to answer the call of our language, regardless of our origins, our particular links, of our class.

Excerpt 4 — From a 1982 letter by Eric M. Maldoff, president of Alliance Quebec, an umbrella group of Québec anglophone organizations, to Québec premier René Lévesque

Camille Laurin, when promoting Bill 101, [said] that commercial signs should mirror Quebec society. As we have told you on so many previous occasions, we can only conclude that your vision of Quebec society is gravely distorted. Where do [anglophones] appear in your mirror? The legislation renders us invisible, which is unacceptable. The signs law is a symbol of the greatest importance to the English-speaking community of Quebec. It casts doubt on our legitimacy and raises questions concerning our right to be present, our right to be visible, our right to receive services in our language, and our right to communicate with each other. There is ample justification for fearing that there may be a "dark plot to put down the anglophones."

Summing Up

As you progress through this course, you will encounter many opportunities to analyze information from a variety of sources. Following the steps in this feature can help you do this.

How have people reconciled contending nationalist loyalties?

VOICES

Self-determination is a right which belongs to peoples. It does not belong to states. It is a right of all peoples. It is universal and non-divisible; that is, either you have it or you do not. It is not a right that is given to peoples by someone else. Please understand, you may have to fight to exercise this right, but you do not negotiate for the right of self-determination because it is yours already.

— Matthew Coon Come, Cree leader and former national chief of the Assembly of First Nations, in documents filed with the UN Commission on Human Rights, 1992

Reconciling can mean coming to terms with the past or mending a broken relationship. When two friends have a serious disagreement, an act of **reconciliation** can help resolve their differences and bring them together again. Similarly, when peoples or nations disagree, or when their nationalist loyalties lead them to pursue contending goals, an attitude of reconciliation can bring them together and enable them to coexist in peace.

But when two contending nations cannot achieve reconciliation, the outcome can be serious. The inability to resolve differences may lead to damaging political struggles and even outright war.

Aboriginal Peoples in Canada

For decades, Canadian governments tried to force First Nations, Inuit, and Métis to abandon their culture and traditions and to assimilate into mainstream society. Over the past decades, this policy has changed, as governments have recognized Aboriginal and treaty rights. But although these rights are now enshrined in the Charter of Rights and Freedoms, many First Nations, Inuit, and Métis continue to face an uphill struggle in their quest to control their own destiny.

Figure 3-13 Oka and Kanesatake

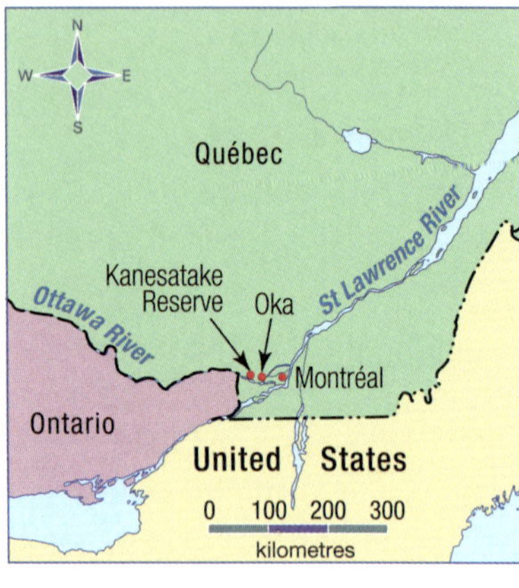

The Oka Crisis

In 1990, a group of Mohawks on the Kanesatake reserve, near the Québec village of Oka, set up a roadblock and a camp in nearby woods. Their goal was to stop the expansion of a golf course onto land the Mohawks claimed as their own and considered sacred. The Québec government refused to talk to the protesters while the roadblock was in place — and the protesters refused to remove the barricade. This standoff went on for four months.

Then, on July 11, the Sureté du Québec, Québec's provincial police force, was ordered to disperse the protesters. Shots were fired and a police officer was killed.

The violence made national — and international — headlines. Other First Nations set up their own barricades to support the protest. As the crisis deepened, the Québec government called in the army. More than 2500 Canadian soldiers moved in and gradually began to cut off the protesters' communications with the outside world. The protest finally ended on September 26.

Many protesters faced criminal charges, but nearly all were found not guilty. Although the federal government later bought the disputed land and transferred ownership to the Mohawks, the crisis left a legacy of bitterness among the people of Kanesatake and other Aboriginal people.

Create a list of the stakeholders in the Oka crisis. What contending nationalist loyalties divided them?

Figure 3-14 This famous photograph is one of the most enduring images of the Oka crisis. It shows Canadian soldier Patrick Cloutier nose to nose with masked protester Brad Larocque. What ideas make this picture so powerful? What contending loyalties are displayed?

The Royal Commission on Aboriginal Peoples

The Oka crisis was a wakeup call for the federal government, and in 1991, Prime Minister Brian Mulroney responded by setting up the Royal Commission on Aboriginal Peoples. Mulroney appointed four Aboriginal and three non-Aboriginal people to sit on the commission, which was chaired by Georges Erasmus, a former national chief of the Assembly of First Nations, and Justice René Dussault of the Québec Appeal Court. The commissioners' goal was to answer this question: What are the foundations of a fair and honourable relationship between the Aboriginal and non-Aboriginal people of Canada?

The commissioners listened to more than 2000 people, visited 96 communities, talked to numerous experts, and reviewed mountains of research before publishing their groundbreaking five-volume report in 1996.

Titled *People to People, Nation to Nation*, the report condemned the treatment of Aboriginal peoples and summed up the commissioners' main conclusion with these words: "The main policy direction, pursued for more than 150 years, first by colonial then by Canadian governments, has been wrong."

The report urged Canadians to view First Nations, Inuit, and Métis in a radically different way — as nations with a right to govern themselves in partnership with Canada. It said:

> [Aboriginal peoples] are political and cultural groups with values and lifeways distinct from those of other Canadians. They lived as nations – highly centralized, loosely federated, or small and clan-based – for thousands of years before the arrival of Europeans. As nations, they forged trade and military alliances among themselves and with the new arrivals. To this day, Aboriginal people's sense of confidence and well-being as individuals remains tied to the strength of their nations. Only as members of restored nations can they reach their potential in the twenty-first century.

A **royal commission** is an important tool used by governments to deal with complicated issues. It is an independent public inquiry established to examine an issue, hear testimony from people involved, and recommend ways of coming to a resolution. Although royal commissions make recommendations, governments are not required to follow them.

Web Connection

To read more of *People to People, Nation to Nation*, go to this web site and follow the links.

www.ExploringNationalism.ca

Statement of Reconciliation

The findings of the Royal Commission on Aboriginal Peoples led the federal government to issue a Statement of Reconciliation in 1998. This document expressed regret for Canada's history of suppressing Aboriginal culture and values and weakening the identity of Aboriginal peoples. "We must recognize the impact of these actions on the once self-sustaining nations that were disaggregated [broken up], disrupted, limited or even destroyed by the dispossession of traditional territory, by the relocation of Aboriginal people, and by some provisions of the Indian Act," the statement said. "We must acknowledge that the result of these actions was the erosion of the political, economic and social systems of Aboriginal people and nations."

Aboriginal people reacted to the statement with mixed feelings. Some viewed it as a step forward, but others viewed it as nothing but empty words. Can a statement like this be an important part of the reconciliation process? Can it have a negative effect?

Against the backdrop of these historical legacies, it is a remarkable tribute to the strength and endurance of Aboriginal people that they have maintained their historic diversity and identity.

— Canadian government, Statement of Reconciliation, 1998

Land Claims

The Royal Commission on Aboriginal Peoples identified the use and control of land as the source of "the most intense conflicts between Aboriginal and non-Aboriginal people." The commission called on the government to change its approach to Aboriginal land claims.

Figure 3-15 James Bay and Northern Québec Agreement

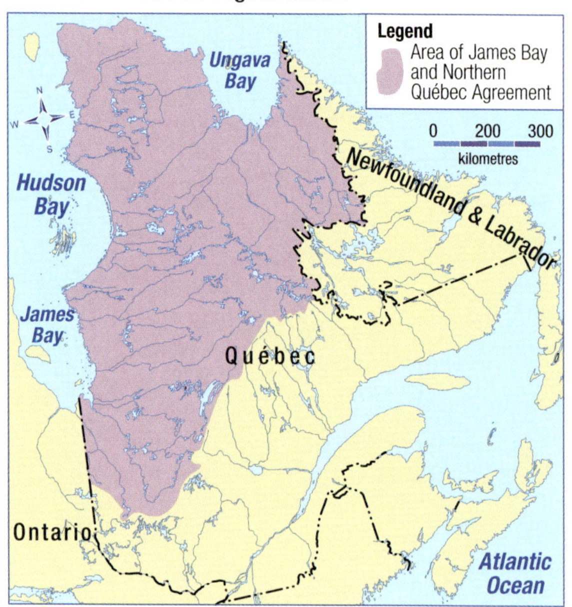

Settling land claims has always been a long, involved process. The timeline in Figure 3-16 shows how long it can take to settle just one claim — and what can happen even after agreement is reached. The James Bay and Northern Québec Agreement of 1975 was the first modern comprehensive land-claim settlement in Canada. Since then, a few other claims have been settled. But by late 2007, about 800 remained unresolved.

On June 29, 2007, the Assembly of First Nations organized the National Day of Action to highlight various issues, including outstanding claims. On that day, Phil Fontaine, national chief of the AFN, told an Ottawa audience that First Nations are fed up with the slow pace of negotiations. "Since the first treaty was signed with us in 1701, our peoples have believed that co-operation must pave the way to progress," Fontaine said. "We like to believe that all Canadians feel this way. Consider where that attitude has gotten us. Obviously, not very far."

First Nations are losing patience, Fontaine added. "Many of our communities have reached the breaking point . . . People are so tired and fed up with this type of existence — especially when all around them is a better life . . . and hope. Living without hope is perhaps the worst aspect of life for so many of Canada's First Nations peoples. That lack of hope plays out in many ways. Desperation breeds abuse, suicide, crime, civil disobedience."

Think about the Oka crisis, the Royal Commission on Aboriginal Peoples, the government's Statement of Reconciliation, and land claims. With a partner, create a T-chart. In the first column, show each event or issue. In the second column, rate whether the event or issue helped or hindered Aboriginal peoples' attempts to reconcile contending nationalist loyalties. Include an explanation of the rating scale you used.

Figure 3-16 James Bay — The Road to Settlement

TIME IMMEMORIAL	1971	1973	1975	1989	2002	2007
Cree and Inuit inhabit the lands east of Hudson Bay and James Bay.	Québec premier Robert Bourassa announces the James Bay Project, which will involve building huge power-generating dams on northern Québec rivers.	Cree Nation takes Québec government to court because dams will flood land in their traditional territory and destroy their traditional way of life.	Lawsuit forces Québec and federal governments to bargaining table. With the Cree and Inuit, they hammer out the James Bay and Northern Québec Agreement, covering about 350 000 square kilometres.	Cree take Québec government to court again, claiming that neither Québec nor the federal government is keeping its part of the bargain.	Québec government and Cree agree to share responsibility for and revenues from hydro development on Cree lands.	Federal government settles with Cree Regional Authority, which will take on more responsibility for self-government while the government pays for building necessary infrastructure.

THE VIEW FROM HERE

Most demonstrations on the 2007 National Day of Action were peaceful. But in Ontario, a group of Mohawks from the Tyendinaga reserve, between Toronto and Kingston, blocked CN's main rail line and shut down Highway 401. The next day, a *Globe and Mail* editorial pointed out that this was the action people would recall. "Many Canadians will simply remember that . . . a portion of the nation's busiest highway was closed for hours and passenger rail service from Toronto to Ottawa and Montreal was suspended." Here is how several First Nations people viewed the effectiveness of the day's events.

Shawn Brant, who organized the blockade in Ontario, is a member of the Bay of Quinte Mohawks. He made the following comments in a CBC interview.

> We feel it's only been through these type of actions that First Nations issues have been made a priority for Canadians and have elevated it in priorities for this government. We'll continue to push this button as long as we have outstanding issues and we'll continue to do it until there's some results . . .
>
> There's about $118 million a day in freight that passes down this train line [between Toronto and Montréal] and there's a great deal of commerce that travels down the 401, so I guess if we're evaluating on a monetary sense . . . certainly we've been successful in our campaign.

Marilyn Jensen of the Carcross Tagish First Nation in Yukon is a director, producer, singer, and dancer with First Peoples Performances. Jensen helped organize a peaceful rally in Carcross, but told the CBC that she understands why some First Nations communities felt the need to be more confrontational.

> I wouldn't really say direct action is always an ugly thing. Sometimes it needs to happen so people will hear, so people will notice. All I know is that myself and the group that I am working with, we've planned a peaceful protest. We know that we live here with other people and we respect that. We respect the goings-on in our community and we respect other people, so we're keeping our demonstration, our protest peaceful.

Doug Cuthand, a member of the Little Pine First Nation in Saskatchewan, is a filmmaker, writer, and journalist. In his column in the *Regina Leader-Post*, he warned against interpreting the largely peaceful gatherings as a sign that everything is fine.

> Why the lack of civil disobedience? It's not as if we don't care or aren't upset with our lot within Canada.
>
> It's because we are Canadians and we are a part of a national culture of negotiation and the respect of law . . .
>
> In Saskatchewan we grew up with the knowledge that we have a special agreement with the Crown and, by extension, Canada. The numbered treaties were negotiated in the late 1800s and they called for a partnership and the tools to develop strong communities in the future.
>
> In the beginning we saw ourselves as partners with Canada. The fact that everything went sideways in the treaty implementation only made our leaders all the more adamant that the treaties be recognized.
>
> But don't confuse our orderly conduct as a sign that things are fine. Things are not fine, and we have serious problems after over a century of colonialism and failed promises.

Explorations

1. Think about each speaker's words in the context of reconciling contending nationalist loyalties. What clues can you find in the speaker's words to reveal his or her attitude toward the importance of reconciling nationalist loyalties?
2. Do you think the use of force helps or hurts the reconciliation process?
3. How important is it to achieve reconciliation between contending nationalist loyalties within Canadian society? Explain your response.

1. In Chapter 1, you explored various ideas about ethnic and civic nationalism (pp. 30–33). Choose a nation mentioned in this chapter and explain whether you think the contending loyalties felt by people illustrate civic or ethnic nationalism. Support your opinion by citing evidence.

2. "The Maple Leaf Forever," which was written by Scottish-born Alexander Muir, was wildly popular with Canadians of British heritage from 1867, when it was written, until the mid-20th century. During that time, this song was often described as Canada's unofficial national anthem.

The Maple Leaf Forever

In days of yore, from Britain's shore,
Wolfe, the dauntless hero came,
And planted firm Britannia's flag,
On Canada's fair domain.
Here may it wave, our boast, our pride,
And join in love together,
The thistle, shamrock, rose* entwine
The Maple Leaf forever!

Chorus

The Maple Leaf, our emblem dear,
The Maple Leaf forever!
God save our Queen, and Heaven bless,
The Maple Leaf forever!

* The thistle is an emblem of Scotland; the shamrock is an emblem of Ireland; and the rose is an emblem of England.

a) Examine the first verse and chorus of "The Maple Leaf Forever." Whose loyalties were affirmed by this song? Whose loyalties were ignored? How might this song have strengthened contending nationalist loyalties?

b) At one time, many people were in favour of making "The Maple Leaf Forever" Canada's national anthem. This began to change in the mid-20th century as Canada became more culturally diverse. "O Canada" was proclaimed Canada's national anthem in 1980. With a partner, list two arguments in favour of making "The Maple Leaf Forever" the national anthem. List two arguments against. Be sure that at least one of your arguments mentions contending nationalist loyalties.

3. Examine the following cartoon. Created by Peter Kuch in 1977, it takes a lighthearted look at what might happen when an Inuk in northern Québec tries to obey the new French-language laws by issuing French commands to his sled dogs.

Figure 3-17

Vite, vite, vite. Peter Kuch, 1977. M999.66.19.

Then read the following statement, which expresses the response to Bill 101 of a group of Inuit who live on Hudson Bay in northern Québec.

> We, the Esquimo, have a distinct culture and language, and like all other people, we are convinced that it belongs to us and to us alone to defend our culture. We . . . want the same chances as the Québécois to take the necessary measures to protect our language. And like the Québécois, we do not want the responsibility and the task of passing laws concerning our language and our culture to belong to anyone but ourselves.

a) What do the cartoon and the statement say about how Bill 101 affected the way the Inuit of northern Québec viewed nationalist loyalties?

b) How might the perspectives on nationalist loyalties of the Inuit of northern Québec conflict with the nationalist loyalties of sovereignist Québécois?

c) Write a brief statement explaining whether you think Canadian government policies, such as multiculturalism, and laws, such as the Charter of Rights and Freedoms, help reconcile these contending loyalties. In your statement, include evidence to support your opinion.

Figure 3-18

4. The Inuk in this picture was photographed in 1945 at Mittimatalik/Tununiq, Nunavut. She is holding a board on which her personal number (see p. 71) has been written in chalk. The picture of this young woman was just one of thousands taken by whalers, missionaries, RCMP officers, and other people between the late 1800s and the mid-20th century.

   Many of these photographs are now part of the collection of Library and Archives Canada, but the people shown in the photos remain largely unidentified. Elders, students, families, teachers, and governments are now trying to identify these people through Project Naming (see p. 70).

   Conduct Internet research to find out more about Project Naming. Then write a brief report that sets out
   - the people involved
   - the goals of the project
   - the tasks involved

   Conclude your report by explaining how Project Naming affirms nationalist loyalties and by rating the importance of this project in helping the Inuit reconcile their contending loyalties.

5. Create an inventory of nationalist symbols, events, or activities you encounter over the course of a week. Record your observations on a chart like the one shown on this page. Do not repeat symbols, events, or activities you encounter every day. If, for example, you see the Canadian flag flying outside your school every morning, list this only once. The chart includes some examples to help you get started.

   At the end of the week, write a few sentences that express your feelings about the nationalist symbols and activities you encountered. Were you surprised, for example, by how many you encountered? By how few? Were you comfortable with the number or kinds of symbols you encountered? Were you uncomfortable? Why?

DAY	SYMBOL, EVENT, OR ACTIVITY
Wednesday	Canadian flag at school Sang "O Canada" to start the school day Went to Ukrainian language class Passed framed copy of Charter of Rights and Freedoms at the front door of school
Thursday	

Think about Your Challenge

The challenge for this related issue asks you to create a coat of arms that represents your response to the related-issue question: To what extent should nation be the foundation of identity?

Identify a nationalist loyalty that might contend with one of your loyalties. Think of a symbol or other graphic that you could incorporate into your coat of arms to represent your feelings about reconciling these contending loyalties. Sketch your idea and explain its significance to a partner. You may or may not wish to include this symbol in your final coat of arms.

CHAPTER 4 Reconciling Nationalist and Non-Nationalist Loyalties

Figure 4-1 Demonstrators from an animal rights group called Fourrure Torture — Fur Torture — gather near the Canadian Embassy in Paris, France, to protest the annual commercial seal hunt off Canada's East Coast. The placard reads, "Canada! Stop slaughtering seals." The word covering the Canadian flag means "Shame."

CHAPTER ISSUE

To what extent should people reconcile their contending nationalist and non-nationalist loyalties?

The annual commercial seal hunt off Canada's East Coast is controversial. Environmental groups around the world have lobbied to ban seal products. Countries such as the United States, France, and Mexico have responded to this pressure. And in 2007, the European Union was planning to make it illegal for members to import goods made from seals.

But both the Canadian government and the government of Newfoundland and Labrador defend the hunt. The Newfoundland and Labrador government says the hunt provides essential work for 6000 people and "is intricately linked to our culture, and to our economy, especially for many of the communities along the east and northeast coast of the island, and as a traditional way of life along the coast of Labrador."

Examine the photograph on page 88, then respond to these questions:

- What beliefs are being expressed by the protesters in the photograph? How might these beliefs shape the protesters' identity? Their loyalties?
- If you were an environmentalist in Port au Choix, Newfoundland, and knew that your neighbours relied on income from the seal hunt, how might you respond? Would your response involve contending loyalties?
- The protesters painted the word "Shame" across the Canadian flag. Was this a disrespectful defacement of the flag or a legitimate protest tactic? Does nationalist loyalty shape your judgment? Explain.
- As props, the protesters used stuffed animals that look like harp seal pups. But killing pups has been illegal since 1987. Does this knowledge change your opinion of the protesters' tactics? Of sealing? Why or why not?

KEY TERMS

non-nationalist loyalty

inflation

alienation

segregation

Looking Ahead

In this chapter, you will develop responses to the following questions as you explore the extent to which people should reconcile their contending nationalist and non-nationalist loyalties:

- What are non-nationalist loyalties?
- How can nationalist and non-nationalist loyalties compete?
- How have people reconciled contending nationalist and non-nationalist loyalties?

My Journal on Nationalism

You have explored several examples of contending nationalist loyalties. Can these loyalties be reconciled? Should they be? What does your response to these questions say about you? Use words or images — or both — to respond to these questions. Date your ideas and keep them in your journal, notebook, learning log, portfolio, or computer file so that you can return to them as you progress through this course.

Figure 4-2 When the Colorado Avalanche played the Edmonton Oilers in October 2007, long-time Oiler Ryan Smyth was in an Avalanche uniform. The game was his first in Edmonton since he was traded in February 2007. At the time of the trade, Smyth told reporters, "Edmonton . . . that's where my heart is." What contending loyalties do you think Smyth might have experienced when he returned to Edmonton for this game?

What are non-nationalist loyalties?

Everyone's identity includes individual and collective loyalties. Some of your collective loyalties may be nationalist, and some may be non-nationalist — loyalties that are not embedded in the idea of nation. Loyalty to your family is an example of a **non-nationalist loyalty**.

The importance people assign to their many loyalties can vary with time and circumstances. During World War II, for example, nationalist loyalty was very important to many Canadians. But in the years after the war ended, non-nationalist loyalties often assumed greater importance.

Suppose you grew up in Banff, the hometown of Ryan Smyth, and became a hockey fan. Like many others in town, you enthusiastically followed Smyth's career and, as a result, became a loyal fan of his first National Hockey League team, the Edmonton Oilers. What loyalties might have been involved in your decision to support the Oilers? Would these loyalties have been nationalist or non-nationalist?

In early 2007, Smyth was traded to the New York Islanders and that summer signed with the Colorado Avalanche. How might this have affected your loyalties? Would you have experienced contending loyalties? If so, how might you have reconciled them? Would you have continued to be a Smyth fan, or would you have chosen another player as a favourite? Would you have continued to root for the Oilers, switched your loyalty to the Avalanche, or chosen another team completely? What loyalties might have played an important role in your decision? What other factors might affect your decision? Which of these loyalties would have been nationalist and which would have been non-nationalist?

The Nature of Loyalties

If you were asked to list your loyalties, you might include your family, your close friends, your school, your favourite music, your nation, and so on.

If your list included 20 different loyalties, what might happen when you develop a new loyalty, perhaps to a different sport? Suppose, for example, you developed a new interest in basketball. Would you need to delete an old loyalty to make room for this new one?

If you answered no, you are like most people, who have an unlimited capacity for forming loyalties. A new loyalty does not require them to give up old loyalties, especially when these loyalties do not contend. Think, for example, about your friends. Forming a new friendship does not require you to drop an old friend. Whether you have two or 22 friends, you can remain loyal to them all.

Do you envision your loyalties as an interconnected web, as a hierarchy that ranks them from most to least important, or as an unconnected patchwork?

Distinguishing between Nationalist and Non-Nationalist Loyalties

The dividing line between nationalist and non-nationalist loyalties is not always clear. Take your friends, for example. You may have chosen some friends because you share their interests and others because you enjoy their sense of humour or you grew up as neighbours. Your loyalty to these friends is not embedded in the idea of nation.

But you may also have chosen some friends because you share with them a sense of belonging to a nation. Two Tamil-speaking students who immigrated to Canada from Sri Lanka, for example, may become friends because they share a nationalist loyalty to their language and culture.

Many non-nationalist loyalties fall into one of the categories shown in Figure 4-3. All are loyalties to an idea, a collective, or a group. A regional loyalty, for example, can be understood as a loyalty to the idea of "the West" or to the people of the West.

These loyalties are often interconnected. Religious loyalty, for example, may also involve cultural, racial or ethnic, and ideological loyalties. In addition, these feelings can sometimes develop into the kind of internalized or collective consciousness that becomes a nationalist loyalty. When, for example, the Third Estate in France rebelled against the nobles and clergy, their class loyalty was transformed into nationalist loyalty. And when Tibetans, who are largely Buddhist, express their desire to govern themselves, their religious and regional loyalties are also transformed into nationalist loyalty.

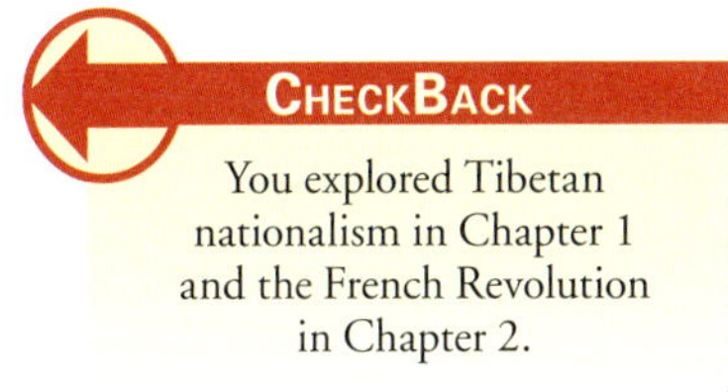

Would loyalty to family, friends, or your school fit into any of the categories in Figure 4-3? Why or why not? What other categories might you add to this chart?

Figure 4-3 Some Non-Nationalist Loyalties

Class Loyalty	Religious Loyalty	Regional Loyalty	Ideological Loyalty	Cultural Loyalty	Racial or Ethnic Loyalty
Loyalty to people from a particular social sector	Loyalty to a religious organization and its beliefs and values	Loyalty to a region and the interests of people living there	Loyalty to shared ideas about how a society should work	Loyalty to a way of life	Loyalty to people of the same racial or ethnic background
Examples – working people, business entrepreneurs	*Examples – Catholic Church, Tibetan Buddhism*	*Examples – the West, the Arctic*	*Examples – Conservatism, Marxism, animal rights*	*Examples – Alberta ranchers, Ukrainian heritage, Siksika heritage*	*Examples – Tutsis, Koreans*

Reflect and Respond

With a partner, return to the chapter-opening photograph of the seal hunt protest (Figure 4-1, p. 88) and choose one character or group mentioned in the questions on page 89. Or choose the Ryan Smyth fan mentioned on page 90.

Discuss the loyalties involved in the situation you chose and create a web or other graphic to show them visually. Use colour and shape to indicate which loyalties are nationalist and which are non-nationalist. Identify contending loyalties by adding connecting lines or another graphic element. Use a numbering system or another method to rate the importance of each loyalty shown. Add a title and a legend to your graphic, and be prepared to explain your judgments.

Explain your graphic to a small group and respond to their questions and comments.

How can nationalist and non-nationalist loyalties compete?

Just as differing nationalist loyalties can compete, so can nationalist and non-nationalist loyalties. This conflict can occur when nationalist and non-nationalist loyalties lead people toward different goals.

When Class and Nationalist Loyalty Compete

Why do people tend to pigeonhole others according to class?

Most societies are divided, either formally or informally, into socio-economic classes. Wealth, status, education level, career choice, ancestry, heritage, ethnicity, or a combination of these factors — and more — often play a role in this division. If people accept these divisions, no conflict occurs. But if people dispute the divisions or believe that one class is favoured over another, conflict may result. The French Revolution is an example of the conflicts that can occur.

Giving Voice to Class Loyalty

Figure 4-4 Maria Dunn has won several City of Edmonton awards and has been nominated for Prairie Music Awards, as well as a Juno Award. How does performance art enable people to both voice their opinions and take action?

Maria Dunn is an Alberta singer-songwriter who has focused her recent writing on the struggles of working people in Western Canada. Her ballad "We Were Good People," for example, tells the story of what happened on December 20, 1932, at the height of the Great Depression.

On that day, about 10 000 desperate farmers, factory workers, and unemployed people had gathered in Edmonton to take part in a peaceful march urging the government to help them. They wanted work, food, and hope for the future. As the marchers turned a corner and headed toward the Alberta legislature, mounted police officers swinging billy clubs rode into the crowd. Twenty-nine people were arrested and many more were injured.

The following are some lines from Dunn's song:

Well the air was almost festive with Christmas trees in view
But as we moved to leave the square and march the Avenue
A sound I'd never heard before turned my heart to lead
The sound of a billy club cracking open heads . . .
We were good people, gathered in the square
It wasn't ease and comfort had driven us there
But they treated us like criminals for showing our despair
Oh I remember well this Bloody Tuesday

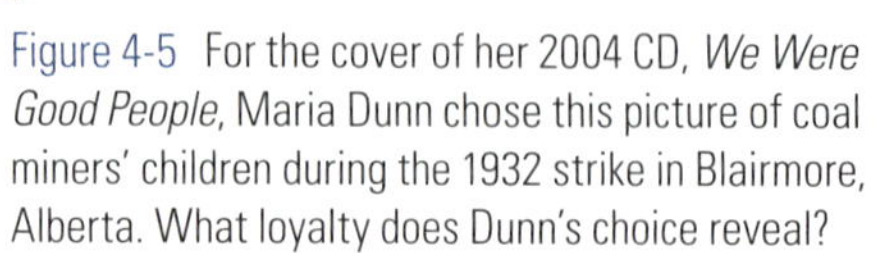

Describe the loyalties that clashed in Edmonton in 1932. How might the outcome have been avoided?

Figure 4-5 For the cover of her 2004 CD, *We Were Good People*, Maria Dunn chose this picture of coal miners' children during the 1932 strike in Blairmore, Alberta. What loyalty does Dunn's choice reveal?

When Religious and Nationalist Loyalty Compete

Because of globalization and worldwide migration, your social studies class may include students with many different religious beliefs. In civic nations such as Canada, where freedom of religion is guaranteed in the Charter of Rights and Freedoms, people with various religious loyalties respect one another's beliefs and coexist peacefully.

But this was not — and is not — always the case. In many countries, religious and nationalist loyalties have come into conflict in the past and continue to do so today.

CHECKFORWARD

You will read more about Iraq in Chapter 5.

Religious Loyalties in Iraq

Since the 2003 United States–led invasion of Iraq and the fall of dictator Saddam Hussein, Iraqis have been divided over how their nation should work. Most Iraqis are Muslims, but they are split into two main groups: Shiites and Sunnis. The two disagree over how to interpret the Qur'an, the Muslim scripture. This disagreement has affected their national loyalties and sparked violent conflict.

Shiites make up about 60 per cent of Iraq's population, while about 35 per cent are Sunnis. This is unusual in the Middle East, where between 85 and 90 per cent of Muslims are Sunnis. Iraq also has a substantial Kurdish population, many of whom are Sunni.

Much of the current religious conflict in Iraq focuses on the role religion should play in the country's political and justice systems. Mansoor Moaddel, an Iranian-born Eastern Michigan University professor who has conducted a series of public opinion surveys in the country, said, "The Kurds and Sunnis dislike religious regimes, while the Shiites have a problem with secular politics [politics in which religion plays no role]."

In 2007, Moaddel conducted another public opinion poll in Iraq. Figures 4-6 and 4-7 show how the Iraqis surveyed responded to two of the questions.

FYI

Many Kurds of northern Iraq regard themselves as a nation because their ethnic origins and traditions are different from those of other Iraqis, who are largely of Arabic heritage. The Kurds live in Kurdistan, a mountainous region that is divided among Iraq, Iran, Turkey, Syria, and Armenia. Most Iraqis speak Arabic, but Kurds speak their own language, Kurdish, and have developed their own distinct traditions and culture.

Examine Figures 4-6 and 4-7. What relationships do you see? Why do you think more Shiites than Sunnis or Kurds would identify themselves as Iraqis first? How might the minority status of Sunnis and Kurds, as well as their opinions about the role of religion in politics, create conflict between their loyalty to their religion and their national loyalty? What factors, besides religion, might affect Kurds' loyalty to the idea of Iraq as their nation?

Which group(s) — Kurds, Sunnis, or Shiites — do you think would be more likely to view religion as a foundation of the Iraqi nation? As a non-nationalist loyalty? Explain your response.

Figure 4-6 Public Opinion Poll, 2007

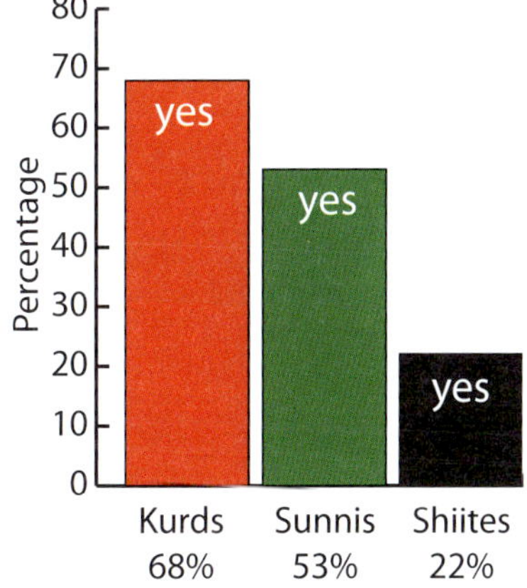

Figure 4-7 Public Opinion Poll, 2007

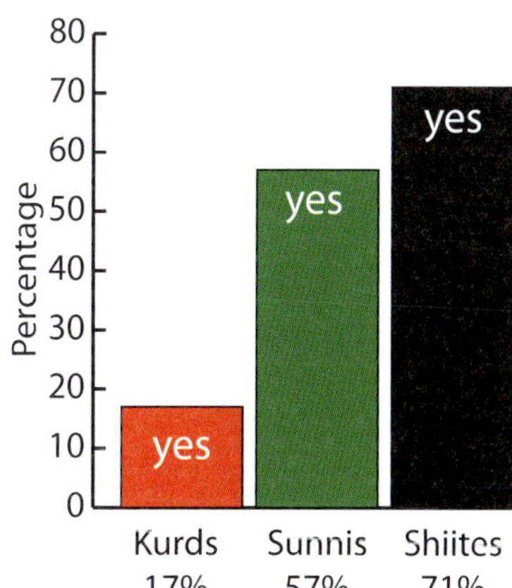

SPINBUSTER

Identifying Spin in the News

SPINBUSTER SPINBUSTER SPINBUSTER SPINBUSTER

"Spin" is a word that is often used to describe how the news is manipulated to shape public opinion by presenting a particular point of view or perspective. Spin often includes elements of bias and propaganda and may involve unsupported opinion, rumour, and even outright lies.

The photograph on this page became one of the enduring images of the war in Iraq. It appeared on the front pages of newspapers around the world, on web sites, and on TV news programs.

Steps to Analyzing and Interpreting Cause-and-Effect Relationships

Step 1: Question assumptions

With a partner, examine the photograph and respond to the following questions:

- If you were a news editor, why would you have chosen to feature this image? What message would you be sending? What loyalties would you be highlighting?
- As a newspaper reader, how would you have responded to the image? What loyalties would have influenced your responses? Would the image have challenged or reinforced these loyalties?

Step 2: Think about bias

With your partner, discuss whether the presentation of the image was biased. The following questions may help focus your thinking:

- What did the news organizations that presented the image have to gain?
- What information might have been left out of the picture? Is it possible that other images presented a conflicting version of the event — and were not used?
- What might you see if you could look beyond the edges of the photograph?

Step 3: Analyze the context

With your partner, analyze how the context of this news story might have affected the way the photograph was interpreted.

- Who told the story that went with the image?
- What might the storyteller have to gain?

Step 4: Be a spinbuster — look for alternative points of view and information

Since this event, journalists and others have questioned what happened. British journalist Robert Fisk, for example, said the event was a "stage-managed photo opportunity."

Others have said that only a few people were in Fardus Square, and most were either journalists or the American marines who pulled down the statue. Still others have claimed that the few Iraqis involved were flown in by the American forces, who planned the event, which took place directly opposite the hotel where the international media were based.

With your partner, discuss whether this information changes your responses to questions in Steps 1, 2, and 3. Make a list of resources you might consult to confirm or challenge claims about the event. Is it possible to find out the truth behind this photograph?

Summing Up

You can use your spinbusting skill to detect bias and propaganda in a variety of situations at school and in everyday life.

Figure 4-8 Soon after American troops entered Baghdad in 2003, Western journalists took this picture of Iraqis pulling down a huge statue of Saddam Hussein in Fardus Square. This action was presented as a symbol of Iraqis' joy at being liberated from the dictator's repressive regime.

When Regional and Nationalist Loyalty Compete

A region may be an area within a country (e.g., the West), an area within a province (e.g., northern Alberta), or even an area that crosses provincial and national boundaries (e.g., the Prairies). People often express their regional loyalty by actively promoting the interests of their region, but this loyalty can sometimes clash with national loyalties. This is what happened in Alberta in 1980.

Oil, Gas, and Regional Loyalty

During the early 1970s, Canada and other countries experienced a prolonged period of **inflation** — rising prices and a drop in the purchasing power of money. By 1978, inflation had eased, but by 1980, the price of oil had risen to $34 (U.S.) a barrel from $14. Canadian manufacturers, who were based largely in Ontario and Québec, as well as consumers across the country, faced high energy bills. Inflation had become a threat again.

In response, Prime Minister Pierre Trudeau's Liberal government introduced the National Energy Program in 1980. The NEP was designed to

- make Canada self-sufficient for energy
- reduce foreign ownership of oil and gas companies operating in Canada
- protect Canadians against high energy costs by setting a Canadian oil price that was lower than the world price

The Trudeau government reasoned that Canada is rich in oil and gas, so Canadians should not have to pay high world prices. Canadian-owned companies were to receive grants for research and development, as well as the right to keep more of their revenues.

But in Alberta, which produced about 86 per cent of Canada's oil, many people were outraged. They protested the federal government's interference in an area of provincial responsibility and warned that the NEP would both prevent Alberta from benefiting from high world prices and seriously harm the Canadian oil and gas industry.

These predictions proved accurate. Many foreign oil companies cut production or shut down their Alberta operations completely to focus on business outside Canada, where they could sell at world prices.

Although the NEP was later dropped, Alberta premier Ralph Klein summed up his view of its effect: "The Alberta economy nose-dived thanks in no small part to the [federal] government's National Energy Program, which drained 50 000 jobs and $100 billion in revenue out of the province."

We view the federal export tax on Alberta oil as contrary to both the spirit and intent of Confederation. It is discriminatory, and is a price freeze on all of Alberta's oil production at immense cost to Albertans.

— Alberta premier Peter Lougheed, opening statement to the First Ministers' Conference on Energy, January 22, 1974

The needs of the federal government to be able to share to a reasonably appropriate degree in the various streams of income across the country [through corporate income tax] are self evident . . . A very high level of provincial royalties obviously erodes the corporate tax base.

— Prime Minister Pierre Trudeau, in a letter to Alberta premier Peter Lougheed, March 12, 1974

Should the resources of each province be shared equally by all Canadians?

Figure 4-9 Tom Innes, a political cartoonist for the *Calgary Herald*, created this cartoon in 1980 as Alberta premier Peter Lougheed (left) and Prime Minister Pierre Trudeau (right) were about to start negotiating the price of Canadian oil. What was Innes predicting would happen? What loyalties do you think motivated Lougheed and Trudeau? How do you think this cartoon would have been received in Alberta? In Ontario? In Québec?

The first time I ever came to the site, I was a 23-year-old kid. I flew into [Fort] McMurray, saw three fights, spent a sleepless night in the hotel, and then came to the [Mildred Lake] site the next morning by boat. I'd never seen anything like it. There it was, sitting in the middle of nowhere. The pilot site was already operational. We worked hard. At the end of the day, we came back to quarters that were very comfortable if not opulent, and ate some of the best meals I've ever eaten.

— *Tom Wild, Syncrude Canada engineer, in* The Syncrude Story: In Our Own Words, *1990*

The Oil Sands and Loyalties

Throughout the 1990s and into the 21st century, business in the oil patch flourished. The price of oil was moving up, and by late 2007, a barrel of crude was selling for more than $95.

In Alberta, this created an economic boom that some likened to a modern-day gold rush. The world oil price was high enough that investing in the costly process of extracting oil from Alberta's oil sands began to make good business sense. This opened vast areas of the province to oil development.

When the oil sands were included in 2007 estimates of total oil reserves, only Saudi Arabia had greater reserves than Canada's 179 billion barrels. Of Canada's total reserves, 175 billion barrels, or 98 per cent, are found in the oil sands.

Developing the oil sands provided many Albertans with new economic opportunities and helped build prosperity in the province. By 2004, for example, more families with annual incomes of $250 000 or more lived in Calgary than in any other Canadian city. But this boom also created challenges. As people moved to Alberta to find jobs, housing was needed. Increased demand caused house prices to skyrocket. This meant that many people had trouble finding an affordable place to live.

Examine the features and graphics on this page and the next. Jot down your immediate responses. Do any of your responses seem to be contradictory? What visual or graphic might you add to the ones on these two pages to help provide a balanced picture of oil sands development? Is it important to provide a balanced picture? Explain your response.

Figure 4-10 Oil Sands in Alberta

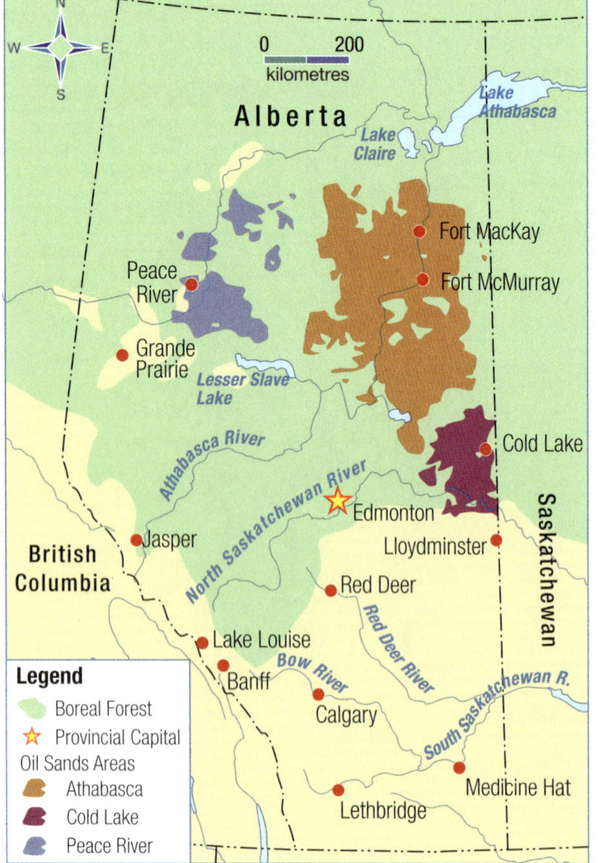

Figure 4-11 These help-wanted signs are a few of the many that appeared along a busy Calgary road in 2007. The high pay offered by the oil industry attracts so many workers that other businesses often have trouble finding employees. The rest of Canada also benefits from oil sands development — through the taxes paid by Albertans, the business opportunities for companies in other provinces, and the jobs for people who move to Alberta. Can supporting Alberta's economic interests express both a regional and nationalist loyalty?

The Oil Sands and Ideological Loyalties

Ideological loyalties can also conflict with nationalist loyalties. Someone who supports oil sands development, for example, may be inspired by both regional and nationalist loyalties. She may believe that developing the oil sands benefits Alberta — and all Canadians — because it provides royalties to the Alberta government, creates a demand for spinoff industries, and ensures that more people are employed and able to pay taxes. Increased tax revenues help the federal government support both social programs and equalization payments to less economically developed provinces.

At the same time, however, other people may believe that the development of the oil sands — and the resulting prosperity — comes at too high a price. These people's ideological loyalty to environmental stewardship and the concept of sustainable prosperity may compete with their regional and nationalist loyalties, which support the idea of a prosperous Alberta and a prosperous Canada.

Examine Figure 4-12. What trends do you see on this graph? How do you think someone who agrees with Ali Abdelrahman, who is quoted in "Voices," would view this graph? How do you think an environmentalist would view this graph? Which view most closely reflects your loyalties? Explain why.

Figure 4-13 Mining for oil sands that lie near the surface involves stripping away the earth to a depth of as much as 100 metres. Estimates suggest that in 2007, strip mining will destroy 3000 square kilometres of boreal forest. Companies are required to restore the areas when they finish mining. What is your response to this information? What might be the response of someone who takes an opposing view? What loyalties might these responses involve?

Figure 4-12 Crude Oil Production in Alberta, Actual and Predicted, 2005

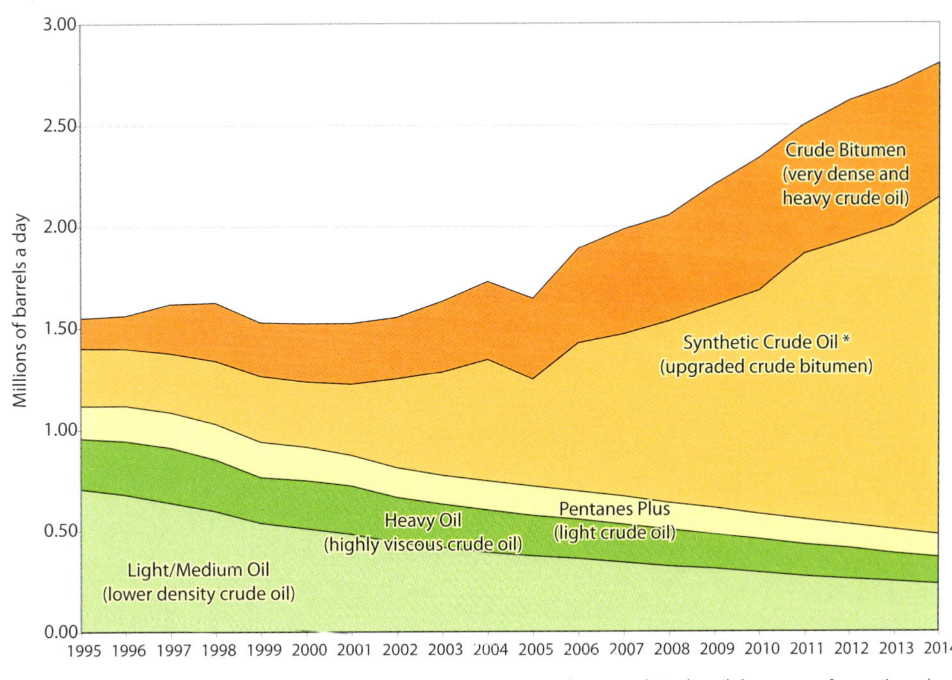

Source: Pembina Institute

* Synthetic crude is the oil that comes from oil sands.

The oil and gas industry is driving the boom for the economy . . . There is a direct effect coming from oil and gas and spilling over to other industries. If you have a healthy economy, that will help other sectors to develop . . . If the whole economy is healthy, that will benefit the province in the long run.

— Ali Abdelrahman, senior economist, Alberta Human Resources and Employment, 2006

To find out more about how oil sands development might be balanced with environmental concerns, go to this web site and follow the links.

www.ExploringNationalism.ca

The Oil Sands and Cultural Loyalties

The development of the oils sands has severely tested the loyalty of some First Nations people to their traditional ways of life and culture. The oil industry provides employment and other economic benefits to First Nations, but it also changes the landscape, making traditional activities such as hunting more difficult.

Strip mining, for example, threatens the Fort McKay First Nation. Andrew Boucher, a Fort McKay Elder, has been hunting and trapping in the area since he was nine years old. But he told a Calgary reporter that Fort MacKay has now become "just a little dot" surrounded by oil sands development. "It's getting worse," he said. "Pretty soon we'll be boxed in here. Our way of life is all screwed up . . . It makes me sick . . . [Trapping is] our way of life, so we'd like to keep it. We don't want to lose our way of life, but we're losing it anyways."

In addition, producing synthetic crude requires a great deal of fresh water, and this affects lakes, rivers, and groundwater supplies in oil sands areas. Melody Lepine, director of the Mikisew Cree First Nation Industry Relations Corp., told *The Nature of Things* that her nation depends on Lake Athabasca, which is fed by the Athabasca River. "We don't want any more water taken out [of the Athabasca River]," Lepine said. "We don't want any more pollution. And we just want to carry on the way we've been carrying on since time immemorial."

Figure 4-14 The exploration sites and lines cut through the boreal forest shown in this aerial photograph are in northern Alberta. To locate and map underground oil sands, companies cut a grid of lines. The grid enables geophysicists to bring vibrator and recorder trucks into the forested areas so they can take measurements.

If 2007 plans go ahead, about 20 per cent of Alberta — 137 000 square kilometres of boreal forest — could be fragmented by well sites, access roads, and pipelines, as well as narrow paths cut through forests to enable trucks carrying measuring equipment to enter an area and conduct seismic tests that map underground oil sands.

Although oil companies are required to restore natural areas when they move on, environmentalists warn that this level of activity in the boreal forest may cause irreversible ecological damage.

Reflect and Respond

Consider the following situations. In each case, identify how nationalist and non-nationalist loyalties might conflict.

- You have just received a "prosperity cheque" from the Alberta government, which is distributing the cheques so Alberta citizens can share in the revenues generated by the oil industry.
- Your family's income depends on the oil industry, and you are the president of a local environmental group.
- The representatives on your First Nation council are withholding drilling rights while they negotiate with an oil company to win better employment opportunities for members of your nation.
- Your family is thinking about buying an SUV.
- Your best friend gets a summer job delivering pizza in Fort McMurray and wants you to join the team.
- A family has moved to Fort McMurray but is living in temporary housing.

THE VIEW FROM HERE

THE VIEW FROM HERE

THE VIEW FROM HERE

The development of the oil sands creates great prosperity, but it also causes environmental damage. This can lead to contending loyalties. Here is how four people have responded to this development.

Melody Lepine is director of the Mikisew Cree First Nation Industry Relations Corp. This First Nation is located on the Athabasca River, about 250 kilometres downstream from Fort McMurray. She made these remarks in 2005.

[The Athabasca River] will just be all dry and contaminated and we'll be scratching our heads 60 years from now thinking we really should have thought about this. Maybe we shouldn't have given away those 10 last water licences. Maybe we should've done more studies, more environmental baseline work research. We don't want to stop development, yet development should be occurring responsibly, weighing both the economic and environmental balance . . .

Peter Lougheed, a former Alberta premier, led the fight against the National Energy Program in the early 1980s. In 2007, he predicted that the clash over oil sands development will divide Canada.

I think the issues we saw before – and I was involved in many of them – were important . . . But they aren't even close to [issues raised by the development of the oil sands] . . .

The government of Alberta, with its acceleration of oil sands operations, will in my judgment be seen as the major villain in all of this in the eyes of the public across Canada . . .

My surmise is that . . . national unity will be threatened if the [Supreme] court upholds federal environmental legislation and it causes major damage to Alberta oil sands and our economy.

Don Thompson is an executive with Syncrude Canada. Syncrude is the world's largest producer of synthetic crude oil from oil sands and supplies about 13 per cent of Canada's oil.

[Syncrude is] a significant generator of economic wealth for Canada. Since we began operations, we have contributed over six billion in royalties, payroll, and municipal taxes to government. And in 2005 alone, our expenditures topped 4.7 billion dollars – the impact of which flowed across the entire country . . . And our land reclamation practices, which include introducing wood bison onto reclaimed land, are recognized sector-wide.

Richard Schneider is senior policy analyst for the Canadian Parks and Wilderness Society in Edmonton and author of *Alternative Futures: Alberta's Boreal Forest at the Crossroads*. He made these remarks in 2003.

Unfortunately we've done a particularly bad job of balancing the needs of development and the needs of the [boreal] forest.

We have some particular problems here because . . . we have forestry and oil and gas development, and agriculture, and the combination of these is what's causing the real concern. For example, in the oil and gas side, we've got upwards of 70 000 kilometres of seismic line being approved for development in a typical year. On top of that, there's well-site clearing, and pipelines put in and roads to every one of those well sites. And so people don't have a good appreciation that the oil and gas industry clears as much forest as the forestry industry does.

Explorations

1. Which speaker's position most closely reflects your own? Is your position based on nationalist or non-nationalist loyalties? What loyalties, if any, does your position compete with?
2. Which speakers do you think demonstrate conflict between their nationalist and non-nationalist loyalties? What are these contending loyalties? Why do they compete?

FOCUS ON SKILLS

Defending an Informed Position

FOCUS ON SKILLS

Leaders of the Dehcho First Nations in the Northwest Territories and the Mikisew Cree and Athabasca Chipewyan First Nations in Fort Chipewyan have called for a moratorium — a temporary suspension — on further development of the oil sands. In 2007, Clayton Thomas-Muller, an Aboriginal activist and a member of the Mathais Colomb Cree Nation (Pukatawagan), called on Indigenous peoples in the area of Alberta covered by Treaties 8 and 11 to support the moratorium. To support his position, Thomas-Muller wrote:

> Over the span of 38 years, Northern Alberta has changed from a pristine environment rich in cultural and biological diversity to a landscape resembling a war zone marked with 200-foot-deep pits and thousands of acres of destroyed boreal forests. Lakes and rivers have been contaminated and groundwater systems drained. The impact of the tar sands industry is what I am talking about. This industry has also resulted in the disruption to the Dene First Nations and their treaty rights, including the cultural disruption to the Cree and Métis communities . . .
>
> In the words of many elders and land-based community members living in the tar sands area, concerns for jobs, housing, income, and economic development have taken priority over the traditional Indigenous values of respecting the sacredness of Mother Earth and protection of the environment.
>
> "The river used to be blue. Now it's brown. Nobody can fish or drink from it. The air is bad. This has all happened so fast," said Elsie Fabian, 63, an Elder in a First Nation community along the Athabasca River.

The proposal for a moratorium is controversial. Suppose you were called upon to decide whether to support this proposal. No matter what you decide, your position is likely to spark disagreement — and you would need to be prepared to defend your decision.

The following steps can help you do this. You can use the same steps to help you defend other positions as you progress through this course.

Defending an Informed Position

Step 1: Decide on a position

With a partner, review the material on the oil sands (pp. 95–98), as well as "The View from Here" (p.99). On the basis of this material, decide whether you would support or oppose a proposal for a moratorium on development in the tar sands. Make a note of the loyalties that would form the basis of your decision, and list arguments that support your position.

Step 2: Consider many points of view and perspectives

With your partner or a small group, brainstorm to create a list of at least four stakeholders — individuals, groups, or organizations — that would be likely to challenge your decision. Create a chart like the one shown on the following page and list the stakeholders you selected in the first column.

Discuss arguments each stakeholder might use against your decision and note these possible arguments in the second column of the chart. In the third column, rate the strength of each argument on a scale of 1 to 5 (1 = weak argument; 5 = strong argument).

Step 3: Respond to the arguments

In the fourth column of the chart, develop responses — or counter-arguments — for each argument. To do this, you may wish to conduct research to find information and statistics to back up your position. Rate the strength of each of your counter-arguments using a scale similar to the one in Step 2.

Step 4: Compare your ideas with a group

With your partner(s), join one or two other pairs or small groups. Compare your charts by discussing the information, notes, and ratings you have included. If necessary, revise your chart to reflect new ideas that resulted from this discussion.

FOCUS ON SKILLS FOCUS ON SKILLS
CUS ON SKILLS FOCUS ON SKILLS FOCUS ON SKILLS

Is a moratorium on development in the tar sands a good idea?

Our Position ______________________________

Our Reasons for Supporting This Position ______________________________

____

Stakeholder Challenging Our Position	Argument(s)	Rating of Argument 1 = very weak 5 = very strong	Our Counter-Argument(s)	Rating of Counter-Argument 1 = very weak 5 = very strong

Some Dos and Don'ts of Effective Counter-Arguments

1. Respond to the validity of the argument, not to the character of the person making the argument.
2. Develop your position through logical arguments.
3. Consider arguments carefully and respectfully. Summarize the other person's point of view or perspective to show that you have listened and understood.
4. Be sure of your facts. Don't claim to know more than you do. Be prepared to conduct further research when you are not sure.

Summing Up

After considering the arguments against your original position, were you tempted to change your mind? As you progress through this course and through life, you will grapple with many issues. Keep an open mind and be prepared to explore alternatives and to compromise when compromising is appropriate.

Figure 4-15 At a Calgary rally staged by Canadians for Kyoto, a protester holds a sign that supports the Kyoto Protocol, which sets out targets for reducing the greenhouse gas emissions that contribute to climate change. Does a gimmick like this help or hinder the protester's argument?

How have people reconciled contending nationalist and non-nationalist loyalties?

Over the course of their lives, many people experience situations in which their nationalist loyalties compete with non-nationalist loyalties because these loyalties have differing goals. When this happens, people have developed various ways of reconciling these contending loyalties. They may, for example,

- live with their contending loyalties
- choose one loyalty over another
- accommodate their non-nationalist loyalties by bringing about change in the nation

If you do not participate in a society's decisions, do you have a right to complain about them?

Living with Contending Loyalties

Faced with a situation in which nationalist and non-nationalist loyalties compete, people may choose to remain uninvolved for a variety of reasons. They may, for example,

- be undecided about how to respond
- believe that living with the contending loyalties is preferable to speaking out or taking action
- believe that, as individuals, they cannot make a difference
- be occupied with other pressing concerns

People who choose to remain uninvolved are sometimes called the silent majority. They are the many people who don't express opinions, even to the occasional pollster who calls on the telephone. But these people may also pay a price for their silence: someone else will make important decisions for them.

Figure 4-16 Falun Gong members in Taipei, the capital of Taiwan, practise the meditation and ritual motions that express the group's beliefs. Falun Gong is legal in Taiwan. But the movement is banned in China, where members are often arrested. How are religious beliefs protected in Canada?

Choosing One Loyalty over Another

When people choose one strong loyalty over another, they risk losing an important part of their identity. In China, for example, the government has outlawed a religious and spiritual movement called Falun Gong or Falun Dafa.

In response to their contending nationalist loyalty and their non-nationalist religious loyalty, some Falun Gong members have chosen to obey their country's laws and stopped practising their religion. Others have chosen to defy their country by practising their religion in secret. If they are discovered, they may be jailed and even tortured.

In both cases, people have been forced to sacrifice an important part of their identity. This can lead to feelings of **alienation** — of being on the outside or left out. When religious or spiritual values and beliefs must be suppressed or hidden, people have a hard time sharing the collective consciousness that comes with feeling as if they belong to their nation.

Finding Ways to Include Nationalist and Non-Nationalist Loyalties

Because the Chinese government has banned Falun Gong, members of this movement face a difficult choice between their religious loyalty and loyalty to their country. But in democratic countries like Canada, people can often find ways to reconcile contending nationalist and non-nationalist loyalties so these loyalties can coexist.

Michaëlle Jean, for example, is a Francophone from Québec and Canada's governor general. Like many immigrants to Canada, Jean has more than one national loyalty. Haitian by birth and Canadian by choice, Jean also applied for — and was granted — French citizenship when she married Jean-Pierre Lafond, who was born in France. But when she was asked to become Canada's governor general, Jean voluntarily renounced her French citizenship so that no one would question her loyalty to Canada.

Jean's appointment was also criticized because she and Lafond seemed to toast Québec independence in a documentary they had appeared in. Jean responded to this accusation by saying that her toast referred to Haiti. She also issued a statement declaring her loyalty to Canada. "I want to tell you unequivocally that both [my husband] and I are proud to be Canadian and that we have the greatest respect for the institutions of our country," the statement said. "We are fully committed to Canada. I would not have accepted this position otherwise . . . [We] have never belonged to a political party or the separatist movement."

At the same time, Jean also has several non-nationalist loyalties, some of which she expressed on her coat of arms. The motto on the coat of arms, "Briser les solitudes," means "Breaking down solitudes." This phrase refers to *Two Solitudes*, a 1945 novel by Hugh MacLennan that explored the idea that Francophone and anglophone Canadians were living together but apart — in two separate solitudes — within the same country.

On her coat of arms (see p. 17), Jean includes both nationalist and non-nationalist symbols. What statement does this make about her identity? What message does Jean's coat of arms send to people who are struggling to reconcile nationalist and non-nationalist loyalties? Is this message appropriate in 21st-century Canada?

The time of the "two solitudes" that for too long described the character of this country is past. The narrow notion of "every person for himself" does not belong in today's world, which demands that we learn to see beyond our wounds, beyond our differences, for the good of all.

— Michaëlle Jean, in her first speech as governor general, 2005

Figure 4-17 When the appointment of Michaëlle Jean to the post of governor general was announced, some people, such as this protester on Parliament Hill, questioned Jean's nationalist loyalty. Is the protester asking a fair question? Should Jean have felt the need to give up her French citizenship?

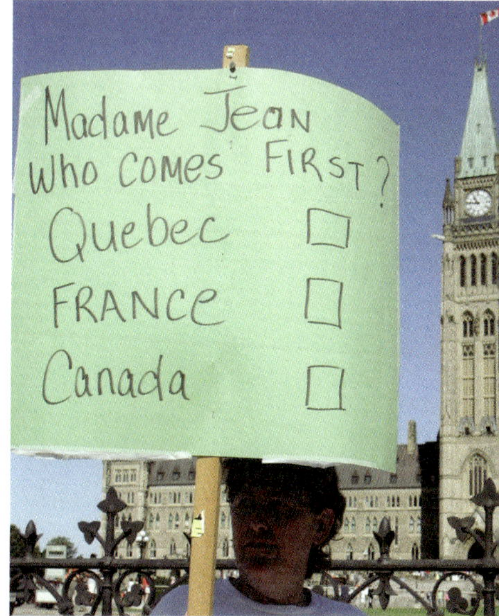

Figure 4-18 In 2006, Michaëlle Jean made an official visit to Haiti, where she was born. Jean spent some of her childhood in the town of Jacmel, where she was welcomed enthusiastically. What loyalties do you think the residents of Jacmel were displaying?

[Wearing] the turban in the RCMP meant an acceptance into Canada's mainstream. To be allowed to wear the turban is a clear indication of getting accepted. I just wanted to join the RCMP as an officer and to be able to work with equal respect and dignity in every way.

— Baltej Singh Dhillon, RCMP officer, in an interview with the India Post, *2002*

Bringing about Change in the Nation

To accommodate non-nationalist loyalties, people who live in democratic countries can try to change their nation. This reconciliation is often achieved by promoting a cause within the context of the nation.

When Baltej Singh Dhillon, for example, challenged the RCMP dress code that required all officers to wear Stetsons, he used options available within Canada to persuade the Mounties to make a reasonable accommodation. These options may not be open to people who do not live in democracies.

But even in democratic countries, people must sometimes seek justice outside the nation. This is what Sandra Lovelace Nicholas, who is featured in "Making a Difference," did when she found that, like thousands of other First Nations women, she had permanently lost her status under the Indian Act.

MAKING A DIFFERENCE

Sandra Lovelace Nicholas
Fighting for First Nations Women

Figure 4-19 Sandra Lovelace Nicholas was awarded the Order of Canada in 1990. In 1992, she received a Governor General's Award in Commemoration of the Persons Case, and in 2005, she was appointed to the Senate.

When Sandra Lovelace Nicholas married a non-Aboriginal American in 1970 and moved with him to California, the Maliseet woman had no idea that she was starting a chain of events that would alter the lives of First Nations men and women across Canada.

A few years later, Lovelace Nicholas and her husband divorced and she returned home to the Tobique First Nation reserve in New Brunswick. But when she arrived, she found that she and her children no longer qualified for the rights and benefits guaranteed in the Indian Act. Though First Nations men who married non-Aboriginal women retained their status and rights, the law stripped First Nations women who married non-Aboriginal men of their status.

Lovelace Nicholas believed this was discrimination. To protest, she set up a tent on the reserve. She then joined reserve mothers who were protesting the lack of housing for women. At the time, all reserve houses were registered in the names of men. The Canadian government had identified them as the heads of households. The protest snowballed into a 100-mile Native Women's Walk from Oka, Québec, to Ottawa.

In Ottawa, Lovelace Nicholas met Prime Minister Joe Clark, who promised action. But nothing happened. First Nations leaders, mostly men, opposed changing the Indian Act, in part because of worries that a change would mean restoring Indian status to thousands of women. They feared that these women would flood back onto reserves and make an already strained housing situation even worse.

So Lovelace Nicholas petitioned the United Nations Human Rights Commission. She said that Canada had violated the International Covenant on Civil and Political Rights, which bans sexual discrimination and guarantees "equal protection before the law" to everyone.

The UN agreed, and in 1985, the federal government finally introduced legislation changing the Indian Act — and 16 000 First Nations women successfully applied to regain their status.

Explorations

1. How can Lovelace Nicholas's actions be interpreted as an attempt to reconcile her non-nationalist loyalty to Aboriginal women with her nationalist loyalties?
2. When people try to change a nation, they often face an uphill battle and may be labelled troublemakers. But later, they are often admired for their courage and wisdom. This is what happened to Lovelace Nicholas. Identify someone else to whom this has happened. Explain the contending nationalist and non-nationalist loyalties this person was trying to reconcile.

Fighting for a Sense of Belonging

In 1957, **segregation** — the forced separation of racial groups — was still common in the American South. But the civil rights movement was gaining strength and laws were changing. That year, 16-year-old Minnijean Brown Trickey and eight other teenagers became the first blacks to attend Central High School in Little Rock, Arkansas.

Angry whites gathered outside the school and screamed taunts and insults as the black students tried to start school, and Arkansas's governor called out the National Guard to block the school's entrance. This went on for days, until U.S. president Dwight Eisenhower sent in the army to protect the teens.

The students, who became known as the Little Rock Nine, were finally able to start classes, but they continued to suffer at the hands of other students. They were spat at, kicked down stairs, and body slammed. Teachers did little to help.

Supported by her belief in non-violence, Brown Trickey took this treatment for five months before she finally reacted strongly. As punishment, she was expelled. Still, she went on to earn a bachelor of arts, and during the Vietnam War moved to Canada with her husband, who was a conscientious objector. In Canada, she continued her education and to fight for a variety of causes. She joined the struggle to save old-growth forests in Ontario's Temagami district and to promote Aboriginal rights.

In some ways, Brown Trickey told an interviewer, her involvement in Aboriginal rights was an accident. "The first people I met when I moved to Toronto were Native Canadians," she said. "I did a bachelor of social work in Native human services, which was great. I learned so much about the similarities of cultures. The main point is that one doesn't really choose a particular issue to work towards. In fact, we are chosen often. That's a good way to be. To me, it means some kind of openness, willingness to work with anyone, any group."

What non-nationalist loyalty were Brown Trickey and the Little Rock Nine trying to reconcile? What might Brown Trickey have in common with Aboriginal peoples in Canada? How might her experience in Little Rock contribute to her interest in the struggle of Aboriginal peoples?

Web Connection

To find out more about the Little Rock Nine and desegregation in the United States, go to this web site and follow the links.

www.ExploringNationalism.ca

Figure 4-20 Soldiers escort the Little Rock Nine to school in 1957. In September 2007, members of the Little Rock Nine (left) gathered to celebrate the 50th anniversary of the successful integration of Little Rock Central High School. Minnijean Brown Trickey (second from left) and the other students have remained fast friends over the years. How might sharing this experience create lasting friendships?

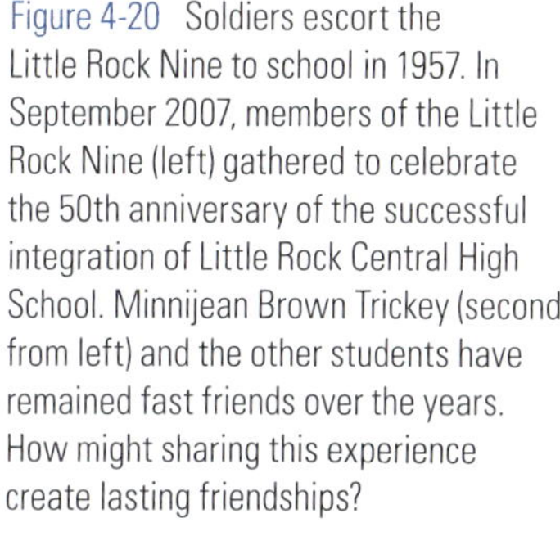

Fighting for Religious Freedoms

Though the Charter of Rights and Freedoms guarantees freedom of religion to Canadians, Canada is a secular state — a country in which religion is separate from politics and government. This does not mean, however, that government actions never affect religious groups, or vice versa.

In 2003, for example, Alberta — like many other provinces — passed a law requiring a photograph on all drivers' licences. But some members of the Wilson Siding Hutterite Colony, a farming community in southern Alberta, believe that the Bible prohibits them from willingly having their picture taken.

Obeying the law would mean violating their religious beliefs, but sticking to their religious beliefs and refusing to have their pictures taken would mean forfeiting their drivers' licences. Losing their licences would hamper the community's ability to continue farming and to interact with other Hutterite communities in the Prairie provinces.

Members of the Wilson colony challenged the Alberta law in court. They argued that the picture requirement violated their religious freedoms, which are guaranteed in the Charter. The court agreed. As a result, an exception was made, and Hutterites were allowed to carry drivers' licences that do not include a photograph — but in late 2007, the case was appealed to the Supreme Court of Canada.

Conduct Internet research to find out what has happened since then.

FYI

Hutterites are a Christian religious community that originated in 16th-century Austria. Members of the community were often persecuted because of their pacifist beliefs and communal lifestyle. As a result, many immigrated to North America, where they hoped to practise their religion in peace. In Hutterite colonies, all property is owned by the community and earnings are pooled. When community members need an item, the community supplies it.

What is at stake here is the future of our country, the interests of Canadian citizens, and most importantly Canada's international reputation for being a leader in human rights where citizens from different ethnic groups are treated no different than other Canadians.

— Maher Arar, at a news conference after returning to Canada, 2003

Making Reconciliation Work

Neither Monia Mazigh nor her husband, Maher Arar, planned to become social activists. The two met when they were students at McGill University, married, and had two children. Mazigh worked as a research assistant and French-language instructor at the University of Ottawa, while Arar was a telecommunications engineer.

But a year after the September 11, 2001, attacks on the United States, the Syrian-born Arar was flying home from a family holiday in Tunisia. On a stopover in New York, he was detained by American officials. After receiving misleading or false information from Canadian officials, the Americans accused Arar of being a terrorist and deported him to Syria. There, he was jailed and tortured.

Over the next year, Mazigh brought her husband's treatment to the attention of the media, which put pressure on the Canadian government to press for Arar's release. Thanks to Mazigh, Arar was finally set free and allowed to return home.

Once Arar was home, he and Mazigh set out to clear his name and ensure that other Canadians never face the same treatment. The two succeeded in pressuring the government to conduct an inquiry to uncover the sequence of events that led to his deportation.

Figure 4-21 Maher Arar and Monia Mazigh consult during a news conference in 2004. How do you think this couple's struggle to win the government's acknowledgement that Arar's rights had been violated may have affected their national loyalty?

The inquiry found no evidence that Arar was involved in terrorism, and in 2007, Prime Minister Stephen Harper formally apologized and announced that Arar would receive $10.5 million in compensation for his ordeal. Arar and Mazigh now live in Kamloops, British Columbia, where Mazigh is a professor of finance at Thompson Rivers University.

Read Maher Arar's words in "Voices" on the previous page. What were his goals in trying to clear his name? What loyalties were involved in these goals? On a scale of 1 to 5 (1 = not very successful; 5 = very successful), rate how successful he was.

To find out more about the Maher Arar case, go to this web site and follow the links.

www.ExploringNationalism.ca

Taking Turns

Is it important to your identity to reconcile your nationalist and non-nationalist loyalties?

The students responding to this question are Jane, who lives in Calgary and is descended from black Loyalists who fled to Nova Scotia after the American Revolution; Rick, who was born in the United States but moved to Fort McMurray with his family when he was 10; and Amanthi, who lives in Edson and whose parents immigrated from Sri Lanka.

Jane

I think my strongest non-nationalist loyalty is to black people everywhere — and this loyalty fits well with loyalty to Canada. After all, the Charter of Rights and Freedoms guarantees that all Canadian citizens are equal. Sure, there are problems, like the police stopping black male drivers just because they think black people are more likely to be criminals, not because they've done anything wrong. So, yes, reconciling my non-nationalist loyalty is important to me because I think our country should be a place where everyone, including me, is really and truly equal.

Rick

I guess you could call me a free spirit. And that's what I like about Alberta — the independent-minded people who are willing to risk doing things on their own. It's all about taking responsibility for your own actions. I don't mind helping out other provinces, which Alberta does through equalization payments. This makes Canada strong, and I feel a strong loyalty to Canada. But if Peter Lougheed's prediction pans out and Canada and Alberta end up in a battle over the oil industry, I'm pretty sure where my loyalty would lie. But I really hope that it doesn't come to that.

Amanthi

I'm a Buddhist, and Buddhists believe in peace and non-violence. But we can be courageous about expressing our convictions. Think about what happened in Burma in 2007 — the thousands of Buddhist monks who marched peacefully to try to persuade the government to become more democratic, even when they probably knew they would be beaten, arrested, and even killed. I sometimes wonder how I would have acted if I'd been faced with the same choice. Take to the streets and try to bring about change or keep my head down and don't rock the boat? I'm lucky to live in Canada, where I don't need to make decisions like this. But I also wish the Canadian government had spoken out more strongly when that happened. I feel a little ashamed of the government's lack of action — and ashamed, too, that I did nothing to change things. Now I need to turn this feeling into positive action.

Your Turn

How would you respond to the question Jane, Rick, and Amanthi are answering? Think about the non-nationalist loyalties you feel most strongly about. Do they compete with your nationalist loyalties? If so, is it important to reconcile these contending loyalties?

THINK...PARTICIPATE...RESEARCH...COMMUNICATE...

1. In her 2007 Canada Day speech, Michaëlle Jean, the country's governor general, issued a challenge to Canadian young people when she said, "I challenge you, the youth of this country, to do everything in your power to make your dreams come true and to make your actions matter. There is no dream too wild or unattainable for those who dare to dream big."
   a) What is your opinion of Jean's challenge?
   b) Return to Mustafa Kemal Atatürk's challenge to the youth of Turkey (p. 33). List two similarities and two differences between Jean's challenge and his.
   c) Think of one dream that you might view as "too wild or unattainable." Explain how trying to realize this dream could help — or harm — you, your community, and your nation.
2. In 1981, at the height of the battle over the National Energy Program, Tom Innes, political cartoonist for the *Calgary Herald*, created the cartoon on this page to express this view of the long negotiations between the Alberta government and the federal government over setting a domestic price for oil. Innes also created the cartoon shown in Figure 4-9.
   a) Identify the characters Innes is lampooning. Who is Pete? Who is Pierre?
   b) Innes titled the cartoon "Team Canada?" What message do you think Innes was trying to convey through his title choice? What is the significance of the question mark in his title? Why did he dress the characters in hockey gear? Why do you think he included a maple leaf as a shoulder emblem for both characters?
   c) Does remaining true to your nationalist loyalty mean accepting the status quo — things as they are? Describe a situation where you think people, including yourself, should try to change the nation to accommodate a non-nationalist loyalty, such as a regional loyalty.
   d) When dealing with serious issues, humour often helps people take themselves a little less seriously by allowing them a moment to pause, step back, and rethink their position. List three reactions Peter Lougheed might have experienced on opening the *Calgary Herald* and seeing Innes's cartoon. Write a sentence explaining a possible reason for each reaction. You might, for example, say that he felt resignation because he believed the situation would never be resolved. Then do the same for Pierre Trudeau.

Figure 4-22 Team Canada?

3. Develop a survey to measure the strength of various contending nationalist and non-nationalist loyalties. Be sure that your survey questions allow for a range of responses. You may, for example, ask respondents to identify the strength of their loyalty to Canada. To do this, you could ask a question like this:

   How would you describe your loyalty to Canada?

   - extremely strong
   - strong
   - not sure
   - weak
   - extremely weak

   To discover whether your respondents feel loyalties that contend with their loyalty to Canada, you might ask a question like this:

   Which of the following do you feel a strong or very strong loyalty toward? Select as many as are applicable.

   - your religion
   - your country of origin
   - your province
   - your gender
   - your nation (please name)
   - other (please list)

   On the basis of responses to this question, you may then wish to test the strength of each of the other loyalties and even ask some questions that compare various loyalties.

   Interview at least 10 people — classmates, teachers, friends outside school, family members — to develop a fair sample.

   Compile a short report that presents and explains your findings. In your report, you may wish to include graphs that show your findings.

4. An epigraph is a quotation at the beginning of a book or a chapter. This quotation often hints at or sums up the theme of the work. As the epigraph for his book *Two Solitudes*, Hugh MacLennan chose this quotation by the Austrian poet and novelist Rainer Maria Rilke: "Love consists in this, that two solitudes protect and touch and greet each other."

   Was MacLennan's choice an appropriate way of thinking about Canada? Explain your reasoning.

5. In this chapter, you have explored nationalist and non-nationalist loyalties, how they can compete, and how some Canadians have chosen to reconcile them.

   Prepare a response to the chapter issue: To what extent should people reconcile their nationalist and non-nationalist loyalties?

   To develop an informed position on this issue, consider some real examples of efforts at reconciliation and whether they have been successful.

   a) In a small group, select some examples of reconciliation efforts and the contending loyalties involved in each. You may draw these examples from *Exploring Nationalism*, your own experience, and other sources. When you have listed about eight examples, review them and consider what might have happened if no reconciliation of loyalties had been attempted.
   b) Drawing ideas from your group discussion, prepare a personal response to the chapter issue.
   c) Share your response with your group. Listen to the responses of other group members. Prepare a group consensus in response to the chapter issue.
   d) Share your group's response with the class and listen to the responses of other groups. Develop a class consensus in response to the chapter issue.

Think about Your Challenge

Consider all the symbols that you have developed for your coat of arms. Each should reflect an aspect of the relationship between your identity and your understandings of nation. Your notes should explain the various symbols, the reasons you chose them, and how they show the relationship between your identity and your understandings of nation.

Ask a partner or your teacher for feedback on this material. On the basis of this feedback and the checklist for success on page 16, create a final version of your coat of arms.

RELATED ISSUE 2

To what extent should national interest be pursued?

Key Issue
To what extent should we embrace nationalism?

Related Issue 1
To what extent should nation be the foundation of identity?

Related Issue 2
To what extent should national interest be pursued?

Related Issue 3
To what extent should internationalism be pursued?

Related Issue 4
To what extent should individuals and groups in Canada embrace a national identity?

Chapter 5

National Interest and Foreign Policy

To what extent do national interest and foreign policy shape each other?

How are nationalism and national interest related?

How has national interest shaped foreign policy?

How has foreign policy shaped national interest?

Chapter 6

Nationalism and Ultranationalism

To what extent can nationalism lead to ultranationalism?

What is ultranationalism?

How does ultranationalism develop?

How have people responded to ultranationalism?

Chapter 7

Ultranationalism and Crimes against Humanity

To what extent can the pursuit of ultranationalism lead to crimes against humanity?

What are crimes against humanity?

How has ultranationalism caused crimes against humanity?

What are some contemporary consequences of ultranationalism?

Chapter 8

National Self-Determination

To what extent should national self-determination be pursued?

What is national self-determination?

What are some effects of pursuing national self-determination?

What are some effects on Canada of pursuing national self-determination?

What are some unintended consequences of the pursuit of national self-determination?

THE BIG PICTURE

Your personal interests, such as your career choices and your health and well-being, are not fixed. They change constantly — as you change, as your needs change, and as the world around you changes.

You can control some of the events that shape your decisions about what is in your interests. If, for example, you plan to become a health care professional, you can choose an educational path that will improve your chances of achieving this goal.

But not everything that affects your interests is in your control. An unexpected accident, an inheritance, or a life-altering emotional experience may prompt a change in the focus of your interests. You may suddenly need to leave school, adopt a different lifestyle, or develop new interests that have a deeper and more personal meaning. In addition, your ideas about what is in your interests may change as you mature. But no matter how you change, pursuing a course that is in your interests requires planning, thought, and an understanding of the changing influences that affect you.

Like you, countries and nations also have interests, and these interests, too, are shaped by events, some of which cannot be controlled. A global epidemic such as SARS, for example, requires an immediate response that may lead to a shift in priorities. But other interests, such as achieving economic prosperity, can be more closely controlled through specific actions and policies.

In Related Issue 1, you explored understandings of nation, nationalism, and identity. In this related issue, you will expand this understanding by exploring and analyzing the links that connect nationalism, national interest, ultranationalism, crimes against humanity, and the pursuit of national self-determination.

The chart on the preceding page shows how you will progress through the chapters of Related Issue 2. As you explore this related issue, you will come to appreciate

- that pursuing national interest can result in both positive and negative outcomes
- how ideas about national interest can change as circumstances change
- that points of view and perspectives on national interest differ, and that these differences often affect decisions about how national interest should be pursued
- that the pursuit of national interest may involve pursuing national self-determination

Your Challenge

Research and present an investigative report on a nationalist movement. As you explore and develop an informed opinion on this movement, you will also be developing a response to the question for this related issue: To what extent should national interest be pursued?

Checklist for Success

Use this checklist to ensure that your report includes everything necessary to be successful.

My Knowledge and Understanding

☑ My opinion is clearly expressed and supported by reliable, valid evidence.

☑ My report shows my understanding of the issue.

☑ My conclusions are logical and clearly expressed.

My Selection, Analysis, and Evaluation of Information

☑ My information was drawn from a variety of sources that are cited correctly and accurately.

☑ My information reflects diverse points of view and perspectives.

☑ My criteria for judgment are clearly explained.

My Report

☑ My choice of technology is appropriate.

☑ My presentation engages the audience and provides opportunities for audience feedback.

☑ My presentation is respectful of others.

Your Investigative Report

As you explore and analyze the ideas presented in this related issue, you will develop an understanding of nationalist movements, how they can evolve, and how they can reflect people's needs, interests, and aspirations. The movement you select may be one you encounter in *Exploring Nationalism* or one you search out for yourself. As you explore this movement, you will arrive at — and present — an informed opinion on the extent to which people should pursue national interest.

You will use technology to present the results of your investigation in the form of a video documentary, a computer software presentation, an e-zine or blog, an audio report, or a photographic essay — or in another format of your choosing. In addition to presenting your informed opinion on the movement, your report will include background, interviews, a summary of the current status of the movement, and your predictions about how the movement is likely to evolve in the future.

What Your Report Will Include

No matter how you choose to present your investigative report, it should include the following elements and answer some of the following questions:

- **Background and key events** — What events, ideas, people, and forces sparked the movement? Have conditions stayed the same? Have conditions improved? Deteriorated? Was Canada involved?
- **People** — Who are the key people involved? Who supports or opposes the movement? What are their stakes in the outcome? Who is hurt or helped? Who is overlooked? Is anyone involved who should not be?
- **Current status** — What is the status of the movement today? How has the movement affected nations and countries, leaders, and people and their neighbours? Canada and Canadians?
- **Predictions** — What is likely to happen and why? How will what happens affect the people involved? How will it affect Canada and Canadians?

Preparing Your Report

Step 1

Choose a nationalist movement and decide on the form your report will take. This decision will affect the kind of information you collect and how you collect it.

Step 2

The conclusion of your report will respond to the Related Issue 2 inquiry question: To what extent should national interest be pursued? Set criteria to help you make judgments in response to this question (e.g., Has pursuing national interest benefited the nationalist movement I chose?). As you progress through this related issue and conduct research, be prepared to adapt, revise, and refine your criteria.

Refer to the prologue (pp. 9–11) for tips on the inquiry process and to "Focus on Skills" (pp. 34–35) for tips on developing inquiry questions that will help guide your research. You may wish to begin by using some of the questions set out on page 112. As you progress through this related issue and find out more about the movement, be prepared to adapt and revise these questions.

Step 3

As you progress through the four chapters of this related issue, keep notes on the information you have gathered. Collect graphics and pictures, and conduct interviews if this is possible. To help organize this material, you may wish to record information on a chart like the one shown.

Step 4

At key intervals as you progress through this related issue, ask a partner or your teacher for feedback on the progress of your research, your conclusions, and your presentation format.

As you near the end of the four chapters in this related issue, begin organizing your material into the format you have chosen. As you assemble information, graphics, interviews, pictures, and notes, keep the related-issue question clearly in focus. Your informed opinion on this question will provide the foundation of your investigative report.

TO WHAT EXTENT SHOULD NATIONAL INTEREST BE PURSUED?

Nationalist Movement ____________________

Aspect of Report	Information	Notes and Sources
Background and key events		
People		
Current status		
Predictions		

Research Tip

When using a search engine to conduct online research, type in the names of the key people involved in the movement, as well as the name of the movement itself. This may provide additional and more varied points of view and perspectives. You may also wish to type in the names of other groups related to the movement you chose.

CHAPTER 5 National Interest and Foreign Policy

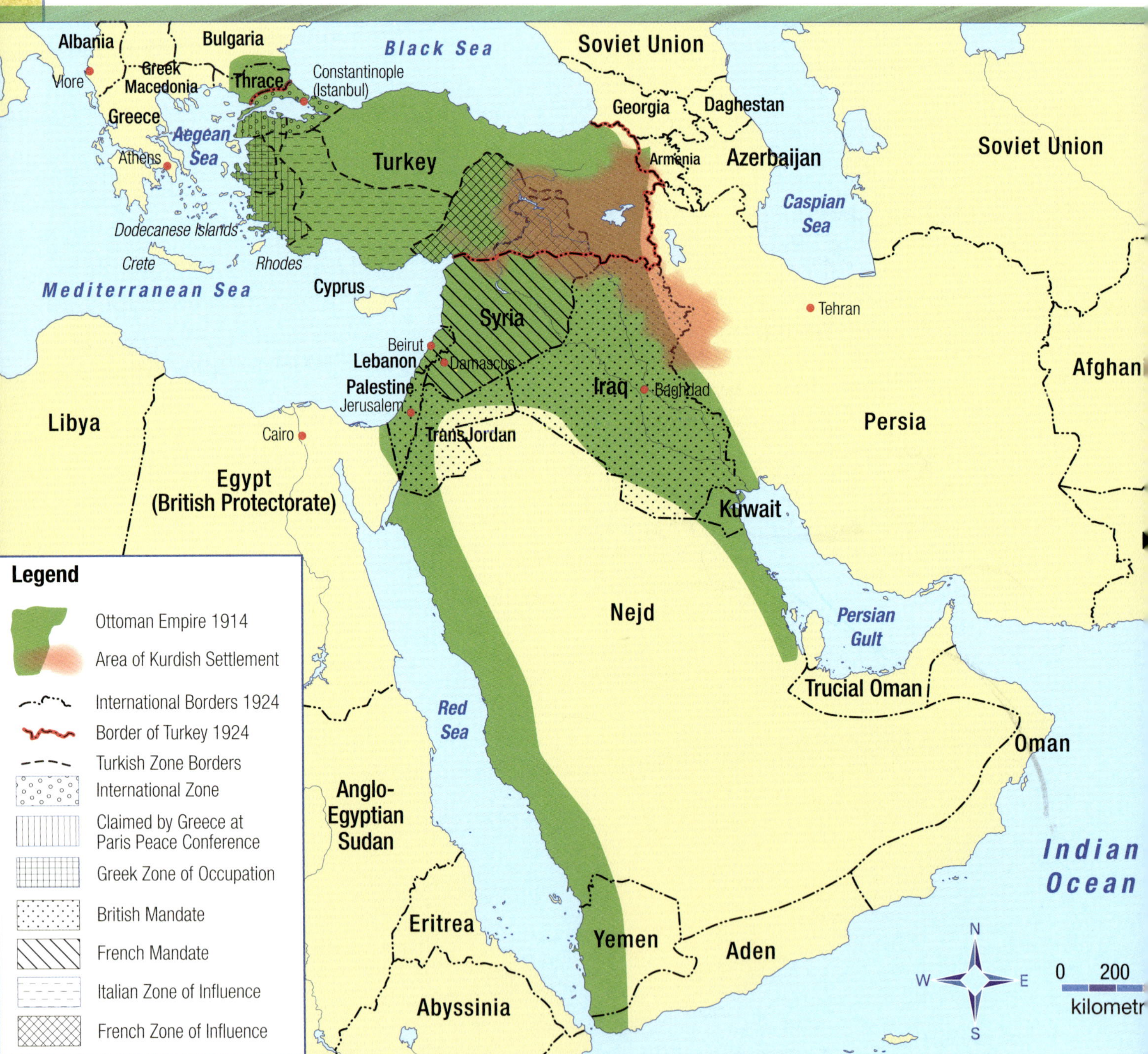

Figure 5-1 This map shows the Middle East before and after World War I. When the war started in 1914, many of today's Middle Eastern countries were part of the Ottoman Empire. After the war ended in 1918, this empire was dissolved and new countries were carved out.

CHAPTER ISSUE

To what extent do national interest and foreign policy shape each other?

THE TREATIES that were drawn up after World War I changed the Middle East dramatically. The Ottoman Empire had dominated the region since the 13th century. At the beginning of the war in 1914, this empire included about 14 million Turks, as well as smaller groups, such as Arabs, Armenians, and Kurds. These minority groups were often denied basic rights.

In World War I, the Ottoman Empire fought on the side of Germany. When the war ended, Britain, France, and the United States were the three most powerful countries among the victors. They dissolved the Ottoman Empire and created new countries by dividing up the Middle East.

Suddenly and without consultation, the peoples who had been part of the Ottoman Empire lived in new nation-states, with new borders and different governments. The area known as Kurdistan, for example, was home to Kurds, a people who shared a culture, history, and language. This area was divided up among the newly created countries of Iraq, Persia (now Iran), Syria, and Turkey.

Examine the map of the Middle East on the previous page and respond to the following questions:

- How might the non-Turkish peoples of the old Ottoman Empire have reacted to the changes made by Britain, France, and the United States?
- What might Britain, France, and the U.S. have gained by creating these new nation-states in the Middle East?
- What nationalist emotions might the changes have aroused?
- How do you think Turks, Arabs, Kurds, and Armenians would have felt about the British and French administrators who controlled their new countries?

KEY TERMS

national interest

peacekeepers

peacemaking

policy

domestic policy

foreign policy

gross domestic product

Looking Ahead

In this chapter, you will develop responses to the following questions as you explore the extent to which national interest and foreign policy shape each other:

- How are nationalism and national interest related?
- How has national interest shaped foreign policy?
- How has foreign policy shaped national interest?

My Journal on Nationalism

Look back at the notes you recorded about nation, identity, and nationalism in Related Issue 1. Use words or images — or both — to express how your understandings of nationalism changed as you progressed through that related issue. Date your ideas and keep them in your notebook, learning log, portfolio, or computer file so that you can return to them as you progress through this course.

How are nationalism and national interest related?

Figure 5-2 Israelis shop at the Mahne Yehuda market in Jerusalem. Many Israelis share ethnic and civic national ties. How might this photograph show people's interest in economic stability and quality of life?

Think about criteria you might use to decide on actions that will best serve your interests now — and in the future. To do this, you probably need to explore various factors and ask yourself questions such as the following:

- How important is my physical safety and personal security?
- How important is my economic well-being and future prosperity?
- How important are my values, beliefs, and culture?

Sometimes, figuring out the course of action that is in your best interests is a matter of personal choice. When, for example, you selected the courses you would take this year, was your decision based on whether you enjoy the subjects or on whether the subjects would help you prepare for your future career? Or on other criteria?

Your interests are not always independent of those of others. You are a member of a family and a community. You cannot always make decisions based only on what will benefit you. You may need to consider the interests of your family and your community. In choosing, for example, the educational path that will best prepare you for a future career, your decision about what is in your own interest may be affected by your family's financial resources, the needs of your wider community, or your need for financial security.

Figure 5-3 In October 2006, the people of Riyadh, Saudi Arabia, paraded camels through the street to celebrate Eid al-Fitr, the end of the fasting of Ramadan. How does this photograph show people's interest in promoting their beliefs, values, and culture?

Figure 5-4 In August 2006, this young citizen of Beirut, Lebanon, waited on a bus that would take her family to safety. A conflict between Israeli armed forces and fighters with Hezbollah, a militant political party in Lebanon, had hurt civilians on both sides. How might this photograph show people's interest in safety and security?

Aspects of National Interest

Like individuals, people who govern democratic communities and nations make decisions based on what is in the community's or nation's interests. Whether a people's nationalism is based on a shared ethnicity and culture or shared beliefs and values, they want certain benefits for themselves and their communities. These benefits — their **national interest** — may focus on one or more of the following:

- economic prosperity — This includes stable employment and a decent standard of living. Governments acting in the national interest try to provide these economic benefits in various ways. They may, for example, pass laws ensuring that citizens are not exploited in the workplace. They may also enter into trade treaties with other nations.
- security and safety — Measures to maintain national security and physical protection include laws that protect citizens within the country, as well as secure borders that can be defended against intruders. Governments acting in the national interest try to ensure the personal safety of citizens, peacefully resolve differences with other countries, and control who enters the country.
- beliefs and values — These include affirming and promoting citizens' values, beliefs, and culture. Governments acting in the national interest try, for example, to safeguard and respect the shared worldviews, ways of life, traditions, and languages of their citizens.

With a partner, discuss several ways in which an educated population is both in people's personal interest and in the national interest. You may wish to use yourselves as examples. Share your ideas with another pair.

The world has changed in profound ways since the end of the cold war, but I fear our conceptions of national interest have failed to follow suit. A new, broader definition of national interest is needed in the new century, which would induce states to find greater unity in the pursuit of common goals and values. In the context of many of the challenges facing humanity today, the collective interest is the national interest.

— *Kofi Annan, while secretary-general of the United Nations, in "Two Concepts of Sovereignty,"* The Economist, *1999*

Changing Views of National Interest

Just as people's understandings of nationalism may differ, their opinions on what is in the national interest may differ. The Israelis shopping in the Jerusalem market in Figure 5-2 might be concerned about stability in the supply and price of food. But the girl waiting to be evacuated from Beirut (Figure 5-4) is probably much more concerned about her government's ability to ensure her family's safety.

National interest is not static and unchanging. Events inside a country — a catastrophic storm or the loss of an essential industry — can change people's opinion about what is in the national interest. Events outside a country — the sudden flare-up of armed conflict between neighbouring states or the peaceful settlement of this conflict — can also change people's priorities.

Figure 5-5 On October 9, 2007, an Iraqi woman helped the Red Crescent Society by carrying boxes of supplies for people in Baghdad. The society conducts relief operations in many Islamic countries. On the same day, four bombs killed at least 12 people and wounded more than 60 in Baghdad. How does this photograph illustrate various ideas expressed by Kofi Annan in "Voices" about collective and national interests?

Differing Views of National Interest

People often decide what is in the national interest based on their understanding of nation and national identity. Many Canadians, for example, take pride in Canada's reputation as a nation of **peacekeepers** — armed forces that maintain peace by keeping enemies apart until a crisis can be resolved through diplomacy and negotiation. As a result, these Canadians may base their decisions about what course of action is in the national interest on whether it will promote peace in the world. But other Canadians believe that Canada's peacekeeping role should shift to **peacemaking**, which allows soldiers to use force for reasons other than self-defence. This is what has happened in the conflict in Afghanistan.

CheckForward

You will read more about the debate over peacekeeping and peacemaking in Chapters 10, 12, and 14.

In other countries, people's ideas about the national interest often demand a strong military that can defend the country's interests against hostile forces. Condoleeza Rice was the United States' secretary of state in 2007. She said that when her country's interests are at stake, the American military "must be able to meet decisively the emergence of any hostile military power."

The government of China also believes that a strong military is essential. The government-controlled newspaper *China Daily* reflected this view when it said, "China's military might is meant to safeguard its own security and stability. It is meant to deter the hostile elements of Cold War mentality who attempt to threaten China's national interests with force."

Can a national government ever represent the interests of all citizens through a single national policy?

Kofi Annan, the former secretary-general of the United Nations, believes that the interdependence of nations in today's globalized world has expanded the meaning of national interest. But John Spritzler, a Harvard University research scientist, believes that there is no such thing as common national interests — even within a country. He says that "working class Americans have interests and values that conflict with the interests and values of America's very wealthy and powerful families. What benefits one typically harms the other: high unemployment, job insecurity, low wages."

With a partner, reread Kofi Annan's statement in "Voices" on page 117. What do you think he meant? Compare what Annan said with the preceding words of John Spritzler. Explain how these two views on national interest differ.

Figure 5-6 On November 18, 2007, Canadian soldiers took part in a ramp ceremony to honour Private Michel Lévesque, who was killed in Afghanistan. Canada's Armed Forces are actively engaged in fighting in Afghanistan because the government decided that this action is in the country's national interest. How does this government policy compete with many Canadians' vision of the country as a nation of peacekeepers?

National Interest and Arctic Sovereignty

National interest often involves claiming sovereignty over territory. This is the case in the Arctic, where five countries — Canada, the United States, Denmark, Norway, and Russia — claim sovereignty to islands and the seabed.

In August 2007, Russia claimed part of the 1800-kilometre Lomonosov Ridge, which runs under the Arctic Ocean. The Russian government says that this ridge is an extension of its continental shelf. Russian scientists mapped part of the ridge, collected soil samples, and planted a flag on the ocean floor at the North Pole in a symbolic claim to the natural resources that may be buried there. Canada disputes this claim.

According to the UN Convention on the Law of the Sea, countries have sovereignty over 22.2 kilometres of sea beyond their coastline and control of the resources in and under the sea for 370 kilometres. Proving that the seabed is an extension of its continental shelf may give a country rights to harvest resources in a larger area.

Two factors have highlighted the importance of claiming sovereignty in the Arctic. The first is climate change, which is causing Arctic ice to melt. This melting may open the Northwest Passage — a water route connecting the Atlantic and Pacific oceans — to year-round commercial navigation, substantially shortening the distance ships must travel between Asia and Europe. The Northwest Passage is claimed by Canada, but other countries, including the United States, say that it is international.

Find the Northwest Passage in Figure 5-7. What arguments might the federal government use to support the idea that claiming the Northwest Passage is in Canada's national interest? Rate the strength of Canada's claim to this sea route on a scale of 1 to 5 (1 = very weak; 5 = very strong).

The second factor that has made Arctic sovereignty an issue is the discovery of extensive oil, natural gas, gold, tin, and diamond deposits in the Arctic seabed. The United States Geological Survey, for example, suggests that 25 per cent of the world's undiscovered oil and gas resources may lie in the Arctic.

Figure 5-7 The Arctic

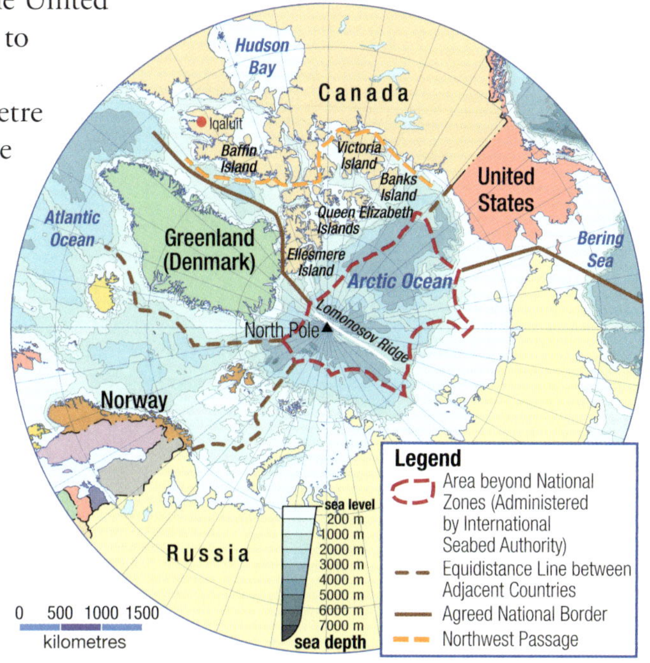

Figure 5-8 Roger Hitkolok of Kugluktuk, Nunavut, is a Canadian Ranger. About 1300 Rangers, who are under the command of the army, provide a Canadian military presence in the Arctic. Does this military presence serve Canada's national interest? Explain your response.

Reflect and Respond

National governments often make a decision about what is in the national interest, then work to persuade citizens to support it. With a partner, choose either peacemaking or Arctic sovereignty and list five strategies the government could use to "sell" the idea to Canadians. Explain how each strategy would be effective.

Building Consensus

FOCUS ON SKILLS

In August 2007, Prime Minister Stephen Harper announced that Canada would protect the sovereignty of its Arctic territory by

- sending new patrol ships
- increasing aerial surveillance
- expanding the Canadian Rangers
- building a Canadian Forces Arctic training centre in Resolute Bay, Nunavut
- establishing a deep-water docking and refuelling port at Nanisivik, Nunavut

Suppose your class was asked to come up with a recommendation in response to this statement: Because Arctic sovereignty is important to the national interest, the Canadian government should aggressively pursue Canada's claim to the Northwest Passage.

To do this, you will need to build a consensus — a general agreement. Building consensus is a collaborative process that involves exchanging ideas, listening carefully to others, and finding a response that everyone can live with. You will begin by developing a group consensus, then move on to build a class consensus.

Steps to Building Consensus

Step 1: Set up and organize the process

In a small group, choose a moderator who will keep group members focused on the task and ensure that the discussion moves smoothly. In addition, choose a recorder to keep track of group members' points of view as you move toward consensus.

On a sheet of paper, create a chart like the following to track your group's progress.

Protecting Canada's Claim to the Northwest Passage

Point of View	Reasons for This View	Group Members' Comments	Possible Compromises among Various Views
1			
2			
3			
4			

Step 2: Explore and evaluate possible responses

Recall what you have already read about Arctic sovereignty, then read the points of view and perspectives presented on the following page. Decide on your own response to the statement and present it to the group. Then listen while other group members state — and give reasons for — their view. The recorder should note views and reasons on the chart.

Once everyone has stated his or her position, analyze and evaluate each view by asking questions like these:

- What would be the short- and long-term effects of decisions based on this view?
- To what extent would this response resolve the issue?
- Which response is the most practical and workable?

Step 3: Compromise and negotiate

Try to narrow down the alternatives and work toward a compromise. Remember that there may be more than one reasonable way to pursue national interest in this situation. Group similar responses and identify responses that differ from the majority opinion. Discuss conditions or limits that you could add to your group response to accommodate various views.

Step 4: Call for consensus

When it seems that group members agree, the moderator should ask whether anyone still has concerns. If no one raises concerns, the moderator can declare that consensus has been reached.

Step 5: Work toward a class consensus

Present your group's consensus to the class and follow similar steps to arrive at a class consensus.

Prime Minister **Stephen Harper**, in a speech at Resolute Bay, Nunavut, on August 10, 2007.

> Even Canadians who have never been north of 60 feel [the sense of "romantic patriotism"' inspired by the Arctic]. It's embedded in our history, our literature, our art, our music – our Canadian soul. That's why we react so strongly when other countries show disrespect for our sovereignty over the Arctic . . . Protecting national sovereignty – the integrity of our borders – is the first and foremost responsibility of the national government.

Franklyn Griffiths, a Canadian political scientist and expert on Canadian–Russian affairs in *The Globe and Mail* on November 8, 2007.

> Some say [that Canada] must now engage the U.S. in a negotiation to secure the outright recognition of our Arctic sovereignty claim. I say the best way to endanger a sovereignty that's well in hand is to pick a fight with the U.S. Navy and stick to it. This we would do in seeking to make the United States bow on the law when we are secure in the benefits of de facto [already existing, though it may not be official] control of the Northwest Passage.
>
> The Prime Minister should instead begin to offer leadership in helping us Canadians lay our Arctic sovereignty obsession to rest. He should engage not the United States in the name of Arctic sovereignty, but the people and government of Nunavut in the name of Arctic stewardship.

Michael Byers, University of British Columbia professor, in his 2007 book, *Intent for a Nation: What Is Canada For?*

> Canada, by fate and geography, is destined to be an Arctic country. Climate change and the global demand for natural resources are only accelerating the process, while introducing international elements – such as an ice-free Northwest Passage and a continental shelf dispute with Russia – that previous generations could not have imagined . . . In the North, the Inuit and other indigenous peoples are our sentinels, soldiers and diplomats. It is time for southern Canadians to look up, way up, and provide serious support for their efforts to build a true North strong and free.

Mary Simon, president of Inuit Tapiriit Kanatami, the national organization representing Inuit, in *The Walrus*, November 2007.

> For the Inuit, [the Arctic] is our homeland, the place where we want to be. For all Canadians, the Arctic must become part of daily life, not just a remote region with beautiful icescapes and polar bears. It is a place where people live, where families are raised, where problems need solving, and where resources exist that will continue to nurture people and finance this wonderful place called Canada. We are here and we will stay. We are also here to work with governments as stewards and guardians of this homeland.

From an online poll conducted in August 2007 by **Angus Reid Global Monitor** to find out what Canadians think about Arctic sovereignty.*

Do you agree or disagree with the following statements?	Agree	Disagree	Not sure
Canada should invest heavily on securing sovereignty over its Arctic territory.	75%	16%	10%
Russia represents a bigger threat than the United States to Canada in matters related to Arctic sovereignty.	53%	29%	19%
I have confidence in the government of Stephen Harper to secure Canada's Arctic sovereignty.	44%	43%	13%
Canada should plant a flag on the Arctic's seabed.	51%	33%	16%

* Figures have been rounded.

Summing Up

You will encounter other situations in which reaching a consensus is important. Following this process will help find solutions that everyone can accept.

How has national interest shaped foreign policy?

A **policy** is a plan of action that has been deliberately chosen to guide or influence future decisions. Your school, for example, probably has policies to guide decisions about what is in the individual or collective interests of the students and staff. One policy may state that students and staff must treat each other with dignity and respect. Other policies may deal with rules about plagiarism and attendance.

A country's government is responsible for developing both **domestic policy** and **foreign policy**.

- domestic policy — Guides decisions about what to do within the country. In Canada, domestic policy may guide decisions about changing federal laws, settling Aboriginal land claims, and spending tax revenues.
- foreign policy — Guides decisions about official relations with other countries. Foreign policy, which is often called external relations or foreign affairs, may involve co-operating with international organizations such as the United Nations, signing treaties, establishing trade relations with foreign states, and taking action on human rights, world health, and environmental issues.

When terrorist threats are regular occurrences, when acts of genocide are visible in our living rooms, when crossing international borders becomes an anxiety-ridden challenge, when frightening diseases and environmental issues have no boundaries, when our economic survival depends so starkly on access to the market of a single foreign power, Canadians begin to realize that foreign policies actually have some relevance to their personal lives.

— Allan Gotlieb, former Canadian ambassador to the United States, 2004

Foreign policy decisions may have relatively short-term effects on a limited number of people or long-term effects on millions of people. Some foreign policy decisions made at the end of World War I, for example, are still affecting the world today. Many people believe that the turmoil in Middle Eastern countries relates directly to the foreign policy decisions of the United States and European countries as they pursued their national interests at the end of World War I.

Figure 5-9 shows how domestic and international events shape — and are shaped by — nationalism, the pursuit of national interest, and foreign policy. All can awaken nationalist feelings. These feelings can cause citizens to revise their opinions about what is in the national interest. In response to these changing ideas, governments may alter their foreign policies.

With a partner, examine Figure 5-9. Then think about Canada's policy of pursuing its claim to the Northwest Passage. Create a similar diagram, but replace "Foreign Policy" with "Claiming Northwest Passage." In the other bubbles, replace the general connections with specific connections related to the Northwest Passage.

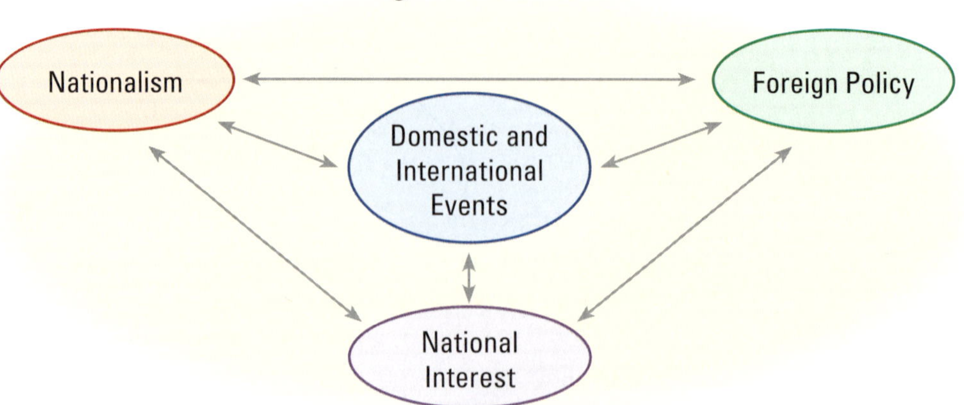

Figure 5-9 Nationalism, National Interest, and Foreign Policy

National Interest and World War I Peace Settlements

World War I was fought in Europe, the Middle East, Asia, and Africa. On one side were the Central Powers, led by Germany; on the other were the Allies, led by Britain. The world had never experienced such a wide-ranging and deadly war. Millions of people died, and the financial cost was enormous.

Before World War I, nationalism had flourished in Europe. Many historians believe that nationalism and people's beliefs about their national interest were important causes of this war.

European governments, for example, believed that expanding their territory in Europe, as well as their colonial possessions, was in their national interest. This belief was a foundation of their foreign policy, which led them to form alliances with other European countries. Alliance members agreed to help one another when one country was threatened. This system of alliances was one factor that brought so many countries into the war so quickly.

Figure 5-10 Gavrilo Princip, a member of a Serbian nationalist group, assassinated Archduke Franz Ferdinand of Austria-Hungary and his wife when they visited Sarajevo, capital of Bosnia and Herzegovina. Bosnia and Herzegovina was part of the Austro-Hungarian Empire. Princip's action sparked the events that drew members of European alliances into war with one another as each country tried to protect its national interests.

Most people affected by World War I had had no say in the decision to go to war. If you lived in the Ottoman, Russian, or Austro-Hungarian empires, for example, you were at war when your rulers declared war. If you lived in Canada, you were included in Britain's declaration of war. Your national interests were not considered.

After more than four years of brutal fighting, an armistice — truce — was declared at 11 a.m. on November 11, 1918, and the war ended.

Treaty Negotiations in France

World War I was fought over sovereignty and territory, economic interests and security, and nationalism and national identity. These issues also dominated the discussions at the peace talks that took place in Paris, France, from 1919 to 1920.

The victorious Allies, especially France and Britain, wanted to punish Germany by imposing harsh conditions. Prime Minister David Lloyd George of Britain, Prime Minister Georges Clemenceau of France, and President Woodrow Wilson of the United States led the most powerful Allied countries. As a result, they made many of the treaty decisions that had far-reaching effects on millions of people.

The financial, military, and territorial penalties imposed on Germany and the Central Powers were severe. The Treaty of Versailles required Germany to reduce its military strength, pay war reparations — compensation — of $30 billion, give up territory in Europe as well as its colonies, and accept responsibility "for causing all the loss and damage" that had affected the Allies.

Read "FYI" and think about what happened to Germany and Canada at the peace conference in Paris. How would you describe the nationalist feelings that might have been evoked in the two countries? Can some nationalist feelings be healthy, while others are unhealthy? If not, why not? If so, what makes the difference?

Web Connection

To find out more about the events set in motion by Gavrilo Princip's actions, go to this web site and follow the links.

www.ExploringNationalism.ca

FYI

Before World War I, Britain still controlled Canada's foreign policy. This is why Canada was automatically at war when Britain declared war. But Canada made an important contribution to the Allied victory, so Prime Minister Robert Borden demanded — and won — the right to attend the Paris Peace Conference and sign the peace treaty as an independent country.

MAKING A DIFFERENCE

Woodrow Wilson
Visionary or Dreamer?

MAKING A DIFFERENCE MAKING A DIFFERENCE MAKING A DIFFERENCE

As World War I raged in January 1918, American president Woodrow Wilson presented a road map for ending the war and establishing long-lasting peace. Wilson called his plan the Fourteen Points.

Wilson believed that the Fourteen Points would make the world safe "for every peace-loving nation which, like our own, wishes to live its own life, determine its own institutions, and be assured of justice and fair dealing by the other peoples of the world as against force and selfish aggression."

Under Wilson's plan, countries would negotiate treaties openly, navigate the seas freely, engage in equal trade, and require fewer war weapons. Colonized peoples would be consulted when colonial claims were decided. Borders would be changed to recognize peoples' sense of nation.

The Fourteen Points did not require Germany to pay reparations, and German leaders supported Wilson's plan. But the Allies began to change Wilson's plan nearly as soon as the armistice was signed. Among the changes were demands that Germany pay reparations and accept guilt for starting the war. Many Germans were bitterly disappointed by this turn of events — and this disappointment sparked the lasting bitterness that would become one of the chief causes of World War II.

One of Wilson's key proposals called for the creation of the League of Nations. This international organization would ensure "political independence and territorial integrity to great and small states alike." Rather than maintain a balance of power between equally armed enemies, the League of Nations would ensure that countries co-operated in the interest of their collective security.

Some people called Wilson a dreamer. They said that he had not thought through how his proposals would work. French prime minister Georges Clemenceau, for example, called Wilson's plan "the fourteen commandments of the most empty theory." Other critics said Wilson's idea for the League of Nations did not take into account longstanding nationalist fears and hatreds that would prevent countries from trusting their security to an outside organization.

In the end, political opponents in Wilson's own country turned public opinion against him and the U.S. refused to sign the Treaty of Versailles or join the League of Nations.

Figure 5-11 In 1919, *The Literary Digest*, a weekly current events and public opinion publication that was a forerunner of *Time* magazine, published these cartoons on the League of Nations. What opposing views of the League do the cartoons present?

Explorations

1. The first three of Woodrow Wilson's Fourteen Points called for
   - open diplomacy and no secret deals between nations
   - freedom of the seas for all countries
   - open and equal trade among nations

   Comment on these proposals in light of your current understanding of nationalism and globalization. List points that show how — and why — these ideas have or have not emerged in today's world.

THE VIEW FROM HERE

The Treaty of Versailles was controversial. Some people believed that it was too harsh. Others, such as Ferdinand Foch, the Allies' supreme commander, who had accepted the German surrender on November 11, 1918, believed that it was too lenient. Foch feared that Germany would rebuild its military strength. He said, "This is not a peace treaty. It is an armistice of 20 years."

Here is how three people have evaluated the Treaty of Versailles at different times.

In 1919, **John Maynard Keynes**, who would later help shape international economic policies, was part of the British delegation at the Paris Peace Conference after World War I.

> The future life of Europe was not [the treaty writers'] concern; its means of livelihood was not their anxiety. Their preoccupations, good and bad alike, related to frontiers and nationalities, to the balance of power, to imperial aggrandizements, to the future enfeeblement of a strong and dangerous enemy, to revenge, and to the shifting by the victors of their unbearable financial burdens on to the shoulders of the defeated.

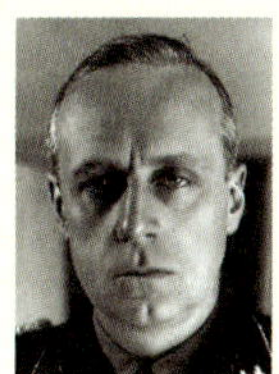

Shortly after the start of World War II in 1939, **Joachim von Ribbentrop**, the foreign minister in Adolf Hitler's Nazi government, blamed the Treaty of Versailles for provoking the German invasion of Poland.

> The Führer [Hitler] has done nothing but remedy the most serious consequences which this most unreasonable of dictates in history [the Treaty of Versailles] imposed upon a nation and, in fact, upon the whole of Europe, in other words repair the worst mistakes committed by none other than the statesmen of the Western democracies.

In 2001, Canadian historian **Margaret MacMillan** published an award-winning book, *Paris 1919,* which examined how peace was negotiated.

> With different leadership in the Western democracies, with stronger democracy in Weimar Germany [a common name for Germany between 1919 and 1933], without the damage done by the Depression, the story might have turned out differently. And without Hitler to mobilize the resentments of ordinary Germans and to play on the guilty consciences of so many in the democracies, Europe might not have had another war so soon after the first. The Treaty of Versailles is not to blame. It was never consistently enforced, or only enough to irritate German nationalism without limiting German power to disrupt the peace of Europe. With the triumph of Hitler and the Nazis in 1933, Germany had a government that was bent on destroying the Treaty of Versailles.

Explorations

1. What common thread weaves through the words of all three speakers and writers?
2. What evidence supports the idea that revenge was a motive in the Treaty of Versailles?
3. How did the Treaty of Versailles fan the flames of nationalism in Germany? If Woodrow Wilson's Fourteen Points had been accepted as the basis of the Treaty of Versailles, do you think Germans would have felt differently? Explain your judgment.

National Interests after World War I

CheckForward

You will read more about the situation after World War I in Chapter 6.

Once World War I ended, many Canadians turned their attention to domestic concerns. The war had created an industrial boom, but this died out, and many returning Canadian veterans had trouble finding work. This created unrest, and people's personal, collective, and national interests began to focus more on what was happening at home and less on events in other countries. Domestic issues became more important than foreign policy concerns.

A similar shift in priorities took place in many other countries that had been involved in the war. Belgium and France, deeply in debt, focused on rebuilding cities, towns, and farms. Britain had serious problems in its empire, especially in India. There, Mohandas Gandhi was leading a nationalist program of peaceful civil disobedience that was hurting an already battered British economy.

Unity among the Allies, who had created the Treaty of Versailles, soon disappeared. The French, who had the most to gain from a successful treaty, were unable to enforce it on their own.

I am directed by the Government of Great Britain to inform you that you may rest assured that Great Britain has no intention of concluding any peace in terms of which the freedom of the Arab people from German and Turkish domination does not form an essential condition.

— Henry McMahon, British high commissioner in Egypt, to Sharif Husayn ibn 'Ali of Mecca, December 1915

Nationalism and National Interests in the Middle East

In the years before World War I, Arabs in the Ottoman Empire had suffered political, cultural, and linguistic persecution at the hands of the ruling Turks. During the war, Arab nationalism — based on shared traditions, religion, language, and history — had been growing. The Arabs' goal was self-government. To further this dream, they had helped the Allies fight the Turks and Germany in the Middle East. In return, they had been promised an independent homeland.

From 1916 to 1918, Prince Emir Faysal, a son of Sharif Husayn ibn 'Ali of Mecca, had led Arab fighters against the Ottoman Turks and helped the British gain control of Palestine in 1917. But at the time, Faysal did not know that Britain and France had secretly agreed to divide up the Middle East and control it themselves. Although Faysal travelled to Paris in 1919 to try to persuade the treaty negotiators to keep their promise to his people, he was unsuccessful.

The Arabs have long enough suffered under foreign domination. The hour has at last struck when we are to come into our own again . . . Why should not the Arabs rule the country where they live and have lived for countless generations? Why should we not be masters in our own house?

— Faysal, son of Sharif Husayn ibn 'Ali, at the Paris Peace Conference, 1919

Why might these foreign powers be in a position to control the national destiny of Arabs? If you were an Arab who had been promised self-government after World War I, how do you think you would have responded to the broken promises of Britain and France? How might this situation have affected your feelings of nationalism and your future attitude toward these countries?

Figure 5-12 T.E. Lawrence, also known as Lawrence of Arabia, was a British officer who played an important role in the Arab rebellion against the Turks and came to passionately support Arab independence. At the Paris Peace Conference, Lawrence tried unsuccessfully to persuade the British and French to keep their promise to their Arab allies. What conflicting loyalties might Lawrence have felt?

Treaties in the Middle East

The Treaty of Versailles was not the only treaty negotiated after World War I. Other treaties gave France control over the territory and the peoples of Syria and Lebanon, while Britain was granted control over the territory and peoples of Cyprus, Iraq, and Palestine, which included Transjordan. Today, much of Palestine has become Israel and the country of Jordan has emerged out of Transjordan.

Although the United States was not involved, U.S. president Wilson supported Britain and France. Neither he nor Clemenceau nor Lloyd George paid much attention to earlier promises or to the national interests of the Middle Eastern peoples who would be affected by their actions. The Allies were concerned only with their own national interests.

As a result of the mechanized warfare that had been introduced in World War I and the growing popularity of the automobile, oil was becoming a more important commodity. And the Middle East was rich in oil. France and Britain believed that controlling much of the Middle East would promote their nationalist interests by securing trade with the region — and a ready source of oil.

But Arab nationalists throughout the region were outraged by what happened. They became even angrier when the British enacted the Balfour Declaration, which promised to set up "a national home for the Jewish people" in Palestine. Arab nationalists viewed these actions as a betrayal of promises that had been made to them.

After the war, a nationalist party led by Mustafa Kemal set up a republic in Turkey. The new government refused to accept the European peace treaty and won independence for Turkey in 1923. Turkey was admitted to the League of Nations in 1932, the same year as Iraq and six years after Germany.

CheckBack

You read about Mustafa Kemal and Turkish nationalism in Chapter 1.

Figure 5-13 To gain Faysal's support, the British arranged for him to be crowned king of Iraq in 1921. T.E. Lawrence wrote that Faysal "looks like a European, and very like the monument of [English king] Richard I at Fontevrault." Why do you think Lawrence might have placed this particular spin on Faysal's appearance?

Reflect and Respond

In *Paris 1919*, Margaret MacMillan wrote: "The peacemakers of 1919 made mistakes . . . By their offhand treatment of the non-European world, they stirred up resentments for which the West is still paying today . . . In the Middle East, they threw together peoples, in Iraq most notably, who still have not managed to cohere into a civil society."

Explain how the foreign policies of Britain and France after World War I — as well as their pursuit of their national interests — might have helped create the resentments MacMillan identified.

If you had been an adviser at the Paris Peace Conference, would you have recommended that the United States, Britain, and France follow a different policy? Explain your response.

GEOREALITY

Oil and National Interest in Iraq

GEOREALITY GEOREALITY GEOREALITY

Until World War I, the world had paid little attention to the country that is now known as Iraq. But as the 20th century unfolded, geography — in the form of vast oil reserves — ensured that Iraq would assume greater and greater importance on the world stage.

Some experts estimate that nearly 25 per cent of the world's oil reserves are located in Iraq. These reserves could serve the country's national interest by providing economic prosperity for the country's 27.5 million people. But oil has not brought prosperity to Iraqis. From the end of World War I to the present, the struggle to control Iraq's oil has caused wars, civil conflict, and invasions.

The most recent invasion took place in March 2003, when Iraq was attacked by 300 000 soldiers from the United States, Britain, and a coalition of other countries. U.S. president George W. Bush and British prime minister Tony Blair said the purpose of the invasion was to protect their countries' national security by deposing Iraqi dictator Saddam Hussein and destroying Iraq's weapons of mass destruction — WMDs. Saddam was captured and executed — but no WMDs were found. Four years later, about 150 000 coalition troops remained in Iraq, along with more than 100 000 people who worked for private military contractors.

Iraq after World War I

After World War I, Iraq was one of the new Middle Eastern nation-states that the Allies carved out of the former Ottoman Empire. These new countries were created to serve the national interest of Britain and France, which needed Middle Eastern oil to fuel their cars, trucks, factories, and military vehicles.

Over the course of the 20th century, many countries came to depend on oil produced in Iraq and other Middle Eastern countries. To ensure that they could sell their oil at a single price — and to sustain their own economies — Middle Eastern oil producers, including Iraq, formed the Organization of the Petroleum Exporting Countries in 1960.

In 1990, Saddam invaded neighbouring Kuwait in an attempt to take over that country's oil fields. This invasion, which became known as the Persian Gulf War, was condemned by the United Nations and foiled by a U.S.-led coalition. After that, Saddam was rumoured to be stockpiling WMDs to use against Israel and other countries. Though Saddam denied the rumours, the UN sent inspectors to search for these weapons.

Figure 5-14 Iraq

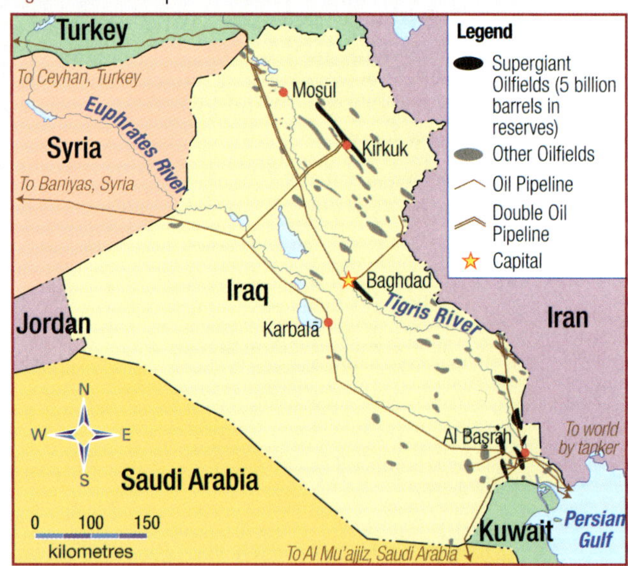

Figure 5-15 Iraq, 1920 to 2005

1920	1932–1979	1979	1980–1988	1990–1991	2003	2005
Britain controls Iraq after World War I	Iraq gains partial independence but internal struggle for control continues	Saddam Hussein seizes power	Iraq is at war with Iran	Iraq invades Kuwait and is defeated by U.S.-led coalition of United Nations forces	U.S. and Britain invade Iraq and establish a coalition government that includes men, women, Sunnis, Shiites, Kurds, and one Christian	Elections take place in Iraq

U.S. National Interest and Foreign Policy

After September 11, 2001, when al-Qaeda terrorists attacked the United States and killed 2819 people, Americans became worried about their personal security. In response, Bush announced a "war on terror" and vowed to track down al-Qaeda members and their leader, Osama bin Laden.

By March 2003, Bush had convinced many Americans that invading Iraq was in their national interest because Saddam planned to sell WMDs to al-Qaeda. Bush was joined by Britain and some other countries. But the UN, whose inspectors had found no WMDs, refused to support the invasion. Without UN approval, Canada and other countries refused to join the U.S. Still, the invasion went ahead.

Noam Chomsky, a professor at the Massachusetts Institute of Technology, said that the decision to invade Iraq had little to do with terrorism. "The real reason for the invasion, surely, is that Iraq has the second largest oil reserves in the world, very cheap to exploit, and is at the heart of the world's major hydrocarbon resources," Chomsky said.

But U.S. vice-president Dick Cheney said that America would be safer when Iraq no longer offered "safe havens for terrorists or places where people can gather and plan and organize attacks against the United States."

By 2007, opinion polls showed that a majority of Americans opposed the Iraq war and did not believe that keeping troops in Iraq increased their security.

Iraqi National Interest and Foreign Policy

By the end of 2007, Saddam had been deposed and executed, and Iraqis had elected a government. But safety and security were a major concern. Every day, Iraqis experienced deadly violence as coalition, ethnic, and religious forces clashed. In 2006, 34 452 Iraqi civilians were killed. More than 36 000 were wounded. About 60 000 people a month were forced from their homes.

Iraq's **gross domestic product** — the value of all goods and services produced in a country every year — was only $1900 a person. By comparison, Canada's GDP was $35 700 a person. Iraqis also lacked adequate health care, water, food, electricity, and sewage disposal.

A 2006 opinion poll conducted in Iraq found that about 90 per cent of respondents believed that they had been better off before the invasion. About 70 per cent wanted coalition forces to leave the country.

Factions inside and outside Iraq continued the struggle for control of its oil. By February 2008, 70 international companies were preparing to compete for the rights to develop the country's oil reserves. The Iraqi government's challenge was to find a way to ensure that the country's oil resources would be used to improve its citizens' economic prosperity and quality of life.

Figure 5-16 On May 1, 2003, under a banner that said "Mission Accomplished," U.S. president George W. Bush gave a famous speech suggesting that the United States had achieved its goals in Iraq. Four years later, American cartoonist M.e. Cohen created this cartoon to mock Bush's pronouncement. What message do you think Cohen was sending? Explain your response.

Explorations

1. Examine the timeline in Figure 5-15. Choose three events that relate directly to national interest. Explain whose national interests were involved and what these interests were.
2. Many historians believe that the developed world's need for oil created — and destroyed — Iraq. Comment on this conclusion.
3. Is pursuing the economic and security interests of one country an appropriate reason for that country to invade another country? Is there a right or wrong answer to this question? Explain your response.

How has foreign policy shaped national interest?

Nationalism, foreign policy, and national interest can be understood as a complex and constantly changing web. Though the pursuit of national interest often shapes foreign policy, foreign policy can also shape national interest. A government's policies can affect its citizens' safety and security, their economic future, and even their values and culture. When Austria-Hungary declared war on Serbia in 1914, for example, that single foreign policy decision affected the Austro-Hungarian people's personal security, their economic prosperity, and their culture for decades to come.

The Mashco Piro and Nahua are among several nomadic peoples who choose to isolate themselves deep in Peru's rainforests. When these peoples do come into contact with outsiders, disaster is often the result. In 1984, for example, loggers kidnapped four Nahua people, who caught the flu from their captors. When the Nahua returned to their community, they infected others. The infection ripped through the community and killed half the Nahua.

Foreign Policy and Contending National Interests in Peru

A country's foreign policy may benefit some communities but have negative effects on others. This is what is happening in Peru.

In 2007, the Peruvian government decided that it would be in the national interest to auction land in the Amazon rainforest to foreign-owned oil companies for development. The wealth generated by oil exploration and extraction could help Peruvians, whose GDP in 2006 was $6600 a person.

But the land in question forms part of the traditional territory of the Mashco Piro, an Indigenous people who shun contact with outsiders. The Mashco Piro do not want to move to another part of the forest or become part of the outside world.

Peruvian law says that if Indigenous people live in a region, the land must be kept for their use. But this law can be set aside if the land is used in a way that contributes to the country's national interest — and Perupetro, Peru's government-owned oil company, has since auctioned off some of the land to Spanish and American oil companies.

In September 2007, the Peruvian government signed the United Nations Declaration on the Rights of Indigenous Peoples as part of its foreign policy. The declaration says that Indigenous peoples have the right not only to territories and resources they have traditionally owned, occupied, and used, but also to own, use, develop, and control territories and resources that they possess by reason of traditional ownership or other traditional occupation or use.

Consider the contending national interests involved in the use of the Peruvian rainforest. Keep in mind, too, that rainforests help to check global climate change. Does this make everyone in the world a stakeholder in the debate over how the rainforest is used? With a partner, discuss this question — and how you might try to reconcile the contending national interests of the Mashco Piro, Nahua, and other Peruvians. How are the rights of the Mashco Piro, Nahua, and other peoples supported by the Declaration on the Rights of Indigenous Peoples?

Figure 5-17 This photograph of a Mashco Piro shelter and campfire was taken in Peru's Alto Purús National Park. The 600 or so Mashco are a nomadic people who are so elusive that very few people have had contact with them.

9/11 and Canada in Afghanistan

The 9/11 attacks on the United States killed 2982 people, including 24 Canadians. It was generally believed that the Taliban rulers of Afghanistan were hiding and protecting Osama bin Laden and other members of al-Qaeda, which had claimed responsibility for the attacks.

As a result, the United Nations agreed that the United States and its allies were entitled to invade Afghanistan to destroy the Taliban and track down bin Laden. Han Seung-soo, president of the General Assembly, announced that the 9/11 attacks had threatened international peace and security and that the United States had "the inherent right of individual or collective self-defence as recognized by the Charter of the United Nations." The UN authorized the North Atlantic Treaty Organization — NATO — to organize this mission, which started in 2001.

As part of its foreign policy after World War II, Canada had helped found NATO. The treaty that created NATO in 1949 said that an attack on one member would be considered an attack on all. As a result, forces from Canada and other countries, including the United States and Britain, went to Afghanistan under the NATO banner.

The Taliban government fell, and Canadian forces helped keep peace while a new government was organized. But when the U.S. invaded Iraq in 2003, many of the American troops in Afghanistan were reassigned to Iraq. This reduced the size of the NATO force in Afghanistan. To make up this shortfall, other countries, such as Canada, increased the size of their force and expanded their role to include active combat.

This foreign policy shift was controversial. Most Canadians had opposed the Iraq invasion, and some now charged that the decision to increase the number of Canadian troops in Afghanistan was a way of helping the government solve a difficult problem: how to appear to support its American ally's war on terror while responding to public opinion by staying out of the war in Iraq.

Jean Chrétien was prime minister when the government decided not to join the American-led invasion of Iraq. Read "Voices." Why do you suppose Chrétien regards this decision as a "great moment for Canada"? What statement does this decision make about Canadians' view of their national interests and foreign policy?

Figure 5-18 A month before the U.S. launched its invasion of Iraq, people around the world organized a day of protest against the American plans. In Canada, where a majority of people supported the government's decision not to join the invasion, demonstrations took place in 70 towns and cities. What national interests do you suppose these Canadians were supporting?

For the independence of the country, saying no to the Americans on the war [in Iraq] was a great moment for Canada. Of course, it was not without risk. Suppose the war in Iraq had been a great success, I think it would have been a bit embarrassing for me. But I thought [the Americans] were wrong and I said so.

— Jean Chrétien, former prime minister, in an interview, 2007

Figure 5-19 The Canadian government declared September 14, 2001, a day of mourning for those who had died in the September 11 attacks on the United States. In Ottawa, up to 80 000 people attended a Parliament Hill rally to show their support for the victims of the attack. How did the attacks affect Canadians' views on their country's national interests and foreign policies?

Figure 5-20 This cartoon by Michael de Adder appeared in the Halifax *Daily News* in April 2007. What do you think the cartoonist is saying about the debate over Canada's foreign policy with respect to Afghanistan?

Debate over Afghanistan

As the fighting in Afghanistan dragged on, Canada and its NATO allies realized that they must place greater emphasis on creating a democratic, self-sufficient society in that country. In addition to making the country more secure, this meant helping Afghans rebuild their economy, political processes, medical facilities, and armed forces and police. But these goals proved difficult to achieve. Taliban and al-Qaeda fighters were using guerrilla tactics to disrupt the lives of the Afghan people and battle NATO forces. By mid-March 2008, 81 Canadian soldiers and one diplomat had been killed in the fighting, and it looked as if the death toll would continue to rise. The continuing conflict created a debate in Canada over whether — and how long — Canadian troops should remain in Afghanistan.

According to Canadian Women for Women in Afghanistan, a Calgary-based organization, the debate over Afghanistan revolved around the following issues:

- the validity of Canada's mission
- the financial cost of the mission
- the combat role of Canadian forces
- the threat to the lives of Canadian forces
- the relationship with the other forces operating in Afghanistan
- the length of the mission

Canadian politicians disagreed over how to resolve these issues. NDP leader Jack Layton believed that a military role was "not the right mission for Canada." He said, "Canadians want a foreign policy rooted in fact, not fear, one that is uniquely independent, not ideologically imported. And one that leads the world into peace, not [one that] follows the U.S. into wars."

But Michael Ignatieff, deputy leader of the federal Liberals, disagreed. He said that Canadians and their NATO allies were trying to stabilize the country "at the request of the Afghan people." And Prime Minister Stephen Harper said, "Canada went into Afghanistan for very real reasons of national security and international security. Because as 9/11 showed, if we abandon our fellow human beings to lives of poverty, brutality and ignorance, in today's global village, their misery will eventually and inevitably become our own."

In July 2007, The Strategic Counsel surveyed Canadians to find out what they thought of Canada's policies in Afghanistan. Examine the poll results, shown in Figure 5-20. With a partner, discuss whether asking questions like these is appropriate when Canadian troops are fighting overseas.

Figure 5-21 Canadian Opinion on Afghanistan, July 2007

Do Canadians support or oppose sending troops to Afghanistan?

Response	%
Total supporting	36%
Strongly support	7%
Support	29%
Oppose	31%
Strongly oppose	27%
Total opposing	59%
Don't know	5%

What do Canadians think is the main reason for our involvement in Afghanistan?

Response	%
Canada is in Afghanistan mainly because of pressure from the U.S. in response to the attack on 9/11	44%
Canada is in Afghanistan because it has an obligation within the broader international community to respond to the threat of global terrorism	53%
Don't know	3%

Canadian casualties: Is it the price we have to pay, or is the price too high?

Response	%
This is the price that must be paid	36%
Price is too high	60%
Don't know	4%

Source: The Strategic Counsel

National Interests and Rights for Women

When the Taliban controlled Afghanistan, girls were not allowed to go to school and women were not allowed to have careers. Although the new NATO-backed government created a ministry of women's affairs to change this situation, Taliban resistance was causing concern. In September 2006, the Taliban took credit for assassinating Safia Ama Jan, an official with the women's ministry.

Sima Samar was Afghanistan's first minister of women's affairs. In 2007, she headed the Afghanistan Independent Human Rights Commission, which monitors the progress of government agencies and other institutions toward implementing human rights laws and policies. Samar said that changing Afghanistan will take time. "We started in 2001 with no systems at all," she said. "We have accomplished a lot . . . Democracy is a process — it doesn't come because you shout at it. You have to deal with the weak points and you can't have it without the participation of half the population [women]."

Figure 5-22 During the Taliban regime, Sima Samar, a doctor, ran clinics and schools for girls and women in Afghanistan. In response to death threats, she said, "Go ahead. Hang me in the public square and tell the people my crime — I was giving papers and pencils to the girls."

Taking Turns

Has Canadian foreign policy in Afghanistan supported the national interests of the Afghan people?

The students responding to this question are Pearl, who lives in St. Albert and whose great-great-great grandfather immigrated from China to work on the Canadian Pacific Railway; Jean, a Francophone student who lives in Calgary; and Violet, who is a member of the Paddle Prairie Métis Settlement.

Pearl

We need to do more to help girls and women in Afghanistan. Sima Samar's story shocked me. Can you imagine not being able to go to school just because you're a girl? Afghan women need better health care and education, and they need protection. Canadian policies in Afghanistan should help Afghan women learn about their rights. And the Canadians should help the Afghan government enforce these rights.

Jean

I think that we should get out of Afghanistan — right now. I don't agree with our government's foreign policy. We aren't really helping the Afghan people; we're fighting with them. And don't we have enough problems with security and inequality in our own country without meddling in other countries' affairs? We need to take care of our own national interests first. Then maybe we can go and help people in other countries.

Violet

My big brother is in the Princess Patricias, and he did a tour in Afghanistan. I support Canada's foreign policy on Afghanistan and the work that Canadian troops are doing over there. They're taking care of our national interests because they're making the world safer for everyone. It wasn't easy for my brother and the other soldiers to go so far away to try to help people enjoy the kinds of freedoms that we take for granted in Canada. Sometimes, though, I worried about my brother and I missed him — a lot.

How would you respond to the question Pearl, Jean, and Violet are answering? Do views they did not mention affect your response? What does this discussion show about the complications involved in balancing foreign policy decisions with the pursuit of national interest?

1. With a partner, create a chart like the one shown.
   a) In the first column, list five priorities (e.g., Arctic sovereignty) that you believe governments in Canada should actively pursue because they are in the national interest.
   b) In the second column, provide several reasons for each choice.
   c) In the third column, list the stakeholders affected by each choice.
   d) In the fourth column, identify one government action or strategy that could help promote the priority.
   e) Compare your chart with that of another pair. Revise your chart to reflect changes in your views as a result of this discussion.

2. Review the chart you completed in response to Question 1. On the basis of your list of priorities, the reasons for the choices, and the stakeholders you identified, write a short essay explaining the extent to which Canada should — or should not — pursue its national interests.
   a) Begin by deciding whether any nation should actively pursue its national interests. You may decide, for example, that it depends on the national interest, on events in the country and elsewhere, and the national and international effects that would result. Establish criteria to help you judge whether pursuing national interests is the most effective course for the government and the people living in Canada.
   b) With your criteria in mind, review the material in this and other chapters of *Exploring Nationalism* and use this material as examples to support your arguments.

Canada's National Interests

Priority	Reasons for Choice	Stakeholders	Action or Strategy
1.			
2.			
3.			
4.			
5.			

3. With a partner, review the responses to the opinion poll on Canada's involvement in Afghanistan (Figure 5-21, p. 132). Then choose one of the actions or strategies you identified in Question 1.

   Make up three statements or questions that you could present to the public to help you measure the degree of support for the action or strategy you identified. Each question or statement should highlight an aspect of the national interest and provide respondents with a number of options for indicating the strength of their response. If, for example, your strategy recommended an increased military presence in Canada's North, your statement might say:

   A strong military presence in the Arctic is essential to protect Canada's security? Do you

   a) agree strongly

   b) agree somewhat

   c) disagree somewhat

   d) disagree strongly

   e) don't know

   Check your statements or questions by responding yourselves to ensure that they will elicit the types of responses you are seeking.

   Poll at least 10 people. They could include family, friends, classmates, teachers, or other people willing to respond. Tabulate your results in charts similar to those shown on page 132.

   On the basis of these results, prepare a recommendation for the government. If you wish, you may explain why you believe the poll results turned out as they did.

4. Examine the cartoon in Figure 5-23. It explores Canadian national interests and the North. Then respond to the following questions:
   - What "story" is the cartoonist telling?
   - How does this story reflect a Canadian national interest?
   - What position on the national interest do you think the cartoonist is taking? As evidence, give specific examples shown in the cartoon.
   - What sense of Arctic sovereignty as a national interest do the scene and setting evoke?
   - Do you think the cartoonist believes Canada should pursue a more aggressive policy in the North? Explain your response.

Figure 5-23

Think about Your Challenge

Your challenge for this related issue is to prepare an investigative report on a historical or contemporary nationalist movement to help you respond to the related-issue question: To what extent should national interest be pursued? Now is the time to start conducting research so that you can choose a movement. Begin putting together ideas that will help you track down sources.

You should also decide on the form your report will take. This decision will affect the kind, amount, and format of the information you gather. Prepare a chart to help you organize this information (an example is shown on p. 113).

CHAPTER 6 Nationalism and Ultranationalism

Figure 6-1 The map shows the Soviet Union in 1938, just before World War II started. The poster, which was created by the government of the Soviet Union, shows dictator Joseph Stalin with Azerbaijanis, one of the many peoples who were part of the country. The slogan — in Azerbaijani — urges people to support the Soviet Union's new constitution. Stalin controlled the Soviet Union from the late 1920s until his death in 1953.

CHAPTER ISSUE

To what extent can nationalism lead to ultranationalism?

THE POSTER ON THE PREVIOUS PAGE shows Premier Joseph Stalin and the people of Azerbaijan, which was part of the vast Soviet Union. The Soviet Union included the present-day country of Azerbaijan, as well as Russia, Ukraine, Tajikistan, Kazakhstan, Georgia, Turkmenistan, Uzbekistan, and Armenia. Though the poster depicts Stalin as a kindly figure, the reality was very different. Under Stalin's rule, between 20 and 60 million people were executed or died in state-created famines, forced-labour camps, and deportations.

For a quarter-century, Stalin controlled the Communist Party — and the Soviet Union. Stalin decided on the country's national interests and set domestic and foreign policies — and forced people to focus their national loyalty on him.

Examine the poster and map, then respond to the following questions:

- How did the artist portray Stalin in the poster?
- What purposes are served by the other figures in the poster?
- What is the poster's underlying message? Why would conveying this message be important in a dictatorship?
- After examining the map, what conclusions can you draw about the peoples who were included in the Soviet Union?
- What difficulties might a dictator experience when trying to control a vast country that contains people of so many different backgrounds?

KEY TERMS

ultranationalism

propaganda

appeasement

conscription

LOOKING AHEAD

In this chapter, you will develop responses to the following questions as you explore the extent to which nationalism can lead to ultranationalism:

- What is ultranationalism?
- How does ultranationalism develop?
- How have people responded to ultranationalism?

My Journal on Nationalism

Look back at the notes you recorded at the beginning of Chapter 5. Compare your current views on nationalism with those you have already recorded. Is your point of view changing? If so, how? Date your ideas and add them to the journal, notebook, learning log, portfolio, or computer file you are keeping as you progress through this course.

What is ultranationalism?

CheckBack

You read about various understandings of nationalism in the prologue and Chapter 1.

Some people believe that nationalism is the most powerful political force in the world — even when they do not agree on exactly what nationalism is. In *Jihad vs. McWorld: Terrorism's Challenge to Democracy*, Benjamin Barber highlighted this disagreement when he wrote: "There is old nationalism and new nationalism, good nationalism and bad nationalism, civic nationalism and ethnic nationalism, nationalism as the forge of great states and nationalism as their coffin . . . the nationalism of the liberal nation-state and the nationalism of . . . parochial politics and tribalism."

People also disagree on when nationalism becomes **ultranationalism**, an extreme form of nationalism. At some point, ultranationalists move from valuing their own nation and its interests to hostility toward people of other nations. This hostility can endanger international peace.

People may agree that ultranationalism includes elements of racism and fanaticism and that it can lead to conflicts, but they do not always draw the line between nationalism and ultranationalism in the same place. Whether people label a belief or policy nationalistic or ultranationalistic sometimes depends on the nation they belong to. Some might view the actions of people in their own group as patriotic, while claiming that similar actions by other peoples are ultranationalistic. Building a strong military, for example, may be viewed as nationalistic in one country — but ultranationalistic in another.

Figure 6-2 When the killers of Hrant Dink went on trial, many Turks gathered outside the courthouse. They carried signs saying, "We are all Hrant Dink" and "We are all Armenians." What collective idea were they expressing?

Ultranationalism may be associated with a fanatical belief in the rights of your own group and a fear and loathing of anyone who challenges those beliefs. In January 2007, for example, Hrant Dink, a Turkish journalist who was also a member of Turkey's Armenian minority, was murdered. The teenager accused of the murder was thought to belong to a Turkish nationalist group.

Dink had angered some nationalists in his country by writing about the massacre of hundreds of thousands of Armenians by Turks in 1915, under cover of World War I. Because of his writing, the journalist had been convicted in 2006 of publicly insulting "Turkishness, the Republic or the Grand National Assembly of Turkey" and had received a six-month suspended sentence.

Dink's conviction and murder sparked heated debate in Turkey about free speech, ethnic tensions, and extreme nationalism. Would you describe Dink's murder as an act of ultranationalism? Does discussing this issue help you decide where to draw the line between nationalism and ultranationalism? Explain your response.

Russian Ultranationalism

Some people believe that drastic economic and social changes that result in unemployment and poverty can spark extreme nationalism. In these circumstances, people's interest in personal security, economic security, and the values of their own group can become all-important.

When the Soviet Union disintegrated in 1991, for example, Russia and 14 other independent republics emerged. But the transition was difficult, and insecurity about the future bred hatred of people who were different, especially immigrants and asylum seekers. In 2006, Alexander Verkhovsky of Moscow's SOVA Centre for Information and Analysis — a non-governmental organization that monitors racist violence in Russia — said, "Most of our population supports the idea of 'Russia for Russians,' which means for ethnic Russians, not for Russian citizens."

[In a crisis] people come to believe that they want security at any cost and that human rights, the broad range of human rights — equality, social and economic rights, all civil liberties and freedoms — are a luxury that will come after security is ensured, which of course is a very big mistake.

— Louise Arbour, UN high commissioner for human rights, on the resurgence of the Taliban in Afghanistan, 2007

Russia under Stalin

At the beginning of the 20th century, Russia was an absolute monarchy. The Russian Revolution in 1918 resulted in the assassination of the czar and royal family and launched a civil war that brought even more suffering to millions of people who had already endured great hardship during World War I.

By 1928, Joseph Stalin, a communist, had emerged as the country's leader. One of Stalin's first acts was to confiscate land owned by farmers and create collective farms owned by the state. Those who objected were executed, and an estimated five million people were deported to forced-labour camps in Siberia or Central Asia.

Why might establishing democracy in a country without a tradition of democratic government be difficult?

Stalin wanted to replace the loyalties of the 100 distinct national groups in the Soviet Union with Soviet nationalism. Any group that objected was persecuted as a "criminal nation." According to Nobel Prize–winning Russian author Aleksandr Solzhenitsyn, Stalin's system of forced national deportations "would fasten its pitiless talons on any nation pointed out to it."

The treatment of Ukrainians was especially brutal. When Ukrainian farmers refused to give up their land, Stalin confiscated their crops. As a result, up to 10 million Ukrainians starved to death in the 1930s. Stalin also outlawed the use of the Ukrainian language in public. Ukrainians were the largest group of political prisoners in the forced-labour camps.

Stalin also rid the Communist Party of anyone accused of being an "enemy of the people." Thousands of Russians were executed, and millions more were sent to slave-labour camps. Included among the exiles were a man who took down a portrait of Stalin to paint a wall, and Ukrainian artist Nikolai Getman, who was in a café when another artist drew a cartoon of Stalin.

Figure 6-3 This lithograph, which was created by the French artist Gignoux in 1931, is titled *The Siberian Gulag*. "Gulag" is an acronym that comes from the Russian words for "administration of corrective labour camps."

Propaganda and Ultranationalism

Figure 6-4 In this 1938 photograph, German children read an anti-Jewish book titled *The Poisonous Mushroom*. Joseph Goebbels said, "The foundations must be laid early in life. Following the Führer's teaching, we are setting a new ideal for the education of our youth."

Propaganda refers to information and ideas that are spread to achieve a specific goal. The information and ideas are often misleading and dishonest. Extreme nationalists use propaganda to manipulate strong human emotions — especially fear and insecurity — and persuade people to behave in certain ways. Propagandists often

- call their opponents names (e.g., "terrorists," "fanatics") designed to arouse people's anger and fears
- play down their own failures and defeats or use words that hide the true meaning of their actions (e.g., calling their own wars "holy" or "just," or referring to death camps as "concentration camps")
- use respected symbols to appeal to people's values and beliefs (e.g., religious symbols, family images, or a national flag)
- appeal to people's fears when trying to persuade them to support particular actions (e.g., claiming that strict law and order is the only way to ensure peace and save a nation)

The poster of Stalin that opens this chapter is an example of Soviet propaganda. At the same time as millions of people were being sent to forced-labour camps, Stalin's propagandists were creating posters, slogans, songs, speeches, newspaper articles, and banners glorifying extreme nationalism and presenting Stalin as a caring father of the Soviet peoples.

In Germany, the Nazis used newspapers, radio, and film to promote extreme nationalism. Joseph Goebbels, Hitler's minister for public enlightenment and propaganda, established a huge propaganda organization that controlled all forms of the media. Goebbels was a gifted speaker who consistently preached the supremacy of the German people and hatred for Jews, whom he called the incarnation of evil.

Figure 6-5 German troops force Jewish women and children out of a house in Warsaw, Poland. People in the Warsaw ghetto had tried to resist German efforts to deport them to death camps, where six million Jews were murdered. How do you think the propaganda shown in the photograph in Figure 6-4 might have influenced the treatment of Jewish people in this photograph?

Reflect and Respond

Propaganda often inflames people's prejudices and feeds on emotions such as fear, guilt, and patriotism. List three criteria you could use to decide whether a government message provides important information required by citizens or is propaganda designed to sway public opinion.

How does ultranationalism develop?

Various factors and events often combine to transform nationalism into ultranationalism. Among these are social and economic crises, the emergence of a charismatic authoritarian leader, and national traditions and myths that promote feelings of superiority.

Web Connection

To find out more about the Great Depression, go to this web site and follow the links.

www.ExploringNationalism.ca

Countries in Crisis

The Great Depression of the 1930s provided fertile ground for the growth of extreme nationalism. Around the world, people suffered economic losses that affected the pursuit of their national interests.

On October 29, 1929, share prices on the New York Stock Exchange dropped drastically. This sudden crash caused economic turmoil in many countries. People lost their savings as banks suddenly closed. Unemployment rose as companies laid off workers. Governments had a hard time taking care of the needs of citizens who had no work and no money to buy food or pay for a place to live.

FYI

To try to pay the war reparations demanded by the Treaty of Versailles, the German government printed huge amounts of money. As a result, the mark — Germany's money — became almost worthless. In 1918, a loaf of bread cost two marks. By 1924, this price had risen to six million marks. People struggled to survive.

Germany after World War I

After the end of World War I, Germany became a republic. Men and women had the right to vote for members of the new parliament. But during the 1920s, no political party won enough votes to run a successful government.

When the Great Depression started in 1929, it hit Germany especially hard. The country was still struggling to recover from the war, trying to pay reparations and make up for the loss of colonies that had been taken away by the victorious Allies. Germany was also deeply in debt to the United States, which had lent the government money to help rebuild the country.

In the early 1920s, Germany suffered through a period of extreme inflation — rising prices and a sharp drop in the buying power of money. German money became almost worthless while prices increased more than 100 times. In the 1930s, German prosperity depended on trade with other countries. But to try to protect their own industries during the Depression, many of those countries stopped importing German goods. As a result, German industries laid off workers. The standard of living of many Germans was destroyed, and many people faced homelessness and starvation.

As economic conditions grew worse, some Germans began to look for a strong leader who could fix the country, and Adolf Hitler's National Socialist German Workers' Party — the Nazi Party — started to gain support. After many failed attempts, Hitler was elected to lead Germany in 1933.

Figure 6-6 The son of a powerful Nazi official gives the Nazi salute. Like other dictators, Adolf Hitler demanded that people obey him without question — and children were indoctrinated early. Why would indoctrinating children be important in a dictatorship?

Once in power, Hitler dissolved the parliament and declared the start of the Nazi Reich, or empire, with himself as dictator. The state ruled in all matters: economic, social, political, military, and cultural. Freedom of the press and freedom of assembly were suspended, and postal, telegraph, and telephone communications were no longer private.

FOCUS ON SKILLS

Assessing the Validity of Information

FOCUS ON SKILLS

During crises such as economic depressions and war, people often face hard times. When a country's national interests demand that its citizens sacrifice their quality of life and even life itself, leaders often appeal to people's feelings of nationalism, patriotism, and national identity. Both Joseph Goebbels, Nazi Germany's minister for public enlightenment and propaganda, and Winston Churchill, the British prime minister during World War II, used radio — the mass medium of the day — to broadcast inspiring, nationalistic messages to the public. Excerpts from their speeches appear on the following page.

To judge the validity of the information in speeches like these, you must analyze the historical context of the speech and assess the speaker's degree of bias and objectivity. The following steps can help you do this.

Steps to Assessing the Validity of Information

Step 1: Review your previous knowledge

When assessing the validity of new information, start with what you already know. Work with a partner to jot down points in response to the following questions:

- What do you know about nationalism during the Great Depression and World War II?
- What do you know about attitudes toward nationalism and national identity at that time?
- What experiences have been related to you by family and friends?
- What is your own experience of how people pursue their national interest during times of crisis?

Step 2: Practise applying assessment criteria

With your partner, examine the questions in the checklist on this page. Discuss how each question could help you assess the validity of the information included in the two speeches.

On a sheet of paper, in your notebook, or in a computer file, create two copies of the checklist. Then, with your partner, read the excerpts from the speeches of Joseph Goebbels and Winston Churchill. Complete one checklist for each excerpt. To answer some questions, you may need to conduct additional research.

When you have completed both checklists, rate the overall validity of the information in each speech. You may wish to use a rating scale of 1 to 5 (1 = not very valid; 5 = highly valid).

Step 3: Discuss your assessment with other students

When you finish, discuss your assessment with another pair. Be on the lookout for new insights into assessing the validity of the information in these speeches. If necessary, revise your own responses as you deepen your understanding.

You might also wish to discuss the effectiveness of each speech in achieving its purpose.

Validity of Information Checklist

Information Source ______________________

Criterion	Question	Resp
Reliability	Who is the author?	
	Why did the author write this piece?	
	Has the author written other material on this subject?	
	What is the author's reputation for reliability?	
Context	When and where was the piece written?	
	Who is the target audience?	
	What medium was used to deliver the message?	
	What effect might the choice of medium have on the target audience?	
Bias	What are the author's main arguments or interpretations?	
	What preferences or dislikes does the author express? Provide at least one example.	
	What persuasive or propaganda techniques does the author use? Provide at least one example.	
	What powerful words and phrases does the author use? Are they used in a positive or negative manner?	
Objectivity	What is the purpose of the message?	
	Is the information based on fact, or does the message appeal mainly to emotions?	
	Is the language of the piece objective or emotionally charged?	
	Does the piece present alternative points of view and perspectives?	
Evidence	What evidence does the author present to support the arguments?	
	Can the evidence be checked against other accounts?	
	Does the author overgeneralize, stereotype, or exaggerate?	
	Are relevant facts left out?	

FOCUS ON SKILLS FOCUS ON SKILLS
CUS ON SKILLS FOCUS ON SKILLS FOCUS ON SKILLS

Joseph Goebbels, minister for public enlightenment and propaganda in Nazi Germany, gave a speech honouring Adolf Hitler's forthcoming 50th birthday. Goebbels spoke in April 1939, a few months before the beginning of World War II.

In an unsettled and confused world, Germany tomorrow celebrates a national holiday in the truest sense of the word. It is a holiday for the entire nation. The German people celebrate the day entirely as a matter of the heart, not of the understanding.

Tomorrow the Führer finishes his 50th year. The entire German nation takes pride in this day, a pride in which those peoples who are friendly with us also take deep and hearty part. Even those who are neutral or oppose us cannot ignore the strong impact of the events. Adolf Hitler's name is a political program for the entire world. He is almost a legend. His name is a dividing line. No one on earth can remain indifferent to his name. For some, he represents hope, faith, and the future; for others, he is an exemplar of confused hatred, base lies, and cowardly slander.

The highest that a person can achieve is to give his name to an historical era, to stamp his personality indelibly on his age. Certainly the Führer has done that. One cannot imagine today's world without him . . .

Adolf Hitler has influenced not only the historical development of his country, but one can say without fear of exaggeration that he has given all of European history a new direction, that he is the towering guarantee of a new order for Europe.

The German people know that the Führer has restored [Germany] to its rightful position in the world. The Reich stands in the shadow of the German sword. Germany's economy, culture, and popular life are blooming under a security guaranteed by the army. The nation, once sunk into impotence, has risen to new greatness.

Nearly two years after the beginning of World War II, British prime minister **Winston Churchill** gave the following speech to Allied representatives, who were meeting in London, England.

What tragedies, what horrors, what crimes has Hitler and all that Hitler stands for brought upon Europe and the world! The ruins of Warsaw, of Rotterdam, of Belgrade are monuments which will long recall to future generations the outrage of unopposed air bombing applied with calculated scientific cruelty to helpless populations . . .

But far worse than these visible injuries is the misery of the conquered peoples. We see them hounded, terrorized, exploited. Their manhood by the million is forced to work under conditions indistinguishable in many cases from actual slavery. Their goods and chattels are pillaged or filched for worthless money. Their homes, their daily life are pried into and spied upon by the all-pervading system of secret political police which, having reduced the Germans themselves to abject docility, now stalks the streets and byways of a dozen lands. Their religious faiths are affronted, persecuted or oppressed in the interest of a fanatic paganism devised to perpetuate the worship and sustain the tyranny of one abominable creature. Their traditions, their culture, their laws, their institutions, social and political alike, are suppressed by force or undermined by subtle, coldly planned intrigue . . .

Hitler may turn and trample this way and that through tortured Europe. He may spread his course far and wide and carry his curse with him. He may break into Africa or into Asia. But it is here, in this island fortress, that he will have to reckon in the end. We shall strive to resist by land and sea . . . With the help of God, of which we must all feel daily conscious, we shall continue steadfast in faith and duty till our task is done.

Summing Up

As you progress through this course, you will often need to assess the validity of information by analyzing and evaluating reliability, context, bias, objectivity, and evidence. The politicians, critics, writers, speakers, artists, and photographers you will encounter will have various points of view and perspectives on the meaning of nationalism and on how national interest should be pursued in various circumstances.

Figure 6-7 Hirohito became the emperor of Japan when his father died in 1926. Hirohito was worshipped as *arahitogami*, a god who is human. How might the idea of the emperor as a demigod — a being who is partly divine — feed into the development of ultranationalism?

Japan after World War I

During World War I, Japan supported the Allies, and after the war, Japanese exports to Europe and the United States increased. But when the Great Depression started, these trading partners tried to support their own industries by limiting imports and Japanese people lost their jobs. Then, in 1932, a massive failure of the rice crop caused famine throughout the country.

Japanese ultranationalists blamed the country's politicians for the economic crisis. They were further enraged when the United States, Canada, and Australia shut out Japanese immigrants. To try to obtain raw materials and markets for Japanese products, Japan invaded Manchuria, in northeastern China, in 1931.

By 1937, the military controlled the Japanese government and Japan was at war with China. Military leaders brought back traditional warrior values, such as obedience to the emperor and the state, and created a cult around the emperor, Hirohito.

Taking Turns

How might a crisis affect people's sense of nationalism and national identity?

The students responding to this question are Pearl, who lives in St. Albert and whose great-great-great grandfather immigrated from China to work on the Canadian Pacific Railway; Blair, who lives in Edmonton and whose heritage is Ukrainian, Scottish, and German; and Amanthi, who lives in Edson and whose parents immigrated from Sri Lanka.

Pearl

My great-grandfather was born in Canada, but he had family in China — and they have told him what it was like when Japan invaded. China was in such chaos that he didn't hear from some of his relatives for years. Sometimes he worried that they had all been killed. He told me that people were really scared, and yeah, some people betrayed their friends and neighbours to get on the good side of the Japanese. But lots of people didn't. People helped one another whenever they could. Even strangers. So in some ways, the hardships drew people together — and deepened their sense of Chinese national identity.

Blair

The way my great-uncle Dmytro tells it, what people in Ukraine went through in 1932 to '33 was caused by Stalin's fear of Ukrainians' strong nationalist loyalties — and these ties still exist, even though we're scattered in different countries. Ukrainians were resisting Stalin in the 1930s, and to force them to do what he wanted, he took the grain from the farmers. He just let them starve. That famine was definitely created by someone who hated my nation, but it sure didn't destroy it. Just the opposite.

Amanthi

I liked what Louise Arbour said about what people do in a crisis. If you didn't have food or a safe place to live, you might not be so concerned about things like equality and freedom — and even national identity. You'd have more important concerns. In some ways, just talking about national identity is a luxury that people like us here in Canada enjoy. I'll bet that if we lived in a one-party state that controlled the media, we wouldn't even hear a voice like Arbour's. If what she said wasn't what the government wanted people to hear, then her words wouldn't be broadcast in the media or put in a textbook.

Your Turn

How would you respond to the question Pearl, Blair, and Amanthi are answering? Explain the reasons for your answer.

Charismatic Leaders

During the 1920s and 1930s, ultranationalist dictators emerged in the Soviet Union, Italy, Germany, and Japan. These leaders inspired enthusiasm and devotion in their followers — and fear in anyone who questioned their leadership or policies. Opposition was squelched with deadly force.

Figure 6-8 Using powerful public address systems, careful staging, and skilful architectural design, Hitler whipped up support for his ultranationalist policies at mass rallies. This rally, which took place in Nuremberg in 1938, was for the Hitler Youth Movement. Why would Hitler consider it so important to inspire German youth to form a loyalty to him personally?

Adolf Hitler in Germany

In Germany, Adolf Hitler promised that he would restore people's national pride by making their country the leading nation on Earth. A skilled speaker who knew how to capture the attention of an audience, Hitler said he would do this by

- refusing to recognize the Treaty of Versailles
- rebuilding Germany's armed forces and reclaiming lost territories
- restoring the superiority of the "Aryan race" — white Europeans of which the Germanic and Nordic peoples were the "purest" examples

Nazi propaganda experts used radio, movies, public address systems, and giant posters to keep Hitler's image and message before the public. The Nazis issued carefully planned releases to newspapers and distributed pamphlets and flyers. Party members organized central and neighbourhood mass meetings attracting audiences of up to 100 000. At these meetings, crowds chanted, "Today Germany, tomorrow the whole world."

Hirohito and Tojo in Japan

In the years leading up to World War II, ultranationalists worked to rid Japan of democracy and to make the country a one-party state ruled by the military. Although Emperor Hirohito — the Son of Heaven — was revered, he was not involved in politics. The commanders of Japan's armed forces decided on the country's national interests and made most of the decisions that took Japan into World War II.

Military leaders, for example, made the decision to invade China and to capture territory belonging to other countries. They wanted raw materials to keep Japanese industries going, as well as markets for Japanese products. They justified this territorial expansion by saying that Japan was only doing the same thing as the United States and the colonial powers of Europe had already done. In 1941, General Tojo Hideki became prime minister and transformed Japan into a military dictatorship. An aggressive ultranationalist, Tojo promised that the country would dominate Asia through military might.

Figure 6-9 Tojo Hideki, who led Japan into World War II, served as prime minister from 1941 to 1944. Raised in a family with a long warrior tradition, Tojo had worked his way up through the ranks and believed that Japan's destiny was to dominate Asia.

SPINBUSTER

Analyzing Propaganda

Germany and the Soviet Union are not the only countries that have used propaganda to persuade citizens to act in the national interest. During World War II, the Canadian government created the Wartime Information Board to control information and inspire support for the war effort. One of the board's strategies was to create propaganda placing a positive spin on the war effort.

Figure 6-10 This World War II poster, which was produced by Canada's Wartime Information Board, was designed to appeal to Canadians' fear of their enemies. It highlighted the need to protect women and children, who were depicted as the country's most vulnerable citizens.

Figure 6-11 In September 1942, the *Montreal Gazette* published this cartoon, titled "Speaking of Sacrifice." It contrasted the sacrifices of Canadian civilians with what happened to soldiers during the disastrous raid on Dieppe, France. There, 900 Canadians were killed, more than 1000 were wounded, and 1900 were taken prisoner.

Steps to Analyzing Propaganda

Step 1: Examine the materials

Examine the illustrations on this page. Create a chart like the one shown on this page and use it to analyze these materials.

Step 2: Assess the effectiveness of the materials

Re-examine the materials in light of your analysis. In a small group, discuss which of the pieces

- is most persuasive. Give reasons for your choice.
- most honestly reflects the facts. Cite evidence to support your opinion.
- least honestly reflects the facts. Cite evidence to support your opinion.

Step 3: Draw conclusions

In a small group, discuss whether you would classify both pieces as propaganda. Is using propaganda justified during wartime? At other times? Justify your response.

Summing Up

You can use your spinbusting skill to detect and analyze propaganda in a variety of situations at school and in everyday life.

Analyzing Propaganda

Item (e.g., poster, radio announce-ment) **and Source**	**Audience** (Who is the target of the mes-sage?)	**Purpose** (What actions is the piece pro-moting?)	**Persuasion Techniques** (What words and images are used to persuade? What emotions does the piece appeal to?)

Instilling Ultranationalist Values

The dictatorships in the Soviet Union, Germany, Italy, and Japan promoted extreme nationalist values. Domestic and foreign policies fostered these values, and the military and police were strengthened to protect them. Education was used as a propaganda tool to instil these values in the young. Culture, art, and the media were used to serve the ultranationalists' goals and to drown out opposing voices.

To find out more about the Nazi persecution of the Jewish people and how this persecution led to the murder of six million Jews, go to this web site and follow the links.

www.ExploringNationalism.ca

Ultranationalist Values in Germany

During the 1930s, German ultranationalist propaganda often focused on the glories and nationalist values of the past. The operas of Richard Wagner glorified a mythic time of German greatness and were much in favour, while modern art and music were condemned. Books were destroyed if they did not follow the approved nationalist line.

The "master race" of German people were called on to build an empire — the Third Reich — that would last for a thousand years. For this to happen, Nazi leaders said, Germany must rid itself of anyone, such as socialists, Jews, Roma, homosexuals, and people with disabilities, who were considered "inferior" or who challenged the state's perspective.

From elementary school through university, students were taught Nazi values and shielded from ideas that challenged these values. History books were rewritten to glorify Germany's past, and in the summer of 1933, ultranationalist university students burned books as part of an "action against the un-German spirit."

The night of November 9–10, 1938, became known as *Kristallnacht* — the Night of Broken Glass. Gangs of Nazi thugs destroyed Jewish synagogues, businesses, community centres, and homes throughout Germany and Austria. They beat up Jewish people, broke windows, and desecrated cemeteries.

Figure 6-12 A Berlin synagogue burns on *Kristallnacht*. How did this event foreshadow what would happen to Jews under Nazi rule in Germany?

Soon afterwards, Hitler's government passed laws taking away the basic rights of Jewish people. They could no longer own property or businesses. Jewish children were expelled from schools and universities, and Jews could not be doctors, lawyers, or university professors. They were also forbidden to own automobiles or have a driver's licence.

More than a hundred years before Hitler came to power, the German poet and playwright Heinrich Heine had written, "Wherever they burn books, they will also, in the end, burn human beings." Why do you suppose Heine made this link? Do you think it is accurate?

Figure 6-13 The books burned at this ceremony at a German university included works by playwright Bertolt Brecht, physicist Albert Einstein, political theorist Karl Marx, psychoanalyst Sigmund Freud, and poet and playwright Heinrich Heine. How would destroying writings like these have helped foster the growth of ultranationalism?

This fall, when the destiny of the Empire is being decided, through His Majesty's summons I have been ordered to the Tsuchiura naval aviation unit as a naval preparatory student. It is an extremely great joy and honour for our family. In life I am a defender of the divine land and through death I become a guardian spirit of the state. While my body may scatter over the skies of the South Seas like cherry blossoms, my soul eternally remains in and protects the land of our ancestors . . . During these extraordinary times for the nation, what a joy it is to be summoned as a soldier.

— Gihei Watayama Mikoto, 21, Japanese naval officer killed in action in the East China Sea, November 1944

Ultranationalist Values in Japan

Just as the Nazis promoted a return to the mythical values of Germany's past, so, too, did the military leaders who controlled Japan. Ultranationalists promoted a return to ancient values that were woven into the country's social and political fabric. Those values included worship of the emperor as a demigod and the belief that the Japanese people are superior to all others and have a mission ordained by heaven to expand beyond the borders of their country.

At the same time as foreign policy officials were assuring the world that Japan wanted peace, the ultranationalists who were gaining more and more control within the country prepared for war.

In the 1930s, Japan's educational system was based on *The Way of Subjects*, published by the Japanese education ministry. Students were taught to idealize the past, to take pride in their race and culture, and to practise duty and obedience as the highest virtues. Western books, ideas, values, and culture were scorned, and the ideals of Nazi Germany were praised. Militarism and national defence were priorities. Fanatic militarists preached a doctrine that included contempt for death, exaltation of victory, and blind obedience.

Warriors of the past and present were honoured. The national Japanese religion, Shinto, was used to unite the nation around the emperor. Shinto teaches that the souls of the dead remain in the land of their birth and that they protect the living. Today, at the Yasukuni Shrine in Tokyo, warriors and soldiers are remembered and worshipped as *kami*, spirits who have become gods. Many people who have died for Japan — including Tojo Hideki and others who were later executed as war criminals — are honoured there. As a result, the shrine is controversial.

Every year, hundreds of thousands of Japanese people visit the shrine. Some Japanese people want Tojo's name removed, but members of the ruling party, including Prime Minister Junichiro Koizumi, continue to visit the shrine to pay their respects to the *kami*.

Figure 6-14 When it became obvious that Japan was losing the war, kamikaze pilots began crashing their planes into Allied ships. These pilots are receiving headbands during a ceremony marking the launch of a suicide mission. How was the pilots' action related to ultranationalism?

Reflect and Respond

Review the events described in this section. Explain how the Soviet Union under Joseph Stalin, Japan under its military leaders, and Germany under Adolf Hitler followed a similar course in the years between World War I and World War II. Link these similarities to the shift to ultranationalism in each country. You may wish to create a Venn diagram to highlight the similarities.

In your view, when did each country cross the line that separates nationalism and ultranationalism? Cite evidence to support your position.

How have people responded to ultranationalism?

Ultranationalism infects all aspects of a country's life: social, economic, political, cultural, and spiritual. Ultranationalists prey on people's fears and use propaganda to spread hatred. In countries around the world, people have found it difficult to find peaceful ways of overcoming extreme nationalist values and beliefs.

They came first for the Communists, and I didn't speak up because I wasn't a Communist.

Then they came for the Jews, and I didn't speak up because I wasn't a Jew.

Then they came for the trade unionists, and I didn't speak up because I wasn't a trade unionist.

Then they came for the Catholics, and I didn't speak up because I was a Protestant.

Then they came for me, and by that time, no one was left to speak up.

— Attributed to Martin Neimoeller, German Lutheran pastor and anti-Nazi activist who spent eight years in a German concentration camp

Appeasement as a Response to Ultranationalism

In the years before World War II, many people in countries that had experienced the terrible costs of World War I and the Great Depression believed that avoiding another war was one of their most important national interests. As a result, they hoped that **appeasement** — giving in to demands — was the best policy when Adolf Hitler and the Nazis began to expand Germany's territory in Europe.

Germany had been expanding its European territory since 1935. Finally, in 1938, British prime minister Neville Chamberlain, French prime minister Edouard Daladier, and Italian prime minister Benito Mussolini met Hitler to discuss Germany's recent takeover of the Sudetenland. Before World War I, Germany had controlled this region, but the Treaty of Versailles had awarded it to Czechoslovakia. In return for Hitler's promise not to expand further, Chamberlain, Daladier, and Mussolini agreed to allow the takeover to go unchallenged. In Britain, Chamberlain explained that "the peoples of the British Empire were at one with those of Germany, of France, and of Italy" in "their anxiety, their intense desire for peace."

Not everyone agreed that appeasement would work. Winston Churchill, who was at the time a member of Parliament in Chamberlain's Conservative Party, condemned the agreement, saying, "An appeaser is someone who feeds a crocodile — hoping it will eat him last." He also said Chamberlain, Daladier, and Mussolini "had to choose between war and dishonour. They chose dishonour; they will have war."

Early in 1939, Hitler took over the rest of Czechoslovakia. Churchill had been proven right. Appeasement had failed.

An old saying suggests that hindsight is 20/20; in other words, it is easy to look back at the past and judge people's decisions. Examine the map in Figure 6-15 and identify the territories Germany took over between 1935 and 1939. In 1938, when Germany took over the Sudetenland, would you have agreed with Neville Chamberlain's or Winston Churchill's response? What criteria would you have used to support your position?

Figure 6-15 Expansion of Germany, 1933–1939

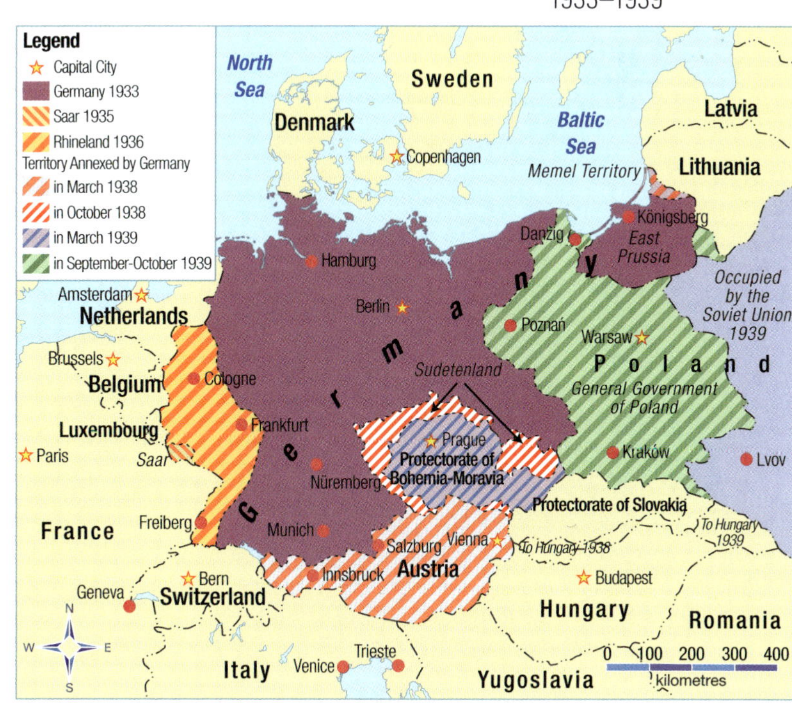

The dynamic leaders of the inter-war years — Hitler, Mussolini, the Japanese militarists — sneered at the League [of Nations], and ultimately turned their backs on it. Its chief supporters — Britain, France and the smaller democracies — were lukewarm and flaccid.

— *Margaret MacMillan, Canadian historian, in* Paris 1919

Failure of the League of Nations

By 1934, 58 countries, including Canada, Britain, and France, were members of the League of Nations, which had been created after World War I. League members agreed to help one another and to take action to maintain peace.

If one country invaded another, League members could

- order the aggressor to leave the other country's territory
- impose trade sanctions — penalties — on the aggressor
- use military force against the aggressor

But member countries were not required to provide troops to stop aggression — and the idea of joint military action soon became an empty threat.

When Japan invaded Manchuria in 1931, for example, China appealed to the League for help. The League condemned the invasion, but Japan responded in 1933 by resigning its membership. After that, League members could not agree on what action to take — and ended up doing nothing.

Ethiopia

After World War I, Italy suffered some of the same problems as Germany. Promising to restore Italy's power and prestige, Benito Mussolini, an extreme nationalist and a gifted speaker, was appointed prime minister in 1922 and soon established himself as a dictator. Like Hitler in Germany and Stalin in Russia, Mussolini ruled through fear. His policies included suppressing all opposition, instilling absolute loyalty, and conquering other territories.

Italy had fought on the side of the Allies in World War I, and Italian ultranationalists had expected to be rewarded. As a result, they were angry when the Treaty of Versailles failed to give Italy control of the independent African country of Ethiopia or the territory it claimed in Europe.

In October 1935, Mussolini ordered Italian forces to invade Ethiopia. Both Italy and Ethiopia were members of the League of Nations, and in June 1936, Haile Selassie, the Ethiopian emperor, travelled to League headquarters in Geneva, Switzerland, to plead for help.

In response, the League called for trade sanctions against Italy, but these failed when many countries, including the United States, ignored them. Britain and France were afraid to strictly enforce the sanctions because they feared driving Mussolini into an alliance with Germany and Japan. As a result, Ethiopia received no international support.

In the 1930s, Germany, Japan, and Italy expanded their territory in pursuit of ultranationalist goals while the world did little but watch. Do you think World War II could have been prevented if Canada and other countries had responded more forcefully?

Figure 6-16 In his 1936 speech to the League of Nations, Haile Selassie told members about the poison gas that Italian planes had sprayed on the "soldiers, women, children, cattle, rivers, lakes and pastures" of his country. How might the people who are the victims of a more powerful country's extreme nationalistic and expansionist foreign policies respond?

War as a Response to Ultranationalism

On September 1, 1939, Adolf Hitler launched an invasion of Poland — and Britain and France finally realized that appeasement was not working. On September 3, the two countries declared war on Germany. World War II had begun.

After a special session of Parliment, Prime Minister William Lyon Mackenzie King announced on September 10 that Canada, too, was at war. "There is no home in Canada, no family and no individual whose fortunes and freedom are not bound up in the present struggle," King said in a radio address to all Canadians. "I appeal to my fellow Canadians to unite in a national effort to save from destruction all that makes life itself worth living and to preserve for future generations those liberties and institutions which others have bequeathed to us."

Examine King's words. How were they crafted to appeal to the emotions of Canadians and to inspire support for the war effort? Were they propaganda? Explain the reason for your judgment.

After World War I, the Canadian government had taken steps to make Canada more independent. By the time World War II broke out in 1939, Canada's foreign policy was no longer tied to that of Britain, as it had been in 1914. This meant that Canada was not automatically included in Britain's declaration of war on Germany.

By introducing propaganda and official censorship, tactics that are also used in dictatorships, was the Canadian government starting down the path to ultranationalism?

Total War

Canada's national interest now focused on the war effort. With the declaration of war, the tone of the language used to describe the country's involvement in international affairs also changed. The government began implying that Germany was the evil enemy, and Canadians were told that they were fighting for "the freedom of mankind."

Government policies focused on what King called "a total effort for a total war," in which "the security of each individual is bound up in the security of the nation as a whole." Under conditions of "total mobilization," Canadians were encouraged to support the war effort by joining the armed forces or by working in essential industries and other civilian activities.

By the end of September 1939, more than 58 000 Canadians had enlisted in the armed forces. Propaganda campaigns were launched to recruit people and persuade them to invest in war bonds, which helped finance the war effort. No employer was allowed to hire anyone who did not have a permit from an employment office, and employment could be restricted to specific locations or industries considered essential to the war effort.

Official censorship was also introduced to ensure that no essential information fell into the hands of the enemy. Government censors, for example, approved every speech broadcast on the CBC and examined stories published in newspapers and magazines. Military censors read all letters from members of the armed forces, as well as letters to soldiers in enemy prisoner-of-war camps. Anything that revealed too much was blacked out.

Figure 6-17 This poster, published by the Wartime Information Board, portrays a soldier with a machine gun, a male worker with a rivet gun, and a female worker with a hoe. What message was this poster designed to convey? Would you classify this poster as propaganda? Why or why not?

Figure 6-18 Recruitment posters like this were a common sight during World War II. What Canadian myths does this poster recall? What emotions do you think it was intended to arouse?

Conscription in Canada

The leaders of Germany, Italy, Japan, and the Soviet Union believed that **conscription** — compulsory military service — was in the national interest. They considered a strong military essential both for national defence and for carrying out their expansion plans.

But conscription was not limited to dictatorships. During World War I, the Canadian government, too, had introduced conscription. But this law had left the country bitterly divided. Many farmers, for example, had worried about what would happen to their farms if they were forced to enlist.

The fiercest opposition, however, came from Québec Francophones, who felt no strong connection to Britain — or to France. In addition, many Francophones were farmers who shared the concerns of farmers elsewhere. Francophones also faced a language barrier because English was the language of the army. Despite this, Francophones had volunteered in about the same ratio as anglophones. What Francophones objected to was forced military service, and violent protests had erupted in both Montréal and Québec City.

When World War II started, Prime Minister William Lyon Mackenzie King was aware of the resentments caused by conscription during World War I. Still, he introduced a limited form of conscription, though he promised not to send conscripts overseas. They would be used only to defend Canada.

CheckForward

You will read more about internments in Chapter 13.

But as the war dragged on, Canadian casualties mounted, and not enough volunteers were enlisting to replace them. King faced a problem, and in 1942, he decided to hold a special vote to ask Canadians' permission to break his promise.

When the votes were tallied, 63 per cent of voters supported King, but this was not the whole story. As predicted, the country was sharply divided: 79 per cent of anglophones had favoured the plan, but 85 per cent of Francophones had opposed it.

Internment in Canada

During World War I, many Canadians became caught up in the racism and extreme nationalism of the period. Thousands of people of German and Ukranian background were interned as enemy aliens. During World War II, wartime propaganda depicted Germans, Italians, and Japanese people as the enemy — and Canadians of German, Italian, and Japanese background were often discriminated against because of this.

Even before World War II, Canadians of Japanese descent had been subjected to discrimination, especially in British Columbia, where many had settled. They were, for example, not allowed to vote or to enter certain professions. After Japanese forces attacked Pearl Harbor and Hong Kong in December 1941, things became even worse.

Figure 6-19 Though discrimination often made it hard for people from visible minority groups to join the armed forces, some Japanese Canadians, such as Shin Takahashi (left) and Toru Iwaasa (right), managed to serve in the Canadian army. What statement might these soldiers' actions make about their national loyalty?

In 1942, Japanese Canadians who lived within 160 kilometres of Canada's Pacific coast were rounded up and transported to internment camps in the British Columbia interior or to farms on the Prairies. Internment camps were like prisons. The government seized Japanese-owned homes, property, and businesses and sold them at bargain prices — then used the money from the sales to pay the costs of keeping people in the camps.

Is it fair to compare conscription and the treatment of Canadians of Japanese descent with Joseph Stalin's actions in the Soviet Union or Adolf Hitler's actions in Germany? Explain your reasoning.

FYI

No Japanese Canadian was ever charged with disloyalty to Canada, and in September 1988, the government apologized and offered compensation for the property seized during World War II.

MAKING A DIFFERENCE

Joy Kogawa
Shedding Light on a Shameful Story

When Joy Kogawa published *Obasan* in 1981, the award-winning book took many Canadians by surprise. It was the first novel to focus on the internment and dispersal of Japanese Canadians during World War II, and it raised public awareness of the discrimination and injustices that had been suffered.

Although the book is a novel, not an autobiography, Kogawa had first-hand knowledge of many of the experiences of her characters. Born in Vancouver in 1935, she and her family were among the 22 000 Japanese Canadians interned during World War II.

In 1942, when Kogawa was six years old, her family home was confiscated, and she and her parents were forced to move to Slocan, a ghost town in the Rocky Mountains. There, Kogawa spent the war years. When the war ended, the family was forced to move again, this time to Coaldale, Alberta, where her mother, who had been a kindergarten teacher, and her father, an Anglican minister, worked as field labourers to survive.

Like Kogawa, Naomi, the narrator of *Obasan*, was a child when her family was exiled to a ghost town in the interior of British Columbia. After the war, the family was not allowed to return to the coast but was sent to live in southern Alberta.

Figure 6-20 After the publication of *Obasan*, poet and novelist Joy Kogawa became active in the movement seeking redress for Japanese Canadians. Since then, she has become an ardent Canadian nationalist who helped organize a national-unity march in Québec.

In the book, Naomi writes about what it was like when she and her family first learned that they would be forced out of their home.

> Our beautiful radios are gone. We had to give them up or suffer the humiliation of having them taken forcibly by the RCMP. Our cameras . . . all are confiscated. They can search our homes without warrant.
>
> But the greatest shock is this: we are being forced to leave. All of us. Not a single person of the Japanese race who lives in the "protected area" will escape . . .
>
> It breaks my heart to think of leaving this house and the little things that we've gathered through the years – all the irreplaceable mementos – our books and paintings – the azalea plants, my white iris . . .

Explorations

1. Joy Kogawa is a member of the Order of Canada, an award given by the governor general to recognize "outstanding achievement, dedication to the community, and service to the nation." If you had gone through Kogawa's experiences, would you have accepted this award? Explain the reasons for your response.
2. Is it fair to judge past actions from the perspective of today's knowledge and understanding? Explain the reasons for your response. List three criteria that could be used to judge past actions fairly.

Peacekeeping

In response to the destruction caused by World War II, the United Nations was formed to help keep peace in the world. At first, UN missions involved only observation, but in 1956, a crisis over the Suez Canal highlighted the need for a different approach.

The privately owned canal, which links the Red and Mediterranean seas, was built in the 19th century. In 1956, it was owned by a British and French company. The canal meant that goods — especially oil — could move between Asia and Europe more quickly and cheaply because ships no longer had to travel all the way around Africa. Ships paid fees for using the canal, and profits went to the company's shareholders.

In 1956, the Egyptian government seized the canal. The government believed that it was in Egypt's national interest for the Egyptian people, not the company's shareholders, to benefit from the canal.

Examine the map in Figure 6-21. Why do you think the Egyptian government might have felt entitled to take over the Suez Canal? Would you classify this action as nationalistic or ultranationalistic? Explain your response.

In response to the Egyptian government's action, Israeli, British, and French forces invaded the canal zone. The Soviet Union supported Egypt and threatened to attack Britain and France. Suddenly, the world was on the brink of another war.

Should peacekeeping forces carry guns?

At the time, Lester B. Pearson was Canada's minister of external affairs. Pearson proposed that the UN send an emergency force to keep peace in the canal zone while diplomats negotiated a resolution to the crisis.

The UN welcomed Pearson's idea, and within days, a UN force made up of soldiers from various countries, including Canada, was in the canal zone. The hostile countries withdrew and a peaceful solution was found.

This venture marked the start of international peacekeeping. For his work, Pearson was awarded the Nobel Peace Prize in 1957.

Figure 6-21 Suez Canal

Today, peacekeepers' responsibilities range from establishing and keeping peace to nation building, which helps countries in crisis make the transition to more democratic forms of government. Because Canadian governments believe that a peaceful world is in Canada's national interest, participating in peacekeeping missions is an important part of the country's foreign policy. By 2007, Canada had taken part in more than 60 peacekeeping missions, helping to implement 170 peace settlements. In many cases, these missions were responses to ultranationalist actions.

THE VIEW FROM HERE

According to the United Nations, "Peace is the most essential product of nation building." But "nation building" — like the words "nation" and "nationalism" — can mean different things to different people. Here is what three thinkers have said about nation building today. Two of the thinkers refer specifically to Afghanistan, where NATO forces were part of a UN-approved mission.

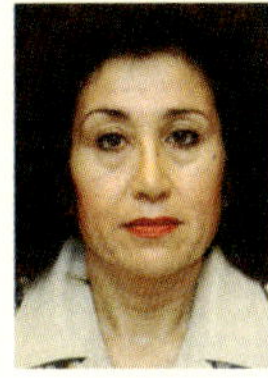

Sima Wali, who fled Afghanistan under the Taliban regime, is president of Refugee Women in Development. Wali said the following in 2002, during a UN-sponsored discussion on support for Afghan women.

> [Women's] rights as more than half of the Afghan population are threatened when partial solutions, instead of long-term engagement toward nation building, are offered . . . Anything less than a commitment from the world community to restore the rights granted to Afghan women is tantamount to succumbing to the discounting of the needs and aspirations of 67 per cent of Afghan society . . . Afghan women have fought for human rights at grave risk to themselves and their families. Fiercely dedicated to a vision of dignity, safety, and freedom, their dream to participate in the rebuilding of their own shattered lives, and that of their nation, is dependent on your commitment to help make that dream a reality.

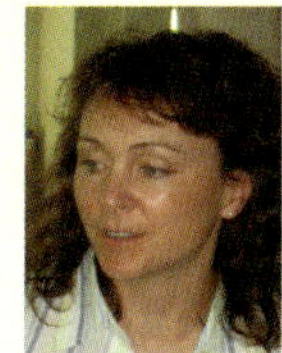

Karin von Hippel, co-director of the Post-Conflict Reconstruction Project of the Center for Strategic and International Studies in Washington, D.C., wrote the following in 2000.

> The promotion of democracy is based on the assumption that democracies rarely go to war with each other and that an increase in the number of democratic states would therefore imply, and indeed encourage, a more secure and peaceful world.
>
> Nation building, which really means state building, has over the years signified an effort to construct a government that may or may not be democratic, but preferably is stable. Today, nation building normally implies the attempt to create democratic and secure states . . . A strategy for rebuilding and democratizing states after intervention must incorporate three fundamental elements. It needs to re-establish security, empower civil society and strengthen democratic institutions, and co-ordinate international efforts.

Michael Ignatieff, a Canadian member of Parliament and historian, wrote the following in 2002. Ignatieff was commenting on the mission of American forces in Afghanistan.

> America's entire war on terror is an exercise in imperialism. This may come as a shock to Americans, who don't like to think of their country as an empire. But what else can you call America's legions of soldiers, spooks and Special Forces straddling the globe? . . .
>
> Nation building has become the cure of choice for the epidemic of ethnic civil war and state failure that has convulsed the developing world since the end of the long imperial peace of the cold war. The nation-building caravan has moved from Cambodia in 1993, where the United Nations supervised an election; to Dili, in East Timor, where it tried to create a government for a country left devastated by the departing Indonesian militias. Wherever the traveling caravan of nation builders settles, it creates an instant boomtown, living on foreign money and hope. But boomtowns inevitably go bust.

Explorations

1. Which thinker's view do you agree with most strongly? Explain why.
2. Reread each of the quoted excerpts. From each, choose several words or phrases that indicate the speaker's or writer's level of concern. Explain each of your choices in a phrase or a sentence.
3. Return to the criteria you identified for judging past actions fairly (p. 153). Apply these criteria to the situation in Afghanistan to decide whether the nation-building mission there is an appropriate use of NATO resources and whether Canada should be participating in this mission.

THINK...PARTICIPATE...RESEARCH...COMMUNICATE...

1. The shift from nationalism to ultranationalism is often accompanied by an increase in propaganda. But when does information become propaganda?
   a) Return to the three criteria you created to judge whether a government statement is simply information required by citizens or propaganda designed to promote ultranationalism (p. 140). Share your criteria with a partner and, if necessary, revise them to take into account the ideas you discussed.
   b) On your own, think of a topic related to Canada's national interest (e.g., taxation or the role of Canadian troops in Afghanistan). Create two different statements on this topic — one that is strictly informational and another that is propaganda. Test each statement against your criteria.
   c) Share your statements with your partner. Using your criteria, decide which of your partner's statements is information and which is propaganda.
   d) With your partner, develop a statement that expresses your understanding of propaganda.
2. Prepare a persuasive argument of at least three paragraphs in response to this question: Should a government ever use propaganda to persuade citizens to support its idea of the national interest?

   In your opening paragraph, include a statement that sets out your understanding of propaganda. You developed this understanding in response to Question 1.

   Include the criteria you used to arrive at this understanding.

   Continue with specific examples to support your position, and conclude by clearly restating your position.
3. When people get to know "the other" through sharing art, literature, sports, ideas, and other aspects of their lives, cross-cultural understanding is promoted. When people understand and accept diversity, it becomes more difficult to spread ultranationalist propaganda.

   Some people say that geniuses are people whose creative efforts not only changed the world in which they worked but also made lasting contributions that extended beyond their own world and culture. The artist Pablo Picasso, for example, is sometimes described as a genius because his works changed the art world — the world in which he worked — and the way people viewed art. In addition, his influence is lasting — he died in 1973, yet his works continue to influence the world today. His influence also extended beyond his own culture — Picasso was Spanish, but his art was embraced by people the world over. People from many different cultures could communicate more effectively through a shared understanding of his art.

   From this chapter, select one person who meets the criteria expressed by this understanding of genius. Explain this person's ideas, how this person changed the world in which she or he worked, and how this person made lasting contributions that extended beyond his or her own culture. When making your selection, remind yourself that not all geniuses are people who can be admired.
4. Return to the map of the Soviet Union in Figure 6-1 (p. 136). Why do you suppose the Soviet Union was set up as a union of socialist republics rather than as a single country that erased the borders between the republics?

   In your response, include ideas relating to ultranationalism.

5. Read "What Do I Remember of the Evacuation" by Joy Kogawa.
   a) In a short paragraph, tell the story related in Kogawa's poem in your own words.
   b) Kogawa's poem presents several competing views — between ages, between loyalties, between outcomes, and between points of view. List three of these conflicts. Explain them in terms of nationalist and ultranationalist ideologies.
   c) Many elements of both information and propaganda appear in this poem. Using the criteria you developed earlier, decide whether this poem is simply a remembrance of things past or a statement of propaganda — or both. Explain your conclusions.
   d) Using this poem as the basis of your answer, state the extent to which nationalism can lead to ultranationalism.

What Do I Remember of the Evacuation

Joy Kogawa

What do I remember of the evacuation?
I remember my father telling Tim and me
About the mountains and the train
And the excitement of going on a trip.
What do I remember of the evacuation?
I remember my mother wrapping
A blanket around me and my
Pretending to fall asleep so she would be happy
Though I was so excited I couldn't sleep
(I hear there were people herded
Into the Hastings Park like cattle
Families were made to move in two hours
Abandoning everything, leaving pets
And possessions at gun point.
I hear families were broken up
Men were forced to work. I heard
It whispered late at night
That there was suffering) and
I missed my dolls.
What do I remember of the evacuation?
I remember Miss Foster and Miss Tucker
Who still live in Vancouver
And who did what they could
And loved the children and who gave me
A puzzle to play with on the train.
And I remember the mountains and I was
Six years old and I swear I saw a giant
Gulliver of Gulliver's Travels scanning the horizon
And when I told my mother she believed it too
And I remember how careful my parents were
Not to bruise us with bitterness
And I remember the puzzle of Lorraine Life
Who said "Don't insult me" when I
Proudly wrote my name in Japanese
And Tim flew the Union Jack
When the war was over but Lorraine
And her friends spat on us anyway
And I prayed to God who loves
All the children in his sight
That I might be white.

Think about Your Challenge

At this point, you should have decided on the format of your investigative report on a nationalist movement. You should also have started filling in the chart (see p. 113) you are keeping to help plan your report.

Return to page 112 and review the elements required to complete your report successfully. These include the back story about the movement, the people involved, the movement's current status, and predictions about whether and how this movement is likely to affect people in the future. Ask a partner or your teacher for feedback on your ideas and work so far. Adjust your material in light of the feedback you receive.

CHAPTER 7 Ultranationalism and Crimes against Humanity

Figure 7-1 On August 6, 1945, an American plane dropped an atomic bomb on the Japanese city of Hiroshima. About 70 000 people died instantly, and the city lay in ruins. The photograph at the bottom shows the mushroom cloud created by the bomb. The building in the photograph at the top left was the closest structure to the blast to remain standing — and its ruins have been preserved and transformed into the Hiroshima Peace Memorial (bottom right). On August 6 every year, people commemorate the devastating event by floating paper lanterns on the river that flows past the memorial.

CHAPTER ISSUE

To what extent can the pursuit of ultranationalism lead to crimes against humanity?

In May 1945, Germany surrendered and the Second World War was over in Europe. But Japanese troops were still fighting in the Pacific, though they had been falling back. American leaders were preparing to invade Japan in the fall of 1945. Many Americans believed that the Japanese commanders were so dedicated that they would never surrender. If they fought to the bitter end, millions of Japanese civilians and soldiers, as well as thousands of Americans, would die.

So on August 6, 1945, the United States dropped an atomic bomb on Hiroshima. Three days later, a second atomic bomb was dropped on Nagasaki — and Japan surrendered. World War II was completely over.

No American lives were lost in the bombings, but the damage to the two Japanese cities was on a scale the world had never seen before.

Examine the photographs on the previous page, then respond to the following questions:

- What do you feel when you look at the photograph of the destruction of Hiroshima?
- Invade Japan or drop the atomic bombs? Were these the only alternatives available to American leaders? Was there another way World War II could have been ended quickly?
- Was dropping the atomic bombs an appropriate response to Japanese ultranationalism?
- Was dropping the atomic bombs on Hiroshima and Nagasaki an act of ultranationalism?

KEY TERMS

genocide

crimes against humanity

war crimes

Holocaust

ethnic cleansing

Looking Ahead

In this chapter, you will develop responses to the following questions as you explore the extent to which ultranationalism and crimes against humanity are related:

- What are crimes against humanity?
- How has ultranationalism caused crimes against humanity?
- What are some contemporary consequences of ultranationalism?

My Journal on Nationalism

Look back at the journal entry you made at the beginning of Chapter 6. Has your understanding of nationalism changed since then? Explain how. Using words or pictures — or both — express your current ideas on nationalism and ultranationalism. Date your ideas and keep them in your journal, notebook, learning log, portfolio, or computer file so that you can return to them as you progress through this course.

What are crimes against humanity?

We knew the world would not be the same . . . I remembered the line from the Hindu scripture, the Bhagavad-Gita. Vishnu is trying to persuade the Prince that he should do his duty and to impress him [Vishnu] takes on his multi-armed form and says, "Now, I am become Death, the destroyer of worlds." I suppose we all thought that one way or another.

— J. Robert Oppenheimer, director of the American project that developed the atom bomb, when he heard about Hiroshima, 1945

People's dedication to their nation can help it grow and prosper, and strong, charismatic leaders can instill feelings of pride. But passionate nationalism and strong leaders can also lead to the excesses of ultranationalism when one group of people commits crimes against other groups.

When Japanese soldiers invaded the Chinese city of Nanjing in 1937, for example, they murdered an estimated 300 000 men, women, and children on orders from the highest ranks of the Japanese military. Nanjing's streets were littered with dead bodies.

Years later, Hong Guiying, a survivor of the massacre, told her story: "I was only seven when the Japanese troops invaded Nanjing, and my family lived at Jishan Village at that time. I saw with my own eyes the Japanese army killing many people of Nanjing with bayonets. Both my father and uncle were killed by Japanese army with bayonet[s]. The house of my family was burnt, and the cattle for plowing was seized away. Many of our neighbors were killed."

Figure 7-2 A mother and child sit amid the destruction in Hiroshima four months after the bomb was dropped. Many of those who lived through the atomic blast died later of starvation or radiation sickness.

In the closing days of World War II, American scientists like J. Robert Oppenheimer, who is quoted in "Voices," developed an atomic bomb. The United States dropped two of these bombs on Japanese cities, and by the end of 1945, up to 140 000 Japanese people had died. In later years, radiation from the bomb continued to make people sick, and thousands more died of leukemia and other forms of cancer.

Hiroshi Sawachika, a doctor, estimated that on the day of the bombing, he treated up to 3000 victims in his hospital on the outskirts of Hiroshima. "I felt as if once that day started, it never ended," Sawachika recalled later. "I had to keep on and on treating the patients forever . . . I learned that the nuclear weapons which gnaw the minds and bodies of human beings should never be used. Even the slightest idea [of] using nuclear arms should be completely exterminated [from] the minds of human beings. Otherwise, we will repeat the same tragedy. And we will never stop being ashamed of ourselves."

The massacre in Nanjing and the dropping of atomic bombs on Japan, along with other horrific events, have fuelled a debate over how the world should respond.

Naming the Crimes

Events like the massacre that occurred in Nanjing sparked many of the countries that belong to the United Nations to agree on definitions of genocide, crimes against humanity, and war crimes.

- **Genocide** refers to the killing of members of a national, ethnic, racial, or religious group; causing serious bodily or mental harm to members of the group; and deliberately inflicting on the group conditions of life calculated to bring about its physical destruction.
- **Crimes against humanity** refers to widespread or systematic attacks against a civilian population — murder, extermination, enslavement, deportation, imprisonment, torture, rape or sexual slavery, enforced disappearance of persons, and the crime of apartheid.
- **War crimes** refers to wilful killing, torture, or inhuman treatment; wilfully causing great suffering; and intentionally directing attacks against the civilian population or against those who are involved in a humanitarian or peacekeeping mission.

These definitions were written by the International Criminal Court, a permanent court that was conceived by the UN in 1998 and supported by many countries, including Canada. With specific legal definitions of these crimes, the ICC can both try and judge people accused of "the most serious crimes of international concern."

Although the ICC is an international court, the countries that support it believe they are operating in their national interest. Peace in the world and security of persons are considered to be in the interest of all countries — and, by extension, so is bringing to justice those who break the peace and deny people's security of person.

With a partner, discuss what Canadian national interests are served by the country's support of the ICC. Develop a statement that supports or opposes Canada's commitment to the ICC — and explain the reasons for your judgment.

In the twentieth century, genocide and mass murders — all crimes against humanity — have killed an estimated 60 million men, women and children — more than were killed in battlefields in all the wars from 1900 to 2000.

— *Barbara Coloroso, author and educator, in* Extraordinary Evil: A Brief History of Genocide, *2007*

How would arriving at definitions of terms like "genocide," "crimes against humanity," and "war crimes" make a difference?

Figure 7-3 Estimated Victims of Genocide and Mass Murders in the 20th Century

National Group	Number Killed
Armenians	1.5 million
Bengalis	1.5 million
Burundians	250 000
Cambodians	1.7 million
Chinese	25 million
East Timorese	200 000
Guatemalans	200 000
Ibos	1 million
Indonesians	500 000
Jews	6 million
Kosovars	10 000
North Koreans	2 million
Roma and Sinti	250 000
Russians	25 million
Rwandans	800 000
Slavs	6 million
Sudanese	2 million
Ugandans	500 000
Ukrainians	3 million

Source: Genocide Watch, 2008

Ultranationalism and Crimes against Humanity

Hate has a nearly limitless ability to dehumanize its victims, shutting down the most basic human capacities for sympathy and compassion.

— Rush W. Dozier Jr., journalist and author, in Why We Hate*, 2002*

Just as nationalism can lead to ultranationalism, ultranationalism can lead to racism and to treating people as if they are less than human. A bigot or racist who treats a particular group of people with contempt may have taken the first step toward treating members of the entire group inhumanely.

Ultranationalists may start by segregating the people they despise, perhaps by excluding them from certain areas, forcing them to live in ghettos, and denying their rights as citizens. The movements of victims of bigotry and racism are often restricted, and they may be pushed to the margins of society and blamed for things that go wrong in a country. Their culture is often destroyed, and they may be deported from their homeland and even murdered. In an ultranationalist state, laws allow actions like these to be carried out as official government policy.

Create a diagram that shows how nationalism, ultranationalism, and racism can be connected.

Bigots and racists are often afraid of the truth. The Turkish journalist Hrant Dink, for example, was killed because he told the story of the Armenian genocide that had taken place during World War I. In Turkey, official state policy denies that this massacre took place and the law makes it a crime to speak of the Armenian genocide.

Figure 7-4 In 1944, these Jewish women and children had just arrived at the Auschwitz-Birkenau death camp. They had been classified by the Nazis as "not fit for work" and waited in a field outside Crematorium IV. They were killed shortly after this picture was taken. Most of the people who entered Auschwitz had little idea of the fate that awaited them.

In ultranationalist states, genocide and crimes against humanity are state-sponsored acts of murder. The murderers believe that these acts promote their national interest. But although the laws that exclude ethnic groups or condemn them to death may be state policy, the crimes are carried out by individuals and the victims are individuals. The child in the centre of Figure 7-4 had a name and a family. The German soldiers who carried out the killings at Auschwitz-Birkenau also had names and families.

Reflect and Respond

Revisit your responses to the questions (p. 159) that opened this chapter. On the basis of the definitions of crimes against humanity, genocide, and war crimes, as well as what you have read and discussed so far, do you wish to revise your answers to any of the questions? Explain why or why not.

How has ultranationalism caused crimes against humanity?

In the past, ultranationalist sentiments and beliefs have caused people to commit crimes against humanity, genocide, and war crimes. Some nation-states — including Germany, Turkey, Japan, and the Soviet Union — had approved these crimes and created policies that encouraged them. As a result, some ethnic nations have nearly disappeared.

Around the world, people study these crimes to try to understand why they happened and what can be done to ensure that they do not happen again.

Peer pressure involves the desire to feel a sense of belonging by going along with group actions. To what extent do you think peer pressure is a factor in motivating ordinary people to commit crimes against humanity, genocide, or war crimes? Explain your judgment.

Web Connection

To find out more about individuals and organizations that are working to prevent genocide, go to this web site and follow the links.

www.ExploringNationalism.ca

Genocide in Turkey — 1915

In the early 20th century, the country that emerged as Turkey in 1922 was still part of the Ottoman Empire. Islam was the official religion, but the empire included many Armenians. Most Armenians were Christians who had maintained their national identity, language, and culture even though they had lived under Ottoman rule for hundreds of years. As a result of their choice to affirm their identity, Armenians often suffered discrimination. In the late 1800s, some Armenian nationalists began fighting for self-determination. They lost this fight, and the Turks killed thousands in the aftermath.

Is a nation that refuses to acknowledge guilt for crimes against humanity doomed to repeat these crimes?

Turkish nationalism became more extreme during World War I, as Turks fought on the side of Germany against the British, Russians, and their allies. When some Armenian nationalists sided with the Russians, they were branded traitors.

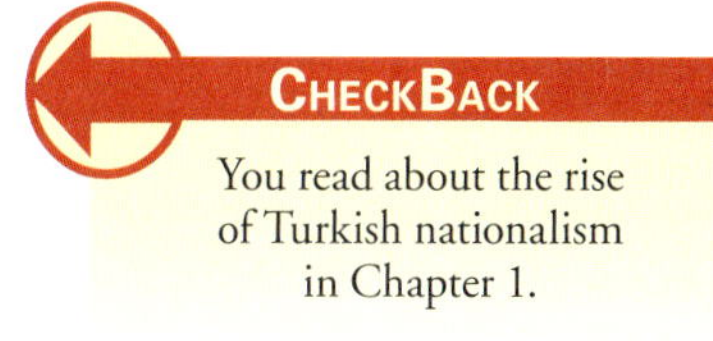

Examine the map in Figure 7-5. Why might some Armenian nationalists look to Russia as a natural ally?

In 1914, the Young Turks — an ultranationalist political party that controlled the Ottoman-Turkish government — issued orders calling for the massacre of Armenians. The orders, which are often called the "Ten Commandments," included the following instructions:

- Apply measures to exterminate all males under 50, priests, and teachers; leave girls and children to be Islamized.
- Carry away the families of all who succeed in escaping and apply measures to cut them off from all connection with their native place.
- Kill off in an appropriate manner all Armenians in the army — this to be left to the military to do.

Figure 7-5 Routes of Armenian Forced Marches, 1915

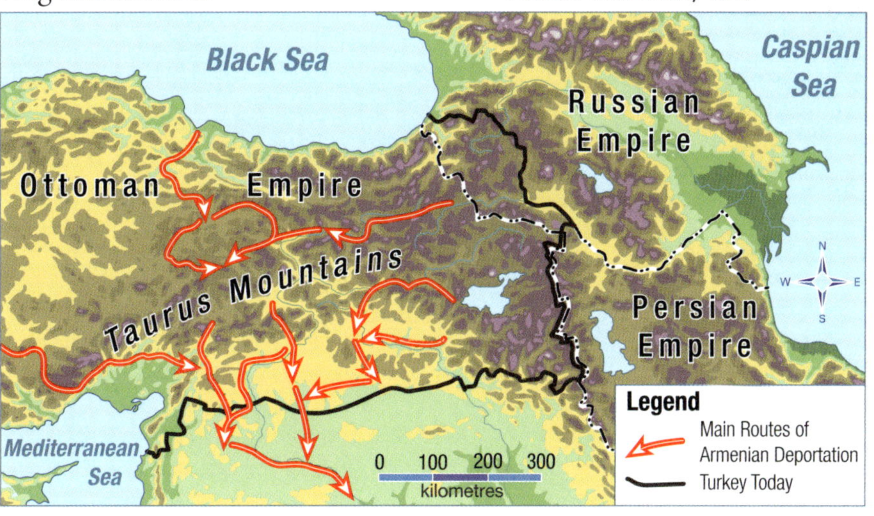

There was a place near Mush where three rivers come together and pass under a bridge . . . My mother went there . . . and saw hundreds of our men lined up on the bridge, face to face. Then the soldiers shot at them from both sides . . . The Turks took the clothes and valuables off the bodies and then they took the bodies by the hands and feet and threw them into the water.

— Mayreni Kaloustian, Armenian genocide survivor, 1992

State-Sponsored Crimes

On April 24, 1915, Turkish soldiers began carrying out the orders they had been given. Armenian community leaders were arrested. Hundreds of thousands were murdered, and the army began the forced deportation of many more. Without food or water, people were forced to walk over mountains and through barren regions toward Syria and the present-day country of Iraq. Though some Turks tried to help and shelter Armenians, fewer than 100 000 of the country's 2 million Armenians survived the slaughter.

Henry Morgenthau Sr. was the American ambassador to Constantinople, now Istanbul. Morgenthau and other foreign observers witnessed and documented the events. In letters to Washington, Morgenthau called the marches a "new method of massacre," with caravans of Armenians "winding in and out of every valley and climbing up the sides of nearly every mountain — moving on and on, they scarcely knew whither, except that every road led to death."

During the war, France and Britain pledged to hold the Ottoman government responsible for the deaths of the Armenians. But after the war, little was done. Turkey did find some of the leaders guilty of murder, but they had all escaped to Germany by the time the trial was held in 1919.

Figure 7-6 In 2005, Armenians and others rallied in various cities around the world to commemorate the 90th anniversary of the genocide. At a rally in New York City, Anne Zartarian held a picture of her father as a child with his two siblings, who both died in the genocide. Why might it be important to Armenians that the genocide be recognized? Why might it be important to Turks to deny that it happened?

Recognizing the Armenian Genocide

Today, many people label this massacre of Armenians a genocide. Canada was one of the first countries to officially support this designation. In 2004, Parliament adopted a motion that said, "This House acknowledges the Armenian genocide of 1915 and condemns this act as a crime against humanity."

The Turkish government admits that many Armenians died in 1915 and 1916, but it denies that the deaths were planned. Turkish officials say that the deaths were caused by inter-ethnic violence and the war.

British journalist Robert Fisk, who has studied the Middle East extensively, says that many Germans witnessed the Armenian genocide, because Germany and Turkey were allies during World War I. Fisk believes that this genocide — and the lack of international action to bring to justice those responsible — provided the model that Adolf Hitler drew on when he initiated the genocide of Jews during World War II. In *The Great War for Civilisation*, Fisk reported that Hitler told a newspaper editor as early as 1931, "We intend to introduce a great resettlement policy . . . remember the extermination of the Armenians."

Famine in Ukraine — 1932–1933

Before the Russian Revolution of 1917, much of Ukraine had been ruled by Russia for nearly 150 years. During the 19th century, Ukrainian nationalism was on the rise, and in 1918, after the revolution, Ukraine tried unsuccessfully to declare independence.

Large areas of Ukraine are ideal for growing wheat, and the region was known as the breadbasket of Europe. Prosperous *kulaks* — farmers who owned land and livestock — were among the strongest supporters of the independence movement. But when Joseph Stalin took control of the Soviet Union in the late 1920s, he decreed that Ukraine's farmland was to belong to the state and that the people were to work the land on collective farms. Many *kulaks* resisted, often by burning their crops and killing their livestock rather than turn them over to the state.

Stalin responded in 1932 by shipping the Ukrainian wheat crop to Russia. Much of this wheat was then sold in foreign markets to raise the cash Stalin needed to build the Soviet army and carry out his plans to modernize the country. Stalin then sealed Ukraine's borders — no one could get out to buy food and no food could get in.

Soviet troops seized the seed grain and remaining food on Ukrainian farms. Anyone caught hiding grain or not co-operating was either executed or deported to forced-labour camps. By the end of 1933, Soviet granaries were full of Ukrainian wheat but between three and seven million Ukrainians had starved to death or been killed by Soviet authorities.

Rumours about the disaster circulated, but Soviet authorities censored news reports, and few outsiders knew what was happening. In fact, as Ukrainians were dying, Western newspapers were praising Stalin's drive to modernize the Soviet Union.

Figure 7-7 Halyna Panasiuk, who now lives in Winnipeg, lived through the famine in Ukraine. At the age of nine, she became used to seeing the dead in her village of Horbinci. She told her story in a 2007 documentary film, saying, "I want people to know the truth because there are still people who are denying what happened. I lived it."

Figure 7-8 In November 2005, Ukrainians gathered at a monument in Kiev, Ukraine's capital, to remember victims of the famine of the 1930s. Why would it be important to Ukrainians to build a memorial like this to honour those who died in the famine?

Some people believe that contemporary mass communication systems will make genocide impossible. Write an e-mail or text message responding to this position.

Recognizing the Ukrainian Genocide

Stalin always denied that he had deliberately starved the Ukrainian people. And even after his death in 1953, Soviet leaders continued to deny that the famine was caused by the state. In November 2006, the Ukrainian parliament declared that the *Holodomor* — the famine plague — was an act of genocide against Ukrainians. But Russia does not accept this judgment.

Still, many historians agree that Soviet policies caused the Ukrainian famine. In 2003, the Canadian Senate adopted a motion calling on the federal government to recognize the famine as a genocide, and in 2007, the Manitoba government declared that it was a genocide.

Shoah — The Holocaust

IMPACT

In 1938, Josef Pitel of Parczev, Poland, was preparing to immigrate to Israel. Before he left, family members gathered for the photograph shown in Figure 7-9. The Pitels were Jews — and when the Nazis invaded Poland, they rounded up the Pitels, along with hundreds of thousands of other Polish Jews, and sent them to Treblinka, a death camp. There, the Pitels were murdered in 1943. At the end of the war, Josef was the only family member still alive.

Figure 7-9 Josef Pitel, the man standing at the right in this family photograph, immigrated to Israel just before the outbreak of World War II. Of the 26 people in the photograph, Pitel was the only survivor. He carried this photograph to Israel with him, and it is now part of Jerusalem's Yad Vashem museum archive of images and names of those who died in the Holocaust.

Genocide

The **Holocaust** — or *Shoah* in Hebrew — is the term used to describe the genocide of about six million Jews during World War II. When the war began, about nine million Jews lived in the 21 countries that were invaded by Germany. Only about three million of these Jews were still alive in 1945.

The ultranationalistic dream of Adolf Hitler, the Nazi dictator, was to build a German empire of pure Aryans. "Aryans" was the word the Nazis used to describe members of the white race. In addition to Jews, the Nazis persecuted and killed millions of Roma and Slav peoples, Communists, homosexual men, people with disabilities, Freemasons, and Jehovah's Witnesses.

International Response to the Threat

During the 1930s, the rest of the world largely ignored what was happening in Germany. Many countries were struggling with the Great Depression. They wanted to avoid war and did not consider intervening to be in their national interest.

In addition, anti-Semitism was common in many countries, including Canada. In early 1939, for example, more than 900 Jewish refugees tried to flee Germany on a ship named the *St. Louis*. Canada was one of the countries where they tried to land, but no country was willing to accept them.

Frederick Blair, who oversaw immigration in Canada, explained the country's refusal. "If these Jews were to find a home [in Canada], they would likely be followed by other shiploads," he said. "No country could open its doors wide enough to take in the hundreds of thousands of Jewish people who want to leave Europe: the line must be drawn somewhere." In the end, the *St. Louis* was sent back to Europe, where many of its passengers died in Nazi death camps.

Still, people in some countries did intervene. The city of Shanghai in China, for example, accepted tens of thousands of Jewish refugees. And many people in German-occupied Denmark hid Jews at great personal risk and smuggled thousands to safety in neutral Sweden.

Growing Awareness

As World War II dragged on, the international community learned more about the genocide. In August 1942, Gerhart Riegner, the United States' representative at the World Jewish Congress in Switzerland, told his government that the Nazis intended to exterminate all the Jews of Europe. At first, Riegner was not believed, and even after his information was verified, little was done to help the thousands who were dying in the camps every day.

Some people argued that the Allies should bomb the camps and the rail lines leading to them. But others said that doing this would also kill the Jewish people in the camps and on the trains.

In April 1945, Allied forces liberated the German death camps, such as Auschwitz-Birkenau, Buchenwald, and Bergen-Belsen. The liberators found thousands of prisoners suffering from disease and starvation. In some camps, bodies had been piled in the open and left unburied. It was clear that these camps had been used for the sole purpose of killing people. Around the world, people learned the extent of the horror through photographs and radio and newspaper reports.

Why Remembering Matters

In 1986, Holocaust survivor Elie Wiesel won the Nobel Peace Prize for his work in the cause of peace and human rights. In his acceptance speech, Wiesel remembered family members, teachers, and friends who had died at the hands of Nazi ultranationalists. He spoke of why remembering genocide matters.

> I remember: it happened yesterday, or eternities ago. A young Jewish boy discovered the Kingdom of Night. I remember his bewilderment, I remember his anguish. It all happened so fast. The ghetto. The deportation. The sealed cattle car. The fiery altar upon which the history of our people and the future of mankind were meant to be sacrificed.
>
> I remember he asked his father: "Can this be true? This is the 20th century, not the Middle Ages. Who would allow such crimes to be committed? How could the world remain silent?"
>
> And now the boy is turning to me. "Tell me," he asks, "what have you done with my future, what have you done with your life?" And I tell him that I have tried. That I have tried to keep memory alive, that I have tried to fight those who would forget. Because if we forget, we are guilty, we are accomplices.
>
> And then I explain to him how naïve we were, that the world did know and remained silent. And that is why I swore never to be silent whenever wherever human beings endure suffering and humiliation. We must take sides. Neutrality helps the oppressor, never the victim. Silence encourages the tormentor, never the tormented. Sometimes we must interfere. When human lives are endangered, when human dignity is in jeopardy, national borders and sensitivities become irrelevant. Wherever men and women are persecuted because of their race, religion, or political views, that place must – at that moment – become the center of the universe.

Figure 7-10 Elie Wiesel stands in front of a photograph of himself and other prisoners. The picture was taken by an American soldier five days after Buchenwald was liberated. Wiesel, who was 17 at the time, is in the bottom right-hand corner of the picture, which now hangs in the Yad Vashem Holocaust memorial in Jerusalem.

Explorations

1. Do the responses of Canada and the international community to the treatment of Jews before and during World War II affect your view of Canada as a caring country? Explain why or why not.
2. Should the many governments and individuals who did nothing to stop the persecution of Jews and others in Germany be considered guilty of crimes against humanity? Explain your response.
3. The guards at the Nazi death camps, the contractors who built the death chambers, the clerks who registered the numbers tattooed on every Jew, and many more people involved in Adolf Hitler's extermination program were all ordinary citizens with spouses, children, mothers, fathers, boyfriends, girlfriends, and neighbours. With this in mind, explain whether you think similar crimes against humanity could happen in Canada. Provide reasons for your judgment.

The Bombing of Hiroshima and Nagasaki — 1945

Policies designed to support national interest are often intended to protect the physical security of a nation and its people, to ensure their economic stability and prosperity, and to protect and promote their values, beliefs, and culture.

Many people argued that dropping the atom bombs on Hiroshima and Nagasaki in 1945 was in the United States' national interest. Some U.S. military experts had estimated that as many as 250 000 Americans might die in an invasion of Japan. These experts warned that ultranationalist warrior values would prevent Japanese soldiers and civilians from surrendering — and that dropping the bombs would save American and Japanese lives.

CheckBack

You read about aspects of national interest and national policies in Chapter 5.

U.S. president Harry S. Truman made the final decision to drop the bombs. Truman believed that it was important to end the war and save as many lives as possible. In an address to the country immediately after the bombing of Hiroshima, he said that the United States would completely destroy Japan's power to wage war only if American forces destroyed "every productive enterprise the Japanese have above ground in any city." These enterprises included docks, factories, and communication systems.

Should U.S. President Harry S. Truman have been accused of war crimes for dropping the two atomic bombs on Japan?

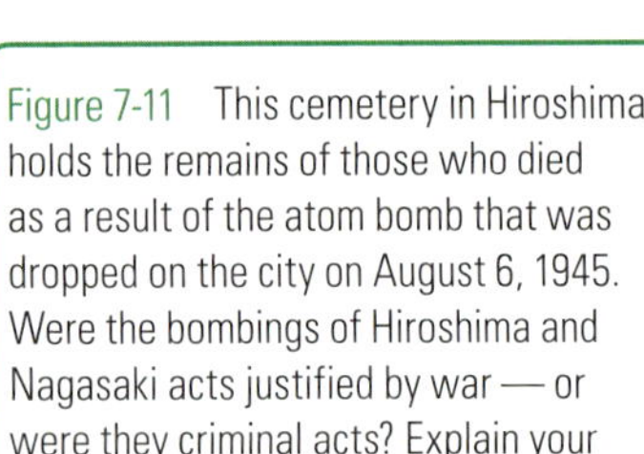

Some of the scientists who had helped build the atomic bomb asked Truman to warn Japan about what was coming. They suggested demonstrating the bomb's destructive force in an uninhabited place — perhaps in Tokyo Bay — so that Japanese leaders would realize the weapon's potential.

General Dwight D. Eisenhower, who had commanded the victorious Allied forces in Europe and who would go on to become president, disagreed with Truman's decision to drop the bomb. Eisenhower said that he had grave misgivings about the action. He believed that Japan was already defeated and said, "Our country should avoid shocking world opinion by the use of a weapon whose employment was . . . no longer mandatory as a measure to save American lives."

Figure 7-11 This cemetery in Hiroshima holds the remains of those who died as a result of the atom bomb that was dropped on the city on August 6, 1945. Were the bombings of Hiroshima and Nagasaki acts justified by war — or were they criminal acts? Explain your response.

Reflect and Respond

With a small group, return to the definitions on page 161. Choose the Armenian genocide, the famine in Ukraine, or the Holocaust. With your group, discuss how ultranationalism caused the crime you chose.

Sum up your discussion in a brief statement and appoint one group member to read it to the class. Be prepared to respond to questions from your classmates.

THE VIEW FROM HERE

Arguments about whether dropping an atomic bomb on civilians was justified began even before the *Enola Gay*, a B-29 Superfortress bomber, dropped the first bomb on Hiroshima at 8:16 a.m. on August 6, 1945. Since then, the debate over whether dropping this bomb was in the national interest of the United States — or of humanity — has continued.

Leó Szilárd, an American physicist of Hungarian descent, was involved in the Manhattan Project, the program that developed the atom bomb. He made the following remarks in a 1960 interview with *U.S. News and World Report*.

> Let me say only this much to the moral issue involved: Suppose Germany had developed two bombs before we had any bombs. And suppose Germany had dropped one bomb, say, on Rochester and the other on Buffalo, and then having run out of bombs she would have lost the war. Can anyone doubt that we would then have defined the dropping of atomic bombs on cities as a war crime, and that we would have sentenced the Germans who were guilty of this crime to death at Nuremberg and hanged them?

In 1995, **Mitsuo Okamoto**, a professor of peace studies at Shudo University in Hiroshima, made these comments when a controversy erupted in the United States over the Smithsonian Institution's plans to exhibit the *Enola Gay* and photographs of victims of the atomic bomb. Some American war veterans protested portraying the Japanese people as victims.

> If it is difficult for a defeated nation like Japan to admit her sins, it must be far more difficult for a victorious nation like the U.S. to admit. To show the *Enola Gay* without showing the tragedy of Hiroshima is to blind people to history. To show Hiroshima without showing Japanese aggression of Asian countries is to abandon historical responsibility.

Oliver Kamm is a British journalist whose columns appear in *The Guardian*. The following excerpt is from a column he wrote on August 6, 2006, the 51st anniversary of the Hiroshima bombing.

> Hiroshima and Nagasaki are often used as a shorthand term for war crimes. That is not how they were judged at the time. Our side did terrible things to avoid a more terrible outcome. The bomb was a deliverance for American troops, for prisoners and slave labourers, for those dying of hunger and maltreatment throughout the Japanese empire – and for Japan itself. One of Japan's highest wartime officials, Kido Koichi, later testified that in his view the August surrender prevented 20 million Japanese casualties.

Explorations

1. Create a T-chart like the one shown and list arguments for and against dropping the atomic bombs on Hiroshima and Nagasaki.

Arguments for and against Dropping the Atomic Bombs	
For	Against

2. Which side — for or against — do you believe is supported by stronger arguments? Explain the reasons for your judgment.
3. Since the bombings of Hiroshima and Nagasaki, the world's nuclear powers have been involved in many wars, but nuclear weapons have never again been used in warfare. Why might a nuclear power involved in a war decide that it is not in its national interest to use nuclear weapons?

What are some contemporary consequences of ultranationalism?

Since the end of World War II, many countries have tried to find ways to eliminate the extreme forms of nationalism that lead to crimes against humanity and genocide. They realize that it is in all countries' — and all peoples' — national interest to eliminate these crimes because they threaten the peace, security, and well-being of all peoples in all countries.

Bringing Criminals to Justice

After the League of Nations failed to prevent the horrors of World War II, world leaders were determined to create an international body that would preserve peace in the world. They believed that a forum where conflicts could be resolved peacefully was in every nation's interest — and the United Nations emerged from these discussions.

In 1945, the UN was in its infancy and had no permanent court to try war criminals. As a result, the victorious Allies set up the international military tribunals that tried German and Japanese individuals and government organizations for crimes against peace, war crimes, and crimes against humanity.

Since then, the UN has been criticized for taking too long to respond to situations in which ultranationalist states or groups within states commit crimes against humanity. For the UN, trying to accommodate the demands of all its member countries — each focused on its own national interests — has been a challenge. Although the UN's founding principles are designed to prevent crimes that are often motivated by ultranationalism, some people believe that the UN has failed to deal with contemporary cases of genocide, crimes against humanity, and war crimes.

The International Criminal Court

In 1948, the UN established a committee to work toward creating an international criminal court, a task that took more than 50 years to complete. One of the chief stumbling blocks was the debate over how the court would operate without infringing the sovereignty of member states. Persuading countries to agree on the laws the court would be responsible for enforcing was another challenge.

The statute creating the International Criminal Court was finally signed by 60 countries in 2002. By early 2008, 45 more countries had signed on. The ICC is sponsored by, but operates independently of, the UN. It is a court of last resort, which means that it will not act if those accused of genocide, crimes against humanity, and war crimes are tried fairly in a national court.

Examine Figure 7-12. The United States, China, and many other countries have not recognized the ICC and refuse to co-operate with it. With a partner, suggest reasons that might explain this choice. Work with your partner to develop two arguments that might persuade these countries to change their mind.

Figure 7-12 Signatories to the International Criminal Court Statute

Some Signatories
Afghanistan
Bosnia and Herzegovina
Cambodia
Canada
France
Germany
Japan
Britain

Some Non-Signatories
China
India
Indonesia
Pakistan
Turkey
United States

Crimes against Humanity in the Former Yugoslavia

At the Paris Peace Conference of 1918–1919, various nations in the area known as the Balkans were merged into a single country called Yugoslavia. Though these nations often shared a history of bitter fighting with one another, their peoples coexisted more or less peacefully until the early 1990s.

By the late 20th century, Yugoslavia was a tightly controlled communist state. When the Soviet Union started to collapse in the late 1980s, nationalist and ultranationalist sentiments bubbled to the surface. In 1991, Slovenia and Croatia declared independence, and Macedonia and Bosnia and Herzegovina followed in 1992. Serbia and Montenegro formed the Federal Republic of Yugoslavia under the leadership of the Serbian ultranationalist Slobodan Milošević.

Figure 7-13 Yugoslavia, 1990

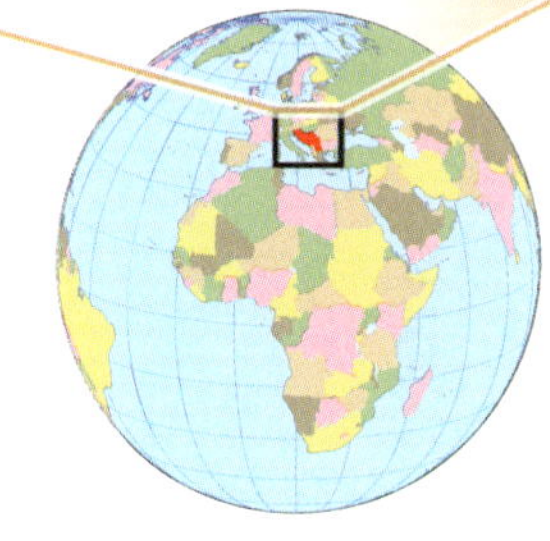

Serbian Ultranationalists and the Siege of Sarajevo

Slobodan Milošević believed that Serbs formed an ethnic nation and that everyone else should be expelled from Serbian territory. He called the expulsion process **ethnic cleansing**, a code word or euphemism designed to make what was happening seem more socially acceptable. But in reality, Serbs were killing non-Serbs. Milošević also sent Serbian forces to help ultranationalist Bosnian Serbs drive non-Serbs out of Bosnia and Herzegovina. There, non-Serbs were harassed. They were not allowed to meet in public places, move to another town without permission, or travel by car.

Sarajevo, the capital of Bosnia and Herzegovina, had once been an integrated city where Orthodox Serbs, Catholic Croats, and Bosnian Muslims lived and worked together. But soon after Bosnia and Herzegovina declared independence, Serbian ultranationalist forces besieged the city. The siege continued until February 1996. During that time, citizens faced constant bombardments and sniper attacks. Internationally renowned centres of Muslim culture — including the National and University Library and the Oriental Institute — were destroyed.

In June 1992, the United Nations Security Council warned Serbian forces to stop attacking Sarajevo — or face military action. Although UN peacekeepers were sent to the country and tried to deliver humanitarian relief and establish safe areas where people were protected, the killing continued. The UN forces had been ordered to remain neutral so they could continue to get food to the besieged city.

Some people believed that the UN did not do enough to stop the massacre of the citizens of Sarajevo. By thc time the siege was finally lifted on February 29, 1996, the death toll in the city had risen to more than 11 000.

Figure 7-14 In 1993, these women were running across a Sarajevo street nicknamed "Sniper Alley." Serb nationalist forces on the hills around the city shot at civilians as they tried to go about their daily lives.

Web Connection

To find out the latest developments at the Criminal Tribunal for the Former Yugoslavia, go to this web site and follow the links.

www.ExploringNationalism.ca

In 1993, the UN Security Council established the International Criminal Tribunal for the Former Yugoslavia. In 2002, Milošević was put on trial for genocide and crimes against humanity, but he died before the end of his trial. The tribunal charged Radovan Karadžić, the Bosnian Serb leader, and Ratko Mladić, Karadžić's army chief, with similar crimes, but the two remained at large in early 2008.

General Dragomir Milošević — no relation to Slobodan Milošević — had commanded the Bosnian Serb forces that besieged Sarajevo. In 2007, the tribunal found him guilty of five counts of murder, inflicting terror, and committing inhumane acts. He was sentenced to 33 years in prison.

MAKING A DIFFERENCE

Louise Arbour
Speaking Out for Human Rights

MAKING A DIFFERENCE
MAKING A DIFFERENC
MAKING A DIFFERENCE

When Montréal-born Francophone Louise Arbour was appointed chief prosecutor of the international criminal tribunals for the former Yugoslavia and Rwanda in 1996, she faced an uphill battle. The tribunals had made little progress in bringing to justice those accused of genocide, and some critics questioned whether Arbour would be able to change this situation.

But by the time she stepped down in 1999, Arbour had silenced her critics. On her watch, Slobodan Milošević and others on various sides of the conflicts had been charged with genocide and crimes against humanity for their roles in the killings. In September 2007, Arbour said that the significance of the charges "was to really capture the world's attention on this new tool that the international community had equipped itself with, which is the law, international criminal law." Arbour also spearheaded efforts to establish the permanent International Criminal Court.

In 1999, she left the UN when Prime Minister Jean Chrétien appointed her to the Supreme Court of Canada. In 2004, she left the Supreme Court to serve a four-year term as the UN's high commissioner for human rights.

As high commissioner, Arbour's job was to investigate human rights violations. She condemned, for example, the American government's treatment of terrorism suspects in its Guantanamo Bay prison, saying that holding prisoners there without trial violates their human rights.

Figure 7-15 As chief prosecutor of the International Criminal Tribunal for the Former Yugoslavia, Louise Arbour carried out investigations in the field. In this photograph, she and a team of forensic experts view the grave of a teenage girl who was allegedly executed by Serb forces in Celine, Kosovo. This girl was among 57 village residents whose bodies were thrown into nine graves after they were allegedly executed.

Arbour's passionate stand on this and many other human rights issues earned criticism from various quarters, but human rights groups supported her enthusiastically. A spokesperson for Amnesty International, for example, said that the criticism was a tribute to her work: "She's been outspoken. She's been unflinching in challenging human rights violations in big and powerful countries as well as in countries not so big and not so powerful."

Explorations

1. Comment on Louise Arbour's belief that international criminal law is an effective tool in fighting crimes against humanity.
2. Create a motto that captures Arbour's passion for human rights.

Crimes against Humanity in Rwanda

CHECKFORWARD

You will read more about Rwanda and Roméo Dallaire in Chapter 10.

The country now known as Rwanda is home to two ethnic groups: Hutus and Tutsis. Although Hutus formed the majority, Tutsis held much of the political power — because they were favoured by the Belgians, who had controlled the country when it was a colony.

After Rwanda gained independence in 1962, this imbalance in power sparked decades of civil conflict. Eventually, the majority Hutus gained control of the country, but the struggle between the two groups continued. Many Rwandans can neither read nor write, and radio is the most popular form of mass communication. Hutu ultranationalists used this medium to wage a propaganda campaign against Tutsis. Some broadcasts urged killing all Tutsis, and specific people were sometimes labelled enemies of the nation and singled out as targets of death squads. Once these "enemies" had been murdered, their killers were often congratulated on air.

Figure 7-16 Rwanda

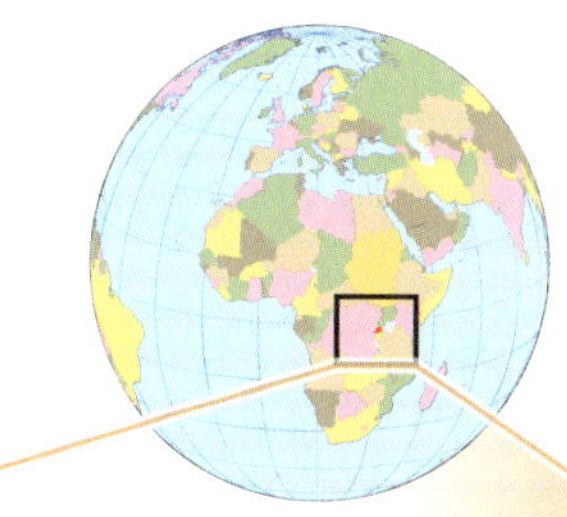

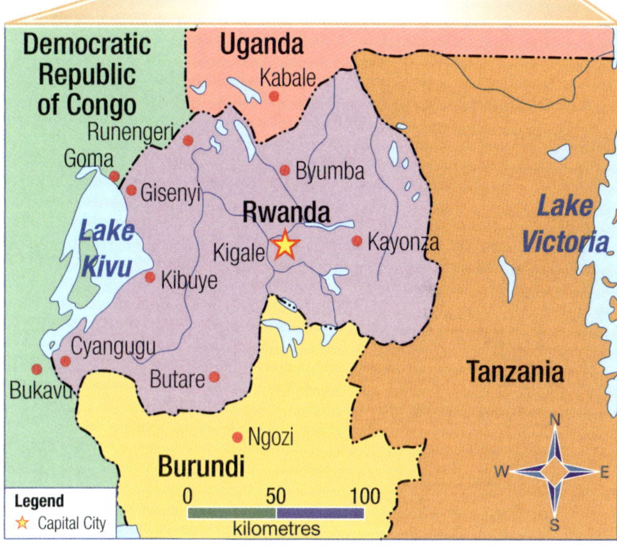

In 1993, the United Nations sent a small force of 2600 soldiers under the command of Canadian general Roméo Dallaire to keep the peace in Rwanda. But in April 1994, an airplane carrying President Juvénal Habyarimana was shot down. Though the assailants were never identified, Hutus blamed Tutsi extremists — and an orgy of killing followed. By the time the slaughter stopped, an estimated 800 000 people — about 10 per cent of Rwanda's population — had been murdered. More than 90 per cent of the dead were Tutsis.

The small group of UN peacekeepers had been powerless to stop the slaughter. Dallaire had repeatedly asked the UN for more help, but his pleas were rejected. UN members still believed that the role of peacekeepers was to prevent conflict between countries rather than to interfere in internal conflicts — even to protect the lives of innocent civilians. Later, Boutros Boutros-Ghali, who was UN secretary-general at the time of the genocide, said that the organization's lack of action was one of the greatest failures of his life.

The genocide in Rwanda raised fundamental questions about the role of the UN and how far it should go to prevent genocide. This genocide also helped generate support for a permanent international criminal court.

Figure 7-17 At one time, government-issued identity cards like the one held by this man labelled people Tutsi or Hutu. The cards, which were abolished in 2004, were introduced by the Belgians, who controlled Rwanda after World War I. During the genocide, Hutu killing squads used the cards to help them identify Tutsi victims.

Analyzing Cause-and-Effect Relationships

FOCUS ON SKILLS

This chapter has explored how various aspects of ultranationalism have caused genocide, crimes against humanity, and war crimes — in Turkey, Ukraine, Nazi-occupied Europe, Serbia, Bosnia and Herzegovina, and Rwanda. You have also explored various effects of those crimes and genocides.

When Rwandan president Juvénal Habyarimana's plane was shot down in April 1994, for example, the Hutu slaughter of Tutsis began. But was Habyarimana's death the sole cause of the genocide?

When considering how to respond to the question, ask yourself questions like these:

- To what extent were aspects of Hutu ultranationalism a cause of the genocide?
- How much did the hate messages broadcast on radio contribute to the mass murders?
- What role was played by the identity cards introduced by the Belgian colonial ruler?

Considering these questions can help you understand how complex cause-and-effect relationships can be. The following steps can help you sort out these complexities.

Steps to Analyzing Cause-and-Effect Relationships

Step 1: Review what you know

Work with a small group to respond to the following questions, which will help you clarify your current opinions and assumptions. As you discuss your responses, refer to examples you have read about in this chapter, as well as relevant notes from your journal on nationalism. Assign a record keeper to keep track of the group's ideas.

- How is ultranationalism related to genocide and crimes against humanity? How can various aspects of ultranationalism become causes of these crimes?
- Which is the most powerful cause of crimes against humanity? Which is the deadliest cause?
- How did aspects of ultranationalism actually move the perpetrators of the crimes toward their goal? What, for example, are the consequences of treating a targeted group with contempt? How can contempt progress to inhumanity and even to genocide?
- What were the immediate effects of the crimes against humanity or genocide? What were the long-term effects?

Step 2: Trace the causes and effects

From this chapter, select one example of a genocide or crime against humanity. Each group member should choose a different example. Work on your own to analyze how aspects of ultranationalism caused the example you chose and led to some of the effects of that crime. A graphic organizer like the one on the following page will help you analyze the complexity of the causes and effects. You can use the organizer to record, organize, understand, and interpret your information and opinions. If necessary, add more boxes as necessary to show your conclusions about causes and effects.

THINKING TIP

As you analyze the causes and effects of the event you chose, keep in mind that the links between events are sometimes coincidental, not causal. Suppose, for example, that the streetlights came on, then your doorbell rang, and right after that, a friend sent you a text message. This sequence of events is coincidental, not causal — one event did not cause the next. When analyzing cause-and-effect relationships, always ask this question: Did Event A *cause* Event B, or did Event B simply happen after Event A?

As you conduct your analysis, make sure your evidence is reliable; logical; relevant to the relationship you are exploring; sufficient to justify your conclusions; representative of a valid, objective, and unbiased selection of causes and effects; and plausible (see "Thinking Tip" on the previous page).

If necessary, conduct further research to verify your conclusions. Note questions you would like to discuss with the other members of your group when you get back together.

Step 3: Consolidate your findings

Return to your group and review your analyses together. Search for patterns and for common causes and effects. At this point, you might ask the recorder to consolidate your conclusions and organize your findings.

Decide on the criteria you would use to rank — in order of importance — the causes and effects. What were the most significant ways in which ultranationalism led to crimes against humanity and genocide? What were the most significant effects — short- and long-term?

Step 4: Interpret your findings

When you have reached a consensus about the conclusions of your analyses, work together to write a brief summary of your position on the extent to which ultranationalism has caused crimes against humanity and genocide. Present your position to your classmates. Listen to other groups' presentations and note convincing arguments that you might add to your group's conclusion.

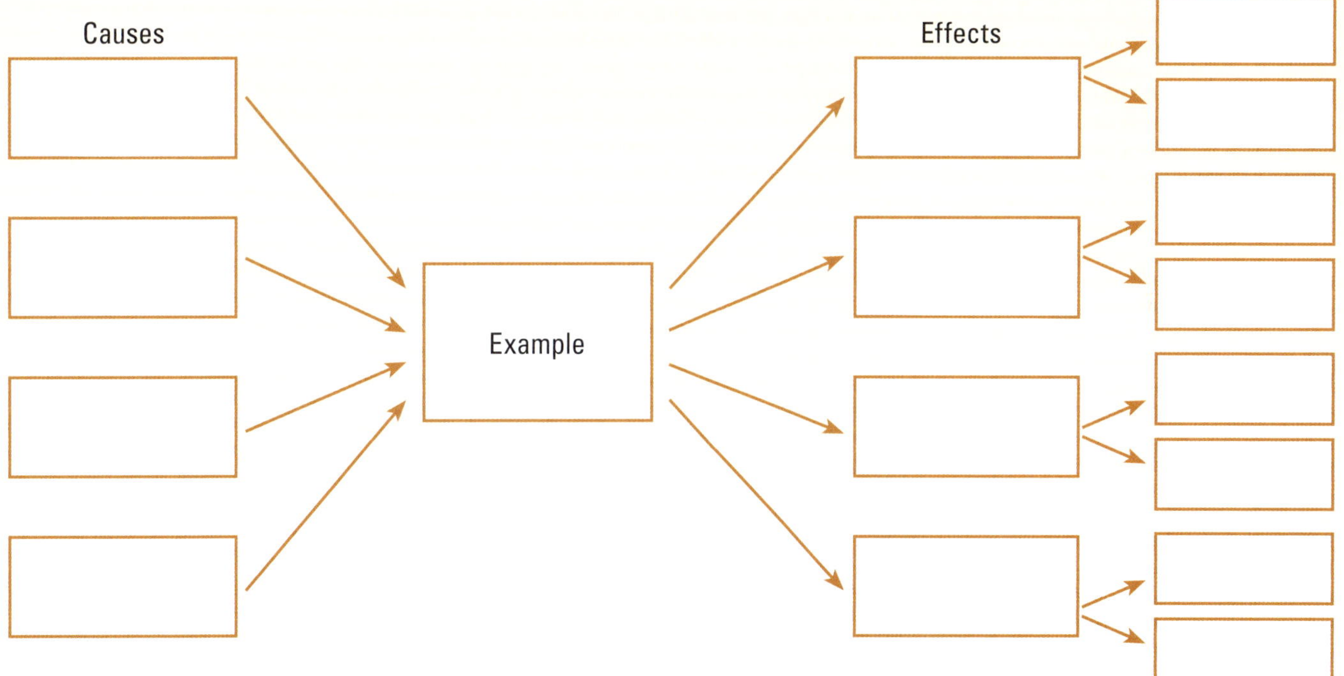

Summing Up

As you progress through the rest of this course, you will encounter many situations in which analyzing causes and effects will help you explore the extent to which nationalism should be embraced. Following the steps set out in this activity will help you analyze and interpret those issues. It will also help you successfully complete the challenge for this related issue.

Acting for Good in the Face of Evil

Sometimes, ordinary people do extraordinary things by standing up for good in the face of evil, such as crimes against humanity and genocide. Oskar Schindler, Feng Shan Ho, and Paul Rusesabagina are examples of people who did this — but the list includes thousands of others.

Figure 7-18 The story of Oskar Schindler, pictured here in 1962, was made into the 1993 Hollywood movie *Schindler's List*. When it was released, this movie sparked controversy because Jews disagreed over whether Schindler was a hero or villain. What might have been the source of this disagreement?

Oskar Schindler

Oskar Schindler was a businessperson who hoped to benefit when the Nazis invaded Poland. He became a member of the Nazi Party and a Nazi spy, and he ran enamel and munitions factories that helped the Nazi war effort. He employed more than 1200 Jews as slave labourers in his Krakow factory. But when the Nazis emptied Krakow's Jewish ghettos and sent the inhabitants to death camps, Schindler did everything he could to protect those who worked in his factory.

He lied, charmed, offered bribes, and spent his own fortune to save Jews from being sent to the Plaszow death camp. For his efforts, the Nazis arrested him several times — but Schindler persisted. He even managed to rescue 1000 people who had already been sent to the Gross-Rosen and Auschwitz death camps. By the end of the war, Schindler was broke, but he had saved the lives of many Jewish men, women, and children.

Figure 7-19 Manli Ho is shown with a picture of her father, Feng Shan Ho, at the opening of a United Nations exhibit called Visas for Life: The Righteous Diplomats. The exhibit honours diplomats such as Feng Shan Ho, who risked their jobs — and lives — to help Jews escape the Nazis.

Feng Shan Ho

When Germany took over Austria in 1938, the Nazis extended their vicious anti-Semitic policies to that country's Jewish population. Many Jews wanted to escape, but they were not allowed to leave Austria unless they had boat tickets or entry visas to other countries — and these were hard to come by. Most countries, including Canada, accepted very few Jews fleeing Nazi-occupied countries.

But the Chinese consul in Vienna, Feng Shan Ho, issued visas to Shanghai to Jews who asked for them, even if the people planned to travel somewhere else once they had left Austria. To Ho, the important thing was to help them escape danger.

At the time, visas were not required to enter Shanghai, but Ho issued them anyway because Nazi authorities required — and accepted — them. When Ho's boss told him to stop, the consul defied orders and continued giving out visas. As a result of his actions, Ho lost his job in Vienna, but not before he had helped about 18 000 Jews escape.

Years later, Ho explained the reason for his actions: "I thought it only natural to feel compassion and to want to help. From the standpoint of humanity, that is the way it should be."

Paul Rusesabagina

When the Rwandan genocide began in 1994, Tutsis and moderate Hutus took shelter in the Hôtel des Mille Collines in the centre of Kigali, the country's capital. Paul Rusesabagina, the hotel manager, had a chance to escape, but he chose to stay, saying, "If I leave tomorrow, I will never again in my life be a free man. I will be a prisoner of my own conscience."

While harbouring the fugitives, Rusesabagina negotiated with and bribed officers of the Rwandan killer squads to buy time for the people he was protecting. He also telephoned and faxed people of influence outside the country to try to get help. On two occasions when the hotel was surrounded by the Hutu military, he managed to contact the French foreign ministry, which pressured the Kigali government to order a withdrawal. When the killing finally ended, none of the 1200 people whom Rusesabagina was protecting had been harmed.

Figure 7-20 Paul Rusesabagina was of mixed Hutu and Tutsi heritage, but his wife was a Tutsi. After the Rwandan genocide, he and his family fled to Belgium. His story was dramatized in the Hollywood movie *Hotel Rwanda*.

Taking Turns

Are crimes against humanity a thing of the past or could they happen again?

The students responding to this question are Rick, who was born in the United States but moved to Fort McMurray with his family when he was 10; Violet, a Métis who is a member of the Paddle Prairie Métis Settlement; and Amanthi, who lives in Edson and whose parents immigrated from Sri Lanka.

Sure, they'll happen again. Look at the number of countries that are ruled by dictators — who don't care about rights as long as they stay in power. But crimes against humanity won't happen on the same scale as the Holocaust. Too many agencies and organizations are dedicated to protecting human rights. Even so, look at what happened in Rwanda, and you can see how long it takes for the world to act.

Forget the future — crimes against humanity are happening right now. They're happening at Guantanamo Bay, where the United States has held suspected terrorists without trial for years. I think they're happening in the Gaza Strip in the Middle East, too. The U.S. isn't a military dictatorship, and neither is Israel or Palestine, but crimes against humanity are still happening. The UN needs to change its ideas about peacekeeping. It needs to be more active about preventing these crimes, instead of just rushing in afterwards and punishing the criminals.

I'm optimistic. With the UN and NGOs working to improve conditions for people and defuse political conflicts, maybe crimes against humanity will happen less often. If the media can work on getting out the news about dangerous situations, people will find out about problems earlier. Then countries can work together to make sure a situation like Sarajevo doesn't happen again. I also think that technologies like Facebook and blogs can make a big difference in spreading the word about dangerous situations.

How would you respond to the question Rick, Violet, and Amanthi are answering? Do you agree with any of their views? Which position do you agree with most, and how would you add to it? What facts would you bring into the discussion? Explain your response.

1. You and a small group have been assigned the task of developing a new United Nations protocol, or procedure, to govern when — and how — the UN should intervene to prevent genocide and crimes against humanity. With your group, brainstorm to develop guidelines that will
   - determine when an act of ultranationalism has led to crimes against humanity
   - establish the steps the UN will follow before intervening
   - establish criteria the UN will use to decide when to send in troops
   - clearly define the role of UN troops (i.e., whether or when they will be allowed to use force)
   - decide which countries will supply the troops
   - set out conditions that must be in place before the UN will agree to relinquish control and withdraw the troops
2. With a partner, choose a historical example of genocide or crimes against humanity. You may choose an example you read about in this chapter or conduct research to discover another example. Then conduct research into a contemporary example. Create a graphic organizer that compares the causes and effects of the two examples you selected. Present your analysis, including the graphic organizer, orally or in writing.
3. Suppose an international human rights group has accused a Canadian citizen of involvement in crimes against humanity in a civil war that is now over. The group wants this woman to be charged and brought before the International Criminal Court. The woman says she is innocent and refuses to appear at the ICC. She wants to plead her case in a Canadian court.

   The ICC has requested that Canada, as a country that supports the ICC, arrest the suspect and send her to The Hague, Netherlands, where the ICC is located. The citizen is demanding that the government protect her from foreign powers. What should the Canadian government do? Explain the reasons for your response.
4. Noam Chomsky, an American linguist, political activist, and philosopher, believes that "ultranationalism" is a powerful word that is often used to place an unfair negative spin on the efforts of movements in developing countries to pursue their national interests. In his 1993 book, *What Uncle Sam Really Wants*, Chomsky wrote:

   > In one high-level document after another, U.S. planners stated their view that the primary threat to the new U.S.-led world order was Third World nationalism – sometimes called ultranationalism: "nationalistic regimes" that are responsive to "popular demand for immediate improvement in the low living standards of the masses" and production for domestic needs.
   >
   > The planners' basic goals, repeated over and over again, were to prevent such "ultranationalist" regimes from ever taking power – or if, by some fluke, they did take power, to remove them and to install governments that favor private investment of domestic and foreign capital, production for export and the right to bring profits out of the country. (These goals are never challenged in the secret documents. If you're a U.S. policy planner, they're sort of like the air you breathe.)

   a) On the basis of what you have read in this chapter, explain why labelling actions "ultranationalistic" can carry powerful negative connotations. Explain how these connotations could be used to generate negative propaganda.

   b) In Chapter 5, you read about Iraq and its oil fields. Suppose the Iraqi government decided to take control of its oil fields and use the profits gained from selling its oil to improve education, health care, communications, transportation, and living conditions in the country.
      - Jot points the Iraqi government could use to place a positive spin on this action. Include the phrase "national interest" in your points.
      - Jot points that the American government could use to place a negative spin on the Iraqi government's action. Use the word "ultranationalist" in your points.

Think...Participate...Research...Communicate...

c) Think about whether "ultranationalism" is a useful word — or is its meaning so murky that it always arouses suspicion that it is being used as propaganda? Summarize your thoughts in a sentence or two.

5. In this chapter, you explored responses to this issue question: To what extent can the pursuit of ultranationalism lead to crimes against humanity?

   With a partner, prepare a response to this question. Your response may be presented as a short essay; a computer software presentation; a series of visuals, which you may create or find in books, magazines, or newspapers, or on the Internet; or in another format of your choosing. Your response should

   - include a clear explanation of your understanding of ultranationalism
   - explain the criteria you would use to judge whether an action is a crime against humanity
   - provide both historical and contemporary examples
   - clearly state your position on the issue and support it with logical reasons

   Present your response to the class and be ready to answer questions from your classmates.

6. The cartoon on this page was created by Jason Love. It depicts the artist's response to nationalism. Examine the cartoon and complete the following activities:

   a) What is the cartoon's message?

   b) In a short paragraph, explain your opinion of the cartoon, its message, and the images the artist chose.

   c) Create a cartoon — or describe the elements you would include in a cartoon — that depicts responses to ultranationalism. Remember to avoid hurtful and stereotypical words and images.

Figure 7-21

Think about Your Challenge

To help you respond to the related-issue question — To what extent should national interest be pursued? — the challenge for this related issue asks you to prepare an investigative report on a historical or contemporary nationalist movement.

Review the research you have completed so far. Make notes about the connections between the movement you are investigating and the national interests the movement is pursuing. Identify the national interests involved and who stands to gain or lose if these interests are pursued. Predict whether the movement is likely to lead to ultranationalism.

Discuss these notes with a partner or your teacher. Revise your notes on the basis of the feedback you receive. Prepare to start putting together your report as you progress through Chapter 8.

CHAPTER 8 National Self-Determination

Figure 8-1 On October 16, 2007, the 38th session of the Canadian Parliament opened when Governor General Michaëlle Jean delivered the throne speech. On March 26, 1990, representatives of the Cree and Inuit peoples of the James Bay region of Québec paddled a combined canoe-kayak to Parliament Hill to protest Hydro-Québec's plans to expand its giant hydroelectric project (top left). On March 20, 2008, protesters demanding freedom for the Tibetan people marched on Parliament Hill (top right).

CHAPTER ISSUE

To what extent should national self-determination be pursued?

CANADIANS HAVE MANY AVENUES for expressing opinions about what is in their national interests. They express their interests, for example, when they vote for representatives on municipal councils, in provincial or territorial legislatures, and in Parliament. At the beginning of each parliamentary session, the political party that has received enough support to form a government prepares a throne speech that sets out its goals for the forthcoming session.

Canadians can also take their concerns directly to Ottawa. This is what representatives of the James Bay Inuit and Cree did in 1990 when they tried to resolve their land-claim dispute with the Québec government. Canadians may also voice their concern for the national interests of people who cannot speak for themselves. In early 2008, for example, demonstrators in Tibet were arrested for speaking out in favour of self-determination — and Canadians who supported their cause demonstrated on Parliament Hill.

Examine the photographs on the previous page and respond to the following questions:

- What national interests does each photograph illustrate?
- How do these photographs represent the complexities that arise when the interests of one group or nation clash with those of another?
- Why would the Cree and Inuit in 1990 and the advocates of a free Tibet in 2008 go to Ottawa, the home of Canada's Parliament, to protest?

KEY TERMS

decolonization

successor state

Looking Ahead

In this chapter, you will develop responses to the following questions as you explore the extent to which national self-determination should be pursued:

- What is national self-determination?
- What are some effects of pursuing national self-determination?
- What are some effects on Canada of pursuing national self-determination?
- What are some unintended consequences of the pursuit of national self-determination?

My Journal on Nationalism

Look back at the journal entry you recorded at the beginning of Chapter 7. Has your understanding of nationalism changed since then? Explain how. Using words or pictures — or both — express your current ideas on nationalism. Date your ideas and keep them in your journal, notebook, learning log, portfolio, or computer file so that you can return to them as you progress through this course.

WHAT IS NATIONAL SELF-DETERMINATION?

CHECKBACK

You read about national self-determination in Chapter 1 and about the former Yugoslavia in Chapter 7.

CHECKFORWARD

You will read more about the former Yugoslavia in Chapter 10.

When a people pursue national self-determination, they are trying to gain — or keep — the power to control their own affairs. They believe it is in their collective interest to make their own decisions about what will benefit them.

At one time, for example, Kosovo was part of Yugoslavia. When the Yugoslav federation broke up in the 1990s, the area became a province of Serbia. Then, in February 2008, Kosovo's government declared independence.

About 90 per cent of Kosovars are ethnic Albanians; most of the rest are ethnic Serbians. Most Albanian Kosovars are Muslims, but most Serbian Kosovars are Christians who belong to the Serbian Orthodox Church. These religious divisions are closely connected to ethnic divisions, and Kosovo has endured centuries of religious and ethnic conflict.

In the 1990s, the conflict between the two groups became so violent that the United Nations sent NATO troops to administer the province. UN forces were still in control when independence was declared.

Though most Albanian Kosovars celebrated their declaration of independence, members of the Serbian minority were afraid of losing their rights and their ancient traditions and culture, which date from the 14th century.

Figure 8-2 Albanian Kosovars (left) celebrated their declaration of independence from Serbia in February 2008. They waved the Albanian flag because most Kosovars are ethnic Albanians and Kosovo did not yet have its own flag. The next day, Serbian Kosovars (right)protested. "Serbia Forever" and "Kosovo is Serbia" were two of the slogans used by ethnic Serbians, who wanted Kosovo to remain part of Serbia.

Self-Determination in 1918

As World War I was drawing to a close in 1918, American president Woodrow Wilson supported what he called the "free self-determination of nations." Wilson hoped this principle would lead to lasting peace in Europe.

But in the treaties negotiated after the war, it became clear that the victorious Allies' concept of self-determination did not apply to everyone. It did not extend to nations, such as those in Yugoslavia, that had been part of the Ottoman Empire or the Austro-Hungarian Empire.

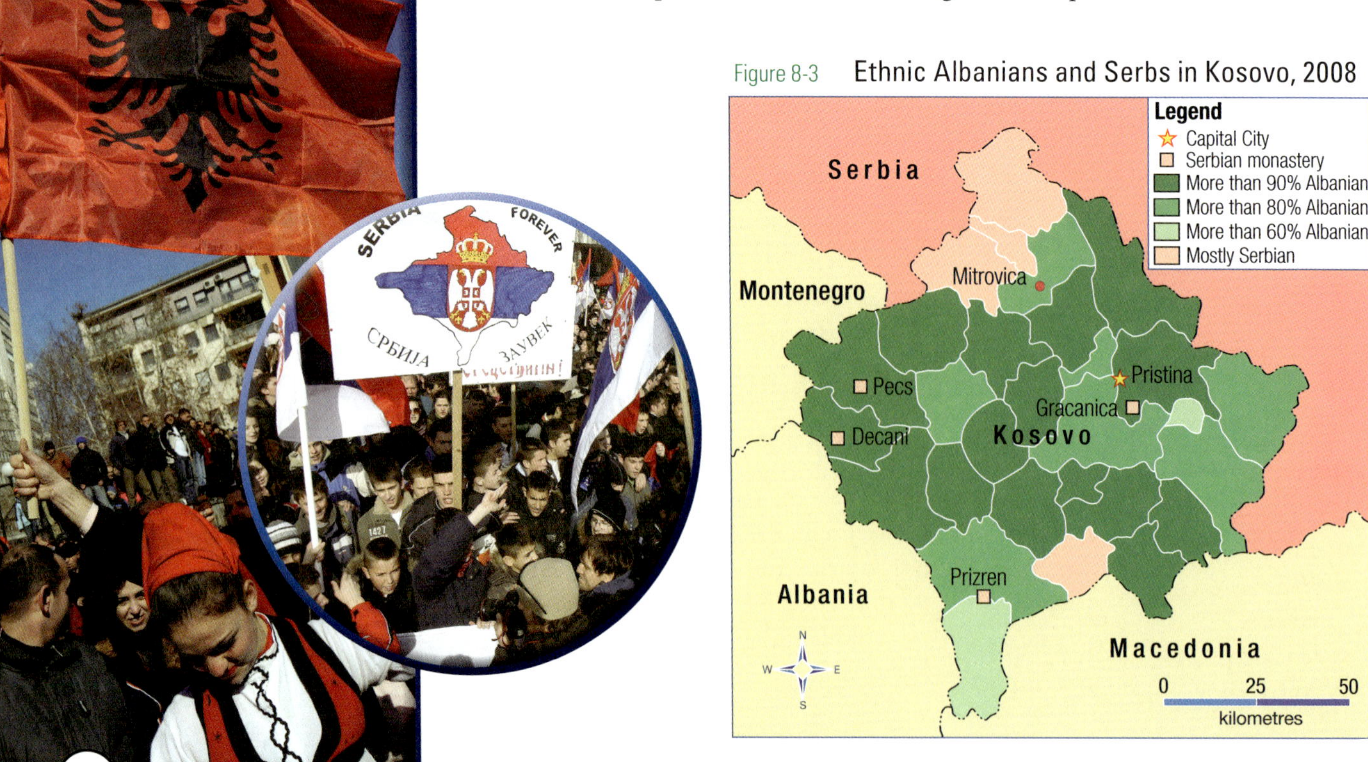

Figure 8-3 Ethnic Albanians and Serbs in Kosovo, 2008

Self-Determination and Nation-States

American historian Louis L. Snyder believed that the desire for self-determination underpins the right of a people to freely choose how they will be governed. But Snyder also acknowledged that just as the idea of self-determination can unify people, it can also drive them apart. On the nation-state level, self-determination helps people see their nation as "unique and indivisible," but on the group or collective level, the pursuit of self-determination can disrupt a nation-state if some people do not believe that the state represents their interests or supports their goals.

The debate over who has the right to self-determination — and what this right means — is reflected in the charter of the United Nations. According to the charter, one of the UN's purposes is "to develop friendly relations among nations based on respect for the principle of equal rights and self-determination of peoples, and to take other appropriate measures to strengthen universal peace."

In addition, all nation-states that belong to the UN are to have "sovereign equality." But the UN leaves unanswered the question of what happens when peoples within nation-states want self-determination.

According to the International Court of Justice, which was established in 1945 as part of the UN, the right to self-determination is held by peoples as well as by governments. This means that the principle of the sovereignty of a nation-state can sometimes conflict with a people's right to self-determination. Kosovo's declaration of independence, for example, was viewed by some countries — including China and Russia — as a threat to Serbia's integrity and status as a nation-state.

Soon after Kosovo declared independence, the UN Security Council held emergency sessions to discuss the situation. Russian ambassador Vitaly Churkin urged Security Council members to declare Kosovo's declaration of independence "null and void." On April 1, UN secretary-general Ban Ki-moon said that UN forces would remain in Kosovo until the Security Council decided otherwise; in other words, Kosovo's independence was not accepted by the UN, even though many individual member states, including Britain, France, Germany, Italy, Croatia, Hungary, Canada, and the United States, had recognized the area as an independent country.

Nationalism, reflecting the urge of self-determination, concerns the aspirations of a people, who believe themselves to be united, to rule themselves and not be controlled by others. The kindred ideas of nationalism and self-determination both act as forces for convergence or divergence.

— *Louis L. Snyder,* Encyclopedia of Nationalism, *1990*

Figure 8-4 On February 18, 2008, the United Nations Security Council met at the request of the Russian Federation to discuss the situation in Kosovo. How much should UN recognition matter to nation-states?

Reflect and Respond

With a partner, develop three criteria that would help the United Nations decide when to recognize a new country such as Kosovo. Take into account the UN's position on human rights, on a nation-state's right to sovereignty, and on a people's right to self-determination. Consider, too, the consequences that might result from recognizing a new country.

What are some effects of pursuing national self-determination?

Web Connection

To find out more about how the political map of the world has changed since 1945 and about current decolonization issues before the UN, go to this web site and follow the links.

www.ExploringNationalism.ca

The pursuit of national self-determination is often complicated by the fact that what is in one people's national interest conflicts with the national interests of other peoples. It is also important to define what "a people" is — and this has proven difficult.

According to Javier Leon Diaz, an international human rights lawyer, no precise legal definition of the term "a people" exists. Still, the term is often used to describe groups who

- share a common historical tradition, language, and religion
- identify themselves as a distinct cultural group
- have a traditional connection to a particular territory

But understanding the term "a people" is only the first step toward resolving various peoples' struggle for the right to self-determination.

In Kosovo, for example, the struggle between ethnic Albanians and ethnic Serbs has continued for generations. Both claim the region. Albanians lived in the area as early as the 6th century, and Serbs have been there since at least the 11th century. Serbian Kosovars have longstanding and strong ties with Serbia, while Albanian Kosovars have strong ties with Albania. Between 1974 and 1998, as Albanian nationalism strengthened, tensions between the two groups deteriorated into armed conflict.

With your partner, return to the criteria you developed to help the United Nations decide when to recognize a new country. Decide whether Kosovo meets your criteria. Explain why or why not.

Figure 8-5 Decolonization — Selected States, 1945 and 2008

Colonial Power	Name in 1945	Status in 2008
Belgium	Belgian Congo	Independent states of Democratic Republic of Congo, Burundi, and Rwanda
France	French Indochina	Independent states of Cambodia, Laos, and Vietnam
France	French West Africa	Independent states of Bénin, Burkina Faso, Côte d'Ivoire, Guinea, Mali, Mauritania, Niger, Sénégal, and part of Togo
Italy	Somaliland	Independent state of Somalia
Netherlands	Indonesia	Independent state of Indonesia
Portugal	East Timor	Independent state of Timor-Leste
Britain	Rhodesia	Independent states of Zambia and Zimbabwe
Britain	British India	Independent states of India, Pakistan, Bangladesh, and Sri Lanka

Decolonization and Self-Determination

Colonies are ruled by the government of another country. When Britain declared war on Germany in 1914, for example, Canada was no longer a British colony but had not yet achieved full independence. Because Britain still controlled its foreign policy, when Britain declared war, Canada was also at war.

Decolonization refers to what happens when a colonial power withdraws from a colony. The people of the former colony may then form a sovereign nation-state. A strong link between decolonization and the idea of national self-determination is built into the charter of the United Nations. Decolonized countries can join the UN and exercise sovereignty under international law.

But decolonized peoples must often deal with the after-effects of colonization. Colonial powers often forced peoples who were once separate — with different languages, religions, traditions, and cultures — into a single colony. When decolonization occurs, violent conflicts such as that in Rwanda may arise.

Decolonization in Indochina

European colonial powers — Portugal, Spain, Britain, the Netherlands, and France — began colonizing Southeast Asia in the 1500s. By the late 1800s, France ruled Vietnam, Laos, and Cambodia and had renamed the region French Indochina.

When Japan invaded the region during World War II, many people became committed to the idea of independence. In Vietnam, Ho Chi Minh, a communist leader, and the Viet Minh independence movement fought against the Japanese and continued the fight against the French when they reoccupied the country after the war.

The war between the Vietnamese and the French, who had considerable American support, went on until 1954, when French forces were defeated. Afterwards, Vietnam was divided in two: the northern Democratic Republic of Vietnam was a communist state supported by China and the Soviet Union, while the Republic of South Vietnam was supported by the United States and other Western powers. Vietnam became a battleground in the Cold War between the two superpowers.

The peace treaty had called for elections to take place in South Vietnam. But no election was ever held. Instead, South Vietnam was ruled by a series of dictators who were supported by the U.S. and opposed by communist Viet Cong guerrilla fighters.

Figure 8-6 North and South Vietnam

The Vietnam War

By 1965, the U.S. had escalated its support of the South Vietnamese government by sending more than 200 000 American troops to the country. Over the next four years, the number of American troops rose to 500 000 and the war was expanded into neighbouring Cambodia.

In the U.S., supporters of the war argued that stopping the spread of communism in the region was in the American national interest. As early as 1954, President Dwight D. Eisenhower had used his domino theory to explain how the communist regimes of China and Russia, if not checked, would take over all of Southeast Asia. "You have a row of dominoes set up," Eisenhower said. "You knock over the first one, and what will happen to the last one is the certainty that it will go over very quickly." Other war supporters said that American soldiers were fighting for the freedom of the Vietnamese people.

But opposition to American involvement grew in the U.S. during the 1960s. Some opponents said that American forces had no right to interfere in a dispute between the peoples of Vietnam. Other war critics spoke of the damage caused by U.S. forces, the loss of American lives, and the physical and economic losses of the Vietnamese people.

[One of the casualties] of the war in Vietnam is the principle of self-determination . . . Whether we realize it or not, our participation in the war in Vietnam is an ominous expression of our lack of sympathy for the oppressed, our paranoid anti-Communism, our failure to feel the ache and anguish of the have nots. It reveals our willingness to continue participating in neo-colonialist adventures.

— Martin Luther King Jr., civil rights leader, in a speech, 1967

Cambodia, Justice, and the Pursuit of National Self-Determination

Sometime before morning the guards took her. I was seven years old; Daravuth was four. Little did I know that would be the last time I would see my mother. The light went out. Eternal night. Life is but a breath.

What seemed like several hours later, my older brothers returned to us. The prison was eerily empty. "Here, take your crying siblings with you. You're free to go home," a guard instructed my older brothers. My mother's blood purchased our freedom. We made our way back to our grandfather's village.

— Theary Seng, Cambodian lawyer and activist, 2005

Among the rights of a people seeking self-determination is the right to security. If they want to bring to justice those who committed crimes against them, international law enables them to do so.

Cambodia, for example, had once been part of French Indochina. From 1975 to 1979, the country was ruled by Pol Pot, a brutal communist dictator who led a movement called the Khmer Rouge. Up to 1.5 million people were either murdered or died of exhaustion, disease, or starvation when Cambodians were forced from their homes in cities and towns to work on inefficient and poorly run collective farms. Although Pol Pot's government was overthrown by Vietnamese forces in 1979 and Cambodia eventually became a constitutional monarchy, the country remained politically unstable. The Khmer Rouge continued to fight a guerrilla war. In 1993, Cambodians voted for the first time in UN-supervised elections, but peace was not achieved until 1998, nearly 20 years after the genocide.

For Cambodians who survived the Khmer Rouge regime, justice has been very slow. In 2003, the United Nations set up a tribunal to try former Khmer Rouge members accused of genocide and crimes against humanity, but progress has been difficult to achieve.

The tribunal includes both UN-appointed and Cambodian judges, and disagreements have arisen over how to accommodate the standards of international law while respecting Cambodian justice traditions. The fact that some members of the current Cambodian government once belonged to the Khmer Rouge has added a layer of complexity to the process.

Some observers, including Theary Seng, an author, lawyer, and activist whose parents were killed by the Khmer Rouge, say that the trials have been delayed so long that they may now serve little purpose. Many senior Khmer Rouge officials, as well as victims and witnesses, are now dead. Pol Pot, for example, died in 1998, before the tribunal was even established.

Figure 8-7 In May 2007, these Cambodian fine arts students performed during the "Anger Day" ceremony at the Choeung Ek Memorial to the killing fields, near Phnom Penh, the Cambodian capital. Every year, people gather at the memorial to remember those who died at the hands of the Khmer Rouge genocide. How might ceremonies like this strengthen people's desire for self-determination?

International law enables Cambodia to bring to justice those accused of genocide and crimes against humanity. What role should the principle of self-determination play in the trials of Khmer Rouge officials accused of involvement in the genocide? Should Cambodians be able to decide for themselves how to bring these criminals to justice, or should the trials be conducted according to principles established by international law?

Tibet and the Pursuit of National Self-Determination

In 2008, as the opening of the Beijing Summer Olympics drew near, some Tibetans used the occasion to press their demand for national self-determination. The Tibet Autonomous Region, now a province of China, was once part of a separate nation with its own culture, language, traditions, and religion. The region had been largely Buddhist since the seventh century. From the mid-17th century until the Chinese invasion in the mid-20th century, Tibet was ruled by dalai lamas, who held political as well as spiritual power.

In 1950, a time when many countries were emerging from colonial rule, China invaded Tibet. The Chinese took control of the government, suppressed the Buddhist religion, and destroyed monasteries. Thousands of Tibetan civilians and monks were killed. The Dalai Lama and his government appealed to the United Nations for help, but the UN Security Council decided that the dispute was between China and Tibet and did not intervene. In the decades since, Tibetan protests against Chinese rule have been put down with force.

Over the years, some UN members have spoken out against the Chinese takeover. In 1959, 1961, and 1965, members of the General Assembly passed resolutions upholding the Tibetan people's right to self-determination. Individual politicians have also spoken out against the invasion. In 1959, Indian prime minister Jawaharlal Nehru said, "It is morally not right for a country to lay full or partial claim on its neighbouring state . . . the last voice regarding Tibet should be the voice of the Tibetan people and nobody else's."

You explored Tibetan nationalism in Chapter 1.

The armed invasion of Tibet for the incorporation of Tibet in Communist China through sheer physical force is a clear case of aggression. As long as the people of Tibet are compelled by force to become a part of China against their will and consent, the present invasion of Tibet will be the grossest instance of the violation of the weak by the strong. We therefore appeal through you to the nations of the world to intercede on our behalf and restrain Chinese aggression.

— Dalai Lama, to the United Nations, 1950

In the 21st century, Tibetans worried about assimilation. When the Qinghai–Tibet Railway was completed in 2006, it opened Tibet to a flood of Chinese immigration. Tibetans have protested that this resettlement violates international law, which bars occupying powers from transferring parts of their own populations into the occupied territory.

If the Chinese resettlement program results in a Chinese majority in Tibet, should the Tibetan people still be able to exercise their right to self-determination? Explain your response.

Figure 8-8 A Tibetan exile carries a picture of the Dalai Lama during a protest rally in Srinager, India, in March 2008. Chinese law forbids Tibetans to possess photographs of the Dalai Lama, and visitors are forbidden to take his picture into Tibet.

Predicting Likely Outcomes

FOCUS ON SKILLS

As part of the decolonization process, the United Nations has supervised plebiscites in former colonies such as Togo and Papua-New Guinea. These plebiscites are intended to discover "the freely expressed will of the people" about how they want to be governed.

But the situation becomes more complex when a colonial power has moved people from the home country into the colony — and changed the colony's demographic structure. This transfer of large numbers of people can change a nation's culture and traditions and affect the outcome of a vote on self-determination.

Suppose you are asked to predict a likely outcome to this question: How is the increased settlement of Chinese people in Tibet likely to affect Tibetans' pursuit of national self-determination?

No one can be certain of the answer to this question, but you may be able to reach an informed opinion. How would you develop a prediction that is informed and based on reliable and valid evidence? In your research, whose views on this issue would you consider knowledgeable and authoritative? The following steps can help you answer these questions and predict a likely outcome.

Steps to Predicting Likely Outcomes

Step 1: Review your prior knowledge

Begin by jotting notes about what you already know about various aspects of the situation in Tibet.

- What do you know about Tibet, China, and colonization and decolonization in general? Review the sections of this chapter that deal with decolonization and the pursuit of national self-determination. In addition, review the notes you have made in your journal at the beginning of every chapter.
- What has happened when similar population shifts have occurred elsewhere? Review your knowledge of what has happened to peoples in similar situations (e.g., Québécois, Aboriginal peoples in Canada, and Albanian and Serbian Kosovars).
- What concepts relating to your exploration of nationalism might be relevant in predicting a likely outcome in Tibet? You may wish to consider concepts such as national identity, ethnic nationalism, national interest, domestic policy, and the relationship between nationalism and the pursuit of national interest.
- What is your point of view as you start this inquiry? You may, for example, believe that a plebiscite would not be the most effective way of finding out what Tibetans want.

Step 2: Use a point-proof-comment organizer to conduct research

Create a point-proof-comment organizer similar to the one shown on the following page to help you organize your research and prepare to make and support a prediction. For each point noted on the organizer, record a proof and your comment on how this might affect your prediction.

Start your research by reading the comments on the following page. You may also need to conduct additional research. Where could you locate a variety of relevant, useful, up-to-date, and authoritative resources? How will you ensure that you are considering a number of perspectives and points of view? If you conduct additional research, continue to use your point-proof-comment organizer to organize the evidence you gather.

Step 3: Make your prediction

Review your notes and your point-proof-comment organizer. Which arguments are most reliable and authoritative?

Write a paragraph that states your prediction, explains why you are making it, and supports it with reliable evidence. If you are undecided, explain the factors that have contributed to your indecision. Share your paragraph with a classmate or your teacher. Edit your work based on their feedback.

Sources

1. On February 8, 2008, **Xinhua**, China's official news agency, issued a report on the number of passengers travelling from China to Lhasa, the Tibetan capital.

   More than 5.95 million people had traveled on the Qinghai-Tibet railway by the end of 2007 since the highest rail route in the world opened in July 2006. The passenger flow accounted for 43 percent of all tourists visiting Tibet Autonomous Region in southwest China during the period, according to the autonomous regional tourism bureau. The operation of the railway line has greatly boosted tourist growth in this landlocked plateau, which registered a record of 4.02 million tourists from other places in China and overseas last year, an annual increase of 60.4 percent, official statistics show.

2. On March 18, 2008, the **Dalai Lama** issued a news release on his official web site.

   Whether it was intended or not, I believe that a form of cultural genocide has taken place in Tibet, where the Tibetan identity has been under constant attack. Tibetans have been reduced to an insignificant minority in their own land as a result of the huge transfer of non-Tibetans into Tibet. The distinctive Tibetan cultural heritage with its characteristic language, customs and traditions is fading away. Instead of working to unify its nationalities, the Chinese government discriminates against these minority nationalities, the Tibetans among them.

3. On March 18, 2008, the **Chinese embassy** in the United States issued a news release.

   Liu Jianchao [a Chinese foreign ministry spokesperson] emphasized that the Chinese Government will unswervingly safeguard the national sovereignty and territorial integrity of China, promote development and stability in Tibet and protect the safety of life and property of people of all ethnic groups in Tibet. No force will stop development and progress in Tibet. Any attempt to split China will be firmly opposed by the Chinese people of all nationalities including the Tibetan compatriots and is doomed to fail.

Point-Proof-Comment Organizer Chinese Immigration and Tibet	
Point	
Proof	
Comment	
Point	
Proof	
Comment	

Summing Up

Whenever you are faced with choices, the ability to think ahead and predict likely outcomes is an important skill. A point-proof-comment organizer is a handy way to organize your thoughts in many situations and can help you make informed predictions.

Figure 8-9 In 1930, Mohandas Gandhi and his supporters were photographed as they launched a campaign of non-violent civil disobedience against British control of India.

Figure 8-10 India, Pakistan, and Kashmir at Partition, 1947

Successor States

A **successor state** — or states — is a country created from a previous state. When the Soviet Union collapsed in the early 1990s, for example, 15 successor states emerged as Lithuanians, Estonians, Latvians, Russians, and other peoples asserted their right to national self-determination.

According to the United Nations' charter and international law, people who lived in a predecessor state — the state that existed before the successor state or states came into existence — have a right to nationality in the successor state or the right to choose their nationality if the predecessor state is divided into more than one state.

India as a Successor State

During the time Britain controlled what are today the independent nation-states of India, Pakistan, Bangladesh, and Sri Lanka, the colonizers exerted more and more control over the lives of the Indigenous peoples of this large area. Like the Hudson's Bay Company, which controlled Rupert's Land in Canada, the British East India Company controlled much of India.

In the early 1800s, the East India Company's grip on India began slipping, and in 1858, without consulting the peoples involved and with no regard for their national interests or right to self-determination, the British government took over and established direct rule over what they called British India. During this time, which was called the Raj — a word that comes from the Hindu word for "reign" — the peoples of India had no real political power. Their efforts to pursue national self-determination were ignored or put down.

But during the first half of the 20th century, Indian nationalist movements gained strength, and the people began to speak out for independence and their right to govern themselves. In 1919, the British rulers had allowed Indians a national parliament elected by a select number of the wealthiest people in the country, but this parliament had little real power.

Examine the map in Figure 8-10. This map shows how colonial India was divided when it finally achieved independence in 1947. Does the division of India into India and Pakistan, which included both East and West Pakistan, appear to be logical? Explain your response.

Non-Violent Protest

During the 1920s, Mohandas Gandhi's non-violent and non-co-operation movement for Indian independence attracted many followers. Gandhi fostered Indian nationalism and believed that independence could be won without bloodshed. The increasing number of people who joined Gandhi's campaigns through the 1930s and 1940s amazed and frightened India's British rulers.

I want freedom immediately, this very night, before dawn, if it can be had. You may take it from me that I am not going to strike a bargain with the [British] Viceroy for ministers and the like . . . Here is the mantra, a short one, that I give you. Do or die. We shall either free India or die in the attempt.

— Mohandas Gandhi, at the start of his Quit India movement against the British, August 8, 1942

The Creation of Pakistan

In the late 1800s, Indians formed the Indian National Congress, or Congress Party, to work toward independence. At first, Muslims and Hindus, the two dominant groups in the colony, worked together in this party. But by 1906, some Muslims were beginning to resent the control exercised by the Hindu majority. They formed the All India Muslim League and declared that when the British left, it would be in the interest of Muslims to form their own separate nation-state.

In early 1940, Muhammad Ali Jinnah, leader of the Muslim League, declared that this separate state would be called Pakistan. He insisted that Muslims and Hindus were two separate nations. In a 1944 letter to Gandhi, Jinnah wrote that Muslims are "a nation with our own distinctive culture and civilization, language and literature, art and architecture, names and nomenclature, sense of value and proportion, legal laws and moral codes, customs and calendar, history and traditions, aptitudes and ambitions."

Gandhi, who advocated a united India, disagreed. He believed that Muslims and Hindus were one nation. He told Jinnah, "A Bengali Muslim speaks the same tongue that a Bengali Hindu does, eats the same food, has the same amusements as his Hindu neighbour."

In the months leading up to independence, conflict between Muslims and Hindus grew violent. On August 15, 1947, India achieved independence, and two days later, Pakistan became the second successor state to what had been British India. In both countries, Hindus and Muslims, who had once lived and worked together peacefully, went on rampages. At least a million people were killed, and millions of refugees tried to escape to safety. Muslims went on the long hard journey from India to Pakistan, and Hindus went on the equally long hard journey from Pakistan to India.

Think about your understandings of nationalism and national self-determination. Do you agree with Jinnah's or Gandhi's position on a united India? Explain your response.

Figure 8-11 In September 1947, soon after the partition of India, thousands of Muslim refugees waited to leave for Pakistan in convoys that would give them some protection against attacks by Hindus.

Kashmir

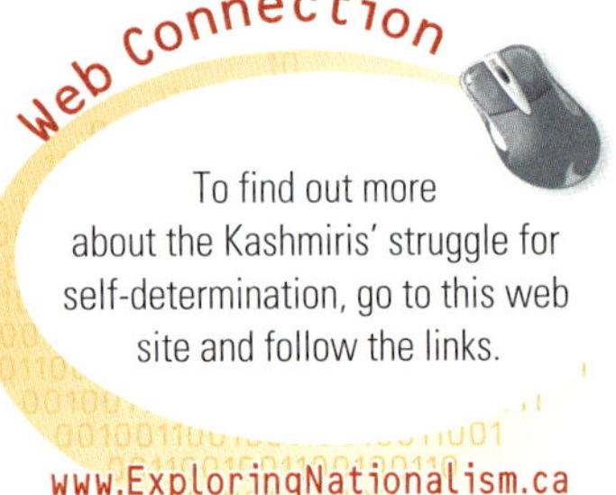

Sometimes a people's desire for self-determination can be lost in the decolonization and successor state processes. What has happened in Kashmir since the British left India is one example of such a loss.

Long before the British took over Kashmir, the Kashmiri people lived in a clearly defined territory in the northwestern Himalaya Mountains. The people of the region speak Kashmiri, a distinct language. They also identify themselves as a distinct cultural group.

In 1947, British, Indian, and Pakistani leaders agreed that the people of Kashmir should have the right to decide whether to join India or Pakistan. In 1948, the United Nations Security Council decided that Kashmiris should vote on the issue in a plebiscite.

Whose wishes were not considered in the decision to hold a plebiscite? What options do you think Kashmiris might have added to the list?

But in the meantime, India invaded Kashmir and took control of much of the Kashmiris' traditional territory. Despite the UN's repeated demands, the promised plebiscite has never been held, and fighting between India and Pakistan has continued on and off in the area ever since.

Figure 8-12 A Kashmiri woman watches as relatives of people who have disappeared in Indian-occupied Kashmir take part in a protest in Srinagar in April 2008. Do you think these disappearances would strengthen or weaken Kashmiris' desire for national self-determination?

The part of Kashmir controlled by India includes more than twice as many Kashmiris as the section controlled by Pakistan. Kashmiris have resisted Indian control, and violent conflicts have arisen repeatedly over the decades. Though the original plebiscite was to ask Kashmiris whether they wanted to join India or Pakistan, many nationalist leaders in Kashmir are now calling for complete independence.

In 2007, the Association of Parents of Disappeared Persons estimated that 10 000 Kashmiris have been "disappeared" — captured by Indian forces and never seen again. Villages in the area along the dividing line between Pakistani- and Indian-controlled Kashmir have been destroyed by shelling. Civilians have been killed, and the survivors have been forced to flee their ruined homes. On both sides of the border, the military presence is a constant reminder that Kashmiris live in occupied territory.

Reflect and Respond

You have read about a number of examples of peoples who have pursued national self-determination and how this pursuit affected them and others. Choose one example (e.g., Tibetans). Create a chart like the one shown. For the people you chose, note at least three positive and three negative consequences of their pursuit of national self-determination. For each consequence, cite an example or proof.

Positive and Negative Consequences of the Pursuit of Self-Determination
People ______________________

Positive Outcomes	Example or Proof	Negative Outcomes	Example or Proof

What are some effects on Canada of pursuing national self-determination?

Colonization in Canada began in the early 1600s when Samuel de Champlain brought settlers to New France. Canadian historian Christopher Moore says that Champlain's action transformed what had been occasional contacts with the Aboriginal peoples of North America into "a permanent European presence in Canada."

Canada was colonized first by the French and then by the British. As more settlers arrived, Aboriginal peoples became a minority. Their territory was taken over, and their right to self-determination was suppressed. But in 1982, Canada established its new Constitution, which affirmed Aboriginal and treaty rights. For some Aboriginal peoples, however, the decolonization process was just beginning.

In Canada today, as in many other countries, two of the UN's core values offer conflicting views of self-determination. On the one hand, UN member countries have the right to sovereignty; on the other hand, the peoples within those countries have the right to control their own affairs and make decisions in their collective interests.

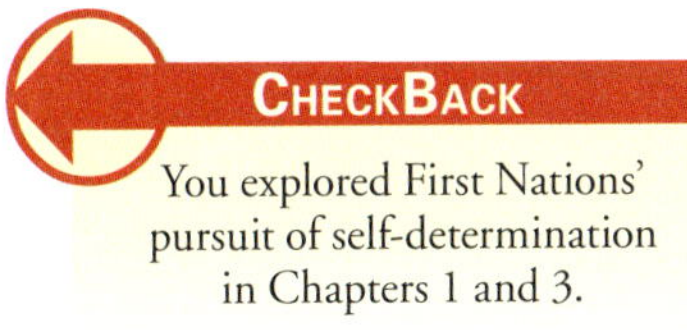

You explored First Nations' pursuit of self-determination in Chapters 1 and 3.

First Nations Pursuit of Self-Determination

According to the Assembly of First Nations, self-determination involves the right of a people to freely

- determine their political status and pursue their economic, social, and cultural development
- dispose of and benefit from their wealth and natural resources

This AFN statement echoes the Declaration on the Rights of Indigenous Peoples, which was adopted by the United Nations in 2007.

But no international principles govern what happens when a people's right to pursue self-determination conflicts with a nation-state's right to sovereignty. *People to People, Nation to Nation*, the 1996 report of the Royal Commission on Aboriginal Peoples, made it clear that Aboriginal peoples' pursuit of self-determination does not involve seeking independence from Canada — but it does include the right to self-government. The report concluded that "self-determination includes governance, so Indigenous peoples are entitled to choose their own forms of government, within existing states."

Many First Nations people believe that self-determination must include changing the balance of political and economic power between First Nations and the Canadian government. In their view, exercising economic power involves making decisions within their communities on economic development and education, as well as providing jobs and industries. First Nations have proposed new laws and institutions to bring about these changes. In 2005, for example, the Canadian government passed a law designed to support institutions that help First Nations communities promote economic growth through investments and job creation.

Poverty, poor health, under-education and high mortality rates all indicate the long-term impacts of the colonization mind-set. It is the Aboriginal peoples' conception of their needs and interests which must be the starting point — the real [meaning] of the term "self-determination."

— Marlene Buffalo, Samson Cree Nation, in People to People, Nation to Nation*, 1996*

[Canada's] constitutional recognition of indigenous governments stands as testimony to a tolerant society that celebrates diversity and rewards those who strive for a better life.

— Justin Ferbey, Carcross Tagish First Nation, in The Globe and Mail*, 2008*

Education and Renewal

To safeguard their social development and culture, some First Nations have established schools where young people can be educated in their own language according to traditional values and knowledge.

Amiskwaciy Academy in Edmonton, for example, enriches the core Alberta curriculum by incorporating Aboriginal teachings and offering optional courses that reflect Aboriginal traditions and values. Elders are available to share their wisdom with students.

Why don't the federal and provincial governments simply honour the original First Nations' treaties?

The First Nations University of Canada in Saskatchewan also focuses on teaching First Nations culture and history. Students can take courses in Indigenous studies, intercultural leadership, and First Nations languages. Science programs incorporate Indigenous knowledge, and students enrol in social work courses designed to promote the healing of First Nations people who have suffered cultural loss.

Inuit Pursuit of Self-Determination

The creation of Nunavut in 1999 is an example of how the Canadian government and Aboriginal communities in Canada can reach agreement on issues involving the pursuit of national self-determination and self-government. The Nunavut Land Claims Agreement, a modern treaty between the government and the Inuit, covers nearly two million square kilometres — 20 per cent of Canada's land mass — and sets out the rights of the Inuit to share in decisions about how their land and its resources are managed and used.

Iqaluit is Nunavut's capital, but key government departments are located in communities across the territory. The government does not have political parties — decisions are made by consensus.

Education in Nunavut promotes Inuit culture, traditions, and languages while helping young people develop the skills needed to develop economically. At Nunavut Arctic College's three campuses and at 24 widely dispersed community learning centres, for example, students prepare for their role in contemporary society at the same time as they learn to respect Inuit values and traditional knowledge. In some cases, Arctic College customizes training programs to help young people take on responsibilities in specific fields, such as municipal government, fisheries, mining, tourism, and mental health.

In a small group, discuss the positive outcomes that can result from creating schools like Amiskwaciy Academy, First Nations University of Canada, and Nunavut Arctic College.

Figure 8-13 On April 1, 1999, this mother and child watched the swearing-in ceremony for members of the Legislative Assembly of Nunavut. Indigenous peoples in South Africa, New Zealand, and South America are using the Nunavut Land Claims Agreement as a model for their own pursuit of self-government and self-determination.

Inuit Tapiriit Kanatami

Inuit Tapiriit Kanatami, which represents Inuit people in Canada, was largely responsible for the creation of Nunavut. The organization was founded as the Inuit Tapirisat of Canada in 1971 to promote the interests of Inuit people and to advocate for self-determination for all peoples.

Today, Inuit Tapiriit Kanatami continues to try to help Inuit people pursue their distinct collective interests and decide for themselves what they want their future to be. The organization manages the Inuit Broadcasting Corporation, operates airlines, and invests in northern businesses. Rosemarie Kuptana, a former president of the organization, explained that Inuit "continue to value our language, to hunt, to trap, to practise customary adoption, and to have a collective identity that is different from other peoples in Canada."

Web Connection

To find out more about Inuit Tapiriit Kanatami, go to this web site and follow the links.

www.ExploringNationalism.ca

MAKING A DIFFERENCE

Zacharias Kunuk
Telling the Truth of What Happened

MAKING A DIFFERENCE MAKING A DIFFERENCE MAKING A DIFFERENCE

As a young child in the late 1950s, Zacharias Kunuk lived with his family on the land, hunting and fishing in the traditional Inuit way. But when he was nine years old, his life changed forever. The Canadian government started settlement programs, and his family was forced to move to Igoolik, on the northwest coast of Baffin Island.

Kunuk grew up listening to the hunting stories told by his father and friends, and in 1981, when Kunuk was 24, he traded some soapstone carvings for a video camera. "What I wanted to do," he told *Ascent* magazine, "was go hunting with my father and videotape it and at the end of the day, he's drinking tea with his hunting buddies. I wanted to see it and show it."

This marked the beginning of Kunuk's filmmaking career, and in 1983, he went to work for the Inuit Broadcasting Corporation, a regional public broadcaster that produces original programming, much of it in Inuktitut. Kunuk's first feature film was called *Atanarjuat* in Inuktitut or *The Fast Runner* in English. Kunuk said that his goal was to tell the "truth of what happened" in Inuit culture. The film, which tells a traditional Inuit story, won international and Canadian awards.

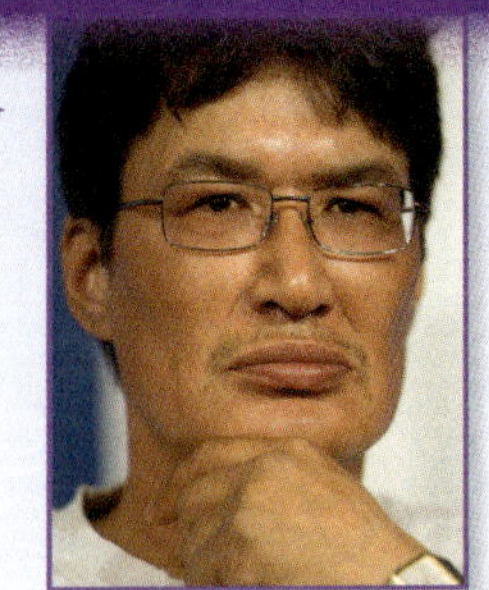

Figure 8-14 Zacharias Kunuk founded Igloolik Isuma Productions, Canada's first independent Inuit film production company. Kunuk's 2001 feature, *Atanarjuat: The Fast Runner*, marked the first time a Canadian movie had been written, produced, directed, and acted by Inuit.

The actors in the film were the Inuit of Igoolik, most of whom knew the story the film was based on. The people of Igloolik also made the traditional caribou clothes and tools used in the film. With no written script, the production was collaborative. Everyone discussed how scenes should be shot.

Kunuk described his goal to *Video Art in Canada*: "We are putting a point of view out to the world. Using video is one tool. People are watching, people are listening."

Explorations

1. The actors in *Atanarjuat: The Fast Runner* spoke Inuktitut. When the film was screened, subtitles in English and other languages were added. What statement do you suppose Zacharias Kunuk was making when he decided to film the dialogue in Inuktitut?
2. In 2008, Kunuk and co-producer Norman Kohn started a YouTube-like web site where Indigenous filmmakers can present their works to audiences. Development of the site was funded by a loan from one of the birthright corporations set up under the Nunavut Land Claims Agreement. Develop three arguments Kunuk and Cohn might have used when persuading the corporation to support their initiative.

It feels good to be able to say that I was doing nothing wrong when I shot that moose to feed my family, especially when I was in an area where our people have been hunting and fishing for generations. That is where and how, by hunting, trapping and fishing, that I and our people have always made our living.

— Alfred Janvier, Métis resident of La Loche, Saskatchewan, 2008

Métis Pursuit of Self-Determination

On March 11, 2008, the Alberta government withdrew a charge of hunting out of season against Alfred Janvier of La Loche, Saskatchewan. Janvier, a Métis, was charged in March 2005 when he shot a moose while travelling from Saskatchewan to Chard, Alberta, to visit his sister.

Janvier fought the charge on the grounds that, as a Métis, he had a constitutional right to harvest the moose and that this right extended across provincial boundaries because Métis traditional territories existed before provincial boundaries were drawn. The issues raised by the case were important to the Métis because harvesting rights are connected with other land-use issues, such as rights to land where oil is being extracted from tar sands.

In 2005, the Métis National Council had appeared before the United Nations Human Rights Committee to argue that Canada has done little to recognize and protect Métis people's right to self-determination. And when the UN General Assembly adopted the Declaration on the Rights of Indigenous Peoples in 2007, the Métis National Council applauded this.

The Canadian Constitution recognizes Métis as one of three Aboriginal peoples who possess Aboriginal and treaty rights. How might the Declaration on the Rights of Indigenous Peoples support the Métis's pursuit of national self-determination?

Figure 8-15 **Métis Settlements in Alberta**

In Alberta, Métis people have experienced some success in pursuing national self-determination. The Métis Association of Alberta was formed in 1932, and in 1938, the provincial government passed the Métis Population Betterment Act. This act established the first — and only — legislated land base for Métis people in Canada. The Alberta government retained ownership of the land, but the settlement associations were granted a degree of self-government.

When the Métis gained constitutional recognition in 1982, Métis people in Alberta pressed harder to win outright ownership of the settlement lands and the right to pursue their own economic, social, and cultural policies. In 1990, Alberta responded by granting title to 500 000 hectares to the people of the Métis settlements. The Métis Association of Alberta, now renamed the Métis Nation of Alberta, continues to fight for the right to self-determination and self-government. The Alberta settlements are still the only constitutionally protected Métis lands in Canada.

How might the Alberta law that recognizes the Métis's right to control large tracts of land affect other Albertans? List at least three positive and three negative effects. Share your list with a partner.

Québec and National Self-Determination

Pursuing national self-determination is often a long, complex process that can spark conflict. Francophone Québécois identify themselves as a distinct cultural group. They share a language, a historical tradition, and a traditional territory. Though Québec remained part of Canada in 2008, the pursuit of sovereignty by many Québec Francophones leaves the province's status in the country uncertain.

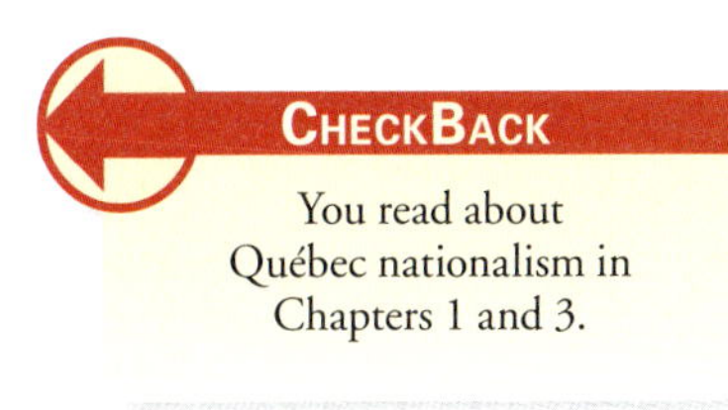

The situation in Québec is an example of how one nation's pursuit of self-determination may impinge on another nation's pursuit of the same goal. Eleven distinct Aboriginal peoples live in Québec. Each has its own claim to self-determination and self-government.

CheckForward

You will read more about the Québécois pursuit of self-determination in Chapter 15.

Sometimes, the interests of these Aboriginal peoples clash with the interests of Québec separatists. During the debate over the 1995 sovereignty referendum, for example, some Aboriginal groups said that if Québec seceded from Canada, they would secede from Québec.

Events in distant countries can also affect questions of self-determination. When Kosovo declared independence from Serbia in February 2008, for example, Canada waited a month before recognizing the new country. Some observers suggested that the delay was caused by the federal government's fear that recognizing Kosovo's sovereignty might encourage the Québec sovereignist cause.

Dušan Bataković, Serbia's ambassador to Canada, warned that recognizing Kosovo set a dangerous precedent. "Can you imagine, for instance, if the Québec parliament declared its unilateral independence the same way the Kosovo parliament did?" he asked. "Would they recognize, in Ottawa, Québec as an independent country or not?"

Figure 8-16 Aboriginal Nations in Québec, 2004

Reflect and Respond

Select one nation that has been pursuing national self-determination in Canada. Note two positive and two negative effects on Canada of this group's pursuit of national self-determination. Support each of your points with logical evidence.

THE VIEW FROM HERE

In October 2006, the Québec wing of the federal Liberal Party voted to recognize Québec as a nation. On November 22, in response to a Bloc Québécois motion that the House of Commons declare Québec a nation, Prime Minister Stephen Harper introduced a motion recognizing that "the Québécois form a nation within a united Canada." On November 27, the House of Commons endorsed the motion by a vote of 266 to 16. Here is what three people said as debate raged over the situation.

On November 23, 2006, Prime Minister **Stephen Harper** responded to Bloc Québécois leader Gilles Duceppe's suggestion that the motion be amended to say that Québécois form a nation "that is currently within Canada."

The true intention of the Bloc leader and the sovereignist camp is perfectly clear. It is not to recognize what the Québécois are, but what the sovereignists would like them to be.

To the Bloc, the issue is not that Québec is a nation – the National Assembly has already pronounced on that; the issue is separation. To them, "nation" means "separation" . . .

The real question is simple: do the Québécois form a nation within a united Canada? The answer is yes. Do the Québécois form a nation independent from Canada? The answer is no, and it will always be no.

On November 27, 2006, Assembly of First Nations national chief **Phil Fontaine** cautioned members of Parliament to bear in mind "the right of self-determination and self-government" held by First Nations in Canada.

The Assembly of First Nations calls upon all Members to make it clear that the Motion with respect to the Quebecois in no way derogates [detracts] from, and in no way diminishes or modifies the unique status and rights of First Nations and their unique place in the past, present and future of this land.

This status and these rights of First Nations include inherent rights of self governance recognized under the laws of Canada and under international law, recognition and safeguarding of aboriginal, treaty and constitutional rights and the right and capacity to continue to live on their traditional and treaty territories and to develop their own distinctive languages and cultures.

On November 29, 2006, **Clément Chartier**, president of the Métis National Council, spoke about the Métis resolution supporting the recognition of Québécois as a nation within a strong and united Canada.

The Métis Nation has long been recognized as a partner in building and defending a strong and united Canada. We value Canada's diversity and believe that the recognition of distinct nations within Canada, such as the Québécois and the Métis Nation, strengthens our bonds to Canada and to each other.

Our nationhood and our rights have already been recognized and protected within the highest law of this land – the Constitution. We have and continue to believe that recognition and respect for the diversity that exists within this country is important.

Explorations

1. In your own words, explain Phil Fontaine's concern. Do you think his concern was justified? Explain your response.
2. In a short written essay, photo essay, display, computer software presentation, or another format of your choice, explain to someone unfamiliar with Canada what Clément Chartier was referring to when he mentioned "Canada's diversity." Be sure to include the term "self-determination" in your presentation.

What are some unintended consequences of the pursuit of national self-determination?

A people's pursuit of national self-determination sometimes results in unintended consequences for others. The partition of India, for example, was an outcome Mohandas Gandhi did not foresee when he began his campaign for Indian self-determination.

In the struggle for self-determination, people sometimes lose their homes, personal security, economic prosperity, the necessities of life, and even life itself. Those who are forced to leave their homeland may also lose their cultural heritage.

When people are trying to achieve or maintain national self-determination, safeguarding their culture and beliefs is often linked to safeguarding the territory that is tied to their identity. Kosovar Serbs, for example, have strong ties to ancient churches and monasteries in Kosovo. James Lyon, a senior adviser to the International Crisis Group, which works to prevent and resolve deadly conflict, spoke of what this loss meant to Kosovar Serbs. "Kosovo plays an integral role in Serbian identity," Lyon said. "Without Kosovo, they suffer an identity crisis that is much more serious than just losing territory."

Figure 8-18 Refugees* from Selected Countries, 2006

Country of Origin	Number of Refugees Recognized by the United Nations
Afghanistan	2 107 519
Bosnia and Herzegovina	199 946
Cambodia	17 995
Iraq	1 450 905
Myanmar (Burma)	202 826
Occupied Palestinian Territory	334 142
Russian Federation	159 381
Rwanda	92 966
Turkey	227 232
Vietnam	374 279

* Estimates of refugees often vary.
Source: United Nations Refugee Agency, *Statistical Yearbook 2006*

Refugees

While people in some countries are fighting for or gaining the right to self-determination, other people are being forced from their homes. By 2006, nearly 32 million people around the world were living as refugees. They had been forced to leave their home country because of persecution, war, or other threats. To escape, some refugees must travel long distances on foot or in unsafe boats, and they usually face an uncertain future or even attacks by extreme nationalists who do not want to offer them shelter.

Once they are out of immediate danger, refugees' main priorities are often to find food, shelter, and health care. If refugees are able to return home, they often find homes, roads, schools, and hospitals in ruins. They have few prospects of earning a living. In addition, their country's justice system may have been shattered, and they may have little or no police protection.

Why doesn't the UN just step in and quickly solve the refugee dilemma?

Figure 8-17 Visoki Dečani Monastery in Kosovo is one of the holy sites revered by Kosovar Serbs. In 2006, UNESCO warned that the monastery, which is a World Heritage Site, was in danger of being lost through neglect and destruction. Should this danger concern only Serbs — or the world?

Should Canada and other developed countries take in more refugees?

Host Countries

The countries to which refugees flee may themselves be experiencing internal conflicts, and some refugees even find themselves fleeing from one conflict zone to another. A sudden influx of refugees can overwhelm the resources of a host country — and create resentments.

Host countries are not required to allow refugees to stay and become citizens, and in time, many refugees are forced to leave. Some host countries give refugees money to encourage them to do this. Australia, for example, gives refugee families about $8000 (U.S.), and some European countries provide the equivalent of $4000 (U.S.) a person.

Figure 8-19 Canadian artist John Larter created this cartoon in 1999. What is Larter's message? Do you agree or disagree? Why?

The United Nations and some countries help by supplying aid to some host countries. Non-governmental organizations, such as the Red Cross, the Red Crescent, and Oxfam, also provide relief and other services to refugee camps and help refugees with development when they return home.

Afghan Refugees

Afghans form the largest single group of refugees in the world. Some refugees have fled Afghanistan, while others remain in the country but have fled areas of conflict or areas that are under Taliban control. Pakistan, which borders Afghanistan, has received the most Afghan refugees — more than two million by 2008. Some Afghans have lived in Pakistani refugee camps since 1979, when they fled the Soviet invasion of their country. Iran, another of Afghanistan's neighbours, has taken in about 1.5 million Afghans. These estimates include both refugees who are registered with the UN and unregistered refugees.

Neither Pakistan nor Iran is a wealthy country. Supporting refugees, even with the help of the UN and NGOs, often challenges their national economic interests. In Iran, the GDP is $12 300 a person. In Pakistan, the GDP is even lower — $2600 a person. By comparison, Canada's per-capita GDP in 2007 was estimated at $38 200.

Afghan refugees often face difficult choices. In early 2008, for example, Pakistan decided to close its largest refugee camp. Afghan refugees were forced to decide whether to try to return home or move to another camp. If they returned home, they faced continuing conflict and economic hardships.

Figure 8-20 Afghan refugees prepared to leave a Pakistani refugee camp and return to Afghanistan. They had collected construction materials to take with them so they could start rebuilding their homes. Is paying refugees to return home a positive way of offering help or a ploy to get rid of them — or both? Explain your response.

But refugees who stayed would continue to live in difficult conditions with little hope of relief. Maulvi Sahib Toti, a refugee from Kunar province in eastern Afghanistan, explained: "There is very little opportunity to earn a living where we come from, and above that, there is a sense of insecurity." But moving to another camp in Pakistan could increase the sense of dislocation that the refugees have already experienced, Toti said. "Our problem is that we want to make a single decision that is long-lasting for us."

In May 2007, Iran forced 85 000 refugees to return to an area where Taliban and coalition forces were actively fighting and where few basic services were available. Adding to the burden of looking after the refugees, both Pakistan and Iran had experienced an increase in terrorist activities. Both countries threatened to use force, if necessary, to get rid of Afghan refugees.

Taking Turns

How has the pursuit of national self-determination affected you?

The students responding to this question are Violet, a Métis who is a member of the Paddle Prairie Métis Settlement; Jane, who lives in Calgary and is descended from black Loyalists who fled to Nova Scotia after the American Revolution; and Blair, who lives in Edmonton and whose heritage is Ukrainian, Scottish, and German.

Violet

My great-grandfather was a member of the original Métis association in 1932, and my grandmother fought for the Alberta Métis settlements all through the 1980s. So my family has been pursuing Métis self-determination for a long time. Grandmother keeps telling my brothers and me that we're not there yet. She says it's now up to us to finish the job that she and our ancestors started.

Jane

I think that gaining self-determination for all peoples is going to take a long, long time. I agree with Martin Luther King Jr. when he said that by going into Vietnam, the Americans didn't even think about the Vietnamese people's right to self-determination. But there's another side to that story. He also said that the American government used up so much of its money on that war that it didn't have any left to help poor people at home.

Blair

Well, the "pursuit" angle in this question gets pretty complicated. Has any nation ever managed to get self-determination free and clear without a battle and without a whole lot of baggage left over? In my family, they still tell stories about the battles the Ukrainians had to fight to get their rights — even in Canada! And as for my Scottish relatives, they say they've been fighting for a constitution since 1707. In 2008, the Scots are still taking polls to decide whether to hold a referendum on independence from Britain.

How would you respond to the question that Violet, Jane, and Blair are answering? Do any of their responses reflect your experience of self-determination? How do their responses demonstrate the complexity of the pursuit of national self-determination?

THINK...PARTICIPATE...RESEARCH...COMMUNICATE...

1. In this chapter, you have explored responses to this issue question: To what extent should national self-determination be pursued? Work in a small group to complete the following tasks:
   a) Deconstruct the issue question to discover its meaning. This process should involve examining the key phrases that make up the question. When you analyze, for example, the phrase "national self-determination," your analysis should clearly express your understandings of the words "national" and "self-determination," as well as the phrase "national self-determination." Record your conclusions in point form.
   b) From this chapter, select an example of a nation seeking self-determination. On the basis of your group's understanding of the issue question, decide whether this nation should continue pursuing self-determination. Provide reasons for your decision.
   c) Share your findings with another group. Compare your group's deconstruction of the issue question, as well as your decision on what the nation should do.
   d) On the basis of this discussion, re-examine the decision you reached. Decide whether you wish to revise or stick with your decision.
   e) Use your decision to prepare a final statement indicating, in general terms, when nations should — and should not — pursue self-determination.
2. Examine the cartoon in Figure 8-21 on this page. It was created by artist Bob Krieger and published shortly after Prime Minister Stephen Harper introduced a motion stating that Québécois are a nation within a united Canada.
   a) What does the hornets' nest represent? What images support your conclusion?
   b) What is Krieger's message? Do you agree with his view? Explain why or why not.
   c) Explain why you think Krieger used the symbol of a hornets' nest. Do you believe this is appropriate? Explain your judgment.
   d) What other symbol(s) might Krieger have used to make the same point? Explain how your choice sends the same message.
3. According to Statistics Canada, Aboriginal peoples are the fastest-growing segment of Canada's population. If population growth rates continue at the same pace, the size of Canada's Aboriginal population could equal that of the non-Aboriginal population in about 2100. Review "Focus on Skills: Predicting Likely Outcomes" (pp. 188–189). Then predict how the growth in Canada's Aboriginal population might affect the following issues:
   a) treaty resolution
   b) employment and education opportunities
   c) Aboriginal self-determination and self-government
   d) an area of interest to you

Figure 8-21

4. Kashmir was promised a plebiscite to decide its political future, but no plebiscite has ever been held. Review the situation in Kashmir.

   a) Prepare a statement that sets out the issue Kashmiris should be deciding. Ensure that your statement indicates the choices available and predicts the possible consequences of each choice.

   b) Write the plebiscite question that you would put to Kashmiris. The question should offer a clear choice and provide some details about the effects of their choice. Voters should be able to answer the question by marking yes or no on a ballot. The following are examples of plebiscite questions that various governments have used:

   April 27, 1942 — Canadians voted on whether to release Prime Minister William Lyon Mackenzie King from his promise not to send conscripts overseas. This was the plebiscite question: Are you in favour of releasing the Government from any obligations arising out of any past commitments restricting the methods of raising men for military service?

   May 26, 1997 — People who would eventually live in Nunavut voted on the makeup of the legislature. This was the plebiscite question: Should the first Nunavut Legislative Assembly have equal numbers of men and women MLAs, with one man and one woman elected to represent each electoral district?

   September 2, 1997 — Newfoundlanders voted on whether to change the province's education system. This was the plebiscite question: Do you support a single school system where all children, regardless of their religious affiliation, attend the same schools where opportunities for religious education and observances are provided?

5. Read the following quotations. The first was a comment by the Dalai Lama in 2001; the second was a comment by Mao Zedong in 1931, when he was establishing the foundation for the emergence of China as a united communist country. Based on your knowledge of events in Tibet over the past decades, describe and comment on the changes in China's attitude toward sovereignty and national self-determination.

   Dalai Lama, March 2001

   > If the Tibetans are truly happy the Chinese authorities should have no difficulty in holding a plebiscite in Tibet. Already some Tibetan non-governmental organizations are advocating a referendum in Tibet. They argue that the best way to resolve this issue once and for all is to allow the Tibetans inside Tibet to choose their own destiny through a freely held referendum. They demand to let the Tibetan people speak out and decide for themselves. I have always maintained that ultimately the Tibetan people must be able to decide the future of Tibet. I would in fact whole-heartedly support the result of such a referendum.

   Mao Zedong, November 1931

   > The Soviet Government of China recognizes the right of self-determination of the national minorities in China, their right to complete separation from China and to the formation of an independent state for each national minority.

Think about Your Challenge

To help you develop a response to the related-issue question — To what extent should national interest be pursued? — your challenge for this related issue involves preparing an investigative report on a historical or contemporary nationalist movement.

You have been gathering information and collecting material as you have progressed through this related issue. Organize these materials into the format you have chosen and write the first draft of your report. Show this draft to a classmate, a family member, or your teacher. Use their feedback and "Checklist for Success" on page 112 to revise your report.

RELATED ISSUE 3

To what extent should internationalism be pursued?

Key Issue
To what extent should we embrace nationalism?

Related Issue 1
To what extent should nation be the foundation of identity?

Related Issue 2
To what extent should national interest be pursued?

Related Issue 3
To what extent should internationalism be pursued?

Related Issue 4
To what extent should individuals and groups in Canada embrace a national identity?

Chapter 9

Nations, Nations-States, and Internationalism

To what extent does involvement in international affairs benefit nations and states?

What are some common motives of nations and states?

How do the motives of nations and states shape their responses to the world?

What are some understandings of internationalism?

How does internationalism benefit nations and states?

Chapter 10

Foreign Policy and Internationalism

To what extent can foreign policy promote internationalism?

How do countries set foreign policy?

How can states promote internationalism through foreign policy?

How does Canadian foreign policy try to balance national interest and internationalism?

Chapter 11

Internationalism and Nationalism

To what extent do efforts to promote internationalism through world organizations affect nationalism?

How have changing world conditions promoted the need for internationalism?

How have the United Nations' changing international responses affected nationalism?

How do the responses of various international organizations affect nationalism?

Chapter 12

Internationalism and Global Issues

To what extent can internationalism effectively address contemporary global issues?

What are some contemporary global issues?

How has internationalism been used to address contemporary global issues?

Is internationalism always the most effective way of addressing contemporary global issues?

The Big Picture

To stay alive, you must breathe, drink, and eat. You have no choice. But in other situations, you may face many choices. When this happens, what motivates you to choose one course of action over another? What motivates you, for example, to study instead of going to a movie with friends — or vice versa? What motivates you to take an after-school job — or not?

Understanding your motives and how they affect your choices enables you to make decisions that are in your best interest. In the same way, understanding the motives of nations and nation-states can help you understand the forces that affect decisions made by governments. In the four chapters of this related issue, you will explore some of these forces, the choices they present to peoples and governments, the decisions that governments have made as a result, and how these decisions have affected international relationships. You will also analyze and evaluate the motives that lie behind foreign policy decisions and how nations and countries adjust to changing world conditions while balancing their national interest against the need to respond to and resolve global issues.

In developing your understanding of the relationships that connect people, groups, and governments to the international community, you will also explore the motives that encourage individuals, groups, and countries to participate in international organizations, both governmental and non-governmental — and how international participation can affect nations, nation-states, and the international community.

The chart on the preceding page shows how you will progress through the chapters of Related Issue 3. As you explore this related issue, you will come to appreciate

- that the relationships among countries are complex and dynamic
- that individuals, groups, and countries participate in international organizations for a complex variety of reasons
- that a country's foreign policies can affect you and others both directly and indirectly
- that changing world conditions and globalization have affected international participation on an individual, regional, and national level — and have sparked a shift in the relationships among individuals, groups, and countries

Your Challenge

Participate in an international summit convened to respond to the international water crisis. The summit will focus on this issue: Should management of the world's water resources be taken out of the hands of national governments and turned over to an international body?

As you explore responses to this question, you will also be responding to the question for this related issue: To what extent should internationalism be pursued?

Checklist for Success

Use this checklist to ensure that your presentation includes everything necessary to be successful.

My Knowledge and Understanding

☑ My position on the issue is clearly stated.

☑ My facts are clearly presented.

☑ My position is supported by reliable, valid evidence.

My Selection, Analysis, and Evaluation of Information

☑ My information was drawn from a variety of reliable sources that are cited correctly and accurately.

☑ My information reflects diverse points of view and perspectives.

☑ My criteria for judgment are clearly explained.

My Presentation

☑ My presentation engages the audience and provides opportunities for audience feedback and interaction.

☑ My presentation is respectful of others.

☑ My presentation is supported by interesting graphics and uses technology appropriately.

Some Background Information

The 2007 report of the World Water Council, a non-governmental organization that tracks and responds to water-related issues, predicted that, by 2020, the world will need 17 per cent more fresh, clean water than is now available. Predictions like this led Ismail Serageldin, a former vice-president of the World Bank and founder and former chair of the Global Water Partnership, to declare in 1999 that "the wars of the [21st] century will be about water."

Experts believe that less than 0.08 per cent of the earth's water is suitable for human use. The rest is salt water or frozen at the poles. Kevin Conway of the International Development Research Centre said: "If we were to imagine all the earth's water in a 1000-litre bucket filled to brimming, the fraction that is fresh water and not locked in ice is a mere 25 millilitres. Rough estimates place South America's share of that total at about half. Asia gets almost 6.25 millilitres, leaving the remainder — another 6.25 millilitres — for everyone living in North and Central America, Europe, Australia, Africa, and the Middle East."

Conway believes in community-based water management and does not believe that international action will resolve the crisis. "It is at [the local level] that the effects of water scarcity are most keenly felt, and it is here that solutions must be implemented," he has said.

But Robert Svadlenka, who has studied the crisis, believes that international action is essential. "Like the air we breathe, [water] is something that we often take for granted. Once assumed unlimited in supply, now even developed nations are realizing its limits. It is the most precious of all resources, an essential component of almost every human activity, and vital to the health of all ecosystems . . . And it is running out."

Water by the Numbers

- By 2025, 20 per cent more water than is now available will be needed to support the additional 3 billion people who will live on Earth.
- Aquifers, which store water underground, supply 1/3 of the world's water and are being pumped out faster than nature can replenish them.
- Half the world's rivers and lakes are seriously polluted.
- Major rivers, such as the Yangtze, Ganges, and Colorado, do not flow to the sea anymore because of dams and upstream water taking.

Preparing for and Participating in the Summit

Step 1

In a group of five or six, refer to the chart titled "Summit Stakeholders and Goals." Assign one stakeholder to each group member. At the summit, the group member will play the role of her or his assigned stakeholder.

Work with your group to organize a process for exchanging views. You may, for example, decide that each stakeholder will open with a one-minute statement, then have three minutes to present supporting arguments. This can be followed by a two-minute question-and-answer session. To close, each stakeholder may have a minute to present counter-arguments, suggestions for compromise, or a final appeal for support.

Step 2

Work independently to prepare a presentation of your stakeholder's position. Start by developing three or four inquiry questions to help guide your research. If you are representing the delegation from Canada, for example, one of your questions might ask how Canada can balance its international responsibilities and its national interest.

Step 3

Decide how you will make your case to other stakeholders, whose goals may be different from yours. Prepare your presentation.

Think about the positions other stakeholders are likely to present. Use your research to prepare counter-arguments.

Step 4

Convene your summit. When the presentations and follow-up are complete, work with your group to try to achieve consensus. Discuss the success of the process you used and prepare a media release summing up your conclusions. If your group was unable to achieve consensus, your release should say this — and explain why.

Step 5

Share your media release with the class. As a class, discuss whether an international summit is an appropriate forum for dealing with the water crisis.

Summit Stakeholders and Goals

Stakeholder	Goals
United Nations	To set criteria for an international body to monitor water use by member states To persuade member states to participate To develop creative incentives to persuade member states to comply
Canada	To retain sovereignty over water To show understanding of the crisis and willingness to help by offering aid and expertise
An Environmental Group	To set up an international panel to ensure that the world's water supply is respected and benefits everyone To ensure that individual countries seek the panel's approval for large-scale water programs To develop trade penalties or sanctions to force countries to comply
A Developing Country (Choose a country such as China, India, or Zambia.)	To gain access to enough fresh, clean water to support the country's citizens To ensure that everyone in all countries has access to enough water
Think Global, Act Local (Group dedicated to local, grassroots action)	To ensure that solutions focus on local actions To involve top scientists in working with local communities and countries to tailor solutions to fit local circumstances
Interior Alliance (Southern Carrier, St'at'imc, Secwepemc, Nlaka'pamux, and Okanagan peoples of British Columbia)	To ensure that water is accessible to First Nations To promote First Nations' inherent rights to care for lands and water as environmental stewards To promote First Nations' rights to participate on a government-to-government basis in decisions affecting resources

CHAPTER 9 Nations, Nation-States, and Internationalism

Figure 9-1 This photograph of Earth was taken by American astronaut William Anders on December 24, 1968, just as the crew of *Apollo 8* emerged from their first orbit around the dark side of the moon, which appears at the right. It was the first photograph of Earth taken from deep space.

CHAPTER ISSUE

To what extent does involvement in international affairs benefit nations and states?

WHEN THE PICTURE on the previous page was published, it created a sensation. Human beings had never before seen a picture of Earth taken from deep space. To many, the planet appeared as a glowing jewel with no sign of human habitation. American nature photographer Galen Rowell, for example, called this picture "the most influential environmental photograph ever taken."

And Pulitzer Prize–winning American poet Archibald MacLeish wrote: "To see the earth as it truly is, small and blue and beautiful in that eternal silence where it floats, is to see ourselves as riders on the earth together, brothers on that bright loveliness in the eternal cold — brothers who know now they are truly brothers."

Examine the photograph, then respond to these questions:

- How does the photograph suggest that the earth is a community in which everyone shares the same future?
- How does it suggest that humanity must deal with challenges, not only as individuals, but also as nations, nation-states, and a global community?
- Why do you suppose Galen Rowell called this picture "the most influential environmental photograph ever taken"?
- How do Archibald MacLeish's words capture the essence of the photograph's meaning? How do his words reflect the time he lived in?
- If you set out to take a picture that would capture the essence of MacLeish's words, what might you choose to photograph?

KEY TERMS

needs

wants

isolationism

unilateralism

bilateralism

multilateralism

supranationalism

internationalism

LOOKING AHEAD

In this chapter, you will develop responses to the following questions as you explore the extent to which international affairs benefit nations and states:

- What are some common motives of nations and states?
- How do the motives of nations and states shape their responses to the world?
- What are some understandings of internationalism?
- How does internationalism benefit nations and states?

My Journal on Nationalism

Look again at the photograph on the previous page. Think about how you could use photographs to express your current ideas about nationalism. Date your ideas and keep them in your journal, notebook, learning log, portfolio, or computer file so that you can return to them as you progress this course.

Figure 9-2 Abraham Maslow's Hierarchy of Human Needs

SELF-ACTUALIZATION
personal growth, fulfilment, etc.

ESTEEM NEEDS
achievement, confidence, self-esteem, respect, etc.

LOVE AND BELONGING NEEDS
friendship, affection, family, relationships, etc.

SAFETY AND SECURITY NEEDS
protection, security, order, law, etc.

BASIC SURVIVAL NEEDS
air, food, water, shelter, warmth, health, sleep, etc.

WHAT ARE SOME COMMON MOTIVES OF NATIONS AND STATES?

Think about the range of human activity on this planet and what motivates people to take action. Psychologists believe that people are motivated by both needs and wants.

Needs are the basic elements — food, water, shelter, health — required for survival. **Wants** are things that people desire, regardless of whether the desired object contributes to their survival. People may, for example, want a cellphone, a fulfilling job, or to dress in the latest fashion, but they do not *need* these things to survive.

Both needs and wants are powerful motivators that encourage people to go to school, to practise a skill, or to work at a job.

Psychologist Abraham Maslow believed that human needs follow a universal pattern or hierarchy. He said that all humans are motivated to meet their basic survival needs — located at the bottom of the pyramid shown in Figure 9-2. Once these needs are met, people begin to be concerned about safety and security, which are the next level up in the hierarchy. And once people satisfy their need for safety and security, they turn their attention to other motivators, such as love, self-esteem, and personal growth and fulfilment.

Think about the motivators listed in Figure 9-2. Why do you think Maslow chose to show these needs as a hierarchy? How well are your needs at each level being met? How might this situation change in five years?

Maslow's theory is not universally accepted. Some critics believe that human nature is too complex to depict as the kind of hierarchy he envisioned. They say, for example, that some humans are born with a powerful need to help others and that, in some cases, this need may override their own need for safety and security.

FYI

In 1938, Abraham Maslow spent time with the Siksika who lived near Calgary. Maslow came to admire the Siksika people, and his observations of their culture challenged his previous understandings about how human nature develops and influenced his theory of human needs.

Figure 9-3 Afghan children greeted these Canadian soldiers as they patrolled outside their base near Kandahar. List factors that might motivate someone to join the Armed Forces. Classify each factor as a want or a need.

Motives of Successful Nations and Nation-States

Just as the behaviour of individuals is motivated by a complex variety of needs and wants, so, too, are the actions of nations and nation-states. Nations are made up of human beings and nation-states are made up of — and governed by — human beings. Successful nation-states, especially those with democratic governments, are often motivated by the need to serve their citizens by providing economic stability, peace and security, self-determination, and humanitarian activities.

The needs and wants that motivate nation-states do not operate in isolation. They overlap, combine, and build on one another in a complex relationship.

Confidence in the economy and in our long-term economic growth demands even greater co-operation to ready a comfort zone of optimal national security. Without a "secure economy," businesses will struggle to grow and earn profits and the revenues for governments will be at risk.

— *John Reid, president, Canadian Advanced Technology Alliance, 2006*

Economic Stability

People and nation-states face similar economic questions about the future. Individuals may worry, for example, about being able to support their family. As a result, they are motivated to find jobs that provide economic stability. Finding this kind of job may require learning a trade or staying in school long enough to earn the educational qualifications needed to pursue a specific career. Nations may take similar steps to prepare for the economic future.

Economic stability depends on a number of factors, including high employment. High employment promotes economic stability because people who have jobs have more money to spend. When people spend more money on goods and services, they create demand — and demand requires more goods and services. The demand for more goods and services means that employers are likely to hire more workers. This creates more jobs and leads to high employment.

High employment helps create prosperity for individuals and also for governments, which are able to collect more taxes and use the proceeds to pay for government services.

Examine the graphic in Figure 9-4, which shows the positive effects of high employment. Use this graphic to explain to a partner how high employment can promote economic stability. Work with your partner to create a similar graphic to show the opposite: how high unemployment might negatively affect economic stability.

Figure 9-4 Positive Effects of High Employment

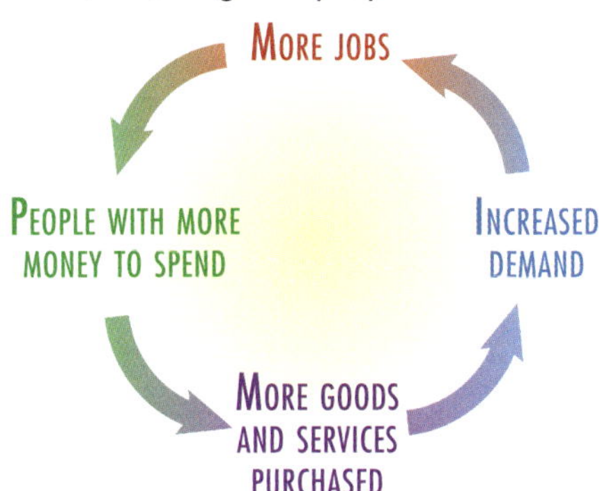

Figure 9-5 Largely because of high oil revenues, the construction industry in Alberta is booming. What workers might be able to get jobs at this Calgary construction site? How might the construction boom lead to positive and negative effects for construction workers and society?

Peace and Security

Is it ever possible for a government to meet all the peace and security needs of a country's citizens?

Psychologist Abraham Maslow believed that safety and security is the second-most-important human need. It is hard to be happy or to live a satisfying life when faced with violence or conflict. People want safe streets, they want their possessions to be secure, and they want to live free of fear of suffering physical or psychological harm.

People who live in countries where they do not feel safe may be unable to attend school or work productively — and citizens who feel insecure are more likely to oppose the government. In addition, countries need well-educated, well-trained workers because a skilled and experienced workforce helps create economic prosperity. This need motivates governments to try to ensure the safety and security needs of citizens.

In countries like Canada, where the Charter of Rights and Freedoms guarantees security of the person, security is considered a human right that the government must provide. People also have access to a legal system that helps keep the peace and settle disagreements fairly and safely.

Like individuals, nation-states are also motivated by concerns about national peace and security. Wars kill and injure people, cause immense grief, destroy property, and deprive people and countries of economic stability. People around the world want to be free of war and to feel protected against ruthless governments that seek conquests.

Figure 9-6 These women are among the 60 000 people who live in the Otash refugee camp in the Darfur region of Sudan, where 2.5 million people have been displaced by fighting between government forces and rebels. What might be some long-term effects of the lack of peace and security created by the civil conflict in Sudan?

Independently and collectively, states have taken steps to promote peace and ensure that their citizens can live in safety. Canada, for example, belongs to a number of organizations whose goals involve ensuring national security. These include the North Atlantic Treaty Organization, an alliance of more than 25 countries, including Canada. NATO's purpose is to safeguard the freedom and security of its members. The North American Aerospace Defense Command is a Canada–United States partnership that is responsible for defending North American air space. The United Nations is an organization dedicated to improving world peace and stability.

Why would countries be motivated to co-operate with other nation-states to ensure peace and security? Would a country with a strong military — such as the United States — be motivated as strongly as nation-states whose armed forces are smaller?

Self-Determination

Most people agree that it is important to control their own lives. People want to make their own decisions about friends, relationships, education and work, and how to spend their free time. For many people, the greatest benefit of adulthood is an increased level of self-determination, which allows them to control their own fate.

Nations and nation-states also want to control their own fate and may try to do this by seeking either self-determination or outright sovereignty. This is what has happened in the former Soviet Union. Since this huge political union started to collapse in the late 1980s, 15 sovereign nation-states have emerged.

Indigenous peoples around the world are also fighting to achieve greater self-determination. In the colonial era, many Indigenous peoples lost control over their own lives to imperial powers. Today, they are seeking to determine for themselves the future course of their lives. For some, this means seeking sovereignty; for others, it means seeking self-determination within a larger nation-state.

In 2005, the Carcross Tagish First Nation of Yukon successfully negotiated a self-government agreement with Canada. The nation's Tagish and Tlingit Elders drafted a statement — in Tagish, Tlingit, and English — describing why the agreement is so important. The following is some of what they said:

> We who are Tagish and we who are Tinglit, our heritage has grown roots into the earth since the olden times. Therefore we are part of the earth and the water. We know our Creator entrusted us with the responsibility of looking after the land into perpetuity, and the water, and whatever is on our land, and what is beneath our land. So those coming after us, we will give them that responsibility into perpetuity. Our elders have assigned us the task of showing respect to things. Therefore, we will look after our land as they have told us to do, as did our elders . . .
>
> We will be the bosses of our land . . . and all the resources of this land, as we have agreed on. We will be our own masters. We who are the Tagish, and we who are the Tlingit, will protect our land . . . we will reform the way we work with the government. We will work together with mutual respect, and act truthfully [toward each other].

Reread the words of the Carcross Tagish Elders. What understanding(s) of nation do these words reflect? How do the Elders view their relationship with the other levels of government in Canada?

CheckBack

You read about understandings of nation in Chapter 1.

How can Aboriginal peoples within Canada, or in any country, be a nation within a nation?

Figure 9-7 Members of the Carcross Tagish First Nation demonstrate in Carcross, Yukon, during the 2007 National Day of Action. This First Nation negotiated a self-government agreement with the Canadian government in 2005. Why might members of this First Nation have believed that participating in the National Day of Action was still important?

Humanitarianism

In December 2006, an earthquake under the Indian Ocean created a huge tsunami — tidal wave — that struck parts of Southeast Asia. About five million people in Indonesia, India, and Sri Lanka were directly affected. Canadians responded by donating millions of dollars to help tsunami victims, while some Canadians chose to go help the sick and injured and to help rebuild villages, schools, and hospitals.

Family members, neighbours, friends, and people living together in communities are often motivated to help one another. Neighbours, for example, may help out when there is illness in a family or when someone is injured in an accident. People are also often motivated to help those who are less fortunate, even when they do not know them personally. High school students, for example, often organize food drives for the local food bank, as well as campaigns to raise money for charitable and humanitarian causes.

Many nation-states also take action to relieve suffering and protect the innocent. Natural disasters, disease, war, and conflict can all cause tremendous suffering. In these situations, many countries offer humanitarian aid, which may include providing money and supplies, as well as accepting and sheltering refugees. Every year, the Canadian government directly sponsors more than 7000 refugees. Private groups, which are responsible for the people they sponsor for a year after their arrival, sponsor several thousand more.

Re-examine Abraham Maslow's hierarchy of human needs (Figure 9-2). Which category do you think includes people's need to help others? How might offering humanitarian aid benefit nations and countries?

Figure 9-8 Alan Hoti, a Kosovo refugee, is greeted by his uncle at Thompson Airport in Manitoba. Members of St. John's United Church in Thompson collected the items necessary for three refugee families from Kosovo to establish themselves in Canada. In what way does sheltering refugees require both individual and state humanitarianism?

In 2006, refugee agencies run by the United Nations provided aid to about 14 million people around the world. These refugees were fleeing war, disasters, or persecution.

Reflect and Respond

How might the needs of wealthy countries differ from those of poor countries?

Reflect on what you have read in this chapter so far and rank the motives of developed and developing countries in order of importance from most to least. Record your choices and explain the criteria you used to make your judgments.

Then think about some of the common needs and motives of nations and states. How similar are they to the common needs and motives of individuals? How does this information show that nations and states are human entities?

THE VIEW FROM HERE

THE VIEW FROM HERE
THE VIEW FROM HERE
THE VIEW FROM HERE

When countries are unable to meet the needs of their citizens, they may be classified as "failed states." But what causes a state to fail? Does the cause lie within the failed state or with the world community? Here is how three people have attempted to answer these questions.

Robert I. Rotberg is a professor of public policy at Harvard University and president of the World Peace Foundation. The following excerpt is from his contribution to *When States Fail: Causes and Consequences*.

State failure is largely man made, not accidental. Cultural clues are relevant, but insufficient to explain persistent leadership flaws. Likewise, institutional fragilities and structural flaws contribute to failure . . . but those deficiencies usually hark back to decisions or actions of men (rarely women). So it is that leadership errors across history have destroyed states for personal gain; in the contemporary era, leadership mistakes continue to erode fragile polities [countries] in Africa, the Americas, Asia, and Oceania that already operate on the cusp of failure.

Erin Simpson is a former policy officer with the Canadian Council for International Co-operation. In this excerpt from an article published in *Peace Magazine*, Simpson examines the role of rich countries and failed states.

Obsessed as rich countries are with stabilizing the world's "failed and fragile states," the idea that these same rich countries are key causes of "failed states" is not on the table. The "failed states" frame ignores the international community's responsibility for the conflict and weak governance – past, present, and (unless things change) future. If we accept . . . that our world is an interconnected system, and that conflicts arise from both outside and within a society, then we will stop debating *whether* or *how* to get involved in the world's troubled areas. The international community is inherently involved, both in originating and responding to problems.

Jean-Pierre Lindiro Kabirigi is a consultant with the Pole Institute, a non-governmental organization based in Rwanda. The following comments are from a 2005 speech titled "Failed States in Sub-Saharan Africa — Causes, Consequences, and Possible Interventions."

On several occasions, many analysts have thought that the solutions to recover peace in the Democratic Republic of Congo have to be found out from outside, especially by protecting the country from its cumbersome neighbours. Although the involvement of Congo's neighbours accounts somehow for the Congo's disastrous state, it is important to point out that before their arrival, the DRC was already a failed state. Moreover, such analysis ignores how much the Congo's elites have played an important role to damage their own country. Congo nationals co-operated themselves with the invaders in what made foreign looting of the DRC possible. In my opinion, what Congo lacks the most is not international assistance. What it profoundly needs is patriotism of the elites.

Explorations

1. Cite one criterion each speaker or writer used to define a "failed state."
2. Which view do you think is the most persuasive? What criteria did you use to make this judgment?
3. Explain how the ideas expressed in these excerpts are linked to the motivations of nations and states: peace and security, economic stability, self-determination, and humanitarianism.

Botswana and Zimbabwe Similar Geography, Different Results

Botswana and Zimbabwe are neighbours in southern Africa. The two countries share a border and many economic and geographic features. Despite these similarities, the two countries have evolved very differently. Botswana enjoys much greater political stability and economic prosperity than Zimbabwe.

In 2007, the Fund for Peace, a non-governmental organization devoted to preventing war and easing the conditions that cause war, ranked 177 countries on its annual index. Zimbabwe's risk of failure was considered the fourth-highest in the world, while Botswana ranked 119th. By comparison, Canada ranked 168th and is considered relatively successful.

Similar Colonial Histories

Both Botswana and Zimbabwe were British colonies, and in both, the economy was controlled by the white minority. When the two countries gained independence, both were rich in natural and human resources, with great potential for the future. Zimbabwe was a major agricultural exporter, although most land was owned by members of the white minority. Botswana had a strong cattle- and meat-exporting economy, which was in the hands of local peoples.

Botswana achieved independence peacefully in 1966 and became a parliamentary republic. For the next five years, the country remained financially dependent on Britain. But development took off after the discovery of diamonds in 1967, and the country is now the leading exporter of gem-quality diamonds. This improves the government's ability to provide services to the people.

In contrast, the white minority in Zimbabwe refused to give up control, and this led to a long and violent civil war that divided the country along racial lines. As a result, Zimbabwe did not achieve independence until 1980.

Figure 9-9 Botswana and Zimbabwe

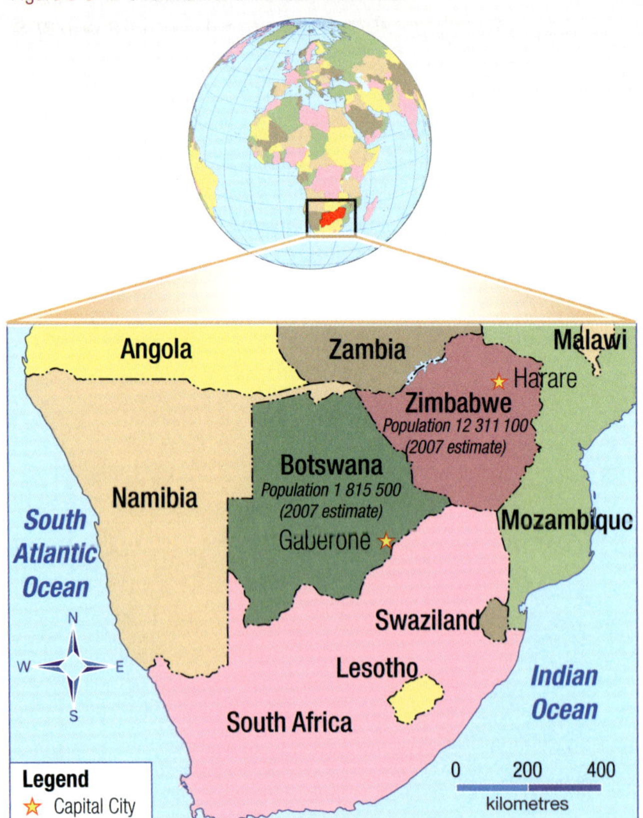

Figure 9-10 Botswana and Zimbabwe — A Comparison

Category	Botswana	Zimbabwe
GDP per person (2006)	$10 900 (U.S.)	$2100 (U.S.)
Inflation rate	11.5% (2006)	1033.5% (2006) 24 000% (2007)
Life expectancy at birth	50.58 years	39.5 years
HIV/AIDS rate	37.3%	24.6%
Population per physician	3477	17 439
Population per hospital bed	635	1959
Educational expenditures as share of GDP	9.3%	11.1%
Number of students per teacher – primary school	27	39
Number of years of compulsory school	10	7
Number of Internet users	60 000	1 220 000
Number of telephone land lines	136 900	331 700
Number of cellphones	979 800	832 500
Number of televisions per 1000 people	27	36
Number of motor vehicles per 1000 people	92	50

Differing Quality of Life

Robert Mugabe, who has led Zimbabwe since independence, was praised at first as a leading figure in African democracy. But this did not last. Although Zimbabwe is officially a parliamentary democracy, Mugabe gradually established a one-party state by violently stifling opposition and trampling the rights of citizens.

In 2000, Mugabe seized the farms of white landowners and handed the property to members of his government and other supporters. Soon afterwards, agricultural production plummeted and exports dropped drastically. Foreign and local investment dried up, and the country's economy slowed down dramatically.

As more and more Zimbabweans began to feel the effects of the economic downturn, the number of people living in makeshift urban slums and shantytowns swelled. Crime shot up, and in 2005, Mugabe's government ordered a crackdown on these areas. Police and security forces evicted people from their homes, setting whole communities ablaze and beating anyone who resisted. By 2006, the homes and livelihoods of an estimated 570 000 people had been destroyed and they had become internally displaced persons.

By the end of 2007, unemployment in Zimbabwe stood at 80 per cent and inflation had skyrocketed to an estimated annual rate of 24 000 per cent — and some economists suggested that the rate was even higher. The situation was so desperate that in July 2007, Mugabe ordered businesses to reduce prices or be seized by the government. Businesses were forced to open, and riots erupted as people tried to buy the few available goods. Gasoline, bread, and other basic commodities quickly sold out, and no new supplies were available.

Meanwhile, Botswana has experienced four decades of political stability and its economy is one of the most dynamic in Africa. And even though the country's rate of HIV/AIDS infection is one of the highest in the world, the Botswana government has put in place one of the most progressive programs in Africa for dealing with this disease.

Figure 9-11 In November 2007, Godfrey Chirenje (right) of Harare waited in line for three hours to buy the loaf of bread he is carrying. By January 2008, the price of bread had risen to as much as a million Zimbabwean dollars a loaf.

As the situation in Zimbabwe became worse, thousands of Zimbabweans flooded into Botswana in search of work. But they were not welcomed. Botswana's unemployment rate was already higher than 20 per cent, and the government did not want its citizens to lose jobs to foreigners.

In 2003, Botswana began building an electric fence along its 500-kilometre border with Zimbabwe. The official reason for building the fence was to stop the spread of foot-and-mouth disease among livestock. In 2003, Botswana lost 13 000 cattle to the disease, which the government claimed was brought across the border from Zimbabwe. But Zimbabweans argue that this rationale is nothing but window dressing. They say that the fence, which is four metres high, is clearly intended to keep people out — and the barrier remains a source of tension between the two countries.

Explorations

1. To meet citizens' needs, nation-states must provide peace and security, economic stability, self-determination, and humanitarian activities. How do the stories of Botswana and Zimbabwe demonstrate the importance of meeting these needs?
2. Examine Figure 9-10 and explain how these statistics highlight the differences in the quality of life of citizens of Botswana and Zimbabwe. How do you think these statistics might affect the sense of nationalism felt by the people of each country?
3. How might living next door to a failing state affect the citizens of a country such as Botswana? Is building an electrified fence an appropriate way of protecting its sovereignty and meeting the needs of its citizens? Explain your response.

Decision Making and Problem Solving

FOCUS ON SKILLS

Experts studying decision making and problem solving have found that decisions made in a systematic way tend to result in more positive outcomes. One strategy that contributes to improved decision making and problem solving is brainstorming, a technique that involves generating alternative ideas.

The story of Botswana and Zimbabwe shows that not all nation-states are successful. When a country is unable to meet the needs of its citizens, it is at risk of failure. A failing state, for example, may be unable to provide citizens with public services, such as basic health care, including vaccinations and other preventive measures. Inadequate health care places citizens at risk of dying prematurely.

According to the 2007 Failed States Index, Zimbabwe was in a state of social, economic, and political crisis. This index rates each country on the basis of 12 indicators divided into three categories (see Figure 9-12). A total score is then calculated. This score estimates a country's risk of failure.

Suppose a delegation from Zimbabwe has approached your group to help develop a plan for improving the quality of life in their country. You and your group must decide on the most effective way of doing this.

Steps to Decision Making and Problem Solving

Step 1: Establish a goal

In a small group, think about the factors that place Zimbabwe at risk of failure and what help would be most significant for Zimbabweans. To do this, you may wish to review the information in Figure 9-9 (p. 216) and Figure 9-12 on this page. Having a specific goal in mind will help you develop an effective strategy that will bring positive results.

Do you, for example, want to help internally displaced people find homes? Or improve health care or education? Once your goal is set, you can focus on developing a strategy to help Zimbabweans achieve it.

Step 2: Consider the complex issues that underlie the question

Complexities such as sovereignty enter the picture. Interfering in the affairs of another country is difficult. Think about how you would feel in the same position. Many Canadians, for example, resent it when Americans suggest ways that Canada might be improved.

Because of the colonial experience, people in many African countries view help from former colonial powers and wealthy Western countries as interference. Keep the issue of sovereignty in mind as you generate and evaluate ideas. If necessary, conduct additional research to comfirm your ideas.

Figure 9-12 Indicators Used to Calculate a State's Risk of Failure

Social Indicators
1. Mounting demographic pressures
2. Massive movement of refugees or internally displaced persons, creating complex humanitarian emergencies
3. Legacy of vengeance-seeking group grievance or group paranoia
4. Chronic and sustained human flight
Economic Indicators
5. Uneven economic development along group lines
6. Sharp or severe economic decline or both
Political Indicators
7. Criminalization or delegitimization (removal of legitimate status) of the state, or both
8. Progressive deterioration of public services
9. Suspension or arbitrary application of the rule of law and widespread violation of human rights
10. Security apparatus operates as a "state within a state"
11. Rise of factionalized elites
12. Intervention of other states or external political actors

Step 3: Brainstorm ideas

Appoint one group member to lead a brainstorming session and another to record ideas. Then brainstorm to generate as many ideas for achieving your goal as possible.

Make sure that everyone in your group has an opportunity to contribute to the discussion. Listen carefully. You may come up with a new idea after hearing someone else's suggestion. At this stage, do not worry about whether ideas are "right" or "wrong," practical or impractical. You never know where an idea will lead the group.

Step 4: Evaluate alternatives

When you finish brainstorming, return to your original goal and set criteria to help you judge which idea will most effectively help you achieve this goal. You may choose to include some of the indicators used to calculate a state's risk of failure (Figure 9-12) among your criteria. You may also choose your own criteria.

The following are some common criteria:

- Will the idea work? (Is it practical?)
- Is the idea fair? (Is it legal and respectful?)
- What are some possible consequences? (Both positive and negative.) Will the effects be short- or long-term? How many people will be helped?

A chart like the following can help you evaluate each idea.

Step 5: Make a decision

With your group, review your evaluation of alternatives and decide which idea will achieve your goal most effectively. Over the course of this discussion, you may decide to combine two or more ideas.

Choose a reporter to present your idea to the class and explain the criteria your group used to arrive at your decision. Be prepared to answer classmates' questions about your choice.

Evaluating Brainstorming Alternatives

Idea	Strengths	Weaknesses

Summing Up

As you progress through this course, you will encounter many opportunities to practise decision-making and problem-solving skills. You can use similar steps to help you do this.

HOW DO THE MOTIVES OF NATIONS AND STATES SHAPE THEIR RESPONSES TO THE WORLD?

The responses of nations and states to world events are often motivated by a complex range of factors linked to people's needs. A country in which people want peace and security, for example, may choose to withdraw from contact with other nation-states and focus on its own affairs. This response, which may help people feel protected against the threat of war, was common during the Great Depression — and it gave leaders like Adolf Hitler the opportunity to expand their territory and crush opposition without interference from the international community.

CHECKBACK

You read about the rise of ultranationalist movements in Chapters 5, 6, and 7.

When deciding how to respond to the world, countries may choose from a range of possibilities, including isolationism, unilateralism, bilateralism, multilateralism, and supranationalism. Like responses to all complex issues, each choice can generate both positive and negative effects.

Isolationism

As the world becomes more globalized, are countries likely to choose isolationism more or less often?

True **isolationism** means that a country completely opts out of participating in international social, economic, political, and military affairs. Until 1854, Japan, for example, had followed an isolationist policy for more than two centuries. During this time, Japan's isolation was so complete that foreigners were barred from entering the country and trade with other countries was discouraged.

How might a policy of complete isolation benefit a country or nation? How might it hurt?

The nearly complete isolationism practised by Japan is rare. More commonly, countries choose to follow an isolationist policy in one area but not in others. Switzerland, for example, refuses to take sides in disputes with other countries and has not joined military alliances. But this country also maintains diplomatic ties with other countries and is a member of the United Nations. And Switzerland has joined other countries in environmental and economic agreements.

Figure 9-13 In 1853, an American fleet under the command of Commodore Matthew Perry landed at Yokohama, Japan. Perry's goal was to persuade Japan to start trading with the United States, and in 1854, the two countries negotiated a trade agreement that ended Japan's isolation from the world.

Unilateralism

Countries are sometimes motivated to respond to events on their own, or unilaterally. **Unilateralism** became an issue during the nuclear arms race, which pitted the United States and its allies against the Soviet Union and its allies. When the arms race began after World War II as part of the Cold War, people feared that nuclear war would destroy life on Earth. Countries began to discuss arms reduction and even full disarmament — the destruction of all nuclear weapons by all countries.

But these discussions did not go well. As a result, some argued that disarming unilaterally — without an international agreement — would be the best way to protect the planet.

Is isolationism a valid response to world issues?

The students responding to this question are Rick, who was born in the United States and moved to Fort McMurray when he was 10; Blair, who lives in Edmonton and whose heritage is Ukrainian, Scottish, and German; and Pearl, who lives in St. Albert and whose great-great-great grandfather immigrated from China to work on the Canadian Pacific Railway.

A country can no more be isolationist than a family living in the middle of a city can live in isolation from everyone else. In any community, things are interconnected. You couldn't escape the connections, even if you wanted to. The clothes you wear, the food you eat, the tools you use all connect you to other people. And then there are services like electricity, water, phones, cable TV, garbage collection — they're all provided by other people. So even if you don't talk to people and think you're completely isolated, you're still connected to others by a huge network. The question shouldn't ask whether isolationism is a valid response. It should ask whether isolationism is even possible. I say that it isn't — and the same is true for countries.

My neighbours can live any way they want, and so can I. As long as we stay on our own side of the fence, it's nobody else's business what I do. Isolationism among countries is like us minding our own business. If a country doesn't want to have contact with other countries, that's their right. In fact, maybe the world would be better off if more countries were isolationist and didn't try to stick their noses into other countries' business. We don't like others telling us how to deal with minorities or the seal hunt or taxes, so why do we think we have a right to tell other countries how to handle their own affairs? We should all just look after our own lives.

I came across a piece of writing that I think expresses how people can't live in isolation. It was written by an Englishman, John Donne, in the 17th century. The language is old-fashioned, and it talks about "man" when it means all people, but that was how they spoke 400 years ago. The "bell" Donne talks about is the church bell that used to be rung when someone died. Here's what he said: "No man is an island entire of itself; every man is a piece of the continent, a part of the main. If a clod be washed away by the sea, Europe is the less, as well as if a promontory were, as well as if a manor of thy friends or of thine own were. Any man's death diminishes me, because I am involved in mankind, and therefore never send to know for whom the bell tolls; it tolls for thee."

How would you respond to the question Rick, Blair, and Pearl are answering? Explain the reasons for your response.

Figure 9-14 The Nanticoke Generating Station on Lake Erie in Ontario is the largest coal-fired power plant in North America — and the largest source of toxic air pollution in Canada. In 2005, this plant released more than 17 million tonnes of the greenhouse gases that contribute to global climate change. Why is bilateral co-operation important when it comes to environmental issues?

Bilateralism

When two countries are motivated by the same issue or need, they may take bilateral action. **Bilateralism** refers to agreements between two countries. In 1991, for example, Canada entered into a bilateral agreement with the United States in an attempt to solve the problem of acid rain — precipitation that has been turned acidic by air pollutants such as sulfur dioxide. These pollutants are emitted into the atmosphere by vehicles and industry, such as coal-burning power generating plants.

Acid rain affects the environment and the economy because it destroys life in lakes and rivers, damages buildings, and hurts crops. It is carried across borders on air currents, so pollutants generated in the United States may fall as acid rain in Canada and vice versa.

The Canada–United States Air Quality Agreement requires the two countries to work toward reducing toxic emissions that cause acid rain and to co-operate on conducting scientific research into the problem.

Multilateralism

Countries may also choose to take a multilateral approach to solving problems. **Multilateralism** involves several countries in working together on a given issue. Middle powers — countries such as Canada, Australia, and Chile, which are not superpowers but still exercise a degree of influence on world affairs — have traditionally chosen multilateral solutions. The influence of middle powers is increased when they stand together. Powerful international organizations such as the United Nations and the World Trade Organization are multilateral in nature.

How might multilateral actions increase the influence of middle powers?

Figure 9-15 Most members of the European Union have given up their national currency and adopted the euro, the common currency of the EU. But other EU members, such as Britain and Denmark, have chosen not to do this. Would you vote to give up Canadian money and adopt a North American currency if it seemed to promise more economic stability?

Supranationalism

Supranationalism is an approach that involves agreeing to abide by the decisions of an international organization made up of independent appointed officials or representatives elected by member states. Many academics view the European Union as a supranational organization because, when they join, member states must give up some control over their own affairs and adhere to EU policies.

In the EU, decisions are made by the majority and are rarely unanimous. Still, all members must abide by the majority decision, so countries must sometimes go along with policies and actions they disagree with.

Reflect and Respond

Is unilateral disarmament a good idea? List the pros and cons for Canada of unilaterally disarming and giving up its armed forces. You might consider how this would affect Canadian sovereignty and foreign policy, as well as what could be done with the money saved.

What are some understandings of internationalism?

The photograph of Earth at the beginning of this chapter suggested that humanity has one home and belongs to one community. This worldview suggests that all people are equal members of the world community and that people's common interests are more important than their differences.

J. Michael Adams and Angelo Carfagna reflected this view when they wrote in *Coming of Age in a Globalized World*: "The power of the nation-state in relation to international forces, particularly regarding economic issues, has declined. To succeed, people must think globally and deal with institutions and individuals throughout the world."

For many people, thinking globally means embracing **internationalism**. Internationalists believe that all members of the global community accept collective responsibility for the challenges that face the world — and that the varying motives of nations and nation-states must be respected in the search for solutions.

Read Socrates' words in "Voices." How might these words define Socrates as an internationalist?

I am not an Athenian or a Greek, but a citizen of the world.

— Socrates, Greek philosopher, 5th century BCE

Brock Chisholm, a Canadian doctor, was the first director general of the World Health Organization. A World War I veteran, he was a general in the Canadian Army Medical Corps during World War II, and in 1944, he was appointed Canada's deputy minister of health. One of Chisholm's main concerns was peace. He believed that it is important to teach children to care for and respect the rights of others and to become citizens of the world.

The World Health Organization

The World Health Organization was established in 1948 as an agency of the United Nations. The WHO is an example of an organization that takes an internationalist approach. Human health is a concern that knows no borders. Contagious diseases can quickly spread around the world and threaten everyone.

WHO staff co-ordinate information about diseases such as influenza, malaria, smallpox, tuberculosis, and AIDS. They also collect statistics on nutrition, population planning, sanitation, and the health of mothers and children.

One of the WHO's greatest triumphs has been the eradication — the complete destruction — of smallpox, a disease that had killed tens of millions of people over the course of human history. A worldwide vaccination campaign began in 1966. By the end of the 1970s, WHO officials had declared that the last case of smallpox had been found and that the disease was eradicated. This internationalist activity provided people everywhere with more security and stability.

Figure 9-16 A nurse in protective clothing stands outside the room of a patient with severe acute respiratory syndrome, or SARS, at a Toronto hospital. SARS first appeared in China in 2002 and spread to a number of countries, including Canada, where it killed 44 people in Toronto. The WHO monitored the outbreak and co-ordinated worldwide measures to control the spread of the disease. Why is an internationalist approach to health problems important?

Figure 9-17 Paralympic racer Chantal Petitclerc (top) of Montréal is just one of many Canadian Olympians who act as athlete ambassadors for Right to Play. They help children, such as these youngsters (bottom) playing on a destroyed tank in Kuito, Angola. From 1975 to 2002, Angola was divided by a bitter civil war during which as many as 20 million landmines may have been planted.

Right to Play

Individuals can also practise internationalism through non-governmental organizations, or NGOs. The creation of NGOs is often inspired by individuals and groups who see a need that is not being met by governments.

In Canada, for example, play is part of life for children. But children in war-torn regions of the world often have nowhere to play. Landmines may have been planted, and children who play in these areas run the risk of setting off an explosion that can disable or kill them. Abandoned military equipment and spent ammunition and artillery shells may also make it impossible for children to do something as simple as kick around a ball.

In the early 1990s, this situation caught the attention of Olympic athletes and organizers. They were led by Johann Olav Koss, a Norwegian speed skater who had won four Olympic gold medals and donated much of his winnings to humanitarian organizations that tried to improve life for children in developing countries. These early initiatives led to the creation in 2003 of Right to Play, an international NGO dedicated to ensuring that children everywhere enjoy the same human rights as those in wealthier countries.

In countries such as Angola, which went through a brutal civil war, Right to Play uses games and sport to educate children about HIV/AIDS and healthy living. It also trains local and international volunteers to start and maintain programs. Reports show that the benefits of the programs include improved school attendance and leadership skills, as well as increased strength, flexibility, and endurance, and greater acceptance of and respect for others.

Is the right to play safely a basic human right that should be enjoyed by all children? All adults?

The Arctic Council

The Arctic Council is another example of an organization that takes an internationalist approach to resolving issues. Formed in 1996, its members include countries with territory in the Arctic: Canada, Denmark — including Greenland and the Faroe Islands — Finland, Iceland, Norway, the Russian Federation, Sweden, and the United States.

The council also includes permanent representatives of six organizations representing Indigenous peoples who live in the Arctic regions of member states. This combination of government and Indigenous peoples' representatives is a unique form of internationalism.

The Arctic Council promotes sustainable development and is dedicated to protecting the region's fragile environment. A priority is monitoring and supporting research on the effects of climate change in the Arctic.

Web Connection

To find out more about the Arctic Council's work on sustainable development and environmental protection, go to this web site and follow the links.

www.ExploringNationalism.ca

Reflect and Respond

List five issues that require international co-operation to resolve, then rank them from most to least important. Explain each choice and the reasons for your ranking.

Clara Hughes
Supporting Children's Right to Play

MAKING A DIFFERENCE
MAKING A DIFFERENCE
MAKING A DIFFERENCE

When Clara Hughes won gold and silver medals at the 2006 Winter Olympics, she startled Canadians by donating $10 000 of her own money to Right to Play. She also challenged other athletes, organizations, and individuals to do the same — and they responded. By the end of 2006, Canadians had donated nearly $500 000 to the NGO.

Hughes believes that sport can change children's lives. It certainly did for her. Born in Winnipeg in 1972, she grew up playing a variety of sports, including ringette, hockey, volleyball, soccer, and softball. But when she hit her early teens, she seemed to be headed for trouble. She had started hanging out with kids whose choices were drawing them down a destructive path.

Hughes's interest in sports pulled her away from this path. "Competitive sport gave me the discipline I lacked as a teenager and gave me something worthwhile to focus on — it got me out of trouble!" she told *Pedal* magazine.

Hughes's Olympic dream began in 1988 when she was 16 years old. Watching the Winter Games on television, she fell in love with speed skating and took up the sport. But she was also a cyclist, and when it became obvious that she could compete internationally in this sport, she decided to focus on cycling.

This choice paid off when she won two bronze medals at the 1996 Olympic Summer Games. But speed skating was Hughes's first love, and in 2000, she returned to her favourite sport. After training for just seven weeks, she made the Canadian national team — and went on to win a bronze medal at the 2002 Winter Olympics.

In 2003, Hughes became an athlete ambassador for Right to Play. Then, at the 2006 Winter Olympics in Torino, Italy, she won her silver and gold medals and issued her challenge. As an ambassador for Right to Play, she has travelled to many of the poorest, war-torn regions of the world. She has helped set up play and sport programs for children and has become a high-profile advocate of children's rights.

Figure 9-18 In 2006, Clara Hughes (top) became the only Canadian athlete to win medals at both the Summer and Winter Olympics. That year, Hughes and cross-country skier Beckie Scott threw the first pitch at a Toronto Blue Jays game. Wearing their Right to Play jackets, the two Olympic champions seized the opportunity to grab some publicity for the organization.

Explorations

1. In what ways might athletes such as Clara Hughes be viewed as internationalists?
2. How might organizations like Right to Play benefit individuals and countries?

How does internationalism benefit nations and states?

Scarred and armed with experience we intend to take better measures this time to prevent a renewal in the lifetime of our children or grandchildren of the horrible destruction of human values which has marked the last and present World Wars. We intend to set up a world organization [the United Nations] equipped with all necessary attributes of power in order to prevent future wars or their planning in advance by restless or ambitious nations.

— *Winston Churchill, British prime minister, to the British House of Commons, 1945*

The two world wars of the 20th century did a great deal to promote internationalism. Many countries decided that the only hope of preventing another disastrous large-scale war was to join together as a world community. These countries believe that managing the world's affairs with greater openness and co-operation, as well as an acceptance of collective responsibility, will improve security and prosperity for all.

Peace and Security

As World War II drew to a close, the international community was concerned with maintaining peace and security and ensuring that a similar devastating war never happened again. Because the League of Nations, formed after World War I, had not achieved its main goals, countries founded a new international body: the United Nations.

With representatives from 192 countries, the UN provides a forum for discussing disputes and airing the grievances and concerns of member states. Though the UN has not prevented all armed conflict, there has not been another world war.

Read Winston Churchill's words in "Voices." Has the UN functioned as Churchill thought it should?

Economic Stability

Figure 9-19 A lone woman walks down a street in Warsaw, Poland, in 1946. Like Warsaw, much of Europe was in ruins at the end of World War II. How would rebuilding Europe help the entire world enjoy greater peace, security, and economic stability?

Representatives of the countries that gathered to found the UN also created two international financial bodies: the International Bank for Reconstruction and Development, which is now part of the World Bank, and the International Monetary Fund, or IMF. Both are affiliated with the United Nations. Their purpose was to help Europe and Asia recover from the devastating economic effects of the war and to promote financial stability throughout the world.

Two years after the war ended, countries also created the General Agreement on Tariffs and Trade to promote economic stability by streamlining international trade. In 1995, the World Trade Organization evolved out of the GATT. Both had similar goals, but the WTO was also intended to be an independent body that could help resolve trade disputes.

By the 1980s, both the World Bank and the IMF had turned their attention to helping developing countries. But critics such as John Phiri, founding director of the NGO Global Justice Zambia, believe that all three bodies are dominated by the United States and other Western countries, which block the efforts of developing countries to achieve prosperity.

"The poverty which is going on in Africa is not natural, it is being manufactured by very selfish people in the WTO, IMF and World Bank," Phiri told the *Zimbabwe Herald*. "Rich countries continue to dominate global politics for their own interest. These institutions work on one principle — the high standard of living of rich nations is dependent on the low standard of living in the developing poor countries."

Indigenous Self-Determination

At the beginning of the 20th century, many regions of the world were colonies of European countries. As the century unfolded, however, many colonized territories achieved independence. The creation of the UN and the adoption of the Universal Declaration of Human Rights after World War II accelerated this process.

But when colonizing powers granted independence, the voices of Indigenous peoples were often ignored. In the last half of the 20th century, Indigenous peoples in many countries began demanding their rights, including the right to self-determination. To help achieve their goals, they began working together in various international organizations, such as the International Working Group on Indigenous Affairs.

They also lobbied the United Nations, which established the Permanent Forum on Indigenous Issues in 2000. And in September 2007, after more than 20 years of negotiation, the UN General Assembly adopted the Declaration on the Rights of Indigenous Peoples. This declaration confirmed Indigenous peoples' right to self-determination.

Four countries — Canada, the United States, Australia, and New Zealand — voted against adopting the declaration. Canada's representative argued that clauses relating to territories and resources were too broad and vague and might interfere with treaties that had already been negotiated.

Web Connection

To read more about the struggles of Indigenous peoples, go to this web site and follow the links.

www.ExploringNationalism.ca

Today's real borders are not between nations, but between powerful and powerless, free and fettered, privileged and humiliated. Today, no walls can separate humanitarian or human rights crises in one part of the world from national security crises in another.

— Kofi Annan, secretary general of the United Nations, 2002

Humanitarianism

International initiatives also help countries respond more quickly to humanitarian emergencies. On December 26, 2004, for example, an earthquake on the floor of the Indian Ocean created a huge tsunami that devastated the coastal areas of many Southeast Asian countries. Entire villages and towns were swept away, and more than 200 000 people in 11 countries were killed.

The world had not experienced a natural disaster of this scale in decades, but international humanitarian and relief agencies such as the Red Cross and Médecins Sans Frontières quickly swung into action. They supplied medical help, clean water, food, and supplies. Governments and individuals also responded with donations of money and supplies for rebuilding.

At one time, the global community would not have known about a disaster like this until a great deal of time had passed. Is the world better off because people know?

Figure 9-20 A village near the coast of Sumatra lies in ruins after a huge tsunami struck Southeast Asia on December 26, 2004. International agencies — agencies based outside any single state — arrived on the scene quickly. What benefits do states and nations receive from such organizations?

1. Think about the chapter issue: To what extent does involvement in international affairs benefit nations and states? In a short paragraph or in point form, comment on how each of the following relates to this issue:
   a) Poet Archibald MacLeish's statement that people are "riders on the earth together" (p. 209).
   b) Abraham Maslow's hierarchy of needs (p. 210).
   c) The statement by Elders of the Carcross Tagish First Nation: "Therefore we are part of the earth and the water" (p. 213).
   d) Jean-Pierre Lindiro Kabirigi's statement that what the Democratic Republic of Congo profoundly needs is "patriotism of the elites" (p. 215).
   e) John Donne's statement, which is quoted by Pearl: "And therefore never send to know for whom the bell tolls; it tolls for thee" (p. 221).
   f) Socrates's statement in "Voices": "I am not an Athenian or a Greek, but a citizen of the world" (p. 223).
   g) Kofi Annan's statement in "Voices": "Today, no walls can separate humanitarian or human rights crises in one part of the world from national security crises in another" (p. 227).

2. In 2000, Raoni Metyktire, chief of the Kayapo, who live in Brazil's Amazon rainforest, went on a world tour to try to encourage people to join the battle to stop the destruction of the rainforest. He said:

> I came to you 10 years ago to explain my concerns regarding the destruction of the Amazon rainforest. I talked to you about the fires, the burning sun, and the strong winds that would blow if man continued to destroy the forest.
>
> You have supported me and given me the means to mark out the boundaries of our ancestral lands. This has now been done: it is an enormous area, full of wildlife, flowers and fruit. It is the most beautiful forest.
>
> Above all, to all those who have given us money or help, I want to say on behalf of the Kayapo people thank you. Nambikwas – meikumbre . . . We all breathe the same air, we all drink the same water, we all live on the same planet. We must all protect it.
>
> People have started to trespass on our land again. The woodcutters and gold miners do not respect the reserve's boundaries. We do not have the means to protect this enormous forest of which we are the guardians for you all.

With a partner or small group, think about the meaning of this statement. Work through the steps to decision making and problem solving ("Focus on Skills," pp. 218–219) to reach a decision about whether the international community should support the Kayapo in their battle to persuade Brazil to do more to save the rainforest.

- Establish a goal.
- Consider the complex issues that underlie the question.
- Brainstorm ideas.
- Evaluate alternatives.
- Make a decision.

Be prepared to share your decision, and the criteria you used to reach it, with the class. Reflect on the process you used to reach this decision.

3. Non-governmental organizations such as Right to Play, the Red Cross, and Médecins Sans Frontières represent a form of internationalism that goes beyond nations and states. List three points that people on each side might argue in a debate on the following statements:
   a) International NGOs such as Right to Play can do more for people than nations and states can.
   b) International NGOs such as Right to Play have no lasting effect on people in developing countries.
   c) People trust international NGOs such as Right to Play to provide humanitarian aid more effectively than governments do.
   d) Humanitarian aid could reach people faster and more effectively if international NGOs worked more closely with national governments.
4. Patrice Lumumba helped the Republic of Congo win independence from Belgium in 1960 and served as the country's first prime minister. He said, "Without dignity there is no liberty, without justice there is no dignity, and without independence there are no free men."

   In a paragraph for each of the following motives of nations and nation-states, explain how Lumumba's message supports the idea that nation-states serve their citizens most effectively when they meet citizens' needs in these areas:
   - economic stability
   - peace and security
   - self-determination
   - humanitarianism
5. For the next week, scan newspapers, magazines, and online news services to find examples of unilateral, bilateral, and multilateral responses to world events or issues. You may also watch TV news or listen to radio news broadcasts.

   Choose one example and prepare an oral or written presentation that explains the event or issue and why you classified the response as unilateral, bilateral, or multilateral. Predict whether the response is likely to result in a positive, negative, or mixed outcome.

   Save your response. As time permits, track the event or issue as it evolves to find out whether your prediction was accurate. Share your prediction and the actual results with a partner. Discuss why you think your prediction was — or was not — accurate.

Think about Your Challenge

Look back at the challenge for this related issue. It asks you to play the role of a delegate to an international summit convened to respond to the international water crisis.

With your group, review the list of summit stakeholders suggested in the challenge (pp. 206–207). If you wish, you may add to this list. Decide which roles members of your group will play. This will provide you with the point of view or perspective needed to begin collecting information for the presentations that you and members of your group will make.

CHAPTER 10 Foreign Policy and Internationalism

Figure 10-1 This collage shows various views of Canada's peacekeeping monument near Parliament Hill in Ottawa. Canada is the only country that has created a monument to peacekeeping forces. The name of the monument, *Reconciliation*, illustrates the central purpose of peacekeeping: to keep the peace long enough for reconciliation to take place.

CHAPTER ISSUE
To what extent can foreign policy promote internationalism?

Reconciliation, Canada's peacekeeping monument, was designed by sculptor Jack Harman, urban designer Richard Henriquez, and landscape architect Cornelia Oberlander. The monument depicts three peacekeepers — two men and a woman — keeping watch from a wall amid the debris of war. In front of them, a grove of young trees symbolizes peace. In 1988, United Nations peacekeepers won the Nobel Peace Prize for 40 years of tireless effort to keep the peace in various parts of the world. This monument commemorates Canada's contribution to those missions.

Examine the collage carefully, then respond to the following questions:

- What is your initial response to the collage of the peacekeeping monument? Does your sense of national identity influence your response?
- What does the existence of the peacekeeping monument say about Canada?
- Why is the name of this monument significant? What other names might have been chosen for this monument?
- The peacekeeping monument is located in Ottawa, Canada's capital and a city that hosts many tourists. What message might this monument convey to visitors from other countries?

KEY TERMS

economic sanctions

collective security

gross national income

tied aid

Looking Ahead

In this chapter, you will develop responses to the following questions as you explore the extent to which foreign policy can promote internationalism:

- How do countries set foreign policy?
- How can states promote internationalism through foreign policy?
- How does Canadian foreign policy try to balance national interest and internationalism?

My Journal on Nationalism

Look again at the collage of the peacekeeping monument. Think about how you could use a collage to express your current ideas about nationalism. Date your ideas and keep them in your journal, notebook, learning log, portfolio, or computer file so that you can return to them as you progress this course.

How do countries set foreign policy?

People living in communities elect leaders, set goals, make and obey laws, settle disputes, and find ways to live together in peace. Some people interact easily with others, but some prefer to live a more isolated existence. Nation-states make similar decisions about how they will live in the world with other countries. These decisions may include whether they will enter into bilateral or multilateral agreements and treaties, as well as how they will try to settle disputes with other states. Decisions about how to deal with other countries are part of a country's foreign policy.

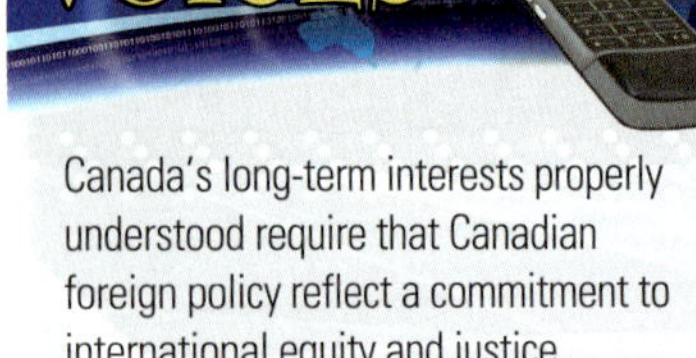

Canada's long-term interests properly understood require that Canadian foreign policy reflect a commitment to international equity and justice.

— *Cranford Pratt, political scientist, in* International Journal, *1996*

Although politicians, diplomats, and experts in foreign relations may set and handle foreign policy, their decisions touch people's everyday lives. If you think about your own life, for example, you will find evidence of Canada's foreign policy in action.

- Much of the food you eat comes from outside the country.
- Many of your clothes, shoes, and other possessions are made outside Canada.
- Many of the television shows you watch and much of the music you listen to is not Canadian-made.
- Your family income may rely on working for a company whose headquarters are in another country or whose profits rely on international sales.
- If you vacation outside Canada, the rules you must follow to gain entry to the country you have chosen are a result of foreign policy decisions.

These aspects of your life — and many more — are the result of agreements the Canadian government has made with other countries.

Figure 10-2 Canadian hockey star Sidney Crosby talks to the media in August 2007 while launching his fall collection of clothing. At the time, this gear was available only in Canada, and many American hockey fans wanted to know when they could get it in the United States. How might the foreign policy of the two countries affect whether U.S. hockey fans will get their wish?

Influences on Foreign Policy Decisions

Do ordinary voters have enough information to make judgments about foreign policy decisions?

In countries ruled by a dictator, an absolute monarch, or a military junta — a committee of military leaders — setting foreign policy is relatively easy. This is because leaders like these can make decisions without consulting the people of their country. But in democracies, setting foreign policy is a more complex process that must reflect the beliefs, values, and goals of the country's citizens. Individuals, groups, and collectives influence government decisions on foreign policy.

Figure 10-3 on the following page shows some influences on Canada's foreign policy. Which groups do you think have the greatest influence? Should non-governmental groups, such as the Canadian Association of Petroleum Producers, be able to influence Canada's foreign policy?

Figure 10-3 Some Influences on Canada's Foreign Policy

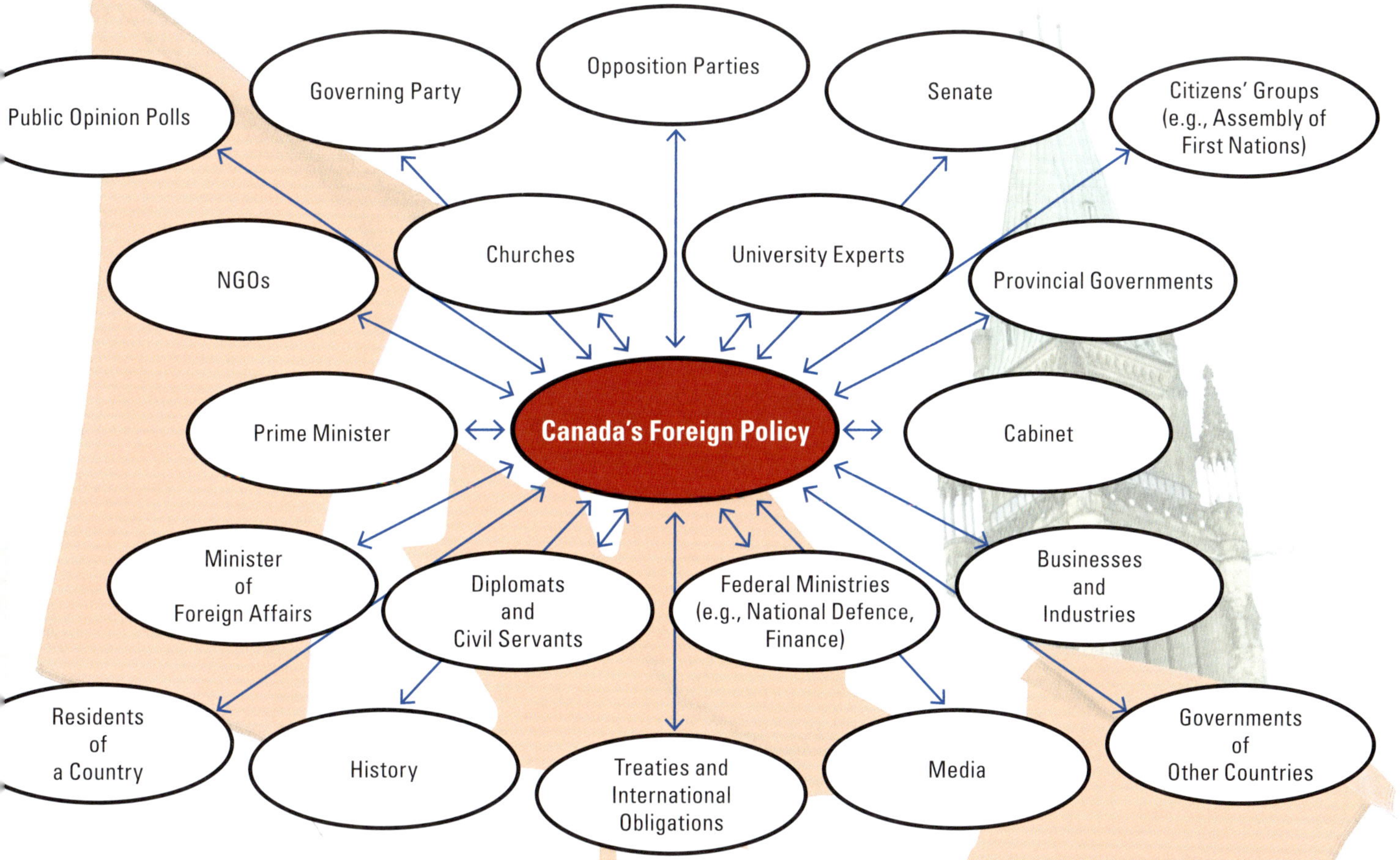

In democracies, citizens influence foreign policy by exercising their right to speak freely and vote. Citizens may also use the power of numbers to influence government. They may join organizations such as the Council of Canadians, which often speaks out on foreign policy issues that affect Canadians, and Amnesty International, which focuses on human rights.

Still, some individuals and groups exercise more influence than others. In Canada, the prime minister, the Cabinet, and members of Parliament who belong to the party in power are highly influential.

Foreign Policy Goals

Setting goals helps people plan for the future. Goals are something to aim for, and they can form the basis of an action plan that helps people achieve them. Think about your own goals in life and what you will need to do to meet them. With clear goals in mind, you can develop a blueprint for your future. Without goals, designing this blueprint is harder.

In the same way, clear foreign policy goals help guide the actions of governments. In 1995, Foreign Affairs and International Trade Canada published a review of Canadian foreign policy. This report highlighted the importance of setting goals that reflect the values of a country's citizens. It said, "Only states with clear objectives, acting on a strong domestic consensus, will be able to deploy significant influence and play an effective role in this new world."

Web Connection

To find out more about the position taken by the Council of Canadians on various foreign policy issues, go to this web site and follow the links.

www.ExploringNationalism.ca

THE VIEW FROM HERE

How much does the public influence the Canadian government's foreign policy decisions? Has the public become more — or less — important in making these decisions? Here is how three people have responded to these questions.

Joe Clark is a former prime minister of Canada. He made these remarks in a 1994 speech to the Institute of International Studies at the University of California, Berkeley.

A generic change has taken place in the context in which foreign policy is decided in developed democracies . . . If foreign policy was once a preserve of elites, it is now very much public policy which must take account of publics which are more knowledgeable, more assertive, and for good or for ill, more influenced by modern media . . . In my own country, which modestly claims to have invented peacekeeping, images out of Bosnia-Herzegovina have caused public opinion now to support Canada pulling out, whatever the consequences for the United Nations, whatever the consequences for the victims of the conflict. That has never happened before in Canada, and to their credit, members of Parliament in a very recent debate took a longer view. But any military engagement requires a longer view, and the combination of television and populism pulls in other directions. Public opinion is rarely a deterrent for peace-breakers, and it would be a terrible irony if it became one for peacemakers.

In 2003, when **Bill Graham** was minister of foreign affairs, he issued a paper titled "A Dialogue on Foreign Policy." In this document, Graham invited Canadians to comment on "the direction, priorities, and choices for Canada in the world."

The future of Canada's foreign policy lies in building on our distinctive advantages in a time of great change and uncertainty. Our diverse population makes us a microcosm of the world's peoples; our geography and population give us broad global interests; our economy is the most trade-oriented among the G7 nations; and our relationship with the United States is extensive and deep. With these and other assets, Canadians recognize that we have a unique basis for asserting a distinctive presence in the world. They also believe that in these times of enormous change, Canada must take stock of how we want to approach new and continuing international challenges. To represent the values, interests and aspirations of Canadians as we confront these challenges, our country's foreign policy must draw as broadly as possible on the views of our citizens.

Wilfried von Bredow is a foreign policy specialist at Marburg University in Germany. In 2001, von Bredow collaborated with the Centre for Canadian Studies at Mount Allison University in New Brunswick to create an online publication titled *Canada's Place in World Affairs*. This excerpt is from the publication.

The foreign policy of a country pursues the national interests of that country or, more precisely, what the current government perceives as the country's national interests . . . In a democratic society, individuals and groups are invited and encouraged to take part in the process of defining national interests and setting priorities. Foreign policy decision making is not confined to a small elite of people, but open to public debate. As a result, these decisions reflect the internal differences of opinion of the various political points of view.

Explorations

1. Identify the common threads in all three points of view.
2. In what ways might the media have a positive or negative influence on foreign policy?
3. In a country as diverse as Canada, is it ever possible to achieve consensus on a foreign policy? Explain the reasons for your response.

Foreign Policy in a Globalizing World

Figure 10-4 A Beijing man flies a kite in Tiananmen Square on December 27, 2007, a day when air pollution in China's capital reached hazardous levels. Governments around the world have encouraged China to take steps to reduce pollution. How is pollution in China an international issue?

Until the end of World War II, governments and diplomats were the main players in international affairs. But since then, the increasing pace of globalization has changed international politics and reduced the role played by nation-states in international affairs. As this has happened, multinational corporations and international business, labour, and humanitarian organizations have come to play increasingly important roles.

In an online publication titled *Canada's Place in World Affairs*, foreign policy specialist Wilfried von Bredow identified one result of this trend: "One of the many consequences of this process [globalization] is the decline of the state's importance as an actor, both within the country and in the international arena. Not all states are equally concerned with the effects of globalization, but all are touched by it in some way."

Von Bredow and others also believe that the changes brought about by globalization have blurred the boundaries between domestic and foreign policy. They have suggested that domestic and foreign policy are now so closely linked that it is often hard to distinguish between the two. Domestic policy is foreign policy and foreign policy is domestic policy.

This view is supported by the federal department of foreign affairs and international trade. In its 1995 review of Canada's foreign policy, it said:

> International trade rules now directly impact on labour, environmental and other domestic framework policies, previously regarded as the full prerogative of individual states. The implementation of international environmental obligations, for instance, could have major domestic implications for producers and consumers and impact on both federal and provincial governments. At the same time, in a world where prosperity is increasingly a function of expanding trade, foreign policy will be driven more than ever by the domestic demand for a better, freer and fairer international environment for trade.

Should multinational corporations have any say in a country's foreign policy?

At one time, foreign affairs and international trade were assigned to two separate federal departments, each with its own Cabinet minister. But in 1982, the two departments were combined into one: Foreign Affairs and International Trade Canada. How did this action reflect changes in the world? How might this pairing affect Canada's approach to foreign affairs and international trade? Would these effects be positive or negative?

Reflect and Respond

Cranford Pratt, a political scientist at the University of Toronto, has said that Canada's foreign policy should reflect a commitment to international equity and justice (see "Voices," p. 232). Think about each of the following imaginary scenarios. For each, list three criteria that Canadian officials could apply to promote international equality and justice.

- Canada and Chile want to negotiate a new trade agreement.
- Zimbabwe wants to buy a Canadian nuclear reactor to increase the country's power-generating capacity.
- A multinational corporation based in the United States wants to buy a large Canadian Internet service provider.

Canada has been participating in the enforcement of UN sanctions against Iraq for 10 years, and our contribution is viewed as crucial by our allies. This operation will further strengthen Canada's military relationship with the United States and reaffirm our commitment to peace and stability in this region.

— Art Eggleton, Canada's defence minister, 2000

The combined effects of the "Gulf War" and the international embargo have killed 1.5 million men, women, and children in Iraq in the last 12 years. Among the victims are 750 000 children under 5 years old, according to UNICEF. The last two co-ordinators for the United Nations Humanitarian Program in Iraq have resigned to protest this embargo.

— Canadian Network to End Sanctions in Iraq, May 5, 2003

How can states promote internationalism through foreign policy?

When setting foreign policy goals, most countries try to balance their national and international interests. Taking an internationalist approach to solving problems can sometimes mean giving up control over aspects of sovereignty, and countries are often reluctant to do this.

When a Liberal government was in power, for example, Canada signed on to the Kyoto Protocol, an international agreement to reduce the greenhouse gases that are a major factor in global climate change. But when a Conservative government took over the reins in early 2006, Prime Minister Stephen Harper backed away from this pledge in favour of a "made-in-Canada" plan to deal with the problem.

Countries can use foreign policy to promote internationalism in several ways, such as through peacekeeping, through international law, and through foreign aid.

Promoting Peace

One of the most powerful ways states can use their foreign policy to promote internationalism is by supporting initiatives that encourage world peace. Because peace and economic stability often go hand in hand, countries such as Canada may develop foreign policies that encourage struggling states to become economically successful and self-supporting.

But this strategy raises many questions.

- Should a country that receives Canadian help be encouraged to introduce policies that reflect Canadian values, even when these conflict with the values of the country's people?
- How can the effectiveness of initiatives be measured?
- Will the money and resources reach the people who need them or fall into the hands of corrupt officials?

In addition, countries sometimes try to promote peace by imposing economic sanctions on a state. Economic sanctions involve cutting off trade with a country in an effort to force it to follow a particular course of action.

Figure 10-5 An Iraqi child receives a polio vaccination in 2000. Polio had been nearly eradicated in Iraq before the UN imposed sanctions, but medical supplies were included on the list of sanctioned goods. As a result, polio re-emerged as a serious childhood illness. Who would you blame for this — Saddam Hussein or the countries supporting sanctions?

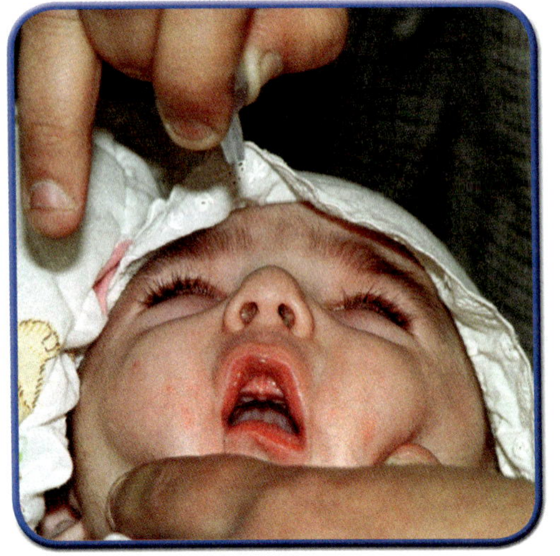

In 1990, for example, the United Nations imposed **economic sanctions** on Iraq. The goal was to force dictator Saddam Hussein to co-operate with the UN, though some said they were actually designed to make life so uncomfortable for Iraqis that they would rebel and oust Saddam from power.

Economic sanctions are controversial. In many cases, they are ineffective because a country has allies that help it get around the sanctions. Critics also argue that sanctions hurt a state's citizens, rather than its government.

Read "Voices" on this page. It presents two different views on the effectiveness of the economic sanctions imposed on Iraq. Canada participated in these sanctions. Were they an effective foreign policy tool? Explain your response.

Peacekeeping and Internationalism

When countries join the United Nations, they agree to support the actions of the Security Council. The Security Council is the UN's most powerful decision-making body. The UN charter requires all members to keep armed forces available for use by the Security Council. With this power, the Security Council hopes to protect the **collective security** of all UN members.

Many Canadians are proud of Canada's reputation for taking part in peacekeeping missions — and that a Canadian introduced peacekeeping to the world. Lester B. Pearson, who would later become prime minister, was Canada's minister of external affairs in 1956, when an international dispute arose over control of the Suez Canal. This waterway, which runs through Egypt, is a vital link that shortens the shipping route between Asia and Europe.

As the crisis brought the world to the brink of war, Pearson suggested that the UN ask countries that were not involved in the dispute to contribute troops to an emergency force. This force would keep peace in the area while a solution was negotiated. The UN endorsed Pearson's proposal, and the crisis was peacefully defused.

This action became a model for future UN peacekeeping missions in countries around the world — and Pearson was awarded the Nobel Peace Prize for his efforts.

Since 1956, Canadian forces have taken part in about 50 peacekeeping missions in various countries. How has this participation helped shape Canada's national identity and foreign policy?

To find out more about Canada and peacekeeping, go to this web site and follow the links.

www.ExploringNationalism.ca

Should the United Nations have its own permanent army that could be used for peacekeeping and peacemaking?

When and How Peacekeepers Are Used

Peacekeepers are not peacemakers. Peacekeepers are sent to conflict zones only after a ceasefire has been negotiated. Their role is to set up a buffer zone between the warring groups and to observe and report on what happens.

Peacekeepers help carry out agreements reached by the UN and governments that have negotiated these agreements. They also try to protect people involved in humanitarian efforts, such as providing food, shelter, and medical care to people caught up in conflicts. UN peacekeepers may provide security, but they can use force only in self-defence.

Troops involved in peacekeeping missions must adhere to the following guidelines:

- Consent — Peacekeepers must respect the sovereignty of the host country.
- Impartiality — Peacekeepers must not take sides.
- Self-Defence — Peacekeepers may use force only to defend themselves.

How might limiting peacekeepers' use of force make it difficult to ensure that warring groups comply with international agreements? Do you agree with this requirement? Why or why not?

Figure 10-6 A Canadian soldier wearing the blue helmet that identifies him as a UN peacekeeper chats with a young Muslim girl in Bosnia in 1994. The Bosnian mission was especially difficult and dangerous for Canadian peacekeepers, who often found themselves under fire from one side or the other. What might this photograph tell you about the way Canadian peacekeepers were viewed?

CheckBack

You read about the conflicts in Yugoslavia and Rwanda in Chapter 7.

Voices

I could tell [the peacekeepers] to do things, but they would check with their country. The troops are under my operational command, but they remained under the ultimate command of their nations, so . . . if a national capital feels that a [rescue] mission is unwarranted, or too risky, or something, the soldiers can turn around and say, "No, I can't do it."

— General Roméo Dallaire, commander of UN forces in Rwanda, 1994

Questioning the Role of Peacekeeping

Most peacekeeping missions have been successful, but several failures in the 1990s raised questions about the effectiveness of peacekeeping as a foreign policy tool.

One of the failures occurred in the former Yugoslavia. In June 1992, the first UN peacekeepers, including Canadian troops, arrived in the region. Despite their presence, the fighting and killing often continued. In many cases, the peacekeepers were helpless to act because of their limited numbers, lack of military power, and orders to avoid using force. As a result, they were often ineffective in preventing genocide.

In 1994, UN peacekeepers were again unable to prevent genocide. In 1993, the UN had sent 2600 troops, including 400 Canadians, to Rwanda under the command of Canadian general Roméo Dallaire. Their mission was to ensure that Rwanda's two main ethnic groups — Hutus and Tutsis — respected a peace agreement. But in 1994, the conflict reignited as Hutus started murdering Tutsis.

Dallaire had warned UN officials of the risk of genocide. He had also requested more peacekeeping troops and permission to seize Hutu weapons. Dallaire's warnings were ignored, and his requests were denied. Although the peacekeepers did as much as they could, they were unable to stop the slaughter.

Over a 100-day period, more than 800 000 Rwandans, mostly Tutsis, were killed. Because Dallaire's warnings had been ignored, the UN force was too small, and troops were forbidden to intervene in the conflict.

Read Dallaire's words in "Voices." What questions does his statement raise about the role of peacekeepers?

After the failure of peacekeeping in the former Yugoslavia and in Rwanda, critics suggested that traditional ideas about peacekeeping should be abandoned in favour of more active peacemaking, such as the tactics used by the multinational UN force that pushed Iraqi invaders out of Kuwait in 1991. The goal of peacemaking is to end armed conflict and human rights abuses. Peacemakers are not limited in the same way as peacekeepers. They need not remain neutral, they may shoot to kill, and their presence does not require the consent of the country they are sent into.

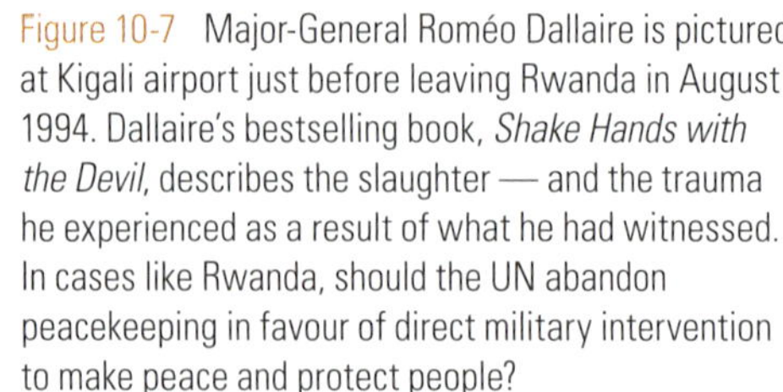

Figure 10-7 Major-General Roméo Dallaire is pictured at Kigali airport just before leaving Rwanda in August 1994. Dallaire's bestselling book, *Shake Hands with the Devil*, describes the slaughter — and the trauma he experienced as a result of what he had witnessed. In cases like Rwanda, should the UN abandon peacekeeping in favour of direct military intervention to make peace and protect people?

International Law and Agreements

International co-operation is essential when the national interest or foreign policy goals of one country conflict with those of another. To help resolve the disputes arising from these conflicts, a body of international law has developed. International law is based on international treaties, agreements, and conventions; UN resolutions; and widely accepted international practices.

International law is interpreted by the UN's International Court of Justice, or World Court. The World Court tries to settle international disputes peacefully — but some countries are reluctant to recognize its authority or abide by its decisions.

In some cases, this is because governments do not want to surrender the right to make decisions based on their own national interest. The United States, for example, has refused to accept the authority of the World Court since 1986. At that time, the court ruled that the U.S. had violated a number of international laws by helping rebels who were trying to overthrow the government of Nicaragua.

A contemporary expression of internationalism and the common heritage of humankind was expressed in the UN's Antarctic Treaty of 1959. The treaty said, "It is in the interest of all mankind that Antarctica shall continue forever to be used exclusively for peaceful purposes and shall not become the scene or object of international discord."

The International Law of the Sea

The United Nations Convention on the Law of the Sea is an example of an agreement that has become part of international law. This agreement sets out rules for the high seas — waters that lie beyond the territorial waters of any country. It defines territorial waters as those extending 22 kilometres from a country's coast and gives coastal countries, such as Canada, the exclusive right to control fishing, mining, and the environment in an area up to 370 kilometres from shore.

The Law of the Sea has been controversial, and Canada did not ratify — accept — this convention until 2003. One reason for the delay was concern over the future of fishing on the Grand Banks.

The Grand Banks are formed by an underwater shelf that extends up to 730 kilometres off the southeast coast of the island of Newfoundland. At one time, this area formed the world's richest fishing grounds, but technological advances in the late 20th century led to overfishing, often by large European vessels. Overfishing reduced fish stocks and destroyed the livelihood of many Newfoundlanders.

To revitalize the fishing industry and enable fish stocks to rebound, Canada believes that it must regulate fishing on the entire Grand Banks. As a result, the Canadian government is working to support Canada's claim to control the entire continental shelf in this area.

Conduct research to find out how Canada's case for extending its control of the continental shelf has progressed since 2008.

Web Connection

To find out more about Canada's position on the Law of the Sea, go to this web site and follow the links.

www.ExploringNationalism.ca

Figure 10-8 In 1995, Fisheries Canada created an international uproar when it seized this Spanish fishing trawler in international waters. The trawler was taken to St. John's, Newfoundland. The Canadian government accused the ship's crew of violating fishing rules by catching immature turbot. Was this seizure justified? Why or why not?

FOCUS ON SKILLS

Persuading, Compromising, and Negotiating to Resolve Conflicts and Differences

The Convention on the Law of the Sea was developed by building consensus. No part of the convention was adopted by a majority vote. All countries that have ratified it have agreed to accept all parts. Ratifying countries have also accepted a process for settling disputes.

For Canada, fishing on the Grand Banks remains an issue. About one-third of this rich fishing area lies outside the 370-kilometre zone defined by the Law of the Sea. Foreign vessels — mostly European — have continued to fish in this area, and many have ignored rules Canada has put in place to maintain fish stocks. As a result, fish stocks have declined dramatically over the past decades.

Suppose your class were asked to draft an international convention to govern fishing on the Grand Banks. To arrive at a consensus on an agreement like this, you would need to take into account the national interests of various countries, as well as the interests of a number of groups. Collaboration, persuasion, negotiation, and compromise would be necessary. The following steps can help you develop the persuading, negotiating, and compromising skills necessary to collaborate to achieve consensus.

Steps to Persuading, Compromising, and Negotiating to Resolve Conflicts and Differences

Step 1: Decide on the stakeholders and assign roles

International agreements can be effective and widely accepted only if they take into account the interests of all stakeholders. In a small group, examine the map of the Grand Banks in Figure 10-9, then brainstorm to create a list of the stakeholders who would have an interest in a convention on fishing in this area. Identify the interest of each stakeholder. A chart like the one shown on this page can help you do this.

Your list is likely to include the government of Canada, as well as fishers from Newfoundland and Labrador. But who else would have an interest in an agreement on fishing on the Grand Banks?

Assign a group member to play the role of each stakeholder. If your list includes more stakeholders than group members, decide on the most important stakeholders and assign roles only for these. Ensure that the stakeholders you choose represent a range of views.

In role, choose a chair to guide the discussion and to ensure that everyone participates and stays on task.

Step 2: Clarify each stakeholder's position on the issue and goals

In role, stakeholders should jot notes outlining the reasons they are concerned about fishing on the Grand Banks and what measures they think will resolve these concerns. A stakeholder representing Newfoundland fishers, for example, may say that he or she wants to ensure that fish stocks rebound so that Newfoundlanders can once again make a living by fishing. This stakeholder may suggest a ban on all foreign fishing on the Grand Banks.

Then give each stakeholder one minute to express her or his position to the group.

Fishing on the Grand Banks

Stakeholder	Interest

Step 3: Identify points of agreement

Once everyone has spoken, identify points of agreement. Everyone, for example, may agree that increasing fish stocks on the Grand Banks is in the interest of all stakeholders. On this basis, draft a statement that summarizes the issue and identifies what the group hopes to achieve during the negotiating session.

During this phase of the activity, your goal is to achieve consensus on common ground and to express this in your statement. As a result, your statement may be very general.

Step 4: Persuade, negotiate, and compromise

With the group's statement in mind, discuss and try to reach consensus on specific actions that would help achieve the goals expressed in your statement.

In the role of your assigned stakeholder, you must be prepared to

- persuade — try to win over other stakeholders through reasoning and persistence
- compromise — give up something you want to meet the needs of another stakeholder
- negotiate — achieve consensus through discussion and agreement

In a discussion like this, give and take is essential. Listen carefully to what is said by other stakeholders. Ask questions to clarify meaning or ask people to expand on what they have said. Look for areas of agreement — and build on these.

Express disagreement with sensitivity. Use "I" messages to express your concerns. Rather than blaming or criticizing the statements of another stakeholder, explain your own position and try to find common ground.

Figure 10-9 Grand Banks

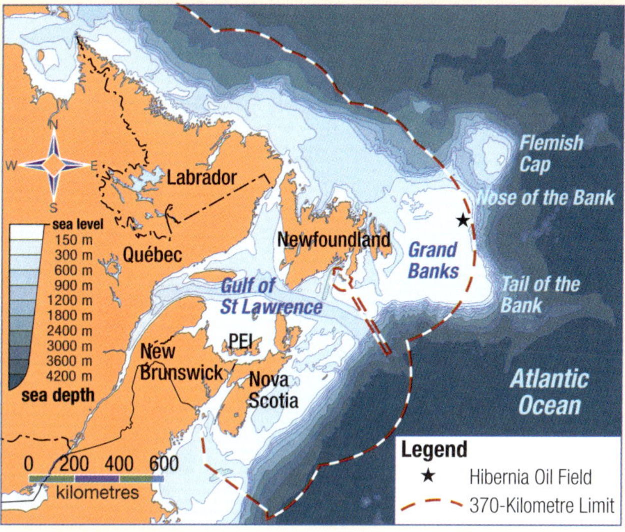

Step 5: Summarize your progress

The goal of your negotiating session is to achieve consensus on actions that will accommodate — to a reasonable extent — the differences in the views of the various stakeholders. When your allotted time for discussion is up, the chair should summarize areas of agreement on specific actions, as well as areas of continuing disagreement.

Some groups may have reached a complete consensus, but others may have reached only partial agreement. Still, this partial agreement could provide the foundation for future negotiating sessions.

Step 6: Present the results of your discussion to the class

The chair of each group should summarize the results of their discussion for the class, outlining areas of agreement and disagreement. Allow time for class members to ask questions and suggest strategies and solutions that worked for their group.

Summing Up

Reflect on the role play you just completed. Which strategies worked most effectively in your group? Did classmates suggest other strategies that you could try next time? Understanding strategies for persuading, compromising, and negotiating can help you and others to find common ground in many different situations.

International Agreements and the Arctic

CheckBack

You read about the debate over Arctic sovereignty in Chapter 5.

The importance of the Convention on the Law of the Sea was highlighted in the summer of 2007. Russian scientists had been exploring the Arctic for months to discover the extent of mineral and energy resources under the ice. Then Russia announced that its expedition had planted a capsule containing a Russian flag 4200 metres below sea level at the North Pole.

The Arctic is Russian. We must prove the North Pole is an extension of the Russian coastal shelf.

— Artur Chilingov, Arctic explorer and leader of the Russian expedition to plant a flag under the North Pole, 2007

Though some people dismissed the flag planting as a publicity stunt, it renewed interest in the competing claims to territory in the Arctic. Since the 1920s, for example, Russian maps have marked large parts of the Arctic as Russian territory.

The Canadian, Danish, Norwegian, and American governments challenge Russia's claims. Canada, for example, says that the waters separating its Arctic islands are frozen for most of the year. Inuit hunters spend some of the year working and even living on this ice. The government maintains that their activity has turned this ice into an extension of Canada's territory.

But according to the Law of the Sea, the area around the North Pole is in international waters because it is located beyond the 370-kilometre limit of all five countries with Arctic claims. This international area is administered by the International Seabed Authority, which was established under the Law of the Sea.

The Law of the Sea allows the five countries with territory in the Arctic to file claims to extend their domain — if they can prove that their continental shelves are geographically linked to the Arctic seabed. As a result, the Russian action has sparked a flurry of scientific activity as all five countries rush to find evidence supporting their own claims to parts of this zone.

Do these competing claims to Arctic sovereignty illustrate the success or failure of internationalism?

Figure 10-10 This satellite photograph of Lancaster Sound in the Northwest Passage between Canada and Greenland was taken in September 2007. As a result of global climate change, this passage may become clear enough of ice to permit safe commercial shipping for at least part of the year. If this happens, how might it affect Canadian foreign policy in the Arctic?

Figure 10-11 A Russian deep-diving miniature submarine is lowered into the Arctic Ocean on August 2, 2007. This mini-submarine was one of two that descended 4200 metres to the ocean floor as Russia staked its claim to much of the Arctic's oil and mineral wealth. Why might an international solution to the issue of Arctic sovereignty be necessary?

Foreign Aid and Internationalism

Countries also promote internationalism by delivering foreign aid. Every year, billions of dollars are transferred from developed to developing countries for humanitarian and other purposes. This money may be used to provide medical supplies, food, clothing, and building supplies. Foreign aid may also be directed toward infrastructure projects, such as sewage treatment facilities and road building.

Foreign aid has the greatest impact when countries co-ordinate their foreign aid policies. This internationalist approach involves both the countries giving the aid and those receiving it in making decisions about the most effective use of foreign aid dollars. This helps avoid delays created by debates over where funds should be directed.

Read Roger Riddell's words in "Voices." How do his words reflect his support of an internationalist approach to foreign aid? Do you support this approach? Why or why not?

Waves of evidence suggest that successful development and the greatest hope of a permanent escape from poverty lie in aid that is rooted in the lives of people, that addresses their needs in relation to their priorities, and that is undertaken with their participation.

— *Roger C. Riddell, senior research fellow, Overseas Development Institute, 1996*

MAKING A DIFFERENCE

Jenna Hoyt
The Power of One

MAKING A DIFFERENCE MAKING A DIFFERENCE MAKING A DIFFERENCE

When Ottawa-born nursing student Jenna Hoyt first visited Ethiopia in 2003, she was stunned by the misery she saw. "For a while, I thought this couldn't actually be a place on Earth where people suffer like this," Hoyt told the *Ottawa Citizen*.

Ethiopia is one of the poorest countries in Africa. Incomes are low, infectious disease rates are high, and about two-thirds of people are illiterate. UNICEF estimates that as many as 150 000 children work and live on the streets of Addis Ababa, the country's capital. As a result, Ethiopia — like Zimbabwe — ranks high on the Failed States Index.

When Hoyt returned to Canada, she created the Little Voice Foundation. As its motto, the foundation adopted the words of politician and philosopher Edmund Burke: "Nobody made a greater mistake than they who did nothing because they thought they could only do a little."

The mission of Little Voice is to support communities in developing countries through education, health care, housing, and hospice facilities. Hoyt began raising money, and in February 2006, the foundation opened a primary school in Addis Ababa. In Ethiopia, most schools charge fees of about $6.70 a month. This sum is beyond the means of many families, and more than a third of Ethiopian children cannot afford an education.

Figure 10-12 Jenna Hoyt poses with students and staff at the Little Voice School. When she graduated with a nursing degree in 2008, Hoyt planned to live permanently in Africa.

By September 2007, Little Voice volunteers had raised enough money that the school was able to offer free schooling to all its 200 students. Little Voice was also able to open a second school, and in July 2006, Little Voice also opened a home for about 30 street children.

Hoyt says that all Little Voice programs are run by "people from the community for the benefit of community." She believes strongly that one person — one little voice — can make a difference in the world.

Explorations

1. As many as 150 000 children live on the streets of Addis Ababa. Do you believe that providing schooling for 200 of these children and a home for about 30 more can make a difference? Explain your response.
2. How does the story of Jenna Hoyt and the Little Voice Foundation reflect an internationalist perspective?
3. Why might it be important for Little Voice projects in Ethiopia to be operated and run by Ethiopians?

Canada should have been number 1 [to meet Lester Pearson's foreign aid challenge]. It is the home of 0.7.

— *Jeffrey Sachs, director of the United Nations Millennium Project, 2005*

Once an undisputed symbol of solidarity with those struck down by misfortune and adversity, humanitarian assistance is now vilified by many as part of the problem, feeding fighters, strengthening perpetrators of genocide, creating new war economies, fuelling conflicts and perpetuating crises.

— *Clare Short, British politician, 1998*

The 0.7 Per Cent Solution

In 1969, former Canadian prime minister Lester B. Pearson, who had a continuing interest in international affairs, challenged the world's richest countries to spend 0.7 per cent of their gross national income on foreign aid. **Gross national income** — or GNI — refers to the total value of the goods and services produced by a country in a year, whether inside or outside the country's borders.

So far, only Denmark, Luxembourg, the Netherlands, Norway, and Sweden have met — or exceeded — Pearson's target. The foreign aid spending of most developed countries is well below this mark. In 2006, for example, Canada's foreign aid amounted to 0.33 per cent of GNI, about half the targeted amount.

Not everyone agrees that Canada should spend more. Many foreign policy experts, including Josée Verner, Canada's minister of international co-operation, believe that the country should focus on delivering aid more effectively, rather than on spending more money.

Criticism of Foreign Aid Policy

Humanitarianism is often the main motive for providing aid to other countries. But other motives can also inspire nation-states to offer aid. These may include strategic and political interests, as well as historical relationships between the giving and receiving countries.

Sometimes, help is offered in the form **tied aid**. When aid is tied, strings are attached. Donor countries may, for example, issue credits that require the country receiving the aid to buy goods and services only from them.

This strategy has been criticized because donor countries may not offer the highest-quality goods and services at the cheapest price. When aid is provided with no strings attached, the receiving country can buy from any source — including other developing countries. This increases trade and development in the countries that need it most.

Figure 10-13 In 2006, Afghan women called for continued food distribution. The Canadian International Development Agency co-ordinates the distribution of Canadian aid. CIDA's priorities for aid distribution are democratic governance, private sector development, health, education, equality between women and men, and environmental sustainability. Do these priorities reflect Canadian values?

Ensuring that aid reaches the people who need it is another challenge. Corrupt officials in the receiving countries sometimes seize aid money and supplies instead of distributing it to needy citizens. In addition, delays and errors often slow the delivery of aid. This can result from the size and complexity of some foreign aid projects. Ghana, for example, receives aid from a variety of sources. As a result, the Ghanaian government must deal with several dozen NGOs, 15 major donor countries, and a number of UN agencies that all have different priorities and accountability requirements. These varying requirements can overwhelm a government's resources.

Reflect and Respond

Should donor countries place restrictions on the way foreign aid money is spent?

Present your response in the form of an essay of at least five paragraphs. Ensure that your position is supported by information and examples.

How does Canadian foreign policy try to balance national interest and internationalism?

Like other countries, Canada tries to develop foreign policy that balances the national interest and internationalism. Building strong relationships with other countries is important, but promoting the interests of Canadian citizens is just as important. Foreign Affairs and International Trade Canada is the federal department responsible for administering foreign policy.

Striking a balance between national interests and internationalism can be difficult. Events such as natural disasters and the September 11, 2001, attacks on the United States can change the world unexpectedly. In addition, the conditions that formed the basis of an agreement may change in a way that makes the agreement ineffective, or one or more states may violate the rules of an international agreement. In cases like these, governments must re-evaluate their foreign policy priorities to promote the interests of citizens while maintaining their reputation in the world community.

Figure 10-14 A haze of smog enveloped Ottawa in the summer of 2007. Smog is a mixture of gases formed when pollutants emitted by industries combine with the exhaust from cars, trucks, and other gasoline-powered engines. How can combatting smog combine a country's national and international interests?

Figure 10-15 sets out Canada's continuing foreign policy goals as they were defined in 2007–2008. These priorities are expressed in general terms. Identify an example that shows how each supports Canada's national interest while promoting internationalism. If you could add a priority to this list, what would it be? Explain how your addition would promote both the national interest and internationalism.

Figure 10-15 Canada's Continuing Foreign Affairs and International Trade Priorities, 2007–2008

1. A safer, more secure, and prosperous Canada within a strengthened North American partnership.
2. Greater economic competitiveness for Canada through enhanced commercial engagement, secure market access, and targeted support for Canadian business.
3. Greater international support for freedom and security, democracy, rule of law, human rights, and environmental stewardship.
4. Accountable and consistent use of the multilateral system to deliver results on global issues of concern to Canadians.
5. Strengthened services to Canadians, including consular, passport, and global commercial activities.
6. Better alignment of departmental resources (human, financial, physical, and technological) in support of international policy objectives and program delivery both at home and abroad.

IMPACT

Canada and Peacekeeping — Myth and Reality

IMPACT

Ever since Lester B. Pearson proposed resolving the 1956 Suez crisis by forming an international peacekeeping force, Canadians have regarded themselves as a nation of peacekeepers. International public opinion polls have also found that people in many other countries view Canada in this light.

From 1956 to 1990, this vision of Canada was accurate. In those years, Canadians participated in all UN peacekeeping missions. But in the 1990s, the number of UN missions increased, and Canada did not have the resources to take part in them all. Still, the country's commitment to peacekeeping remained strong. The statistics in Figure 10-17 show this commitment.

Canadian Peacekeepers in the Former Yugoslavia

Canada's most extensive peacekeeping mission occurred in the former Yugoslavia during the 1990s. As the Cold War ended, Slovenia, Croatia, and Bosnia demanded independence and the Yugoslavian federation started to disintegrate. Serbia opposed the independence movements, and fierce fighting erupted as ethnic and religious groups turned on one another.

Figure 10-16 Soldiers carry the coffin of Canadian peacekeeper Mark Bourque during a ceremony in Port-au-Prince, Haiti, in December 2005. Bourque and another peacekeeper were ambushed as they drove through a conflict area in this troubled country. Is it right to put Canadians in harm's way for the sake of peacekeeping?

Hundreds of thousands of refugees fled for their lives. People were homeless and hungry. The UN Security Council recognized that this crisis threatened world peace, and the UN negotiated several ceasefires so that peacekeeping forces could be sent in. But there was little peace to keep.

Canadian troops were part of the UN protection force in Bosnia and Croatia. In Croatia, the government allowed armed groups to invade areas under UN protection and commit atrocities. Although Canadian peacekeepers witnessed and reported many of the atrocities, the UN forbade them to intervene.

Then, in September 1993, about 875 members of the 2nd Battalion of the Princess Patricia's Canadian Light Infantry were ordered to an area of Croatia known as the Medak Pocket. The PPCLIs' mission was to protect several Serbian villages against attack by Croatian troops. When the Croatians opened fire with machine guns and heavy artillery, the Canadians were forced to defend themselves. The PPCLIs pushed the Croats out of the area — and earned the Canadians a rare award from the UN.

Figure 10-17 Canada's Peacekeeping Record

Number of Canadian who served on peacekeeping missions, 1956–2006	125 000
Number of Canadian peacekeepers killed	108
Canada's most extensive peacekeeping mission	Croatia and Bosnia in the 1990s — 1600 troops and police
Number of Canadians serving as peacekeepers worldwide in 2006	100

Source: UN Peacekeeping Project, United Nations Association in Canada

The Peacekeeping Debate

The events at the Medak Pocket helped spark a continuing debate in the world community over the effectiveness of the UN tradition of peacekeeping — and whether the idea of peacekeeping was out of date and should be replaced by peacemaking.

This debate became even more intense after the failure of the UN to prevent the Rwandan genocide in 1994.

More and more Canadians began to question whether Canada should continue to participate in UN peacekeeping missions. In 2006, for example, retired Canadian major-general Lewis MacKenzie, who had commanded UN peacekeepers in Bosnia, told a forum on the future of peacekeeping that he wanted "to get rid of the Canadian myth" of peacekeeping. Mackenzie said that peacekeeping is "the most misunderstood and abused term in this country."

Political columnist Jim Travers disagreed. "Peacekeeping ranks up there with hockey . . . It is important in [Canadians'] self-definition," Travers told the forum. "Where peacekeeping wobbled off the track and remains off the track is that peacemaking is an aggressive and smug export of Canadian values." To get peacekeeping back on track, he said, "We need to make a difference, not just a cheap political statement, make a genuine effort to help."

Figure 10-18 Selected Arguments for and against Canada's Continued Participation in UN Peacekeeping Missions

For	Against
Canada has a long, proud history of peacekeeping.	This does not mean it must continue to do so.
Peacekeeping helps define Canada in the international community.	In 2006, Canada's contribution to peacekeeping ranked 55th out of 108 contributing countries.
Peacekeeping helps set Canada apart from the United States.	Canada has strong ties with many countries besides the United States.
Canadians draw part of their identiy from their vision of the military as peacekeepers, not warriors.	The nature of armed conflict has changed, and UN peacekeepers are no longer as respected by combatants as they once were.
Peacekeeping has successfuly maintained world peace by enabling warring sides to find solutions.	Peacekeeping has not rid the world of conflict. Wars and armed conflicts throughout the world have continued to result in millions of casualties.
The UN plays the most important role in maintaining global peace and security.	Military alliances such as the North Atlantic Treaty Organization have also played an important role in protecting collective security.

Explorations

1. After World War II, many Nazis accused of committing war crimes claimed that they were only following orders. This defence was not accepted. But what about peacekeepers who witness murder and do nothing because their orders bar them from intervening?

   Suppose a peacekeeper were charged with failing to take action to prevent a war crime. List an argument that could be used by each of the following:

   a) the peacekeeper's lawyer

   b) the prosecutor who laid the charge

   c) the judge deciding on the peacekeeper's guilt or innocence

2. A soldier who fails to obey an order may be court-martialled and face a prison term. This means that peacekeepers who disagree with orders face a difficult choice. Should an option besides obeying or disobeying be open to peacekeepers? If so, explain what it should be. If not, explain why not.

3. Is peacekeeping an important part of Canada's national identity or a myth created for political purposes? Explain your response.

Someone steps on a landmine somewhere every 20 minutes. Landmines kill 72 people every day: 90 per cent of victims are civilians and 40 per cent are children. Landmines cost as little as $3 (U.S.) to make but up to $1000 (U.S.) to remove. Estimates suggest that more than 45 million landmines are still in place around the world.

Landmines and Foreign Policy

Controlling weapons of war is difficult, but it is an important internationalist goal. Hundreds of millions of landmines, for example, have been used in conflicts around the world. Troops often plant them to protect their bases, and they are a cheap and effective tool in guerrilla wars. But these weapons remain in the ground long after a war has ended. They pose a threat to civilians and are costly and dangerous to remove.

In 1980, the United Nations Convention on Inhumane Weapons tried to establish rules for using landmines. One of the rules said that mines must be removed at the end of a war. When this convention was largely ignored, the UN tried to implement an outright ban in 1996. But only 14 countries endorsed the ban.

In 1992, a small group of NGOs asked American activist Jody Williams to start a campaign against landmines. Williams worked with the group to found and build the International Campaign to Ban Landmines, an organization that is supported by more than 1400 NGOs in 90 countries.

What does Williams's action reveal about the ability of individuals to influence foreign policy and bring about change?

Figure 10-19 Landmines in the World, 2006

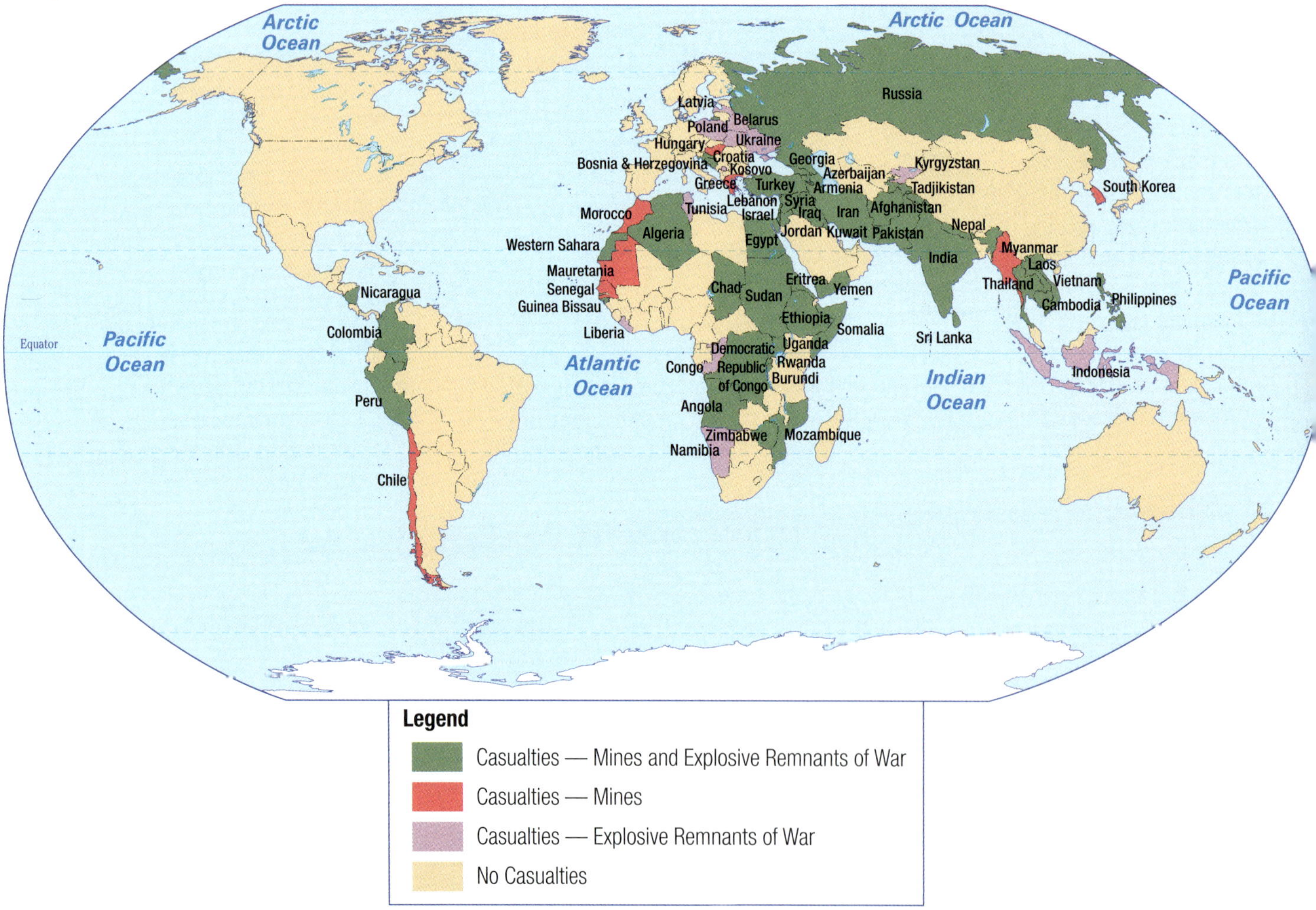

Legend

- Casualties — Mines and Explosive Remnants of War
- Casualties — Mines
- Casualties — Explosive Remnants of War
- No Casualties

Source: Landmine Monitor Report 2006

The Ottawa Treaty

In 1997, Williams and Canadian foreign affairs minister Lloyd Axworthy organized an international meeting in Ottawa. This resulted in the drafting of a convention that is often called the Ottawa Treaty. This treaty banned the use of landmines and required governments to contribute to removing existing mines.

By mid-2007, 157 countries, including Canada, had signed this treaty. But the United States, China, Russia, and India had refused to sign, saying that landmines are necessary for defence.

In 2002, Canada, the European Union, and the United States committed $94 million (Cdn) to clearing landmines in Afghanistan. Seven thousand Afghans were trained to remove the mines, but Taliban fighters have continued to plant them. Mines have killed or wounded dozens of Canadian soldiers and thousands of Afghan citizens.

➡ Does Canada's position on landmines strike a balance between national interest and internationalism? Does this reflect Canadian identity?

Web Connection

To find out more about the International Campaign to Ban Landmines, go to this web site and follow the links.

www.ExploringNationalism.ca

Taking Turns

In a globalizing world, should national interest be the focus of foreign policy?

The students responding to this question are Harley, a member of the Kainai Nation near Lethbridge; Jane, who lives in Calgary and is descended from black Loyalists who fled to Nova Scotia after the American Revolution; and Amanthi, who lives in Edson and whose parents immigrated from Sri Lanka.

Harley

We have to look beyond ourselves and our own community. September 11, 2001, showed that our safety can be threatened by people who live on the other side of the world, so Canadian foreign policy should reflect the fact that security is an international concern. We now live in a global village, and we have to consider that those in need on other continents are also part of our community. We should expect our foreign policy to reflect these realities.

Jane

It's naive to tie ourselves to some vague idea of internationalism. We can clearly reach a consensus only on what's best for Canada's national interest. This is real and this is now. If we look out for ourselves, Canada will continue to be a safe haven for others — and in the end, this will be good for the world. This is a diverse country founded on strong values and the rule of law. Too many other countries are run by dictators or have values that conflict with ours. Let them fight among themselves while we take care of ourselves.

Amanthi

I think that international solutions to problems related to the environment, human rights, and poverty have a good chance of working and should be part of Canada's foreign policy. It's in our national interest to have a stable economy in a peaceful world — and what happens in other countries eventually affects Canada. So internationalism is in our own national interest.

Your Turn

How would you respond to the question Harley, Jane, and Amanthi are answering? Do views they did not mention influence your response? What does this discussion show about the complex process of balancing national interest and internationalism?

1. In this chapter, you explored this issue: To what extent can foreign policy promote internationalism?

   With a partner, identify and deconstruct the elements of this question. To help you do this, return to the prologue (pp. 4–5) and discuss the following questions. Then respond to the chapter-issue question.

   The following will help you shape your response. Be sure to include the ideas brought out in the bullets that accompany each element of the question, as well as other factors you consider important. You may present your completed response as an essay, a series of "interviews" between a reporter and an "expert," a media report, or in another format — or you may choose to use computer presentation software.

   a) To what extent . . .
      - What limits are suggested by this phrase?
      - Does this phrase allow us to respond, "Not at all"?
      - Can an answer to a question that starts this way ever be complete?

   b) . . . can . . .
      - Does this verb imply "should"?
      - What is the difference between something that *can* be done and something that *should* be done?

   c) . . . foreign policy . . .
      - What goals should foreign policy promote?
      - What role should Canada's national interest play in developing foreign policy?
      - How closely should Canada's international aid be tied to foreign policy goals?

   d) . . . promote . . .
      - What does "promote" mean?
      - What other verbs might have been used instead? Why was "promote" chosen?

   e) . . . internationalism?
      - What is our understanding of internationalism?
      - What are some positive and negative effects on Canada of internationalism?
      - How has internationalism affected Canadian foreign policy?
      - Can — or should — foreign policy be used to promote internationalism?

2. The graph in Figure 10-20 shows the Canadian government's contributions to foreign aid in selected years.

   a) Comment on the trends the graph reveals.

   b) Prepare a short briefing paper setting out your observations on the trends and offering your advice to the government officials who decide how much should be spent on foreign aid.

   c) Some of Canada's foreign aid takes the form of goods, such as wheat, computers, and building supplies. Other aid takes the form of services, such as technical support, expert advice, training programs, and teachers. Are these effective ways of delivering foreign aid? Explain your answer.

   d) The following proverb is often attributed to the ancient Chinese philosopher Laozi. Comment on Canada's foreign aid in light of Laozi's words.

   > Give a man a fish and you feed him for a day. Teach him how to fish and you feed him for a lifetime.

Figure 10-20 Percentage of Canada's GNI Dedicated to Government Foreign Aid, 1950–2005

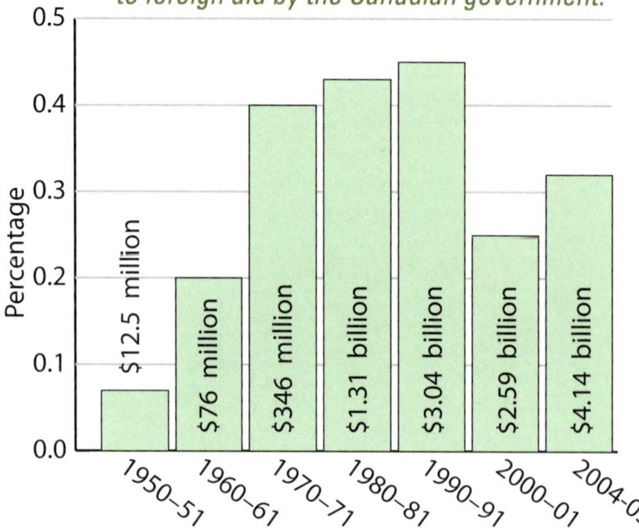

Note: Figures rounded to nearest million.
Source: Canadian International Development Agency

3. Read the three quotations that follow. Then write a short piece setting out the concerns identified by these observers and expressing your opinion on how the Canadian government might respond to these concerns.

Engineers Without Borders, 2008

> Receiving tied aid is costly and inefficient; in receiving tied aid, countries are automatically limited in their ability to seek appropriate, low-cost goods and services . . . Canadian aid often ends up right back in the pockets of Canadian corporations, rather than where it is needed most.

Walter Williams, economist and columnist, 2005

> The worst thing that can be done is to give more foreign aid to African nations. Foreign aid goes from government to government. Foreign aid allows Africa's corrupt regimes to buy military equipment, pay off cronies and continue to oppress their people.

William Easterly in *The White Man's Burden: Why the West's Efforts to Aid the Rest Have Done So Much Ill and So Little Good*, 2006

> [A worldwide tragedy for people who are poor has been that] the West spent $2.3 trillion on foreign aid over the last five decades and still had not managed to get twelve-cent medicines to children to prevent half of all malaria deaths. The West spent $2.3 trillion and still had not managed to get four-dollar bed nets to poor families. The West spent $2.3 trillion and still had not managed to get three dollars to each new mother to prevent five million child deaths.

4. Examine the cartoon by Kjell Nilsson-Mäki in Figure 10-21.
   a) In point form, describe Nilsson-Mäki's message.
   b) On the basis of your current understanding of foreign aid, do you think this message is justified? Explain your answer.
   c) Create a drawing or cartoon that expresses your informed opinion about foreign aid. Your graphic might express your opinion on the amount of aid given by Canada, the kind of aid, the effect of aid on Canada's foreign policy, or some other aspect of aid.

Figure 10-21

"Not only did the American banks give us billions in reconstruction loans, they also threw in this lovely toaster."

Think about Your Challenge

For this challenge, you are preparing a presentation as a delegate to a mock international summit to find solutions to the world water crisis. At this stage, decide on a format for presenting your ideas to the summit. You may choose to write a speech, to create large visuals and charts, to use computer software to generate materials, or to use a combination of methods.

Continue to refer to your inquiry questions as a guide to your research. The format of your presentation will be decided in large part by the kind of information you have collected.

CHAPTER 11 Internationalism and Nationalism

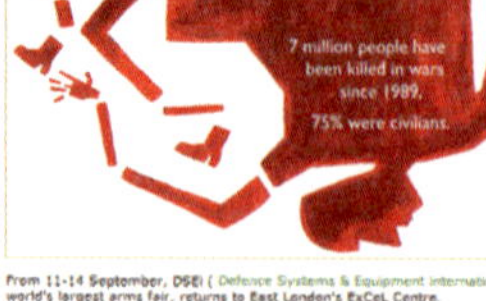

Figure 11-1 Artillery shells (top right) are just some of the weapons on display at the Defence Systems and Equipment International Exhibition and Conference, which takes place every two years in London, England. The DSEi exhibition, one of the world's biggest arms fairs, also draws protests like the one shown in the photograph. The poster at the bottom was produced by Disarm DSEi, a group dedicated to ending the arms trade.

CHAPTER ISSUE

To what extent do efforts to promote internationalism through world organizations affect nationalism?

THE INTERNATIONAL ARMS TRADE is big business. Though estimates vary, some experts say that countries around the world spend more than $200 billion a year on weapons. At the biannual Defence Systems and Equipment International Exhibition and Conference in London, England, more than 1200 manufacturers display their wares — for both private and government buyers.

Many groups and governments say that arms fairs serve an important purpose. Arms fairs provide an opportunity to assess and buy technologically advanced weapons that help promote safety and security and protect a country's sovereignty. But critics argue that these fairs promote war and threaten everyone's security by making weapons easily available.

Examine the images on the previous page, then respond to the following questions:

- Can buying and manufacturing weapons be a purely defensive strategy?
- What benefits and risks might states face when buying and selling weapons on the international market?
- How can the sale of weapons promote — and threaten — world peace?
- Should the arms trade be regulated? If so, who should be responsible for regulating it? If not, why not?
- Why might organizers have chosen to highlight the word "defence" in the fair's name? Is this name accurate? Explain your response.

KEY TERMS

voluntary balkanization

responsibility to protect

common human heritage

trickle-down effect

LOOKING AHEAD

In this chapter, you will respond to the following questions as you explore the extent to which efforts to promote internationalism through world organizations affect nationalism:

- How have changing world conditions promoted the need for internationalism?
- How have the United Nations' changing international responses affected nationalism?
- How do the responses of various international organizations affect nationalism?

My Journal on Nationalism

Look again at the images on the previous page. Think about images you could use to express your current ideas about nationalism and internationalism. Date your ideas and keep them in your journal, notebook, learning log, portfolio, or computer file so that you can return to them as you progress through this course.

How have changing world conditions promoted the need for internationalism?

In a world of near instant communications, the nation-state is irrelevant. One of the outward symbols of its existence is the national border, staffed by uniformed officials checking papers and manning barricades. But what use are such border controls in the world of the Internet, for example?

— *Kenichi Ohmae, author and business strategist, in* The Globalist, *2005*

As the world becomes more and more globalized, many challenges can no longer be confined within the borders of a single country. In November 2002, for example, a farmer in China died of a disease that was not identified at the time. Three months later, an American travelling to Singapore from China died of the same illness, and several people who treated him also became sick. The outbreak spread from there, and by the time the disease — eventually dubbed severe acute respiratory syndrome, or SARS — was contained in July 2003, the illness had been reported in 26 countries, including Canada.

The challenges presented by diseases such as SARS, as well as threats such as terrorism and climate change, demand that countries co-operate to find multilateral solutions. In addition, the ease and speed of travel between countries, as well as rapid advances in communication technology, also promote internationalism. Citizens around the world can now communicate with one another independently; they no longer need to rely on their government to speak for them. As a result, some observers, such as Kenichi Ohmae, believe that the borders between countries are becoming meaningless.

Countries that support internationalism accept collective responsibility for some of the world's problems and work together to solve them. As the world globalizes, many people believe that international approaches to meeting challenges are more important than ever.

If nation-states are irrelevant and unworkable, as some observers suggest, does this mean that even talking about nation and national identity is also irrelevant?

Global Communication

In the 1960s, Canadian media philosopher Marshall McLuhan was one of the first to understand the information revolution and to predict the impact of electronic information systems on human society, and especially on the nation-state. In his famous 1967 book, *The Medium Is the Massage*, McLuhan wrote: "Electric circuitry has overthrown the regime of 'time' and 'space' and pours upon us constantly and continuously the concerns of all other men. It has reconstituted dialogue on a global scale. Its message is Total Change, ending psychic, social, economic, and political parochialism. The old civic, state, and national groupings have become unworkable."

Figure 11-2 An Indian fisher uses a cellphone to call the market to see which merchant will give him the best price for his catch. Cellphones are just one of the devices that are changing the way the world does business. Do technological advances like the cellphone support or threaten traditional ways of life such as this fisher's?

The Global Village

The creation of the Internet — as well as the development of satellite and fibre optic communications, cellphones, and other communication innovations — seems to support McLuhan's predictions about the effects of the information revolution. It is now possible for people to form groups independent of — and parallel to — the state. Some people even argue that these groups have become entirely new "nations." As McLuhan predicted, technology has ended the psychological, social, political, and economic isolation of many parts of the world.

In his writing, McLuhan described how electronic mass media collapse space and time, the barriers that had stood in the way of human communication. The disappearance of these barriers has meant that people can now relate to one another on a global scale. They live in what McLuhan called a "global village." How might people's ability to communicate directly with one another promote internationalism?

Has the Internet truly created a global village or merely a series of small, isolated online communities?

FYI

Many of the states in the mountainous Balkan Peninsula were once part of the Ottoman Empire. The peninsula takes its name from *balkans*, a Turkish word for mountains. After World War I, these states were united into the country of Yugoslavia. But the rugged landscape made communication difficult and kept peoples isolated. As a result, they were often hostile to one another — and the term "balkanize" entered English.

Voluntary Balkanization

McLuhan's idea of the world as a global village — a single collective of citizens with common interests — is not accepted by everyone. Marshall Van Alstyne, a professor of information economics at Boston University, and Erik Brynjolfsson, a management professor at the Massachusetts Institute of Technology, have studied the social effects of the Internet. Their research has shown that Internet users seek out connections with like-minded individuals whose values are similar to their own. As a result, these people become less likely to trust important decisions to those whose values differ from their own.

Van Alstyne and Brynjolfsson call this phenomenon **voluntary balkanization**. "Balkanization" refers to the separation of people into isolated and hostile groups. Van Alstyne and Brynjolfsson are concerned that the resulting loss of shared experiences and values may harm the structure of democratic societies.

In their 2004 book, *Electronic Communities: Global Village or Cyberbalkans?*, they wrote:

> Because the Internet makes it easier to find like-minded individuals, it can facilitate and strengthen fringe communities that have a common ideology but are dispersed geographically. Thus, particle physicists, oenophiles [wine enthusiasts], Star Trek fans, and members of militia groups have used the Internet to find each other, swap information and stoke each others' passions. In many cases, their heated dialogues might never have reached critical mass as long as geographic separation diluted them to a few parts per million. Once like-minded individuals locate each other, their subsequent interactions can further polarize their views or even ignite calls-to-action.

Think about the way you communicate through the Internet. Does this communication open people's minds by bringing individuals into contact with a diverse group, or does it close people's minds because they have attached themselves to like-minded communities?

Figure 11-3 Some parents and educators worry that communicating electronically isolates young people at a time when socializing is important for the development of their identity. Do you think this concern is valid?

Effects of Technology on Citizenship and Democracy

We've expanded to the point where all the world will be connected — we're going to have to get on with each other.

— Tim Berners-Lee, developer of the World Wide Web, 2007

Darin Barney, a professor of communication studies at McGill University, has written extensively about the relationship between technology and citizenship. Barney does not believe that whether people have access to digital technology is the real issue; rather, he says that the issue is whether technology can empower people and contribute to their autonomy, or independence.

In an online interview, Barney told the editor of a blog:

> Even after we all have a broadband connection and we are all Internet and computer literate, the real digital divide will remain: the divide between those for whom digital technology serves as an instrument of power (probably a small minority), and those for whom it serves as an instrument of powerlessness (probably a majority).
>
> Contemporary technological discourse traps us with the assumption that access, or even access with skill, necessarily constitutes empowerment and liberation. I think this is a dubious proposition given the history of modern technological systems, almost all of which have served to reinforce, rather than to democratize, existing distributions of political and economic power . . . Equal access to a technology of disempowerment, or a technology configured to disempower, can undermine democracy instead of contributing to it.

Think about Barney's words. How might digital technology serve as an instrument of power? How might it serve to disempower people?

Figure 11-4 A Japanese man holds a portable device with an earphone plug and a screen as he participates in testing the Tokyo Ubiquitous Technology Project in March 2007. The $8.7-million (U.S.) project, which is supported by the Japanese government, involves sending messages to shoppers from 1200 computer chips lodged in lampposts, subway station ceilings, and sidewalks. The messages contain maps, store guides, and quick history lessons. How might this use of technology reinforce national interest rather than internationalism?

Reflect and Respond

Some people believe that globalization has made it impossible to retreat from internationalism.

Write a four- to six-paragraph blog response to this view. State your position clearly and provide examples to support it. Conclude with a statement that sets out your prediction for the future of internationalism.

How have the United Nations' changing international responses affected nationalism?

CheckBack

You read about the conflicts in Rwanda and the former Yugoslavia in Chapters 7 and 10.

The debate over the effectiveness of peacekeeping and peacemaking shows that not everyone agrees that internationalism is the key to bringing peace to the world. Aggressive states, failed states, and revolutionary movements have challenged the international order and the goals of the United Nations.

In 2003, the UN was nearly 50 years old and the high-profile failure of peacekeeping missions such as those in the former Yugoslavia and Rwanda, as well as changing world conditions, had led some people to question the effectiveness of the organization. As a result, the UN decided to re-examine its goals. Kofi Annan, who was secretary-general at the time, said that the organization needed to adapt to changes in the world.

> We have come to a fork in the road. This may be a moment no less decisive than 1945 itself, when the United Nations was founded.
>
> At that time, a group of far-sighted leaders, led and inspired by [United States] President Franklin D. Roosevelt, were determined to make the second half of the 20th century different from the first half. They saw that the human race had only one world to live in, and that unless it managed its affairs prudently, all human beings may perish.
>
> So they drew up rules to govern international behaviour, and founded a network of institutions, with the United Nations at its centre, in which the peoples of the world could work together for the common good.
>
> Now we must decide whether it is possible to continue on the basis agreed then, or whether radical changes are needed.

The UN report *A More Secure World* stated that intervention in the internal affairs of sovereign states should occur only when

- there is a defined threat
- the purpose of intervention is clear
- the intervention is the Security Council's last resort
- only appropriate means are used
- the reasons for the intervention are examined and reported to the Security Council

A panel of diplomats and international leaders examined the future of the UN, and in 2004, they produced a report titled *A More Secure World: Our Shared Responsibility.* The report recommended that the UN relax its longstanding tradition of staying out of internal conflicts — conflicts that occur within countries. It said that the UN has a **responsibility to protect** people when states violate or fail to uphold the rights and welfare of their own citizens. This intervention could take the form of humanitarian operations, monitoring missions, diplomacy, or — as a last resort — military force.

This recommendation was controversial. Some viewed it as a direct challenge to sovereignty and nationalism. Why might some states regard UN intervention in a country's internal affairs as interference?

Figure 11-5 The flag of the United Nations was still flying after a car bomb blast near UN offices in Algiers, the capital of Algeria, on December 11, 2007. Another blast damaged an Algerian government building. A group linked to al-Qaeda claimed responsibility for the bombings and said that the attacks were aimed at "the Crusaders and their agents, the slaves of America and the sons of France." Do incidents like this suggest that internationalism no longer works?

Iran's Conflict with the UN

The UN's new direction was challenged almost immediately by a situation that had been simmering for some time.

Although a number of counties, such as the United States, Russia, Britain, France, China, India, and Pakistan, have already developed nuclear weapons, the UN is trying to limit the spread of these weapons because of the threat they pose to world peace.

Iran had signed the Nuclear Non-Proliferation Treaty, which was designed to prevent the spread of nuclear weapons while allowing countries to develop nuclear facilities for peaceful purposes, such as generating electrical power. The International Atomic Energy Agency, an arm of the United Nations, monitors whether countries are observing the terms of the treaty.

In 2003, the IAEA reported that for 18 years, Iran had been secretly enriching uranium. Enriched uranium can be used both to generate nuclear power and to build nuclear weapons.

The secrecy of the Iranian program aroused the suspicions of Western members of the IAEA, which called on the country to stop enriching uranium. The Iranian government refused, maintaining that it is merely pursuing its national interest by developing the ability to generate nuclear power. Iranian officials also said that Iran should be free to control this process without outside interference.

Mahmoud Ahmadinejad, the country's president, has called for the destruction of Israel, denied that the Holocaust happened, and threatened the United States. In light of Ahmadinejad's statements, Iran's assurances have failed to convince many in the world community. Many observers believe that the goal of the Iranian program is to develop nuclear weapons for use against Israel and other countries, including the United States.

The UN Security Council called on Iran to stop its nuclear program — and imposed sanctions when the Iranian government refused. Some observers believe that this disagreement has the potential to escalate rapidly. For this reason, they believe that it poses the most pressing threat to world peace.

The Iranian nation will not succumb to bullying, invasion and the violation of its rights.

— Mahmoud Ahmadinejad, president of Iran, October 2007

Figure 11-6 Nuclear Facilities in Iran

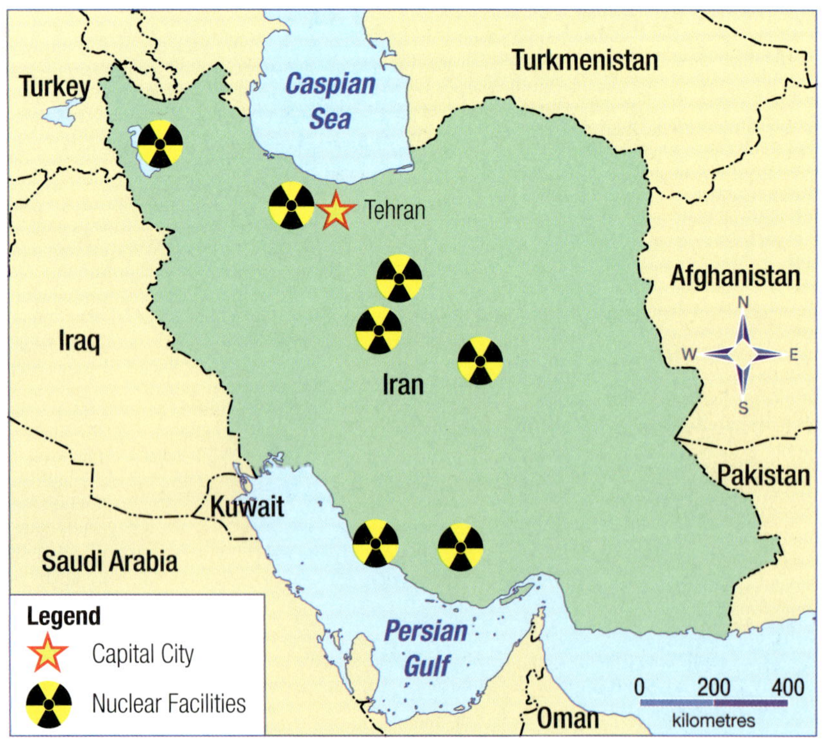

Figure 11-6 shows the location of nuclear facilities in Iran. If the United States, Russia, Britain, France, China, India, Pakistan, North Korea, and possibly Israel already have nuclear weapons, is it fair to stop Iran from developing them? If Iran is planning to develop nuclear weapons, is this a situation in which the UN should intervene to exercise its responsibility to protect? Explain your response.

Analyzing Spin in Official Documents

In 2003, Zahra Kazemi, an Iranian-Canadian journalist, was arrested for taking photographs during a protest outside a prison in Tehran, Iran's capital. Kazemi died while in custody. The Iranian government claimed at first that she had suffered a stroke. When Canadian officials protested, it was eventually determined that she had been tortured and murdered.

An Iranian official was charged with the murder, but he was acquitted — and the Iranian court declared Kazemi's death an accident. Unsatisfied with this outcome, Canada recalled its ambassador to Iran and used the United Nations Human Rights Council as a platform for denouncing Iran's human rights record.

In response, Iran published a 70-page document challenging Canada's record on protecting human rights. This booklet was distributed to members of the UN body. Some of Iran's claims are set out in Figure 11-7.

Steps to Analyzing Spin in Official Documents

Step 1: Analyze the claims

With a partner, examine the claims that appear in Figure 11-7. Discuss

- whether the claim was biased
- whether there was any truth to the claim
- the factors that shaped your judgment about the bias and truth of the claims

As you do this, consider what — if anything — the Iranian government had to gain by publishing these claims.

Step 2: Assess the validity of the claims

With your partner, create a T-chart like the one shown. In the first column, record each of Iran's claims. In the second column, record your assessment of the validity of the claim and note the criteria you used to support your judgment. You may need to conduct some additonal research.

Iran's Claims about Canada	Assessment of the Evidence and Validity of the Claims (1 = completely inaccurate; 5 = completely accurate)

Figure 11-7 Some of Iran's Claims about Canada

Claims about Canada

- Canada violates the rights of women and does not promote or protect women's rights.
- Canada's violation of the rights of Aboriginal people is a serious cause for concern.
- Canadian police routinely strip-search and beat prisoners.

Step 3: Be a spinbuster — look for alternative points of view and information

When news of Iran's claims was broadcast, Ezat Mossallanejad, an Iranian-born analyst and researcher at the Canadian Centre for Victims of Torture, said that his centre has gathered evidence of widespread human rights abuses in Iran: "There is maltreatment of children, rape of women and torture. Iran is ruled by a tyrannical government, and accountable to no one." But he also added: "Canada is not blameless, and we have recorded cases of maltreatment. But the situations are not comparable."

With your partner, discuss whether the Iranian claims should be dismissed as propaganda or treated as a wakeup call by Canadians who have grown smug about Canada's human rights record. Or would you take a completely different position?

Summing Up

As you progress through this course, you can use your spinbusting skill to analyze and assess the validity of statements made in various documents.

The concept of a common human heritage is a powerful one. It reaffirms that human beings, despite their differences, belong to a single species. While cultures may vary, and languages differ enormously, our songs express a shared human sentiment. Such an idea invites us to visit the great temple complex of Khajuraho, or Granada in Spain or the Great Wall of China, and say this belongs to us, and it is our common heritage, there for us to preserve and respect.

— Shobita Punja, writer and teacher who has worked on projects to preserve India's cultural heritage, 2000

Protecting the Common Human Heritage

In 1945, the UN created the United Nations Educational, Scientific and Cultural Organization. UNESCO promotes international co-operation in the fields of education, science, culture, and communication and works to create respect for the shared values and dignity of every civilization and culture. Part of its mandate involves preserving the **common human heritage**, such as world heritage sites, traditional skills and knowledge, and the arts.

UNESCO has established a list of human cultural features that are important to all people, regardless of where they live. UNESCO believes that peace will be promoted if people know about and help preserve this common human heritage. In addition, acknowledging a common human heritage may help promote responsible global citizenship.

UNESCO has identified many natural and human-made sites around the world as world heritage sites. The pyramids of Egypt are an example. These sites, regardless of where they are located, are considered important to all the peoples of the world. UNESCO has also identified masterpieces of humanity's oral and intangible cultural heritage, such as the Azerbaijani mugham, a traditional musical form.

But deciding exactly what should be classified as part of the common human heritage can present challenges. Whales, for example, are an important part of the natural heritage of this world. So, too, are elephants, walruses, and many other animals. Some people reason that if these animals were respected as part of the common heritage of humans, more might be done to protect the environment that sustains them.

Examine the elements of the common human heritage in Figure 11-9 and think about your own community. What aspects of the common human heritage exist within your community? Consider both tangible and intangible aspects, as well as natural and human-made aspects.

Figure 11-8 A pod of killer whales swims near North America's Pacific coast. Whales travel the world's oceans and are not restricted to a particular site, region, or country. Would the international community do more to protect these mammals, as well as other animals, if they were considered part of the natural heritage?

Figure 11-9 Common Human Heritage

Material Culture

World Heritage Sites

14 Sites in Canada

Examples
- Dinosaur Provincial Park
- Head-Smashed-In Buffalo Jump
- Waterton Glacier International Peace Park
- Rideau Canal

812 Sites around the World

France—Chartres Cathedral
Lebanon—City of Tyre
Mali—City of Timbuktu
Mexico—Town of Uxmal

Common Human Heritage

Intangible Culture

Examples
- Festivals
- Arts
- Music
- Traditional Skills and Knowledge
- Beliefs and Traditions
- Oral Traditions
- Languages

Identifying the Common Human Heritage

One challenge facing UNESCO is to identify sites and intangible masterpieces that have outstanding value to humanity. A cultural site, for example, might show creative genius, or it could have exerted great architectural influence. It could also be associated with ideas and beliefs of universal significance. A natural site may exemplify a major stage in the earth's history, contain the natural habitat of a threatened species, or be a setting of exceptional beauty.

In Canada, 14 world heritage sites have been designated. Most are natural sites, such as parks and glaciers, but four are cultural: the historic district of Old Québec City, the Old Town of Lunenburg in Nova Scotia, the Rideau Canal, and L'Anse aux Meadows in Newfoundland and Labrador. L'Anse aux Meadows contains the remains of a 1000-year-old Viking colony and is believed to be the first European settlement in North America.

Although Canadians may value the 14 sites that have received UNESCO's world heritage designation, are these places part of the culture and heritage of all humanity? Explain your response.

Web Connection

To find out more about UNESCO's world heritage sites, go to this web site and follow the links.

www.ExploringNationalism.ca

Threats to the Common Human Heritage

Sovereign states control what goes on within their own borders. They may dam rivers, allow the building of roads and housing developments, and decide whether — and how — to affirm and promote culture. UNESCO's designation of world heritage sites, as well as masterpieces of humanity's oral and intangible cultural heritage, provides safeguards that protect these elements of the common human heritage.

But UNESCO's safeguards can interfere with the plans of nation-states. In 2001, for example, Afghanistan's Taliban rulers destroyed two ancient statues of Buddha, the revered religious leader. Taliban leaders said they were destroying these "idols" in the name of Islam and ignored an international protest against the destruction. Balancing the need to preserve the common human heritage against the national interest of a particular nation-state is a challenge that UNESCO continues to struggle with.

Figure 11-10 The Taliban, which controlled Afghanistan at the time, ordered this huge, ancient statue of Buddha destroyed. Today, the Afghan government and others are working to rebuild this statue and another that was also destroyed. Should works of art like this be considered the property of the state in which they are located, or are they part of everyone's heritage?

Reflect and Respond

Although the United Nations is an international organization, it relies on the co-operation of member countries to achieve its goals. Though the UN can exert pressure on member countries, it has no military arm and cannot force states to go along with its policies.

With a small group, create an action plan that consists of a series of steps the UN could follow when trying to persuade a country's government to adhere to a UN policy.

FOCUS ON SKILLS

Using Debate to Persuasively Express Informed Views

One of UNESCO's goals is to preserve the common human heritage. But this goal is sometimes controversial because it can pit national interests against international interests. Was Afghanistan's Taliban government, for example, within its rights to destroy the ancient Buddha statues? Or should UNESCO have had the power to step in and stop the destruction?

To consider the issue of whether national or international interests should prevail in situations like this, you will participate in an informal debate. The following steps will help you persuasively express your informed view.

Steps to Using Debate to Persuasively Express Informed Views

Step 1: Choose sides

In a group of six to eight, draw lots or use another method to divide the group into two subgroups. One subgroup will develop an informed position supporting a nationalist view; the other will develop an informed position supporting an internationalist position.

You will work with members of your subgroup to develop arguments supporting your position. Your goal is to inform and persuade the other side.

Step 2: Get ready for the debate

With your subgroup, brainstorm to create a list of arguments that support your position. Then decide on the most effective order for presenting these arguments.

- Assign each group member an area to research. The goal is to find information and ideas that support your arguments.
- Set a time for completing research.

Step 3: Prepare arguments and counter-arguments

Rejoin your subgroup and discuss the results of your research. Choose the information and ideas that support your position most effectively. Then work together to consider arguments that might be presented by the other subgroup and prepare effective counter-arguments.

When preparing both arguments and counter-arguments, refer to the tips on the following page. They will help you increase the effectiveness of your arguments and counter-arguments.

Step 4: Hold the debate

Your teacher will explain the format you will use to conduct your informal debate.

Step 5: Evaluate the arguments and presentations

As the members of your group make their presentations, use a checklist like the one shown on the following page to evaluate the effectiveness of their arguments. What criteria might you add to the checklist?

When the debate is over, share your evaluation with other group members. Discuss whether you were swayed by the strength of the arguments or the effective use of tools of persuasion — or both.

Figure 11-11 The historic Prince of Wales Hotel is a landmark in Waterton Lakes National Park. In 1931, this park was united with Glacier National Park in Montana to form the first international peace park. The purpose was to emphasize that international co-operation is required to protect natural areas. But what might happen if the government decided to sell the park because the money was needed to support a program that was in the national interest?

Summing Up

As you progress through this course and through life, you will often want to persuade others to share your point of view. When this happens, keep in mind the persuasion strategies you have learned — and be prepared to use them.

FOCUS ON SKILLS FOCUS ON SKILLS
CUS ON SKILLS FOCUS ON SKILLS FOCUS ON SKILLS

Dos and Don'ts of Effective Persuasion

Professionals have identified tools that boost the persuasive power of arguments. They have also identified pitfalls to watch out for. As you prepare your arguments, keep the following dos and don'ts in mind.

Dos

☑ Support your arguments with relevant, accurate facts. Present enough supporting facts to persuade, but be aware that too many facts can confuse and dissuade.

☑ Anticipate and acknowledge the counter-argument. This adds power to your arguments by showing that you have considered — and refuted — other points of view.

☑ Refer to authorities and respected sources (e.g., "A 2005 UNESCO report found that . . . "). Doing this can inspire confidence in your arguments.

☑ Use comparisons to support your position (e.g., "This is similar to . . ."). This provides the audience with a reference point that helps them understand your position.

☑ Appeal to values that are important to people. Values such as honesty, duty, and friendship can be very persuasive.

☑ Suggest alternatives (e.g., "It is also possible to . . .").

☑ Pose questions, then provide the answer (e.g., "Could the Buddhas have been saved by using military force? No, because who would send soldiers to die for a carved rock?").

☑ Include effective figures of speech, such as metaphors (e.g., "This proposal is a gold-medal winner . . .").

☑ Use the respectful speaking and listening skills you have developed over the years. These include making eye contact, paying attention to your posture, modulating your voice, monitoring your language carefully, and respecting the other person's point of view. No matter how right you believe you are, you can often gather important information from listening carefully to other opinions and ideas.

☑ Display sensitivity to your audience. Watch for clues in their body language.

Don'ts

☒ Use inappropriate humour. What one person finds funny, someone else may find offensive or insulting.

☒ Monopolize the floor. Know when to stop talking.

☒ Criticize the person making the arguments. Focus on countering the arguments. Targeting the speaker is disrespectful — and can undermine your position in the eyes of the audience.

☒ Repeat points excessively. A point may be extremely important, but take care not to repeat it so often that it loses its power.

Effective Persuasion Checklist

Persuasion Strategies	Very Effectively	Somewhat Effectively	Ineffectively
Supported position with facts			
Acknowledged counter-arguments			
Referred to authorities and respected sources			
Used comparisons to support position			
Appealed to important values			
Suggested alternatives to strengthen position			
Posed questions and provided answers			
Used figures of speech			
Spoke and listened respectfully			
Displayed sensitivity to audience			
Used appropriate humour			
Avoided monopolizing the floor			
Focused on arguments, not the person			
Avoided excessive repetition			

How do the responses of various international organizations affect nationalism?

Many of the forces that shape globalization — trade, safer and faster transportation, and improved communications — also shape the growth of internationalism. Each of these forces increases contact among countries at both governmental and non-governmental levels.

But some people believe that this increased contact is a double-edged sword. It encourages internationalism and co-operation among countries, but it may also erode the sovereignty of nation-states.

Read James Warburg's words in "Voices." What is he saying about the future of nation-states in an era of internationalism? Do you agree? Explain your position to a partner.

Voices

A world which fails to establish the rule of law over the nation-states cannot long continue to exist. We are living in a perilous period of transition from the era of the fully sovereign nation-state to the era of world government.

— *James Warburg, former financial adviser to U.S. president Franklin Roosevelt, in* The West in Crisis, *1959*

Economic Organizations

In a 1963 speech, United States president John F. Kennedy said, "As they say on my own Cape Cod, a rising tide lifts all the boats."

This idea has become the driving force behind the many international trade agreements that have been negotiated over the past few decades. Supporters of these agreements believe that as the economies of developed countries become stronger and more prosperous, a **trickle-down effect** is created.

Why would a country ever agree to join the WTO when this organization's rules may decrease a government's ability to make its own decisions?

Trickle-down theory suggests that when people in developed countries have more money to spend, they will buy goods and services offered by businesses in less developed countries — and this spending will help strengthen the economy of the developing world. Many international economic organizations, such as the World Trade Organization and the European Union, support this principle.

The World Trade Organization

In 1948, 23 countries, including Canada, signed the General Agreement on Tariffs and Trade, which set out rules governing how member states would conduct trade. In 1995, the GATT became the World Trade Organization, which includes more than 150 countries.

Pascal Lamy, the WTO's director general, said that "reducing trade barriers has been, is and will remain essential to promote growth and development, to improve standards of living and to tackle poverty reduction."

But not everyone believes that the WTO helps the world. Some believe that this organization threatens national identity and the ability of countries to pursue their national interest. WTO rules can be enforced through economic sanctions, and this gives the organization enormous power that can be used to override the wishes of national governments.

Figure 11-12 In 2007, Indonesian farmers gathered to protest WTO director general Pascal Lamy's visit to their country. The farmers believe that WTO rules will prevent their government from protecting domestic agriculture and that this will destroy their livelihoods. Is the WTO the most appropriate target for protests like this?

Maude Barlow, for example, is a Canadian critic of the WTO. Barlow has reminded Canadians that the WTO classifies water as a commodity that can be traded. She insists that this means that the WTO can force Canada to export water to the United States, even if the Canadian government believes that this is not in Canada's national interest.

The European Union

After years of negotiating, the European Union became an official supranational body in 1991. In addition to promoting peace, security, and justice, the EU is dedicated to creating one of the largest free-trade zones in the world by integrating the economies of member countries. As a result, most obstacles standing in the way of the free movement of goods and people across the national borders of member countries have been removed. Supporters of the EU argue that the size of the European trade zone gives member countries the economic power necessary to play an important role in world trade.

One of the obstacles to freer trade within the EU was national currencies, such as the British pound, the French franc, and the Italian lira. To overcome this, most member countries have adopted the euro as a common currency.

Felipe González Márquez, a former prime minister of Spain, believes that adopting the euro will encourage the people of European countries to view themselves as a community. "The single currency is the greatest abandonment of sovereignty since the foundation of the European Community," he said. "We need this united Europe . . . We must never forget that the euro is an instrument for this project."

But not everyone agrees with González Márquez. Britain and Denmark, who are both EU members, have resisted adopting the euro. One of the factors contributing to this resistance is their citizens' belief that accepting the euro will lead to a loss of national identity and sovereignty.

Although EU members have successfully liberalized trade, the idea of adopting a constitution that applies to all EU members remains controversial. One of the sticking points in the constitutional debate involves the sovereignty of national governments. The proposed EU constitution said, for example, that once member countries have signed agreements with the EU, they cannot pass national laws that violate these agreements. In early 2008, EU politicians were considering reforming the proposed constitution to overcome some of the objections that have stood in the way of its adoption.

Examine the map of the EU in Figure 11-13. Both World War I and World War II began as conflicts between European countries and spread around the world. Do you believe that co-operating in the EU reduces the chances that another war will start in the same way? Explain your response.

Web Connection

To find out more about the countries that belong to the European Union, go to this web site and follow the links.

www.ExploringNationalism.ca

FYI

The EU by the Numbers

Member states: 27

Estimated population (2008): 492 000 000

Official languages: 23

Europe Day: May 9 (the day the union was first proposed)

Cities where the European Parliament meets: 2 (Brussels, Belgium, and Strasbourg, France)

Figure 11-13 The European Union, 2008

Cultural and Language-Based Organizations

Many groups whose members share a common bond, such as language or cultural links, have formed international organizations that extend well beyond national borders. These groups, such as Indigenous peoples and Francophones, are acting internationally to find ways to combine their voices to affirm and promote their national identity in their individual countries. Some groups, such as the Inuit Circumpolar Conference, are non-governmental, while others, such as la Francophonie, are governmental. And the Arctic Council involves representatives of both governments and non-governmental organizations.

Early Indigenous Peoples' Initiatives

In 1973, representatives of many Indigenous peoples who live in the world's circumpolar region met at the Arctic Peoples Conference in Copenhagen. This conference marked the beginning of international co-operation among Indigenous peoples — and helped inspire the formation of groups such as the World Council of Indigenous Peoples and the Inuit Circumpolar Conference.

Spearheaded by George Manuel, a Shuswap from British Columbia, the World Council of Indigenous Peoples was one of the first international groups to focus on Indigenous rights. Though the WCIP disbanded in 1996, it played an important role in developing the Declaration on the Rights of Indigenous Peoples.

The Inuit Circumpolar Conference represents about 160 000 Inuit who live in the Arctic regions of Canada, Alaska, Greenland, and Russia. The council's General Assembly meets every four years. Its goals include promoting the interests and rights of the Inuit — and all Indigenous peoples — as well as strengthening the cultural bonds that unite them.

Figure 11-14 Inuit hunters Joshua Kango and Meeka Mike follow polar bear tracks across the snow-covered ice of Frobisher Bay near Tonglait, Nunavut. Older Inuit remember spending up to 10 months a year on the land, but global climate change has reduced this time so that six months is now the upper limit in many areas. How might the issue of global climate change highlight the importance of the Arctic Council?

The Arctic Council

In 1991, representatives of the world's eight Arctic countries — Canada, Denmark, Iceland, Finland, Norway, Sweden, the United States, and Russia — met in Finland to discuss strategies for protecting the fragile Arctic environment. This meeting also included representatives of the Indigenous peoples who live in the Arctic.

Five years later, the Arctic Council emerged from this initiative. Mary Simon, an Inuk from Nunavik, had been appointed Canada's first ambassador for circumpolar affairs in 1994. In this position, Simon led the movement to create the council.

The Arctic Council broke new ground by combining in its membership representatives of Arctic Indigenous groups and representatives of the governments of the eight Arctic countries. Some observers have predicted that this breakthrough — including non-state nations as official members — will lead to a new era of co-operation and inspire other governmental organizations to broaden their focus in a similar way.

Think about the United Nations and its attempts to promote world peace. If the UN, like the Arctic Council, allowed non-state nations to become members, would this be a step forward? Explain your response.

La Francophonie

La Francophonie — l'Organization internationale de la Francophonie — was originally an organization of countries in which French is an official language. Although la Francophonie's members include only governments, they are not always national governments. Canada, for example, is a member, but so are the provinces of Québec and New Brunswick.

Although la Francophone is committed to promoting the French language and cultural and linguistic diversity, in recent years, the organization has reached out beyond language to include governments that share a vision of international co-operation and support for human rights. In Macedonia, for example, French is not an official language, yet this country is a member of la Francophonie.

Though la Francophonie passes resolutions, they do not have the force of law and members are not required to abide by them. Still, these resolutions often influence governments to change their policies.

MAKING A DIFFERENCE

Mary Simon
A Life Devoted to Activism

MAKING A DIFFERENCE
MAKING A DIFFERENCE
MAKING A DIFFERENCE

Mary Simon cut her political teeth in the 1970s, when she joined the Northern Québec Inuit Association to fight Hydro Québec's plans to build the huge James Bay power generating project. This battle eventually led to the landmark James Bay and Northern Québec Agreement. Since then, Simon has continued to promote the cause of the peoples of the Arctic.

The daughter of a Hudson's Bay Company manager and an Inuk, Simon was born in Kangiqsualujjuaq, on the eastern shore of Ungava Bay in the Nunavik region of northern Québec. She believes that a childhood spent immersed in traditional Inuit culture helped create her strong relationship to the land.

But Simon's father also ensured that his children had opportunities to learn English as a second language. "This fluency in English was one of the springboards to my 'career' in the political development of Nunavik," she has said.

Simon's activism led to involvement in the Inuit Circumpolar Conference, and she was elected president of this organization in 1986. She also played an important role in ensuring that Aboriginal people's rights were protected in the 1982 Canadian Constitution.

Figure 11-15 Mary Simon has published a book titled *Inuit: One Arctic — One Future*. For her work on Arctic issues, Simon has been awarded the Order of Canada, the National Order of Québec, the Gold Order of Greenland, and a National Aboriginal Achievement Award.

When Prime Minister Jean Chrétien appointed Simon Canada's first ambassador for circumpolar affairs in 1994, she spearheaded the initiative to create the Arctic Council and became its first chair. She is now president of the Inuit Tapiriit Kanatami, an organization that represents the 53 000 Inuit of Canada's North.

Simon has seen great changes in people's attitudes toward the Arctic. "As recently as 25 years ago, the Arctic regions were hardly on the political environmental agenda," she said. "Now hardly a day goes by without a news story on the Arctic," she said.

Explorations

1. Would you describe Mary Simon as a nationalist or an internationalist — or both? Cite evidence to support your judgment.
2. Would membership in international organizations like the Inuit Circumpolar Conference and the Arctic Council be likely to strengthen or weaken the Inuit sense of national identity? Explain your response.

Security Organizations

Countries have always formed defensive military alliances to ensure their security. When the Cold War began, for example, the countries of Western Europe and North America feared the military threat posed by the powerful, communist-controlled Soviet Union. To protect themselves, they formed the North Atlantic Treaty Organization, or NATO, in 1949. Canada was a founding member of this organization.

NATO members agreed that an attack on one member would be considered an attack on them all. When the Soviet Union started collapsing in the late 1980s, NATO's role began to evolve to include peacekeeping and peacemaking. By 2008, for example, armed forces from Canada and other NATO members were deeply involved in a peacekeeping and peacemaking mission in Afghanistan.

Other countries have formed similar military alliances. The Collective Security Treaty Organization, for example, includes Russia and other former Soviet republics.

Taking Turns

How much sovereignty should Canada be willing to give up for the sake of pursuing internationalism?

The students responding to this question are Rick, who was born in the United States but moved to Fort McMurray with his family when he was 10; Jean, a Francophone student who lives in Calgary; and Pearl, who lives in St. Albert and whose great-great-great grandfather immigrated from China to work on the Canadian Pacific Railway.

Working with other countries is a good idea, but I think Canada needs to be careful about giving up too much sovereignty. The Kyoto Protocol is an example. My dad works in the oil patch, and he says it would be disastrous if Canada accepted Kyoto. He thinks Stephen Harper's made-in-Canada solution is the answer — and I agree. But I also think that the Kyoto process was important. It really focused everyone's attention on global climate change.

I think it's best to look at things case by case. Lots of Francophone Canadians are glad that Canada takes part in la Francophonie. It helps raise awareness of language and cultural issues, especially in countries like this, where Francophones are a minority. But this is no reason to allow la Francophonie to tell Canadians what we should do to affirm and promote cultural groups. We can make these decisions for ourselves.

We should definitely listen to international opinion, because, like it or not, Canada is part of a world community. When making decisions, it always helps to have lots of opinions, and belonging to international organizations helps us find out about the perspectives of others. It's like brainstorming in class. The more ideas people throw into the pot, the more likely they are to come up with a solution that suits everyone. So pursuing internationalism is like a giant brainstorming session. And in a multicultural country like Canada, this kind of brainstorming is really important.

Your Turn

How would you respond to the question Rick, Jean, and Pearl are answering? Explain the reasons for your answer.

THE VIEW FROM HERE

Is pursuing internationalism the only appropriate course in today's globalized world? Or does internationalism mean giving up too much control? Here is how four thinkers have responded to these questions.

Eric Kierans was a Canadian economist, politician, and writer who held many posts in both the Québec and Canadian governments. In 1983, Kierans gave the annual Massey Lecture, which focused on the role of the nation-state in a globalizing world.

> Globalism, therefore is specialization – but specialization means an ever-growing dependency. Nations become famous for making the wings of a plane but not the fuselage, for mining the ore but not milling it, for cutting down the trees but importing the furniture. Gone is the balanced growth that would enable the state to offer the wide range of career opportunities to a youth educated at great expense . . . Since each nation's resources have been placed in an international pot and its manpower assigned some partial and specialized role, the nation's freedom to create the instruments necessary to the achievement of its own priorities has been sharply reduced.

Andrew Herod is a geographer and specialist in international affairs at the University of Georgia. He has written widely about internationalism, especially as it concerns labour. Herod wrote the following in a 2003 article titled "Geographies of Labor Internationalism."

> Globalization is transforming the spatial organization of the world economy. In particular, it is leading to the "shrinking globe" phenomenon and the speeding up of social interaction between places across the planet . . . Where globalization may encourage some workers to engage in traditional international solidarity campaigns it might also, paradoxically, lead others to focus on highly local campaigns, the consequences of which can quickly be spread far and wide as a result of the growing spatial interconnectivity of the planet that globalization has augured.

J. Michael Adams and **Angelo Carfagna** of Fairleigh Dickinson University in the United States frequently collaborate on projects that focus on global education and world citizenship. This excerpt is from *Coming of Age in a Globalized World*, a 2006 book that was one of their collaborative projects.

> We agree that the nation is a great source of emotional attachment, and that emotional ties across borders can sometimes be difficult to build. But [an argument that nationalism is the most universally legitimate political value] ignores the need for a broader international consciousness in today's age, as well as the many international causes that have inspired great passion – from efforts to abolish slavery, to movements that enhance women's and children's rights, to environmental campaigns . . .
>
> Even without a shared culture, we have a shared commitment to addressing common concerns and problems. This commitment is the foundation for our international community and for world citizenship, illustrated particularly in the work of the United Nations and the development of international law and treaties in the second half of the twentieth century.

Explorations

1. In your own words, restate the main idea presented in each of these quotations.
2. Which of the ideas expressed do you think is the most powerful? The most logical? Why?
3. Do any of these speakers see a positive future for nationalism and internationalism? Explain your response.

1. Imagine that a large historic site in your community has attracted the attention of the federal government, which has proposed asking UNESCO to designate it a world heritage site. The property was once the rural home of a community resident who went on to become a world-famous artist. The site includes heritage buildings, and archeological digs have found important evidence of early Aboriginal settlements. Designation as a world heritage site means the property would be preserved and maintained as it is. No changes could be made.

   But your community has grown, and the property is now in a very desirable suburban location. Housing and services are badly needed to keep up with rapid population growth. A developer has applied to tear down the heritage buildings and replace them with an apartment building, townhouses, a community centre that includes a library, and a palliative care facility for people who are terminally ill. The project would support the community's economy by creating short- and long-term employment opportunities and by helping to meet the community's housing and social needs. As a result, it is supported by many in the community.

   Others, however, support the call to make the property a world heritage site. They argue that this prestigious designation would also support economic growth by attracting tourists to the community. They say that a community that ignores its past loses its future and believe that celebrating community heroes, such as the artist, celebrates the great potential in everyone.

   Before deciding whether to go ahead with the request, the federal government has asked the community to respond.

   a) In a group of six to eight, follow the steps developed in "Focus on Skills" (pp. 262–263) to prepare for an informal debate on the federal government's proposal. Half the group will argue in favour of the world heritage designation, while the other half will argue against it.

   b) Hold the debate in the format selected by your teacher. Then evaluate the arguments and presentations made by each side.

   c) When your evaluation and discussion are complete, work as a full group to prepare a position paper in response to the proposal.

   d) Share your position with other groups. Did one side or the other predominate? Discuss the reasons this might — or might not — have occurred.

2. Create a poster, a political cartoon, or some other visual to express your thoughts on whether the pursuit of internationalism must automatically lead to conflict with national interests. Through this visual, you will be responding to the chapter-issue question: To what extent do efforts to promote internationalism through world organizations affect nationalism?

   Your visual can focus on any topic, such as voluntary balkanization, the effects of communication technology, or the responsibility to protect. Display your work on a bulletin board or in some other area of the classroom. Be prepared to explain and defend the position presented in your visual.

3. The motto of the European Union is "United in diversity." In an essay of no more than five paragraphs, discuss whether this might also be an appropriate motto for Canada.

   - In the opening paragraph, state your position: whether this motto is appropriate for Canada and how you will go about supporting your position.
   - In the middle paragraphs, support your position by providing convincing reasons that cite examples from your community, province, and the country as a whole.
   - In the final paragraph, sum up your arguments and state your conclusion.

4. The poster shown in Figure 11-16 is a reproduction of the cover of a late 19th-century German socialist pamphlet. The woman at the top represents Freedom (*Freiheit*). She is shown extending her welcome to all the peoples of the world. The words on the banner say, "Workers of the world unite." This motto is attributed to the famous socialist thinker Karl Marx.
   a) Each person depicted in the poster represents a continent. Explain why you think the creator of the artwork made these choices.
   b) What does this poster say about nationalism and internationalism?
   c) If you were to revise this poster to send the same message to contemporary audiences, what images would you select? How would you present them?

Figure 11-16

Think about Your Challenge

Your challenge for this related issue is to participate in a mock international summit on the world water crisis. Review the material in this chapter and the activities you completed as you progressed through the chapter. Continue to make notes about ideas that could be useful in completing the challenge. Your notes might include

- how the tools of effective persuasion could help you during the conference
- how changing world conditions have promoted the need for internationalism
- how the United Nations might play a role in reconciling contending national interests
- how responses from other international organizations could play a role in resolving this crisis

CHAPTER 12 Internationalism and Global Issues

Figure 12-1 This cartoon by Arcadio Esquivel was published in the Panamanian newspaper *La Prensa* and comments on predictions that the world's supply of fresh, clean water is dwindling.

CHAPTER ISSUE
To what extent can internationalism effectively address contemporary global issues?

CANADA HAS MORE FRESH, clean water than any other country on Earth — and many Canadians take access to water for granted. They think nothing of taking long showers, watering lawns, and washing cars. The average Canadian uses about 335 litres of water a day, much more than people in most other countries. The French, for example, use only about 150 litres a day.

At the same time, many people in the world have little or no access to clean drinking water. The cause may be geography, poverty, population growth, or conflict — but this lack of water can be deadly. People may die.

Many internationalists argue that water is a basic human need and that the earth's resources, especially water, belong to everyone and should be shared by countries with abundant clean water. Some even predict that access to clean water will become the next major source of conflict in the world.

Examine the cartoon on the preceding page, then respond to the following questions:

- What is the message of the cartoon?
- Is water a resource like oil? Should private corporations be able to take water and sell it wherever there is a demand?
- Should Canada's water be reserved for Canadians, or are water-rich countries like Canada obligated to share their water with other countries?
- Why might some people predict that unequal access to clean water will become a source of conflict?

KEY TERMS

absolute poverty

odious debt

LOOKING AHEAD

In this chapter, you will develop responses to the following questions as you explore the extent to which internationalism can effectively address contemporary global issues:

- What are some contemporary global issues?
- How has internationalism been used to address contemporary global issues?
- Is internationalism always the most effective way of addressing contemporary global issues?

My Journal on Nationalism

Review your journal entries so far. Think about access to water and record your thoughts on whether an internationalist approach is required to avoid conflict over water. Date your ideas and keep them in your journal, notebook, learning log, portfolio, or computer file so that you can return to them as you progress through this course.

What are some contemporary global issues?

Figure 12-2 **Canada's Pollution Record among OECD Members — Some Key Indicators***

Indicator	Canada's Rank
Greenhouse gas emissions	26th of 29
Energy consumption	28th of 30
Carbon monoxide generated	28th of 28
Water consumption	29th of 30
Nuclear waste generated	30th of 30
Average distance travelled by road vehicles	29th of 30

* Because reliable data were not available in all categories, not all rankings are out of 30.

Source: Sustainable Planning Research Group, Simon Fraser University, The Maple Leaf in the OECD: Comparing Progress toward Sustainability

Increasing globalization has cast a worldwide spotlight on issues that might, at one time, have concerned only a limited number of people. When a giant tsunami hit Southeast Asia in 2004, for example, news of the destruction started flashing around the world in minutes. Events like this show that the world's people are more connected than ever. This connectedness has fostered an awareness that issues such as climate change, the spread of disease, and access to water affect everyone.

Climate Change

Ocean currents and prevailing winds pay no attention to boundaries. This means that pollution generated in one country can be carried elsewhere — and the effects of pollution can be felt well beyond a country's borders.

Examine the map in Figure 12-3. Does this map reinforce the need for an international approach to resolving the challenges of climate change? Explain your response.

The Kyoto Protocol, which was proposed in 1997, is an international attempt to reduce the greenhouse gas emissions that are a key contributor to global climate change. Developed countries that signed this protocol, including Canada, agreed to reduce greenhouse gas emissions by 20 per cent by the year 2020. But Canada has since announced that it will not meet its Kyoto targets –– largely because estimates have suggested that doing so could cost the economy $51 billion.

To some people, this backing away from Kyoto suggests that Canada will continue to be one of the worst polluters among the world's developed countries. A Simon Fraser University study published in 2005 by the David Suzuki Foundation examined the environmental records of the 30 countries that belong to the Organisation for Economic Co-operation and Development. Some of the indicators that resulted in Canada's overall low ranking of 28th are shown in Figure 12-2. Only Belgium and the United States ranked lower than Canada.

Figure 12-3 **World Ocean Currents and Prevailing Winds**

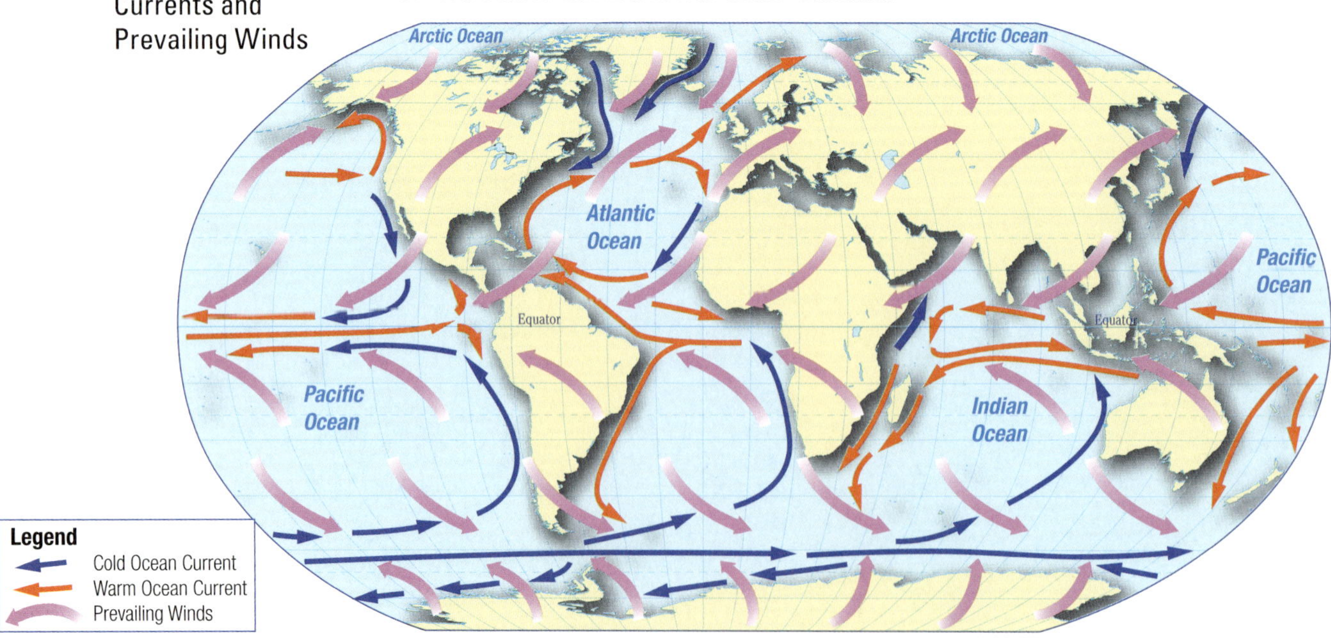

The Spread of Disease

The spread of deadly diseases is also a contemporary global issue, though it is not a new one. Throughout history, diseases have devastated various peoples. In the 14th century, the Black Death spread across Asia, Europe, and Africa, killing up to 125 million people. This notorious plague is still considered the deadliest epidemic ever.

And when World War I ended in 1918, soldiers returning from the trenches of France and Belgium brought a killer flu virus with them. Some historians estimate that this virus killed as many as 50 million people around the world, including more than 50 000 Canadians.

In the past, diseases often took a long time to spread from place to place, but this is not the case today. Just as goods and people can now move quickly and easily around the world, so can diseases — and this increases the potential danger. Between November 2002 and July 2003, for example, SARS spread to 26 countries and killed nearly 800 people.

Every year, one billion people travel by plane and in so doing provide viral hitchhikers [with] unprecedented opportunities. In the 19th century, steam ships took a couple of months to spread trouble; now it can be done in less than 12 hours. The concentration of people in megacities also guarantees rapid dispersion [of viruses].

— Andrew Nikiforuk, journalist and author of Pandemonium, *2006*

International Efforts to Stop the Spread of Disease

The World Health Organization, a United Nations agency, is at the centre of international efforts to identify, monitor, and control health threats, including deadly diseases. During the SARS epidemic, for example, WHO officials helped co-ordinate measures that limited the spread of this disease and prevented the outbreak from infecting more people.

CHECKBACK

You read about SARS and the World Health Organization in Chapters 9 and 11.

According to the WHO, the epidemic of 1918 was the last major influenza pandemic, though severe flu outbreaks also occurred in 1957 and 1968. A pandemic is an epidemic that affects many people over a large geographic area.

On the basis of past experience, the WHO expects three or four flu pandemics to occur every 100 years. As a result, WHO officials have warned that the arrival of the next pandemic, which could kill as many as seven million people, is only a matter of time.

In response to this threat, the WHO has set up the Global Outbreak Alert and Response Network. This international group links health organizations in various countries, plans and co-ordinates international responses, and ensures that technical help is ready to swing into action when an outbreak occurs.

Is an international organization such as the WHO essential to controlling 21st-century pandemics — or should countries be left alone to take unilateral action that is in their own national interest?

Figure 12-4 Fear gripped many Canadian communities during the 1918 flu epidemic. Many people, such as these telephone operators in High River, wore masks to try to shield themselves against infection.

Avian Influenza

WHO officials have predicted that avian influenza, or bird flu, is likely to cause the next deadly pandemic. Bird flu is spread by infected birds that carry the disease wherever they fly. Though many varieties of bird flu exist, only one — the H5N1 strain — has so far infected human beings.

The H5N1 strain, which is similar to the virus that killed so many in 1918, first appeared in poultry in Hong Kong in 1997. Eighteen people who had been in close contact with the infected birds caught the disease, and six died. To contain the outbreak, health officials ordered the slaughter of Hong Kong's entire domestic poultry population, about 1.5 million birds.

Since then, outbreaks of the H5N1 strain have been reported in other Asian countries and as far west as Turkey, Greece, and Romania. In every case, health officials limited the outbreak, though the death rate among people who contracted the disease was high.

Figure 12-5 When a strain of bird flu was found at free-range poultry farms in British Columbia, officials with the Canadian Food Inspection Agency swung into action. Even though the flu was not the deadly H5N1 strain, farms were quarantined, millions of domestic birds were slaughtered, and health officials took precautions to keep health workers and the public safe.

Still, some medical experts believe that the WHO's warnings about a bird flu pandemic are alarmist. Richard Schabas, for example, is a former chief medical officer of health for Ontario. Referring to a WHO warning in 2007, Schabas told CBC News: "This is the third time the WHO has told us we were on the brink of an avian influenza pandemic. They said it in 1997 and they were wrong. They said it a year ago and they were wrong."

Is it fair to label as "alarmist" the WHO's predictions of a bird flu pandemic? Explain your response.

Voices

It's a very important question: do you get to have this water just because you live [in Canada], just because your parents were born here or whatever, and other people don't get water just because they live somewhere where there isn't any? How fair is that? Not fair.

— Maude Barlow, chair of the Council of Canadians and co-founder of the Blue Planet Project, 2007

Access to Water

Estimates suggest that Canada has up to 20 per cent of the world's fresh water but just 0.5 per cent of the world's population. As a result, most Canadians have access to plenty of clean water.

But most people in the world do not. In 2006, the United Nations reported that 1.1 billion people had inadequate access to water and more than 2.5 billion had inadequate access to sanitation. In addition, nearly 2 million children died of diseases caused by unclean water and poor sanitation.

Because access to clean water is an important health issue, some people argue that water-rich countries like Canada should share their water, and in 2002, a United Nations committee declared that access to clean water is a fundamental human right. Canada was the only country to oppose this resolution.

Control over Water

Countries control the water within their borders and make their own decisions about how to use it. These decisions may include selling water, diverting water to generate hydroelectric power, and making rules about dumping sewage into fresh water. But as the world's supply of fresh water declines, water-rich countries are expected to face increased international pressure to share this resource.

The Canadian government discourages bulk water exports, but environmentalists and others fear that this policy may be challenged by the World Trade Organization and the terms of the North American Free Trade Agreement. In early 2008, the University of Toronto's Munk Centre for International Studies called on the federal government to introduce strict new laws barring the transfer of water out of the country. "This may be one of the last opportunities for Canada to effectively control its water, to have sovereign control over its water," said Adèle Hurley, director of the centre's program on water issues.

Supporters of this approach say that water is a sovereignty issue and that Canada must act to protect its national interest in this area. But others believe that Canada is trying to tighten control over its water at a time when world water shortages are increasing.

If water were declared an international resource that is owned by all humanity, how would nation-states be affected?

Figure 12-6 The recently built Three Gorges Dam on the Yangtze River in China is the world's largest dam. It was built to generate electricity, store water for irrigating crops, control floods, and improve inland navigation. Some critics say that the dam will increase the accumulation of pollutants and interfere with the quality and amount of water flowing into the ocean.

Figure 12-7 The Oldman River Dam, located on the Oldman River near Pincher Creek, Alberta, was built to generate electricity and supply irrigation water to reduce the severity of droughts in the area. But the project became controversial when it was opposed by members of the Piikani Nation and the Friends of the Oldman River Society, an environmental group. Despite this opposition, the project went ahead and the dam was completed in 1992.

Reflect and Respond

In March 2004, columnist Wendy R. Holm of the magazine *Country Life in BC* wrote: "Whether you love the NAFTA or hate the NAFTA is not the point. Whether you support or oppose water exports is not the point. The point is sovereignty. Canada must have absolute discretion over the management of her water resources. In perpetuity."

With a partner, prepare point-form notes you could use as the basis of a written response supporting or opposing Holm's position.

How has internationalism been used to address contemporary global issues?

How can it be in a country's national interest to try to solve problems in other countries?

Web Connection

To find out more about the world's least developed countries and the percentage of the population that lives on less than a dollar a day, go to this web site and follow the links.

www.ExploringNationalism.ca

Suppose you wanted to take a course that is offered only at a school outside your neighbourhood. Would you make the decision to change schools on your own, or would you involve your family? What factors would influence who to involve in your decision?

Some issues, such as which school you attend, can be resolved individually or as a family, but other issues are too complex for individuals to handle on their own. In fact, many contemporary global issues are so complex that even national governments are unable to deal with them. This is why many countries choose to work with the international community to tackle challenges such as poverty, hunger, disease, debt, climate change, human rights, and conflict.

Internationalism and Poverty

Poverty often causes other problems, such as hunger, disease, and conflict. In 2006, the World Bank estimated that more than a billion of the world's 6.65 billion people live in absolute poverty. The United Nations defines **absolute poverty** as a "condition characterized by severe deprivation of basic human needs, including food, safe drinking water, sanitation facilities, health, shelter, education and information. It depends not only on income but also on access to services."

Oxfam, an international NGO, has identified the following causes of poverty:

- Lack of education. In many countries, schools charge fees that are beyond the means of many families. People who have not received a basic education have trouble finding jobs and may become locked into a cycle of poverty.
- Lack of access to resources. Millions of farmers do not have the resources — land, water, credit, and access to markets — needed to survive.
- Conflict and war. People in various countries have been displaced by war. People who have fled their homes often find it impossible to work and earn money.
- Trade rules. Farmers, labourers, and factory workers can be affected by international trade rules, such as high tariffs and bans on certain imports. These rules can interfere with people's ability to sell their goods and services.
- Discrimination. Within countries, members of minority groups often have limited access to jobs, resources, and government help.

Figure 12-8 This child is helping his parents locate recyclable material in a garbage dump in southwestern China. Estimates suggest that more than 85 million Chinese people live in absolute poverty. Should the level of poverty in China be an international concern?

In your own words, explain the meaning of "cycle of poverty," which appears in the first bullet. If necessary, create a diagram to make your ideas clear.

Internationalism and Hunger

Hunger, malnutrition, and starvation are often direct results of poverty. In his book *Global Problems and the Culture of Capitalism*, Richard Howard Robbins wrote, "The great dilemma is how to create economic, social, and political conditions to ensure that everyone has access to food or the means to acquire it."

In recent decades, the dilemma identified by Robbins has become the focus of international efforts. In November 1996, for example, the United Nations organized the first World Food Summit. Delegates from 185 countries and the European Community met in Rome and concluded this summit with a vow to reduce by half the number of hungry people in the world. They set 2015 as the target date for achieving this goal.

This goal was reinforced in 2000, when the United Nations identified eradicating extreme hunger and poverty as one of its millennium development goals. Though some progress has been made, change is happening very slowly — and experts predict that efforts will likely fall well short of targets.

Non-governmental organizations also act internationally to reduce hunger and eliminate its causes. The VERITAS Foundation, for example, is an American-based NGO dedicated to fighting child hunger, destitution, and illiteracy on a local, national, and global scale. In 2007, this organization raised more than $100 000 in response to UNICEF's urgent appeal for food, shelter, and books for children in Afghanistan.

Hunger Free World, an NGO based in Japan, fights hunger by delivering aid and providing teachers and educational programs that promote self-sufficiency. One of its projects involves establishing links between high schools in Japan and high schools in developing countries.

Identify two or three important steps Canadians could take to help eliminate poverty and hunger in the world. For each step, explain whether individual, group, or government involvement is necessary to carry it out.

Hunger in Canada

Developing countries are not the only ones where hunger is a problem. Canada, for example, is one of the world's wealthiest countries. Its booming economy has led to a decline in the percentage of Canadians who live in poverty. Despite this decline, experts estimate that about 11 per cent of Canadians still live below the poverty line. Between 1989 and 2007, for example, the number of people using food banks increased by 91 per cent, and in March 2007 alone, more than 720 000 people relied on food banks to feed themselves and their families.

If 11 per cent of Canadians live in poverty, should Canadians focus on solving their own problem before worrying about poverty in the rest of the world?

To give money is an easy matter in any man's power. But to decide to whom to give it, and how much and when, and for what purpose and how, is neither in every man's power nor an easy matter. Hence it is that such excellence is rare, praiseworthy, and noble.

— *Aristotle, Greek philosopher, 4th century BCE*

World Hunger by the Numbers

Frequency of starvation deaths: 1 every 4 seconds

Number of children who die of starvation: 6.57 million a year

Number of people who are chronically hungry: 850 million (1 in 7)

To find out more about international efforts to eradicate hunger, go to this web site and follow the links.

www.ExploringNationalism.ca

One of the worst things about AIDS is that it just never stops — you scramble to find the money to get medical treatment for a sister or a husband who falls sick, and then it's not enough and that person dies and you go into debt to pay for the funeral, and then you have a couple more orphans to try to find school fees for and you don't get a crop in the ground because you're dealing with all this, and then there's no food and you can't go to the city to look for work because you're nursing someone else. There is no respite.

— Stephanie Nolen, Canadian journalist and author, 2006

Internationalism and Disease

Just as poverty contributes to hunger and malnutrition, so it also contributes to disease. Malnourished people cannot fight disease as effectively, and people who are poor often have neither the education necessary to understand disease prevention nor the money to buy medicines. In addition, their governments often cannot afford to supply citizens with the kind of health care that many Canadians take for granted.

HIV and AIDS in Africa

In developed countries such as Canada, a diagnosis of AIDS was once considered a death sentence. This is no longer the case, as science has developed drugs that enable people with the virus to survive. In addition, preventive strategies have helped slow the spread of the disease. In 2006, only about 0.3 per cent of Canadians had AIDS.

Things are different in developing countries. In sub-Saharan Africa, for example, about 1.6 million people died of AIDS in 2007 and an estimated 22.5 million were living with the virus. Few Africans with AIDS can afford treatment, and many countries lack the medical resources to cope with what has become a pandemic.

In response, the United Nations appointed Canadian politician and diplomat Stephen Lewis special envoy for HIV/AIDS in Africa, a post he held until 2006. Lewis believes that AIDS and poverty are the most significant threats to the world today.

"Disease breeds poverty because it completely destroys the income of a family and poverty breeds disease because nobody has anything to eat, and immune systems grind down," Lewis told an interviewer. "So the interlinking of poverty and disease is probably the major issue on the planet. The most distinct manifestation of the issue is HIV and AIDS because you can't possibly think of anything where 25 million people have already died and 40 million people are infected."

Lewis's efforts, as well as those of the World Health Organization, individuals, groups, and governments, have highlighted the challenge of HIV/AIDS in Africa and elsewhere. At the UN World Summit in 2005, for example, leaders pledged to achieve universal access to treatment by 2010.

As a step toward this goal, governments have relaxed rules so that generic drug companies can make cheaper AIDS drugs and distribute them in developing countries. Non-governmental organizations such as the Stephen Lewis Foundation, the Gates Foundation, and the Clinton Foundation have launched awareness, prevention, and treatment programs.

Though these measures have helped, they have not solved the problem. At the end of 2006, only about 28 per cent of the people who needed treatment for AIDS were receiving it.

Web Connection

To learn more about efforts to combat AIDS in Africa, go to this web site and follow the links.

www.ExploringNationalism.ca

Figure 12-9 These children at a hospital in Pretoria, South Africa, either contracted AIDS from their parents or are at risk of developing the disease. They are among an estimated 11 million African youngsters who were orphaned when their parents died of AIDS.

Internationalism and Debt

Suppose you earn $3000 a month — but your expenses, including loan payments, total $4000 a month. What would your financial position be at the end of a year?

The same thing can happen to countries. Jamaica, for example, borrowed heavily from private banks, the World Bank, and the International Monetary Fund. The Jamaican government believed it could repay these loans as the economy grew and tax revenues increased.

But the economy did not perform as expected, and making payments became difficult. Nearly half Jamaica's tax revenue went to pay interest on the loans. In addition, conditions attached to the World Bank and IMF loans required the country to reduce spending by cutting services provided to citizens.

Other developing countries face similar problems. Commenting on the IMF's record, economist Lester Thurow wrote, "Historically, the IMF has been very good at restoring financial stability (its primary job) but horrible at restoring domestic prosperity (its secondary job)."

When the World Bank and the IMF lend money to a country, should they have the right to dictate how that country manages its national budget?

Web Connection

To find out more about how debt relief has helped countries in Africa, go to this web site and follow the links.

www.ExploringNationalism.ca

Odious Debt

In 1927, the Soviet thinker Alexander Sack coined the term **odious debt**. Sack wrote, "If a despotic power incurs a debt not for the needs or in the interest of the State, but to strengthen its despotic regime . . . this debt is odious." Sack said that these debts are owed by the regime, not the people of the country — and the people should not be required to repay them if the regime falls.

Probe International, an NGO that monitors Canada's delivery of foreign aid, uses Sack's term to describe debts that meet the following criteria:

- The debt was incurred without the consent of the people of the state.
- The debt did not benefit the people of that state.
- The lender was aware of these two conditions.

Organizations such as Probe International, as well as many governments, believe that countries should not be forced to repay odious debts. But other people, such as economist William Easterly, disagree. "Despite its overwhelming popularity among policymakers and the public, debt relief is a bad deal for the world's poor," Easterly wrote. "By transferring scarce resources to corrupt governments with proven track records of misusing aid, debt forgiveness might only aggravate poverty among the world's most vulnerable populations."

In response to pressure, some wealthy countries have begun forgiving loans they have made to developing countries. They believe that this relief will improve developing countries' chances of achieving economic stability.

With a partner, decide whether you agree with Probe International's or William Easterly's position on repaying odious debt. Explain how you arrived at your judgment.

Figure 12-10 Jamaica's beaches are a popular destination for tourists like those in the top photograph. These tourists are unlikely to visit the slums of Kingston, Jamaica's capital. There, poverty has sparked violence, and army vehicles like those in the bottom photograph often patrol the streets.

Internationalism and Climate Change

The Arctic ice cap is melting much faster than predicted — about 30 years ahead of forecasts. If melting continues at current rates, the Arctic Ocean could be nearly free of summer ice by 2020. This melting would speed up the pace of global climate change.

Climate change may be the most pressing environmental issue of the 21st century. A combination of factors contribute to climate change. High energy use in North America, for example, creates the greenhouse gas emissions that are a major contributor to climate change. In South America, cutting down tropical rainforests to make room for farming, ranching, and mining destroys trees that absorb carbon dioxide and help reduce the effects of climate change.

These factors — and others — contribute to the melting of the polar ice caps. Many scientists believe that this melting will increase the pace of climate change and cause destructive flooding along the coasts of all continents. The international community acknowledges that climate change affects everyone and has begun to work together to introduce measures to slow its pace.

In 1972, the United Nations Conference on the Human Environment established the United Nations Environment Programme to provide leadership in dealing with environmental issues. This international organization works with businesses, governments, independent scientists, and local communities to promote partnerships to establish and enhance sustainable products, procedures, and development.

The Kyoto Protocol is another international attempt to deal with climate change. Developed countries that signed the protocol agreed to reduce their domestic production of greenhouse gases to meet specific targets, but no specific targets were set for developing countries, such as China and India.

Some opponents of Kyoto believe that the failure to hold developing countries to the same standards as developed countries was unfair. Others emphasized the economic costs of meeting the Kyoto targets. John Howard, who was prime minister of Australia at the time, argued that meeting the Kyoto goals would place Australia at a disadvantage because its businesses and industries compete with those of China and India, which are not required to meet the same emission standards. Howard believed that Australian jobs would be lost as industries struggled to cut emissions.

Figure 12-11 This cartoon by artist Bill Greenhead sends a strong environmental message. What is the message? If everyone shares this planet, should all countries not take equal responsibility for preventing climate change?

Figure 12-12 Ecological Footprint of Selected Countries, 2003

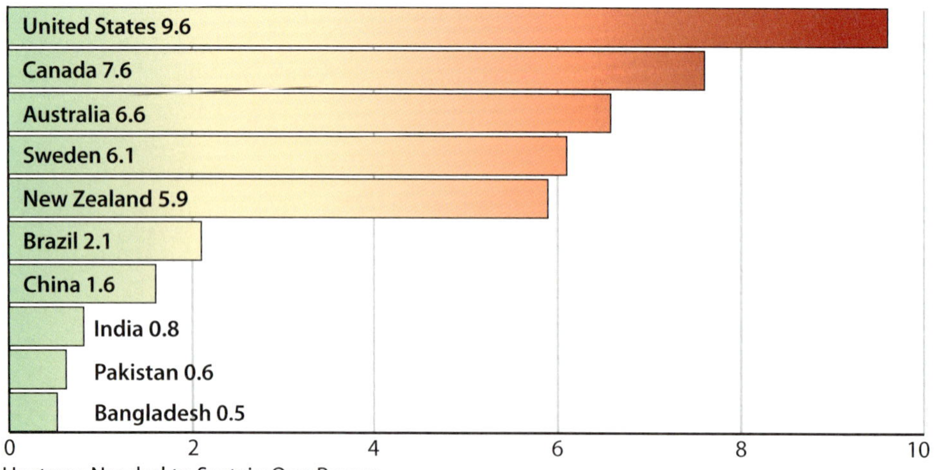

Canada and the United States voiced similar objections. The U.S. and Australia refused to endorse the protocol. And although Canada signed the agreement, Prime Minister Stephen Harper rejected it when he was elected in 2006. The difficulty of persuading countries to agree to the Kyoto Protocol shows how hard it can be to achieve international agreement and co-operation, even when countries agree that an issue is extremely important.

Examine the data in the graph in Figure 12-12. Does this graph support arguments that developing countries such as India and China should not be required to meet the same Kyoto standards as developed countries such as the United States and Canada? Explain your response.

MAKING A DIFFERENCE

Sheila Watt-Cloutier
Defending the Right to Be Cold

MAKING A DIFFERENCE MAKING A DIFFERENCE MAKING A DIFFERE

When Sheila Watt-Cloutier was growing up in Kuujjuaq, a community on the Koksoak River in northern Québec, she and her friends never wore shorts and T-shirts in summer. It was just too cold.

But things have changed. Many summer days are now so warm that Kuujjuaq residents often go down to the river to cool off.

Watt-Cloutier does not view this as an improvement. She believes that the Inuit have the right to be cold — and she has devoted her life to defending this right by raising awareness of climate change.

After attending McGill University, Watt-Cloutier's work focused on health, social, and youth issues — and this led to involvement in regional, national, and international Inuit organizations. She served as chair of the Canadian Inuit Circumpolar Council and later as chair of the international body.

In her work with the ICC, she helped negotiate a ban on the use of toxic chemicals. These chemicals have polluted the Arctic food chain and accumulated in the bodies of Inuit. The breast milk of many Inuit mothers, for example, is so contaminated that they have been advised either not to breastfeed or not to eat meat killed in the hunt.

The Inuit are on the land every day, and for years, they have been noticing changes. Ice forms later in the year and breaks up earlier. Traditional winter and summer travel routes have changed because the ice pack is different. And animals such as polar bear, caribou, and seals, which the Inuit rely on, have changed their habits.

Figure 12-13 Environmental activist Sheila Watt-Cloutier has won many awards, including a National Aboriginal Achievement Award, the Governor General's Northern Medal, and the United Nations' Mahbub ul Haq Award for Human Development. In 2007, she was nominated for the Nobel Peace Prize.

Watt-Cloutier believes that these changes are linked to changes that are happening elsewhere — and that her people are the early warning system for the rest of the world. "Connectivity is going to be the key to addressing these issues, like contaminants and climate change," she told an interviewer for *Grist*, an online environmental magazine. "They're not just about the contaminants on your plate. They're not just about the ice depleting. They're about the issue of humanity. What we do every day — whether you live in Mexico, the United States, Russia, China . . . can have a very negative impact on an entire way of life for an entire people far away from that source."

Explorations

1. How do Sheila Watt-Cloutier's words demonstrate the importance of an international approach to resolving environmental issues? Do you agree with her?
2. Watt-Cloutier shows that the actions of one person can matter, even when dealing with global issues. Identify one action you could take to have a positive effect on reducing global climate change and explain the effects of your action.

Internationalism and Human Rights

There is a known crisis in Myanmar and it degrades humanity as a whole when the international community ignores it. We must address the lack of international interest, access and information — and recognize that these factors are interrelated.

— *Sara Brooks, development specialist, in the* Human Rights Tribune, *2006*

After the horror of the World War II Holocaust, the international community recognized the importance of working together to prevent similar abuses from happening again. As a result, the United Nations adopted the Universal Declaration of Human Rights in 1948. This document set out rights and freedoms that everyone is entitled to.

Why would listing specific universal human rights, such as "life, liberty, and security of person," be considered an important step in limiting future abuses?

When a country violates the rights of its own citizens or the citizens of another nation-state, the UN can take action against the violator. But political alliances come into play, and achieving consensus on the actions to take — and even whether violations have occurred — is not easy.

Before the UN can take action, all five permanent members of the UN Security Council — China, France, Russia, Britain, and the United States — must agree. A majority of other Security Council members must also agree. If even one permanent member vetoes — rejects — a proposal, the UN cannot act.

Figure 12-14 Myanmar (formerly Burma)

Human Rights in Myanmar

In 2007, people in Myanmar, which has been under military rule since 1962, began a series of peaceful protests to demand a greater say in how their country is run. Buddhist monks, who are widely respected for their moral leadership, led the demonstrations.

The government responded by ordering the army to fire on the unarmed protestors. Thousands of people were killed, and thousands of monks were arrested and have not been seen since.

When images of the brutal crackdown reached the world via cellphones and the Internet, the UN Security Council met to debate a resolution calling on Myanmar to release all political prisoners, begin dialogue, and stop abusing people's human rights. China and Russia vetoed the proposal, arguing that the events in Myanmar posed no threat to international peace and security. As a result, the UN took no action.

Does the UN's failure to take action to help the people of Myanmar suggest that it is as ineffective as the League of Nations, which you read about in Chapter 6?

Internationalism and Conflict

One of the chief goals of the United Nations and other international organizations is to help countries work together to ensure peace and security in the world. But issues affecting peace and security are often complex and not easily resolved. As a result, the world community often struggles to chart an effective course of action.

Almost invariably, we discuss Darfur in a convenient military and political shorthand — an ethnic conflict pitting Arab militias against black rebels and farmers. Look to its roots, though, and you discover a more complex dynamic. Amid the diverse social and political causes, the Darfur conflict began as an ecological crisis, arising at least in part from climate change.

— Ban Ki-moon, UN secretary-general, 2007

Conflict in Darfur

The conflict in the Darfur region of western Sudan shows how complex causes can spark violence and make maintaining peace difficult. About 60 per cent of Darfuris are farmers, and most are black people. Many of the rest are nomadic or semi-nomadic herders whose background is largely Arabic. In recent decades, the region has been plagued by droughts. As the countryside became more arid, the two groups began competing for land.

This competition turned violent in March 2003, when the Sudan Liberation Army and other rebel groups began attacking government targets in Darfur. The SLA claimed that Sudan's government, which is dominated by Arabs, favoured Arabs over black farmers. Since then, a brutal civil war has raged. Government-backed troops and members of Arabic Janjaweed militias have been accused of genocide for systematically killing black Sudanese peoples. By 2007, an estimated 200 000 people had been killed and about 2.5 million had fled their homes.

The UN tried negotiating with the Sudanese government, and the Security Council imposed economic sanctions on the country. In addition, the International Criminal Court began to investigate war crimes and issued arrest warrants for a government minister and a Janjaweed leader. Despite these actions, the violence continued.

In 2004, the African Union — an organization made up of countries in Africa — sent peacekeepers to Darfur, but this force was too small to be effective. After intense negotiations, the Sudanese government agreed to allow a joint force of UN and African peacekeepers into the country in 2008.

Figure 12-15 Sudan

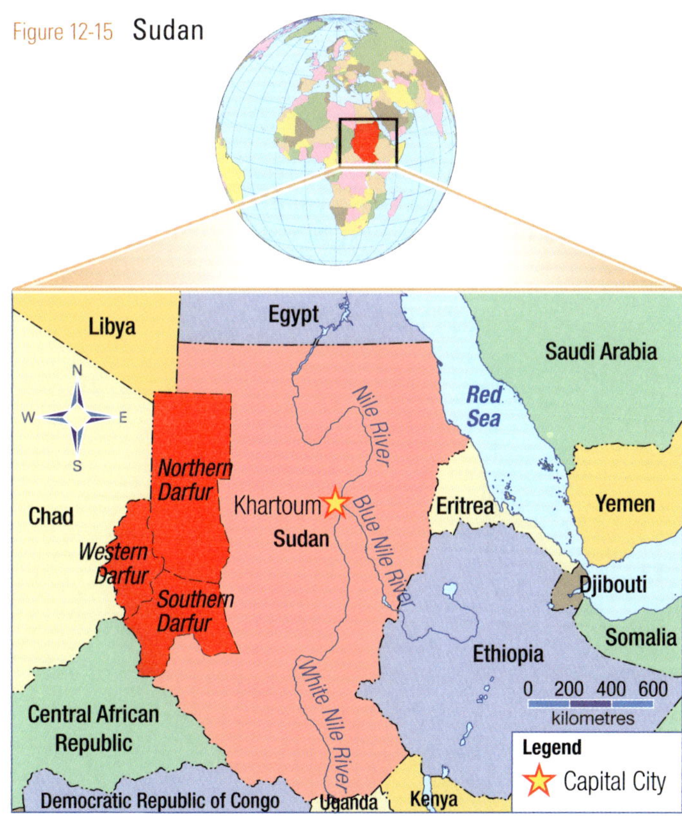

Reflect and Respond

With a partner, create a rating system that includes criteria for judging the success of international efforts to combat poverty, hunger, disease, debt, climate change, human rights, and conflict. Then use your system to create a report card that rates the success of internationalism. Include a statement that predicts the future of internationalism.

Communicating Effectively to Express a Point of View

FOCUS ON SKILLS

Figure 12-16 Peter Mansbridge has anchored *The National*, CBC's flagship newscast, since 1988. Watch a national news broadcast on a Canadian network and pay careful attention to the pace at which the announcers speak.

Making oral presentations is common not only in school but also in business, government, clubs, churches, and volunteer groups. A classroom presentation may involve one or more speakers, and it may take several forms.

Learning to effectively express a point of view is an important skill. The following steps can help you practise this skill.

Steps to Communicating Effectively to Express a Point of View

Step 1: Select a topic and format

With your partner, return to the report card you created for "Reflect and Respond" on page 285 of *Exploring Nationalism* and select one topic (e.g., poverty, hunger, disease, debt, climate change, human rights, or conflict). This topic will become the focus of a two-minute presentation that expresses and justifies your evaluation of the success of international efforts in the area you have chosen.

Decide on a format for your presentation. You may choose to make a speech, use computer presentation software, create a video, or combine several of these formats — and others that you may prefer.

Step 2: Conduct research

With your partner, review the material on your topic in *Exploring Nationalism* and conduct additional research to expand your knowledge. Record the details of all sources you consult.

Step 3: Prepare your presentation

Because you cannot possibly cover everything on the topic in two minutes, carefully select the details you will emphasize to achieve the maximum impact and to effectively convey your informed opinion.

- Develop an introduction, supporting details, and a conclusion.
- Decide how you and your partner will work together to present your evaluation.
- Prepare a list of equipment you will need (e.g., an overhead projector), arrange to have it on hand, and make sure you know how to operate it.
- Prepare answers for questions you think your classmates may ask.
- Save research material you do not plan to use in the presentation. This may come in handy when classmates ask questions.

FOCUS ON SKILLS FOCUS ON SKILLS CUS ON SKILLS FOCUS ON SKILLS FOCUS ON SKILLS

Step 4: Rehearse your presentation

With your partner, practise your presentation. As you rehearse, coach each other, using the checklist on this page as a guide. Your classmates will use the same checklist to evaluate your presentation skills.

Step 5: Make your presentation

Present your views and answer questions posed by your classmates. When your classmates make their presentations, use the checklist like the one on this page to evaluate their skills.

Presentation Dos and Don'ts

Skill	Often	Sometimes	Rarely
Speaking Skills			
• Varied tone of voice and emphasized important points			
• Spoke clearly (could be heard by everyone)			
• Paused at end of sentences and didn't rush			
• Pronounced terms without stumbling			
• Was prepared to answer questions from audience			
Body Language			
• Faced the audience			
• Stood straight and didn't lean on podium or table			
• Spoke to audience rather than reading from notes			
• Used gestures effectively rather than fidgeting			
• Made eye contact with various audience members			
Group Skills			
• Co-ordinated speaking role with partner			
• Shared speaking load with partner			
Use of Audiovisual Aids			
• Used well-designed, easy-to-read materials			
• Arranged equipment so audience could see easily			
• Knew how to use equipment			

Summing Up

As you progress through this course, you will have many opportunities to express a point of view — and you can use the skills you have practised to do this effectively. These skills are important not only in school but also in many other situations.

Is Internationalism Always the Most Effective Way of Addressing Contemporary Global Issues?

Web Connection

To learn more about the UN's millennium development goals and their current status, go to this web site and follow the links.

www.ExploringNationalism.ca

In 2000, the UN established eight international targets — its millennium development goals. These goals, which were to be achieved by 2015, included reducing poverty by 50 per cent, ensuring that all children have access to primary education, and combating diseases such as HIV/AIDS. By 2008, it had begun to look as if none of these goals would be reached.

Does the fact that the world is unlikely to achieve any of the UN's millennium development goals suggest that international attempts to solve the world's problems are a failure?

International Trade

International trade and economic globalization are often held out as the solution to the world's problems. Many economists and experts in international relations believe that trade improves economic prosperity, contributes to stability and security, and fosters peaceful relations among countries. Policy analysts Gerald P. O'Driscoll Jr. and Sara J. Fitzgerald expressed this idea when they wrote: "Countries that trade with each other are far less likely to confront each other on the battlefield than are countries with no trade relationship."

This view is reflected in the policies of the World Trade Organization, which was established to promote and regulate international trade. The WTO maintains that a world trade system promotes peace by helping to resolve disputes, stimulate economic growth, and reduce inequality. According to the WTO, the system "does reduce some inequalities, giving smaller countries more voice, and . . . freeing the major powers from the complexity of having to negotiate trade agreements with each of their numerous trading partners."

Figure 12-17 This cartoon was created for *The Post* of Zambia by Trevor Ford, who was also known as Yuss. What message was Yuss sending about the effectiveness of the UN's millennium development goals? Do you agree with this point of view? Why or why not?

But this view has been challenged. Critics argue that the WTO and international trade place developing countries at a disadvantage.

John Madeley, a professor at the London School of Economics, for example, believes that international trade rules benefit only developed countries. "Under economic globalization, poor countries have liberalized and rich countries have continued to protect. The result has been a flow of cheap, often subsidized, goods to developing countries, which has cost millions of their farmers and industrial workers their jobs," he said. "Free trade cannot be fair to the poor. With no barriers to trade, the poor swim in the same economic stream as the transnational corporations that account for two-thirds of world trade."

Internationalism and Nation-States

People are divided over the effects of internationalism on the future of nation-states. Some, such as Joseph Stiglitz, a Nobel Prize–winning economist who was once a senior vice-president at the World Bank, believe that international trade and financing policies have caused great suffering and reduced the decision-making power of national governments.

Stiglitz is especially critical of the structural adjustment programs of institutions like the World Bank and the International Monetary Fund. In return for loans, these institutions often require the governments of developing countries to introduce changes that may include opening up markets to outside investment and reducing budget deficits by lowering government spending on social programs such as education and health care.

In 2002, Stiglitz told the *New York Times Magazine* that the IMF "undermines the democratic process, because it dictates policies."

Taking Turns

Is internationalism the only way to address contemporary global issues?

The students responding to this question are Rick, who was born in the United States but moved to Fort McMurray with his family when he was 10; Violet, a Métis who is a member of the Paddle Prairie Métis Settlement; and Jane, who lives in Calgary and is descended from black Loyalists who fled to Nova Scotia after the American Revolution.

Rick

I say that individual action is more important than action by nation-states because it can cut through or go around the roadblocks and delays created whenever governments try to do things. Take action on your own — change to energy-saving light bulbs, use less water, drink fair-trade coffee, sign an online petition . . . do anything. The power of one can solve lots of problems if everyone takes personal responsibility.

Violet

When it comes to issues like disease, lots of evidence says that internationalism is effective. We need to build on the successes of international groups like the World Health Organization. Developing countries can't do everything on their own — and it's in our interest to make sure that they're peaceful and prosperous. They provide markets for our goods, and if they struggle, our stability and prosperity is affected. So the international community needs to find solutions — and I think it's doing that, even if progress is slow.

Jane

I don't know. I'm not sure that internationalism is really working, at least the way things are set up now. If I were an optimist, I suppose I'd say that things are improving, even if it's only gradually. But if I were a pessimist, I might say that the developed world is taking advantage of the developing world — and developing countries won't put up with this forever. It's bound to create resentment, and what happens when this resentment boils over?

How would you respond to the question Rick, Violet, and Jane are answering? Explain the reasons for your answer.

Decline versus Shift

In his book *Fortune Favors the Bold: What We Must Do to Build a New and Lasting Global Prosperity*, Lester Thurow wrote that the power of individual nation-states to control their own destiny is declining.

> In the 20th century, governments came to think of themselves as economic air traffic controllers controlling the flows of their economies. With globalization this power is disappearing for governments large and small. Governments are still important in the knowledge-based economy, but instead of being air traffic controllers of economic events within their borders, governments are increasingly having to become airport builders constructing runways to attract global economic activity to locate within their borders.

The unregulated internationalization of capital is now being followed by the internationalization of peoples' movements and organizations. Building peoples' international organizations and solidarity will be our revolution from within: a civil society without borders. This internationalism or "globalization from below" will be the foundation for a participatory and sustainable global village.

— *From* Global Pillage to Global Village, *a joint report of nearly 80 American groups opposed to the North American Free Trade Agreement, 1993*

Some people, however, view this change not as a decline in the power of nation-states, but as a sign of a shift that may change the way people view themselves in the world. In a 1997 article in the magazine *Foreign Affairs*, international affairs specialist Jessica Matthews wrote that "a novel redistribution of power among states, markets, and civil society" has taken place.

By "civil society," Matthews means non-government and non-business groups that include non-governmental organizations, community groups, faith-based groups, and universities. In the view of many, civil society helps link citizens, nation-states, and international organizations — and these links provide individuals with unprecedented opportunities to influence policy and events at local, regional, national, and international levels.

Matthews views these changes as a positive development in the history of nation-states. She wrote:

> National governments are not simply losing autonomy in a globalizing economy. They are sharing powers – including political, social, and security roles at the core of sovereignty – with businesses, with international organizations, and with a multitude of citizens' groups . . . The steady concentration of power in the hands of states that began in 1648 with the Peace of Westphalia is over, at least for a while . . . International standards of conduct are gradually beginning to override claims of national or regional singularity. Even the most powerful states find the marketplace and international public opinion compelling them more often to follow a particular course.

Figure 12-18 This cartoon, titled "Blind Nationalism," was created by the Cuban cartoonist Ares. What message is Ares sending? How do you think Ares might view the decline in the power of the nation-state?

Like Matthews, philosopher and political activist Noam Chomsky believes that individuals have the power to pressure national governments and the international community to find solutions to the world's problems. Chomsky said, "States are not moral agents, people are, and can impose moral standards on powerful institutions."

What do you think? Is what is happening a decline in the power of nation-states or a shift in the way governments operate? Make your own prediction about what might happen as a result. Would the result you predicted be a postive or negative development for the world?

THE VIEW FROM HERE

For many people, the United Nations represents internationalism at work. But will the UN remain a useful tool for dealing with global issues in the 21st century? Here is how three people with a vital interest in the UN have responded to this question.

Gareth Evans is a former Australian politician who has served on the UN Secretary-General's Advisory Committee on the Prevention of Genocide and Mass Atrocities. He said the following in a speech to Foreign Affairs Canada in 2005.

No organization in the world embodies as many dreams, yet delivers as many frustrations, as the United Nations. This year we have seen both abundantly at play. There are plenty who are justifiably now skeptical that the UN and its member states will ever be capable of responding to the challenge of reform . . . But we have no alternative but to keep on trying – all of us.

Srgjan Kerim is the former foreign minister of Macedonia. In 2007, when he was elected president of the United Nations General Assembly, he urged members to form partnerships and make globalization more inclusive.

It is possible, I believe, to forge a new culture of international relations, by demonstrating the courage to rise above ourselves. The UN needs be at the forefront of building a new culture of international relations based on greater trust and mutual co-operation and fairer economic consensus . . . Achieving this will necessarily tend to further . . . devolve sovereignty, particularly at the individual and international level.

Since 1978, writer and novelist **Shashi Tharoor** has served the UN in a variety of roles. The following is an excerpt from an article published in a 2005 issue of the *New Internationalist*. In it, Tharoor argues that the UN was not created to take humanity to heaven but to save it from hell.

The UN is not simply a security organization; it is not a sort of NATO for the world. When the present crisis has passed, the world will still be facing (to use Secretary-General Kofi Annan's phrase) innumerable "problems without passports" that cross all frontiers uninvited; weapons of mass destruction and terrorism, certainly, but also the degradation of our common environment, contagious disease and chronic starvation, human rights and human wrongs, mass illiteracy and massive displacement.

These are problems that no one country, however powerful, can solve on its own – as someone once said about water pollution, we all live downstream. They cry out for solutions that, like the problems themselves, cross frontiers.

Explorations

1. In a phrase or single sentence, capture the message of each quotation.
2. Does a common thread run through the words of Gareth Evans, Srgjan Kerim, and Shashi Tharoor? If so, explain what it is. If not, explain the differences.
3. With a partner discuss this statement: If the United Nations did not exist, people would have to invent it.

1. Marhall McLuhan used the phrase "global village" to express his belief that the people of the world were becoming more closely linked than ever. Explain how McLuhan's concept of a global village affects nationalism. Can nationalism continue to exist in a global village? Is the idea of nationalism out of date — or is it more important than ever?

2. Research the relationship between development of the Alberta oil sands and global climate change. Briefly state your position on each of the following aspects of this relationship:
   a) an international environmental issue
   b) Alberta's responsibility to the global community
   c) Canada's response to the growing international movement calling for reductions in greenhouse gas emissions

3. Work with a group of three or four to design and create a poster promoting international action on one of the global issues explored in this chapter (poverty, hunger, disease, debt, climate change, human rights, and conflict) or a global issue of great importance to the group.

   Create a statement that outlines the motivation, aim, and message of the poster. Present your poster to the class.

4. For decades, singer-songwriter and political activist Bob Geldof has been involved in celebrity events designed to raise awareness of and eliminate poverty. During a speech accepting the 2005 Man of Peace award, which was presented in Rome, Geldof said: "We live in a broken world which has never been healthier, wealthier, or freer of conflict, but 500 kilometres south of here, they die of want . . . It's not only intellectually absurd, it's morally repulsive."

   What was Geldof referring to when he said, "500 kilometres south of here"?

   In your own words, explain Geldof's message. In your statement, be sure to note the relationship between Geldof's words and the need for international action on global issues.

5. According to the United Nations' charter, this international organization is responsible for protecting the citizens of the world. But UN rules, which allow any of the five permanent members of the Security Council to veto proposed actions, often interfere with the UN's ability to meet this responsibility.

   Create a cartoon, drawing, or electronic presentation that lampoons — makes fun of — this situation. Remember to use respectful words and images. Stereotypes are unacceptable. Humour should result from the situation, not from the characters in the cartoon.

6. Examine the cartoon on this page and note its title.
   a) What is the artist's message about the state of the world today?
   b) Express your view of this message by writing a caption for the cartoon.
   c) Refer to an issue explored in this chapter and explain how this cartoon sums it up.

Figure 12-19 Our World Today

Think about Your Challenge

Your challenge for this related issue is to participate in a mock international summit on the world water crisis. Review the notes you prepared as you progressed through the chapters of this related issue, then begin preparing your presentation for the conference. Decide what you hope to achieve and how you will go about achieving this goal, then select the material you will present to other delegates and assemble the visual materials you plan to use. As you prepare, you may wish to review this chapter's skill focus: communicating effectively to express a point of view (pp. 286–287).

Think about the arguments, positions, and ideas other delegates are likely to make. Make notes about possible responses.

RELATED ISSUE 4

To what extent should individuals and groups in Canada embrace a national identity?

Key Issue
To what extent should we embrace nationalism?

Related Issue 1
To what extent should nation be the foundation of identity?

Related Issue 2
To what extent should national interest be pursued?

Related Issue 3
To what extent should internationalism be pursued?

Related Issue 4
To what extent should individuals and groups in Canada embrace a national identity?

CHAPTER 13

VISIONS OF CANADA

To what extent have visions of Canadian identity evolved?

↕

What is Canada?

How and why did early visions of Canada emerge?

To what extent did various early visions of Canada meet people's needs?

How is the evolution of various visions of Canada reflected in the country today?

CHAPTER 14

CANADIAN IDENTITY

To what extent have attempts to promote national identity been successful?

How have symbols and myths been used to promote a national identity?

How have institutions been used to promote a national identity in Canada?

How can government programs and initiatives be used to promote a national identity?

How can individuals promote a national identity?

CHAPTER 15

THE QUEST FOR CANADIAN UNITY

To what extent should Canadian national unity be promoted?

What is national unity?

How does the nature of Canada affect national unity?

How has the changing face of Canada affected national unity?

CHAPTER 16

VISIONS OF NATIONAL IDENTITY

To what extent should I embrace a national identity?

What are some possible visions of nation?

What are some possible visions of Canada?

What is your vision of national identity?

THE BIG PICTURE

As you explored the first three related issues, you developed understandings of the concepts of identity, nation, nation-state, nationalism, and internationalism. In the process, you may have come to understand that you are a member of at least one nation — and perhaps several.

Some experts in fields such as political philosophy and history take a dim view of nationalism, arguing that contending nationalist loyalties cause much of the conflict in the world as nation struggles against nation. Those who hold this view believe that nationalism is a negative force that leads to an us-versus-them worldview.

Others view nationalism more positively. They argue that a sense of nation and nationalism creates bonds among people and that these bonds foster security and well-being. From this base, they argue, nations can develop, prosper, and confidently play a role in world affairs, offering aid, expertise, and a model for other nations to follow.

No matter which vision of nation and nationalism you subscribe to, nationalism affects your life. In Canada, many nations coexist, though their goals sometimes conflict. Some nations are even dedicated to changing the country's structure. For Canada and Canadians, this diversity presents both challenges and opportunities — and you will explore some of these as you progress through this related issue.

Lester B. Pearson, a former prime minister and winner of the Nobel Peace Prize, identified these challenges and opportunities when he said that Canadians have choices: "whether we live together in confidence and cohesion; with more faith and pride in ourselves and less self-doubt and hesitation; strong in the conviction that the destiny of Canada is to unite, not divide; sharing in co-operation, not in separation or in conflict; respecting our past and welcoming our future."

The chart on the previous page shows how you will progress through Related Issue 4. As you explore this related issue, you will come to appreciate that

- developing a national identity is a process with a past, a present, and a future
- national identity is complex and multi-faceted
- people have differing visions of their national identity
- these differing visions affect the way people view their nation and nationalism

Your explorations in this related issue will challenge you to develop your own understandings of the complexities of nationalism in Canada — and to decide the extent to which you wish to embrace nationalism.

Your Challenge

Participate in a four-corners debate that discusses, analyzes, and evaluates responses to the question for this related issue: To what extent should individuals and groups in Canada embrace a national identity?

You will then work with the class to build a consensus in response to the key course question: To what extent should we embrace nationalism?

Checklist for Success

Use this checklist to ensure that you are well-prepared for the debate.

My Knowledge and Understanding

☑ My criteria for judgment show my understanding of the issue.

☑ My criteria for judgment are clearly explained.

☑ My opening position is based on my criteria.

☑ My arguments are thoughtful and based on sound evidence.

My Selection, Analysis, and Evaluation of Information

☑ My information is drawn from a variety of sources.

☑ My evidence is relevant, valid, reliable, and free of bias.

☑ My evidence shows that I have considered a variety of points of view and perspectives.

☑ My sources and references are cited correctly and accurately.

My Presentation of My Position

☑ I support my position with graphics and other material.

☑ I listen carefully and respond thoughtfully to new ideas.

☑ I am prepared to change my position as new ideas and logical challenges are presented.

A Four-Corners Debate

As you progress through the four chapters of this related issue, you will develop understandings of, as well as opinions and ideas about, the extent to which individuals and groups in Canada should embrace a national identity. These ideas, along with the notes you have been keeping in your journal on nationalism, will help you prepare to take part in a four-corners debate on this statement:

> Individuals and groups should embrace a national identity.

Before the debate begins, you will see four signs — Strongly Agree, Agree, Disagree, and Strongly Disagree — posted in the four corners of the classroom. These signs indicate levels of agreement and disagreement with the debate statement.

At the beginning, you will take a position under the sign that best represents your opening position on the debate statement — and you will have an opportunity to present evidence and arguments to persuade others to support your position. You will also have an opportunity to listen to, consider, and ask questions about the views of others, as well as to decide whether their arguments are convincing enough to persuade you to change your position.

Your teacher will explain the debate procedure in more detail.

Preparing for the Debate

At the end of each chapter, you will have an opportunity to think about and start preparing the material needed to complete this challenge.

As you progress through the chapters, think about criteria you can use to guide your choice of an initial informed position. Basing your decision on strong, insightful criteria will help you develop and defend your position on the debate statement. It will also help you ask and answer powerful questions, listen thoughtfully and respectfully to the ideas of others, and evaluate and respond to the informed positions of others.

Steps to Your Challenge

Step 1

To prepare an informed position on an issue, it is important to analyze the issue and try to understand the relationships between the parts and the whole. Examine the parts of the debate statement. Who, for example, are "individuals" and "groups"? Does this refer to all Canadians, to the members of a particular nation within Canada, to the students in your classroom — or to some other individuals and groups? And what does the word "embrace" mean? Does it mean complete acceptance of a particular view? Does it allow for critical thought?

In developing your informed position, you will explain your understanding of the various aspects of the debate statement. These understandings will affect the criteria you develop, the judgment you reach, and the way you approach the debate statement.

Step 2

Develop a starting position. Do you strongly agree, agree, disagree, or strongly disagree with the debate statement? The ideas you encounter as you progress through this related issue and those you have recorded in your journal, as well as the criteria you develop, will help you arrive at a position — and decide whether you need to carry out additional research before deciding what position to take. You should also choose graphics and other materials to help support your position.

When the debate begins, you will be asked to move to the area of the classroom with the sign that best represents your position. The number of students taking each position will be counted.

Step 3

Present your position — and be prepared to answer questions and to listen as others present their position.

During the debate, you will have an opportunity to change your position. Be prepared to identify the arguments that persuaded you to stick with your original position or make a change.

Step 4

When the debate concludes, stay with the group under the sign that represents your final position. With this group, extend your discussion to develop a consensus on the key course issue: To what extent should we embrace nationalism?

Develop a statement that summarizes your consensus and record this on the chalkboard or a sheet of chart paper. Then work with the class to achieve consensus on the same issue. If achieving consensus is not possible, develop a statement that reflects the majority and minority views on the issue.

Step 5

On the basis of the statement you developed in Step 4, decide as a class whether this course provided you with the information and opportunities necessary to develop an informed response to the key course-issue question. If you would recommend changes, explain what these would be.

Challenge Tips

To get the most out of a four-corners debate, consider these pointers.

Listen Actively	Think Critically	Participate Respectfully
Make notes about what others say so that you can fine-tune your response. Deconstruct key phrases and ideas presented by others to ensure that you understand their message. Treat disagreement as an opportunity to learn about other points of view and perspectives that you can build on.	Be open to the idea of changing your opinion when you encounter valid evidence and sound arguments. Be strong-willed enough to maintain a position you believe in without being stubborn. Be aware of your own biases.	Be willing to accept that others believe in their position as strongly as you believe in yours. Be open to new ideas and extend to others the same respect you expect. Be willing to explore new ideas. Be careful to focus on the ideas, not the person.

CHAPTER 13 Visions of Canada

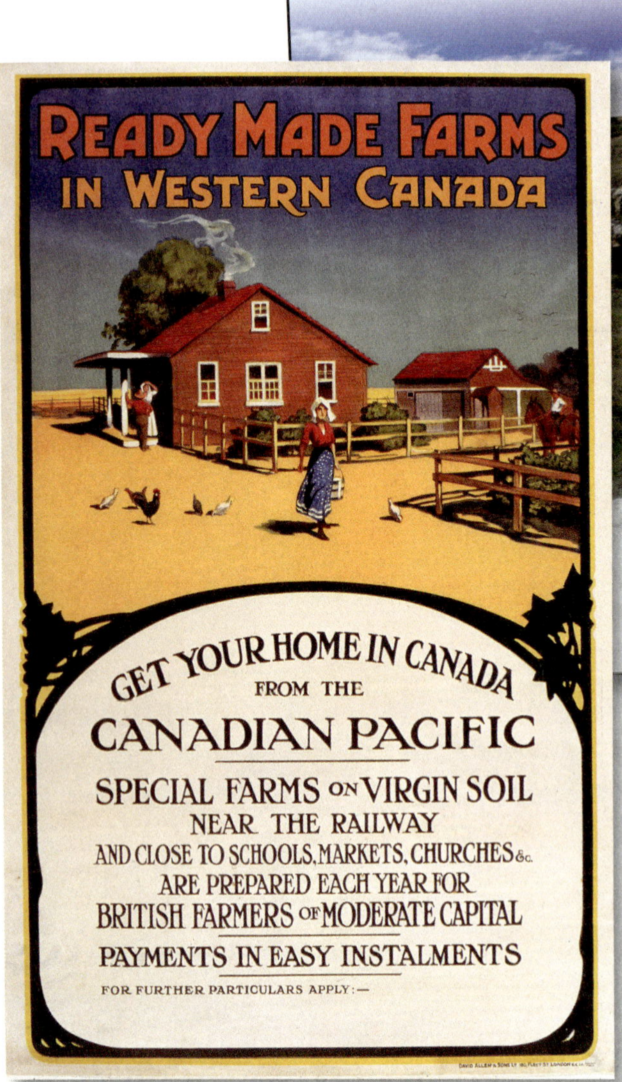

Figure 13-1 At different times, the posters on this page have been used to promote aspects of Canada. The Canadian Pacific Railway poster at left was created in the early 20th century and was designed to attract British farmers to Canada. The poster in the middle is a contemporary poster used by Alberta's Ministry of Tourism, Parks, Recreation and Culture. And the poster at the top was used to advertise Expo 67, a world's fair held in Montréal to celebrate Canada's centennial. All were created to give people at home and abroad a sense of Canada and its values.

CHAPTER ISSUE

To what extent have visions of Canadian identity evolved?

THE POSTERS ON THE PREVIOUS PAGE represent visions of Canada. Each is from a different time in the country's history, but all three offer idealized answers to this question: What is Canada?

When individuals, groups, businesses, and governments try to capture the identity of a country in a single image, their visions frequently differ, often because their goals differ. The poster created by the Canadian Pacific Railway, for example, was designed to attract settlers to the West. It shows a Canada that railway officials believed would appeal to British immigrants.

Examine the images on the previous page and think about how they reflect evolving visions of Canada. Then respond to the following questions:

- What does each poster tell you about the image of Canada those who commissioned it wanted to convey?
- Can a single poster or image provide enough information about a country or people to represent everyone? Should it be required to do this? What elements of Canadian identity do you believe have been left out of each poster?
- To what extent do you think the posters show a real, imagined, or purposely fabricated view of Canadian identity?
- Do any of the images match your vision of Canada? If so, how? If not, what image(s) would you include on a poster advertising Canada?

KEY TERMS

responsible government

Looking Ahead

In this chapter, you will respond to the following questions as you explore the extent to which visions of Canada have evolved:

- What is Canada?
- How and why did early visions of Canada emerge?
- To what extent did various early visions of Canada meet people's needs?
- How is the evolution of various visions of Canada reflected in the country today?

My Journal on Nationalism

Keeping in mind the visions of Canada represented in the posters on the previous page, use words or images — or both — to express your current ideas on changing visions of national identity. Date your ideas and keep them in your journal, notebook, learning log, portfolio, or computer file so that you can return to them as you progress through this final related issue.

What is Canada?

It is our outrageous dimensions that give shape and reason to our identity as Canadians. While no single factor forms a nation's character, winter's dominance, and the North that symbolizes it, rank among Canada's most potent influences.

— Peter C. Newman, historian and journalist, 1990

National identity involves a sense of belonging to a collective or community. When a nation has a clearly defined identity, individuals and groups who have internalized this identity are much more likely to affirm and promote a single identifiable identity.

Nationalism and identity are often related. People may define themselves in terms of the identity of the collective or nation to which they feel most closely connected. And just as aspects of your personal identity change as you grow and reconsider your values and goals, so, too, do aspects of national identity.

Which do you find easiest to define — your personal, group, collective, or national identity? Explain your response.

Differing Visions of Canada

Canadians have been trying to define Canada's identity since before Confederation. Some, for example, argue that certain beliefs, values, and traditions make Canadians different from citizens of other countries. Others say that Canada includes many identities. Still others argue that there is no such thing as a Canadian identity. Those who believe this say that Canada is so big and includes people from so many cultural backgrounds that Canadians have little in common. Though they acknowledge the existence of a nation-state called Canada, they do not believe that a Canadian nation exists.

Some, such as comedian Mike Myers, argue that Canadians are best described as "not being" something else. They say, for example, that Canadians are "not American" or "not British." Myers once said, "Canada is the essence of not being. Not English, not American, it is the mathematic of not being."

Others prefer to describe what Canadians "are." Political journalist Susan Delacourt, for example, wrote: "Bilingualism, multiculturalism, and religious and political pluralism are all part of the complicated mix that we call Canadian society . . . To be Canadian means to be willing to shrug off your own identity so you can imagine what it's like to be someone else."

When Delacourt wrote about being willing to "shrug off" your own identity, did she mean that you must abandon your identity? Explain your response.

Figure 13-2 Until 1965, Canada did not have its own official flag. In 1964, Prime Minister Lester Pearson suggested that Canada adopt a design. In the bottom photograph, a committee that reviewed thousands of designs meets to narrow down the choices. In the other photograph, a university student presents his choice to Pearson. Do you think the flag that was finally adopted adequately reflects Canada's identity, or would another design be more appropriate?

Canadian Identity and Geography

Canadian history is full of stories about how people have struggled to either tame or adapt to nature. Novelist Margaret Atwood, for example, has said that "survival" is the word that distills "the essence" of Canada. Some have argued that Canadians are defined by their country's vast open spaces, its relatively small and widely dispersed population, its climate, and its northerliness. Like Peter C. Newman, who is quoted in "Voices" on the previous page, these people believe that Canada's rugged geography is fundamental to the Canadian spirit.

Web Connection

To see photographs of sites linked to Albertan and Canadian identity, go to this web site and follow the links.

www.ExploringNationalism.ca

One Canada

In 1956, John Diefenbaker, who would later become prime minister, said, "I have one love — Canada; one purpose — Canada's greatness; one aim — Canadian unity from the Atlantic to the Pacific." Those who identify with Diefenbaker's vision of one Canada believe that Canadians, regardless of their ethnic, cultural, language, and regional differences, are committed to living together as a civic nation in one political unit: the nation-state that began at Confederation.

One of the derivations proposed for the word Canada is a Portuguese phrase meaning "nobody here." The etymology of the word Utopia is very similar, and perhaps the real Canada is an ideal with nobody in it. The Canada to which we really do owe loyalty is the Canada that we have failed to create . . . our identity, like the real identity of all nations, is the one that we have failed to achieve. It is expressed in our culture, but not attained in our life . . . the uncreated identity of Canada may be after all not so bad a heritage to take with us.

— Northrop Frye, Canadian professor and literary critic, in The Modern Century*, 1967*

Pluralistic and Multicultural

The Canadian government describes one element of Canada's identity as "bilingual within a multicultural context." People who support this vision say that Canada's diversity *is* its identity. They believe that Canadians respect and encourage differences. This vision of Canada implies that Canadians are free to maintain their traditional cultures and languages — because Canada is a mosaic of identities.

Communities and Nations within a Nation

In 1979, Joe Clark, who was then leader of the Progressive Conservative Party, said, "Governments make the nation work by recognizing that we are fundamentally a community of communities." And in 2006, Prime Minister Stephen Harper proclaimed that the Québécois constitute a "nation within a united Canada." This statement acknowledged that the Québécois have a collective identity that is different from that of other peoples in Canada — but it also says that they are still part of the larger Canadian nation. These visions of Canadian identity suggest that many different national identities coexist within Canada.

Does the existence of many differing visions of Canadian identity mean that trying to define Canada is an exercise in futility?

Reflect and Respond

Use words or pictures — or both — to describe the identity of one of the groups or collectives that you are part of. You may, for example, choose your family, school, club, or community. Illustrate the characteristics that distinguish your group from others.

Then review the visions of Canadian identity offered by various people. Which of the visions of Canada do you think most closely reflects the country today? Explain your response. If you think that none of these visions captures today's Canadian identity, identify another vision that you think is more accurate.

How do you think this vision will change as Canadian identity evolves over the next 25 years?

Comparing Various Narratives

FOCUS ON SKILLS

Narratives relate past events — and often reveal what was important to a culture at a particular time. A narrative may reveal an individual's point of view, or it may reflect the perspective of an institution or collective.

The narrator's point of view may also affect how she or he remembers an event. As a result, narratives written by different people about the same event may be very different. American editor and writer Tom Bissell said, "This does not make the authors of those narratives liars; it makes them servants of fallible human memory and perception."

Your description of a school event, for example, may be different from that of a classmate. The purpose of your narrative may also affect your description. In an e-mail message to a friend, you might describe an event one way. But an account written for your community newspaper would probably be different.

The narratives on the following page set out two visions of Canadian national identity. The following steps can help you examine, compare, and analyze these narratives — and others you will encounter as you progress through this final related issue.

Steps to Comparing Various Narratives

Step 1: Ask questions

To effectively compare narratives, you must sift through the words and identify the narrators' points of view or perspectives. A chart like the one on this page can help you do this.

Step 2: Read the narratives

Each of the two narratives on the following page comments on national identity in Canada. Read both to develop a sense of what they say. Then read them again. This time, jot point-form notes in response to the questions on the chart.

Were you able to answer all the questions? If not, read the pieces a third time. Fill in responses you may have missed, and make notes about information you still need to know and questions you would like to ask the writers.

Step 3: Practise comparing

Examine your notes or chart to find similarities and differences. As you do this, asking yourself questions like the following can help deepen your understanding:

- Does the narrator believe that nationalism is an internalized feeling or that it springs from external sources, such as political groups, books, school, the Internet, and various media?
- Do the narratives include statements that suggest that the writers agree — or disagree — with each other?

Narratives do not always include all the information needed to conduct an effective comparison. After reading the narratives, ask yourself the following questions:

- What further evidence would I like to see in support of the views presented?
- Do I need to know more about the narrators, the context in which the narratives were written, or the sources the narrators used? Where would I begin to look for this missing information?

Comparing Various Narratives

Questions	Richard Gwyn	Edward Greenspon
What is the writer's purpose?		
Who is the audience?		
What is the context? (e.g., When, where, and why was the piece written? What was the narrator's occupation at the time? What groups did the narrator belong to?)		
How does the narrative fit with what I already know?		
Does the narrative reflect an objective reality or a well-accepted interpretation of events?		
What biases are evident?		
Does the narrative support or challenge my own biases?		
Does the narrator's use of language affect my judgment of the narrative's validity?		
What elements of the narrative are convincing — or unconvincing?		

FOCUS ON SKILLS FOCUS ON SKILLS
CUS ON SKILLS FOCUS ON SKILLS FOCUS ON SKILLS

Narrative 1

Richard Gwyn is a journalist and political commentator. Born and raised in Britain, Gwyn lives in Britain and Canada. The following excerpt is from his 1996 book, *Nationalism without Walls: The Unbearable Lightness of Being Canadian*, which describes how Canada and Canadians changed when Brian Mulroney was prime minister from 1984 to 1993.

> All nation-states exist therefore as exercises in the collective imagination. They exist because their people want to have something they can call their own . . .
>
> Nation-states then fulfilled themselves by protecting their citizens . . . [but] most nation-states have done a good deal more for their citizens: They have looked after them, economically and socially . . .
>
> Our provider-state is being hollowed out . . . An entire new generation of young people and middle-aged self-employed are learning how to provide for themselves so that they no longer need the kind of state that's been around for half a century . . . The Canadian state . . . will never again be there for us in the way it has been throughout the lifetimes of almost all Canadians now alive . . .
>
> Nation states continue to command loyalty because people want to belong to them. How long, though, can this loyalty be sustained once it becomes clear that nation-state governments no longer possess the authority and power to reciprocate loyalty? . . .
>
> We aren't rooted in ethnicity. Our history no longer engages us. Almost all of our protective external walls have crumbled . . .
>
> Without a common ethnic identity, without much remembered (or imagined) history, without external walls, the Canadian community either exists as a political entity within which all who live here act as citizens . . . or there is no particular reason for the Canadian community to continue to exist at all.

Narrative 2

Born in Montreal, **Edward Greenspon** studied journalism at Carleton University and completed a master's degree in politics and government at the London School of Economics. Greenspon was editor-in-chief of *The Globe and Mail* when several of this newspaper's writers fanned out across the country to find out what young Canadian adults were thinking and doing. The following excerpt is from Greenspon's foreword to the resulting book, which was published in 2004 and titled *The New Canada*.

> A new confidence has taken hold among Canadians and with it a new form of nationalism is flowering. This is not the exclusionary economic nationalism of old – not the "we must close the shutters against American influence" kind – nor is it the exclusionary ethnic form of nationalism so often evident in other places around the world.
>
> Rather, Canada is indeed blazing the trail of 21st-century nations: globally engaged, socially liberal, culturally diverse. After years of struggling for an international identity, Canada has found its unique voice in the chorus of nations.

Vocabulary Tip

"To compare" means to examine and analyze similarities and differences.

"To contrast" means to examine and analyze only differences.

Summing Up

As you complete this final related issue, you will encounter many examples of narratives that recount events from various points of view and perspectives. Using the comparison strategies you have learned will help you compare these narratives and gain a deeper understanding of ideas and events that have affected Canadians' sense of national identity.

How and Why Did Early Visions of Canada Emerge?

Web Connection

To find out more about Robert Baldwin, Louis-Hippolyte LaFontaine, and responsible government, go this web site and follow the links.

www.ExploringNationalism.ca

Concepts of independence and freedom, as well as a desire for self-determination, often provide a foundation for the national identity of former colonies. Think, for example, about the United States. The chorus of its national anthem concludes with these words: "the land of the free, and the home of the brave." Many Americans identify strongly with these words.

Canada also evolved from a desire for independence, freedom, and self-determination. Step by step, through rebellions, elections, skirmishes, and debates, Canada gained independence from Britain. As this happened, Canada's citizens conceived many visions of what the country was — and what it could be.

Does any phrase from "O Canada" resonate with Canadians in the same way as the final chorus of "The Star-Spangled Banner" resonates with many Americans? Explain your response.

Working Together to Achieve Responsible Government

In the early decades of the 19th century, many colonists in British North America wanted a greater say in their own affairs, which were controlled by Britain. In 1841, the British government merged Upper Canada, which was mostly anglophone, and Lower Canada, which was mostly Francophone, into a single province called Canada. Upper Canada, which is today southern Ontario, was renamed Canada West, and Lower Canada, which is today southern Québec, was renamed Canada East.

Figure 13-3 This monument on Parliament Hill in Ottawa commemorates the achievements of Robert Baldwin (left) and Louis-Hippolyte LaFontaine. The monument was created in 1914 by Walter Allward, who also designed the Vimy Memorial. What message(s) might a monument to Baldwin and LaFontaine be intended to convey to Canadians?

The new province had one legislative assembly, made up of an equal number of representatives from Canada West and Canada East. But the population of Canada East was much higher than that of Canada West, and English was the only language allowed in the legislature. The British plan was to assimilate Francophones into anglophone culture.

In response, Louis-Hippolyte LaFontaine, a political leader from Canada East, joined forces with Robert Baldwin of Canada West to demand **responsible government** — a government that answered to the people rather than to British-appointed governors. In addition, LaFontaine wanted Francophone culture to survive — and Baldwin supported this goal.

The two knew that they would need to set aside their cultural differences and find a way of co-operating. Baldwin expressed this idea in a letter to LaFontaine: "There is, and must be, no question of races." By 1848, the two had succeeded. French was restored as an official language of the legislature, and in the following years, Britain also granted responsible government to other North American colonies, such as New Brunswick.

Baldwin and LaFontaine's successful bicultural initiative and their vision of Canada as an anglophone–Francophone partnership became a model for future generations.

Confederation: A New Vision of Canada

In 1861, a civil war erupted in the United States as the states in the North and the South fought over differing visions of their country. When this war ended in 1865, some Americans believed that Canada should be annexed — incorporated into the United States. In 1866, the American House of Representatives even passed an act proposing that the U.S. take over all Britain's colonies in North America. In addition, the Fenians, a militant Irish-American group, were conducting armed raids into Canada. Their goal was to capture and hold the British colonies until British forces withdrew from Ireland.

At the same time, the economy of British North America was suffering because of restrictive trade laws put in place by Britain and the U.S. And Francophones in Canada East were also afraid that their voices were being drowned out by the flood of immigration to Canada West, which had grown so much that Francophones were outnumbered by anglophones.

To deal with these issues, a new coalition of political leaders emerged in the 1860s. Led by John A. Macdonald and George-Étienne Cartier, their goal was to achieve independence and preserve Canada, including the French language and culture. They envisioned a union of Britain's North American colonies — and after long negotiations, a new country called Canada was created in 1867. It comprised the former province of Canada — which was divided into two new provinces, Ontario and Québec — as well as Nova Scotia and New Brunswick.

The British North America Act, which created Canada, defined two levels of representative and responsible government. The federal government was to look after national affairs, and the four provincial governments would manage their own regional affairs. This arrangement ensured that Québec could affirm and promote the French language and culture of the province's Francophones.

At Confederation, Canada was a different country from what it is today. But as circumstances changed, and as events influenced people and policies, new visions of what it meant to be Canadian began to emerge.

Examine the illustrations on this page. Describe your reaction to both. If a map similar to that in Figure 13-5 appeared in an American newspaper today, how would you respond?

Why were the voices of First Nations people not part of this process?

Figure 13-4 This 1869 cartoon shows an early vision of Canada as a forceful country resisting American annexation. The bulldog is a British symbol. How would you interpret the presence of the man and the bulldog in the background?

Figure 13-5 This tongue-in-cheek portrayal of North America under U.S. control appeared in the *New York Times* in 1888.

THE VIEW FROM HERE

In the years before Confederation, various visions of Canada emerged. Here are the ideas of three different people.

In 1849, **Shingwaukonse** led the Anishinabé who lived near Sault Ste. Marie, Ontario. Concerned that the government had allowed mining companies to move onto his people's land, Shingwaukonse expressed a vision that protected his people's rights while allowing the mining companies to continue doing business — under specific conditions.

> The Great Spirit, we think, placed these rich mines on our lands, for the benefit of his red children,* so that their rising generation might get support from them when the animals of the woods should have grown too scarce for our subsistence. We will carry out, therefore, the good object of our Father, the Great Spirit. We will sell you the lands, if you will give us what is right and, at the same time, we want pay for every pound of mineral that has been taken off our lands, as well as for that which may hereafter be carried away.

* Shingwaukonse was using the language that was common at the time.

Antoine-Aimé Dorion was a Québec lawyer and politician. He favoured uniting Canada East and West but opposed a larger confederation. In 1865, Dorion's views sparked a debate over whether Canada should be a union of two nations — British and French — or a federation of equal provinces.

> This scheme proposes a union not only with Nova Scotia, New Brunswick, Prince Edward Island, and Newfoundland, but also with British Columbia and Vancouver's Island . . . It is evident . . . that it is intended eventually to form a legislative union of all the provinces . . . Perhaps the people of Upper Canada* think a legislative union a most desirable thing. I can tell those gentlemen that the people of Lower Canada* are attached to their institutions in a manner that defies any attempt to change them in that way. They will not change their religious institutions, their laws, and their language, for any consideration whatsoever.

* Though the names of Upper and Lower Canada had been officially changed, many people continued to use these former names.

Irish-born **Thomas D'Arcy McGee** was a Montréal politician, journalist, historian, and poet who supported Confederation. In 1860, McGee concluded a speech to the Legislative Assembly of Canada with the following words.

> I have spoken . . . with a sole, single desire for the increase, prosperity, freedom and honour of this incipient Northern nation . . . I look to the future of my adopted country with hope, though not without anxiety. I see in the not remote distance one great nationality, bound, like the shield of Achilles, by the blue rim of ocean.
>
> I see it quartered into many communities, each disposing of its internal affairs, but all bound together by free institutions, free intercourse, and free commerce.
>
> I see within the round of that shield the peaks of the western mountains and the crests of the eastern waves – the winding Assinaboine, the five-fold lakes, the St. Lawrence, the Ottawa, the Saguenay, the St. John and the Basin of Minas – by all these flowing waters in all the valleys they fertilize, in all the cities they visit in their courses, I see a generation of industrious, contented moral men, free in name and in fact – men capable of maintaining, in peace and in war, a constitution worthy of such a country.

Explorations

1. In a single sentence for each, summarize the vision of Canada presented by these speakers.
2. Which of these early visions continue to be reflected in today's notions of Canada? Explain the connections you have detected.

Evolving Visions of Canada

As Canada's territory and population expanded after Confederation, visions of the country began to evolve. John A. Macdonald's dream of a country stretching from sea to sea, for example, became reality when the Canadian Pacific Railway opened Western Canada to settlement. But at first, few people were interested.

To pave the way, the federal government negotiated treaties with the First Nations of the West. Many traditional Aboriginal lands became government property and First Nations peoples were moved to reserves.

Nevertheless, only a trickle of immigrants arrived in the West before Wilfrid Laurier became prime minister in 1896. Laurier believed that an unsettled West meant an undefended West, and his Liberal government decided to do more to attract settlers.

Clifford Sifton, minister of the interior in Laurier's government, was handed responsibility for achieving this goal. At first, Sifton wanted only British and American immigrants because he believed they would make the best homesteaders — so he established immigrant-recruiting offices in England and the United States.

But the Prairie population was still not increasing fast enough, so Sifton also set up immigration offices in non-English-speaking European countries. As a result, communities of Poles, Germans, Ukrainians, Finns, Norwegians, and others began to appear on the Prairies.

As more people arrived in the West, new provinces were created and joined Confederation. The Prairie population grew from a sparse 1.3 million people in 1911 to 2 million by 1921. In Alberta, the population density in 1901 averaged 0.29 people per 2.6 square kilometres; by 1921, this had increased to 2.37 people.

This dramatic population increase changed the identity of Canada. As the country became more multicultural, people of British background were no longer the dominant cultural group. Francophones were also affected. Most of the non-English-speaking immigrants chose to learn English, which meant that Francophones became an even smaller minority.

Let me tell you, my fellow countrymen, that all the signs point this way, that the 20th century shall be the century of Canada and Canadian development . . . Canada shall be the star towards which all men who love progress and freedom shall come.

— Wilfrid Laurier, prime minister of Canada, 1904

Figure 13-6 Clifford Sifton was the government minister responsible for attracting settlers to the West. In 1903, he authorized the publication of a book of cartoons providing information for settlers. The cover cartoon, shown in the photograph, depicts John Bull, representing England, and Uncle Sam, representing the United States, carrying bags of money to invest in Western Canada. What image of Canada did this cartoon portray?

Reflect and Respond

Think about how immigration in the early 20th century changed Canada's national identity and laid the foundation for today's multicultural society. In an increasingly globalized world, does diversity provide a solid foundation for building a national identity?

Create a T-chart like the one shown. Then think about countries like Japan and Korea, in which people share similar ethnic and cultural roots. In the first column, list the advantages of situations like this. Then think about Canada's diversity — and in the second column, list the advantages of situations like this.

With a partner or small group, discuss your T-chart. If necessary, revise your chart to reflect ideas arising from this discussion.

Similarity, Diversity, and National Identity	
Advantages of Ethnic and Cultural Similarity	**Advantages of Ethnic and Cultural Diversity**

To what extent did various early visions of Canada meet people's needs?

By the time Clifford Sifton's immigration push came to an end in the early 20th century, Canada had been set on the path toward multiculturalism. But the way was not always smooth, and in a vast and varied country, some groups believed that their needs were not being met.

Challenges and Opportunities for Francophones

Figure 13-6 Languages in Canada

Language	1867*	1931*	2001*
French	31%	27%	23%
English	61%	56%	60%
Other	8%	17%	18%

* Percentages have been rounded.

Do the patterns suggested by the statistics in Figure 13-6 suggest that the arrangement worked out at Confederation should be changed?

As the ratio of Francophones in the Canadian population shrank during the early 20th century and as new, largely English-speaking provinces joined Confederation, the power and influence of Québécois began to decline. The partnership that had marked the Baldwin–LaFontaine and Macdonald–Cartier coalitions in the 1800s seemed to be collapsing under the weight of an influx of immigrants who were either already English speakers or chose to learn English.

As a result of their status as a shrinking minority, many Québec Francophones came to believe that they had three options:

- accept their new position within Canada
- promote a vision of Québec as a strong, autonomous province within Canada
- promote a vision of a sovereign Québec

The Growth of French-Canadian Nationalism

In the decades after Confederation, many Québécois were suspicious of government policies that encouraged immigration. They believed that most immigrants would integrate into anglophone society and that Francophones would be outnumbered. This possibility threatened their position as equal partners in Confederation.

Henri Bourassa, for example, was at various times between 1896 and 1932 a member of Parliament or a member of the Québec legislature. Bourassa believed that equality between Francophone and anglophone cultures in Canada was essential if Francophones were to continue to support Confederation. For Bourassa, this meant that Québécois must have a high degree of control over their own affairs.

Figure 13-7 On May 24, 1917, Montréal residents took to the streets to protest conscription. This was just one of many anti-conscription protests that took place in Québec. Outside Québec, opposing conscription was often interpreted as unpatriotic. Was this a fair assessment?

But as Canada's identity changed, Bourassa became increasingly anti-British. During World War I, for example, he helped lead Francophone opposition to conscription, saying that people of French heritage should not be required to fight in "Britain's wars."

Though some anglophones and allophones — immigrants whose first language is neither English nor French — were against conscription, opposition was strongest among Francophone Québécois. This drove a wedge between many Québec Francophones and much of the rest of Canada. Many Francophones believed that their interests were being ignored.

Wilfrid Laurier was no longer prime minister, but he was concerned about the divide created by the conscription issue. In a 1917 letter to a friend, he wrote, "The racial chasm which is now opening at our feet may perhaps not be overcome for many generations."

Québec nationalism is rooted in the desire of Francophone Québécois to affirm and promote their identity and French heritage. The Catholic religion was an important part of this heritage, and for much of the first half of the 20th century, Lionel Groulx, a professor, priest, and historian, was at the centre of a nationalist movement with the church as its focus. Groulx believed that a separate state might be necessary to achieve freedom and independence.

CheckBack

You read about the Québec sovereignty movement in Chapter 3.

Since the Quiet Revolution, the focus of Québec nationalism has shifted away from religion. According to a 2004 poll, 83 per cent of Québec respondents identified themselves as Catholic — but 66 per cent also said that religion was unimportant in public life. And 59 per cent said it was unimportant in private life.

When the conscription issue arose again during World War II, the debate was nearly as divisive as it had been in World War I — and some Canadians began to question the possibility of a unified country.

Canada emerged from World War II as an increasingly urban industrial country. In 1901, for example, 37 per cent of Canadians lived in cities; by 1951, this number had risen to 62 per cent. Like many other Canadians, Québécois also moved to cities.

How might moving to a city affect people's sense of identity?

Long-serving Québec premier Maurice Duplessis had picked up on the ideas of Groulx and others. In the mid-20th century, Duplessis fought for greater autonomy and focused Québécois on the traditional values of church and community. But by the time he died in 1959, many Francophone Québécois were ready to embrace what came to be called the Quiet Revolution. They wanted to modernize Québec by improving social programs and the education system — but they also wanted to affirm and promote the French language and the culture of the province's Francophones.

To achieve their goals, many believed that Québec must control immigration, social programs, industry, job creation, language laws, and some aspects of foreign policy. For some, sovereignty was the only solution — and in 1968, René Lévesque and others founded the Parti Québécois to promote independence.

In the same year, Pierre Trudeau was elected prime minister. Trudeau was Québécois, but his vision of the country was federalist. He believed in "two official languages and a pluralist society" — and in 1969, his government passed the Official Languages Act, which protected the language rights of all Francophones in Canada.

The debate over Québec's place in Canada continues to evolve. For many Québécois, the challenge is to maintain their distinct identity in a continent of non-Francophones. For the federal government, the challenge is to unite a diverse country while accommodating a changing population.

Figure 13-8 John Collins of the *Montreal Gazette* created this cartoon in 1964. What message about Canadian unity was Collins sending? Does this message remain relevant today?

Web Connection

To find out more about Canadian immigration over the years, go to this web site and follow the links.

www.ExploringNationalism.ca

Immigration and the New Canada

Until the 1960s, Canadian policies favoured immigrants from Northern Europe and the United States. The experiences of immigrants from other places, such as China, Caribbean countries, and Italy, were often difficult and sometimes traumatic. Many of these immigrants felt as if they were excluded from visions of Canada and were not regarded as Canadians, even when they had been born in Canada or had lived in Canada for many years.

Taking Turns

What vision of Canada meets your needs?

The students responding to the question are Harley, a member of the Kainai Nation near Lethbridge; Rick, who was born in the United States but moved to Fort McMurray with his family when he was 10; and Jane, who lives in Calgary and is descended from black Loyalists who fled to Nova Scotia after the American Revolution.

Harley

My people belong to our own nation. But the Kainai are also connected to Canada because of the treaty our ancestors signed with the British queen. Some Elders think that this deal was broken. My grandmother tells me how her culture and language were stolen when the government forced her to go to residential school. Canada hasn't always served the needs of the Kainai — or even taken the needs of my people into consideration. Still, I think that we can be both Kainai and Canadian. I think that a truly pluralistic Canada — a nation of many nations, each with loyalty to their nation and to Canada, and with true respect for other nations — could meet my needs.

Rick

E pluribus unum — out of many, one — is the American motto, and that says it all. One thing I like about the States is that nearly everyone wants to be part of one nation. This isn't true of Canada. So many groups want to have their own identity or to separate that it's hard to keep the country together. But then I think about what's happening here in Fort McMurray, where people from all over Canada, and from others places, too, are working hard toward a goal: pulling oil out of the tar sands. Everyone in this country, no matter where they come from, is working hard to make Canada the best place it can be, for everyone. We're all moving forward together.

People talk about Canada as a multicultural country, but this vision doesn't match the reality — and the reality sure doesn't serve *my* needs. I look at my family's past and see how they were treated in the United States and then how hard it was for them when they arrived in Nova Scotia. Even today, it isn't easy to be black in North America, even in a supposedly multicultural society like Canada's. The Soviet Union split up and Czechoslovakia divided in two when circumstances changed. Maybe the same thing should happen in Canada, because Confederation is an idea whose time has passed.

How would you respond to the question Harley, Rick, and Jane are answering? Explain the reasons for your response. How important is it for Canadians to have a single coherent vision of themselves as a nation?

Not Wanted in Canada

When navvies were needed to help build the Canadian Pacific Railway, Chinese immigrants were welcomed to Canada. In 1885, however, the federal government introduced the Chinese Immigration Act, which imposed a head tax of $50 on Chinese people who wanted to come to Canada. This tax rose to $100 in 1900, and by 1904, it was $500. Finally, in 1923, the government banned nearly all immigration from China.

Discriminated against by the government, Chinese Canadians, as well as immigrants from other Asian countries, were not allowed to vote or to hold certain jobs until after World War II. In the communities where they settled, they also suffered discrimination — and as a result, they often turned to one another for support. Many settled together in urban neighbourhoods, called Chinatowns, and formed alliances like the Chinese Consolidated Benevolent Foundation in British Columbia.

Black immigrants from the United States suffered similar discrimination. Attracted by Clifford Sifton's advertising campaign, one group of black Americans immigrated to Saskatchewan in 1905. Others followed them to the Prairies to escape racism in their home states. This alarmed some Canadians, and the government tried to discourage these black immigrants. Advertising was removed from black American communities, and they were subjected to stricter medical tests than other immigrants.

In 1911, Prime Minister Wilfrid Laurier even banned the immigration of blacks for a year. Laurier's order said that the "Negro race . . . is deemed unsuitable to the climate and requirements of Canada." This order was never enforced, because blacks stopped trying to immigrate to Western Canada.

These Chinese and black immigrants were excluded from visions of Canada at the time. So were many other groups, such as Doukhobors, Jews, and Ukrainians.

This discrimination continued for decades. Finally, in 1962, changes to the Immigration Act opened Canada's doors to people from all over the world. And in 1971, the federal government adopted a policy of "multiculturalism within a bilingual framework," which once again altered Canada's identity. Despite this official policy, many immigrants and Canadians continue to believe that their needs are not being met.

I am in prison because I covet riches
Driven by poverty I sailed over here on the choppy sea.
If only I did not need to labour for money,
I would already have returned home to China.

— Anonymous poem written on a cell wall in the federal immigration building in Victoria, B.C.

Web Connection

To find out more about redress for the Chinese immigration policies of the 20th century and how the Canadian government responded in 2006, go to the following web site and follow the links.

www.ExploringNationalism.ca

Figure 13-9 Thomas Mapp and his family immigrated to Edmonton from Kansas in 1906. Along with a number of other black families, they later moved to a homestead in Amber Valley, where this photograph was taken in 1925. Why would immigrants tend to gather in communities with others of the same background?

IMPACT

The Ukrainian Experience in Canada

IMPACT

Alexander and Anna Szpak and their three children were among the first wave of Ukrainian immigrants who swelled the population of the Prairies between 1900 and 1914. Like the Szpaks, many of the newcomers set to work carving out homesteads, a challenge that was filled with hardship. For the Szpaks and others who did not speak English, things were even harder. Many of their neighbours neither understood nor appreciated their traditions and customs — and they often felt isolated and lonely.

Immigration

The Szpak family came from western Ukraine and settled in northeastern Alberta, where Alexander paid $10 for 64.7 hectares under the Dominion Lands Act. In return for this land, the Szpaks were required to clear a certain amount of property every year and to construct buildings. The work was backbreaking and life was hard. One winter, for example, both a son and a daughter died of tuberculosis.

Alexander was used to farming and hard work, but he found the soil and climate challenging. When the farm could not support his family, he travelled to Barkerville, British Columbia, to work in a gold mine. After working there for some time, he returned to the farm, where he began raising and selling draft horses.

Discrimination

Like nearly 200 000 other Ukrainian immigrants, members of the Szpak family left behind a familiar identity to embrace a new one. But they often met hostility in their new country. Although Clifford Sifton believed that Ukrainians were the kind of hard-working, farm-savvy immigrants needed on the Prairies, many anglophone Canadians disagreed. Led by Conservative politicians, some English-language newspapers ridiculed the Ukrainian newcomers and called them names.

Harassment by newspapers, politicians, and neighbours made it hard for Ukrainian immigrants to integrate into their new communities and to get to know townspeople and neighbours whose heritage was not Ukrainian. In addition to the language barrier, immigrants from Ukraine also faced criticism for retaining their traditional customs and style of dress.

Figure 13-10 This photograph of a sod house was taken near Viking, Alberta, in the early 20th century. The first house of many Prairie homesteaders was either built completely of sod, like the one pictured, or had a sod roof.

Internment

When World War I started in 1914, attitudes toward Ukrainian immigrants became even more hostile. At the time, Ukraine was part of the Austro-Hungarian Empire, which was allied with Germany. As a result, many immigrants from both Germany and parts of Austria-Hungary were labelled "enemy aliens" and required to register with the government, carry identity cards, and report to police at regular intervals.

About 80 000 Ukrainian immigrants found themselves classified as enemy aliens, and another 5000 were interned in 24 forced-labour camps across the country. Though some Canadians spoke out against this internment, many of the internees were forced to remain in the camps until 1920, two years after the war ended.

Assimilation and Reclamation

Embittered and beaten down by their treatment, many of these Ukrainian immigrants lost or abandoned their history, culture, and language — their identity — as they tried to fit in to Canadian society. But today, many descendants of these immigrants are rediscovering the past, recognizing their rich heritage, and embracing traditions that were once integral to Ukrainian identity. Harvey Spak, for example, is Alexander and Anna Szpak's grandson. An Alberta artist and filmmaker, Spak uses a changed spelling of the family name. He told the story of his grandparents and other Ukrainian immigrants in "The Fullness of Time: Ukrainian Stories from Alberta," an episode in a documentary series about the immigrant experience in Canada.

Figure 13-11 Internment Camps, 1914–1920

Explorations

1. With a partner, create a dialogue between Alexander or Anna Szpak and a recent immigrant to Canada. Include at least three exchanges — either questions or comments — that focus on comparing attitudes toward Ukrainians in the early 20th century with attitudes toward immigrants today. Ensure that your dialogue refers to the identity and the needs of immigrants. Present your dialogue to a small group or the class.
2. Build a family tree. You may focus on your own family or another family, or you may create a fictitious family. Fill in as many generations and details as you can.

On your family tree or in your detailed notes, identify dates that are significant in world, national, or regional history — and whether these events influenced the identity of the people on your family tree. Were they, for example, forced to move because of a war or conflict? Choose one element of your family tree to share with your classmates through a brief oral presentation, a computer software presentation, or a bulletin-board display.

Asserting Aboriginal Rights

In Canada, Aboriginal nationalism revolves around the rights to self-determination, to self-government, to their relationship with the land, and to traditional ways of life, which may include hunting, fishing, and trapping. In the case of First Nations, many leaders say that these rights were negotiated in treaties — and many First Nations people have argued that the treaties give them the right to govern themselves within Canada. If nationhood and self-determination mean creating separate and independent laws, which will take precedence — the laws of a First Nation or the laws of Canada?

As a historical nation, not a tribe, the Métis were and remain in the vanguard of asserting self-government rights as an Aboriginal people in Canada.

— *John Weinstein, adviser to Métis leaders, in* Quiet Revolution West: The Rebirth of Métis Nationalism, *2007*

Métis Self-Government

John A. Macdonald's vision of an expanded Canada was made possible by the government's 1870 purchase of Rupert's Land from the Hudson's Bay Company. But Macdonald's vision ignored the views of the Métis people living in the Red River area of what is now Manitoba. At the time, the Métis made up more than half the population of this area.

After taking up arms in 1869 and 1870, the Métis — with Louis Riel leading an independent provisional government — forced the federal government to address their concerns. Macdonald responded by pushing the Manitoba Act through Parliament. This act created the province of Manitoba, recognized the French and English languages as equal, upheld Aboriginal rights, and provided 566 500 hectares of land specifically for Métis people.

But disagreements arose over how to distribute this land. And while Manitoba's lieutenant-governor and the Métis wrangled over this, settlers started arriving — and the flood of immigration shifted the balance so that the Métis were outnumbered by people of European heritage.

The Métis felt cheated, and disagreements about land and rights to self-government continued until Riel led a second uprising in 1885. Riel was executed for his role in this resistance, and the Métis dream of self-determination was shattered.

Figure 13-12 Métis leader Louis Riel (seated at centre) and members of his provisional government posed for this photograph in 1870. For decades, most history books identified the Métis uprising of 1885 as the North West Rebellion. But recently, more people have been calling it the North West Resistance. What does this change suggest about visions of Canada?

Today, the Constitution recognizes the Métis as an Aboriginal people with a common history and traditional lands and culture, and they have re-emerged as a nation that desires self-determination. But unlike First Nations people, the Métis were never forced onto reserves, so their land base is scattered.

John Weinstein identified the problem in *Quiet Revolution West: The Rebirth of Métis Nationalism*: "The Métis of Red River and the North-West spurned the protection of the Crown as a price for retaining some of their land and resource rights because it thwarted their ability to be self-governing. In the end, Canada used the Métis demand for more — that is, responsible government for the West in the form of Métis-majority provinces — as an excuse to give them less, much less."

Treaties, the Indian Act, and Self-Determination

In 1876, Parliament passed the Indian Act, which gave the federal government control over every aspect of the lives of First Nations people. The act defined who was an "Indian" and denied full citizenship rights to "Indians." First Nations people were allowed to become full citizens — but only if they gave up their treaty rights.

The Indian Act was presented as a way to protect First Nations' well-being, which had been guaranteed in treaties, but it was also designed to encourage assimilation. Read the words of Ovide Mercredi and Mary Ellen Turpel in "Voices." How did First Nations' understanding of their relationship with Canada differ from the government's understanding?

Over the years, the Indian Act was amended many times — but First Nations people were rarely consulted about the changes. Then, in the 1970s, First Nations united in the National Indian Brotherhood, the forerunner of the Assembly of First Nations, to persuade Prime Minister Pierre Trudeau and Minister of Indian Affairs Jean Chrétien to abandon their proposal to end the federal government's treaty obligations. This battle marked the beginning of a new period of Aboriginal political strength.

Today, many First Nations are in the process of settling land claims, which often involve asserting their rights to traditional lands and to govern themselves. The Nisga'a of northwestern British Columbia, for example, had never signed a treaty, though they had been trying since 1890. Between 1927 and 1951, they could do nothing because a law made it illegal for First Nations to raise money to support land claims.

Once this law was repealed, the Nisga'a challenged the government in court. This action went to the Supreme Court of Canada, which ruled in 1973 that Aboriginal rights and title to land exist even if the government does not recognize them. In 1982, Canada's Constitution confirmed these rights.

The groundbreaking Supreme Court ruling paved the way for the settlement of land claims. The Nisga'a Final Agreement was one of the most important — and controversial. Some people believed that it gave the Nisga'a too much autonomy, while others believed that the Nisga'a had given up too much.

The First Nations view our relationship today as a continuation of the treaty relationship of mutuality where neither side can act unilaterally without consultation. This partnership is symbolized by the grandfather of all treaties, the Iroquois Confederacy Gus-wen-tah or two-row wampum between your ancestors and those of the Iroquois . . . First Nations and Europeans would travel in parallel paths down the symbolic river in their own vessels. The two-row wampum, which signifies "One River, Two Vessels," committed the newcomers to travel in their vessel and not attempt to interfere with our voyage.

— Ovide Mercredi and Mary Ellen Turpel, in In the Rapids — Navigating the Future of First Nations, *1993*

CHECKBACK

You read about the rise of First Nations' nationalism during the 1970s in Chapter 2.

Figure 13-13 With other Nisga'a, Gary Alexcee, chief councillor of the village of Gingolx, celebrates passage of the Nisga'a Final Agreement in 2000. The agreement recognized the Nisga'a claim to 2019 square kilometres and their right to make their own decisions about social policy and resource development. The agreement also provided money to develop conservation measures and social and education programs.

Reflect and Respond

Early visions of Canada often ignored or actively discriminated against people whose language, culture, traditions, or ethnicity did not match mainstream ideas about the country. Choose one group who encountered this prejudice.

Then examine the Charter of Rights and Freedoms. If the Charter had existed at the time the group you chose encountered the prejudice, which clauses would have protected members of the collective against this prejudice?

Jot point-form notes about your ideas, then use these notes to write a statement that sums up your ideas.

How is the Evolution of Various Visions of Canada Reflected in the Country Today?

VOICES

One of the biggest changes in Canada over the past twenty years has been the emergence of a more deeply entrenched pan-Canadian national identity. Young Canadians, at least outside Quebec, are far more likely than older Canadians to define themselves as Canadian first, rather than in terms of their province.

— Matthew Mendelsohn, political scientist, 2005

As circumstances changed over time, visions of Canadian identity also changed. At one time, the dominant anglophone vision of the country tended to overshadow other possible visions. But in the last half of the 20th century, this began to change. French and English were confirmed as official languages, and Canada became an officially multicultural country.

A 2003 poll by the Centre for Research and Information on Canada found that 54 per cent of those surveyed agreed that multiculturalism made them feel proud to be Canadian. This sense of pride was even higher among people aged 18 to 30 — 66 per cent of respondents in this group took pride in Canada's multiculturalism.

The Founding Nations Debate

For many years, schools taught students that Canada was created by the French and British. This popular catch phrase ignored Aboriginal peoples, who had lived in what is now Canada long before the Europeans arrived and the nation-state of Canada was created.

As the Aboriginal contribution to Canada became more widely recognized, some people began to refer to "three founding nations": Aboriginal people, French, and British. But not everyone accepts this idea. Some people argue that Aboriginal peoples were not a homogeneous — uniform — nation and did not participate in founding the nation-state of Canada in the same way as the French and English. The concept of three founding nations also excludes the contributions of immigrants from countries that were neither French nor British.

➡ In a small group, brainstorm to come up with a catch phrase to replace "three founding nations" and accurately describe the contribution of the diverse peoples who have created the Canadian nation.

Figure 13-14 Immigrants' Sense of Canadian Identity

Do you identify yourself as Canadian? Percentage Who Answered Yes.			
Immigrant Group	Arrived before 1991	Arrived 1991–2001	Second Generation
Black	27.2%	13.9%	49.6%
Chinese	42.0%	30.6%	59.5%
South Asian	32.7%	19.1%	53.6%
Other visible minorities	32.8%	17.4%	60.6%
Total visible minorities	34.4%	21.4%	56.6%
White immigrants	53.8%	21.9%	78.2%

Source: Institute for Research on Public Policy

The Multiculturalism Debate

Though many Canadians take pride in Canada's reputation as a diverse and multicultural society, a 2007 study by the Institute for Research on Public Policy showed that recent immigrants who belong to visible minority groups integrate more slowly into Canadian society than their white counterparts and feel less Canadian.

➡ The responses of various immigrant groups to one of the study's questions are shown in Figure 13-14. Examine this chart. What patterns can you identify? Do these patterns influence your opinion about the success of multiculturalism in Canada? Do they influence your understanding of Canadian national identity?

Studies like the one shown in Figure 13-14 have sparked debate over the success of Canada's multicultural policies — and the wisdom of promoting diversity. Political commentator John Ibbitson believes that multiculturalism has helped Canada attract immigrants — and immigrants have helped the country's economy. "Multiculturalism . . . will be the all-important key to Canada's prosperity in the twenty-first century," Ibbitson wrote in *The Polite Revolution: Perfecting the Canadian Dream.*

Other cultural commentators, such as Neil Bissoondath, believe that the policy has failed. "The architects of the policy . . . were blind to the fact that their exercise in social engineering [manipulating people to take certain actions] was based on two essentially false premises," Bissoondath wrote in the *New Internationalist.* "First, it assumed that 'culture' in the larger sense could be transplanted. Second, that those who voluntarily sought a new life in a new country would wish to transport their cultures of origin."

Debates like the one over multiculturalism suggest that visions of Canada continue to evolve. Is this debate a sign of a healthy or an unhealthy society? Explain your response.

I was born and bred in this amazing land. I've always considered myself a Canadian, nothing more, nothing less, even though my parents come from Italy. How come we have acquired a hyphen? We have allowed ourselves to become divided along the line of ethnic origins, under the pretext of the "Great Mosaic."

— Laura Sabia, feminist and columnist, 1978

MAKING A DIFFERENCE

Neil Bissoondath
Challenging Multiculturalism

When successful novelist Neil Bissoondath published his 1994 non-fiction book, *Selling Illusions: The Cult of Multiculturalism in Canada*, it sparked an uproar. In the book, Bissoondath — an immigrant himself — argued that multiculturalism is not as successful as many would like to believe. He charged that multiculturalism highlights the differences that divide Canadians rather than the similarities that unite them. As a result, it undermines a unified vision of Canada and encourages the isolation and stereotyping of cultural groups.

Born in Trinidad to a family with roots in India, Bissoondath immigrated to Canada in 1973 to study French literature — and was shocked by what he found. "I was seeking a new start in a land that afforded me that possibility," he wrote in the *New Internationalist.* "I was not seeking to live in Toronto as if I were still in Trinidad — for what would have been the point of emigration?"

Figure 13-15 In his fiction, novelist Neil Bissoondath often deals with global themes that focus on identity. His book *The Worlds Within Her* was nominated for a Governor General's Award in 1998.

Since *Selling Illusions* was published, Bissoondath has become an outspoken critic of official multiculturalism. At the same time, however, he believes that Canada must continue to welcome immigrants and to combat racism, sexism, and other forms of discrimination.

To offset the effects of multiculturalism, he says that Canadians must develop a new vision of the country — "A Canada where no one is alienated with hyphenation. A nation of cultural hybrids, where every individual is unique and every individual is a Canadian, undiluted and undivided."

Explorations

1. In your own words, summarize Neil Bissoondath's argument against multiculturalism. On a scale of 1 to 5, rate your level of agreement with his view (1 = disagree completely; 5 = agree completely). Explain the criteria you used to support your judgment.
2. "Sacred cow" is a term that describes ideas or institutions that are considered immune to criticism. In Canada, multiculturalism is often viewed as a sacred cow. Should people be allowed to challenge multiculturalism? Should people be allowed to challenge any sacred cow? Explain your judgment.

1. During the 1957 federal election campaign, economic adviser Merrill Menzies helped the Progressive Conservative Party develop its platform and strategy. Menzies offered voters a new vision of Canada. In his introduction to this vision, Menzies referred to John A. Macdonald's 19th-century National Policy, which included uniting Canada by building the CPR, attracting immigrants to the West, and protecting Canadian industry with high tariffs. Here is some of what Menzies said:

> From Confederation until the 1930s, there was a powerful unifying force in the nation . . .
> This unifying force was the challenge and the development of the West. It engendered a powerful but not xenophobic [foreigner hating] nationalism and was made possible and given shape and direction by Macdonald's National Policy. [Since then], we have had no national policy – and we have had no transcending sense of national purpose, no national myth, no unifying force. That is why I have proposed a new national policy – the NEW FRONTIER POLICY; a new national strategy . . . a new national myth – the "North" in the place of the "West."

   In a small group, discuss the possible meaning of the North as a "new frontier" and respond to the following questions:
   - On the basis of your knowledge of the development of Western Canada, what might a plan for the North look like?
   - What challenges and benefits could be expected when implementing this plan?
   - How might the Aboriginal peoples of the North respond?

   Jot notes about your responses, then discuss whether your group supports Menzies' idea. Share your group's conclusions with the class, explaining the reasons for your judgments.

2. With a partner or small group, imagine that you are part of a team developing a vision of Canada to present during a forthcoming election campaign. Choose a political party or a national group — real or imaginary — to represent and jot notes about the Canada your party or group envisions. Create a slogan that will appeal to the nationalistic feelings of the public and encourage them to support your party's or group's ideas.
   a) Brainstorm to create a list of words that will attract the support of citizens. Create a 30-second radio announcement that includes your slogan, as well as some of these words, in a description of your vision of the Canada of the future.
   b) Create a one-page leaflet that does the same thing as the radio announcement. Decide what visual images will effectively support your words.
   c) Make up three questions that your group could include in a survey of support for your vision of Canada. Then survey at least 10 people in your family, school, or community. Try to choose people of varied ages and backgrounds.
      - Collate the responses and create a visual, such as a mind map, graph, or chart, to display them.
      - Explain the similarities and differences you detect in the responses.
      - Identify unusual or unexpected responses.
   d) Write a statement that summarizes the information on your visual (e.g., What does the visual tell you about the responses? Are the responses linked to age, origin, or birthplace?).

3. Create two visual images — one from the past and one in the present — to represent your individual, collective, and national identity. Think back to when you entered Grade 7 or Grade 8 and how you viewed these aspects of your identity. Then think about how your ideas about your identity have changed since then. The following questions may help you develop your visuals:
   - What aspects of your past identity, if any, have you modified, abandoned, or retained?
   - Are particular aspects of your identity more important today than they were several years ago?

   Present your visuals to the class either orally or by posting them on a bulletin board. If you choose to post them, include a statement that sums up what they represent.

4. The poster on this page was created in 1882 by William Notman, a famous Canadian photographer. At the time, sports and physical activities were popular — and were viewed as a way of instilling important values in young people. Canadian sporting groups actively promoted the idea that national identity and physical activity were linked. Examine the poster and respond to the following questions:
   a) How does this poster link national identity and physical activity?
   b) Consider the visions of Canada presented in this chapter. Which vision is linked most closely to this poster? Explain the reason for your judgment.
   c) Does the link between national identity and physical activity continue to exist today? Cite examples to support your response.
5. On the opening pages of this chapter, you were asked to identify images you would include on a poster advertising Canada today. Return to the notes you made in response to this question. After reading the chapter, would you change or replace any of the images you identified? If you would not, explain why not. If you would, explain why — and how.

Figure 13-16

Think about Your Challenge

By now, you have recorded several entries in the journal you are keeping in response to the related-issue question: To what extent should individuals and groups in Canada embrace a national identity?

Think about the criteria you used when making your comments — and start developing a list of criteria to use as a guide when making the judgment that will become your informed position on this issue.

Share your criteria with some of your classmates, and comment on whether you agree with the criteria they have chosen. When this discussion concludes, revise your own criteria to include new ideas that may have emerged from this discussion. Include your list of criteria in your journal and be prepared to make more revisions as you progress through this related issue.

CHAPTER 14 Canadian Identity

Figure 14-1 In 1995, as Québec was preparing for a referendum on sovereignty, CBC Radio host Jowi Taylor began assembling the Six String Nation guitar. It took 10 years to collect the guitar's 63 pieces of wood, bone, metal, and stone from across Canada. Each piece represents an element of the nation's history. The guitar has become a symbol of Canada's past, as well as of Canadian unity.

CHAPTER ISSUE

To what extent have attempts to promote national identity been successful?

WOOD FROM A TREE revered by the Haida of British Columbia, gold from a Stanley Cup ring, and a chip off the oldest kind of rock in the world are all part of the Six String Nation guitar, which was unveiled to audiences across Canada in 2006. Since then, thousands of people have been photographed holding the guitar at festivals, concerts, schools, and other events. And in February 2008, the instrument received its official nickname — Voyageur.

When CBC Radio host Jowi Taylor started the project, his goal was to portray and promote Canada's national identity. To do this, he collected elements that he believes represent what it is to be Canadian.

Creating a national symbol is much like creating a brand with a name people recognize instantly. It announces who Canadians believe they are, how they want to be perceived, and what it means to be part of Canada.

Examine the photograph of the guitar on the previous page, then respond to the following questions:

- Why might the nickname "Voyageur" have been chosen for the guitar?
- Are there any pieces you do not recognize? If so, does this make these pieces less relevant or significant?
- Would a non-Canadian recognize the elements as symbols of Canada?
- If you were choosing pieces for the guitar, what would you pick?

KEY TERMS

institution

LOOKING AHEAD

In this chapter, you will develop responses to the following questions as you explore the extent to which attempts to promote national identity have been successful:

- How have symbols and myths been used to promote a national identity?
- How have institutions been used to promote a national identity in Canada?
- How can government programs and initiatives be used to promote a national identity?
- How can individuals promote a national identity?

My Journal on Nationalism

Using words or images — or both — express your current point of view on the Canadian national identity. Review previous journal entries and identify two or three ideas that have contributed to your current view. Date your ideas and keep them in the journal, notebook, learning log, portfolio, or computer file you are keeping as you progress through this final related issue.

How have symbols and myths been used to promote a national identity?

To find our more about Canada's national symbols, go to this web site and follow the links.

www.ExploringNationalism.ca

When you created a coat of arms in response to the challenge for Related Issue 1, you chose symbols that represented how your understandings of nation shape — and are shaped by — your identity. In similar ways, people and governments often use symbols to portray what they think is important about their country's history, nationhood, and role in the world.

The beaver, for example, is Canada's national animal. As a symbol, it appears on the five-cent piece to represent Canada's history, as well as qualities people have come to associate with Canada and Canadians. And the loon is the source of the name "loonie," the nickname for Canada's $1 coin.

If you were asked to name other animals and birds to represent Canada's national identity, which would you choose? Explain your response.

Just as symbols can portray a nation's identity, so can myths. Many cultures are founded on a creation myth — a story that relates how a place, a city, or a nation and its people came into being. These myths provided ancient peoples with a foundation for their culture, a justification for laws, and unifying stories that all members could claim as their own.

Today, people also turn to myths as a force that unifies and promotes national identity. National myths are stories that promote national values and perspectives. They can include ancient myths, such as stories of the Greek gods of Mount Olympus, and ancient religious texts, such as the Hindu epic poem *Ramayana*, as well as more recent stories. They can also include versions of historical events and personalities, such as stories of early voyageurs canoeing westward, the building of the Canadian Pacific Railway, and the War of 1812 — which Canadians consider a triumph over American invaders and Americans view as their victory.

Many people suggest that the meaning of many of Canada's myths and symbols is to foster pride in the idea that Canadians persevered and overcame obstacles and hardships. As a result, Canadians are a people who are hardworking, ingenious, and determined.

Figure 14-2 Canada's National History Society named its magazine after the beaver, a Canadian national symbol. The beaver provides a link to Canada's fur-trading past and symbolizes qualities that many Canadians take pride in. The cover shown was for a special 2008 edition. The loon and its haunting cry are associated with northern lakes and isolation, and this bird has come to symbolize Canada as the figure on its $1 coin. But when so many Canadians live in urban areas, are these symbols still valid?

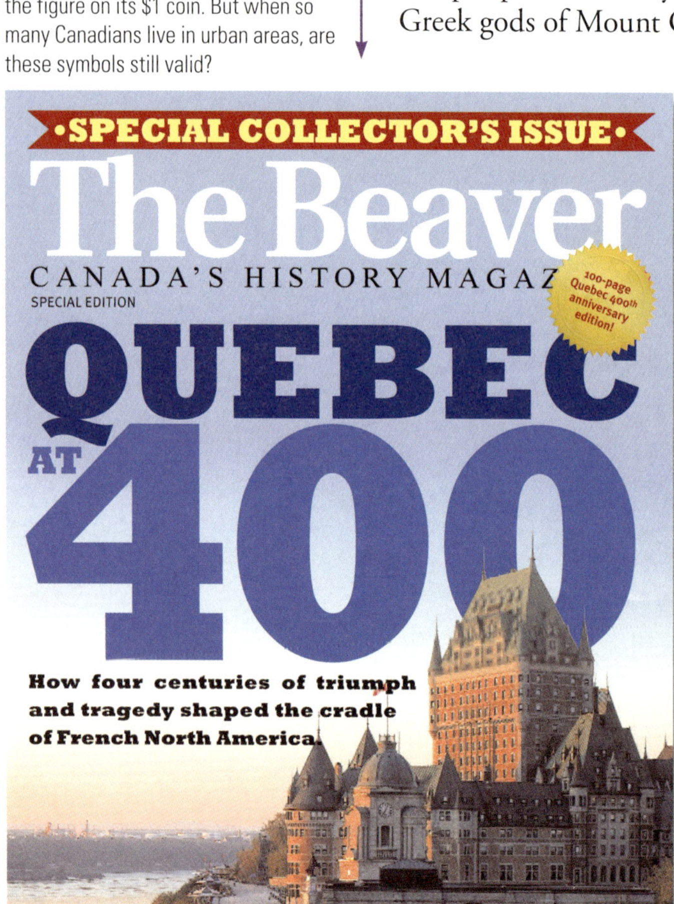

Using National Symbols to Promote Canadian Identity

People in Canada and around the world associate a number of symbols with Canada: the Rocky Mountains, hockey, the Canada goose, and the maple leaf. When a symbol triggers an association — the maple leaf means Canada — then it is successful. Sometimes, however, symbols succeed in more limited ways. The loon, for example, is not widely known as a symbol of Canada, and the Canada goose can be considered a nuisance.

With a partner, list three other symbols of Canada. What do they tell people about the country? Do the symbols you chose accurately represent a Canadian national identity? What aspects of a Canadian national identity are not included in these symbols?

The great passenger trains were a symbol — still are, years after their demise — and symbols do not operate on the level of logic, but of emotion.

— *Peter C. Newman, in* The Canadian Revolution: From Deference to Defiance, *1996*

MAKING A DIFFERENCE

Jowi Taylor and George Rizsanyi
The Six String Nation Guitar

MAKING A DIFFERENCE
MAKING A DIFFERENCE

In 1995, just before the Québec referendum on separation, broadcaster Jowi Taylor decided to promote national unity by creating a symbol of Canada's past and diversity. For 10 years, he worked on the Six String Nation guitar.

Taylor told CBC TV what happened as he began criss-crossing Canada to assemble the elements of the guitar: "Then began a journey that took us to Haida Gwaii, and took us across the country and got a lot of people talking to us with their stories, and [the guitar] became a talking stick for the country."

The guitar includes wood from Pierre Trudeau's canoe paddle, the deck of the *Bluenose II*, Wayne Gretzky's hockey stick, the homes of Alberta cowboy John Ware and basketball inventor James Naismith, the first Ukrainian Orthodox church in Canada, a Saskatchewan grain elevator, and the Saint-Boniface Museum, which was once a convent where Louis Riel went to school.

It also includes a piece of stone from a memorial to Almighty Voice, the Cree leader who led the last armed resistance to European settlement on the Prairies, and a piece of mammoth ivory collected by Sonny MacDonald, a Chipewyan Dene from Forth Smith in the Northwest Territories.

Figure 14-3 Jowi Taylor (left) and Canadian rocker Colin James checked out the Six String Nation guitar before it was played for the first time on Canada Day, 2006. Has this guitar succeeded in becoming a symbol of Canada?

One piece of the guitar is particularly meaningful to guitar maker George Rizsanyi — an inside strut made from a fragment of Pier 21 in Halifax, where he and his family, like many others, had landed in Canada as immigrants.

Rizsanyi believes that the voices of each story in the guitar will combine when it is played, and he hopes this will give Canadians a sense of the richness of their own history. "They will recognize how deep the culture and history of Canada . . . how colourful it is, that we should be proud as Canadians," he told CBC TV.

Explorations

1. Describe how the Six String Nation guitar tries to unite various aspects of Canada. Do you think it succeeds in helping Canadians view themselves as a nation? Explain your judgments.
2. Should this guitar be promoted as a national symbol? How would you suggest doing this?

Using National Myths to Promote Canadian Identity

CheckBack

You read about Ernest Renan's understanding of nation in Chapter 1.

According to the French political thinker Ernest Renan, a nation is unified by two things: shared memories of the past and its people's consent in the present — their desire to live together and affirm their heritage. Shared memories of a common history help unite peoples, but peoples also select the myths they want included in their national memory. An early chapter of Canada's national myth, for example, tells the story of mostly European pioneers who triumphed over nature. The government used this story to create symbols and advertising that attracted settlers to Canada. But in the 21st century, the reality is that more than 80 per cent of Canadians live in urban areas and few live completely off the land.

Who is left out of the myth of the "rugged Canadian" triumphing over nature?

Can Canada continue to call itself a nation of peacekeepers if its forces are small and scattered around the world?

The image of Canadians as peacekeepers is more recent. Although many Canadians, as well as members of the international community, view Canada as a nation of peacekeepers, the numbers tell a different story. In 1991, Canada contributed more than 10 per cent of all UN peacekeeping forces. Sixteen years later, this contribution amounted to less than 0.1 per cent.

Some people believe that as long as myths serve a valid purpose, such as promoting national unity, facts are not important. But others say that national myths may sometimes be based on lies that promote the dominance of one social group over another.

Canadian political scientist Arash Abizadeh summed up this debate in an article in the *Journal of Political Philosophy*. "Against the charge that identity-grounding myths are simply lies and fabrications that represent some particular groups' will to power, others have argued that it is a mistake to understand national histories as a set of truth claims in the fashion of the academic historian," Abizadeh wrote. "Rather, they should be seen as something closer to stories . . . National myths are not lies and fabrications; they are inspiring narratives, stemming from human imagination, in which we tell ourselves who we are or want to be."

Legends are what you tell yourself when you don't know your own history. It's cozy and cuddly, politically inoffensive, and reinforces the hegemony [domination] of the ruling class.

— *John Fitzgerald, Newfoundland historian, quoted in* The Next Canada *by Myrna Kostash, 2000*

Reflect and Respond

Look around your school for images, symbols, and stories that create a sense of group identity and belonging. What, for example, does your school crest or logo represent? Did someone famous attend your school? Are stories about students' achievements in sports or the arts highlighted? What feelings do these images, symbols, and stories inspire in you? Explain your response.

Then examine some Canadian bills. What symbols are used on the $5 bill? On the $10 bill? On the $20 bill? What stories or myths about Canada do they suggest? What might these images tell people in other countries about Canada's national myths?

How have institutions been used to promote a national identity in Canada?

An **institution** is an organization established for and united by a specific purpose — and institutions often use national symbols and stories in a variety of ways to define an identity and promote a sense of belonging.

The activities of various institutions often overlap — and their mission may not be restricted to a single field. Governments, organizations, communities, and individuals may operate — and co-operate in funding — institutions that provide services such as social assistance, education, and cultural events. Public art galleries and museums may be operated by national, provincial, or local governments, often to display national or regional treasures and convey messages about national and regional culture.

If you wanted to tell others about your community or what makes your province unique, what would you say? How would you spread your message?

During a previous visit 32 years ago I said that "I want the Crown in Canada to represent everything that is best and most admired in the Canadian ideal. I will continue to do my best to make it so during my lifetime, and I hope you will all continue to give me your help in this task." I would like to repeat those words today as, together, we continue to build a country that remains the envy of the world.

— Queen Elizabeth II, in an address to the Alberta legislature, 2005

Cultural Institutions

Some cultural institutions honour elements of Canada's heritage and history as a foundation of national identity. The Monarchist League, for example, celebrates Canada's British connection and the country's links to the British crown.

Read Queen Elizabeth II's words in "Voices." Do you agree with the Monarchist League's celebration of Canada's links with the British monarch?

Art galleries such as the National Gallery of Canada in Ottawa often display Canadian art that is the source of strong national symbols. These include paintings by Cornelius Krieghoff, Emily Carr, and members of the Group of Seven. Museums may also display objects from the nation's past that express — and occasionally challenge — people's sense of belonging. The Glenbow Museum in Calgary, for example, has mounted a permanent and online exhibit called Mavericks: An Incorrigible History of Alberta. The publicity for this exhibit says, "Alberta was shaped by Mavericks — men and women who were adventurous, hard-working, and spirited."

What do you think the Glenbow Museum wants visitors to think about when they view Mavericks? How do you think exhibits like Mavericks might affect Albertans' sense of identity?

Other institutions may help athletes, sometimes by sending them to represent Canada at national and international competitions. And still others try to preserve and promote Aboriginal languages, French, and heritage languages.

Web Connection

To view the Glenbow Museum's Mavericks exhibit, go this web site and follow the links.

www.ExploringNationalism.ca

Figure 14-4 The Mavericks exhibit at Calgary's Glenbow Museum showcases the lives of some of Alberta's legendary characters. One is John Ware, shown with his boarhound, Bismark, in 1891. A former slave, Ware became a rancher renowned for his skills. How might the Glenbow's decision to include Ware in the exhibit influence the way Albertans view their province's history? Their sense of identity?

Educational Institutions

In Canada, provincial and territorial governments are responsible for education. At various levels, schools teach courses about Canadian history, culture, and identity. But many other institutions also provide information and education in these areas.

To find out more about the Dominion Institute, go to this web site and follow the links.

www.ExploringNationalism.ca

The Dominion Institute

Founded in 1997, the Dominion Institute uses television, news and electronic media, and school programs to educate people about how Canada's history has shaped the country's identity. Remembering the past is an important part of a nation's identity. Québec's provincial motto — "Je me souviens," or "I remember" — acknowledges this concept.

At the same time, the Dominion Institute's web site notes that only one-third of eligible first-time voters cast ballots in the 2006 federal election, that two-thirds of Canadians have never heard of Vimy Ridge, and that 44 per cent of Canadians believe that D-Day marks the bombing of Pearl Harbor.

Is it important for Canadians to know about Vimy Ridge and what happened on D-Day? Explain your response.

Figure 14-5 This information banner is one of many on the Dominion Institute's web site. How many of the people in the background can you identify? Should Canadians feel pride in the achievements of these people?

The Council of Canadians

CHECKFORWARD

You will read more about Maude Barlow and the Council of Canadians in Chapter 15.

Founded in 1985, the Council of Canadians is Canada's largest citizens' organization. The COC describes its mission as protecting "Canadian independence by promoting progressive policies on fair trade, clean water, energy security, public health care, and other issues of social and economic concern to Canadians." Working with a network of volunteers, the council organizes events and publishes research reports and other material to ensure that people and governments "know the kind of Canada" that Canadians want.

If you wanted to promote Canadian identity, would you choose to work with the Monarchist League, the Dominion Institute, the Council of Canadians, or another institution? Explain your reasons.

Figure 14-6 Maude Barlow, national chair of the Council of Canadians, rallies protesters outside a Canadian Medical Association meeting in 2006. At the meeting in Charlottetown, Prince Edward Island, the CMA was considering various moves that Barlow said would open the door to privatized health care.

Institutions That Seek Influence

Many institutions try to influence not only government policies, but also the way policy is developed. These institutions often promote the interests of a particular group by ensuring that members' voices are heard — and that their stories become part of national myths and identity. To achieve this goal, political institutions may organize public relations campaigns, commission surveys, maintain web sites, and publish books, pamphlets, and magazines.

Aboriginal Organizations

Aboriginal organizations such as the Assembly of First Nations and the Métis National Council, as well as regional groups such as the Métis Nation of Alberta, work with Aboriginal people across Canada. They may, for example, initiate campaigns to improve access to clean water or support traditional hunting rights. But they also promote Aboriginal perspectives and ensure that these are considered when issues of national interest are debated.

How successful do you think Aboriginal organizations have been in ensuring that their peoples' perspectives are included in Canada's national stories? Explain your judgment.

Figure 14-7 At the web site of the Métis Nation of Alberta, you can hear the Métis national anthem and view the organization's magazine, *Otipemisiwak — Voice of MNA*. The magazine's covers often display symbols that are important to Métis identity.

Pollsters and Think Tanks

News organizations, government agencies, and other groups often hire polling companies like Ipsos Reid, COMPAS, and The Strategic Council to provide a snapshot of Canadians' views on particular issues. The results of these surveys can affect, for example, whether a government holds an election or cuts taxes, as well as what people read about and see in the news.

In 1997, for example, the Dominion Institute asked Ipsos Reid to conduct a mock citizenship exam similar to the one immigrants must pass to become citizens — and 45 per cent of respondents failed. When the survey was repeated 10 years later, the results were even worse: 60 per cent of respondents failed, though 70 per cent of immigrants passed.

In response to this survey, the Dominion Institute recommended that high school students across Canada be required to pass a national citizenship exam as a condition of graduation. Do you think this idea would effectively promote a Canadian national identity? Explain your judgment. Should requirements for citizenship include a knowledge of Canada as well as the skills to participate in the democratic process?

Figure 14-8 Dominion Institute–Ipsos Reid's Mock Canadian Citizenship Exam, 1997 and 2007

Selected Questions
What was the main trade controlled by the Hudson's Bay Company?
Who is Canada's head of state?
Which four provinces joined together in Confederation?
What three oceans border Canada?
Name four of the five great lakes.

In addition to polling companies, think tanks such as the Fraser Institute influence government policies and media coverage of national issues. Founded in 1974 by a group of academics and business executives, this independent research and educational institution says its goal is to redirect public attention to the role of competitive markets in meeting the needs of Canadians. It has published reports on privatizing health care and on the environment and has advocated a simpler tax system and abolishing minimum-wage rules. As a result, it is often described as a "right-wing think tank" that serves the interests of businesspeople and conservatives.

Combating poverty, deprivation and exclusion is not a matter of charity, and it does not depend on how rich a country is . . .

Poverty eradication is an achievable goal. By tackling poverty as a matter of human rights obligation, the world will have a better chance of abolishing this scourge in our lifetime.

— Louise Arbour, UN high commissioner for human rights, 2006

There can be no patriotism without permanent opposition and criticism.

— Hannah Arendt, writer and political philosopher, 1963

Economic and Commercial Institutions

Groups representing labour unions, industry associations, chambers of commerce, manufacturers, and other businesses, as well as people who are poor, also try to make their voices heard. One of the ways they do this is by appealing to a particular view of Canada. In addition, some businesses, such as the Hudson's Bay Company, are large and influential enough to be counted as institutions in themselves.

The National Anti-Poverty Organization

Founded in 1971 by delegates of more than 250 groups, the National Anti-Poverty Organization advocates on behalf of people who are poor. NAPO was one of the first non-governmental organizations in the world to be granted the right to appear before the United Nations Committee on Economic, Social and Cultural Rights, and has presented evidence on how Canada has failed to live up to its international human rights obligations.

Examine the words of Louise Arbour and Hannah Arendt in "Voices." Would Arbour and Arendt defend NAPO's right to criticize Canada's human rights record? Do criticisms like those presented by NAPO make Canada stronger or weaker? Explain your response.

The Hudson's Bay Company

Founded in 1670, the Hudson's Bay Company owned and controlled a large part of Canada until 1868. During that time, the Bay issued its own currency, made its own laws, and controlled many aspects of its employees' lives, as well as their livelihood.

Figure 14-9 Canada's wheelchair curling team won the gold medal at the 2006 Paralympics in Turin, Italy. Uniforms for both Olympic and Paralympic athletes were designed and supplied by the Bay. How might this association benefit the Bay?

The Bay's history, including stories of exploration, adventure, and greed, looms large in Canada's national myths. The Hudson's Bay blanket was one of the items traded to Aboriginal trappers for furs, and the blanket became a symbol of the company — and of Canada. The Hudson's Bay Company Archives — historical documents, artwork, photographs, and objects — are now part of Manitoba's provincial archives.

Reflect and Respond

What visions of Canada's national identity are presented by the Monarchist League? The Mavericks exhibit at the Glenbow Museum? The Dominion Institute? The Métis National Council? The Fraser Institute? The National Anti-Poverty Organization? The Bay? What perspectives does each institution present? Prepare an e-mail message to send to each, asking three questions about its vision of Canadian identity and how the institution promotes it.

SPINBUSTER

Identifying Spin in Commercial and Corporate Communications

The Hudson's Bay Company — the Bay — is the oldest continuously operating business in Canada and one of the oldest in the world.

In a report posted on the company's web site, Governor and Chief Executive Officer Jerry Zucker said that in his travels across Canada, he was "struck by the deep sentiment Canadians feel for Hbc . . . This report illustrates the depth and breadth of our commitment to Canada and the communities where we work and live."

Zucker also reported that the company had provided funding for 200 Canadian athletes and established a program for community heritage initiatives. As chair of HBC's History Foundation, Zucker described this as "an opportunity to embrace the collective history of this country."

Steps to Analyzing and Interpreting Commercial or Corporate Communications

Step 1: Question assumptions

With a partner, examine the excerpts from Zucker's report and respond to the following questions:

- If you were a corporate executive, why would you have presented this message? What message would you be sending? What loyalties would you be highlighting?
- As a potential Bay customer, how would you respond to the message? What loyalties would influence your responses? Would the message challenge or reinforce your loyalty to the Bay? To Canada?

Step 2: Think about motives

With your partner, discuss Zucker's motives. The following questions may help focus your thinking:

- What might Zucker gain from sending this message? What might the company gain? Who else would benefit?
- What impression of the company's national identity does Zucker's message leave you with?
- What has been left out of the message? Is it possible that including this information would present a conflicting version of the company's national identity?

Step 3: Analyze the context

With your partner, analyze how the context of Zucker's message might affect the way Canadian consumers respond to the company.

- Does the message promote aspects of Canada's national identity?
- In the context of globalization, is emphasizing the Bay's commitment to Canadian communities, athletes, and history important to Canadian consumers?

Step 4: Be a spinbuster — look for alternative points of view and information

Jerry Zucker bought the Bay in January 2006. Zucker was a South Carolina businessperson, and some might say that the Bay's attempts to remain Canadian — by funding athletes and local history projects and promoting national symbols — are designed to attract consumers by preserving a veneer of Canadian identity.

With your partner, discuss whether this information changes your responses to the questions in Steps 1, 2, and 3. Then answer the following questions:

- Does the citizenship of a company's owner matter? Does it matter where a company's headquarters are located? Where its executives live?
- Why would Zucker have wanted to emphasize the Bay's roots as a Canadian company?
- Should profits from Canadian companies stay in Canada to provide jobs for Canadians?
- Should foreign ownership of Canadian businesses and resources be limited or controlled in some way? If so, why? If not, why not?

Compile a list of resources you might consult to conduct further research on who owns "Canadian" companies.

Summing Up

You can use your spinbusting skill to analyze and interpret a variety of institutional messages at school and in everyday life.

FOCUS ON SKILLS

Writing for Different Purposes and Audiences

FOCUS ON SKILLS

Whenever you write something — an essay, an e-mail message, a job application, or a text message — you write with a specific purpose and audience in mind. The purpose and audience determine the kind of writing required. You might, for example, write a text message to a friend one way and a letter applying for a job another way.

Jerry Zucker's message on page 329 is a good example of writing for a specific purpose and audience. Zucker wanted to assure people that the Bay remains committed to Canada — and to encourage Canadians to support the company.

The following steps will help you focus on an audience and a purpose in your own writing. You can use the same process to help you plan essays and complete other written assignments.

Steps to Writing for Different Purposes and Audiences

Step 1: Think about one purpose and audience

Imagine this scenario: a representative in the United States Congress has suggested in a television interview that Canada should join the United States to create one large country. He argues that Canadians are really no different from Americans and should follow the lead set by Alaska in 1867, when this territory joined the United States. You have been invited to write a guest column for the *New York Times*. You want to explain to American readers that Canadians and Americans are different and that creating one country is not a good idea.

Think about your goal. How will you persuade your audience? What information will you include in your column? Why would you include this information — what is the context? What kind of writing would be most appropriate? Use a chart like the one shown to make notes about what you will write.

Purpose and Audience Subject ________________	
Purpose	
Audience	
Content and context	
Writing style	

FOCUS ON SKILLS FOCUS ON SKILLS FOCUS ON SKILLS FOCUS ON SKILLS CUS ON SKILLS

Step 2: Think about different audiences

Your column has been so successful that you have been asked to present the same arguments in different formats:

- as an opinion piece in *Alberta Venture*, a magazine for Alberta businesspeople
- as a blog for your school's online student magazine
- as an article in *The Beaver*, a magazine published by Canada's National History Society

With a partner, discuss how the varying interests of these audiences might shape your writing. Record your notes on a chart like the one shown on this page.

Step 3: Think about different purposes

With your partner, discuss how your column would change

- if its purpose were to persuade readers that there is no difference between Canadians and Americans
- if its purpose were to persuade Americans that they are no different from Canadians and that the United States should join Canada

Compare your ideas with those of another pair.

Step 4: Write your column

Choose one publication and one purpose. Write a 200-word opinion piece, blog, or article on whether Canada should join the United States.

Step 5: Compare and revise

Compare your piece of writing with that of your partner. Use your partner's feedback to revise your piece if you wish.

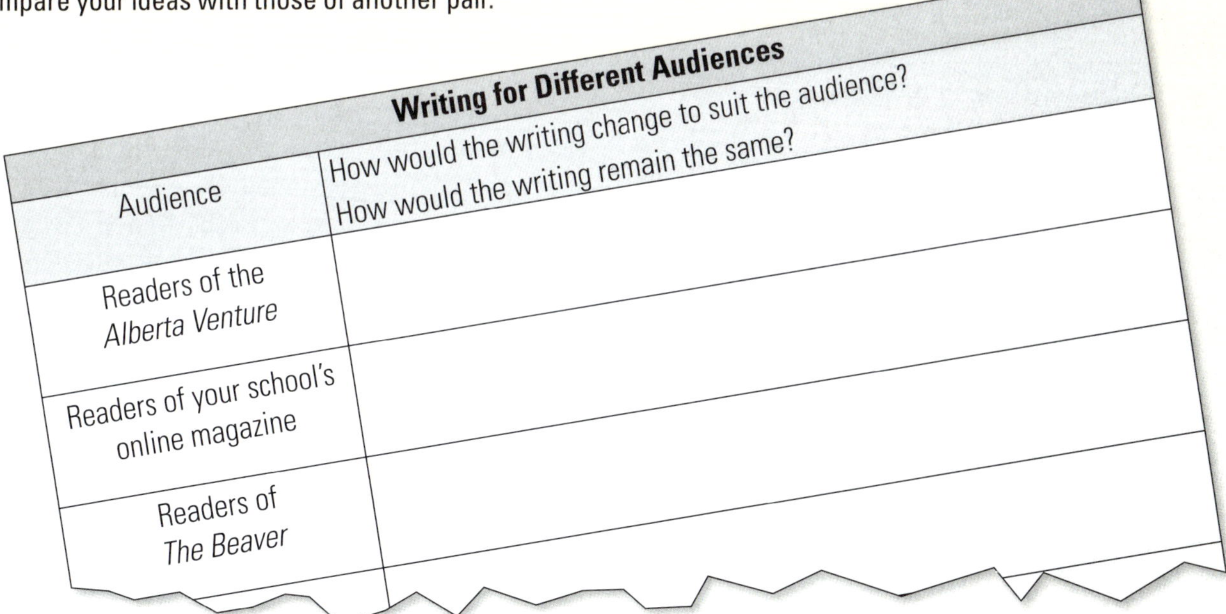

Writing for Different Audiences

Audience	How would the writing change to suit the audience? How would the writing remain the same?
Readers of the *Alberta Venture*	
Readers of your school's online magazine	
Readers of *The Beaver*	

Summing Up

As you progress through this course and through life, you will often be called on to write for different audiences and purposes. Following steps like these will help you write more effectively.

How can government programs and initiatives be used to promote a national identity?

Federal government programs are often used to promote national unity and a sense of Canadian identity. But they frequently spark controversy. The governor general and lieutenant-governors, for example, are symbolic heads of state who represent the British crown. Many believe that these symbols help unite Canada by reminding Canadians of the country's history, but others regard them as remnants of colonialism and believe they should be abolished.

Should Canadian taxpayers be required to foot the bill for promoting Canadian culture?

Although the CBC operates independently of the federal government, about two-thirds of its annual budget comes from government grants. This means that everyone in Canada contributes about $33 a year to keep the CBC operating.

Arts and Cultural Programs

Cultural institutions are important to all peoples, and in Canada, governments support cultural industries through direct funding and by putting in place programs that encourage Canadian involvement in activities such as publishing, film and television, music, and dance.

The CBC, NFB, and CRTC

The Broadcasting Act specifically requires the Canadian Broadcasting Corporation — the Société Radio-Canada, or CBC–Radio Canada — to "be predominantly and distinctively Canadian" and to "contribute to shared national consciousness and identity." The CBC–Radio-Canada promotes Canadian identity by broadcasting programs that all Canadians can listen to, see, and share.

The National Film Board produces films in English, French, and other languages. These films reflect Canadian points of view and perspectives and often win awards — and sometimes they arouse controversy. A 1982 NFB documentary about World War I flying ace Billy Bishop, for example, caused an uproar when it questioned some of Bishop's achievements.

The Canadian Radio-television and Telecommunications Commission regulates and licenses broadcasting in Canada and requires broadcasters to meet Canadian-content quotas. This policy has helped Canadian musicians and performers, as well as TV and film producers, compete in a marketplace dominated by American media — but the need for quotas, and exactly how high they should be, remains controversial.

Figure 14-10 The Canadian War Museum has seven permanent galleries and also hosts special exhibitions, such as Stitches in Time, which appeared in 2008. The 15 quilts by artist Johnnene Maddison evoked the experiences of women on the home front during World War II. Can museums and art galleries contribute to national myths by mounting displays like this? Explain your response.

National Galleries and Museums

The federal government also helps fund museums and galleries, such as the National Gallery of Canada, the Canadian Museum of Civilization, and the Canadian War Museum. All celebrate aspects of Canadian culture and identity.

The Canadian War Museum, for example, commemorates the efforts of Canadians during times of war. The museum attempts to strike a balance between building pride in military achievements and recognizing the horror of war.

Educational Programs

Although education is a provincial and territorial responsibility, the federal government plays an indirect role by providing some funding. And in some areas, such as universities and the education of First Nations students on reserves, the federal government plays a more direct role. Providing an education to students on a reserve is a treaty obligation. At all levels of education, the federal government supports a number of programs that promote a Canadian national identity.

I believe Canada is stronger when our young people are encouraged to live in and learn about another region and devote their skills and energy to local communities in need.

— Justin Trudeau, politician and son of Katimavik co-founder Pierre Trudeau, 2005

Katimavik

Between 1977 and 1986, and again since 1994, the federal government has operated a program called Katimavik — an Inuktituk word that means "meeting place" — to educate Canadian youth through community involvement. The program provides 17- to 21-year-olds with a chance to travel and learn about other regions of Canada while volunteering, developing job skills, living in a group, and developing closer ties with their peers and the country. More than 25 000 young people have volunteered in more than 2000 communities across Canada.

In 2006, Katimavik conducted an assessment of the program's costs and benefits. The study found that every dollar the government spent on the program generated $2.20 in participating communities — and provided participants with opportunities to develop new friendships and personal skills, foster personal growth, and expand their outlook on life in general and toward other cultures. Both Katimavik volunteers and participating communities said they would recommend the program to friends, other communities, and businesses.

Canadian historian, novelist, humorist, and travel writer Will Ferguson was a Katimavik volunteer when he was 19. At the time, he says, Katimavik paid "a dollar a day and all the granola we could eat." Ferguson went on to write and edit many books about Canadian identity, including a humorous memoir about his Katimavik experience: *I Was a Teenage Katima-Victim: A Canadian Odyssey.*

Canada World Youth

Through the Canadian International Development Agency, the federal government also funds a program called Canada World Youth. This international intercultural program involves 17- to 24-year-old Canadian volunteers in community development exchanges with young people in other countries.

Kat Koostachin of Saskatchewan is one of 27 000 young people who have participated in this program since it was founded in 1971. Koostachin said the experience inspired her to pursue an education in international relations. "I . . . now realize how important it is for me to help my own community in Canada. I hope to do this by getting other First Nations youth involved in community work and programs," she wrote.

In 1986, the federal government suspended its funding of Katimavik but reversed this decision in 1994. Are programs like Katimavik and Canada World Youth an appropriate way to spend public money? With a partner, develop three arguments in favour of these programs and three arguments against. Include a statement about Canadian identity in at least one of your arguments.

Figure 14-11 Katimavik volunteer Alistair Thomson (left) worked with these students at Palliser Heights School in Moose Jaw, Saskatchewan, as well as several Chinese participants in Canada World Youth, to create this window painting.

Programs That Promote Peace, Order, and Good Government

CheckBack

You read about the beginnings of the French republic and nationalism in the United States in Chapter 2.

France's republic was founded on the principles of liberty, equality and brotherhood. The United States declared its independence on the basis of "self-evident truths" — people's right to equality, life, liberty, and the pursuit of happiness. Canada's confederation, it is often said, was established to secure peace, order, and good government.

The Royal Canadian Mounted Police

One of the first institutions established to achieve the goals of peace, order, and good government was a national police force. Founded as the North-West Mounted Police in 1873, renamed the Royal Northwest Mounted Police in 1904, and finally the Royal Canadian Mounted Police in 1920, this force provides national, federal, provincial, and even municipal policing.

The force's dress uniform — scarlet tunic, brown riding boots, jodhpurs, and wide Stetson — has become a symbol of Canada, and its Musical Ride has been widely acclaimed since its first public performance in 1901.

Figure 14-12 An RCMP officer in dress uniform stands in front of a mural depicting the Musical Ride. The Musical Ride represents the RCMP's tradition of being a "mounted" police force. Do the dress uniform and the Musical Ride reflect the reality of the Mounties' role in Canada today?

The RCMP's dress uniform has changed very little over the decades. With a partner, list at least three reasons the Mounties might have continued to use this dress uniform.

Immigration and Security Programs

The first government bodies encountered by many visitors and immigrants to the country include Canada Customs and Revenue, Citizenship and Immigration Canada, and the Canada Border Services Agency.

The CCRA ensures that Canadians share in the costs of running the country by collecting taxes equally from everyone. Citizenship and Immigration Canada deals with matters relating to citizenship and immigration, introduces new Canadians to the country, and helps them integrate. The Canada Border Services Agency works with the RCMP, other police forces, and other Canadian government agencies, as well as international agencies, to keep Canadians safe and the borders secure.

In addition, the Canadian Security Intelligence Service, which is Canada's spy service, interacts with police forces and domestic and international agencies to make the country secure from threats.

To find out more about CSIS, go to this web site and follow the links.

www.ExploringNationalism.ca

Economic Programs

Many everyday items used by Canadians across the country, such as money and postage stamps, are provided by government programs and use symbols that promote national unity.

The Bank of Canada and the Royal Canadian Mint

Between 1858 and 1908, Canadian coins were made in Britain. Then a branch plant of the Royal Mint was built in Ottawa to make both Canadian and British gold coins. The federal government took control of the mint in 1931 and created the Bank of Canada in 1934. The mint's coins and bills have carried symbols of Canadian identity — images of the Vimy Memorial, Canadian birds and historical figures, First Nations artworks, Olympic athletes, and Terry Fox — and spread them across the country and around the world.

Figure 14-13 The first Canadian bank notes were printed in 1935 in either French or English, depending on where they would circulate. In 1937, the bank printed the words on the bills in both languages. What does this change in policy suggest about how ideas about Canada's national identity had evolved?

Advertising and Sponsorship

Publicly funded Canada Day celebrations are one way the federal government promotes Canadian identity and unity. A government-run organization called the National Committee helps communities organize and pay for Canada Day celebrations. Since 1985, every province and territory has had a committee that uses federal grants to help co-ordinate these celebrations.

Members of Parliament often hand out flags and maple leaf pins to constituents, and in 1996, the government sponsored what it called the One in a Million National Flag Challenge. The plan was to distribute a million flags to Canadians, who would fly them on Flag Day in 1997. The program cost $15.5 million, or about 50 cents for every Canadian.

Sponsoring athletes — at the Olympic, Paralympic, and Commonwealth Games, for example — and celebrating their achievements is another way the federal government promotes Canada at home and abroad.

When the Canadian Football League was in financial trouble in the late 1990s, the federal government provided funding to place a sticker of the Canadian flag on every player's helmet. Some Canadians complained that the government was bailing out privately owned sports teams. Others said that the government was simply paying for advertising.

Reflect and Respond

Part of the challenge of developing a program to promote a national identity can lie in promoting the program itself. Sometimes it needs broader coverage; other times, the coverage needs to be more tightly focused.

Choose one program, such as Katimavik or sponsoring Paralympic athletes, and work with a partner to develop a promotional campaign aimed at raising the program's profile among high school students across Canada. What arguments would you use to persuade the government that funding your campaign is worthwhile? What methods of advertising and communication would you use? Would you develop a new logo or symbol? What stories would you convey? Work with a partner to map out your campaign, then present and explain your ideas to the class.

VOICES

Oh! The good old hockey game,
Is the best game you can name;
And the best game you can name,
Is the good old hockey game!

— Stompin' Tom Connors, "The Hockey Song," 1971

My profession has taken me to every part of the world, none of them more beautiful than where I live. As a musician, I respond to the harmony and rhythm of life, and when I'm deeply moved it leaves something singing inside me. With a country as large and as full of contrast as Canada, I had a lot of themes to choose from when I wrote the *Canadiana Suite*. This is my musical portrait of the Canada I love.

— Oscar Peterson, musician and composer, 1997

HOW CAN INDIVIDUALS PROMOTE A NATIONAL IDENTITY?

When Canada's unity was threatened by the Québec referendum in 1995, Jowi Taylor was inspired to create the Six String Nation guitar. Taylor's action is an example of how individuals can play an active role in promoting national identity.

Musicians, painters, writers, and others have often used symbols of Canada and drawn on national myths for inspiration. In the process, they have sometimes added new symbols and myths to Canada's story. Many Canadian backpackers, for example, sport Canadian flags on their packs, a strategy that proclaims their sense of identity as they travel the world.

Musicians and Artists

Stompin' Tom Connors has travelled all over Canada, singing his distinctly Canadian songs about hockey, football, soldiers, snowmobiles, sasquatches, and Bud the PEI spud. His most famous composition, "The Hockey Song," has even been called a national anthem.

Jazz pianist Oscar Peterson recognized in the 1960s that being Canadian brought a different note to his chosen form. His *Canadiana Suite*, written in 1964, moves from Eastern to Western Canada, with compositions inspired by the country's regions. Peterson's own favourite was "Wheatland," reflecting the Canadian Prairies.

Roch Carrier is a novelist, playwright, and children's writer whose stories are enjoyed by Francophones and anglophones alike. A quotation from his famous story *The Hockey Sweater* is found on the back of Canada's $5 dollar bill. And award-winning folksinger and actor Tom Jackson, a member of the Cree Nation who grew up on the One Arrow Reserve in Saskatchewan, is also the founder of a concert series that raises money for food banks.

In the 1920s, the Group of Seven painters set out to explore and paint the Canadian landscape in a different way from artists who had been heavily influenced by European tastes and traditions. These painters — and others, such as Emily Carr — created images that reflected their feelings about their country, and their works have come to represent Canada.

Figure 14-14 Jazz musician Oscar Peterson received the Order of Canada in 1973. He was widely acclaimed as an ambassador of Canada and for bringing Canadian culture to the world — and vice versa.

Today, Aboriginal artists like Kent Monkman, a member of the Fisher River Band of Manitoba, often use their art to promote their people's identity. Monkman has written that the reality of Aboriginal peoples was often "painted out of the narratives" created by other artists. "It's worth examining that whole period of art, so purely one-sided, like a big cover-up of what was really happening," he told *The Walrus* magazine. "I try to approach it with humour, focusing on the side of the art culture that is about survival and being able to adapt, and to look forward. It's a very gentle way of making people aware of this huge obliteration of our narratives."

Athletes and Roving Ambassadors

Figure 14-15 Lesley Buttle (left) helps her son, Jeffrey, hold up the gold medal he won at the 2008 World Figure Skating Championship in Göteborg, Sweden.

Government and corporate funding has helped many athletes compete for Canada at all levels of sports. But the dedication and sacrifice of their families, coaches, and other individuals is also invaluable.

Wayne Gretzky's father, Walter, helped his young son hone his skills by building what has been called the most famous backyard hockey rink in the world. And when figure skater Jeffrey Buttle won the world championship in 2008, it was another milestone in a career that began when his mother put him on the ice for the first time at the age of two. Lesley Buttle, says she'll happily "share him with Canada . . . Of course, it would have been nice to share him when it was time to drive all those miles at 5 a.m. But no one's around to share that, only parents."

Whenever people put a flag of their country or an emblem of their school on their backpack, wear a T-shirt that says they are Albertan or Sri Lankan, or drive out of the province in a car with Alberta licence plates, they display where they are from.

Taking Turns

Is promoting national identity my responsibility?

The students responding to this question are Violet, who is a member of the Paddle Prairie Métis Settlement; Blair, who lives in Edmonton and whose heritage is Ukrainian, Scottish, and German; and Jane, who lives in Calgary and is descended from black Loyalists who fled to Nova Scotia after the American Revolution.

I don't need to advertise that I'm Canadian. I don't put flag stickers all over my locker or binders like some kids I know. I'm glad I'm Canadian, but, to be specific, I'm Métis. That's what I tell others I am, because I think this identity is special. I think individuals should promote their own cultures. By showing that you're Métis or Inuit or Québécois or Anglo-Canadian, you're also promoting Canada's multicultural identity.

I definitely think it's my responsibility to promote my identity as a Canadian. I have a Team Canada hockey sweater that I wear a lot. When I wear it, I feel more connected to other Canadians. People smile at me — we seem to have something in common. I also love Canada Day! Every July 1st, I hang a huge flag off our apartment balcony and go down to the park to watch fireworks.This country could use more Canadian spirit. We're all Canadian — let's be proud of that.

Jane

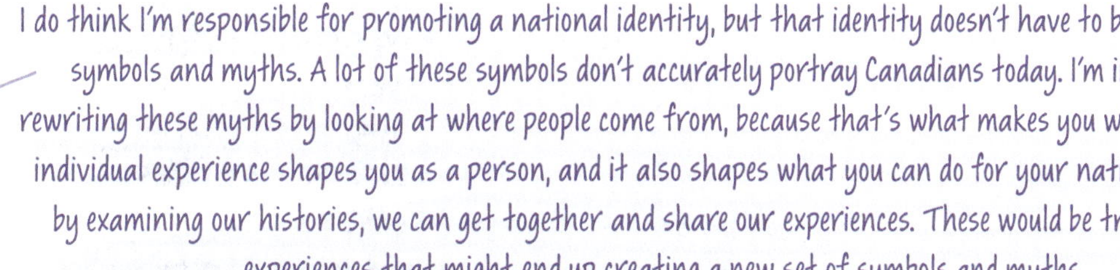

I do think I'm responsible for promoting a national identity, but that identity doesn't have to buy into national symbols and myths. A lot of these symbols don't accurately portray Canadians today. I'm interested in rewriting these myths by looking at where people come from, because that's what makes you who you are. Your individual experience shapes you as a person, and it also shapes what you can do for your nation. If we start by examining our histories, we can get together and share our experiences. These would be truly Canadian experiences that might end up creating a new set of symbols and myths.

How would you respond to the question Violet, Blair, and Jane are answering? Have you ever done something to promote your Canadian identity? What would you consider doing in the future? Explain your responses.

The Greatest Canadians

Pierre Berton wrote 50 books for adults and 22 for children. Many of his works examined the myths and realities of Canada's history and identity. Among his most popular books were histories of the Canadian Pacific Railway, the Klondike, the Great Depression, and the exploration of Canada's North.

Berton was also a television personality and wrote scores of articles, columns, and essays. In many ways, he became as recognizable as some of his subjects. When Berton died in 2004, Mel Hurtig, author, activist, and original publisher of *The Canadian Encyclopedia*, said: "[Berton] hated what he called anti-Canadians — people who put Canadians down and people who weren't proud of their country. I loved him for that."

In 2004, CBC TV asked viewers, "Who is the greatest Canadian?" Viewers nominated 140 000 people, and the debate raged until the top 10 were chosen and a final selection was made. The results are shown in "FYI."

Analyze the list of Canadians in "FYI." What elements of Canadian identity does this list represent? What elements of Canadian identity are missing from this list? Does this list fairly represent Canada? If so, explain how. If not, explain why not. What names would you add to this list? Why would you add them? Who would you delete to make room for them? Explain your choices.

To find out more about CBC's *Greatest Canadian* series, go to this web site and follow the links.

www.ExploringNationalism.ca

The CBC's Top 10 Greatest Canadians

1. Tommy Douglas
2. Terry Fox
3. Pierre Elliott Trudeau
4. Frederick Banting
5. David Suzuki
6. Lester B. Pearson
7. Don Cherry
8. John A. Macdonald
9. Alexander Graham Bell
10. Wayne Gretzky

Figure 14-16 The photograph at top right shows former NDP leader Tommy Douglas, whose efforts to bring pubic health care to Canada earned him recognition as the greatest Canadian in a 2004 CBC contest. In the photograph at left, Pierre Berton sits on CPR Engine 148 during the making of *The National Dream*, a TV series in which Berton narrated the story of how the railway was built.

THE VIEW FROM HERE

To many people, the land, and especially natural areas, are core elements of Canadian identity. But as Canadians become more and more urbanized, will they stop identifying with the outdoors? Here is how three people have responded to this question.

James Outram was a mountain climber and writer who described his impression of the Canadian Rockies in 1906.

There is a wonderful fascination about mountains. Their massive grandeur, majesty of lofty height, splendour of striking outline – crag and pinnacle and precipice – seem to appeal both to the intellect and to the inmost soul of man, and to compel a mingled reverence and love . . . in Canada there still exists that chiefest charm of novelty and adventure, the thrill of climbing virgin peaks, of traversing untrodden valleys, of viewing regions never seen before by human eyes.

Peter C. Newman is a journalist and historian. In *The Canadian Revolution: From Deference to Defiance*, he talks about how contemporary technology has affected Canadians' traditional relationship with the land.

Land-as-Identity became an accepted axiom, with territorial integrity becoming the country's strongest sustaining myth. The trouble with having a national identity defined as an offshoot of nature is that it had so little to do with the Darwinian ethic of the 1980s. For the dwellers in the global village, circa 1995, the new frontier was the electronic territory known as cyberspace. Instead of being the defining element of the country, land had become a mere backdrop to other events. Yet another once-reliable touchstone of the past had vanished.

Chief **Dan George** of the Salish Nation was born in British Columbia and dedicated his life to explaining and sharing his culture with others. A writer and poet, he also acted in movies and television shows. In his poem "My Heart Soars," he described his emotional attachment to the natural environment.

The beauty of the trees,
the softness of the air,
the fragrance of the grass,
speaks to me.

The summit of the mountain,
the thunder of the sky,
the rhythm of the sea,
speaks to me.

The faintness of the stars,
the freshness of the morning,
the dew drop on the flower,
speaks to me.

The strength of fire,
the taste of salmon,
the trail of the sun,
And the life that never goes away,
They speak to me.

And my heart soars.

Explorations

1. What theme links the words of all three writers? Does this theme reflect your ideas about Canadian identity?
2. Do you agree with Peter C. Newman that a touchstone of the Canadian past has vanished? Is this a positive or negative development? Has anything been gained in return? Explain your responses.

1. Choose an institution or government program and work with a small group to develop criteria and a checklist for judging its effectiveness in promoting Canadian identity.

   Your criteria should reflect the aspects of the program that your group finds important and measurable and should help you determine whether the program or institution is achieving its objectives. You may consider, for example, its costs (Is the program cost-effective?) or its profile (Do people know enough about the program? Is the program well-known for the wrong reasons?). Your checklist may look like the one shown on this page.

   Compare your checklist and criteria with those of two other groups. As a result of this discussion, you may wish to revise your checklist.

2. Use the checklist and criteria you developed in response to Question 1 to rate another program or initiative designed to promote an identity. The initiative may be a government program; a commercial advertising campaign; a project to boost school spirit; an event in your community; a celebrity's web site; a new CD release; or a person, place, or event of your choosing. Be prepared to present — and defend — your ratings to the class.

   Write a statement commenting on how effectively the criteria you developed for Question 1 fit your assignment for Question 2. What conclusion(s) can you draw as a result?

3. Work with a partner to create an outline for a documentary film. Your outline can take the form of either a computer software presentation or a storyboard.

   The documentary will focus on your community's identity — on what makes it different or special, in a positive or a not-so-positive way. The goal of the film is to portray your community as you see it — the identity you want to present to the larger world.

   In your outline, explore some of the community's history and stories from its early days. Why is your community located where it is? What tales give the community its richness and character? What people should you interview? What places should you mention? What events should you recount?

   As you work on your outline, keep a journal describing your thoughts on how you chose the images and created the storyline. This journal will form the basis for your documentary's voice-over narration.

Program ______________________		
Criteria	Information	Evaluation (1 = not very effective; 5 = highly effective)

4. Develop a survey to find out what people think about a specific aspect of Canadian identity. You may decide, for example, to choose sports. Your survey might ask respondents to rank a list of sports in order of their importance to Canadian identity, then respond to questions and statements like the following:
   - Do you believe that one of these sports symbolizes Canada? Which one?
   - Do you believe that other Canadians would agree with you?
   - On a scale of 1 to 10 (1 = not important; 10 = extremely important), assess the importance of promoting the sport nationally.

   Your survey should include at least five questions. Ask 10 people — classmates, family members, friends, your teachers — to complete the survey.

   Prepare a summary paragraph explaining how and why you chose your focus and describing your findings. If your survey lends itself to mathematical analysis, you may wish to present the data as a graph that shows the responses as percentages.

5. Write a brief essay in response to this question: Should the government be in the business of promoting Canada to Canadians and the world at large?

   Your opening paragraph should clearly state your position and indicate why you hold it. The middle paragraphs should clearly explain why and how you reached your informed position. To illustrate your arguments, use examples from *Exploring Nationalism*, from other material you have read, and from research you conduct. The final paragraph should sum up your ideas and restate your position.

6. In his 1964 book *Rivers of Canada*, Canadian author Hugh MacLennan wrote:

   > The rivers of Canada are still there, and their appearance and character have changed little or not at all in the last century and a half. It is only our use of them that has altered. Now we fly over them, build dams on them, fish in them for sport, use them for municipal water supplies, and some of them we have poisoned with sewage and industrial effluents . . . But the rivers are as worth knowing as they ever were, though none of us will know them as the voyageurs did.

   Québec City–born Joseph Légaré was one of the first Canadian artists to start developing a distinctively Canadian style. He painted *Les Cascades de la Rivière Saint-Charles à la Jeune-Lorette* in about 1832. His depiction of the falls on the St. Charles River illustrates his love for the rivers of Canada.

   Either paraphrase MacLennan's thoughts or paint a word picture describing Légaré's painting. In your statement, explain how Canada's rivers function as a symbol of national identity.

Think about Your Challenge

By now, you have recorded a number of entries in the journal you are keeping in response to the related-issue question: To what extent should individuals and groups in Canada embrace a national identity?

It is time to start thinking about how this question relates to the course-issue question: To what extent should we embrace nationalism? If you embrace a national identity, are you automatically embracing nationalism? Can you embrace one without embracing the other? Discuss this conundrum with a partner, a small group, or the class.

In your journal, record what you think will be your starting position in the four-corners debate that is the related-issue challenge. Record notes on at least two arguments you will make to support your position.

CHAPTER 15 The Quest for Canadian Unity

Figure 15-1 Figure 15-1 Canada is a vast country whose diverse peoples often feel strong loyalties to their own groups or nations. The illustrations on this page show some symbols that are important to people of various cultures and nations. Canada's diversity means that promoting a sense of national unity is often a challenge.

CHAPTER ISSUE

To what extent should Canadian national unity be promoted?

SUPPOSE YOU AND YOUR CLOSE friends want to do something together but cannot decide what. You have suggested a movie, but your closest friend wants everyone to go to her place to watch some videos on YouTube. Another friend must finish an essay, and two others want to go to the mall to check out a new store. Your goal was to do something together, but your conflicting needs and wants are getting in the way.

The Canadian government often faces similar dilemmas. The government must manage the country and hold it together while accommodating change and attending to citizens' diverse wants and needs. Even when people share similar goals, they may not agree on the most effective way of achieving them.

Examine the collage of images on the previous page, then respond to the following questions:

- What is the main message of the collage? Explain your response.
- Why do you think the Canadian maple leaf flag and the Peace Tower were selected as the underlying image of the collage?
- Is the red maple leaf a strong enough symbol to unite Canada?
- What would you suggest as a symbol that all Canadians can identify with and rally round?
- If you could choose one more symbol to add to this collage, what would it be? What message would it send?
- What is one way to unite a country while promoting diversity?

KEY TERMS

patriated

equalization payments

inherent right

ecozone

economic nationalists

LOOKING AHEAD

In this chapter, you will explore the extent to which Canadian national unity should be promoted as you respond to the following questions:

- What is national unity?
- How does the nature of Canada affect national unity?
- How has the changing face of Canada affected national unity?

My Journal on Nationalism

You are nearing the end of your exploration of nationalism. Review your journal entries and your thinking about nationalism. Note major changes in your thinking, and why you think these changes occurred. Date your ideas and keep them in your journal, notebook, portfolio, learning log, or computer file so that you can return to them as you complete this course.

What is national unity?

Canada is a civic experiment, an attempt to bind diverse peoples together in equality of citizenship. Our citizenship expresses the ideal that all Canadians should stand equal before the trials of life and that all Canadians should benefit equally from life's opportunities.

— Michael Ignatieff, historian and politician, in Maclean's, *2006*

People's feelings of unity — oneness — with others is often closely tied to their sense of identity. Those who feel a common bond with others or who have a strong sense of belonging to a particular group or collective often feel as if they are part of a unified whole.

Think about your school. To what degree do students root for school teams, proudly display school colours, or participate in school-wide projects? Are these things important in promoting a sense of unity in your school community?

When people feel a sense of national unity, they identify with others who belong to the same nation. For many Canadians, this sense of national identity and unity means sharing basic beliefs and values, such as respect for diversity.

But sharing fundamental values and beliefs does not mean that all Canadians speak with a single voice. In a 1971 speech to the Ukrainian Canadian Congress, Prime Minister Pierre Trudeau expressed this idea when he said: "There is no such thing as a model or ideal Canadian. What could be more absurd than the concept of an 'all Canadian' boy or girl? A society which emphasizes uniformity is one which creates intolerance and hate."

CheckBack

You read about the relationship between nationalism and identity, as well as the concept of civic nation, in Chapter 1.

Many thinkers suggest that a society in which diverse people agree to live together according to rules based on specific values and beliefs is a civic nation — and Canada is often cited as an example. In civic nations, promoting national unity often involves trying to achieve consensus.

Forces Affecting National Unity

Is national unity a goal worth pursuing?

The intensity of the sense of national unity felt by a country's citizens waxes and wanes — and this waxing and waning can be influenced by external and internal events. War, for example, is an external force that sometimes inspires people to feel an increased sense of patriotism and unity with other citizens. Sociologists have described this as the rally-round-the-flag effect. Political scientist John Kirton and researcher Jenilee Guebert identified this effect in the aftermath of the 9/11 attacks on the United States. Canadians, too, had died in these attacks, and many Canadians shared Americans' sense of outrage over the murders.

"[Twenty-four] innocent civilian Canadians had been deliberately murdered on 9/11, in the twin towers of a city that was far closer to Canada than Pearl Harbor had been in 1941, when the last bolt-out-of-the-blue attack had hit the soil of its American neighbour," Kirton and Guebert wrote. "The conditions were thus especially ripe for the familiar 'rally effect' to spring to life in Canada, as in so many other countries when they first go to war."

Internal pressures can also affect national unity. In Canada, for example, nations within the Canadian confederation, as well as people seeking to assert their nationhood, have exerted pressure to promote their own loyalties and sense of national identity. This sometimes creates the sense that Canadian unity is fragile.

In 2006, for example, a poll commissioned by *Western Standard* magazine and COMPAS, a public opinion research company, found that nearly one-third of Alberta respondents supported the idea that Canada's Western provinces should explore the idea of forming their own country.

And in 2006, a poll conducted by the Innovative Research Group found that many Canadians believe that Québec will have separated by the year 2020. The results of this poll are shown in Figure 15-2.

Examine the polling results in Figure 15-2. When you consider these figures, along with Albertans' feelings about Western separation, do you agree that Canadians' sense of unity is fragile — or would you argue that these results show Canada's strength? Explain your response.

Figure 15-2 Predictions on Québec Separation

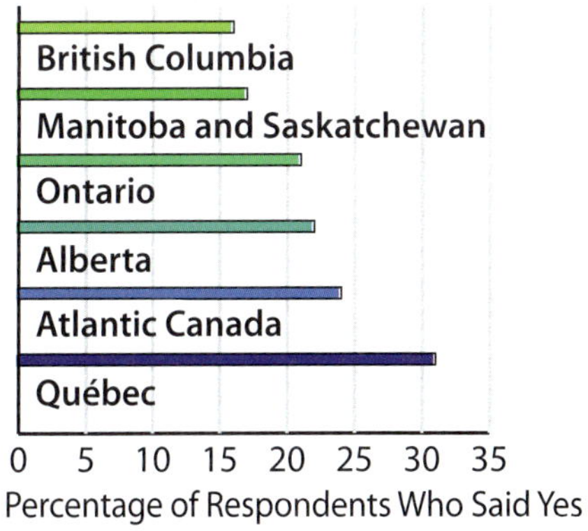

British Columbia
Manitoba and Saskatchewan
Ontario
Alberta
Atlantic Canada
Québec

0 5 10 15 20 25 30 35
Percentage of Respondents Who Said Yes

MAKING A DIFFERENCE

Maude Barlow
Passionately Dedicated to Canadian Unity

MAKING A DIFFERENCE

Figure 15-3 The author of several books, Maude Barlow has been honoured with a two-year Lannan Cultural Freedom Fellowship for 2005 and 2006, as well as the 2005 Right Livelihood Award, also known as the "Alternative Nobel."

While Maude Barlow was growing up in Ottawa, she watched her father campaign for prison reform. A World War II veteran, her father had witnessed wartime atrocities — and had returned home determined to help change the world. His sense of social justice inspired his daughter to follow in his path.

In the 1970s, Barlow ran for the Liberal nomination in an Ottawa riding but was defeated.

This defeat marked a turning point for Barlow. Rather than continue to try to join the system, she decided to work outside it. She wanted the freedom to work with or criticize the government in power and to promote causes she believed in.

In 1985, Barlow and a group of concerned citizens founded the Council of Canadians, a national advocacy group that includes about 100 000 members. The COC's mission was to draw Canadians' attention to what the group perceived as the shortcomings of the Canada–United States Free Trade Agreement, but the group has expanded its activities to include protecting "Canadian independence by promoting progressive policies on fair trade, clean water, energy security, public health care, and other issues of social and economic concern to Canadians."

Barlow's work in these areas sparked an interest in what is happening around the world, and she is a director of the International Forum on Globalization. This think tank examines the benefits and drawbacks of globalization. She also co-founded the Blue Planet Project, a group dedicated to working internationally on water-related issues.

Barlow believes that international laws and bilateral trade agreements must benefit all citizens, not just businesses and political groups. She has criticized what she views as Canada's cozy relationship with the United States, arguing that the country should pursue a more independent course in trade and international affairs.

In all her activities, Barlow acts from a passionate belief in the importance of Canadian sovereignty and the power of individuals to bring about positive change. "I go crazy when I see certain things and I have to find out why they happen," she told CBC's *Life and Times*. "And I have to tell people . . . I have to do something so that other people will also take action."

Explorations

1. Maude Barlow has built a career by working outside Canada's political system. Does the work of people like Barlow help or hurt Canadian unity? Explain your response.
2. Conduct online research to find out more about the Council of Canadians. Would you consider joining this group? Explain the reasons for your judgment.

Canadian National Unity

Canada is the world's second-largest political territory. Its relatively small population is spread over six time zones and regions with vastly different physical characteristics. This means that Canadians may express many different points of view and perspectives on issues. Issues of concern to people in rural Alberta, for example, may not be important to residents of Vancouver or St. John's — and vice versa. In addition, Canadians speak many different languages and come from varied cultural and ethnic backgrounds. Their personal histories and experiences may be very different. This often makes it difficult for anyone to promote national unity by expressing a single vision of Canada.

Within Canada, individuals, groups, and collectives often feel contending loyalties and sometimes have trouble striking a balance between their loyalties. Increasing globalization has further complicated concepts of national identity and unity. Someone who was born in England to Indian and Pakistani parents, then spent her formative years in South Africa before moving to Alberta to pursue a rewarding career, may have a particular view of Canadian unity. This view may be very different from that of an immigrant with a different background and history and from that of someone born and raised in Alberta.

Figure 15-4 These three photographs — of the Newfoundland village of Bonavista, the prairie near Medicine Hat, and the city of Whitehorse — show images of Canada. How do they reflect the difficulty of achieving national unity? How do they reflect the many identities of Canadians?

Reflect and Respond

On a chart like the one shown, list five groups, collectives, or nations to which you feel loyalty. On a scale of 1 to 5, rank each according to its importance to you (1 = not very important; 5 = very important).

List the key goal(s) of each group, collective, or nation. Place an asterisk beside goals that may conflict and be prepared to explain the source of the potential conflict.

Briefly explain whether and how each loyalty promotes or discourages Canadian unity.

My Loyalties

Group, Collective, or Nation	Ranking of Importance	Key Goal(s)	Effect on Canadian Unity

How does the nature of Canada affect national unity?

Maintaining unity in any group is often a challenge. Think about your own experiences with clubs and groups of various kinds. In any group or organization, conflicting forces create divisions between people. People within these groups may have different interests and goals or conflicting personalities and ways of doing things. As people mature and explore new opportunities, old loyalties may be strained and ways must be found to maintain them.

Nations and countries experience similar challenges — and these are magnified in a country as large and diverse as Canada.

With a partner, list four or five of the most difficult aspects of maintaining unity within a group. Jot a note explaining each choice. Place an asterisk beside the aspects that would also make it difficult to maintain national unity.

Canada — a triumph of politics over geography and economics — and sometimes it seems over common sense.

— *Leonard Louis Levinson, in* Webster's Unafraid Dictionary, *1967*

The Geography of Canada

Canada is huge. It stretches from the Arctic and Pacific seacoasts, over tundra and mountains, across prairies, past the Canadian Shield and the St. Lawrence lowlands, to the Appalachian region and the Atlantic coast. The geography of these regions is very different.

As a result, peoples in various regions have differing needs that are often dictated by the geography of the area where they live. These differences often create inter-regional tensions. Explosive economic growth in Alberta, for example, has generated prosperity for many Albertans, but this has affected the Maritimes by persuading skilled workers to move west. And the effects of climate change cause difficulties in the North, but they may benefit farmers in southern Saskatchewan.

Though faster and more efficient transportation and electronic communication have brought Canada's regions closer together and TV often acts as a homogenizing force, major differences continue to stand in the way of national unity.

Examine the cross-section of Canada shown in Figure 15-5. How does this profile illustrate the influence of geography — both positive and negative — on Canadian unity?

Canada by the Numbers

Area: 9 976 634 square kilometres

World rank in size: 2nd

Distance north to south: 4 634 kilometres (Cape Columbia on Ellesmere Island to Middle Island in Lake Erie)

Distance east to west: 5 514 kilometres

Length of coastline: 241 402 kilometres

Number of times France would fit into Canada: 18

Number of times Britain would fit into Canada: 40

Length of border with United States (including Alaska): 8 890 kilometres

Number of climate zones: 11

Number of ecozones: 16

Number of time zones: 6

Figure 15-5 Cross-Section of Landform Regions along Canada–U.S. Border

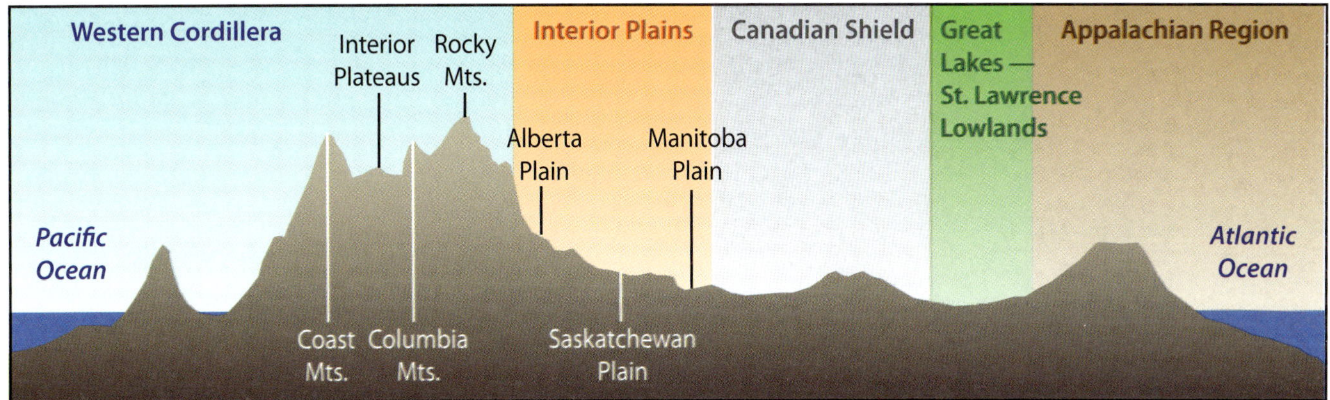

Western Alienation

Regional needs often dictate how the federal government allocates money for federally funded programs. In addition, the federal government's objectives do not always match the goals of people in specific regions. These realities can foster the belief that Confederation has not benefited all Canadians equally. In Alberta and other Western provinces, this belief has sometimes led to feelings of alienation.

These feelings came to a head in 1982, when the battle over the National Energy Program was in full swing. Gordon Kesler, a member of the newly formed Western Canada Concept party, won a provincial by-election in the Alberta riding of Olds-Didsbury. Kesler lost the seat in a general election held a few months later, but his win revealed the depth of some Westerners' feelings of alienation.

You read about the National Energy Program in Chapter 4.

These feelings had led to the founding of Kesler's party, which advocated creating a new country in the territory west of the Ontario–Manitoba border. Although this party continues to exist, its extreme policies, such as ending immigration, have kept it on the margins. Since then, other parties supporting Western separation have also sprung up.

It is imperative to take the initiative to build firewalls around Alberta, to limit the extent to which an aggressive and hostile federal government can encroach upon legitimate provincial jurisdiction.

— Stephen Harper and others, in a letter to Alberta premier Ralph Klein, 2001

The most successful movement to emerge from Alberta led to the founding of the Reform Party — now part of the Conservative Party of Canada — in 1986. With deep roots in rural Alberta, this party was formed under the leadership of Preston Manning. In the 1993 federal election, the party's slogan was "The West wants in." Rather than separation, Reformers wanted a greater voice and more control over decision making in Ottawa.

Read the words of Stephen Harper and others in "Voices" on this page. Once Harper became prime minister, he said that his views on building a firewall had changed. What might have caused him to change his position?

Alienation in Other Regions

Newfoundland and Labrador officially joined Confederation on March 31, 1949 — but the province was nearly equally divided on the wisdom of this decision. In a referendum on the question, 78 323 voted yes and 71 334 voted no. Confederation supporters won by a mere 6989 votes.

At various times, other provinces, such as Québec and Nova Scotia, have expressed deep dissatisfaction with the federal government. In 2007, for example, tensions between the federal government and Newfoundland and Labrador flared up over oil royalties.

Since entering Confederation, Newfoundland and Labrador has been one of the most economically disadvantaged provinces in the country. But offshore oil and gas developments promised to change this. When the province believed that Ottawa was going back on its promise to allow Newfoundland and Labrador to keep most of the royalties from provincial gas and oil industries, Premier Danny Williams was so angry that he ordered the Canadian flag on all provincial buildings lowered to half-mast — a symbolic gesture that declared the death of peaceful arrangements between the two levels of government.

Does this dispute over oil royalties suggest that Alberta has more in common with Newfoundland and Labrador than many people think? Explain your response.

The Federal System and National Unity

In the 1860s, just as Britain's remaining North American colonies were moving toward Confederation, a devastating civil war divided the United States. When this country had been created nearly a century earlier, its Constitution had placed a great deal of power in the hands of the states rather than the central government. The Civil War was, in part, the result of the continuing power struggle caused by this situation.

Having witnessed the destruction caused by the American Civil War, John A. Macdonald and his colleagues were determined not to duplicate the conditions that might lead to a similar conflict in Canada. As a result, they agreed that federal and provincial or territorial governments would share some powers, but the British North America Act placed most key decision-making powers in the hands of the national government. It also specified that powers not mentioned in the act belonged to Ottawa.

But this situation changed in 1982, when the Constitution was **patriated** — transferred from the control of the British government to that of the Canadian government. The 1982 Constitution gave the provinces new rights and powers, such as exclusive control over resource development, which had been a key demand put forward by Alberta.

We have conferred on [the federal government], not only specifically and in detail, all the powers which are incident to sovereignty, but we have expressly declared that all subjects of general interest not distinctly and exclusively conferred upon the local governments and local legislators [the provinces], shall be conferred upon the General Government and Legislature.

— John A. Macdonald, in a speech to the Legislative Assembly, 1865

Equality and Fairness in a Federal System

When citizens believe they are treated fairly and equally, they are more likely to feel a sense of belonging to their country or nation. In a country as large and diverse as Canada, ensuring that all citizens feel as if they are treated fairly and equally presents many challenges — and can affect people's sense of national unity.

Equalization Payments

One of the federal government's jobs is to ensure that public services are available more or less equally to all Canadians, no matter where they live. Since 1957, the Canadian government has used a system of **equalization payments** to achieve this goal.

Under its equalization program, the federal government collects taxes from individuals and businesses across the country. These revenues are then pooled and redistributed to less prosperous provinces, which decide how to spend the money.

The formula for calculating equalization payments is complex and causes frequent squabbles. Prosperous provinces often claim that their taxpayers contribute too much, while less prosperous provinces say that they do not receive enough. Ontario is the only province that has never received equalization payments.

The statistics in Figure 15-6 show the distribution of equalization payments in 2008–2009. Which provinces received no equalization payments? Explain how equalization payments might help or hurt the cause of national unity.

Figure 15-6 Distribution of Equalization Payments, 2008–2009

Province	Payment Received ($ Millions)
Newfoundland and Labrador	$158
Prince Edward Island	$322
Nova Scotia	$1465
New Brunswick	$1584
Manitoba	$2063
Québec	$8028
Total	$13 620

Source: Department of Finance Canada

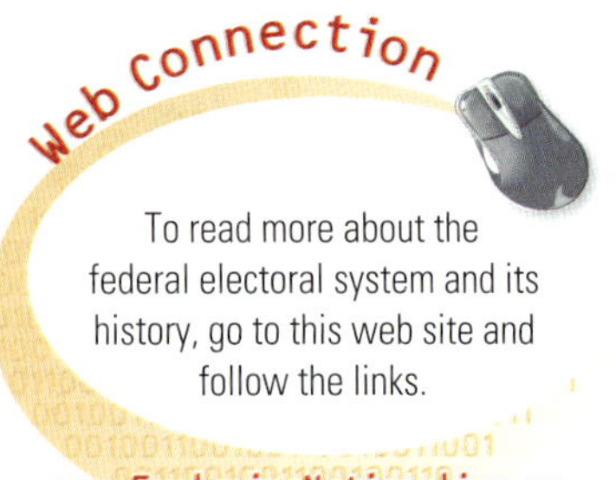

To read more about the federal electoral system and its history, go to this web site and follow the links.

www.ExploringNationalism.ca

Political Representation

Canada's population is spread unevenly across the country, and ensuring that all Canadians and all regions are represented fairly in Parliament presents another challenge to national unity. The geographic, cultural, political, and demographic diversity of Canada's provinces and territories has always demanded a method of representation that is more complex than the concept of one person, one vote. If representation by population were the sole basis for electing members of Parliament, Ontario and Québec — where about two-thirds of Canadians live — would easily dominate. The voices of people in smaller provinces, such as Prince Edward Island, and sparsely populated territories would rarely be heard.

As a result, at Confederation, a compromise was built into the formula for allocating federal seats, and this formula has changed several times over the years to reflect the changing nature of the country. In 1915, for example, Prince Edward Island was guaranteed a minimum of four seats in Parliament.

Examine the data in Figure 15-8 and explain how these figures might be interpreted as positive and negative forces for national unity.

Figure 15-7 Like a growing number of Canadians, Jeff Chiba Stearns is of mixed-race ancestry. His mother's heritage is Japanese, and his father's is European. Some people of mixed ancestry have begun calling themselves Hapa, a Hawaiian word meaning "mixed-race." "Using the word 'Hapa' allowed us to escape from other people's definitions," Stearns told CBC Radio's *The Current*. What do you think this comment meant?

Official Multiculturalism

In the second half of the 20th century, the federal government changed Canada's immigration policies and began to welcome immigrants from many different parts of the world. This changed the character of the country, and in 1971, Canada became the first country to adopt multiculturalism as official government policy. This policy, which was affirmed in the Charter of Rights and Freedoms and enhanced in the Canadian Multiculturalism Act of 1988, is reflected in the country's pluralistic society.

The changes to immigration policies meant that, by 2006, an estimated one in every six Canadians was a member of a visible minority group. This statistic presents unique challenges and opportunities. All governments must find a way of striking a balance between honouring Canada's traditions and fostering a vision of the future that Canadians of all backgrounds and heritages can unite behind and promote.

With a partner, identify three ways that multiculturalism can contribute to national unity. Share your thoughts with the class.

Figure 15-8 Federal Representation in Selected Provinces

Number of MPs	Population (2008 Estimate)	People Represented by Each MP*
Alberta – 28	3.5 million	125 000
British Columbia – 36	4.5 million	125 000
Ontario – 106	13 million	123 000
Prince Edward Island – 4	140 000	35 000

* Rounded to nearest thousand.

Québec Sovereignty and National Unity

One of the greatest challenges to Canadian national unity has been the rise of Québec nationalism — and one of the greatest challenges to Québec nationalism has been the power of the federal government to convince Québécois that Canada is their country. The tension created by these challenges shapes the "Québec issue."

Within Québec, an element of the Francophone population has always sought greater self-determination. In the 1962 provincial election, the Québec Liberal Party voiced this impulse when it adopted the slogan "Maîtres chez nous" — "Masters in our own house." This slogan helped define the Quiet Revolution that occurred during the 1960s and involved a push for greater provincial power and reduced federal control over Québec's affairs.

CheckBack

You read about the Quiet Revolution in Chapters 8 and 13.

Canada will be a strong country when Canadians of all provinces feel at home in all parts of the country, and when they feel that all Canada belongs to them. We wish nothing more, but we will accept nothing less. Masters in our own house we must be, but our house is the whole of Canada.

— Pierre Trudeau, to the Liberal leadership convention, 1968

It is simply difficult — extremely difficult — for someone to become bilingual in a country that is not. And make no mistake. Canada is not a bilingual country. In fact, it is less bilingual today than it has ever been . . . So there you have it. As a religion, bilingualism is the god that failed. It has led to no fairness, produced no unity and cost Canadian taxpayers untold millions.

— Stephen Harper, in the Calgary Sun, *2001*

Challenges for Francophones across Canada

The debate over affirming and promoting the French language and culture often focused on Québec and ignored the struggle of Francophones outside that province. But many provinces, including New Brunswick, Ontario, Manitoba, and Alberta, have significant French-speaking communities, though these communities form only a small part of the total population.

Since 1867, each of these provinces has ruled against the French language at some point. In 1892, for example, the government of the North-West Territories, which included the present-day provinces of Alberta and Saskatchewan, passed a law that only English would be used in the legislature. In 1871, the teaching of French in New Brunswick schools was outlawed. And as recently as 1930, Saskatchewan barred the teaching of French, even outside school hours.

The Royal Commission on Bilingualism and Biculturalism

In response to growing agitation in Québec, the federal government established the Royal Commission on Bilingualism and Biculturalism in 1963. The mission of the B and B Commission was to explore and recommend ways of maintaining national unity while enhancing the dual nature of Canada.

After holding hearings across the country, the commissioners found that

- most Francophones were shut out of positions of economic and decision-making power
- Francophone minorities outside Québec lacked the educational opportunities available to the anglophone minority in Québec
- the language barrier prevented many Francophones from finding government jobs and gaining access to federal services

Figure 15-9 In Ottawa, stop signs and other official signs are printed in both English and French. What message does this send to Canadians? How important is this message? Explain your response.

Does focusing on issues involving English and French take much-needed attention away from issues involving other nations in Canada?

From the beginning, the B and B Commission aroused suspicions in parts of the country. Some people in the West viewed it as a government ploy to force them to learn French. Many in Québec believed that it was designed to divert attention from the province's social and economic problems. And some said that its focus was too narrow because it did not acknowledge the existence of other minority groups, such as Aboriginal peoples.

In response to these criticisms, the federal government acted quickly to implement many of the commissioners' recommendations. Federal funds, for example, were offered to the provinces to encourage them to increase the availability of French-language education, and New Brunswick declared itself officially bilingual. In addition, a federal department of multiculturalism was created — and this led to changes in Canada's policies toward all minorities.

Web Connection

To learn more about the Royal Commission on Bilingualism and Biculturalism, go to this web site and follow the links.

www.ExploringNationalism.ca

Official Bilingualism

One of the most important outcomes of the B and B Commission was the Official Languages Act, which was passed by the Liberal government of Prime Minster Pierre Trudeau in 1969. Its goals were to

- affirm the equal status of English and French
- preserve and develop official language communities in Canada
- guarantee that federal services are available in both official languages
- ensure that anglophones and Francophones have equal opportunities to participate in Parliament and federal institutions, such as the courts and the federal civil service

Figure 15-10 English–French Bilingualism in Canada, 1996–2006

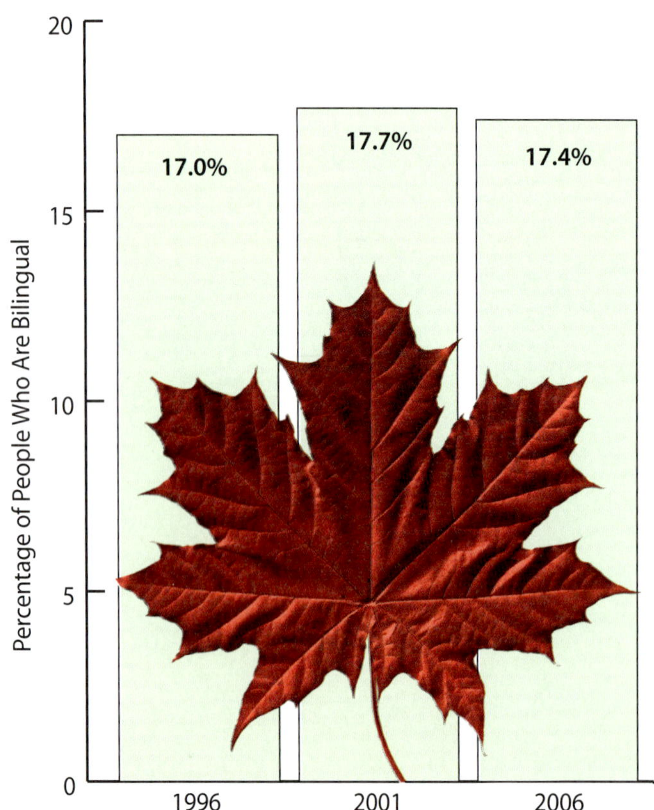

Since then, this act has been changed and strengthened. Official languages were, for example, enshrined in the Constitution Act of 1982. But as immigration began to increase in the last half of the 20th century, the number of languages spoken in Canada also increased. The 2006 census, for example, revealed that 20 per cent of the population speaks at least one non-official language at home. For the government, this has intensified the challenge of promoting official bilingualism.

Examine the data in Figure 15-10. If you were asked to judge the success of official bilingualism on the basis of this graph alone, what conclusion might you reach? What other evidence would you want to examine before making a judgment on this issue? Then read the words of Pierre Trudeau and Stephen Harper in "Voices" on page 351, and consider whether the B and B Commission has had a positive or negative effect on national unity. Show your assessment on a continuum with "negative effect" at one end and "positive effect" at the other. Be prepared to defend your judgment.

THE VIEW FROM HERE

THE VIEW FROM HERE
THE VIEW FROM HERE
THE VIEW FROM HERE

Although Canada patriated its Constitution in 1982, Québec did not sign the agreement. Since then, debate has continued over the wisdom of trying to bring Québec into the Constitution. Two attempts to include Québec have failed, and in a 1995 referendum, Québécois narrowly supported remaining in Canada.

Angus Reid was the founder and chief executive officer of the Angus Reid Group, a polling company. In 1991, Reid argued that it was time to amend the Constitution to maintain Canadian unity.

> I believe we have a unique window of opportunity in Canada to undertake the significant changes that are required to keep this country together. Against the backdrop of emotion, frustration and anger that fill the TV screen each night is an increasing resolve among Canadians to make the changes that are necessary to unite the country.
>
> The way to the future really only has two paths. One involves the development of a new constitution for all of Canada and the other involves the complete separation of Québec and the possible breakup of the rest of Canada.

In his 2007 autobiography, *My Years as Prime Minister*, former prime minister **Jean Chrétien** explained why he decided against another attempt to change the Constitution to accommodate Québec.

> Given that constitutional amendments were just about the last thing I wanted to spend my time on anyway, I immediately abandoned [constitutional change] as dead in the water. I decided instead to ask Justice Minister Allan Rock to prepare a bill on the veto and a resolution on distinct society for presentation as soon as possible to the House of Commons. These two initiatives may not have been entrenched in the Constitution, I argued, but they made it almost impossible politically for any future government to stand up in Parliament and say it was going to ignore the provinces' veto or Quebec's distinct status.

Ovide Mercredi, former national chief of the Assembly of First Nations, has lobbied vigorously for Aboriginal peoples to be involved in any negotiations on constitutional change. He made the following remarks in a 1999 online series of commentaries sponsored by the Dominion Institute.

> How can national unity be achieved without the participation of the aboriginal people who possess a pre-existing title to the very soil that Canada now claims as its territory?
>
> We can all agree that the participation of aboriginal peoples in the restructuring of Canada might bring more challenges in the quest for unity. But to exclude aboriginal peoples, because too many challenges increase the likelihood of failure, is dishonest and cowardly. To favour political expediency rather than to face reality mocks Canada's deeply cherished principles of democracy and fairness for all.

Explorations

1 In your own words, explain the position of each speaker.

2. Québec did not sign the 1982 Constitution. Both the Meech Lake Accord (1987–1990) and the Charlottetown Accord (1992) — attempts to include Québec — failed. Considering your understanding of Canada as a nation, Canada's national interest, and the diversity of Canadian society, what do you think might be the most effective way of achieving unity on this issue?

Confirming or Revising Your View or Opinion

FOCUS ON SKILLS

When economist John Kenneth Galbraith was accused of changing his position, he is reported to have said: "When the facts change, I change my mind. What do you do, sir?"

How would you respond to Galbraith's question? What do you do when new ideas, information, and arguments suggest that a position you have taken should be modified or even reversed? Does changing your mind show flexibility and a willingness to adapt, or does it indicate indecisiveness? Does the importance of the decision play a role in your willingness to revise your position? Would you, for example, be more reluctant to reconsider your point of view on national unity than your opinion about a movie?

As you have progressed through this course, you have been keeping a journal to track your understandings of nationalism. You will use this journal as you work through the following steps, which will help you understand whether, how, and when your understanding(s) of nationalism changed — and to reflect on this process.

Steps to Confirming or Revising Your View or Opinion

Step 1: Review your original and current positions

Return to the journal entry you recorded at the beginning of Chapter 1. It asked you to note your understanding(s) of nationalism. Then reread the journal entry you made at the beginning of this chapter.

Compare the two by using a chart like the one shown on the following page to record point-form notes setting out your original understanding(s) and your current understanding(s). In the third column, identify whether and how your original view has changed or been confirmed.

Step 2: Reflect on the process

You have been encouraged to reflect on your understanding(s) of nationalism at the beginning of each chapter. Skim and scan your journal to trace the evolution of your thinking. Identify points at which your thinking changed and what influenced these changes — or identify evidence that confirmed your original view.

In the fourth column of the chart, enter notes about these influences. You might, for example, include notes such as "new information" (specify what this was), "the opinion of . . ." (specify a knowledgeable person), "a shift in my values" (specify the shift), and "logical arguments" (specify the argument).

In the final column, assess the weight of each influence on a scale of 1 to 5 (1 = somewhat persuasive; 5 = very persuasive) in persuading you to confirm or change your view or opinion.

Step 3: Restate your position

After reviewing your understandings and considering the factors that influenced your thoughts, write a journal entry that sums up the evolution of your thinking. Share this with a partner.

FOCUS ON SKILLS FOCUS ON SKILLS CUS ON SKILLS FOCUS ON SKILLS FOCUS ON SKILLS

Step 4: Practise the skill

Consider this situation. Before World War II, Prime Minister William Lyon Mackenzie King had promised Canadians that conscripts would be required to perform home service only. They would not be sent overseas to join the fighting. But by 1942, Canadian casualties were mounting and voluntary recruitments were not high enough to replace soldiers who had been killed or wounded. Many people, particularly anglophones, were urging King to reverse his position on conscription — but many Francophones were urging him to keep his promise.

King changed his mind and decided to send conscripts overseas, but he wanted to be sure that Canadians supported him. So he called a plebiscite — a special vote on a particular issue — asking Canadians to release him from his promise. On April 7, 1942, about three weeks before the plebiscite was held, he addressed the country and pleaded with people to understand that the situation had changed.

This is what King said.

> The restriction upon the power of the government was necessary at the outset to preserve national unity . . . You know full well that a foremost aim of my public life has been the preservation of the unity of Canada. I must say that under the changed conditions of today, and with Canada's record in war being what it has been over the past two and a half years, I see no reason why the removal of the restriction should weaken unity. I believe firmly that its removal will help overcome a source of irritation and disunity within our own country.

Work with your partner to put yourselves in King's place. To record the evolution of King's thinking and gain an understanding of the process he went through, create a chart similar to the one you completed earlier. Conduct research to find out about conditions when the war began, how things had changed by 1942, and the eventual outcome of King's change of mind.

With your partner, write a short statement that clearly presents the reasoning King used to justify his shift in thinking.

My Understandings of Nationalism

My Original Understanding(s)	My Current Understanding(s)	What Has Changed	What Influenced the Change	Ranking of Persuasiveness of Change 1 = somewhat persuasive; 5 = very persuasive

Summing Up

You are nearing the end of this course, and you will soon be developing your response to the key course-issue question: To what extent should we embrace nationalism? A systematic approach to analyzing the evolution of your thinking, such as the one suggested in this skill focus, can help you clarify your thoughts.

Aboriginal Self-Determination and National Unity

Are sovereignty and self-determination the same thing?

Our governments were recognized in treaties between nations. They were recognized in royal proclamations, constitutions and domestic laws. They were recognized by all the European and Canadian governments that have come and gone over the intervening 500 years. Internationally, the United Nations Declaration on [the] Rights of Indigenous Peoples also recognizes the right to self-government.

— Wilton Littlechild, Ermineskin Cree and Alberta regional chief, Assembly of First Nations, to the Standing Senate Committee on Aboriginal Peoples, 2007

Self-determination involves making your own decisions about what is in your best interests. Doing this often demands a degree of self-government. Aboriginal peoples believe that self-determination is an **inherent right** — a right that exists because they occupied their land and governed themselves for thousands of years before the arrival of Europeans in North America. Striking a balance that satisfies the needs and aspirations of Aboriginal peoples and all Canadians presents unique challenges and opportunities.

Although Canada's 1982 Constitution recognized "Aboriginal rights," it did not define whether these rights included self-determination and self-government. Since then, some politicians, such as Paul Martin, who was prime minister from 2003 to early 2006, have agreed that Aboriginal rights include self-determination, but this was never made official. More recently, the Canadian government has explicitly refused to support the United Nations Declaration on the Rights of Indigenous Peoples, which affirms Aboriginal peoples' right to self-determination — and to self-government in "matters relating to their internal and local affairs."

Over the years, however, the Nisga'a of British Columbia and the Inuit of Nunavut and Nunavik have negotiated agreements that give them a form of self-determination and self-government. When negotiating agreements like these, the federal government's position has been that federal, provincial, territorial, and Aboriginal laws must work in harmony.

Figure 15-11 In 2007, Chief Mike Retasket of the Bonaparte Indian Band in British Columbia addressed a rally on the National Day of Action organized by the Assembly of First Nations. On the stage, organizers included a large Canadian flag. What message might the decision to include this flag have sent?

But Stephen Cornell, a sociologist who is co-director of the Harvard Project on American Indian Economic Development, believes that Aboriginal self-government involves more than local control. "If it were just that, then simply mimicking existing Western modes of governance and policy-making might be good enough," Cornell has written. "These Western modes have their place, but they rest on values and techniques that are often in conflict with values and practices of First Nations. Importantly, self-government is an opportunity to express the unique values and aspirations of the nation itself — to build 'Aboriginality' into law-making and governance and to have shared meaning for the community to which these laws apply."

In your own words, sum up Cornell's position. Compare his statement with the words of Wilton Littlechild in "Voices." On the basis of these statements, what prediction(s) would you make about the future of Canadian national unity and Aboriginal self-determination?

Aboriginal Land Claims and National Unity

In recent decades, some progress has been made toward settling the hundreds of outstanding Aboriginal land claims. The James Bay and Northern Québec Agreement of 1975 started this process, and since then, other claims, such as that of the Nisga'a of British Columbia, have been settled.

Still, for Aboriginal peoples, the pace of settlements has been frustratingly slow. Though specific land claims are not necessarily tied to self-government, the two issues often affect each other. The issue is complicated by the fact that non-Aboriginal Canadians are nearly evenly divided over whether Aboriginal peoples are entitled to self-government. A 2001 National Post–COMPAS poll, for example, found that 49 per cent of respondents believed that Aboriginal peoples are entitled to self-government.

The federal government divides Aboriginal land claims into two broad categories:

- Comprehensive land claims involve traditional lands, such as large parts of British Columbia, where Aboriginal rights and title were never dealt with in treaties or other agreements.
- Specific land claims involve areas where disputes have arisen because treaties have been violated or land has been removed without the consent of First Nations.

The Nisga'a Agreement

When the governments of Canada, British Columbia, and the Nisga'a Nation reached a comprehensive land-claim agreement in 1998, it was hailed as a milestone. Like many B.C. First Nations, the Nisga'a had never signed a treaty, and the agreement confirmed their right to control 2000 square kilometres of traditional territory in the Nass River area. The agreement also affirmed the Nisga'a Nation's right to self-government — to make their own decisions on issues relating to culture, language, public works, land use, health, child welfare, education, and mineral resources.

Through this agreement, the Nisga'a gained a degree of self-determination, but they also recognized the authority of the Canadian government. In what ways might this agreement affect Canadian national unity? Nisga'a national unity?

Figure 15-12 Nisga'a Territory

Nunavut

On April 1, 1999, the political map of Canada changed when a new territory — Nunavut — was created. The government of Nunavut, where 85 per cent of people are Inuit, has gradually taken over responsibility for its own administration. To enhance unity in the territory, *quajimajatuqangit* — traditional Inuit knowledge — plays an important role in developing government policies. Healing circles, for example, are a traditional practice that has become part of the justice system.

Reflect and Respond

Many factors pose challenges to Canadian unity. In response, the federal government has used strategies such as equalization payments to promote national unity. With a partner, list at least five strategies the federal government could put into practice to reinforce Canadian national unity.

Compare your list with that of another pair. With the other pair, develop a combined list of the five strategies you believe are the most practical. State the main reason your group chose each strategy.

GEOREALITY

Nunavik and the New North

GEOREALITY GEOREALITY GEOREALITY

In March 2008, a historic agreement came into force. It created a form of self-government in the northern third of Québec. This area, called the Regional Government of Nunavik, covers nearly 507 000 square kilometres north of the 55th parallel and is home to about 10 000 people, mostly Inuit. The region will remain part of Québec but elect its own government to administer local services such as education and health care.

Announcing the agreement, Prime Minister Stephen Harper said: "It took 30 years to bring it to fruition, but this historic milestone hails the dawn of a new era for the Nunavimmiut [residents of Nunavik]. By resolving the issues of land and resource ownership and usage rights, the agreement creates a stable environment for investment and development that will mean new jobs and business opportunities for people throughout this region."

A Different Model

Unlike other land-claim settlements, the Nunavik agreement sets up a form of parliamentary government similar to the system that already exists in Ottawa and the provinces. The settlement is also unlike other agreements because it is not based on ethnicity. It involves everyone who lives in Nunavik.

The Nunavik regional government will receive funding from both Ottawa and Québec City, but revenues will also come from royalties associated with resource development. This revenue source creates exceptional opportunities for the people of Nunavik, but it also means that they assume responsibility for sustaining the region's fragile environment.

Figure 15-13 Nunavik Region of Québec

Life in the Arctic Ecozones

An **ecozone** is an area of the earth's surface that represents a large ecological zone and has characteristic landforms and climate. The northern tip of Nunavik lies in the Northern Arctic Ecozone, and a small part of the eastern section is in the Arctic Cordillera Ecozone. But most of the region is in the Southern Arctic Ecozone or the Taiga Shield Ecozone. The entire region is dry year-round, with cool summers and very cold winters.

This Arctic environment has always presented special challenges and opportunities to the Inuit, who developed effective strategies for living in the harsh conditions. Traditionally, these strategies relied on hunting and fishing.

Both the Northern and Southern Arctic Ecozones have sensitive ecosystems and limited biodiversity — a small number of different plants and animals. The Northern Arctic Ecozone, for example, includes fewer than 20 species of mammals.

In any sensitive ecosystem, a small change in climate can result in dramatic changes in the area's biodiversity. Though the Inuit way of life has contributed little to the warming that is taking place in the Arctic, climate change threatens the traditional Inuit lifestyle.

The agreement that created Nunavik is unlikely to help the Inuit control climate change, but it may provide the tools they need to adapt to the changes. "Climate change is caused by southerners," Johnny Watt, a former mayor of Kuujjuaq, the region's capital, told *The Walrus* magazine. "It's their fault. All we can do is speak out — that's our main contribution. Otherwise there's no choice but to get used to it."

Changing Traditions

Climate change, population growth, easier and faster transportation and communications, and urbanization have combined to change the traditional Inuit way of life — and these changes have sometimes strained their sense of identity and unity. Before contact with Europeans, for example, Inuit created carvings from the teeth and bones of the animals they had killed. Because the Inuit migrated with the seasons, these carvings often decorated items that had practical uses. They were generally small so that they could be transported easily.

But when people from the South discovered these objects and wanted to buy them, Inuit carvers started making them for sale as works of art. In response to demand, Inuit sculptors began creating carvings that were bigger and heavier. They sometimes also used non-traditional materials.

Figure 15-14 Inuit artists George Pitseolak and Jimmy Pitaloosie created these sculptures for sale.

Bear and Cubs	*Seal*
George Pitseolak	Jimmy Pitaloosie
27.5 cm x 45 cm	33 cm x 21.6 cm
Serpentine	Serpentine
Dorset Fine Arts	Dorset Fine Arts

New Challenges and Opportunities

The growing integration of the economies of northern and southern Canada has created many new challenges and opportunities for the Inuit. In 2003, for example, mining companies spent about $18 million on exploration in the region. A year later, this figure had risen to $30 million — and it continues to grow. This growth has given young Inuit opportunities to train for jobs such as prospecting, mining, operating and maintaining heavy equipment, carpentry, and administration.

Tourism is also a growing industry. Nunavik attracts hunters and fishers from the South, but ecotourism is also becoming important and has created many jobs.

The introduction of jobs that replace traditional lifestyles makes school-based education essential for Inuit youth. But many young people in the North believe they are receiving mixed messages. On the one hand, they are advised to stay in school to improve their chances of landing a job; on the other, they are encouraged to honour and maintain Inuit values and their traditional way of life. These conflicting expectations can create a sense of alienation that makes it difficult for Inuit to maintain a sense of identity.

Figure 15-15 The community of Akulivik, pictured in winter and summer, lies north of the tree line on the eastern shore of Hudson Bay in the Northern Arctic Ecozone. What challenges might this environment present?

Explorations

1. When Stephen Harper announced the Nunavik agreement, he referred to "Nunavimmiut." Explain the significance of Harper's choice of this word rather than the word "Inuit."
2. The agreement that created Nunavik may set a precedent that will lead to similar agreements in other parts of Canada. If it does become a precedent, how would it benefit Aboriginal peoples and Canadian unity? Explain your response.
3. The agreements relating to the Nisga'a, Nunavut, and Nunavik provide three different models for achieving self-determination and self-government. Which do you believe is most effective from the perspective of

   a) Canada

   b) the people of the territory involved

   Explain the reasons for your judgment.

How has the changing face of Canada affected national unity?

Increasing globalization, ease and speed of travel, new technologies, and world events mean that today's Canada is very different from the country that was created in 1867. Many of these changes have reinforced Canadian unity, but people also worry that some of the changes are dividing Canadians and will have a negative effect on national unity.

VOICES

But a nation does not remain a nation only because it has roots in the past. Memory is never enough to guarantee that a nation can articulate itself in the present. There must be a thrust of intention into the future.

— *George Grant, philosopher, in* Lament for a Nation: The Defeat of Canadian Nationalism, *1970*

Emerging Trends

In the 21st century, various trends — both in Canada and internationally — are likely to affect Canadian unity. The effects of some of these trends, such as changing immigration patterns and economic globalization, are already evident.

Immigration

Peoples from around the world have found a home in this country, and the Canadian population increasingly reflects all the nations of the world. The 2006 census provided a snapshot of this "new" Canada.

- Canada's foreign-born population grew four times faster than its Canadian-born population.
- 58.3 per cent of recent immigrants came from Asia, including the Middle East, compared with 12 per cent in 1971.
- More than 20 per cent of Canadians speak neither English nor French as their first language. This was up from 18 per cent in 2001.
- After English and French, Chinese languages are the most commonly spoken.
- The percentage of bilingual (English–French) anglophones outside Québec dropped to 13 per cent from 16.3 per cent in 1996.
- More than 60 per cent of immigrants choose to live in Canada's three largest cities: Montréal, Toronto, and Vancouver. Only 5 per cent settle in rural areas.
- More than 80 per cent of Canadians live in urban centres.

In *The Polite Revolution: Perfecting the Canadian Dream*, John Ibbitson reflected Canadians' overwhelmingly positive view of immigration when he wrote: "Immigrants are vital to Canada, not simply because they help to infill sectors of the economy where there are labour shortages. They are vital because they represent the very future of the economy itself."

In 2006, the British-based polling company Ipsos MORI surveyed people in eight countries, including Canada, to assess attitudes toward immigration. The results are shown in Figure 15-16. Examine these results. How do Canadians' attitudes toward immigrants differ from the attitudes of people in other countries? What might account for this? How might this affect Canadian unity and identity?

Figure 15-16 Immigrant Influence

Overall, would you say immigrants are having a good or bad influence on the way things are going in [country]?

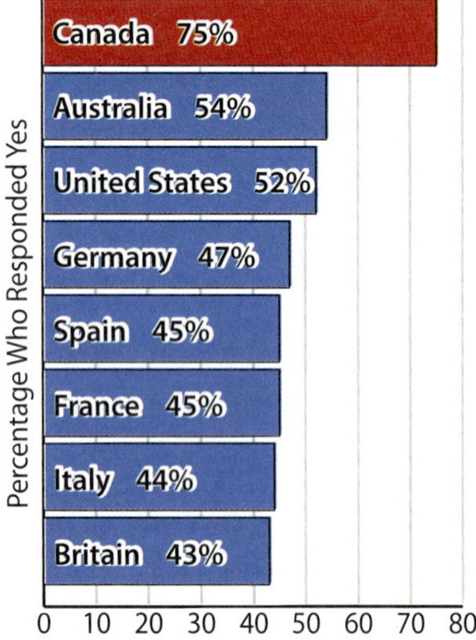

Source: Ipsos MORI International Social Trends Monitor, May 2006

Urbanization

At the beginning of the 20th century, only about 37 per cent of Canada's population lived in urban areas. By 2006, a little more than a hundred years later, this had changed dramatically, as more than 80 per cent of people were urbanites.

In addition, nearly all the 1.8 million immigrants who arrived in Canada during the 1990s settled in urban areas. And about 73 per cent of the new arrivals settled in three large cities: Toronto, Montréal, and Vancouver.

This trend means that Canada's large urban centres are growing rapidly — and this has created challenges. As people move to cities, they require housing and services such as transit and education. In some cities, keeping up with the demand for homes and services has strained resources. It also means that some cities, such as Toronto, have become so large that they are demanding a greater say in decisions that used to be made exclusively by the federal and provincial governments.

Examine the bar graph in Figure 15-17. If this trend continues, how do you think Canada is likely to be affected? Is increasing urbanization likely to unite or divide Canadians? Explain your responses.

Figure 15-17 Proportion of Canada's Population Living in Cities, 1901–2006

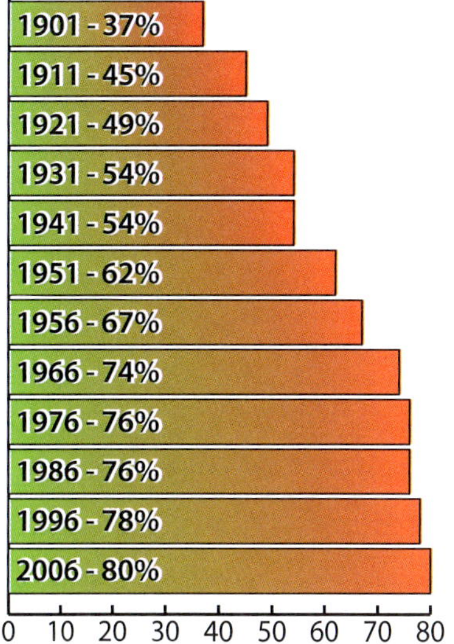

Source: Statistics Canada, Censuses of Population, 1901 to 2006

Aboriginal Peoples

The 2006 census revealed that the number of Aboriginal peoples in Canada topped one million for the first time since the federal government started keeping records. This means that Aboriginal peoples are the fastest-growing segment of the country's population. In the 10-year period between 1996 and 2006, the Aboriginal population increased by 45 per cent, while the non-Aboriginal population increased by only 8 per cent. Aboriginal peoples now make up 3.8 per cent of people in Canada, compared with 2.8 per cent in 1996.

Of the three Aboriginal groups, the greatest growth occurred among those who identified themselves as Métis. Their number increased by 91 per cent. Statistics Canada attributed some of this growth to a higher-than-average birth rate but also pointed out that more people are now willing to identify themselves as Métis.

The 2006 census also revealed that, for the first time, a majority of Aboriginal people — 54 per cent — live in urban areas. Winnipeg is home to the largest concentration of Aboriginal people, who make up 10 per cent of the city's total population. Edmonton is second, and Calgary is fourth.

Examine the information in Figure 15-18 and think about the effects of these trends. How are the growing population and increasing urbanization of Aboriginal peoples likely to affect their sense of national identity? Are these trends likely to strengthen or weaken Canadian unity? Explain your responses.

FYI

In April 2008, the Canadian Senate voted to conduct some of its debates and committee meetings in Inuktitut. The Senate will hire interpreters to translate debates and proceedings that are of particular interest to Nunavut. Though Inuktitut will be the only non-official language allowed at first, the Senate planned to assess the success of this initiative with a view to extending this decision to include other Aboriginal languages. In 2008, seven of Canada's senators had Aboriginal roots.

Figure 15-18 Growth in Aboriginal Populations, 1996–2006

	1996	2006	Percentage Increase
People who identified themselves as Aboriginal	799 010	1 172 790	+46.8%
First Nations	529 040	698 025	+29%
Métis	204 115	389 785	+91%
Inuit	40 220	50 485	+26%

Source: Statistics Canada, 1996 and 2006 Census

Economic Globalization

This is an important moment for Canada. Well below the radar screen and unknown to most Canadians, a serious commitment has now been undertaken by their government to create a North American fortress with a common economic, security, resource, regulatory, and foreign policy framework.

— Maude Barlow, chair of the Council of Canadians, in Too Close for Comfort: Canada's Future in Fortress North America, *2005*

As the world becomes increasing globalized, multilateral trade agreements have become increasingly common. For **economic nationalists** — people who believe that a country's businesses and industries should be protected — these trade agreements are often a double-edged sword. On the one hand, increased trade may generate economic prosperity; on the other, the requirements of these agreements can threaten a country's ability to make decisions that are in the best interests of its citizens.

In the late 1980s, the Conservative government of Brian Mulroney negotiated a free-trade agreement with the United States. In 1994, this agreement was extended to include Mexico. Since then, Canada has also extended free trade to Chile and Colombia, and is negotiating free-trade agreements with China and Europe.

These agreements remain controversial, and Canadians are often divided about their benefits. Ontario, for example, relied on manufacturing jobs to fuel its economy, but free trade meant that manufacturers were free to move their plants to countries where workers' wages and benefits were lower and business rules, such as environmental standards, were less strict. When these plants moved, Ontario workers lost their jobs.

In May 2008, the Conservative government of Prime Minister Stephen Harper made history when it stepped in to prevent the sale of Canadian space technology to an American defence contractor. MacDonald, Dettwiler and Associates — MDA — had planned to sell its space technology division to American-owned Alliant Techsystems for $1.3 billion.

Blocking the sale marked the first time a government had used the Investment Canada Act, passed in 1985, to prevent the sale of a Canadian company to foreign owners. When Canadian businesses valued at more than a specified amount — $295 million in 2008 — are slated to be sold to non-Canadians, this act requires a review of the sale to ensure that it will benefit Canada. Since this act was introduced, Investment Canada has approved nearly 1600 foreign takeovers of Canadian companies.

MDA's space technology division includes the Canadarm; Dextre, a two-armed robot used on the International Space Station; and the Radarsat-2 satellite, which records environmental images and data. Much of the work on these technologies was completed in partnership with the Canadian Space Agency, which funded their development.

Figure 15-19 Dextre, the robot developed by MacDonald, Dettwiler and Associates in partnership with the Canadian Space Agency, cost $200 million and was installed on the International Space Station in March 2008. Dextre can lift nearly 600 kilograms, is capable of sensing the movements of the objects it manipulates, and is expected to perform important tasks in maintaining the station.

News of the proposed sale created an uproar. Marc Garneau, the first Canadian to fly in space and a former head of the Canadian Space Agency, argued that the deal enabled MDA to profit from technology that had been developed at the expense of Canadian taxpayers. But Garneau added that more than economic benefit was involved. "It's an issue that touches on our sovereignty as a country," he said. "The fact is that [Radarsat-2] is very promising technology, which we can sell to the rest of the world . . . we should hold on to it."

The government's action renewed debate over whether — and when — foreign companies should be allowed to take over Canadian businesses. Dominic D'Alessandro, president and chief executive of Canadian-owned Manulife Financial, reflected the views of many Canadians when he told shareholders, "I sometimes worry that we may all wake up one day and find that as a nation, we have lost control of our affairs."

To find out more about the Canadian Space Agency, Canadarm, Dextre and Radarsat-2, go to this web site and follow the links.

www.ExploringNationalism.ca

Taking Turns

Is economic globalization likely to increase — or decrease — Canadians' sense of national unity?

The students responding to this question are Jean, a Francophone student who lives in Calgary; Rick, who was born in the United States but moved to Fort McMurray with his family when he was 10; and Jane, who lives in Calgary and is descended from black Loyalists who fled to Nova Scotia after the American Revolution.

Jean

A sense of national unity? You're joking, right? I don't think Canadians feel a sense of national unity in the first place, so I don't see how economic globalization would affect it one way or the other. I'm not saying this lack of national unity is a bad thing. It means that peoples are free to pursue their own interests — and can be citizens of the world rather than just focusing on Canada.

Rick

My family is pretty involved in the oil business here in Fort McMurray, and you just have to look around to see the benefits of economic globalization. Companies and people from all over the place are at work here — and lots of that is because of economic globalization. Things are booming, and a booming economy helps Canada in lots of ways — like when people are making a good living at good jobs, they feel good about themselves and about their country. They have choices, and they feel more unified. So yes, I would say that economic globalization will increase Canadian unity.

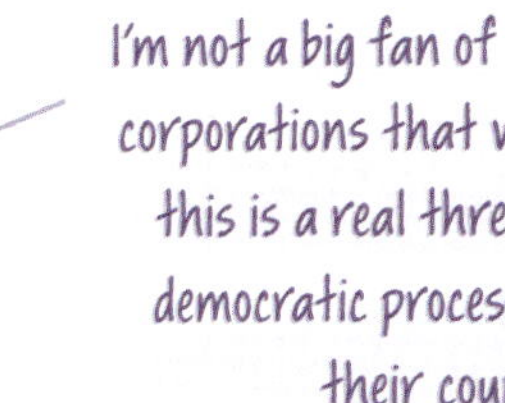

Jane

I'm not a big fan of economic globalization. I think it creates really huge multinational corporations that will one day be more powerful than governments. And I think that this is a real threat to unity and to lots of other things we take for granted, like democratic processes. Will people one day have to decide between a corporation and their country or nation? That isn't going to help national unity.

Your Turn

How would you respond to the question Jean, Rick, and Jane are answering? How important is a sense of national unity? Explain the reasons for your response.

1. In this chapter, you have explored responses to this issue question: To what extent should Canadian national unity be promoted?

   Indira Gandhi, who served several terms as prime minister of India, once said that Canada is proof that "diversity not only enriches but can be a strength." Canada is a large and diverse country that is often viewed as a model because of its ability to unite various peoples. At the same time, many Canadians worry that various forces are pushing the country apart.

   Write a short essay that explains why someone like Indira Gandhi would view Canada as a model. In your essay, comment on whether you believe that this view is accurate and support your judgment with valid evidence.

2. In the 1990s, some people feared that the nation-state of Canada might not continue to exist as it had for more than a hundred years. The Meech Lake and Charlottetown constitutional accords had failed to win public support, and the 1995 Québec referendum on sovereignty was a "near-death experience" for Canadian federalists. In those years, former prime minister Joe Clark wrote a book titled *A Nation Too Good to Lose: Renewing the Purpose of Canada.* In this book, Clark suggested some strategies that ordinary citizens could follow to keep Canada united. The following are some of his suggestions:

Keeping Canada Together

1. Start discussions about Canada. Find some background material that can be circulated and serve as the basis of discussion. Invite a teacher or a community leader or any wise person to serve as moderator.
2. Invite speakers, either to informal neighbourhood discussions or meetings of existing organizations. The point would be to generate more understanding of the Canada you don't yet know.
3. Speak up for your country. Remind your friends and family about the United Nations' judgment that Canada is one of the best places in the world to live in.

   a) On a scale of 1 to 5 (1 = least effective; 5 = most effective], rank Clark's suggestions. In point form, note one justification for each of your judgments.
   b) Which recommendation(s) could be followed in your community or school?
   c) Add two recommendations to the list. Explain the purpose of each suggestion you added.

3. Former prime minister Jean Chrétien and former Québec premier Bernard Landry hold conflicting views on the future of Québec and Canada.

Jean Chrétien, in his memoir, *My Years as Prime Minister*, 2007

> Will independence bring a better form of government for the people of Quebec? In my opinion, no. Will it bring more peace? No. More prosperity? No. More justice? No. Even a better chance of survival of the French language and culture in North America? Again, no.

Bernard Landry, in an interview, 2006

> My sovereignist convictions . . . [are] based on our interests in the future and even with Canadian interests. It's not in the interests of Canada to be constantly fighting Québec's aspirations and trying to centralize when Québec wants to decentralize. Some things must be centralized in Canada, in the interests of New Brunswick and Prince Edward Island, but it's against Québec's interests. So if Québec is out of Canada, Canada will be in a better position to live its destiny and organize itself along values that are good for Canada. At the moment, it's an internal fight: on Constitution, on budget, about everything! It's not good for Canada and not good for Québec.

These remarks were made at different times and in different places. But suppose Chrétien and Landry were participating in a moderated public debate on Canada's and Québec's future. During this kind of debate, the moderator asks questions submitted by news organizations or the public.

   a) Prepare a powerful question to submit during the debate between Chrétien and Landry. Your question might, for example, ask the two to predict the consequences of their vision on Canada, Québec, and the international community.
   b) Take the position of either Chrétien or Landry and list points you would use to respond to the question you have prepared.
   c) Then take the other debater's position and refute your own points.
   d) Of the two positions you have explored, which do you believe is stronger? Explain why.

4. With two other students, brainstorm to create a web of ideas about Canada and the world. Use the following questions to guide your brainstorming session:
   - What does it mean to be a citizen of Canada?
   - What might it mean to be a citizen of the world and of Canada simultaneously?
   - What conflicts may arise between nationalism or national identity and internationalism?
   - What virtues, values, and qualities could Canadians export to the rest of the world?

   Join another group and compare ideas.

   As a class, discuss the various ideas that have been generated.

5. In this chapter, you explored responses to the following inquiry questions:
   - What is national unity?
   - How does the nature of Canada affect national unity?
   - How has the changing face of Canada affected national unity?

   a) Choose one of these questions and develop two or three powerful questions that connect the question you chose to your own experiences. If you chose the final question, for example, you might ask a question like this: How has my life been affected by the changing face of Canada?
   b) Join three or four other students and compare the powerful questions you developed. Discuss whether common themes emerge from this comparison.
   c) On the basis of this discussion, develop three powerful questions that could be asked about any of the inquiry questions explored in this chapter.

Think about Your Challenge

By now, you have had many opportunities to revisit your responses to the related-issue question: To what extent should individuals and groups in Canada embrace a national identity?

Think about these responses and review the notes you made earlier on your starting position for the four-corners debate on the course-issue question: To what extent should we embrace nationalism? Decide whether you wish to stick to this position or revise your opinion.

Once you have firmed up your position, begin recording notes on arguments that will help you persuade others to support this position. Ask a classmate, friend, family member, or another person to listen as you express your arguments and ask this person for feedback. On the basis of this feedback, revise your arguments to make them more effective. In addition, start preparing counter-arguments.

CHAPTER 16 Visions of National Identity

Figure 16-1 Jane Ash Poitras, a Cree-Chipewyan artist from Alberta, created this mural — *Those Who Share Together, Stay Together*. The artwork, which measures 3.7 metres by 4.3 metres, presents her view of Canada's history and her hopes for the country's future.

JANE ASH POITRAS — IN HER OWN WORDS

On her inspiration for the mural

> I thought about Canada being part of Mother Earth, so the middle part shows Canada's landscape, with Québec as the heart of the country and the Maritimes as the birthplace. I also put Native elements on the provincial shields at the top and used a Québec Montagnais design for the Québec section.

On finding ways to live together peaceably and with justice

> We have to be colour blind. For example, I use a lot of colour in my art, but I don't see myself as a Native artist. I see myself as a person. I want to know about other people's heritage, culture, and beliefs, but it doesn't matter what colour they are.

CHAPTER ISSUE

To what extent should I embrace a national identity?

In 1997, Jane Ash Poitras created *Those Who Share Together, Stay Together* for the art gallery of the Confederation Centre of the Arts in Charlottetown, Prince Edward Island. The mural is part of an exhibit titled Telling Stories: Narratives of Nationhood. The gallery explains the purpose of the exhibit this way: "Looking at artistic voices represented across Canada, it becomes clear that our identity — who and what we are as individuals, communities, regions, and a country — can never be told in just one story. The cultures, histories, and relationships among Canadian communities have always been changing."

Poitras captured this spirit when she said, "The world embraces a diversity of cultures with parallels that spring from Mother Earth. Spirituality is in every thread of every nation and it falls to us to find the needle to weave the thread into a testimony of beauty."

Examine the mural on the previous page. As you examine the image, respond to these questions:

- Which world events and histories do you think influenced Jane Ash Poitras as she created this mural?
- Which national identities are represented in the mural?
- How would you interpret Poitras's vision of Canada's future?
- What is the significance of the title of the mural?
- If you were creating a mural showing your vision of Canada's past and future, what images would you include? What title might you give it?
- How would these images represent your vision of your national identity?

KEY TERMS

cosmopolitan

asymmetrical federalism

Looking Ahead

In this chapter, you will respond to the following questions as you explore the extent to which you should embrace a national identity:

- What are some possible visions of nation?
- What are some possible visions of Canada?
- What is your vision of national identity?

My Journal on Nationalism

As you progressed through the previous 15 chapters, you recorded your thoughts on your understandings of nationalism. As you work through this final chapter, try to reach a personal conclusion about the key course issue: To what extent should we embrace nationalism?

What are some possible visions of nation?

CheckBack

You explored understandings of nation and the concept of a civic nation in Chapter 1.

FYI

Manga cartoons originated in Japan, and this style of graphic novel has been exported to the world. But some manga books published recently in Japan have begun to encourage hatred of other cultures. One of these books, titled *The 100 Crimes of China*, described China as the most evil country in the world. Another was titled *Why We Should Hate South Korea*. Though many Japanese people are disturbed by publications like these, the books have found an audience.

National identity is, in general, a collective or group identity that is based on linguistic, ethnic, cultural, religious, geographic, spiritual, or political understandings of nation — and it often combines two or more of these understandings.

In some cases, people combine aspects of these understandings of nation with a concept of themselves as a civic nation. Japan, for example, can be viewed as a civic nation because it has a parliamentary government and a legal system based in civil law. But most Japanese people also share common racial, cultural, and linguistic characteristics. Ethnic Japanese people, for example, make up 98.5 per cent of the population, and 84.5 per cent of Japanese people practise both Shintoism and Buddhism. The language of the country is Japanese.

The national identity of the Japanese people evolved over centuries. For hundreds of years, Japanese people identified mainly with the feudal lords who ruled their region of the country. But in the 19th century, when Japan united against threats of invasion by Britain, Russia, and France, a sense of national identity began to emerge. In the years leading up to World War II, the country's education system emphasized patriotism and respect for traditional culture and beliefs.

This educational emphasis changed after the war, but it began to re-emerge in the early 21st century. In 2006, for example, Japan passed a law requiring teachers to evaluate students' level of patriotism, as well as their interest in learning about their country's traditional culture.

If one measure of your school performance were based on your patriotism and interest in learning about Canadian culture, how would this affect your sense of national identity? Explain your response.

When nations do not have a nation-state of their own, national identity may be based on religious and linguistic, as well as cultural and ethnic, understandings. Tibet, for example, has been Buddhist since the eighth century. The people speak the Tibetan language and follow ancient cultural traditions.

But by 2008, an influx of ethnic Chinese people had changed the makeup of Tibet's population. The Government of Tibet in Exile estimated that ethnic Chinese people outnumbered Tibetans. Many Tibetans want to be free of Chinese control and determine for themselves how their nation will evolve — but this goal may become more difficult to achieve as the region's population continues to change.

Figure 16-2 A pilgrim lights a butter lamp at Tibet's holiest Buddhist shrine, the 1300-year-old Jokhang Temple in Lhasa. Some pilgrims spend years travelling on foot over great distances to reach this shrine. How do actions like this reflect Tibetan national identity?

Pluralism and Diversity

By 2008, more people than ever were migrating around the world. The citizens of many nation-states — including Canada and the United States — come from diverse backgrounds and cultures and bring unique experiences, points of view, and perspectives to their new homes.

A pluralistic society reflects an inclusive approach that is characterized by respect for diversity. It assumes that diversity is beneficial and that cultural, religious, spiritual, ideological, gender, linguistic, environmental, and philosophical groups should enjoy autonomy.

Tolerance, openness and understanding towards other peoples' cultures, social structures, values and faiths are now essential to the very survival of an interdependent world. Pluralism is no longer simply an asset or a prerequisite for progress and development, it is vital to our existence.

— Prince Karīm al-Hussainī, the Aga Khan, philanthropist and spiritual leader of Shia Ismaili Muslims, 2005

Evolving Identities

As people move from one country to another, they also move through a complex web of diverse cultures. This experience can change their individual identity and their sense of national identity. A Canadian doctor, for example, who was born in India of Indian and Pakistani parents may have close ties to family and friends in both countries, and she may maintain these ties through frequent telephone calls and e-mail messages. She may have studied tropical medicine in London, England, and, while there, she may have established ties with other students from many areas of the world. She may be volunteering with Doctors Without Borders in Sudan and share strong humanitarian values with other volunteers who are also working with this organization.

People with a background like this are sometimes described as **cosmopolitan**. They borrow, adopt, and adapt values from many cultures, and they often believe in civic nationalism as a way of upholding pluralistic and cosmopolitan values. According to Canadian historian and politician Michael Ignatieff, "a cosmopolitan, post-nationalist spirit will always depend, in the end, on the capacity of nation-states to provide security and civility for their citizens."

When law and order disintegrated in countries like Rwanda and the former Yugoslavia, pluralism and diversity could not survive. Amartya Sen, who is quoted in "Voices," argues that freedom of choice is the key to balancing conflicting national identities. People can choose different identities if they have the freedom to do this, but if they have no freedom, they may be locked into a particular national identity.

If a person can have only one identity, then the choice between the national and global becomes an "all or nothing" contest. But to see the problem in these stark and exclusive terms reflects a profound misunderstanding of the nature of human identity, in particular its inescapable plurality.

— Amartya Sen, Nobel Prize winner in economics, in Identity and Violence, *2006*

Do you believe that you have only one primary national identity? Or do you feel free to explore and embrace various national identities?

Figure 16-3 In 2006, Prime Minister Stephen Harper and the Aga Khan met to discuss establishing the Global Centre for Pluralism in Ottawa. The centre will help people from around the world study and foster the values, practices, and policies of pluralistic societies. Why might this field of study be important?

Figure 16-4 British Residents Who Were Born Abroad* — Selected Statistics, 2001

Country of Birth	Number	Percentage of New Immigrants Employed
Australia	106 404	91
Bangladesh	154 201	43
Canada	70 145	83
Germany	262 276	69
India	466 416	66
Italy	107 002	73
Iraq	32 251	38
Kenya	129 356	61
Pakistan	320 767	44
South Africa	140 201	82
United States	155 030	68

* "Born abroad" means born outside England, Scotland, and Wales.
Source: BBC News, Institute for Public Policy Research

Pluralism in Britain

Building a pluralistic nation-state that genuinely respects and appreciates diversity can be challenging. In Britain, for example, the 2001 census showed that more than 7.5 per cent of the population was born outside the country. Many of the newcomers had arrived in search of economic prosperity and an improved quality of life.

Examine the data in Figure 16-4. What trends do you note? Return to survey results shown in Figure 15-16 (p. 360). Based on these figures, what conclusions, if any, can you draw? Explain your responses.

Some British people believe that the country's immigration system doesn't work. They believe that the increased population strains public services. Others are afraid that immigrants are changing Britain's traditional national identity. They worry when they see immigrants living in ethnic, cultural, or religious enclaves and remaining separate from mainstream British culture.

Fears like these became more pronounced in July 2005, when four young men detonated bombs on three London subway cars and a bus, injuring about 700 people and killing themselves and 52 others. Three of the bombers were British citizens of Pakistani descent; the fourth arrived from Jamaica as a child.

After the bombings, Trevor Phillips of the British Commission for Racial Equality said that British society is becoming more divided by race and religion: "We are becoming more unequal by ethnicity . . . the aftermath of [the bombings] forces us to assess where we are. And here is where I think we are: we are sleepwalking our way to segregation. We are becoming strangers to each other, and we are leaving communities to be marooned outside the mainstream."

In January 2006, Gordon Brown, who later became prime minister, called on the British people to refocus on the common values that unite them. He said, "We have to be clearer now about how diverse cultures, which inevitably contain differences, can find the essential common purpose . . . without which no society can flourish." The British government began developing programs to promote British unity. One of the initiatives is a test requiring new citizens to show that they understand British history, customs, laws, and values.

Figure 16-5 Monty (Mudhsuden Singh) Panesar, the first Sikh to play for England's national cricket team, was born in England to parents who had immigrated from India. The game of cricket was exported to India — and other colonies of the British Empire — during colonial times. How might the achievements of athletes such as Panesar help increase acceptance of pluralism?

Reflect and Respond

Questions on the British citizenship test deal with issues such as the role of women in society, child labour, the education system, and religious tolerance. Many people support the test, but some have warned that it may become a way of excluding people from British citizenship.

Many of the test questions focus on traditional British values. One question asks, "What and when are the main Christian festivals? What other traditional days are celebrated?" Is it fair to require potential citizens to pass a test like this? Explain your response.

What are some possible visions of Canada?

Even before Confederation, Canada was visualized as a country that embraced a degree of pluralism, though the extent of pluralism was limited. Still, the concept of a pluralistic nation existed as an idea about what the country could become.

On July 1, 1867, politician Thomas D'Arcy McGee, one of the fathers of Confederation, captured this vision when he said: "So long as we respect in Canada the rights of minorities, told either by tongue or creed, we are safe. For so long it will be possible for us to be united. But when we cease to respect these rights, we will be in the full tide towards that madness which the ancients considered the gods sent to those whom they wished to destroy."

Why were there no mothers of Confederation?

Reread McGee's words. How do they reflect the makeup of Canada in 1867? How do they reflect ideas about Canada today?

A few decades later, this vision remained strong. Wilfrid Laurier, the first Francophone prime minister of Canada and who held this post from 1896 to 1911, compared his vision of the country to a cathedral. "It is the image of the nation I would like to see Canada become," Laurier said. "For here I want the marble to remain the marble; the granite to remain the granite; the oak to remain the oak, and out of these elements I would build a nation great among the nations of the world."

As the 20th century unfolded and Canada welcomed more and more immigrants from more and more regions of the world, the country changed — and early visions expanded to include much more diverse ideas about Canadian society.

Today, Canada is often described as a civic nation with a national identity based on shared values and beliefs expressed in law. The values shared by Canadians are enshrined in the Charter of Rights and Freedoms, which is part of the Constitution. The Constitution sets out the kind of country Canadians want to live in and the values and beliefs that bind them together and form an important aspect of Canadian national identity.

Figure 16-6 In 2006, members of visible minority groups made up 16.2 per cent of Canada's population. Toronto, where these commuters were waiting together for public transit, is the most ethnically diverse city in the country. Nearly 47 per cent of Toronto residents are members of visible minority groups.

Figure 16-7 Important Factors When Choosing a Spouse

When choosing a spouse, it is very important, important, not very important, or not at all important that both people share similar . . .

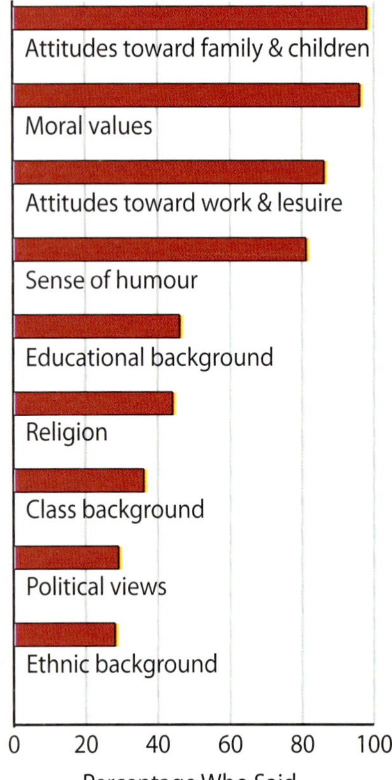

Source: *A New Canada: An Identity Shared by Diversity.* Centre for Research and Information on Canada, October 2003

A Pluralistic Country

When responding to public opinion polls, a high percentage of Canadians consistently identify the country's multicultural and pluralistic nature as something they support and take pride in. These policies are often described as the characteristics that distinguish Canada from other countries.

In a 2008 survey conducted by CTV and *The Globe and Mail*, 88 per cent of respondents said that they believed their community was welcoming to people from visible minority groups. But at the same time, 61 per cent of respondents believed that Canada was doing too much to accommodate the five million Canadians who belong to visible minority groups. This percentage rose to 72 per cent in Québec.

Though people often express concerns about the success of multiculturalism and pluralism, many commentators, such as Edward Greenspon, editor-in chief of *The Globe and Mail*, believe that these policies have promoted the development of a new form of nationalism in Canada. Greenspon wrote that this new nationalism enables people to be who they are while still belonging to a larger group.

For many Canadians, ethnic ties are no longer their first concern. This was illustrated by a 2003 survey that revealed respondents viewed ethnic background as the least important factor when choosing a spouse.

In addition, the 2006 census revealed that 41.4 per cent of Canadians identified their ethnic origins as mixed. This percentage has been rising steadily — in 1996, it stood at 35.8 per cent.

Examine the survey results in Figure 16-7. How would you have responded to each question? On the basis of Canadians' rating of the importance of ethnic background in choosing a spouse, as well as the percentage of Canadians from mixed ethnic backgrounds, what conclusions might you draw about how multiculturalism and pluralism are working? Explain your response.

Diversity in Alberta

According to the 2006 census, Alberta's population grew by 10.6 per cent between 2001 and 2006. During the same period, the population of Canada increased by 5.4 per cent. In 2001, about 6.9 per cent of immigrants to Canada chose to settle in Alberta. By 2006, this figure had risen to 9.3 per cent.

During the same five-year period, Alberta also attracted many migrants from other Canadian provinces and territories. Nearly 227 000 people migrated to Alberta from elsewhere in Canada, while more than 138 600 left the province. This meant that migration from within Canada increased Alberta's population by more than 88 000.

Figure 16-8 In March 2007, Malcolm Mayes, cartoonist for the *Edmonton Journal*, created this cartoon to show the difference between the number of people moving into and out of Alberta. How do you think this demographic change will affect Albertans' individual and group identities?

Many people believe that Alberta's increasing diversity will strengthen the province's communities. But others fear that diversity may result in divisions within or between communities. Some Albertans are also concerned about the portrayal of pluralism policies. Political scientist Yasmeen Abu-Laban believes that the federal government uses multiculturalism and pluralism to forge business and trade links with other countries, rather than "to increase equality at home."

But the manager and staff at Westend Suzuki, an Edmonton car dealership, have found that diversity provides direct economic benefits. In 2007, staff at the dealership spoke English and French, as well as 13 other languages including Punjabi, Italian, Cantonese, and Hindi.

To find out about Alberta government programs designed to promote human rights and diversity, go to this web site and follow the links.

www.ExploringNationalism.ca

MAKING A DIFFERENCE

Zarqa Nawaz
Breaking Down Stereotypes

MAKING A DIFFERENCE MAKING A DIFFERENCE MAKING A DIFFERENCE

When Zarqa Nawaz, creator of the groundbreaking hit CBC TV series *Little Mosque on the Prairie*, was developing the sitcom, one of her goals was to break down stereotypes and bring people together. "I see the show as a way to show young Canadians that it is possible to live in an ethnic community peacefully despite religious differences," she told an online discussion sponsored by *The Globe and Mail*.

Figure 16-9 Zarqa Nawaz's first venture into filmmaking was a short comedy called *BBQ Muslims*. It tells the story of two brothers who are suspected of terrorism after their barbecue explodes. Nawaz has also created a documentary titled *Me and the Mosque*.

The name of Nawaz's show is a play on the title *Little House on the Prairie*, a series of books about a family who settled in the 19th-century American West. The books were later adapted to create a popular TV show. *Little Mosque* is about a Muslim community in the fictional small Saskatchewan town of Mercy. Every episode features the humorous interactions of Muslims with one another — and with non-Muslim townspeople.

Born in England to Pakistani parents, Nawaz immigrated to Canada with her family, who settled in Toronto. She began wearing a hijab when she was in Grade 9 and has attended a mosque most of her life. For the past few years, she has lived in Saskatoon with her husband and children.

Writing a sitcom about a particular ethnic or religious group's experiences in a new environment presents challenges. Nawaz acknowledges that using humour to deal with these issues is risky, but she also believes it can be highly effective.

"I've always reacted to very difficult subjects with humour," she said. "The only way I can deal with these issues is to make them more universal and appeal to a greater number of people, to get across the ridiculousness of what is happening and the paranoia and worry that exists now in the community." Besides, she added, humour can encourage people to think about serious issues.

Nawaz said that her own experience growing up as a Muslim in Canada was positive — and she believes that Canadians have made pluralism work. "The fact that I can be comfortable with my Canadian identity along with my Islamic identity proves to me that it's working."

Explorations

1. Suppose you were asked to create a written pitch outlining an idea for a new TV show that, like *Little Mosque on the Prairie*, derives its appeal from portraying a potentially contentious issue of national identity in a humorous light. Identify the issue you will address (e.g., *Little Mosque* draws some of its humour from the misunderstandings that occur between Muslims and non-Muslims), the setting (e.g., *Little Mosque* places a Muslim community in the middle of the Canadian Prairies), and how it will meet its goal (e.g., *Little Mosque* presents ordinary people in situations that require them to work together). Your pitch should be no longer than one page and should include at least one scenario that could become the basis of an episode. Remember to use respectful language.

A Nation of Many Nations

As Canadians reassess their national identity in the 21st century, some view Canada as a country made up of many nations. Confederations of nations are not a new idea. They existed among some First Nations of North America long before Europeans arrived. According to historian Olive Dickason, by the 1500s, if not earlier, some peoples in North America had agreed that it was in their collective interest to organize themselves into multinational alliances. Their goals were to protect themselves against mutual enemies and to promote trade.

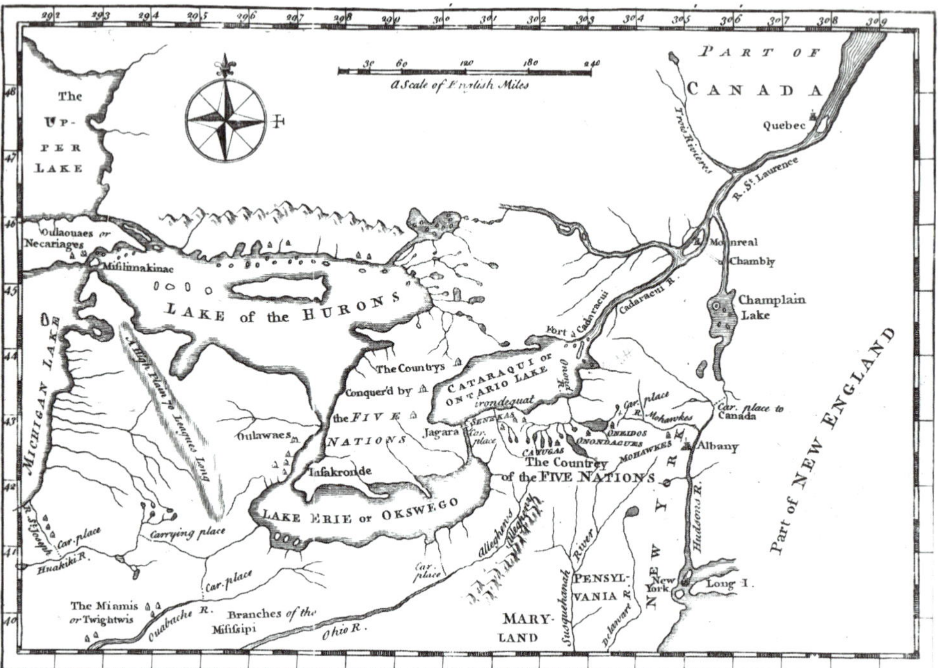

Figure 16-10 This early map shows the territory of the Five Nations of the Haudenosaunee as it was in 1650 in what is today New York State and Ontario.

Among these alliances was the League of Haudenosaunee, also known the Iroquois or Five Nations Confederacy. This was a social and political system that was originally made up of the Mohawk, Oneida, Onondaga, Cayuga, and Seneca Nations. In the early 1700s, the alliance became the Six Nations Confederacy when the Tuscarora Nation joined. Each nation looked after its own internal affairs, but all agreed to work together for mutual protection and trade. The league was ruled by a council of 50 chiefs who represented the people and who met when the need arose.

The league was guided by The Constitution of the Iroquois Nations: The Great Binding Law, Gayanashagowa, which was passed on orally from generation to generation and which outlined the decision-making process. The law included rules about the duties and rights of those who held specific positions, adoption and emigration, the structure of clans, and the role of women in the clans. Action was taken only after the six nations achieved consensus.

VOICES

It is wrong to ignore the historical rights that Aboriginal people still enjoy as self-governing political entities — rights that Canada undertook to safeguard as we were struggling toward nationhood.

—People to People, Nation to Nation: The Report of the Royal Commission on Aboriginal Peoples, *1996*

The dream of a Canada as a uni-national state was always a fiction, a fiction rooted historically in the denigration of French and Aboriginal cultures.

— Will Kymlicka, political philosopher, 1998

Aboriginal Nations Today

The 1996 report of the Royal Commission on Aboriginal Peoples made it clear that Canada is a nation of nations. It said that Aboriginal governments are "one of three orders of government in Canada — federal, provincial/territorial, and Aboriginal."

In a 2003 study of Aboriginal people's participation in the Canadian electoral process, political scientist Alan C. Cairns wrote: "To [the Royal Commission on Aboriginal Peoples] 'nation' was the fundamental unit of analysis, and the relation between Aboriginal peoples and the Canadian State was to be nation-to-nation. Canada was to become a multinational federation in which interactions would be among nations, not citizens."

Though Aboriginal people view themselves as nations whose Aboriginal and treaty rights are confirmed in Canada's Constitution, Aboriginal leaders agree that they wish to remain nations within Canada. But despite the recommendations of the royal commission, progress in achieving their goals has been slow. The Indian Act remains in force, Aboriginal peoples continue to face many challenges, and more than 800 specific land claims have yet to be settled.

In its report, the royal commission said that 66 of its recommendations could be implemented within 20 years. In 2006, on the 10th anniversary of the release of the commission's findings, the Assembly of First Nations issued a report card assessing the federal government's progress toward fulfilling the recommendations — and gave the government a failing grade.

Examine the information in Figure 16-11. Do you think the Assembly of First Nations' initiative in issuing this report card would have helped or hurt the cause of Aboriginal peoples? Explain your response.

Figure 16-11 **AFN Report Card on Government Progress toward Meeting Targets in Selected Areas, 2006**

Royal Commission Recommendation	Status in 2006	Grade
Public inquiry into residential school abuse	No public inquiry, but establishment of the Aboriginal Healing Foundation, the Indian Residential Schools Canada, and the completion of the Indian Residential School Settlement Agreement	B+
Canada-wide framework agreement to guide treaty negotiations	Not implemented	F
New treaties: replace existing comprehensive claims policy, as a broad base for matters to be discussed in treaty negotiations	No national treaty policy	F
Recognition of Aboriginal ownership and management of cultural and historic sites	Some recognition in northern land-claim agreements, but no national direction outside of self-government	C
Parliament and national Aboriginal organizations to jointly designate a National Peoples Day	National Aboriginal Day established as June 21 every year, 1996	A

Source: *Royal Commission on Aboriginal People at 10 Years: A Report Card*, Assembly of First Nations

The Québécois Nation

In recent years, Québec sovereignists have lost support among Québécois voters. In the 2007 provincial election, the sovereignist Parti Québécois placed third and formed neither the government nor the official opposition for the first time since 1973.

A year later, the PQ announced that it was abandoning its plan to hold another sovereignty referendum as soon as possible if the party regains power. Instead, the party pledged to engage the people of Québec in debate about sovereignty issues, the meaning of citizenship in the province, a Québec constitution, and winning from Ottawa power over language, culture, immigration, communications, and employment insurance.

PQ leader Pauline Marois said: "It will always be difficult for a small people speaking French in America, to assume its place, to continue to exist. It cannot be otherwise. There are 300 million anglophones surrounding us. We have to find ways to clearly indicate that in Québec, things happen in French."

With a partner, roleplay a discussion that might have occurred between two Parti Québécois members, one who supported sticking to the party's referendum pledge and the other who supported abandoning it. Raise at least two points to support your position.

Figure 16-12 In the 2007 provincial election, the Action Démocratique du Québec under leader Mario Dumont, pictured here, became the province's official opposition party for the first time since it was founded in 1994. The ADQ is a nationalist party that supports greater autonomy for Québec, but it stops short of advocating outright sovereignty. What does the ADQ's strong showing say about the shift in attitude among Québec voters?

You read about reasonable accommodation in Chapter 3.

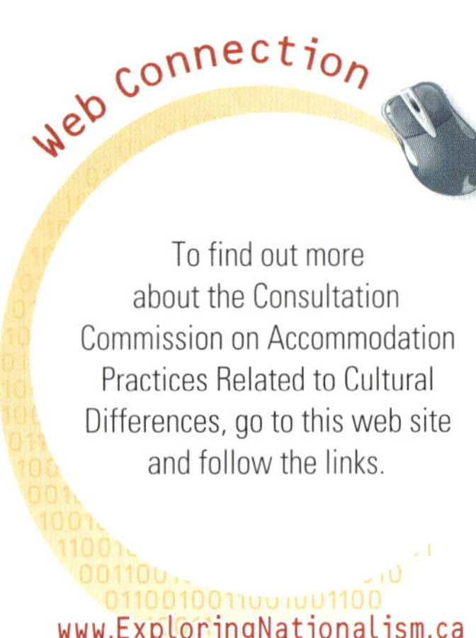

To find out more about the Consultation Commission on Accommodation Practices Related to Cultural Differences, go to this web site and follow the links.

www.ExploringNationalism.ca

Québec and Reasonable Accommodation

In the early 21st century, reasonable accommodation became an issue in Québec when various minority groups became alarmed about what they viewed as a lack of willingness to allow them to affirm and promote their own culture and traditions — and to feel as if they belonged in Québec.

Brigitte Haentjens, an award-winning theatre director who was born in France but who has worked in both Ontario and Québec, summed up the feelings of many immigrants when she told the *Montreal Gazette*: "I can't be Québécois." Haentjens said that she felt more at home among the Francophone minority in Ontario than in mostly Francophone Québec.

The issue of reasonable accommodation came to a head in early 2007 when the council of the small Québec town of Hérouxville adopted a code of conduct for immigrants. Though no foreign-born people live in the town, the code included a ban on accommodating prayer in school and on the extreme and illegal practices of genital mutilation and stoning women. Several nearby towns passed similar codes.

These actions sparked intense debate over how Francophone Québécois could affirm and promote their traditional language and culture while accommodating the needs of immigrants. In response, Québec premier Jean Charest established the Consultation Commission on Accommodation Practices Related to Cultural Differences. The commission's mission was to explore challenges related to reasonable accommodation in the province. The two commission chairs, Gérard Bouchard and Charles Taylor, travelled the province to hear the comments of individuals and groups. Their recommendations were to be delivered at the end of May 2008.

Figure 16-13 In October 2007, Fatima-Zahra Benjelloun of the Islamic Cultural Centre of Québec appeared before the Bouchard–Taylor commission to express her organization's concerns about reasonable accommodation in Québec.

Implications of a Nation of Nations

According to political philosopher Will Kymlicka, Canadians outside Québec view Canada as a single national community that includes all citizens, no matter what their language, ethnicity, or region. But this is not the view of many Québécois.

For thinkers such as Kymlicka, the idea of Canada as a country of many nations requires Canadians to embrace the concept of **asymmetrical federalism**. Under asymmetrical federalism, all provinces and territories would not share power with the federal government in the same way. The differing linguistic and cultural needs of provinces, territories, and regions would be accommodated by allowing them to exercise differing degrees of control in critical areas such as immigration.

Although a degree of asymmetrical federalism already exists in Canada — Québec, for example, already exercises more control over immigration than other provinces — the issue is contentious. Some believe that it could undermine Canadian unity because it threatens the principle of provincial equality.

If Canadians were to embrace asymmetrical federalism, how might this affect Canadian national identity? Explain your response.

THE VIEW FROM HERE

The Canadian Multiculturalism Act of 1988 affirmed that Canadians have a constitutional right "to the equal protection and benefit of the law without discrimination and that everyone has the freedom of conscience, religion, thought, belief, opinion, expression, peaceful assembly and association." But how successful is multiculturalism? Here is how three people have responded to this question.

In 2007, **Michael Adams**, social researcher and co-founder of Environics Research Group, argued that the children of immigrants have no problem reconciling contending national loyalties.

[Children of immigrants] are proud to be Canadians, but they are also proud of their ethnic, religious, racial background. In a lot of the polling, we're asking them to choose between the two. They say, "Well, I feel a deeper attachment to my Muslim status." And then immediately you jump to the conclusion that they don't love Canada.

Well, actually, they do love Canada. And they actually think that, when they say they're proud Canadians, they can also be proud Muslims and also citizens of the world. They're trying to communicate subtle, postmodern multiple identity.

Will Kymlicka, Canada Research Chair in Political Philosophy at Queen's University, wrote the following in his 2007 book, *Multicultural Odysseys: Navigating the New International Politics of Diversity.*

There are a few things we can say with some confidence about the effects of multiculturalism in practice. None of the countries that have moved along the multiculturalist path in the West have subsequently descended into civil war or anarchy, or faced military coups, or suffered economic collapse. On the contrary, even a casual inspection of the list of countries which are "strong" in their commitment to multiculturalism policies shows that they are amongst the most peaceful, stable, and prosperous societies on the planet.

In 2007, **Gilles Duceppe**, leader of the separatist Bloc Québécois, put forward this view of how reasonable accommodation should work in Québec.

Multiculturalism as a model of integration does not work in Québec. Immigrant cultures and beliefs must merge with Québec's culture and beliefs if the latter is to survive. They are coming to a nation with values, a culture, and history. The model developed in Québec reflects that reality. It's in total contradiction with the definition of a Canada that is bilingual and multicultural.

Explorations

1. Complete a chart like the one shown.
   - In the first column, list three key social factors that could be used as measures of the success or failure of multiculturalism (e.g., major civil strife).
   - In the second column, record a criterion based on each factor you identified (e.g., Has multiculturalism caused major civil strife in Canada?).
   - In the third column, record a yes or no response to your criterion (e.g., No).

Judging the Success of Multiculturalism

Key Social Factor	Criterion	Response (Yes or No)	Proof or Example

   - In the final column, provide evidence to support your response (e.g., Millions of people from many countries live together peacefully).
   - Use the information in your chart as a basis of an overall judgment about the success of multiculturalism. Compare your conclusions with those of others.

Two nations have evolved that are utterly alike in almost all of their externals and yet are utterly unalike in their political cultures so that they are as distinct from each other as are the Germans from the French, say, even though both are Europeans just as Canadians and Americans are both North Americans.

— Richard Gwyn, journalist and political commentator, in The 49th Paradox: Canada in North America, *1987*

With blithe lightness of mind we assumed that the world was moving irrevocably beyond nationalism, beyond tribalism . . . toward a global market culture that was to be our new home. In retrospect, we were whistling in the dark. The repressed has returned, and its name is nationalism.

— Michael Ignatieff, historian and politician, in the National Post, *2000*

A Divided Canada

In some cases, successor states have divided into more than one country after achieving independence. This is what happened in India, which divided into India and Pakistan. Later, Pakistan divided again when Bangladesh, which had been East Pakistan, became independent.

In the 1990s, when the separatist movement in Québec was at a peak, it looked as if the division of Canada was an imminent possibility. But Québec has not been the only province or region to consider separation. Some Westerners also advocate withdrawing from Confederation, though supporters of this idea are few and the movement is not nearly as strong as the sovereignist movement in Québec.

What might be some political, economic, and organizational challenges if voters in one province or territory supported leaving Canada? Explain your response.

North American Integration

Canadians have a great deal in common with Americans. Both Canada and the United States are democracies, and English is the dominant language in both countries. Canadians and Americans also dress similarly, listen to the same music, watch the same television programs, and follow many of the same sports — and are indistinguishable in many other ways. As a result, people from other parts of the world are often hard-pressed to tell the difference between citizens of the two countries.

Some people have suggested that Canada should merge with the United States. Though this idea does not enjoy widespread support in either country, some people believe that it is not as far-fetched as it seems. When Canada and the U.S. entered into the Free Trade Agreement, for example, many individuals and groups, such as the Council of Canadians, warned that this economic integration was the first step toward a political merger.

After the attacks on the U.S. on September 11, 2001, the American government's preoccupation with security also influenced Canada. For decades before this, the 6400-kilometre line that divides Canada and the U.S. had been called the longest undefended border in the world — but the United States came to regard it as an opportunity for terrorists to sneak into the United States. As a result, armed patrols now guard the border in many areas and surveillance has been stepped up. In addition, strict rules have been introduced to govern the entry of Canadians into the United States.

Figure 16-14 A communications assistant with the U.S. Border Patrol monitors the border between Canada and the United States from a huge facility in Blaine, Washington. Since 9/11, the United States has introduced high-tech methods to beef up surveillance on its border with Canada.

In 2002, Canada and the U.S. created the Binational Planning Group. The group's goal is to increase co-operation between the two countries in the areas of foreign policy, defence, and security. This involves co-ordinating maritime surveillance, sharing intelligence, and conducting joint military exercises. One of the first steps taken by the group was to bring about a bilateral pact that allows troops from one country to cross the border to help police and firefighters deal with emergencies in the other country.

On a scale of 1 to 5, rate how close you think Canada and the United States are to political union (1 = not very close; 5 = very close). Does your sense of Canadian identity play a role in your response? Explain why or why not.

Do agencies such as the Binational Planning Group and treaties such as NAFTA mean that Canada is already part of the U.S. — even if Canadians don't know it?

Taking Turns

Is North American integration a sound idea?

The students responding to this question are Rick, who was born in the United States but moved to Fort McMurray with his family when he was 10; Harley, who is a member of the Kainai Nation near Lethbridge; and Jean, a Francophone student who lives in Calgary.

Rick

My family immigrated from the States, and we fit right in here in Fort McMurray. My life here isn't very different from what it was like in the States, and people who don't know us have no idea that we were originally American. There are some minor differences between Canadians and American — like the fact that Americans aren't nearly as passionate about hockey — but really, I don't think it would make much difference to most Canadians if Canada and the United States merged. People's lives wouldn't change that much. Canadians are already Americans in everything but name.

I was on the Net and read a speech by Ovide Mercredi, who was once the national chief of the Assembly of First Nations. He said that Canada is already being Americanized and compared this with what happened to Aboriginal peoples when they were colonized. If Canadians want to know what could happen when peoples lose sovereignty and the right to control their own destiny, he said they should look to what has happened to Aboriginal peoples in Canada. Mercredi's speech really impressed me. I wouldn't wish the Aboriginal experience on anyone, so no, I don't support North American integration.

Harley

Jean

As a Francophone, I am completely against North American integration. Francophones are already a minority in Canada, and if Canada joined the United States, we'd be an even smaller minority. Keeping up our language and cultural traditions is hard enough in Canada, where we have a history and the Constitution protects our rights. In the United States, there are no such protections — and we would be swamped.

Your Turn

How would you respond to the question Rick, Harley, and Jean are answering? Explain the reasons for your response. How important is Canadian national identity to you?

Canada and Globalization

The country needs more aggressive strategies to make sure that social mobility is still possible. That is why immigrants come to Canada. Abstract debates about multiculturalism and pluralism mean less to them than being given a real chance to succeed.

— Marina Jiménez, immigration specialist for The Globe and Mail, *2007*

As the world becomes more globalized, Canadians — and others — have begun debating the effects of globalization on nationalism and national identity. Some believe that a sense of national identity will become even more important in the 21st century, while others say that the world has outgrown the idea of national identity and it is time for a new model. For some people, a new model involves global citizenship.

Globalization has made migration to distant places much easier, and Canada is an acknowledged world leader in promoting multiculturalism and cultural pluralism. Canada has evolved — and continues to evolve — on the foundation of the diverse linguistic, cultural, religious, and ethnic identities that make up the country. But Canadians sometimes struggle to reconcile respect for and acceptance of diversity with their desire to foster national unity. The shared ideal of unity in diversity is one of the themes of Jane Ash Poitras's mural, *Those Who Share Together, Stay Together*, which opened this chapter.

Although the word "multicultural" has been used since the 1940s to describe societies that encourage cultural pluralism, the word "multiculturalism" was coined in Canada in 1965 — and has since been adopted by English speakers around the world.

The Canadian ideal of diversity is widely admired, but some people believe that it is just that: an ideal. For immigrants, especially those who belong to visible minority groups, this ideal does not always translate into reality. Today's immigrants, for example, are often much better educated than immigrants of previous generations, but many have trouble finding jobs in their chosen field.

Along with Stuart N. Soroka and Richard Johnston, Keith Banting of the School of Policy Studies at Queen's University conducted a study that included measuring trust among people in ethnically diverse Canadian neighbourhoods. They found that when people from visible minority groups moved into predominantly white areas, the white majority became less trusting. And members of visible minority groups trusted others less when their neighbourhood was largely white than when it was ethnically diverse.

With a partner, discuss who should be responsible for bridging the trust gap in ethnically diverse neighbourhoods. Individuals? Governments? Another group or groups? If Canadians are to be united in a sense of common purpose and identity, is bridging this gap important? Explain your response.

Figure 16-15 Most immigrants settle in Canada's large cities, where street scenes like this are becoming more and more common. If you were using this photograph to illustrate Canadian identity to a non-Canadian, what would you say?

Canada in the World

On the world stage, Canada is often described as a middle power — a country that is not a superpower but does have some ability to influence world affairs. And Canadians often take pride in their country's reputation for leadership in specific areas such as multiculturalism, peacekeeping, and foreign aid.

You read about the role of middle powers in Chapter 9.

A 2008 poll conducted by Environics Research on behalf of a number of organizations, including the CBC and *The Globe and Mail,* found that more than 50 per cent of respondents believe that Canada exerts "some influence" on world affairs. But many, such as author and cultural commentator Neil Bissoondath, question whether this perception is accurate and whether Canada is living up to its reputation as a country that can — and should — play a prominent role in the world.

And in 2008, when a food crisis threatened people, especially those in developing countries, Jeffrey Sachs, American economist and adviser to United Nations secretary-general Ban Ki-moon, accused Canada of abandoning the leadership role it had often played in international development. "We've seen essentially no global leadership from Canada on poverty, hunger, disease, climate change and foreign assistance," Sachs told *The Globe and Mail.*

Sachs added that these actions were the result of Canadian government policies and did not reflect the attitudes of Canadians. "This has been a huge surprise for me as a lifelong admirer of Canada, that we don't see the ambition of the Canadian people manifested in Canada's policies right now," he said.

Should Canadians be alarmed about the views of non-Canadians such as Jeffrey Sachs? Do Sachs's comments affect your vision of Canada? Explain your responses.

Janice Gross Stein, a political scientist who is director of the Munk Centre for International Studies at the University of Toronto, believes that Canada's diversity means that it is in a unique position to make a difference in the world. "Networks of immigrants now connect Canada around the globe," Stein wrote in her contribution to *Great Questions of Canada.* "These networks are invaluable channels as Canada seeks to make its voice heard on international issues. We should lead in developing practices of multiple citizenship to strengthen these connections."

Despite our foreign aid programs and our record in peacekeeping, Canada is a country greatly diminished since the Second World War. The truth is, we carry little weight in the world. Were the Canadian state to disappear tomorrow, many beyond our borders would notice but few would mourn.

— Neil Bissoondath, author and cultural commentator, 2000

Reflect and Respond

To help clarify your thinking on issues relating to visions of Canada, respond to the following questions. In each case, justify your response.

a) Should some elements of multiculturalism and pluralism be sacrificed to promote Canadian identity?

b) Should Canada adopt asymmetrical federalism as a way of ensuring that nations within the country enjoy greater self-determination?

c) Should the number of official languages in Canada be increased to make the country more inclusive?

d) Should Canada become more like the United States to maintain free trade and access to American goods and services?

e) Should Canada try to regain its position as world leader in areas such as peacekeeping and international development?

Compare your responses with those of a small group. Present your conclusions to the class in visual form, perhaps as a graph or diagram.

FOCUS ON SKILLS

Honing Oral, Written, and Visual Literacy

FOCUS ON SKILLS

To understand an issue and reach an informed position, it is important to consider a range of points of view and perspectives. It is also important to understand positions other than your own and to express the arguments of others — even if you do not accept these arguments.

To practise your oral, written, and visual literacy skills in preparation for participating in the debate that concludes this related issue, you will develop a position on this proposal:

Canadian schools should adopt a policy of actively promoting Canadian national identity.

Your position and the reasons for it will depend on your views on issues on nationalism and national identity. You might, for example, decide that you agree, though not strongly. Your reservations may stem from the fact that you identify more strongly with a nation other than Canada, or that you believe that the word "identity" should be changed to "identities." Or you might disagree because you believe that in an interconnected world, a global identity is more realistic than a national identity.

Steps to Honing Oral, Written, and Visual Literacy

Step 1: Develop a position

With a partner, imagine that you are members of your community's school board and you must decide whether to support or oppose the proposal. You might begin by creating a T-chart like the one shown and recording arguments for and against the proposal. Once you decide on a position, you may wish to challenge yourselves by taking a position that you do not personally support.

Canadian schools should adopt a policy of actively promoting Canadian national identity.	
Arguments for	**Arguments against**

Step 2: Create a news release announcing your response

Once you have decided on your position, imagine that you are a representative of your community school board and write a news release announcing the board's position and inviting reporters to a news conference on the issue.

The news release should be no longer than one typed page. When drafting it, consider your audience and purpose. The release should be in formal language and should explain the following:

- the school board's decision
- the reasons for the decision
- the expected results of the decision
- a general statement about your community, province, or country and why the decision makes sense in this context
- details of the forthcoming news conference, including who will attend and where it will be held

Step 3: Prepare for the news conference

To enhance the presentation of your position at the news conference, create a graphic, collage, slogan, or other visual that reinforces your position and acts as a backdrop for your announcement. Think about image(s), picture(s), or words that would create a positive impression in the minds of the audience.

Use the T-chart you created earlier to consider questions that your classmates, who will play the role of reporters, might ask. Thinking about this ahead of time will help you prepare responses.

With your partner, decide on the role each of you will play at the news conference. How will you, for example, introduce yourselves? Will one of you read the statement while the other handles question, or will you share responsibility for answering questions? Will one of you explain the graphic or illustration you created?

When other pairs make their presentations, you will play the role of reporter. Use the arguments you recorded on your T-chart to prepare questions you might ask in this role.

Step 4: Stage the news conference

With your partner, present your position to the news conference. You might choose to sit at a desk at the front of the classroom or to use a lectern, if one is available. Remember to use formal language and to present your statement as if you really are representing the school board.

Read aloud your statement, then answer the reporters' questions.

Step 5: Check your learning

Once you have completed the activity, work with your partner to assess your presentation. To help you do this, create a chart like the one shown on this page.

Assessing Our Presentation
Our Position ______________

Question	Response and Comment
1. Which part of your presentation — the graphic image, the written statement, or responding to questions — do you think was most effective? What made it effective? What would you improve if you had another chance to complete the presentation?	
2. Did the reporters' questions reveal that information was missing from your written statement? If so, what was this information?	
3. Did the reporters raise questions that you had not expected or could not answer? If so, what were they? After reflecting on these questions, how would you answer them now?	
4. After thinking about your responses to the reporters' questions, would you change any of your answers?	
5. What new ideas, points of view, or perspectives on Canadian identity did this activity suggest to you?	
6. After listening to other points of view and responses, have you changed your position on the issue? Why or why not?	

Summing Up

Many activities in this course have helped you hone your oral, written, and visual literacy skills. Once an assignment is complete, reflecting on your performance is important because it enables you to assess where you need to focus your efforts to improve. A chart similar to the one on this page can help you organize this assessment.

What is your vision of national identity?

If you don't have a nation, a country of your own, you have no platform to act in the world . . . In order for us to truly live up to our potential in the world, and this includes reducing international inequalities, Canada must have its own sovereignty, its own freedom to move.

— David Orchard, farmer, lawyer, and Canadian nationalist, in ZNet, *2004*

Global citizenship is when you start to break down the political borders and start to worry about people all over the world. [It's] moving away from the idea of nationalism to the responsibility of the person to the whole world.

— Keen Sung, student delegate to the Global Youth Assembly, Edmonton, 2007

The French philosopher Ernest Renan once said that a nation is "a group of people united by a mistaken view about the past and a hatred of their neighbors." Renan made this remark in the 19th century, when ideas about nationalism were often rooted in concepts such as language, religion, and ethnicity — and before ideas about civic nations had taken hold.

Like most sardonic remarks, Renan's comment involved both bitter humour and a grain of truth. Some people do base their understanding of nation on a specific interpretation of the past and hatred of so-called others. But many more people base their vision on understandings that include a combination of religion, language, geography, ethnicity, spirituality, and civic ideals.

Defining Your Vision

In his foreword to *The New Canada,* Edward Greenspon, *Globe and Mail* editor-in-chief, wrote that Canadians are developing a new ethnicity — "simply Canadian." As proof, Greenspon cited the 2001 census, when 39 per cent of people identified their ethnic origins as Canadian.

Greenspon also wrote: "The 'I am Canadian' marketing phenomenon tapped into something real: Canadians are very proud of their national identity. With no trace of irony, they proudly yell about how modest they are, and patriotically claim that they have no patriotism. Despite our claim to a modest and deferential nationalism, our nationalism has become as emotional and assertive as anyone's."

Reread Greenspon's words. Would you say that he views the attitude he describes as a positive or negative development? Do you agree with his assessment? Why? If Canadians are developing a sense of Canadian ethnicity, how might this affect the idea of Canada as a civic nation that celebrates diversity?

In a famous 1963 speech, American civil rights leader Martin Luther King Jr. used the specific example of his own family to illustrate a broader vision of a civic nation in which all people enjoy equal rights and equal opportunities. King proclaimed: "I have a dream that my four little children will one day live in a nation where they will not be judged by the colour of their skin, but by the content of their character."

Figure 16-16 Martin Luther King Jr. delivers his widely quoted "I Have a Dream" speech in Washington D.C. Five years later, King was assassinated. Is a civic nation the only kind of nation in which King's dream can be achieved?

Citizens of the World

In August 2007, the John Humphrey Centre for Peace and Human Rights, a non-profit organization named for the Canadian who wrote the first draft of the United Nations' Universal Declaration of Human Rights, hosted the Global Youth Assembly in Edmonton. At the assembly, University of Alberta political scientist Andy Knight said: "We are all on the same planet, drinking the same water, affected by the same type of forces. And these things have no respect for national borders. Regardless of diversity and difference, we all have things in common. We are united in that diversity."

This theme — that the peoples the world are united in diversity — has been expressed by many people. In "Voices" on the previous page, for example, Keen Sung, a delegate to the Global Youth Assembly, expresses the idea that nationalism must evolve into a sense of personal international responsibility. And Jeffrey Sachs, who is quoted in "Voices" on this page, has argued that the interconnectedness of people and governments and the complexity of the problems facing humanity today mean that transcending borders is not only possible, but also necessary.

The balancing of internationalist perspectives with a strong sense of national identity may present one of the challenges of the 21st century. Some people may resolve this challenge by embracing nationalism. Others will look outward and embrace internationalism, and still others will try to strike a balance between the two.

To what extent should we embrace nationalism? This is the question that has provided the foundation of *Exploring Nationalism*. Given the nature of the world today — a world that globalization and communication technologies have made smaller than ever — is this the appropriate question? Would you have chosen a different question to examine? Explain your response.

Despite the reveries and fantasies of some, the age of empire is over. Power is already diffusing widely in the 21st century. A new kind of global politics must take shape, built not on U.S. or Chinese pre-eminence, but on global co-operation across regions.

— *Jeffrey Sachs, in* Common Wealth: Economics for a Crowded Planet, *2008*

If all people are citizens of the world, does this mean that national identity is irrelevant?

Figure 16-17 The United Nations' mandate expresses an international ideal by saying that one of its primary aims is "to reaffirm faith in fundamental human rights, in the dignity and worth of the human person, in the equal rights of men and women and of nations large and small." Does your vision of national identity include these ideals?

1. In this chapter, you explored responses to this question: To what extent should I embrace a national identity?

   Based on your understanding of nation and identity, develop a response to this chapter-issue question. Your response may take any form you wish. You may, for example, create a dialogue between two politicians with opposing views, a poem or song, a piece of art, a video documentary, a slogan, or a poster. Present your response to the class and be prepared to justify your position.

2. In the prologue, you read about several interpretations of nationalism. Then, as you began each chapter, you kept a journal that recorded your changing understanding of this concept.
   a) Use the information from these and other sources to write a statement that sums up your current understanding of nationalism.
   b) Deconstruct your understanding by identifying each element included in your statement. Explain why you chose it and how it relates to nationalism.
   c) Share your statement with a partner. Note comments made by your partner. If necessary, revise your statement and notes.
   d) Present your statement to a small group or the class. Be prepared to defend your position.
   e) With the small group or the class, develop a consensus statement to sum up your current understanding of nationalism.

3. A mission statement identifies an organization's goals and often lays out the strategies the organization hopes to follow to achieve these goals. The following are excerpts from the mission statements of three different organizations.
   - **IBM** — At IBM, we strive to lead in the invention, development and manufacture of the industry's most advanced information technologies, including computer systems, software, storage systems and microelectronics.

     We translate these advanced technologies into value for our customers through our professional solutions, services and consulting businesses worldwide.
   - **Alberta Education** — Alberta Education supports schools that are safe, caring, orderly, positive, productive, respectful and free from the fear of physical and emotional harm. A safe and caring environment contributes to successful schools.
   - **Petro-Canada** — To be the leader in the development of some of the purest base oils and innovative, superior products that customers trust for productivity improvements around the world.

   a) In this course, you have explored nationalism and developed your own understandings of this concept. With a small group, develop a mission statement for Canada. Your mission statement should reflect your understanding of nation, set out how you wish Canada to evolve, and take into account Canada's Charter of Rights and Freedoms.
   b) Maintain notes that track your progress toward developing your statement. Reflect on current Canadian laws and how they may need to be changed to reach the goals set out in your mission statement.

      These notes will also help you prepare for the four-corners debate on this statement: Individuals and groups should embrace a national identity.
   c) Share your mission statement with another group. Explain the process you went through to arrive at it. Ask the other group for feedback, and if necessary, revise your statement to reflect the feedback you received. Listen and comment as the other group shares its mission statement with you.
   d) Create a display that highlights your mission statement. Create a wall of statements by posting your mission statement along with those of others in the class. Be prepared to explain your statement and what will be required to achieve the goals it identifies.

4. The key course issue asks: To what extent should we embrace nationalism?
   a) Who is meant by "we" in this question?
   b) What nationalism do you think the question implies?
   c) Explain why you think this issue is — or is not — an important issue to consider.
   d) If you were asked to write an issue question for a course designed to help students develop an understanding of nationalism and its effects on identity, Canada, and other nations within Canada, what would your question say?

5. In a *Globe and Mail* opinion piece, Tom Kent, a former civil servant who served as principal assistant to Prime Minister Lester Pearson, wrote: "Most of us are proud to belong to a nation that welcomes diverse peoples and accepts many cultures. But present law permits, even encourages, confusion of loyalties and plurality of citizenship. The sense of Canadian identity is increasingly diluted."
   a) On the basis of this quotation, identify Tom Kent's position on multiculturalism.
   b) Write a statement on Canadian identity that you think Kent would agree with.
   c) Write a statement of Canadian identity that you think Kent would not agree with.
   d) Which statement would you agree with? Why?
6. Read the excerpts from the poem "I Am a Canadian." This poem was written in 1977 by Duke Redbird, poet, storyteller, actor, broadcaster, and member of the Saugeen First Nation in Ontario.
   a) What national identity is Duke Redbird expressing in this poem?
   b) In Chapter 6, you read about the response of many Turkish people to the assassination of Hrant Dink, who tried to draw attention to the Armenian genocide. People carried signs saying, "I am Hrant Dink." How is Duke Redbird's poem similar in spirit to the sentiments expressed by the Turkish protesters?
   c) Duke Redbird wrote this poem more than 30 years ago. Write a five-line stanza in a similar style. Your goal is to capture your feelings about Canadian identity today.

I Am a Canadian

I'm Sir John A. Macdonald
I'm Alexander Graham Bell
I'm a pow-wow dancer
And I'm Louis Riel
I'm the Calgary Stampede
I'm a feathered Sarcee
I'm Edmonton at night
. . .
I'm a maple tree and a totem pole
I'm sunshine showers
And fresh-cut flowers
I'm a ferry boat ride to the Island
I'm the Yukon
I'm the Northwest Territories
I'm the Arctic Ocean and the Beaufort Sea
I'm the prairies, I'm the Great Lakes,
I'm the Rockies, I'm the Laurentians
I am French
I am English
And I am Métis
But more than this
Above all this
I am a Canadian and proud to be free.

Think about Your Challenge

The second part of the challenge for this related issue asks you to participate in a consensus-building exercise in response to the key course-issue question: To what extent should we embrace nationalism?

Prepare a statement in response to this question. As you participate in the four-corners debate, which makes up the first part of the challenge, adjust your statement to reflect the new information, ideas, points of view, and perspectives you encounter as the debate unfolds.

Glossary

A

absolute poverty A condition characterized by severe deprivation of basic human needs, including food, safe drinking water, sanitation facilities, health, shelter, education, and information. Absolute poverty may depend not only on income but also on access to services.

alienation The experience of feeling left out or being on the outside. People who choose one strong loyalty over another risk alienation from an important part of their identity and from sharing in the collective consciousness of their group.

appeasement Giving in to demands. A foreign policy practised by Britain and the United States when they granted Hitler concessions in an effort to avoid World War II.

asymmetrical federalism The concept that all Canadian provinces and territories may not share power with the federal government in the same way.

B

bilateralism Agreements between two countries to work toward resolving issues that concern both countries.

C

civic nation A nation created by people — no matter what their ethnicity, culture, and language — who agree to live according to particular values and beliefs expressed as the rule of law.

collective consciousness An internal consciousness, or awareness, shared by many people. It may be based on a shared memory of and pride in specific events, which become myths and symbols of belonging.

collective security The condition of protecting all members of a group or collective from danger. The United Nations tries to ensure the collective security of all member states.

common human heritage The cultural inheritance from the past that all people share and that is preserved in world heritage sites, traditional skills and knowledge, and the arts.

conscription Compulsory military service. In Canada during World Wars I and II, the policy was controversial, especially among Francophones in Québec.

contending loyalties Loyalties that compete. People sometimes need to choose among various loyalties based on their commitment to those loyalties.

cosmopolitan Borrowing, adopting, and adapting values from many cultures.

crimes against humanity Widespread or systematic attacks against a civilian population, including murder, extermination, enslavement, deportation, imprisonment, torture, rape or sexual slavery, enforced disappearance of persons, and the crime of apartheid.

cultural pluralism A belief or doctrine that holds that collectives should be encouraged to affirm and promote their unique cultural identity in a diverse society.

D

decolonization The process that occurs in a former colony when an imperial power withdraws. Decolonized countries can exercise sovereignty under international law and can join the United Nations.

domestic policy A plan of action that guides a government's decisions about what to do within a country. In Canada, domestic policy decisions may include changing federal laws, settling Aboriginal land claims, and spending tax revenues.

E

economic nationalists People who believe that a country's businesses and industries should be protected against foreign interests.

economic sanctions The action of cutting off trade with a country in an effort to force it to follow a particular course of action.

ecozone An area of the earth's surface that represents a large ecological zone and has characteristic landforms and climate.

equalization payments Revenues from federal taxes that are paid by the Canadian government to less prosperous provinces to ensure that public services are more or less equally available to all Canadians.

ethnic Racial, cultural, or linguistic characteristics. Many nations come into being because people share a collective identity based on ethnic characteristics.

ethnic cleansing A term that is used to make more socially acceptable the murder or expulsion of an ethnic nation from a territory.

ethnic nationalism Nationalism that is founded on shared ethnicity, culture, and language. People who share these traits may choose to create a nation-state based on their collective identity.

F

federalists People who support a federal system of government. In Canada, people who oppose Québec sovereignty and believe that Québec should remain a Canadian province, ensuring its place in Confederation.

foreign policy A plan of action that guides a government's decisions about its official relations with other countries. Also called foreign affairs or external relations.

G

genocide The killing of members of a national, ethnic, racial, or religious group; causing serious bodily or mental harm to members of the group; and deliberately inflicting on the group conditions of life calculated to bring about its physical destruction.

gross domestic product The value of all goods and services produced in a country in a year.

gross national income The total value of the goods and services produced by a country in a year, whether inside or outside the country's borders.

H

Holocaust The English term used to describe the genocide of about six million Jews by the Nazis during World War II.

I

inflation A rise in prices accompanied by a drop in the purchasing power of money. Increases in the price of goods and services can threaten the economic security and interests of people in a region or country.

inherent right The right to self-determination that exists for Aboriginal peoples in Canada because they occupied the land and governed themselves for thousands of years before Europeans arrived in North America.

institution An organization established for and united by a specific purpose. Institutions provide services such as social assistance, education, and cultural events. They also often use national symbols and stories to define their identity and promote a sense of belonging.

international Between countries or nation-states. Nation-states may co-operate with one another to promote peace and security, trade, health, human rights, and the protection of endangered peoples and cultures.

internationalism The doctrine that all members of the global community accept collective responsibility for the challenges that face the world and that the motives of nations and nation-states must be respected in the search for solutions.

isolationism A policy whereby a country completely opts out of participating in international social, economic, political, and military affairs.

M

multiculturalism A belief, doctrine, or policy that embraces the idea of ethnic or cultural diversity and promotes a culturally pluralistic society.

multilateralism A policy that involves several countries working together to meet challenges and solve problems. The United Nations is multilateral in nature.

N

national interest The interests of the people of a nation. National interest may include economic prosperity, security and safety, and beliefs and values.

nation-state A country that has physical borders and a single government. Nation-states may be based on ethnic nationalism or civic nationalism or a combination of the two.

needs The basic elements — food, water, shelter, health — that humans require for survival.

non-nationalist loyalty A loyalty that is not embedded in the idea of nation. People may be loyal to and identify with family, friends, a region, an idea, a collective or a group, a way of life, and a culture.

O

odious debt A debt that is incurred by a despotic power, not to meet the needs of the people of the country but to strengthen the despotic regime.

P

patriated Transferred from the control of the British government to that of the Canadian government. The patriated Canadian Constitution of 1982 gave the provinces more rights and powers than they had under the British North America Act of 1867.

patriotism Love of country and an interest in its well-being. A sense of loyalty that may be expressed in various ways.

peacekeepers Armed forces who maintain peace by keeping enemies apart until a crisis can be resolved through diplomacy and negotiation.

peacemaking Allowing armed forces that were originally sent to maintain peace in a region of conflict to use force for reasons other than self-defence.

pluralism A belief or doctrine that a society should reflect an inclusive approach that encourages diversity. It assumes that diversity is beneficial and that diverse groups, whether these are cultural, religious, spiritual, ideological, gender, linguistic, environmental, or philosophical, should enjoy autonomy.

policy A plan of action that has been deliberately chosen to guide or influence future decisions.

propaganda Information and ideas that are spread to achieve a specific goal. Extreme nationalists may use misleading and dishonest information to create fear and insecurity and to persuade people to behave in certain ways.

R

reasonable accommodation A legal and constitutional concept that requires Canadian public institutions to adapt to the religious and cultural practices of minorities as long as these practices do not violate constitutional rights and freedoms.

reconciliation An act of resolving differences and repairing relationships that enables people to come to terms with past injustices and to coexist in peace.

responsible government A government that answers to the people rather than to colonial governors. The concept was introduced in Canada by Louis-Hippolyte LaFontaine and Robert Baldwin in the 1840s.

responsibility to protect A doctrine that says the United Nations must protect people within a state when that state violates or fails to uphold the rights and welfare of its own citizens.

rhetoric The art of shaping language to influence the thoughts and actions of an audience.

royal commission An independent public inquiry established by governments to examine complicated issues, hear testimony from people involved, and recommend ways of achieving a resolution.

S

segregation The forced separation of racial groups. Extreme loyalty to one racial group can lead to separate schools and living areas for racial minorities and eventually to ultranationalism and persecution of those minorities.

self-determination The power to control one's own affairs. National self-determination is the power of people within a nation-state or nation to make their own decisions about what is in their interest.

sovereignists In Canada, people who support the idea of Québec's becoming an independent nation-state that can control its own destiny.

sovereignty The political authority to control one's own affairs. Sovereignty may be distinguished from, and can sometimes conflict with, self-determination, which is a people's right to control their own affairs.

successor state A country created from a previous state. By international law, the people who lived in the predecessor state have a right to nationality in the successor state or to choose their nationality if the predecessor state is divided into more than one state.

supranationalism A policy by which countries agree to abide by the decisions of an international organization made up of independent appointed officials or representatives elected by member states.

T

tied aid Help that is given with strings attached. These strings may include agreements that the country receiving the aid will buy goods and services only from the country or organization supplying the aid.

trickle-down effect The theory that when people in developed countries have more money to spend, they will buy goods and services offered by businesses in less developed countries and that this spending will eventually help strengthen economies in the developing world.

U

ultranationalism An extreme form of nationalism. Ultranationalists are often fanatically loyal to their own nation and hostile and racist toward other nations.

unilateralism The policy of a country responding to events on its own without agreements with, or support from, other countries.

V

voluntary balkanization The separation of like-minded people into isolated groups that are hostile to people whose values differ from their own. This separation may result in a loss of shared experiences and values and can harm the structure of democratic societies.

W

wants Things that people desire, regardless of whether the desired object contributes to their survival.

war crimes Wilful killing, torture, or inhuman treatment; wilfully causing great suffering; and intentionally directing attacks against a civilian population or against those who are involved in a humanitarian or peacekeeping mission.

Index

A

A More Secure World, 257
Aboriginal peoples, 61-62, 82-85
assimilation, 61
Cardinal, Harold, 61
contributions to Canada, 316
Fontaine, Phil, 84
inherent rights, 356
land claims, 84, 357
Lepine, Melody, 98, 99
National Day of Action, 84, 85
and national unity, 361
nations today, 374-375
Oka crisis, 82
organizations, 327
population growth, 361
reconciling their loyalties, 82-85
rights, 314-315
Royal Commission on, 83-84, 193, 374, 193. 375
self-determination for, 314-315, 356
spiritual connections to land, 28
women's rights, 104
see also First Nations, Inuit, Métis
advertising, 335
Afghanistan
Canadian soldiers in, 69, 118, 131, 249
invasion of, 131, 132
landmines in, 249
refugees from, 200-201
Taliban in, 131, 132, 139
women's rights in, 133, 155
Africa, HIV/AIDS in, 280
Aga Khan, the, 369
AIDS, 280
air pollution, 235, 245
al-Hussain, Prince Kar m (the Aga Khan), 369
al-Qaeda, 129, 130, 132, 257
Albanian Kosovars, 182, 184
Alberta
diversity in, 372-373
oil and gas industry, 95-100
alienation
of Atlantic provinces, 348
defined, 102
of Western provinces, 348
allophones, 79, 308
Amazon rainforest, 130
ambassadors, roving, 337
American Revolution, 46, 58
Amiskwaciy Academy, 194
anglophones, 305, 352
in Québec, 62-63, 77, 78, 79, 80, 81
Annan, Kofi, 117, 118, 257
annexing Canada, 305
Antarctic Treaty, 239
anti-Semitism, 166
Arar, Maher, 106-107, 334
Arbour, Louise, 172, 328
Arctic Council, The, 224, 266
Arctic ecozones, 358
Arctic sovereignty, 119-121
Armenians, 138, 162, 163-164
art galleries, 325, 332
artists, 336
Ash Poitras, Jane, 366, 367, 380
Carr, Emily, 327, 336
Group of Seven, 327, 336
Légaré, Joseph, 341
Monkman, Kent, 336
Picasso, Pablo, 156
Wieland, Joyce, 18-19
Ash Poitras, Jane, 366, 367, 380
Assembly of First Nations, 70, 193, 327
assimilation, 61, 313
asymmetrical federalism, 376
Atatürk, Mustafa Kemal, 33
athletes, 337
funding for, 325, 329, 337
Hughes, Clara, 225
humanitarian actions, 224, 225
Paralympic, 224, 328, 335
sponsorship of, 328, 335
atomic bomb, 158, 159, 160, 168, 169
Auschwitz-Birkenau, 162, 167, 176
Austro-Hungarian Empire, 123, 182
avian influenza (bird flu), 276

B

B and B Commission, 351-352
Baldwin, Robert, 304
Balfour Declaration, 127
balkanization, voluntary, 255
Barlow, Maude, 264, 276, 326, 345
Barney, Darin, 256
Bastille, storming of the, 44-45, 47, 56
Battle of Beaumont-Hamel, 75
Battle of the Plains of Abraham, 62, 63
Battle of the Somme, 75
Battle of Vimy Ridge, 20, 75
beaver, 322
beliefs and values, 117
expressed by laws, 30, 371
Berton, Pierre, 338
bias, detecting, 48-49, 94
bigotry, 162
bilateralism, 222

bilingualism, 309, 351-352
Bill 101, 78-81, 86
bird flu, 276
Bishop, Billy, 332
Bissoondath, Neil, 74, 317, 381
Black Death, 274
black immigrants, 311
Bloom, William, 36
Bonaparte, Napoléon, 53, 54-55, 56
Boston Tea Party, 58
Botswana, 216, 217
Bouchard, Lucien, 77
Bourassa, Henri, 308
bourgeoisie, 46
Britain
    control over Canada, 59, 123, 151
    control over India, 190-192
    control over Middle Eastern countries, 126, 127
    government of, 370
    parliament, 46, 58
    pluralism in, 370
    tea tax, 58
    wars with France, 47, 58
    in World War I, 123
British North America Act, 305, 349
British worldview in Canada, 60, 86
Brown Trickey, Minnijean, 105
Brynjolfsson, Erik, 255
Bush, George W., 128, 129

C

cahiers de doléances, 51
Callihoo, Victoria, 60
Cambodians, 186
Canada
    as a country, 21
    influence on world affairs, 381
    as a nation, 21
Canada goose, 323
Canada World Youth, 333
Canada-United States Air Quality Agreement, 222
Canadian Broadcasting Corporation (CBC), 332
Canadian Multiculturalism Act, 350, 377
Canadian Pacific Railway, 59
Canadian Radio-television and Telecommunications Commission (CRTC), 332
Canadian Rangers, 119
Canadian Security Intelligence Service (CSIS), 334
Canadian War Museum, 332
Carr, Emily, 327, 336
Carrier, Roch, 336
Cartier, George-Étienne, 305
cause-and-effect relationships, 94, 174
CBC, 332
Charter of the French Language (Québec), 78-81, 86
Charter of Rights and Freedoms, 30, 93, 106, 212, 350, 371
Chartier, Clément, 29, 198
China, 118, 150
    air pollution in, 235
    Falun Gong in, 102
    government of, 102, 118, 203
    invasion of Tibet, 187, 189, 368
    Japan's invasion of Nanjing, 160
    Mao Zedong, 203
Chinese immigrants, 59, 311
Chinese Immigration Act, 311
Chomsky, Noam, 129, 178, 290
Chrétien, Jean, 61, 131, 315, 353, 364
Churchill, Winston, 61, 68, 142, 143, 149, 226
citizens of the world, 385
citizenship
    exam, 327
    oath, 72, 74
civic nationalism, 30-32, 43
Clark, Joe, 234, 301
class loyalties (socio-economic), 91, 92
Clemenceau, Georges, 123, 124, 127
climate change, 274, 282-283
coat of arms, 16-17, 103
collective consciousness, 45, 53
collective identity, 36, 37, 40, 67
comedians, 38
common human heritage, 260-262
communication, global, 254
Communist Party in Russia, 137, 139
Confederation, 305, 307, 308
Confedspread quilt, 18-19
conscription, 152, 308, 309
consensus-building, 120-121
Constitution (1982), 30, 61, 349, 353, 356, 371, 193. 314
contending loyalties, 69, 76-77, 82, 99, 102, 103, 306
Convention on Inhumane Weapons, 248
Convention on the Law of the Sea, 119, 239, 240, 242
cosmopolitan, 369
Council of Canadians (COC), 326, 345
country defined, 21
crimes against humanity, 158-177
Croatia, 246
Crosby, Sidney, 232
CRTC, 332
CSIS, 334
cultural institutions, 325
cultural and language-based organizations, 266-267
cultural loyalties, 91, 96, 97, 98
cultural nationalism, 26
cultural pluralism, 72

D

D-Day, 326
Dalai Lama, 187, 189, 203
Dallaire, Roméo, 173, 238
dams, 277
Darfur, 212, 285
de Gouges, Olympe, 53, 65

death camps, 162, 167, 176
debating
    four-corners, 296-297
    to persuasively express informed views, 262-263
debt, 281
Declaration on the Rights of Indigenous Peoples, 130, 193, 196, 227
Declaration of the Rights of Man and of the Citizen, 52
Declaration of the Rights of Woman and of the Female Citizen, 53, 65
decline vs shift, 290
decolonization, 184-185
Defence Systems and Equipment International Exhibition and Conference, 252, 253
Dextre, 362
Dhillon, Baltej Singh, 73, 104
Diefenbaker, John, 301
Dink, Hrant, 138, 162
discrimination
    against black immigrants, 311
    against Chinese immigrants, 311
    against Jewish immigrants, 166
    against Ukrainians, 312-313
    against women, 104
    racial, 57, 152
diseases
    avian influenza (bird flu), 276
    Black Death, 274
    contagious, 223
    deadly, 275
    flu, 274
    HIV and AIDS, 280
    internationalism and, 280
    linked to poverty, 280
    polio, 236
    SARS (severe acute respiratory syndrome), 223, 254, 275
    smallpox, 223
    spread of, 276
displaced people, 212
diversity, 369-370, 371-373, 380
Doctors Without Borders, 68
domestic policy, 122
Dominion Institute, 326, 327
Douglas, Tommy, 338
Dunn, Maria, 92
Duplessis, Maurice, 309

E

Earth, deep space photo, 208, 209
ecological footprints of some countries, 282
economic and commercial institutions, 328
economic globalization, 362-363
economic nationalists, 362
economic opportunities, 96, 97, 99
economic organizations, 264-265
economic prosperity, 117, 129
economic sanctions, 236, 285
economic stability, 211, 226, 236
ecozones, 358
Edinborough, Arnold, 73
educational institutions, 326
educational programs, government support of, 333
Egypt, 154, 246
Eisenhower, Dwight D., 168, 185
employment, high, 211
Enola Gay (B-29 Superfortress bomber), 169
equalization payments, 349
Estates General, 47, 51
Ethiopia, 150, 243
ethnic characteristics, 26
ethnic nationalism, 26, 31, 32, 43
European Union (EU), 265
Expo, 18, 67

F

failed states, 215
Falun Gong, 102-103
Faysal, Prince Emir, 126, 127
federalists, 77
Feng Shan Ho, 176
Fenians, 305
Ferdinand, Archduke Franz, 123
Fête nationale, Québec, 69
First Nations
    alliances, 374
    Assembly of, 70, 193, 327
    cultural traditions, 26
    Dene Nation, 29
    elders, 98, 100
    Haida, 26
    Indian Act, 315
    land claims, 315
    loyalties of, 70
    Nisga'a, 315, 356
    opposition to oil sands, 98, 99, 100
    schools, 194
    self-determination, pursuit of, 193, 213
    Siksika, 26, 28, 210
    Six Nations Confederacy, 374
    status as nations, 70
    Tagish, 213
    Tlingit, 213
    today, 374-375
    women's rights, 104
    see also Aboriginal peoples
flag
    Canadian, 59, 300, 335
    Quebec's, 342
fleur de lis, 342
flu epidemic of 1918, 274
foreign aid, 243, 244
foreign policy, 122, 129, 130, 151, 230-249
    in a globalizing world, 235
    goals, 233

influences on decisions, 232-233, 234
viewpoints on, 234
four-corners debate, 296-297
Francophones
and bilingualism, 309, 351-352
challenges and opportunities for, 308-309, 351
opposed to conscription, 152, 308
in Québec, 25, 60, 62-63, 77-81, 305
and World War II, 152
Francophonie, l'Organization internationale de la, 267
Fraser Institute, 327
free-trade agreement, 362, 378
French nationalism, 42-57
French Revolution, 44-47, 50-55, 56, 91
French-Canadian nationalism, 308-309

G

Gandhi, Mohandas, 126, 190, 191, 199, 349
Garneau, Marc, 363
General Agreement on Tariffs and Trade (GATT), 226, 264
genocide
of Armenians, 138, 161, 162, 163-164
of Cambodians, 186
of Jews, 162, 166-167
of Tutsis in Rwanda, 173, 177, 238
of Ukrainians, 165
geographic nationalism, 27
geography of Canada, 347
George, Chief Dan, 61, 339
Germans, 140, 141-143, 145, 147, 149
death camps, 162, 167, 176
Hitler, Adolf, 141, 143, 145
Nazis, 140, 141, 143, 145, 147, 148, 176
Giroux, Raymond, 77
Glenbow Museum, 325
global communication, 254-256
global issues
access to clean water, 272, 273, 276
climate change, 274, 282-283
control over water, 277
debt, 281
disease, 280
human rights, 284
hunger, 279
poverty, 278
viewpoints on, 291
global thinking, 223
global village, 255
globalization, 254-256, 269, 346, 362-363, 380-381, 385
Goebbels, Joseph, 140, 142, 143
government, 290
British, 304
of Canada, 59
equalization payments, 349
responsible, 304
support of educational programs, 333
governor general, 332
Jean, Michaëlle, 16, 17, 103, 108, 158
Grand Banks, fishing on, 239
Great Depression, 141
greatest Canadians, 338
Greenspon, Edward, 302, 303, 372, 384
gross domestic product, 129
Group of Seven, 336
Guevara, Ernesto "Che", 45

H

Hapa (mixed race), 350
Harper, Stephen, 20, 25, 62, 74, 107, 120, 121, 132, 198, 369
views on bilingualism, 351
and Canadian space technology, 362
and the Kyoto Protocol, 236
views on Québec sovereignty, 198, 301
head tax, 311
Highway of Heroes, 69
Hindus, 191
Hirohito, Emperor, 144, 145
Hiroshima and Nagasaki, 158, 159, 160, 168, 169
Hitler, Adolf, 141, 143, 145, 149
HIV/AIDS, 280
hockey, 23, 39, 62, 90, 320
Crosby, Sidney, 232
Holocaust, 162-163, 258
host countries, 200
Hoyt, Jenna, 243
Hudson's Bay Company, 328-329
Hughes, Clara, 225
human heritage, common, 260-262
human rights, 172, 259, 284
humanitarianism, 214, 224, 227, 243
Hussein, Saddam, 93, 94, 128, 129, 236
Hutterites, 106
Hutus, 173, 177, 238

I

Ibbitson, John, 30, 31, 72, 317
identity
evolving, 369
individual, 36, 40
and loyalty, 40, 102
and nation, 16, 36, 37, 40
national, 36-39, 40, 300
sacrificing part of one's, 102
viewpoints on, 339
ideological loyalties, 91, 97
Ignatieff, Michael, 31, 32, 62, 63, 132, 155, 373
immigrants
allophones, 79
attracting, 298, 307, 324
black, 311
and Canadian nationalism, 63
difficulty finding jobs, 380

discrimination against, 57, 59, 63
diversity of, 369-370, 371-373
favoured, 310
and nationalism, 72
policies, 350
in Québec, code for, 376
Ukrainian, 312-313
immigration, trends in, 260
India, 126, 190-192
creation of Pakistan, 191
Gandhi, Mohandas, 126, 190, 191
invasion of Kashmir, 192
self-determination for, 190-192, 199
Indian Act, 315
indigenous peoples
Arctic Council representing, 224, 266
Declaration on the Rights of, 130, 193, 196, 227
of Peru, 130, 228
self-determination for, 227
Indochina, 185
inflation, 95
inherent rights, 356
institutions, 325-328
cultural, 325
economic and commercial, 328
educational, 326
political, 327
integration of Canada with United States, 378-379
International Atomic Energy Agency (IAEA), 258
International Bank for Reconstruction and Development, 226
International Criminal Court (ICC), 161, 170, 172, 178
international defined, 21
international law, 239
International Monetary Fund (IMF), 226, 281, 289
international summit, 206-207
international trade, 288
internationalism, 226-227, 243, 245, 294-297
and climate change, 274, 282-283
and conflict, 285
and debt, 281
decline vs shift, 290
and disease, 280
and governments, 290
and human rights, 284
and hunger, 279
and nation-states, 289
and poverty, 278
Internet, social effects of, 255
internment camps in Canada, 152, 153, 313
Inuit, 61
and Bill, 101 86
Circumpolar Council, 266
creation of Nunavut, 62, 194-195
environmental problems facing, 283
Kiviaq, 71
Kunuk, Zacharias, 195
names, 70-71, 87
nationalism, 62
Nunavut, 62, 194-195, 357
on protecting the Arctic, 121
relocation program, 62
response of Québec Inuit to Bill 86, 101
and self-determination, 194-195
Tapiriit Kanatami, 195
Tootoo, Jordin, 62
Iran, 200, 201, 258, 259
Iraq
Hussein, Saddam, 128, 129, 236
oil in, 127, 128-129
people of, 93, 128, 129, 236
isolationism, 220
Israel, 27, 76, 116, 258
Israelis, 116, 118
Italians, 114, 150

J

Jamaica, 281
James Bay and Northern Québec Agreement, 84
Japan, 144, 148, 150, 152
bombing of Hiroshima and Nagasaki, 158, 159, 160, 168, 169
bombing of Pearl Harbor, 152
invasion of China, 160
invasion of Southeast Asia, 185
national identity, 368
Japanese Canadians, 152-153
Jean, Michaëlle, 16, 17, 103, 108, 180
Jerusalem, 28, 116
Jews, 27, 28, 76, 127
discrimination against immigrants, 166
and Feng Shan Ho, 176
and Oskar Schindler, 176
persecution by Germans, 140, 147, 162, 176
Wiesel, Elie, 167
Journal on Nationalism, 19, 43, 67, 89

K

Kashmiris, 192
Katimavik, 333
Kazemi, Zahra, 259
Khan, Sheema, 39
Khmer Rouge, 186
King, Martin Luther, Jr., 185, 384
King, William Lyon Mackenzie, 151, 152, 355
Kiviaq, 71
Klein, Ralph, 95
Kogawa, Joy, 153, 157
Koreans, 26
Kosovo, 182, 183, 184, 197, 199
kulaks, 165
Kunuk, Zacharias, 195
Kurds, 93, 114
Kyoto Protocol, 101, 236, 274, 282

L

LaFontaine, Louis-Hippolyte, 304
land claims, 84, 315, 357
landmines, 248-249
Laurier, Wilfrid, 307, 308, 311, 371
Law of the Sea, 119, 239, 240, 242
League of Nations, 150, 170
Lebanon, 116
Lepine, Melody, 98, 99
Lévesque, René, 78, 309
Libman, Robert, 80
lieutenant-governors, 332
Little Rock Nine, 105
Little Voice Foundation, 243
Lloyd George, David, 123, 127
loon, 322, 323
Lougheed, Peter, 95, 99
Louis XV, king of France, 44, 47
Louis XVI, king of France, 44, 47, 50, 52
Lovelace Nicholas, Sandra, 104
loyalties
    Bill 101 affecting, 80
    and choices, 68, 69, 70-74, 102
    class (socio-economic), 91, 92
    contending, 69, 76-77, 82, 99, 102, 103, 306, 346
    cultural, 91, 98
    of First Nations peoples, 70
    and identity, 40
    ideological, 91, 97
    in multicultural society, 72
    nationalist, 66-88, 91, 107
    nature of, 90
    non-Canadian nationalist, 71
    non-nationalist, 90-91, 103-104, 107
    and patriotism, 69
    racial or ethnic, 91
    reconciling, 82-84, 88-109
    regional, 95-98
    religious, 91, 93, 102-103
    your own, 64

M

Macdonald, John A., 59, 305, 314, 318, 349
McGee, Thomas D'Arcy, 306, 371
MacLennan, Hugh, 103, 109
McLuhan, Marshall, 254, 255
"Maple Leaf Forever, The", 86
Marie Antoinette, 50, 52
Maschco Piro people of Peru, 130
Maslow, Abraham, 210, 212
Maslow's Hierarchy of Human Needs, 210
Mazigh, Monia, 106-107
Medécins Sans Frontières/Doctors Without Borders, 68, 227
Mercer, Rick, 75
Mercredi, Ovide, 316, 353
Métis, 20, 29, 60, 61, 63
    Janvier, Alfred, 196
    organizations, 327
    Riel, Louis, 314
    self-determination for, 196, 198, 314
middle-class people in France (in the 1700s), 46
Middle East
    after World War I, 114, 126
    map before and after World War I, 114
    turmoil related to foreign policy, 122
military, 69, 118
    in Afghanistan, 69, 118, 131, 132, 249
    Princess Patricia's Canadian Light Infantry, 246
Milošević, Slobodan, 171, 172
Monarchist League, 325
money, Canadian, 322, 335
Monkman, Kent, 336
Montferrand, Joseph (Joe Mufferaw), 41
motives, 220-221
Mugabe, Robert, 217
multiculturalism, 72-74, 301, 315-316, 350, 377
multilateralism, 222
museums, 332
Musical Ride, 334
musicians
    Connors, Stompin' Tom, 336
    Peterson, Oscar, 336
Muslims
    Albanian Kosovars, 182
    in France, 57
    in India, 191
    in Iraq, 93
    Jinnah, Muhammad Ali, 191
    Shiite, 93
    Sunni, 93
    women, 39, 57
Mussolini, Benito, 149, 150
Myanmar, 284
myths about Canada and Canadians, 38-39, 57, 59, 60, 247, 322

N

Nahua people of Peru, 130
names
    changing spelling of, 313
    Inuit, 70-71, 87
    in Québec, 25
Napoléon (Bonaparte), 53, 54-55, 56
narratives, comparing, 302-303
nation
    building, 155
    as a civic concept, 30-32, 43
    as a collective concept, 23
    as a concept, 21-22
    cultural understandings, 26
    defined, 21
    ethnic understandings, 26, 31, 32, 43
    geographic understandings, 27
    and identity, 14-39

linguistic understandings, 25
as a patriotic concept, 24
political understandings, 29
relationship to land, 28
religious understandings, 27
spiritual understandings, 28
views on what makes a nation, 22
nation-state(s), 21, 32
and internationalism, 289
and self-determination, 183
sovereign, 184
successful, 211-214
National Anti-Poverty Organization (NAPO), 328
National Day of Action, 84, 85
National Energy Program (NEP), 95
National Film Board (NFB), 332
national identity, 36-39, 40, 300, 368
national interest(s), 117-119, 134
after World War I, 126-127, 129
common, 118
contending, 130
in Peru, 130
to what extent should it be pursued?, 110-113
national myths, 38-39, 59
national pride, 56
national symbols, 56, 87
national unity, 342-365
and Aboriginal peoples, 361
concepts of, 346
feelings of, 344-345
forces affecting, 344-345
geographical factors, 347
and immigration trends, 260
and urbanization, 261
nationalism
civic, 30-32
defined, 21
ethnic, 26, 31, 32, 43
French, 42-47
French-Canadian, 308-309
Inuit, 62
and memories, 56
Métis, 60, 61, 63
political, 29
Québécois, 62-63, 309
supra-, 222, 265
ultra-, 138-141
in the United States, 58
nationalist loyalties, 66-88, 91, 107
nations
motives of, 220-221
successful, 211-214
NATO (North Atlantic Treaty Organization), 131, 132, 212, 268
navvies, 59, 63, 311
Nawaz, Zarqa, 373
Nazis, 140, 141, 143, 145, 147, 148, 176
needs, defined, 210
Newfoundland fisheries, 239
Newfoundland and Labrador oil royalties, 348
Newfoundland Regiment, 75
Newman, Peter C., 300, 301, 339
9/11 attacks, 129, 131, 245, 344
Nisga'a, 315, 356
Noble, Sierra, 20
non-governmental organizations (NGOs), 200, 216, 224, 226, 248, 279, 281
non-nationalist loyalties, 90-91, 103-104, 107
North American integration, 378-379
Northwest Passage, 119, 120, 242
Nuclear Non-Proliferation Treaty, 258
Nunavik, 358-359
Nunavut, 62, 194-195, 357

O

Official Languages Act, 309, 352
oil and gas industry
in Alberta, 95-100
in Iraq, 127, 128-129
National Energy Program (NEP), 95
Newfoundland and Labrador royalties, 348
Organization of Petroleum Exporting Countries, 128
in Peru, 130
possible Arctic resources, 119
Oka crisis, 82
Oldman River Dam, 277
Organization of Petroleum Exporting Countries, 128
Ottawa Treaty, 249
Ottoman Empire, 33, 114, 115, 123, 126, 128, 163, 164, 182
overgeneralizing, 49

P

Pakistan, 191, 200, 201
parades, 66-67
Paris riots, 43
parliamentary democracy, 59
Parti Québécois, 78, 309, 375
patriation of the Constitution, 349, 353
patriotism, 24, 69, 344
peace and security, 212, 226
peacekeepers
Canadian, 118, 154-155, 173, 237, 238, 246-247, 324
myth about, 247
Reconciliation (monument), 230
UN, 171, 237, 238, 324
Pearl Harbor, 152
Pearson, Lester B., 154, 237, 244, 300
people, a, defined 184
People to People, Nation to Nation, 83, 193, 374
performers, 300
Carrier, Roch, 336
comedians, 38
Connors, Stompin' Tom, 41, 336

Dunn, Maria, 92
Lightfoot, Gordon, 59
musicians, 20, 336
Myers, Mike, 38, 300
Noble, Sierra, 20
Peterson, Oscar, 336
Persian Gulf War, 128
Peterson, Oscar, 336
Picasso, Pablo, 156
pluralism, 369-370, 371-373
Pol Pot, 186
Poland, 140, 151, 176, 226
policy, 122
polio, 236
political cartoons, 86, 95, 108, 129, 132, 135, 200, 202, 288
political institutions, 327
political nationalism, 29
political representation, 350
pollsters, 327, 353
pollution
air, 235, 245
in Canada, 274
poverty, 278
prevailing winds, 274
Princess Patricia's Canadian Light Infantry, 246
Princip, Gavrilo, 123
Project Naming, 70, 87
propaganda, 140, 143, 146, 149, 152

Q

Québec
anglophones in, 62-63, 77, 78, 79, 80, 81
contending loyalties in, 77-81
Francophones in, 25, 60, 62-63, 77-81, 197
immigrants, code for, 376
linguistic understanding of nation, 25
reasonable accommodation, 376
self-determination for, 197-198, 351
separation, 345, 378
sovereignty and, 52, 65, 77-81, 197, 309, 351-352
Québécois
cultural identity, 301
Francophone nationalism, 25, 77-81, 309, 376
nation, 375
nationalism, 62-63
Quiet Revolution, 79, 309
Quiller-Couch, Arthur, 23

R

racial or ethnic loyalties, 91
racism, 57, 152, 162
against Jewish people, 140, 147
during World War II, 152
radio broadcasting, 332
RCMP, 73, 104, 334
reasonable accommodation, 73-74, 376
reconciliation, 82
Reconciliation (monument), 230
Red Crescent, 200
Red Cross, 200, 227
refugees, 199-201
regional loyalties, 91, 95-96, 97
Reid, Angus, 353
Reign of Terror, 53
religious freedom, 93, 106
religious loyalties, 91, 93, 102-103
religious nationalism, 27, 28
relocation of Inuit, 62
Renan, Ernest, 22, 384
responsible government, 304
rhetoric, detecting, 48-49
Rice, Condoleeza, 118
Riel, Louis, 314
Right to Play, 224, 225
rights
Aboriginal, 314-315
for Aboriginal women, 104
human, 172, 259, 284
inherent, 356
for women, 104, 133, 155
Rizsanyi, George, 323
Royal Canadian Mint, 335
Royal Canadian Mounted Police (RCMP), 73, 104, 334
Royal Commission on Aboriginal Peoples, 83-84, 193, 374, 375
Royal Commission on Bilingualism and Biculturalism, 351-352
royal commissions, defined 83
rule of law, 30
Rusesabagina, Paul, 177
Russia
Arctic exploration, 242
and Arctic sovereignty, 119
Napoléon's invasion of , 54-55
Russian Empire, 123
Rwanda, 173, 177, 238

S

salons, 46
Samar, Sima, 133
sanctions, economic, 236
Sarajevo, 171-172
SARS (severe acute respiratory syndrome), 223, 254, 275
Saudi Arabian, 116
Schindler, Oskar, 176
Scott, Duncan Campbell, 61
seal hunt protest, 88-89
security
organizations, 268
and peace, 212, 226
and safety, 117
segregation, 105
Selassie, Haile, 150

self-defence, inherent right of individual or collective, 131
self-determination, 29, 82, 163
for Aboriginal peoples, 314, 356
and decolonization, 184-186
for First Nations peoples, 193-194
for Indians (people of India), 190-192, 199
for indigenous peoples, 227
for Inuit peoples, 194-195
for Métis peoples, 196
and nation-states, 183
national, 180-203
for Québec, 197-198, 351
for Tibetans, 187
self-government, 126
Sen, Amartya, 40
separation
of Québec, 345, 378
of Western Canada, 348
Serbians, 171-172, 182, 183, 184, 197, 199, 246
settlers, attracting, 298, 307, 324
Seven Years' War, 47, 62
Shiites, 93
Sieyès, Emmanuel-Joseph, 48, 49
Sifton, Clifford, 307
Sikhs, 73
Siksika, 26, 28, 210
Simon, Mary, 266, 267
Six Nations Confederacy, 374
Six String Nation guitar, 320-321, 323, 336
skills
analyzing cause-and-effect relationships, 174
analyzing information from many sources, 80-81
assessing the validity of information, 142-143
building consensus, 120-121
communicating effectively to express a point of view, 286-287
comparing various narratives, 302-303
confirming or revising your view or opinion, 354-355
decision making and problem solving, 218-219
defending an informed position, 100-101
detecting rhetoric and bias, 48-49
developing effective inquiry questions, 34-35
honing oral, written, and visual literacy, 382-383
persuading, compromising, and negotiating to resolve conflicts and differences, 240-241
predicting likely outcomes, 188-189
quescussions, 34
using debate to persuasively express informed views, 262-263
writing for different purposes and audiences, 330-331
smallpox, 223
Smyth, Ryan, 90
social factors and French nationalism in the 18th century, 45
South Baffin Place Names Project, 70
Southeast Asia, 185
sovereignists, 77, 78
sovereignty
Arctic, 119
Kosovo and, 197
for nations and nation-states, 213
Québec and, 52, 65, 77-81, 197, 309, 351-353
Tibet and, 29
Soviet Union (USSR), 136, 136-139, 165, 213
space technology, 362-363
spin (manipulation of news), 94
analyzing propaganda, 146
in commercial and corporate communications, 329
in official documents, analyzing, 259
sponsorship, 328, 335
Stalin, Joseph, 136, 137, 139, 140, 165
Statement of Reconciliation, 83
stereotyping, 49, 373
strip mining, 97, 98
successor states, 190-192
Sudan, 285
Suez Canal crisis, 154, 246
Sunnis, 93
supranationalism, 222, 265
symbols
on Canadian money, 322, 335
national, 56, 87, 322-323
of various peoples, 342

T

Taliban, 131, 132, 139, 261
Taylor, Jowi, 320-321, 323, 336
technology
effects on citizenship and democracy, 256
Internet, social effects of, 255
used for communication, 254
television broadcasting, 332
Tennis Court Oath, 47
terrorist attacks, 129, 131, 245, 344, 370
think tanks, 327
Third Estate, 47, 48, 91
Thomas-Muller, Clayton, 100
Those Who Share Together, Stay Together, 366, 367, 380
Tibet, 27, 29, 91, 187, 368
Dalai Lama, 187, 189, 203
invasion by China, 187, 189, 368
Tojo Hideki, 145, 148
Tootoo, Jordin, 62
treaties
with Aboriginal peoples, 61, 70, 315
with Middle Eastern countries, 115
negotiated after World War I, 182
Nuclear Non-Proliferation, 258
Ottawa, 249
see also Treaty of Versailles
Treaty of Versailles, 123-125, 126, 141, 145, 150
Trudeau, Pierre, 61, 95, 309, 315, 344, 351

Truman, Harry S., 168
Turkey, 33, 34, 114, 126, 127
  Dink, Hrant, 138, 162
  genocide of Armenians, 138, 162, 163-164
  Young Turks, 163
Tutsis, 173, 177, 238
two solitudes, 103, 109

U

Ukrainians, 139, 152, 165, 312
ultranationalism, 138-157, 158-179
UNESCO, 177, 260
unilateralism, 220
United Nations, 131, 170
  A More Secure World, 257
  Antarctic Treaty, 239
  Committee on Economic, Social and Cultural Rights, 328
  Convention on Inhumane Weapons, 248
  Convention on the Law of the Sea, 119, 239, 240, 242
  creation of, 170
  Declaration on the Rights of Indigenous Peoples, 130, 193, 196
  Environment Programme, 282
  Human Rights council, 259
  International Atomic Energy Agency (IAEA), 258
  peacekeepers, 171
  policy on internal conflicts, 257
  Security Council, 183, 187, 237, 246, 258, 284, 285
  trials for war criminals, 170
  Universal Declaration of Human Rights, 227, 284, 385
United Nations Educational, Scientific and Cultural Organization (UNESCO), 260
United States, 46, 58, 119, 121
  9/11 attacks, 129, 131
  in Afghanistan, 131
  annexing Canada, 305
  bombing of Hiroshima and Nagasaki, 158, 159, 160, 168, 169
  border security, 378
  integration with Canada, 378-379
  in Vietnam War, 185
  war on Iraq, 129, 131
Universal Declaration of Human Rights, 227, 284, 385
urbanization, 261

V

Van Alstyne, Marshall, 255
Vietnam, 185
Vimy Memorial, 20
visions of Canada, 298-319, 368-385
Voltaire, 46, 47
von Bredow, Wilfried, 234, 235

W

wants, defined, 210
war crimes, 161
wars
  American Revolution, 46, 58
  Persian Gulf, 128
  protection from, 212
  Seven Years,' 47, 62
  in the United States, 305
  Vietnam, 185
  see also World War I, World War II
water, access to clean, 272, 273, 276
Watt-Cloutier, Sheila, 283
Western Canada, alienation of, 348
Wieland, Joyce, 18-19
Wiesel, Elie, 167
Williams, Jody, 248
Wilson, Woodrow, 123, 124, 127, 182
women
  Aboriginal, rights for, 104
  in Afghanistan, rights for, 133, 155
  Muslim, 39, 57
  and salons, 46
world affairs, 381
World Bank, 226, 281, 289
World Court, 239
World Health Organization (WHO), 223, 275, 276
World Heritage Sites, 177, 260, 261
world ocean currents, 274
world peace, 236
World Trade Organization (WTO), 226, 264, 288
World War I, 123
  Germany after, 141
  Japan after, 144
  national interests after, 126-127
World War II, 145, 146
  bombing of Hiroshima and Nagasaki, 158, 159, 160, 168, 169
  Canadian efforts, 151
  and Japan, 144, 148, 152, 158, 159, 160, 168
  propaganda, 140, 143, 146, 149, 152

Y

Yugoslavia, 171-172, 182, 246

Z

Zimbabwe, 216-217
Zucker, Jerry, 329, 330

Photo Credits

Realted Issue 1
p14 The Canadian Press (Larry MacDougal); **p**15 left The Canadian Press (*Toronto Sun*/Paul Henry), (Larry MacDougal),top (Michel Spingler); **p**17 The Office of the Secretary to the Governor General; **p**18 National Gallery of Canada (15458), George Whiteside; **p**20 left The Canadian Press (Michel Spingler), Photo courtesy of Veterans Affairs Canada; **p**22 top left clockwise Mary Evans Picture Library/ ALAMY, Mary Evans Picture Library, Photo courtesy of Benedict Anderson; **p**23 The Canadian Press (Larry MacDougal); **p**25 The Canadian Press (*Journal de Montréal*/Raynald Leblanc); **p**26 left The Canadian Press (Lee Jin-man), (Darren Stone), (*Lethbridge Herald*/ Ian Martens); **p**27 The Canadian Press (action press/XINHUA); **p**31 The Canadian Press (Paul Chiasson); **p**33 Photo courtesy Ates Akkor; **p**38 top The Canadian Press (Jason DeCrow), Dallas and John Heaton/Jupiter Images; **p**39 The Canadian Press (Jacques Boissinot); **p**41 Used by permission of Bernie Bedore and Yüksel Hassan; **p**42 arcadio/Cagle Cartoons 21251; **p**44 left Leonard de Selva/CORBIS, The Gallery Collection/Corbis; **p**45 left The Canadian Press (Javier Galeano), Bettman/CORBIS; **p**46 Stefano Bianchetti/Corbis; **p**47 The Gallery Collection/Corbis; **p**50 The Canadian Press (Sony Pictures/Everett Collection); **p**53 Giraudon/Art Resource, NY; **p**56 The Art Archive/Corbis; **p**58 Bettman/CORBIS; **p**59 Canadian Pacific Railway Archives BR 117; **p**60 *Windspeaker*, **p**61 The Canadian Press; **p**62 left The Canadian Press (Andrew Vaughan), (Larry MacDougal); **p**66 top left clockwise The Canadian Press(Fort McMurray Today/Carl Patzel), (*Edmonton Sun*-Darryl Dyck), (*Journal de Québec*/Karl Tremblay), (*Edmonton Sun*-David Bloom), (Larry MacDougal); **p**68 The Canadian Press (Achmad Ibrahim); **p**69 The Canadian Press (Frank Gunn); **p**71 Photo courtesy Kiviaq; **p**72 The Canadian Press (Ryan Remiorz); **p**73 The Canadian Press (*Toronto Sun*/Paul Henry); **p**74 The Canadian Press (Calgary Sun/ Carlos Amat); **p**75 The Rooms Provincial Archives, F46-24/Holloway Studio; **p**78 The Canadian Press; **p**82 The Canadian Press (Shaney Komulainen); **p**85 top left The Canadian Press (Jonathan Hayward), Photo courtesy of Marilyn Jensen, Photo courtesy of Doug Cuthand; **p**87 National Archives Canada e002344280; **p**88 The Canadian Press (Michel Euler); **p**90 The Canadian Press (John Ulan); **p**92 Photo courtesy of Maria Dunn, Glenbow Archives NC-54-4401; **p**94 The Canadian Press (Jerome Delay); **p**95 Glenbow Archives M-8000-624; **p**96 The Canadian Press (Larry MacDougal); **p**97 Chris Evans/ The Pembina Institute; **p**98 David Dodge/The Pembina Institute; **p**99 top left clockwise David Dodge/The Pembina Institute, Photo courtesy of Syncrude Canada/Don Thompson, Photo courtesy of Rob Schneider/Edmonton branch–Canadian Parks and Wilderness Society, The Canadian Press (Dave Buston); **p**101 CCL wikipedia; **p**102 The Canadian Press (Jerome Favre); **p**103 left The Canadian Press (Fred Chartrand), (Jonathan Hayward); **p**104 The Canadian Press (*New Brunswick Telegraph-Journal*/Noel Chenier); **p**105 left The Canadian Press (Danny Johnston), Library of Congress; **p**106 The Canadian Press (Tom Hanson); **p**108 Glenbow Archives M-8000-885;

Realted Issue 2
p110 Fahad Shadeed/AFP/Getty Images; **p**111 top Alfred Eisenstaedt/ Pix Inc./Time & Life Pictures/Getty Images, The Canadian Press (Jeff McIntosh); **p**116 top The Canadian Press (Sebastian Scheiner), Fahad Shadeed/AFP/Getty Images, Patrick Baz/AFP/Getty Images; **p**117 Wissam Al Okaili/AFP/Getty Images); **p**118 The Canadian Press (Bill Graveland); **p**119 The Canadian Press (Jeff McIntosh); **p**123 Leonard de Selva/CORBIS; **p**124 Used by permission University of California, San Diego/Department of History; **p**125 top left Pictorial Press Ltd/Alamy, Hulton Archive/Getty Images, Bill Bolychuk/Margaret MacMillan; **p**126 Bettman/CORBIS; **p**127 Evening Standard/Getty Images; **p**129 Artizans.com COH937; **p**130 Photo courtesy of Chris Fagan; **p**131 left The Canadian Press (Tom Hanson), (*Winnipeg Free Press*/Ken Gigliotti); **p**132 Artizans.com DEA2118; **p**133 The Canadian Press (Martin Gnedt); **p**135 Artizans.com GMAC996; **p**136 International Institute of Social History (IISH) Netherlands; **p**138 The Canadian Press (Serkan Senturk); **p**139 The Siberian Gulag, caricature from 'Le Pelerin', 1931 (colour litho), Gignoux (20th century) Private Collection, Archives Charmet/The Bridgeman Art Library; **p**140 top Stadtarchiv/Nurnberg, Juergen Stroop Photographie, 1943. Photo by Imagno/Getty Images; **p**141 Keystone Features/Getty Images; **p**143 left Bettman/CORBIS, CCL wikipedia; **p**144 Bettman/CORBIS; **p**145 top Topical Press Agency/Getty Images, U.S. Naval Institute; **p**146 left McGill University Library/War Poster Collection WP2.B73.F7, McCord Museum M965.199.3366; **p**147 top Popperfoto.com/Robertstock, The Canadian Press (Everett); **p**148 Time & Life Pictures/Getty Images; **p**150 The Canadian Press (Everett Collection); **p**151 Attack on All Fronts 19730004-030 © Canadian War Museum; **p**152 top The Torch be Yours to Hold It High. 19940001-840 © Canadian War Museum, Glenbow Archives NA-3369-2; **p**153 The Canadian Press(Sharon Doucette); **p**155 top clockwise The Canadian Press (Geert Vanden Wijngaert), Photo courtesy of Karin von Hippel, Senior Fellow, Post-Conflict Reconstruction Project CSIS, Washington, The Canadian Press (Laetitia Deconinck); **p**158 top clockwise The Canadian Press (Stanley Troutman), (Shizuo Kambayashi), (Everett); **p**160 Alfred Eisenstaedt/Pix Inc./Time & Life Pictures/Getty Images; **p**162 Yad Vashem, The Holocaust Martyrs' and Heroes' Remembrance Authority; **p**164 Spencer Platt/Getty Images; **p**165 top The Canadian Press (*Winnipeg Free Press*/Phil Hossack), (Sergei Chuzavkov); **p**166 Yad Vashem, The Holocaust Martyrs' and Heroes' Remembrance Authority; **p**167 Sven Nackstrand/AFP/Getty Images; **p**168 Jodi Cobb/National Geographic Collection/Getty Images; **p**169 left Hank Walker/Time Life Pictures/Getty Images, Photo courtesy of Professor Mitsuo Okamoto; **p**171 Tom Stoddart/Getty Images; **p**172 The Canadian Press (Peter Dejong); **p**173 Gianluigi Guercia/ AFP/Getty Images; **p**176 top Keystone/Getty Images, Stan Honda/ AFP/Getty Images; **p**177 The Canadian Press (Aaron Harris); **p**179 www. cartoonstock.com jlv0033; **p**158 The Canadian Press (Fred Chartrand), insets left (Sean Kilpatrick), (Fred Chartrand); **p**160 left Dimitar Dilkoff/AFP/Getty Images, Carsten Koall/Getty Images; **p**161 Henry Ray Abrams/AFP/Getty Images; **p**164 Tang Chin Sothy/ AFP/Getty Images; **p**165 The Canadian Press (Mukhtar Khan); **p**168 Popperfoto/Getty Images; **p**169 Popperfoto/Getty Images; **p**170 The Canadian Press (Mukhtar Khan); **p**172 Carlo Allegri/AFP/Getty Images; **p**173 The Canadian Press (Adrian Wyld); **p**176 left clockwise The Canadian Press (Sean Kilpatrick), (Tom Hanson), Photo courtesy of the Métis Nation; **p**177 The Canadian Press (Visar Kryeziu); **p**178 top Artizans.com LAR116, Tariq Mahmood/AFP/Getty Images; **p**180 Artizans.com KR1725

Realted Issue 3
p204 The Canadian Press (Irwin Fedriansyiah); **p**205 top The Canadian Press (Tom Hanson), (action press/XINHUA Yichang/ Hubei Province); **p**208 NASA; **p**210 The Canadian Press (Terry Pedwell); **p**211 The Canadian Press (Larry MacDougal); **p**212 The Canadian Press (Alfred de Montesquiou); **p**213 The Canadian Press (*Whitehorse Star*/Vince Federoff); **p**214 The Canadian Press (*Winnipeg Free Press*/Ken Gigliotti); **p**215 top clockwise Photos courtesy of Professor Robert I. Rotberg, Erin Simpson, Pole Institute; **p217** The Canadian Press; **p**220 Bettman/CORBIS; **p**222 top The Canadian Press (Dave Chidley), Àlex Culla i Viñals/iStock; **p**223 The Canadian Press (Kevin Frayer); **p**224 top The Canadian Press (Tom Hanson), Wolfgang Langenstrassen/dpa/Corbis; **p**225 top The Canadian Press (Dusan Vranic), (Frank Gunn); **p**226 Bettman/ CORBIS; **p**227 The Canadian Press (Philip A. McDaniel/USN/ ABACA); **p**230 Bill Williams; **p**232 The Canadian Press (Nathan Denette); **p**234 left Photo courtesy of the Right Honourable Joe Clark; The Canadian Press (Gurinder Osan); **p**235 The Canadian

Press (Oded Balilty); **p**236 The Canadian Press (Jassim Mohammed); **p**237 The Canadian Press (Tom Hanson); **p**238 The Canadian Press (Ryan Remiorz); **p**239 The Canadian Press (Fred Chartrand); **p**242 The Canadian Press (Vladimir Chistyakov), inset NASA/CORBIS; **p**243 Photo courtesy of Jenna Hoyt, Little Voice Foundation; **p**244 The Canadian Press (Musadeq Sadeq); **p**245 The Canadian Press (Fred Chartrand); **p**246 The Canadian Press (Ariana Cubillos); **p**252 The Canadian Press (Kirsty Wigglesworth), inset (Rex Features), DSEI; **p**254 The Canadian Press (M. Lakshman); **p**255 The Canadian Press (Don Denton); **p**256 The Canadian Press (Katsumi Kasahara); **p**257 The Canadian Press; **p**260 The Canadian Press (SplashdownDirect/Matthew Watkinson/Rex Features); **p**261 The Canadian Press (Mildred Dearborn); **p**262 The Canadian Press (Larry MacDougal); **p**264 The Canadian Press (Irwin Fedriansyiah); **p**266 The Canadian Press (Kevin Frayer); **p**267 The Canadian Press (Tom Hanson); **p**269 top clockwise The Canadian Press (Doug Ball), Photo courtesy of Professor Andrew Herod, University of Georgia, Photos courtesy of Kumarian Press; **p**271 Austrian Archives/Magma/ CORBIS;**p**272 Arcadio/Cagle Cartoons; **p**275 Glenbow Archives NA-3452-2; **p**276 The Canadian Press (Richard Lam); **p**277 top The Canadian Press (action press/XINHUA Yichang/Hubei Province), (Larry MacDougal); **p**278 Feature China/ LU DI/epa/Corbis; **p**280 The Canadian Press (Tom Hanson); **p**281 left The Canadian Press (Jeff McIntosh), inset (Brennan Linsley); **p**282 www.cartoonstock.com bgrn647; **p**283 The Canadian Press (Chris Windeyer); **p**286 Photo by Dustin Rabin, courtesy of the Canadian Broadcasting Corporation; **p**288 Trevor Yuss/*Zambia Post*; **p**290 Ares/Cagle Cartoons; **p**291 Photos courtesy of the United Nations Photo Library; **p**293 www.cartoonstock.com mkon106

Related Issue 4

p294 The Canadian Press (Alberto Ramella); **p**295 top The Canadian Press (Tom Hanson), Heiko Wittenborn; **p**298 top clockwise Library and Archives Canada. Reproduced with the permission of the Minister of Public Works and Government Services Canada (2008) Source: Library and Archives Canada/Canadian Corporation for the 1967 World Exhibition fonds/e000988791, Alberta Tourism, Parks & Recreation, Parks Division, Canadian Pacific Railway Archives A.6204; **p**300 left The Canadian Press, Originally photographed by Cliff Buckman, Flag Committee, John Ross Matheson Fonds, Queen's University Archives; **p**304 Andrew Balfour Photography; **p**305 top McCord Museum M994X.5.273.46, Taken from *The Fight for Canada: Four Centuries of Resistance to American Expansionism* by David Orchard. Originally appeared in the Dec.1, 1888, issue of the *New York World*. Used with permission of Citizens Concerned About Free Trade; **p**306 top clockwise The Shingwauk Project/Algoma University College (www.shingwauk.auc.ca), Library and Archives Canada, The Canadian Press (Irma Coucill); **p**307 left Library and Archives Canada PA-027942, Glenbow Archives NA-3818-16; **p**308 Library and Archives Canada C-006859; **p**309 McCord Museum M965.199.267; **p**311 Glenbow Archives NA-316-1; **p**312 Glenbow Archives NA-1758-13; **p**314 Glenbow Archives NA-1039-1; **p**315 The Canadian Press (Tom Hanson); **p**317 The Canadian Press (*Toronto Star*/ Randy Quan); **p**319 McCord Museum II-64974; **p**320 Six String Nation (Sandor Fizli); **p**322 left Reproduced with permission of *The Beaver: Canada's History Magazine*, David Tanaka; **p**323 The Canadian Press (Jonathan Hayward); **p**325 Glenbow Archives NA-266-5; **p**326 top Dominion Institute, The Canadian Press (Charlottetown Guardian/Brian McInnis); **p**327 Reproduced with permission Mètis Nation of Alberta; **p**328 The Canadian Press (Alberto Ramella); **p**332 Photo courtesy of Johnnene Maddison; **p**333 The Canadian Press (*Moose Jaw Times-Herald*/Mark Taylor); **p**334 The Canadian Press (Geoff Howe); **p**335 National Currency Collection, Currency Museum, Bank of Canada, Photography by Gord Carter, Ottawa; **p**336 The Canadian Press (Chuck Mitchell); **p**337 The Canadian Press (J.P. Moczulski); **p**338 top The Canadian Press(Chris Schwarz), Canadian Pacific Railway Archives M.8907; **p**339 top clockwise Mary Evans Picture Library, The Aboriginal Multi-Media Society, Curtis Studio Limited, Toronto; **p**341 Musée national des beaux-arts du Québec, 58.538; **p**344 The Canadian Press (Tom Hanson), insets left clockwise The Canadian Press (Sean Kilpatrick), National Symbols of Ukraine (wikipedia), James Gritz/ iStock, Angsar Walk, Frank Leung/iStock, Collection Musée acadien de L'Université de Moncton; **p**347 Photo courtesy of Maude Barlow/ The Council of Canadians; **p**348 left The Canadian Press (Jonathan Hayward), David Tanaka, The Canadian Press (Chuck Stoody); **p**352 Photo courtesy of Jeff Chiba Stearns; **p**353 The Canadian Press (Fred Chartrand); **p**355 top clockwise Photo courtesy of Dr. Angus Reid, The Canadian Press (*Winnipeg Free Press*/Wayne Glowacki), (Nick Procaylo); **p**358 The Canadian Press(Richard Lam); **p**361 left Photos courtesy of Dorset Fine Arts; Heiko Wittenborn; **p**364 NASA; **p**370 Used by permission Jane Ash Poitras; **p**372 Liu Jin/ AFP/Getty Images; **p**373 The Canadian Press (Tom Hanson); **p**374 The Canadian Press (Tom Hevezi); **p**375 The Canadian Press (J.P. Moczulski); **p**376 Artizans.com MAY1843; **p**377 The Canadian Press (Religion News Service/National Film Board of Canada; **p**378 MPI/ Getty Images); **p**379 The Canadian Press (Jacques Boissinot); **p**380 The Canadian Press (Jacques Boissinot); **p**381 left clockwise Photo courtesy of Michael Adams/Environics, Photo courtesy of Professor Will Kymlicka; The Canadian Press (Ryan Remiorz); **p**382 The Canadian Press (Ted S.Warren); **p**384 The Canadian Press (Steve White); **p**388 The Canadian Press; **p**389 Bill Williams, insets left clockwise The Canadian Press (Nick Procaylo), (*Journal de Québec*/ Karl Tremblay), (Aaron Harris), National Gallery of Canada (15458)

Text Credits

p22 Excerpt from Anderson, Benedict. *Imagined Communities: Reflections on the Origin and Spread of Nationalism.* Revised edition. London and New York: Verso, 1991, pp. 5-7. Used by permission of Benedict Anderson.

p28 "Not Just a Platform for My Dance" by Marilyn Dumont from *A Really Good Brown Girl.* Brick Books, 1996. Used by permission.

p39 Excerpt from "I Was a Teenage Hijabi Hockey Player" by Sheema Khan. Used by permission of the author, Sheema Khan.

p41 Excerpt from "Big Joe Mufferaw" by Stompin' Tom Connors. *Big Joe Mufferaw,* written by Tom C. Connors c1970 Crown-Vetch Music (SOCAN) All rights Reserved.

p63 Quotation: from "The History That Matters Most," Michael Ignatieff. *Great Questions of Canada.* Rudyard Griffiths, ed. Key Porter, 2000, 2007. p. 25. Permission Pending.

p77 Raymond Giroux, "Québec: A Nation Divided" in Kenneth McRoberts & Patrick Monahan, *The Charlottetown Accord, the Referendum, and the Future of Canada.* Toronto: University of Toronto Press, 1993, p. 152. Used by permission.

p80 "Raining on the Parade." Robert Libman. Montreal Gazette. Aug. 28, 2007. Used by permission of Robert Libman.

p81 "Why We Need Bill 101." André Burelle. Montreal Gazette.

p81 Letter of Eric M. Maldoff, president, Alliance Quebec, to René Lévesque, March 22, 1982. *The Dynamics of Ethno-Linguistic Mobilisation in Canada.* Paul Prosperi. Used by permission of Paul Prosperi.

p85 "Aboriginal Day Proved Its Point." Doug Cuthand. Regina Leader-Post. July 9, 2007. Used by permission Doug Cuthand.

p97 Line graph: Crude Oil Production in Alberta. Used by permission Pembina Institute.

p92 Excerpt from "We Were Good People," Maria Dunn. The phrases "We were good people" and "I remember Bloody Tuesday" were taken from a letter written by William Dolinsky in an unpublished letter to the *Edmonton Journal* in 1999 describing what he had witnessed in 1932. ©Maria Dunn and William Dolinsky, 2003.

p121 Poll results: Angus Reid Global Monitor. From an online poll conducted in August 2007 by Angus Reid Global Monitor on Arctic Sovereignty. Used by permission of Angus Reid Global Monitor/ Mario Canseco.

p121 Excerpt from "Our Arctic Sovereignty Is Well in Hand," Franklyn Griffiths. Used by permission of Franklyn Griffiths.

p132 Excerpts from charts showing results of Strategic Counsel survey, July 2007. Source: *The Globe and Mail*/CTV News/The Strategic Counsel. Used by permission of The Strategic Counsel.

p153 "What Do I Remember of the Evacuation", by Joy Kogawa, is reprinted with the permission of the author. It was first printed in *A Choice of Dreams* published by McClelland and Stewart in 1974.

p167 Excerpt from Elie Wiesel's Nobel Peace Prize acceptance speech. Permission Pending.

p303 Excerpt from *Nationalism without Walls.* Richard Gwyn. McClelland and Stewart, 1996. pp. 17, 21, 30. Permission pending.

p303 Excerpt from foreword to *The New Canada.* Erin Anderssen. Foreword by Edward Greenspon. McClelland and Stewart, 2004. pp. 1–2. Permission Pending.

p336 "The Hockey Song", written by Tom C. Connors ©1971 Crown-Vetch Music (SOCAN) All rights Reserved. Used by permission.

p339 "My Heart Soars" © Dan George. From *The Best of Chief Dan George,* Hancock House Publishers. Permission Pending.

p391 Excerpt from "I Am a Canadian" by Duke Redbird. Reprinted by permission Duke Redbird.